SOURCEBOOK ON HISTORY OF EVOLUTION

Revised Printing

Mark A. Largent

University of Puget Sound

KENDALL/HUNT PUBLISHING COM
4050 Westmark Drive   Dubuque, Iowa

Table of Contents

Introduction

The materials in this volume are primary source documents, works written by the historical figures, and are intended to help students understand some of the issues, problems and methods authors have used in exploring the scientific study and the social influences of evolutionary thought. Unlike secondary sources, which are narratives and analyses written about historical subjects, primary sources allow us first hand experience in the approaches and tools historical figures used. At the same time, however, primary sources are considerably more difficult to read, as the concerns, assumptions, and expectations of historical figures are often fundamentally different that those of the modern reader. My goal in presenting these materials is to help students begin to bridge the gap between themselves and the historical subjects in order to make both the subjects' worlds and their own world and little more clear to them.

I owe special thanks to Professors Paul Farber, Mike Osborne, Mott Greene, Diane Paul, Christian Young, and Michael Reidy. Their advice and encouragement substantially influenced the content of this volume. I would also like to thank Professors Sally Gregory Kohlstedt and John Beatty for introducing me to much of this material and for helping me begin to think critically about the history of evolutionary thought and its relationship with Western culture.

Mark A. Largent
University of Puget Sound
August 2004

Section I

*Thoughts on Evolution
before 1859*

Jean Baptiste Lamarck

Zoological Philosophy, 1809

Lamarck (1744-1829) is widely credited with originating a workable theory of evolution a full half-century before Darwin published his theory of natural selection. A Frenchman who lived through the French Revolution, Lamarck was trained as a medical doctor and made significant contributions to the development of the modern museum. In his *Zoological Philosophy,* he argued that organisms could change slowly from generation to generation through the inheritance of acquired characteristics. Abilities or traits that an organism developed throughout the course of its lifetime could be passed in whole or in part to its offspring. In this selection, Lamarck challenged the notion of a species, the idea of which implied that groups of organisms that we call species are inherently fixed and unchanging, and laid some of the groundwork necessary for natural historians to begin considering the possibility that species change over time.

OF SPECIES AMONG LIVING BODIES AND THE IDEA THAT WE SHOULD ATTACH TO THAT WORD

It is not a futile purpose to decide definitely what we mean by the so-called *species* among living bodies, and to enquire if it is true that species are of absolute constancy, as old as nature, and have all existed from the beginning just as we see them to-day; or if, as a result of changes in their environment, albeit extremely slow, they have not in course of time changed their characters and shape.

The solution to this question is of importance not only for our knowledge of zoology and botany, but also for the history of the world.

I shall show in one of the following chapters that every species has derived from the action of the environment in which it has long been placed the *habits* which we find in it. These habits have themselves influenced the parts of every individual in the species, to the extent of modifying those parts and bringing them into relation with the acquired habits. Let us first see what is meant by the name of species.

Any collection of like individuals which were produced by others similar to themselves is called a species.

This definition is exact; for every individual possessing life always resembles very closely those from which it sprang; but to this definition is added the allegation that the individuals composing a species never vary in their specific characters, and consequently that species have an absolute constancy in nature.

It is just this allegation that I propose to attack, since clear proofs drawn from observation show that it is ill-founded.

The almost universally received belief is that living bodies constitute species distinguished from one another by unchangeable characteristics, and that the existence of these species is as old as nature herself. This belief became established at a time when no sufficient observations had been taken, and when natural science was still almost negligible. It is continually being discredited for those who have seen much, who have long watched nature, and who have consulted with profit the rich collections of our museums.

Moreover, all those who are much occupied with the study of natural history, know that naturalists now find it extremely difficult to decide what objects should be regarded as species.

From *Zoological Philosophy,* University of Chicago Press, text originally published 1809.

They are in fact now aware that species have really only a constancy relative to the duration of the conditions in which are placed the individuals composing it; nor that some of these individuals have varied, and constitute races which shade gradually into some other neighbouring species. Hence, naturalists come to arbitrary decisions about individuals observed in various countries and diverse conditions, sometimes calling them varieties and sometimes species. The work connected with the determination of species therefore becomes daily more defective, that is to say, more complicated and confused.

It has indeed long been observed that collections of individuals exist which resemble one another in their organisation and in the sum total of their parts, and which have kept in the same condition from generation to generation, ever since they have been known. So much so that there seemed a justification for regarding any collection of like individuals as constituting so many invariable species. Now attention was not paid to the fact that the individuals of the species perpetuate themselves without variation only so long as the conditions of their existence do not vary in essential particulars. Since existing prejudices harmonise well with these successive regenerations of like individuals, it has been imagined that every species is invariable and as old as nature, and that it was specially created by the Supreme Author of all existing things.

Doubtless, nothing exists but by the will of the Sublime Author of all things, but can we set rules for him in the execution of his will, or fix the routine for him to observe? Could not his infinite power create an *order of things* which gave existence successively to all that we see as well as to all that exists but that we do not see?

Assuredly, whatever his will may have been, the immensity of his power is always the same, and in whatever manner that supreme will may have asserted itself, nothing can diminish its grandeur.

I shall then respect the decrees of that infinite wisdom and confine myself to the sphere of a pure observer of nature. If I succeed in unravelling anything in her methods, I shall say without fear of error that it has pleased the Author of nature to endow her with that faculty and power.

The idea formed of species among living bodies was quite simple, easy to understand, and seemed confirmed by the constancy in the shapes of individuals, perpetuated by reproduction or generation. Such are a great number of these alleged species that we see every day.

Meanwhile, the farther we advance in our knowledge of the various organised bodies which cover almost every part of the earth's surface, the greater becomes our difficulty in determining what should be regarded as a species, and still more in finding the boundaries and distinctions of genera.

According as the productions of nature are collected and our museums grow richer, we see nearly all the gaps filled up and the lines of demarcation effaced. We find ourselves reduced to an arbitrary decision which sometimes leads us to take the smallest differences of varieties and erect them into what we call species, and sometimes leads us to describe as a variety of some species slightly differing individuals which others regard as constituting a separate species.

Let me repeat that the richer our collections grow, the more proofs do we find that everything is more or less merged into everything else, that noticeable differences disappear, and that nature usually leaves us nothing but minute, nay puerile, details on which to found our distinctions.

How many genera there are both among animals and plants, among which the number of species referred to them is so great that the study and determination of these species are well nigh impracticable! The species of these genera, arranged in series according to their natural affinities, exhibit such slight differences from those next them as to coalesce with them. These species merge more or less into one another, so that there is no means of stating the small differences that distinguish them.

It is only those who have long and diligently studied the question of species, and who have examined rich collections, that are in a position to know to what extent species among living bodies merge into one another. And no one else can know that species only appear to be isolated, because others are lacking which are close to them but have not yet been collected.

I do not mean that existing animals form a very simple series, regularly graded throughout; but I do mean that they form a branching series, irregularly graded and free from discontinuity, or at least once free from it. For it is alleged that there is now occasional discontinuity, owing to some species having been lost. It follows that the species terminating each branch of the general series are connected on one side at least with other neighbouring species which merge into them. This I am now able to prove by means of well-known facts.

I require no hypothesis or supposition; I call all observing naturalists to witness.

Not only many genera but entire orders, and sometimes even classes, furnish instances of almost complete portions of the series which I have just indicated.

When in these cases the species have been arranged in series, and are all properly placed according to their natural affinities, if you choose one, and then, jumping over several others, take another a little way off, these two species when compared will exhibit great differences. It is thus in the first instance that we began to see such of nature's productions as lay nearest to us. Generic and specific distinctions were then quite easy to establish; but now that our collections are very rich, if you follow the above-mentioned series from the first species chosen to the second, which is very different from it, you reach it by slow gradations without having observed any noticeable distinctions.

I ask, where is the experienced zoologist or botanist who is not convinced of the truth of what I state?

How great the difficulty now is of studying and satisfactorily deciding on species among that multitude of every kind of polyps, radiarians, worms, and especially insects, such as butterflies, *Phalaena, Noctua, Tinea,* flies, *Ichneumon, Curculio, Cerambix,* chafers, rose-chafers, etc.! These genera alone possess so many species which merge indefinably into one another.

What a swarm of mollusc shells are furnished by every country and every sea, eluding our means of distinction and draining our resources.

Consider again, fishes, reptiles, birds and even mammals; you will see that except for gaps still to be filled, neighbouring species and even genera are separated by the finest differences, so that we have scarcely any foothold for setting up sound distinctions.

Is there not an exactly similar state of affairs in the case of botany, which deals with the other series, consisting of plants?

How great indeed are the difficulties of the study and determination of species in the genera *Lichen, Fucus, Carex, Poa, Piper, Euphorbia, Erica, Hieracium, Solanum, Geranium, Mimosa,* etc., etc.

When these genera were constituted only a small number of species belonging to them were known, and it was then easy to distinguish them; but now that nearly all the gaps are filled, our specific differences are necessarily minute and usually inadequate.

Let us see what are the causes which have given rise to this undoubted state of affairs; let us see if nature affords any explanation, and whether observation can help us.

We learn from a number of facts that, according as the individuals of one of our species change their abode, climate, habits, or manner of life, they become subject to influences which little by little alter the consistency and proportions of their parts, their shape, properties and even their organisation; so that in course of time everything in them shares in these mutations.

In the same climate, very different habitats and conditions at first merely cause variations in the individuals exposed to them; but in course of time the continued change of habitat in the individuals of which I speak, living and reproducing in these new conditions, induces alterations in them which become more or less essential to their being; thus, after a long succession of generations these individuals, originally belonging to one species, become at length transformed into a new species distinct from the first.

Suppose, for example, that the seeds of a grass or any other plant that grows normally in a damp meadow, are somehow conveyed first to the slope of a neighbouring hill where the ground although higher is still rich enough to allow the plant to maintain its existence. Suppose that then, after living there and reproducing itself many times, it reaches little by little the dry and almost barren ground of a mountain side. If the plant succeeds in living there and perpetuating itself for a number of generations, it will have become so altered that botanists who come across it will erect it into a separate species.

The same thing happens in the case of animals that are forced by circumstances to change their climate, habits, and manner of life: but in their case more time is required to work any noticeable change than in the case of plants.

The idea of bringing together under the name of species a collection of like individuals, which perpetuate themselves unchanged by reproduction and are as old as nature, involved the assumption that the individuals of one species could not unite in reproductive acts with individuals of a different species.

Unfortunately, observation has proved and continues every day to prove that this assumption is unwarranted; for the hybrids so common among plants, and the copulations so often noticed between animals of very different species, disclose the fact that the boundaries between these alleged constant species are not so impassable as had been imagined.

It is true that often nothing results from these strange copulations, especially when the animals are very disparate; and when anything does happen the resulting individuals are usually infertile; but we also know that when there is less disparity these defects do not occur. Now this cause is by itself sufficient gradually to create varieties, which then become races, and in course of time constitute what we call species.

To assist us to a judgment as to whether the idea of species has any real foundation, let us revert to the principles already set forth; they show:

1. That all the organised bodies of our earth are true productions of nature, wrought successively throughout long periods of time.
2. That in her procedure, nature began and still begins by fashioning the simplest of organised bodies, and that it is these alone which she fashions immediately, that is to say, only the rudiments of organisation indicated in the term *spontaneous generation*.
3. That, since the rudiments of the animal and plant were fashioned in suitable places and conditions, the properties of a commencing life and established organic movement necessarily caused a gradual development of the organs, and in course of time produced diversity in them as in the limbs.
4. That the property of growth is inherent in every part of the organised body, from the earliest manifestations of life; and then gave rise to different kinds of multiplication and reproduction, so that the increase of complexity of organisation, and of the shape and variety of the parts, has been preserved.
5. That with the help of time, of conditions that necessarily were favourable, of the changes successively undergone by every part of the earth's surface, and, finally, of the power of new conditions and habits to modify the organs of living bodies, all those which now exist have imperceptibly been fashioned such as see them.
6. That, finally, in this state of affairs every living body underwent greater or smaller changes in its organisation and its parts; so that what we call species were imperceptibly fashioned among them one after another and have only a relative constancy, and are not as old as nature.

But objections may be raised to the allegation that nature has little by little fashioned the various animals known to us by the aid of much time and an infinite variation of environment. It may be asked whether this allegation is not refuted by the single fact of the wonderful variety observed in the *instinct* of various animals, and in the marvellous *skill* of all kinds which they exhibit.

Will anyone, it may be asked, venture to carry his love of system so far as to say that nature has created single-handed that astonishing diversity of powers, artifice, cunning, foresight, patience and skill, of which we find so many examples among animals? Is not what we see in the single class of insects far

more than enough to convince us that nature cannot herself produce so many wonders; and to compel the most obstinate philosopher to recognise that the will of the Supreme Author of all things must be here invoked, and could alone suffice for bringing into existence so many wonderful things?

No doubt he would be a bold man, or rather a complete lunatic, who should propose to set limits to the power of the first Author of all things; but for this very reason no one can venture to deny that this infinite power may have willed what nature herself shows us it has willed.

This being so, if I find that nature herself works all the wonders just mentioned; that she has created organisation, life and even feeling, that she has multiplied and diversified within unknown limits the organs and faculties of the organised bodies whose existence she subserves or propagates; that by the sole instrumentality of *needs*, establishing and controlling habits, she has created in animals the fountain of all their acts and all their faculties, from the simplest to instinct, to skill, and finally to reason; if I find all this, should I not recognise in this power of nature, that is to say in the order of existing things, the execution of the will of her Sublime Author, who was able to will that she should have this power?

Shall I admire the greatness of the power of this first cause of everything any the less if it has pleased him that things should be so, than if his will by separate acts had occupied itself and still continued to occupy itself with the details of all the special creations, variations, developments, destructions, and renewals, in short, with all the mutations which take place at large among existing things?

Now I hope to prove that nature possesses the necessary powers and faculties for producing herself that so much excite our wonder.

The objection is still raised however that everything we see in living bodies indicates an unchangeable constancy in the preservation of their form. It is held that all animals whose history has come down to us for two or three thousand years have always been the same, and neither lost nor acquired anything in the perfection of their organs and the shape of their parts.

Not only had this apparent stability passed for an undoubted fact, but an attempt has recently been made to find special proofs of it in a report on the natural history collections brought from Egypt by M. Geoffroy. The authors of the report express themselves as follows:

"The collection has in the first place this peculiarity, that it may be said to contain animals of all periods. It has long been asked whether species change their shape in the course of time. This question, apparently so futile, is none the less necessary for the history of the world, and consequently for the solution of innumerable other questions which are not foreign to the gravest subjects of human worship."

"We have never been in so good a position to settle this question, in so far as concerns a large number of remarkable species and some thousands that are not remarkable. It appears as though the superstition of the ancient Egyptians were inspired by nature for the purpose of leaving a record of her history."

"It is impossible," continue the authors of the report, "to control our flights of imagination, on seeing still preserved with its smallest bones and hair, perfectly recognisable, an animal which two or three thousand years ago had in Thebes or Memphis its priests and altars. But without giving rein to all the ideas suggested by this approach to antiquity, we shall confine ourselves to the announcement that this part of M. Geoffroy's collection shows that these animals are exactly similar to those of to-day." (*Annales du Muséum d'Hist. natur.,* vol. i. pp. 235 and 236.)

I do not refuse to believe in the close resemblance of these animals with individuals of the same species living to-day. Thus, the birds that were worshipped and embalmed by the Egyptians two or three thousand years ago are still exactly like those which now live in that country.

It would indeed be very odd if it were otherwise; for the position and climate of Egypt are still very nearly what they were in those times. Now the birds which live there, being still in the same conditions as they were formerly, could not possibly have been forced into a change of habits.

Furthermore, it is obvious that birds, since they can travel so easily and choose the places which suit them, are less liable than many other animals to suffer from variations in local conditions, and hence less hindered in their habits.

Indeed there is nothing in the observation now cited that is contrary to the principles which I have set forth on this subject; or which proves that the animals concerned have existed in nature for all time; it proves only that they inhabited Egypt two or three thousand years ago; and every man who has any habit of reflection and at the same time of observing the monuments of nature's antiquity will easily appreciate the import of a duration of two or three thousand years in comparison with it.

Hence we may be sure that this appearance of stability of the things in nature will by the vulgar always be taken for reality; because people in general judge everything with reference to themselves.

For the man who forms his judgment only with reference to the changes that he himself perceives,

the eras of these mutations are stationary states which appear to him to be unlimited, on account of the shortness of the existence of individuals of his own species. Moreover, we must remember that the records of his observations, and the notes of facts which he has been able to register, only extend back a few thousand years; which is a time infinitely great with reference to himself, but very small with reference to the time occupied by the great changes occurring on the surface of the earth. Everything seems to him to be *stable* in the planet which he inhabits; and he is led to repudiate the signs which exist everywhere in the monuments heaped up around him, or buried in the soil which he tramples underfoot.

Magnitudes are relative both in space and time: let man take that truth to heart, and he will then be more reserved in his judgments on the stability which he attributes to the state of things that he observes in nature. (See the Appendix, p. 141, of my *Recherches sur les corps vivants.*)

In order to admit the imperceptible changing of species, and the modifications which their individuals undergo according as they are forced to change their habits and contract new ones, we are not reduced to a mere consideration of the very short spaces of time comprised in our observations; for, in addition to this induction, a number of facts collected many years ago throw enough light on the question to free it from doubt; and I can now affirm that our observations are so far advanced that the solution sought for is patent.

Indeed not only do we know the results of anomalous fertilisations, but we also now know positively that a compulsory and sustained alteration in the habitats and manner of life of animals works after a sufficient time a very remarkable mutation in the individuals exposed to it.

Consider the animal which normally lives in freedom in plains where it habitually exerts itself by swift running; or the bird which is compelled by its needs to pass incessantly through large spaces in the air. When they find themselves imprisoned, the one in the dens of a menagerie or in our stables, the other in our cages or back yards, they undergo in course of time striking alterations, especially after a succession of generations in their new state.

The former loses a great part of his swiftness and agility; his body thickens, the strength and subtleness of his limbs diminish, and his faculties are no longer the same; the latter becomes heavy, can scarcely fly, and takes on more flesh in all his parts.

In Chapter VI. of this Part I., I shall have occasion to prove by well-known facts the power of changes of conditions for giving to animals new needs, and leading them on to new actions; the power of new actions when repeated to induce new habits and in-clinations; finally, the power resulting from the more or less frequent use of any organ to modify that organ either by strengthening, developing and increasing it, or by weakening, reducing, attenuat-ing it, and even making it disappear.

With regard to plants, the same thing may be seen as a result of new conditions on their manner of life and the state of their parts; so that we shall no longer be astonished to see the considerable changes that we have brought about in those that we have long cultivated.

Thus, among living bodies, nature, as I have al-ready said, definitely contains nothing but indi-viduals which succeed one another by reproduc-tion and spring from one another; but the species among them have only a relative constancy and are only invariable temporarily.

Nevertheless, to facilitate the study and knowl-edge of so many different bodies it is useful to give the name of species to any collection of like individ-uals perpetuated by reproduction without change, so long as their environment does not alter enough to cause variations in their habits, character and shape.

OF THE SPECIES ALLEGED TO BE LOST

I am still doubtful whether the means adopted by nature to ensure the preservation of species or races have been so inadequate that entire races are now extinct or lost.

Yet the fossil remains that we find buried in the soil in so many different places show us the remains of a multitude of different animals which have ex-isted, and among which are found only a very small number of which we now know any living ana-logues exactly alike.

Does this fact really furnish any grounds for in-ferring that the species which we find in the fossil state, and of which no living individual completely similar is known to us, no longer exist in nature? There are many parts of the earth's surface to which we have never penetrated, many others that men capable of observing have merely passed through, and many others again, like the various parts of the sea-bottom, in which we have few means of discov-ering the animals living there. The species that we do not know might well remain hidden in these various places.

If there really are lost species, it can doubtless only be among the large animals which live on the dry parts of the earth; where man exercises absolute sway, and has compassed the destruction of all the individuals of some species which he has not wished to preserve or domesticate. Hence arises the possibility that animals of the genera *Palaeotherium*,

Anoplotherium, Megalonix, Megatherium, Mastodon, of M. Cuvier, and some other species of genera previ-ously known, are no longer extant in nature: this however is nothing more than a possibility.

But animals living in the waters, especially the sea waters, and in addition all the races of small sizes living on the surface of the earth and breath-ing air, are protected from the destruction of their species by man. Their multiplication is so rapid and their means of evading pursuit or traps are so great, that there is no likelihood of his being able to de-stroy the entire species of any of these animals.

It is then only the large terrestrial animals that are liable to extermination by man. This extermina-tion may actually have occurred; but its existence is not yet completely proved.

Nevertheless, among the fossil remains found of animals which existed in the past, there are a very large number belonging to animals of which no liv-ing and exactly similar analogue is known; and among these the majority belong to molluscs with shells, since it is only the shells of these animals which remain to us.

Now, if a quantity of these fossil shells exhibit differences which prevent us, in accordance with prevailing opinion, from regarding them as the rep-resentatives of similar species that we know, does it necessarily follow that these shells belong to species actually lost? Why, moreover, should they be lost, since man cannot have compassed their destruc-tion? May it not be possible on the other hand, that the fossils in question belonged to species still exist-ing, but which have changed since that time and become converted into the similar species that we not actually find. The following consideration, and our observations throughout this work, will give much probability to such an assumption.

Every qualified observer knows that nothing on the surface of the earth remains permanently in the same state. Everything in time undergoes various mutations, more or less rapid according to the na-ture of the objects and the conditions; elevated ground is constantly being denuded by the com-bined action of the sun, rain-waters and yet other causes; everything detached from it is carried to lower ground; the beds of streams, of rivers, even of seas change in shape and depth, and shift imper-ceptibly; in short, everything on the surface of the earth changes its situation, shape, nature and ap-pearance, and even climates are not more stable.

Now I shall endeavour to show that variations in the environment induce changes in the needs, habits and mode of life of living beings, and espe-cially of animals; that these changes give rise to modifications or developments in their organs and the shape of their parts. If this is so, it is difficult to deny that the shape or external characters of every living body whatever must vary imperceptibly, although that variation only becomes perceptible after a considerable time.

Let us then no longer be astonished that among the numerous fossils found in all the dry parts of the world, and constituting the remains of so many animals which formerly existed, there are so few of which we recognise the living representatives.

What we should wonder at, on the contrary, is finding amongst these numerous fossil remains of once living bodies, any of which the still existing analogues are known to us. This fact, proved by our collections of fossils, suggests that the fossil remains of animals whose living analogues we know are the least ancient fossils. The species to which each of them belongs doubtless has not had time to undergo variation.

Naturalists who did not perceive the changes undergone by most animals in course of time tried to explain the facts connected with fossils, as well as the commotions known to have occurred in different parts of the earth's surface, by the supposition of a universal catastrophe which took place on our globe. They imagined that everything had been displaced by it, and that a great number of the species then existing had been destroyed.

Unfortunately this facile method of explaining the operations of nature, when we cannot see their causes, has no basis beyond the imagination which created it, and cannot be supported by proof.

Local catastrophes, it is true, such as those produced by earthquakes, volcanoes and other special causes are well known, and we can observe the disorder ensuing from them.

But why are we to assume without proof a universal catastrophe, when the better known procedure of nature suffices to account for all the facts which we can observe?

Consider on the one hand that in all nature's works nothing is done abruptly, but that she acts everywhere slowly and by successive stages; and on the other hand that the special or local causes of disorders, commotions, displacements, etc., can account for everything that we observe on the surface of the earth, while still remaining subject to nature's laws and general procedure. It will then be recognised that there is no necessity whatever to imagine that a universal catastrophe came to overthrow everything, and destroy a great part of nature's own works.

I have said enough on a subject which presents no difficulty. Let us now consider the general principles and essential characters of animals.

Name: _____ **Date:** _____

1. How, according to Lamarck, did the increasingly large museum collections encourage him to think differently about species?

2. In what activities do organisms engage that influence their physical selves?

3. Lamarck lists and describes six statements that will allow him to explore the question of whether or not the idea of species has any real foundation. Describe these six statements in your own terms.

    1.

    2.

    3.

4.

5.

6.

4. Why, according to Lamarck, might one mistakenly believe that species are stable entities?

5. How does Lamarck use fossil evidence to support his claim?

George Cuvier

Essay on the Theory of the Earth, 1813

Cuvier (1769-1832) was a French zoologist who studied anatomy and physiology in Germany and developed a system of comparative anatomy, which allowed anatomists to contrast and classify organisms based on their similarities and differences. With his system of comparative anatomy, Cuvier could infer a great deal of information about organisms' structure and habits based only on a few skeletal remains. In this selection from his *Essay on the Theory of the Earth,* Cuvier discussed the significance of the fossil remains of large organisms and argued that some species must have gone extinct, a relatively radical idea for his time. Despite his promotion of the idea of extinction, Cuvier was not an evolutionist. Just the opposite; Cuvier believed that extinction was proof that organisms could not evolve.

HIGH IMPORTANCE OF INVESTIGATING THE FOSSIL REMAINS OF QUADRUPEDS

It is obvious that the fossil remains of the bones of quadrupeds must lead to more rigorous conclusions than any other remains of organized bodies, and that for several reasons.

In the first place, they indicate much more clearly the nature of the revolutions to which they have been subjected. The remains of shells certainly indicate that the sea has once existed in the places where these collections have been formed: But the changes which have taken place in their species, when rigorously enquired into, may possibly have been occasioned by slight changes in the nature of the fluid in which they were formed, or only in its temperature, and may even have arisen from other accidental causes. We can never be perfectly assured that certain species, and even genera, inhabiting the bottom of the sea, and occupying certain fixed spaces for a longer or shorter time, may not have been driven away from these by other species or genera.

In regard to quadrupeds, on the contrary, every thing is precise. The appearance of their bones in strata, and still more of their entire car-cases, clearly establishes that the bed in which they are found must have been previously laid dry, or at least that

dry land must have existed in its immediate neighbourhood. Their disappearance as certainly announces that this stratum must have been inundated, or that the dry land had ceased to exist in that state. It is from them, therefore, that we learn with perfect certainty the important fact of the repeated irruptions of the sea upon the land, which the extraneous fossils and other productions of marine origin could not of themselves have proved; and, by a careful investigation of them, we may hope to ascertain the number and the epochs of those irruptions of the sea.

Secondly, the nature of the revolutions which have changed the surface of our earth, must have exerted a more powerful action upon terrestrial quadrupeds than upon marine animals. As these revolutions have consisted chiefly in changes of the bed of the sea, and as the waters must have destroyed all the quadrupeds which they reached, if their irruption over the land was general, they must have destroyed the entire class, or, if confined only to certain continents at one time, they must have destroyed at least all the species inhabiting these continents, without having the same effect upon the marine animals. On the other hand, millions of aquatic animals may have been left quite dry, or buried in newly-formed strata, or thrown violently on the coasts, while their races may have been still preserved in more peaceful parts of the sea, whence they might again propagate and spread after the agitation of the water had ceased.

From *Essay on the Theory of the Earth,* Edinburgh: William Blackwood, 1813.

Thirdly, this more complete action is also more easily ascertained and demonstrated; because, as the number of terrestrial quadrupeds is limited, and as most of their species, at least the large ones, are well known, we can more easily determine whether fossil bones belong to a species which still exists, or to one that is now lost. As, on the other hand, we are still very far from being acquainted with all the testaceous animals and fishes belonging to the sea, and as we probably still remain ignorant of the greater part of those which live in the extensive deeps of the ocean, it is impossible to know, with any certainty, whether a species found in a fossil state may not still exist somewhere alive. Hence some naturalists persist in giving the name of oceanic or pelagic shells to *belemnites* and *cornua-ammonis,* and some other genera, which have not hitherto been found, except in the fossil state, in ancient strata; meaning by this, that although these have not as yet been found in a living or recent state, it is because they inhabit the bottom of the ocean, far beyond the reach of our nets.

OF THE SMALL PROBABILITY OF DISCOVERING NEW SPECIES OF THE LARGER QUADRUPEDS

Naturalists certainly have neither explored all the continents, nor do they as yet know even all the quadrupeds of those parts which have been explored. New species of this class are discovered from time to time; and those who have not examined with attention all the circumstances belonging to these discoveries, may allege also that the unknown quadrupeds, whose fossil bones have been found in the strata of the earth, have hitherto remained concealed in some islands not yet discovered by navigators, or in some of the vast deserts which occupy the middle of Africa, Asia, the two Americas, and New Holland. But, if we carefully attend to the kinds of quadrupeds that have been recently discovered, and to the circumstances of their discovery, we shall easily perceive that there is very little chance indeed of our ever finding alive those which have only been seen in a fossil state.

Islands of moderate size, and at a considerable distance from the large continents, have very few quadrupeds, and these mostly very small. When they contain any of the larger quadrupeds, these must have been carried to them from other countries. Cook and Bougainville found no other quadrupeds besides hogs and dogs in the South Sea islands; and the largest quadruped of the West India islands, when first discovered, was the *agouti,* a species of the *cavy,* an animal apparently between the rat and the rabbit.

It is true that the great continents, as Asia, Africa, the two Americas, and New Holland, have large quadrupeds, and, generally speaking, contain species proper to each: Insomuch, that, upon discovering countries which are isolated from the rest of the world, the animals they contain of the class of quadrupeds were found entirely different from those which existed in other countries. Thus, when the Spaniards first penetrated into South America, they did not find it to contain a single quadruped exactly the same with those of Europe, Asia, and Africa. The puma, the jaguar, the tapir, the capybara, the lama, or glama, the vicugna, and the whole tribe of sapajous, were to them entirely new animals, of which they had not the smallest idea.

Similar circumstances have recurred in our own time, when the coasts of New Holland and the adjacent islands were first examined. The species of the kangaroo, *phascoloma, dasyurus, peramela, phalanger,* or flying opposum, with the hairy and spinous duck-billed animals denominated *ornithorinchus* and *echidna,*[1] have astonished zoologists by presenting new and strange conformations, contrary to all former rules, and incapable of being reduced under any of the former systems.

If there still remained any great continent to be discovered, we might perhaps expect to be made acquainted with new species of large quadrupeds; among which some might be found more or less similar to those of which we find the exuviæ in the bowels of the earth. But it is merely sufficient to glance the eye over the map of the world, and observe the innumerable directions in which navigators have traversed the ocean, in order to be satisfied that there does not remain any large land to be discovered, unless it may be situated towards the antarctic pole, where eternal ice necessarily forbids the existence of animal life.

Hence, it is only from the interiors of the large divisions of the world already known, that we can now hope to procure any quadrupeds hitherto unknown. But a very little reflection will be sufficient to convince us that our hopes from thence are not much better founded than from the largest islands.

Doubtless, European travellers cannot easily penetrate through vast extents of countries which are either uninhabited, or peopled only with ferocious tribes; and this is peculiarly the case in regard to Africa. But there is nothing to prevent the animals

---

[1]These are new animals of Australia or New Holland, only recently discovered, whose strange conformations, not analogous with the animals of the old world, or of America, have required the adoption of new generic terms by Cuvier and other naturalists.—*Transl.*

themselves from roaming in all directions, and penetrating to the coasts. Even although great chains of mountains may intervene between the coasts and the interior deserts, these must certainly be broken in some parts, to allow the rivers to pass through; and in these burning deserts the animals naturally follow the courses of the rivers. The inhabitants of the coasts must also frequently penetrate inland along the rivers, and will quickly acquire a knowledge of all the remarkable living creatures, even to the very sources of these rivers, either from personal observation, or by intercourse with the inhabitants of the interior. At no period of our history, therefore, could civilised nations frequent the coasts of large countries for any length of time, without gaining some tolerable knowledge of all the animals they contained, or at least of such as were any way remarkable for their size or configuration. This reasoning is supported by well-known facts. Thus, although the ancients seem never to have passed the mountains of Imaus, or to have crossed the Ganges towards the east of Asia, and never penetrated far to the south of Mount Atlas in Africa, yet they were acquainted with all the larger animals of these two grand divisions of the world; and if they have not distinguished all their species, it was because the similarities of some of these occasioned them to be confounded together, and not because they had not seen them, or heard them talked of by others.

The ancients were perfectly acquainted with the elephant, and the history of that quadruped is given more exactly by Aristotle than by Bufon. They were not ignorant even of the differences which distinguish the elephants of Africa from those of Asia.

They knew the two-horned rhinoceros, which Domitian exhibited in his shews at Rome, and had stamped on his medals, and of which Pausanias has left a very good description. Even the one-horned rhinoceros, although its country be far from Rome, was equally known to the Romans; Pompey shewed them one in the circus, and Strabo has described another which he saw at Alexandria.

The hippopotamus has not been so well described by the ancients as the two foregoing animals; yet very exact representations of it have been left by the Romans, in their monuments relative to Egypt, such as the statue of the Nile, the Prenestine pavement, and a great number of medals. It is known that this animal was frequently shown to the Romans, having been exhibited in the circus by Scaurus, Augustus, Antoninus, Commodus, Heliogabalus, Philip, and Carinus.

The two species of camel, the Bactrian and Arabian, were both well known to the ancients, and are very well described and characterised by Aristotle.

The Giraffe, or camelopardalis, was likewise known to the ancients, one having been shewn alive in the circus during the dictatorship of Julius Cæsar, in the year of Rome 708. Ten of them were shewn at once by Gordian III. all of which were slain at the secular games of the emperor Philip.

When we read with attention the descriptions given of the hippopotamus by Herodotus and Aristotle, which are supposed to have been borrowed from Hecatæus of Miletus, we cannot fail to perceive that these must have been taken from two very different animals; one of which is the true hippopotamus, and the other the gnou, or *antilope gnu* of Gmelin's edition of the Systema Naturæ.

The *aper æthiopicus* of Agatharcides, which he describes as having horns, is precisely the Ethiopian hog or *engallo* of Buffon and other modern naturalists, whose enormous tusks deserve the name of horns, almost as much as those of the elephant.

The *bubalus* and the *nagor* are described by Pliny; the *gazella* by Elian; the *oryx* by Oppiann; and the *axis,* so early as the time of Ctesias: all of them species of the antilope genus.

Elian gives a very good description of the *bos grunniens,* or grunting ox, under the name of the ox having a tail which serves for a fly-flapper.

The buffalo was not domesticated by the ancients; but the *bos Indicus,* or Indian ox of Elian, having horns sufficiently large to contain three amphoræ, was assuredly that variety of the buffalo which is now called the *arnee.*

The ancients were acquainted with hornless oxen, and with that African variety of the ox whose horns are only fastened to the skin, and hang down dangling at the sides of the head. They also knew those oxen of India which could run as swift as horses, and those which are so small as not to exceed the size of a he-goat. Sheep also with broad tails were not unknown to them, and those other Indian sheep which were as large as asses.

Although the accounts left us by the ancients respecting the *urus,* or *aurochs,* the rein-deer, and the elk, are all mingled with fable, they are yet sufficient to prove that these animals were not unknown to them, but that the reports which had reached them had been communicated by ignorant or barbarous people, and had not been corrected by the actual observations of men of learning.

Even the white bear had been seen in Egypt while under the Ptolemies.*

Lions and panthers were quite common at Rome, where they were presented by hundreds in the games of the circus. Even tygers had been seen there, together with the striped hyena, and the nilotic

---

*Athenaeis, lib. V.

crocodile. There are still preserved in Rome some ancient mosaic, or tesselated pavements, containing excellent delineations of the rarest of these animals; among which a striped hyena is very perfectly represented in a fragment of mosaic, in the Vatican museum. While I was at Rome, a tesselated pavement, composed of natural stones, arranged in the Florentine manner, was discovered in a garden beside the triumphal arch of Galienus, which represented four Bengal tygers in a most admirable manner.

The museum of the Vatican has the figure of a crocodile in basalt, almost perfectly represented, except that it has one claw too many on the hind feet. Augustus at one time presented thirty-six of these animals to the view of the people.*

It is hardly to be doubted that the *hippotigris* was the zebra, which is now only found in the southern parts of Africa.† Caracalla killed one of these in the circus.

It might easily be shewn also that almost all the most remarkable species of the *simiæ* of the old world have been distinctly indicated by ancient writers, under the names of *pitheci, sphinges, satyri, cephi, cynocephali,* or *cercopitheci.*‡

They also knew and have described several very small species of *gnawers*,§ especially such of that order as possessed any peculiar conformation or remarkable quality; as we find, for instance, the *jerboa* represented upon the medals of Cyrene, and indicated under the name of *mus bipes,* or two-legged rat. But the smaller species are not of much importance in regard to the object before us, and it is quite sufficient for the enquiry in which we are engaged, to have shewn that all the larger species of

quadrupeds, which possess any peculiar or remarkable character, and which we know to inhabit Europe, Asia, and Africa at the present day, were known to the ancients; whence we may fairly conclude, that their silence in respect to the small quadrupeds, and their neglect in distinguishing the species which very nearly resemble each other, as the various species of antelopes and of some other genera, was occasioned by want of attention and ignorance of methodical arrangement, and not by any difficulties proceeding from the climates or distance of the places which these animals inhabited. We may also conclude with equal certainty, that as eighteen or twenty centuries at the least, with the advantages of circumnavigating Africa, and of penetrating into all the most distant regions of India, have added nothing in this portion of natural history to the information left us by the ancients, it is not at all probable that succeeding ages will add much to the knowledge of our posterity.

Perhaps some persons may be disposed to employ an opposite train of argument, and to allege that the ancients were not only acquainted with as many large quadrupeds as we are, as has been already shewn, but that they actually described several others which we do not now know; that we are rash in considering the accounts of all such animals as fabulous; that we ought to search for them with the utmost care, before concluding that we have acquired a complete knowledge of the existing animal creation; and, in fine, that among these animals which we presume to be fabulous, we may perhaps discover, when better acquainted with them, the actual originals of the bones of those species which are now unknown. Perhaps some may even conceive that the various monsters, essential ornaments of the history of the heroic ages of almost every nation, are precisely those very species which it was necessary to destroy, in order to allow the establishment of civilized societies. Thus Theseus and Bellerophon must have been more fortunate than all the nations of more modern days, who have only been able to drive back the noxious animals into the deserts and ill-peopled regions, but have never yet succeeded in exterminating a single species.

---

*Dion. lib. LV.

†Id. LXXVII. Compare also Gisb. Cuperi de Eleph. in nummis obviis. ex. II. cap. 7.

‡See Lichtenstein, Comment. de Simiarum quotquot veteribus innotuerunt formis. *Hamburg,* 1791.

§Cuvier gives this name, *rongeurs,* here translated *gnawers,* to the order denominated glires by Linnæus, owing to their fore-teeth being peculiarly fitted for gnawing the roots, barks, and stems of vegetables.—*Transl.*

Name: _____ **Date:** _____

1. What does Cuvier mean when he uses the term "revolutions?"

2. What is a quadruped?

3. Cuvier argues that there is a very small probability of researchers discovering new species of large quadrupeds. Describe in your own terms three reasons in support of this claim:

1.

2.

3.

Charles Lyell

Principles of Geology, 1830–1833

Lyell (1797-1875) was trained and worked as a lawyer before devoting himself to the emerging science of geology. A Scotsman, Lyell traveled extensively around Europe and collected what he believed was evidence that the Earth had undergone and continued to undergo slow, constant change through erosion and uplift. Between 1830 and 1833 he published *Principles of Geology,* which laid the foundation for modern geology by describing how researchers could, using his notion of slow, continual change, study the inorganic world and extrapolate what it was like in the past. While he believed that the inorganic world changed over time, he did not believe in organic evolution. In this selection, Lyell recounted Lamarck's theory of the inheritance of acquired characteristics and dismissed it as too problematic to possibly be true. In later years, Lyell was a close friend of Charles Darwin and one of the first people to whom Darwin described his theory. Lyell, like so many other prominent nineteenth-century scientists, came to believe that Darwin was right and accepted the notion that the organic work, like the organic world, underwent slow, continuous change over time.

CHANGES OF THE ORGANIC WORLD NOW IN PROGRESS

The last book, from chapters fourteen to thirty-three inclusive, was occupied with the consideration of the changes brought about on the earth's surface, within the period of human observation, by inorganic agents; such, for example, as rivers, marine currents, volcanoes, and earthquakes. But there is another class of phenomena relating to the organic world, which have an equal claim on our attention, if we desire to obtain possession of all the preparatory knowledge respecting the existing course of nature, which may be available in the interpretation of geological monuments. It appeared from our preliminary sketch of the progress of the science, that the most lively interest was excited among its earlier cultivators, by the discovery of the remains of animals and plants in the interior of mountains frequently remote from the sea. Much controversy arose respecting the nature of these remains, the

From *Principles of Geology: The Modern Changes of the Earth and Its Inhabitants Considered as Illustrative of Geology,* New York: D. Appleton & Company, 1857.

causes which may have brought them into so singular a position, and the want of a specific agreement between them and known animals and plants. To qualify ourselves to form just views on these curious questions, we must first study the present condition of the animate creation on the globe.

This branch of our inquiry naturally divides itself into two parts: first, we may examine the vicissitudes to which species are subject; secondly, the processes by which certain individuals of these species occasionally become fossil. The first of these divisions will lead us, among other topics, to inquire, first, whether species have a real and permanent existence in nature? or whether they are capable, as some naturalists pretend, of being indefinitely modified in the course of a long series of generations? Secondly, whether, if species have a real existence, the individuals composing them have been derived originally from many similar stocks, or each from one only, the descendants of which have spread themselves gradually from a particular point over the habitable lands and waters? Thirdly, how far the duration of each species of animal and plant is limited by its dependence on certain fluctuating and temporary conditions in the state of the animate and inanimate world? Fourthly, whether there be proofs of the successive extermination of species in the ordinary course of nature, and whether there be any reason for conjecturing that new animals and plants are created from time to time, to supply their place?

WHETHER SPECIES HAVE A REAL EXISTENCE IN NATURE

Before we can advance a step in our proposed inquiry, we must be able to define precisely the meaning which we attach to the term species. This is even more necessary in geology than in the ordinary studies of the naturalist; for they who deny that such a thing as a species exists, concede nevertheless that a botanist or zoologist may reason as if the specific character were constant, because they confine their observations to a brief period of time. Just as the geographer, in constructing his maps from century to century, may proceed as if the apparent places of the fixed stars remained absolutely the same, and as if no alteration were brought about by the precession of the equinoxes; so, it is said, in the organic world, the stability of a species may be taken as absolute, if we do not extend our views beyond the narrow period of human history; but let a sufficient number of centuries elapse, to allow of important revolutions in climate, physical geography, and other circumstances, and the characters, say they, of the descendants of common parents may deviate indefinitely from their original type.

Now, if these doctrines be tenable, we are at once presented with a principle of incessant change in the organic world; and no degree of dissimilarity in the plants and animals which may formerly have existed, and are found fossil, would entitle us to conclude that they may not have been the prototypes and progenitors of the species now living. Accordingly M. Geoffroy St. Hilaire has declared his opinion, that there has been an uninterrupted succession in the animal kingdom, effected by means of generation, from the earliest ages of the world up to the present day, and that the ancient animals whose remains have been preserved in the strata, however different, may nevertheless have been the ancestors of those now in being. This notion is not very generally received, but we are not warranted in assuming the contrary, without fully explaining the data and reasoning by which it may be refuted.

I shall begin by stating as concisely as possible all the facts and ingenious arguments by which the theory has been supported; and for this purpose I cannot do better than offer the reader a rapid sketch of Lamarck's statement of the proofs which he regards as confirmatory of the doctrine, and which he has derived partly from the works of his predecessors and in part from original investigations.

His proofs and inferences will be best considered in the order in which they appear to have influenced his mind, and I shall then point out some of the results to which he was led while boldly following out his principles to their legitimate consequences.

LAMARCK'S ARGUMENTS IN FAVOR OF THE TRANSMUTATION OF SPECIES

The name of species, observes Lamarck, has been usually applied to "every collection of similar individuals produced by other individuals like themselves." This definition, he admits, is correct; because every living individual bears a very close resemblance to those from which it springs. But this is not all which is usually implied by the term species; for the majority of naturalists agree with Linnæus in supposing that all the individuals propagated from one stock have certain distinguishing characters in common, which will never vary, and which have remained the same since the creation of each species.

In order to shake this opinion, Lamarck enters upon the following line of argument:—The more we advance in the knowledge of the different organized bodies which cover the surface of the globe, the more our embarrassment increases, to determine what ought to be regarded as a species, and still more how to limit and distinguish genera. In proportion as our collections are enriched, we see almost every void filled up, and all our lines of separation effaced! we are reduced to arbitrary determinations, and are sometimes fain to seize upon the slight differences of mere varieties, in order to form characters for what we choose to call a species; and sometimes we are induced to pronounce individuals but slightly differing, and which others regard as true species, to be varieties.

The greater the abundance of natural objects assembled together, the more do we discover proofs that every thing passes by insensible shades into something else; that even the more remarkable differences are evanescent, and that nature has, for the most part, left us nothing at our disposal for establishing distinctions, save trifling, and, in some respects, puerile particularities.

We find that many genera amongst animals and plants are of such an extent, in consequence of the number of species referred to them, that the study and determination of these last has become almost impracticable. When the species are arranged in a series, and placed near to each other, with due regard to their natural affinities, they each differ in so minute a degree from those next adjoining, that they almost melt into each other, and are in a manner confounded together. If we see isolated species, we may presume the absence of some more closely connected, and which have not yet been discovered. Already are there genera, and even entire orders—nay, whole classes, which present an approximation to the state of things here indicated.

If, when species have been thus placed in a regular series, we select one, and then, making a leap over several intermediate ones, we take a second, at some distance from the first, these two will, on comparison, be seen to be very dissimilar; and it is in this manner that every naturalist begins to study the objects which are at his own door. He then finds it an easy task to establish generic and specific distinctions; and it is only when his experience is enlarged, and when he has made himself master of the intermediate links, that his difficulties and ambiguities begin. But while we are thus compelled to resort to trifling and minute characters in our attempt to separate the species, we find a striking disparity between individuals which we know to have descended from a common stock; and these newly acquired peculiarities are regularly transmitted from one generation to another, constituting what are called *races*.

From a great number of facts, continues the author, we learn that in proportion as the individuals of one of our species change their situation, climate, and manner of living, they change also, by little and little, the consistence and proportions of their parts, their form, their faculties, and even their organization, in such a manner that every thing in them comes at last to participate in the mutations to which they have been exposed. Even in the same climate, a great difference of situation and exposure causes individuals to vary; but if these individuals continue to live and to be reproduced under the same difference of circumstances, distinctions are brought about in them which become in some degree essential to their existence. In a word, at the end of many successive generations, these individuals, which originally belonged to another species, are transformed into a new and distinct species.

Thus, for example, if the seeds of a grass, or any other plant which grows naturally in a moist meadow, be accidentally transported, first to the slope of some neighboring hill, where the soil, although at a greater elevation, is damp enough to allow the plant to live; and if, after having lived there, and having been several times regenerated, it reaches by degrees the drier and almost arid soil of a mountain declivity, it will then, if it succeeds in growing, and perpetuates itself for a series of generations, be so changed that botanists who meet with it will regard it as a particular species. The unfavorable climate in this case, deficiency of nourishment, exposure to the winds, and other causes, give rise to a stunted and dwarfish race, with some organ more developed than others, and having proportions often quite peculiar.

What nature brings about in a great lapse of time, we occasion suddenly by changing the circumstances in which a species has been accustomed to live. All are aware that vegetables taken from their birthplace, and cultivated in gardens, undergo changes which render them no longer recognizable as the same plants. Many which were naturally hairy become smooth, or nearly so; a great number of such as were creepers and trailed along the ground, rear their stalks and grow erect. Others lose their thorns or asperities; others, again, from the ligneous state which their stem possessed in hot climates, where they were indigenous, pass to the herbaceous; and, among them, some which were perennials become mere annuals. So well do botanists know the effects of such changes of circumstances, that they are averse to describe species from garden specimens, unless they are sure that they have been cultivated for a very short period.

"Is not the cultivated wheat" (*Triticum sativum*), asks Lamarck, "a vegetable brought by man into the state in which we now see it? Let any one tell me in what country a similar plant grows wild, unless where it has escaped from cultivated fields? Where do we find in nature our cabbages, lettuces, and other culinary vegetables, in the state in which they appear in our gardens? Is it not the same in regard to a great quantity of animals which domesticity has changed or considerably modified?" Our domestic fowls and pigeons are unlike any wild birds. Our domestic ducks and geese have lost the faculty of raising themselves into the higher regions of the air, and crossing extensive countries in their flight, like the wild ducks and wild geese from which they were originally derived. A bird which we breed in a cage cannot, when restored to liberty, fly like others of the same species which have been always free. This small alteration of circumstances, however, has only diminished the power of flight, without modifying the form of any part of the wings. But when individuals of the same race are retained in captivity during a considerable length of time, the form even of their parts is gradually made to differ, especially if climate, nourishment, and other circumstances be also altered.

The numerous races of dogs which we have produced by domesticity are nowhere to be found in a wild state. In nature we should seek in vain for mastiffs, harriers, spaniels, greyhounds, and other races, between which the differences are sometimes so great that they would be readily admitted as specific between wild animals; "yet all these have sprung originally from a single race, at first approaching very near to a wolf, if, indeed, the wolf be not the true type which at some period or other was domesticated by man."

Although important changes in the nature of the places which they inhabit modify the organization of animals as well as vegetables; yet the former, says Lamarck, require more time to complete a considerable degree of transmutation; and, consequently, we are less sensible of such occurrences. Next, to a diversity of the medium in which animals or plants may live, the circumstances which have most influence in modifying their organs are differences in exposure, climate, the nature of the soil, and other local particulars. These circumstances are as varied as are the characters of the species, and, like them, pass by insensible shades into each other, there being every intermediate gradation between the opposite extremes. But each locality remains for a very long time the same, and is altered so slowly that we can only become conscious of the reality of the change by consulting geological monuments, by which we learn that the order of things which now reigns in each place has not always prevailed, and by inference anticipate that it will not always continue the same.

Every considerable alteration in the local circumstances in which each race of animals exists causes a change in their wants, and these new wants excite them to new actions and habits. These actions require the more frequent employment of some parts before but slightly exercised, and then greater development follows as a consequence of their more frequent use. Other organs no longer in use are impoverished and diminished in size, nay, are sometimes entirely annihilated, while in their place new parts are insensibly produced for the discharge of new functions.

I must here interrupt the author's argument, by observing, that no positive fact is cited to exemplify the substitution of some *entirely new* sense, faculty, or organ, in the room of some other suppressed as useless. All the instances adduced go only to prove that the dimensions and strength of members and the perfection of certain attributes may, in a long succession of generations, be lessened and enfeebled by disuse; or, on the contrary, be matured and augmented by active exertion; just as we know that the power of scent is feeble in the greyhound, while its swiftness of pace and its acuteness of sight are remarkable—that the harrier and stag-hound, on

the contrary, are comparatively slow in their movements, but excel in the sense of smelling.

It was necessary to point out to the reader this important chasm in the chain of evidence, because he might otherwise imagine that I had merely omitted the illustrations for the sake of brevity; but the plain truth is, that there were no examples to be found; and when Lamarck talks "of the efforts of internal sentiment," "the influence of subtle fluids," and "acts of organization," as causes whereby animals and plants may acquire *new organs,* he substitutes names for things; and, with a disregard to the strict rules of induction, resorts to fictions, as ideal as the "plastic virtue," and other phantoms of the geologists of the middle ages.

It is evident that, if some well-authenticated facts could have been adduced to establish one complete step in the process of transformation, such as the appearance, in individuals descending from a common stock, of a sense or organ entirely new, and a complete disappearance of some other enjoyed by their progenitors, time alone might then be supposed sufficient to bring about any amount of metamorphosis. The gratuitous assumption, therefore, of a point so vital to the theory of transmutation, was unpardonable on the part of its advocate.

But to proceed with the system: it being assumed as an undoubted fact, that a change of external circumstances may cause one organ to become entirely obsolete, and a new one to be developed, such as never before belonged to the species, the following proposition is announced, which, however staggering and absurd it may seem, is logically deduced from the assumed premises. It is not the organs, or, in other words, the nature and form of the parts of the body of an animal, which have given rise to its habits, and its particular faculties; but, on the contrary, its habits, its manner of living, and those of its progenitors, have in the course of time determined the form of its body, the number and condition of its organs—in short, the faculties which it enjoys. Thus otters, beavers, waterfowl, turtles, and frogs, were not made web-footed in order that they might swim; but their wants having attracted them to the water in search of prey, they stretched out the toes of their feet to strike the water and move rapidly along its surface. By the repeated stretching of their toes, the skin which united them at the base acquired a habit of extension, until, in the course of time, the broad membranes which now connect their extremities were formed.

In like manner, the antelope and the gazelle were not endowed with light agile forms, in order that they might escape by flight from carnivorous animals; but, having been exposed to the danger of being devoured by lions, tigers, and other beasts of prey, they were compelled to exert themselves in running with great celerity; a habit which, in the course of many generations, gave rise to the peculiar slenderness of their legs, and the agility and elegance of their forms.

The camelopard was not gifted with a long flexible neck because it was destined to live in the interior of Africa, where the soil was arid and devoid of herbage; but, being reduced by the nature of that country to support itself on the foliage of lofty trees, it contracted a habit of stretching itself up to reach the high boughs, until its neck became so elongated that it could raise its head to the height of twenty feet above the ground.

Another line of argument is then entered upon, in farther corroboration of the instability of species. In order, it is said, that individuals should perpetuate themselves unaltered by generation, those belonging to one species ought never to ally themselves to those of another; but such sexual unions do take place, both among plants and animals; and although the offspring of such irregular connections are usually sterile, yet such is not always the case. Hybrids have sometimes proved prolific, where the disparity between the species was not too great; and by this means alone, says Lamarck, varieties may gradually be created by near alliances, which would become races, and in the course of time would constitute what we term species.

But if the soundness of all these arguments and inferences be admitted, we are next to inquire, what were the original types of form, organization, and instinct, from which the diversities of character, as now exhibited by animals and plants, have been derived? We know that individuals which are mere varieties of the same species would, if their pedigree could be traced back far enough, terminate in a single stock; so, according to the train of reasoning before described, the species of a genus, and even the genera of a great family, must have had a common point of departure. What, then, was the single stem from which so many varieties of form have ramified? Were there many of these, or are we to refer the origin of the whole animate creation, as the Egyptian priests did that of the universe, to a single egg?

In the absence of any positive data for framing a theory on so obscure a subject, the following considerations were deemed of importance to guide conjecture.

In the first place, if we examine the whole series of known animals, from one extremity to the other, when they are arranged in the order of their natural relations, we find that we may pass progressively, or, at least, with very few interruptions, from beings of more simple to those of a more compound structure;

and, in proportion as the complexity of their organization increases, the number and dignity of their faculties increase also. Among plants, a similar approximation to a graduated scale of being is apparent. Secondly, it appears, from geological observations, that plants and animals of more simple organization existed on the globe before the appearance of those of more compound structure, and the latter were successively formed at more modern periods; each new race being more fully developed than the most perfect of the preceding era.

Of the truth of the last-mentioned geological theory, Lamarck seems to have been fully persuaded; and he also shows that he was deeply impressed with a belief prevalent amongst the older naturalists, that the primeval ocean invested the whole planet long after it became the habitation of living beings; and thus he was inclined to assert the priority of the types of marine animals to those of the terrestrial, so as to fancy, for example, that the testacea of the ocean existed first, until some of them, by gradual evolution, were *improved* into those inhabiting the land.

These speculative views had already been, in a great degree, anticipated by Demaillet in his Telliamed, and by several modern writers; so that the tables were completely turned on the philosophers of antiquity, with whom it was a received maxim, that created things were always most perfect when they came first from the hands of their Maker; and that there was a tendency to progressive deterioration in sublunary things when left to themselves—

——omnia fatis
In pejus ruere, ac retrò sublapsa referri.

So deeply was the faith of the ancient schools of philosophy imbued with this doctrine, that, to check this universal proneness to degeneracy, nothing less than the reintervention of the Deity was thought adequate; and it was held, that thereby the order, excellence, and pristine energy of the moral and physical world had been repeatedly restored.

But when the possibility of the indefinite modification of individuals descending from common parents was once assumed, as also the geological inference respecting the progressive development of organic life, it was natural that the ancient dogma should be rejected, or rather reversed, and that the most simple and imperfect forms and faculties should be conceived to have been the originals whence all others were developed. Accordingly, in conformity to these views, inert matter was supposed to have been first endowed with life; until, in the course of ages, sensation was superadded to mere vitality: sight, hearing, and the other senses were afterwards acquired; then instinct and the mental faculties; until, finally, by virtue of the tendency of things to *progressive improvement;* the irrational was developed in the rational.

The reader, however, will immediately perceive that when all the higher orders of plants and animals were thus supposed to be comparatively modern, and to have been derived in a long series of generations from those of more simple conformation, some farther hypothesis became indispensable, in order to explain why, after an indefinite lapse of ages, there were still so many beings of the simplest structure. Why have the majority of existing creatures remained stationary throughout this long succession of epochs, while others have made such prodigious advances? Why are there such multitudes of infusoria and polyps, or of confervæ and other cryptogamic plants? Why, moreover, has the process of development acted with such unequal and irregular force on those classes of beings which have been greatly perfected, so that there are wide chasms in the series; gaps so enormous, that Lamarck fairly admits we can never expect to fill them up by future discoveries?

The following hypothesis was provided to meet these objections. Nature, we are told, is not an intelligence, nor the Deity; but a delegated power—a mere instrument—a piece of mechanism acting by necessity—an order of things constituted by the Supreme Being, and subject to laws which are the expressions of his will. This Nature is *obliged* to proceed gradually in all her operations; she cannot produce animals and plants of all classes at once, but must always begin by the formation of the most simple kinds, and out of them elaborate the more compound, adding to them, successively, different systems of organs, and multiplying more and more their number and energy.

This nature is daily engaged in the formation of the elementary rudiments of animal and vegetable existence, which correspond to what the ancients termed *spontaneous generation.* She is always beginning anew, day by day, the work of creation, by forming monads, or "rough draughts" (ébauches), which are the only living things she gives birth to *directly.*

There are distinct primary rudiments of plants and animals, and *probably* of each of the great divisions of the animal and vegetable kingdoms. These are gradually developed into the higher and more perfect classes by the slow but unceasing agency of two influential principles: first, *the tendency to progressive advancement* in organization, accompanied by greater dignity in instinct, intelligence, &c.; secondly, *the force of external circumstances,* or of variations in the physical condition of the earth, or the

mutual relations of plants and animals. For, as species spread themselves gradually over the globe, they are exposed from time to time to variations in climate, and to changes in the quantity and quality of their food; they meet with new plants and animals which assist or retard their development, by supplying them with nutriment, or destroying their foes. The nature, also, of each locality, is in itself fluctuating; so that, even if the relation of other animals and plants were invariable, the habits and organization of species would be modified by the influence of local revolutions.

Now, if the first of these principles, *the tendency to progressive development,* were left to exert itself with perfect freedom, it would give rise, says Lamarck, in the course of ages, to a graduated scale of being, where the most insensible transition might be traced from the simplest to the most compound structure, from the humblest to the most exalted degree of intelligence. But, in consequence of the perpetual interference of the *external causes* before mentioned, this regular order is greatly interfered with, and an approximation only to such a state of things is exhibited by the animate creation, the progress of some races being retarded by unfavorable, and that of others accelerated by favorable, combinations of circumstances. Hence, all kinds of anomalies interrupt the continuity of the plan; and chasms, into which whole genera or families might be inserted, are seen to separate the nearest existing portions of the series.

LAMARCK'S THEORY OF THE TRANSFORMATION OF THE ORANG-OUTANG INTO THE HUMAN SPECIES

Such is the machinery of the Lamarckian system; but the reader will hardly, perhaps, be able to form a perfect conception of so complicated a piece of mechanism, unless it is exhibited in motion, so that we may see in what manner it can work out, under the author's guidance, all the extraordinary effects which we behold in the present state of the animate creation. I have only space for exhibiting a small part of the entire process by which a complete metamorphosis is achieved, and shall therefore omit the mode by which, after a countless succession of generations, a small gelatinous body is transformed into an oak or an ape; passing on at once to the last grand step in the progressive scheme, by which the orang-outang, having been already evolved out of a monad, is made slowly to attain the attributes and dignity of man.

One of the races of quadrumanous animals which had reached the highest state of perfection, lost, by constraint of circumstances (concerning the exact nature of which tradition is unfortunately silent), the habit of climbing trees, and of hanging on by grasping the boughs with their feet as with hands. The individuals of this race being obliged, for a long series of generations, to use their feet exclusively for walking, and ceasing to employ their hands as feet, were transformed into bimanous animals, and what before were thumbs became mere toes, no separation being required when their feet were used solely for walking. Having acquired a habit of holding themselves upright, their legs and feet assumed, insensibly, a conformation fitted to support them in an erect attitude, till at last these animals could no longer go on all-fours without much inconvenience.

The Angola orang (*Simia troglodytes*, Linn.) is the most perfect of animals; much more so than the Indian orang *(Simia Satyrus)*, which has been called the orang-outang, although *both* are *very inferior* to man in corporeal powers and intelligence. These animals frequently hold themselves upright; but their organization has *not yet* been sufficiently modified to sustain them habitually in this attitude, so that the standing posture is very uneasy to them. When the Indian orang is compelled to take flight from pressing danger, he immediately falls down upon all-fours, showing clearly that this was the original position of the animal. Even in man, whose organization, in the course of a long series of generations, has advanced so much farther, the upright posture is fatiguing, and can be supported only for a limited time, and by aid of the contraction of many muscles. If the vertebral column formed the axis of the human body, and supported the head and all the other parts in equilibrium, then might the upright position be a state of repose: but, as the human head does not articulate in the centre of gravity, as the chest, belly, and other parts press almost entirely forward with their whole weight, and as the vertebral column reposes upon an oblique base, a watchful activity is required to prevent the body from falling. Children who have large heads and prominent bellies can hardly walk at the end even of two years; and their frequent tumbles indicate the natural tendency in man to resume the quadrupedal state.

Now, when so much progress had been made by the quadrumanous animals before mentioned, that they could hold themselves habitually in an erect attitude, and were accustomed to a wide range of vision, and ceased to use their jaws for fighting and tearing, or for clipping herbs for food, their snout became gradually shorter, their incisor teeth became vertical, and the facial angle grew more open.

Among other ideas which the natural *tendency to perfection* engendered, the desire of ruling suggested itself, and this race succeeded at length in getting the better of the other animals, and made themselves masters of all those spots on the surface of the globe which best suited them. They drove out the animals which approached nearest them in organization and intelligence, and which were in a condition to dispute with them the good things of this world, forcing them to take refuge in deserts, woods, and wildernesses, where their multiplication was checked, and the progressive development of their faculties retarded; while, in the mean time, the dominant race spread itself in every direction, and lived in large companies, where new wants were successively created, exciting them to industry, and gradually perfecting their means and faculties.

In the supremacy and increased intelligence acquired by the ruling race, we see an illustration of the natural tendency of the organic world to grow more perfect; and, in their influence in repressing the advance of others, an example of one of those disturbing causes before enumerated, that *force of external circumstances* which causes such wide chasms in the regular series of animated being.

When the individuals of the dominant race became very numerous, their ideas greatly increased in number, and they felt the necessity of communicating them to each other, and of augmenting and varying the signs proper for the communication of ideas. Meanwhile the inferior quadrumanous animals, although most of them were gregarious, acquired no new ideas, being persecuted and restless in the deserts, and obliged to fly and conceal themselves, so that they conceived no new wants. Such ideas as they already had remained unaltered, and they could dispense with the communication of the greater part of these. To make themselves, therefore, understood by their fellows, required merely a few movements of the body or limbs—whistling, and the uttering of certain cries varied by the inflexions of the voice.

On the contrary, the individuals of the ascendant race, animated with a desire of interchanging their ideas, which became more and more numerous, were prompted to multiply the means of communication, and were no longer satisfied with mere pantomimic signs, nor even with all the possible inflexions of the voice, but made continual efforts to acquire the power of uttering articulate sounds, employing a few at first, but afterwards varying and perfecting them according to the increase of their wants. The habitual exercise of their throat, tongue, and lips, insensibly modified the conformation of these organs, until they became fitted for the faculty of speech.

In effecting this might change, "the exigencies of the individuals were the sole agents; they gave rise to efforts, and the organs proper for articulating sounds were developed by their habitual employment." Hence, in this peculiar race, the origin of the admirable faculty of speech; hence also the diversity of languages, since the distance of places where the individuals composing the race established themselves soon favored the corruption of conventional signs.

In conclusion, it may be proper to observe that the above sketch of the Lamarckian theory is no exaggerated picture, and those passages which have probably excited the greatest surprise in the mind of the reader are literal translations from the original.

Name: _____ **Date:** _____

1. Does Lyell believe that "species have a real existence in nature?" Why or why not?

2. What, according to Lyell, was Lamarck's definition of "species?" How was it different than the definition of species offered by other naturalists?

3. In recounting Lamarck's arguments, Lyell claims there is one especially large flaw. What is it?

4. Other than Lamarck's work, what other argument does Lyell suggest that would account for instability of species and thus the creation of new species?

5. In recounting Lamarck's claims about the transformation of an orangutan into a human, what statements do you think Lyell offered in his attempt to excite "the greatest surprise in the mind of the reader?"

Louis Agassiz

Essay on Classification, 1859

Agassiz (1807-1873) was a Swiss-born naturalist who immigrated to the United States in 1846 and took a position as professor at Harvard University. Agassiz was one of the last great hold-outs against Darwin's theory of natural selection and went to his grave believing that species were real, fixed, and immutable groups of organisms. In this piece, published the same year as Darwin's *On the Origin of Species,* Agassiz upheld one of his central theses: researchers ought to study natural objects free from overarching theoretical notions, including concepts like Darwin's theory of natural selection. As he put it simply, "Study Nature, Not Books."

THE LEADING FEATURES OF A NATURAL ZOOLOGICAL SYSTEM ARE ALL FOUNDED IN NATURE

Modern classifications of animals and plants are based upon the peculiarities of their structure; and this is generally considered as the most important, if not the only safe, guide in our attempts to determine the natural relations which exist between animals. This view of the subject seems to me, however, to circumscribe the foundation of a natural system of Zoology and Botany within too narrow limits, to exclude from our consideration some of the most striking characteristics of the two organic kingdoms of nature, and to leave it doubtful how far the arrangement thus obtained is founded in reality, and how far it is merely the expression of our estimate of these structural differences. It has appeared to me appropriate therefore to present here a short exposition of the leading features of the animal kingdom, as an introduction to the study of Natural History in general and of Embryology in particular, as it would afford a desirable opportunity of establishing a standard of comparison between the changes animals undergo during their growth, and the permanent characters of full-grown individuals of other types, and perhaps of showing also what other points beside structure might with advantage be considered in ascertaining the manifold relations of animals to one another and to the

world in which they live, upon which the natural system may be founded.

In considering these various topics, I shall of necessity have to discuss many questions bearing upon the very origin of organized beings and to touch upon many points now under discussion among scientific men. I shall, however, avoid controversy as much as possible and only try to render the results of my own studies and medications in as clear a manner as I possibly can in the short space of an essay like this.

There is no question in Natural History on which more diversified opinions are entertained than on that of Classification; not that naturalists disagree as to the necessity of some sort of arrangement in describing animals or plants, for since nature has become the object of special studies it has been the universal aim of all naturalists to arrange the objects of their investigations in the most natural order possible. Even Buffon,[1] who began the publication of his great Natural History by denying the existence in nature of any thing like a system, closed his work by grouping the birds according to certain general features exhibited in common by many of them. It is true, authors have differed in their estimation of the characters on which their different arrangements are founded; and it is equally true that they have not viewed their arrangements in the same light, some having plainly acknowledged the artificial character of their systems, while others have

Originally published in 1859.

[1][Georges L. LeClerc de Buffon, 1707–1799.]

urged theirs as the true expression of the natural relations which exist between the objects themselves. But, whether systems were presented as artificial or natural, they have to this day been considered generally as the expression of man's understanding of natural objects, and not as a system devised by the Supreme Intelligence and manifested in these objects.[2]

There is only one point in these innumerable systems on which all seem to meet, namely, the existence in nature of distinct species persisting with all their peculiarities, for a time at least; for even the immutability of species has been questioned.[3] Beyond species, however, this confidence in the existence of the divisions, generally admitted in zoological systems, diminishes greatly.

With respect to genera, we find already the number of the naturalists who accept them as natural divisions much smaller; few of them having expressed a belief that genera have as distinct an existence in nature as species. And as to families, orders, classes, or any kind of higher divisions, they seem to be universally considered as convenient devices, framed with the view of facilitating the study of innumerable objects and of grouping them in the most suitable manner. The indifference with which this part of our science is generally treated becomes unjustifiable, considering the progress which Zoology in general has made of late. It is a matter of consequence whether genera are circumscribed in our systematic works within these or those limits; whether families inclose a wider or more contracted range of genera; whether such or such orders are admitted in a class and what are the natural boundaries of classes; as well as how the classes themselves are related to one another, and whether or not all these groups are considered as resting upon the same foundation in nature.

Without venturing here upon an analysis of the various systems of Zoology—the prominent features of which are sufficiently exemplified for my purpose by the systems of Linnæus and Cuvier,[4]

which must be familiar to every student of Natural History—it is certainly a seasonable question to ask whether the animal kingdom exhibits only those few subdivisions into orders and genera which the Linnæan system indicates, or whether the classes differ among themselves to the extent which the system of Cuvier would lead us to suppose. Or is, after all, this complicated structure of Classification merely an ingenious human invention which every one may shape as he pleases to suit himself? When we remember that all the works on Natural History admit some system or other of this kind, it is certainly an aim worthy of a true naturalist to ascertain what is the real meaning of all these divisions.

Embryology, moreover, forces the inquiry upon us at every step, as it is impossible to establish precise comparisons between the different stages of growth of young animals of any higher group and the permanent characters of full-grown individuals of other types, without first ascertaining what is the value of the divisions with which we may have to compare embryos. My studies in this department for many years have led me to pay the most careful attention to this subject and to make special investigations for its solution.

Before I proceed any further, however, I would submit one case to the consideration of my reader. Suppose that the innumerable articulated animals, which are counted by tens of thousands, nay, perhaps by hundreds of thousands, had never made their appearance upon the surface of our globe, with one single exception: that, for instance, our Lobster (*Homarus americanus*) were the only representative of that extraordinarily diversified type—how should we introduce that species of animals in our systems? Simply as a genus with one species, by the side of all the other classes with their orders, families, etc., or as a family containing only one genus with one species, or as a class with one order and one genus, or as a class with one family and one genus? And should we acknowledge, by the side of Vertebrata, Mollusks, and Radiata, another type of Articulata, on account of the existence of that one Lobster, or would it be natural to call him by a single name, simply as a species, in contradistinction to all other animals?[5] It was the consideration of this supposed case which led me to the investigations detailed below, which, I hope, may end in the ultimate solution of this apparently inextricable question.

Though what I have now to say about this supposed case cannot be fully appreciated before read-

---

[2]The expressions constantly used with reference to genera and species and the higher groups in our systems—as, Mr. A. *has made* such a species *a genus;* Mr. B. *employs* this or that species to *form his genus;* and in which most naturalists indulge when speaking of *their* species, *their* genera, *their* families, *their* systems—exhibit in an unquestionable light the conviction, that such groups are of their own making; which can, however, if the views I shall present below are at all correct, only be true in so far as these groups are *not* true to nature.

[3]Jean Baptiste Lamarck [1744–1829], *Philosophie zoologique* (2 vols., Paris, 1809; 2d ed., 1830); Baden Powell [1796–1860], *Essays on the Spirit of the Inductive Philosophy* (London, 1855). Compare also Sect. xv below.

[4][Carolus Linnæus, 1707–1778; Georges Cuvier, 1769–1832;] cf. Chap. III, Sect. III.

[5][These are Agassiz's terms for the four great branches of the animal kingdom, designations adopted from Cuvier's classifications. Common examples are: Vertebrata (reptiles, mammals); Mollusks (snails, squid); Radiata (starfishes, sea lilies); Articulata (worms, insects).]

ing my remarks in the following chapter respecting the character of the different kinds of groups adopted in our systems, it must be obvious that our Lobster, to be what we see these animals are, must have its frame constructed upon that very same plan of structure which it exhibits now; and, if I should succeed in showing that there is a difference between the conception of a plan and the manner of its execution, upon which classes are founded in contradistinction to the types to which they belong, we might arrive at this distinction by a careful investigation of that single Articulate, as well as by the study of all of them; and we might then recognize its type and ascertain its class characters as fully as if the type embraced several classes, and these classes thousands of species. Secondly, this animal has a form, which no one would fail to recognize; so that, if form can be shown to be characteristic of families, we could thus determine its family. Again: besides the general structure, showing the fundamental relations of all the systems of organs of the body to one another in their natural development, our investigation could be carried into the study of the details of that structure in every part, and thus lead to the recognition of what constitutes everywhere generic characters. Finally: as this animal has definite relations to the surrounding world, as the individuals living at the time bear definite relations to one another, as the parts of their body show definite proportions, and as the surface of the body exhibits a special ornamentation, the specific characters could be traced as fully as if a number of other species were at hand for comparison; and they might be drawn and described with sufficient accuracy to distinguish it at any future time from any other set of species found afterwards, however closely these new species might be allied to it. In this case then we should have to acknowledge a separate branch in the animal kingdom, with a class, a family, and a genus, to introduce one species to its proper place in the system of animals. But the class would have no order, if orders determine the rank, as ascertained by the complication of structure; for, where there is but one representative of a type, there is no room for the question of its superiority or inferiority in comparison to others within the limits of the class, orders being groups subordinate to one another in their class. Yet even in this case, the question of the standing of Articulata, as a type among the other great branches of the animal kingdom, would be open to our investigations; but it would assume another aspect from that which it now presents, as the comparison of Articulata with the other types would then be limited to the Lobster and would lead to a very different result from that to which we may arrive, now that this type includes such a large number of most extensively diversified representatives belonging even to different classes. That such speculations are not idle must be apparent to any one who is aware that, during every period in the history of our globe in past geological ages,[6] the general relations, the numeric proportions, and the relative importance of all the types of the animal kingdom have been ever changing, until their present relations were established. Here then the individuals of one species, as observed while living, simultaneously exhibit characters which, to be expressed satisfactorily and in conformity to what nature tells us, would require the establishment, not only of a distinct species, but also of a distinct genus, a distinct family, a distinct class, a distinct branch. Is not this in itself evidence enough that genera, families, orders, classes, and types have the same foundation in nature as species, and that the individuals living at the time have alone a material existence, they being the bearers, not only of all these different categories of structure upon which the natural system of animals is founded, but also of all the relations which animals sustain to the surrounding world—thus showing that species do not exist in nature in a different way from the higher groups, as is so generally believed?

The divisions of animals according to branch, class, order, family, genus, and species, by which we express the results of our investigations into the relations of the animal kingdom, and which constitute the primary question respecting any system of Zoology seem to me to deserve the consideration of all thoughtful minds. Are these divisions artificial or natural? Are they the devices of the human mind to classify and arrange our knowledge in such a manner as to bring it more readily within our grasp and facilitate further investigations, or have they been instituted by the Divine Intelligence as the categories of his mode of thinking?[7] Have we per-

---

[6]A series of classifications of animals and plants, exhibiting each a natural system of the types known to have existed simultaneously during the several successive geological periods, considered singly and without reference to the types of other ages, would show in a strong light the different relations in which the classes, the orders, the families, and even the genera and species, have stood to one another during each epoch. Such classifications would illustrate, in the most impressive manner, the importance of an accurate knowledge of the relative standing of all animals and plants, which can only be inferred from the perusal even of those palæontological works in which fossil remains are illustrated according to their association in different geological formations; for in all these works the remains of past ages are uniformly referred to a system established upon the study of the animals now living, thus lessening the impression of their peculiar combination for the periods under consideration.

[7]It must not be overlooked here that a system may be natural, that is, may agree in every respect with the facts in nature, and yet not be considered by its author as the manifestation of the thoughts of a Creator, but merely as the expression of a fact existing in nature—no matter how—which the human mind may trace and reproduce in a systematic form of its own invention.

haps thus far been only the unconscious interpreters of a Divine conception in our attempts to expound nature? And when, in our pride of philosophy, we thought that we were inventing systems of science and classifying creation by the force of our own reason, have we followed only, and reproduced, in our imperfect expressions, the plan whose foundations were laid in the dawn of creation, and the development of which we are laboriously studying—thinking, as we put together and arrange our fragmentary knowledge, that we are introducing order into chaos anew? Is this order the result of the exertions of human skill and ingenuity, or is it inherent in the objects themselves, so that the intelligent student of Natural History is led unconsciously, by the study of the animal kingdom itself, to these conclusions, the great divisions under which he arranges animals being indeed but the headings to the chapters of the great book which he is reading? To me it appears indisputable that this order and arrangement of our studies are based upon the natural, primitive relations of animal life—those systems to which we have given the names of the great leaders of our science who first proposed them being in truth but translations into human language of the thoughts of the Creator. And if this is indeed so, do we not find in this adaptability of the human intellect to the facts of creation,[7a] by which we become instinctively, and, as I have said, unconsciously, the translators of the thoughts of God, the most conclusive proof of our affinity with the Divine Mind? And is not this intellectual and spiritual connection with the Almighty worthy our deepest consideration? If there is any truth in the belief that man is made in the image of God, it is surely not amiss for the philosopher to endeavor, by the study of his own mental operations, to approximate the workings of the Divine Reason, learning from the nature of his own mind better to understand the Infinite Intellect from which it is derived. Such a suggestion may at first sight appear irreverent. But who is the truly humble? He who, penetrating into the secrets of creation, arranges them under a formula which he proudly calls his scientific system? Or he who, in the same pursuit, recognizes his glorious affinity with the Creator, and in deepest gratitude for so sublime a birthright strives to be the faithful interpreter of that Divine Intellect with whom he is permitted, nay, with

whom he is intended, according to the laws of his being, to enter into communion?

I confess that this question as to the nature and foundation of our scientific classifications appears to me to have the deepest importance, an importance far greater indeed than is usually attached to it. If it can be proved that man has not invented, but only traced this systematic arrangement in nature, that these relations and proportions which exist throughout the animal and vegetable world have an intellectual, and ideal connection in the mind of the Creator, that this plan of creation, which so commends itself to our highest wisdom, has not grown out of the necessary action of physical laws, but was the free conception of the Almighty Intellect, matured in his thought, before it was manifested in tangible external forms—if, in short, we can prove premeditation prior to the act of creation, we have done once and for ever with the desolate theory which refers us to the laws of matter as accounting for all the wonders of the universe and leaves us with no God but the monotonous, unvarying action of physical forces, binding all things to their inevitable destiny.[8] I think our science has now reached that de-

---

[7a]The human mind is in tune with nature, and much that appears as a result of the working of our intelligence is only the natural expression of that preestablished harmony. On the other hand the whole universe may be considered as a school in which man is taught to know himself, and his relations to his fellow beings, as well as to the First Cause of all that exists.

[8]I allude here only to the doctrines of materialists; but I feel it necessary to add that there are physicists who might be shocked at the idea of being considered as materialists who are yet prone to believe that when they have recognized the laws which regulate the physical world and acknowledged that these laws were established by the Deity, they have explained everything, even when they have considered only the phenomena of the inorganic world, as if the world contained no living beings and as if these living beings exhibited nothing that differed from the inorganic world. Mistaking for a causal relation the intellectual connection observable between serial phenomena, they are unable to perceive any difference between disorder and the free, independent, and self-possessed action of a superior mind, and call mysticism even a passing allusion to the existence of an immaterial principle in animals, which they acknowledge themselves in man. (Powell, *Essays*, pp. 385, 466, 478). I would further remark, that, when speaking of creation in contradistinction with reproduction, I mean only to allude to the difference there is between the regular course of phenomena in nature and the establishment of that order of things, without attempting to explain either; for in whatever manner any state of things which has prevailed for a time upon earth may have been introduced, it is self-evident that its establishment and its maintenance for a determined period are two very different things, however frequently they may be mistaken as identical. It is further of itself plain that the laws which may explain the phenomena of the material world, in contradiction from the organic, cannot be considered as accounting for the existence of living beings, even though these have a material body, unless it be actually shown that the action of such laws implies by their very nature the production of such beings. Life in appropriating the physical world to itself with all its peculiar phenomena exhibits, however, some of its own and of a higher order, which cannot be explained by physical agencies. The circumstance that life is so deeply rooted in the inorganic nature, affords, nevertheless, a strong temptation to explain one by the other; but we shall see presently how fallacious these attempts have been.

gree of advancement in which we may venture upon such an investigation.

The argument for the existence of an intelligent Creator is generally drawn from the adaptation of means to ends, upon which the Bridgewater treatises,[9] for example, have been based. But this does not appear to me to cover the whole ground, for we can conceive that the natural action of objects upon each other should result in a final fitness of the universe and thus produce an harmonious whole; nor does the argument derived from the connection of organs and functions seem to me more satisfactory, for, beyond certain limits, it is not even true. We find organs without functions, as, for instance, the teeth of the whale, which never cut through the gum, the breast in all males of the class of mammalia; these and similar organs are preserved in obedience to a certain uniformity of fundamental structure, true to the original formula of that division of animal life, even when not essential to its mode of existence. The organ remains, not for the performance of a function, but with reference to a plan,[10] and might almost remind us of what we often see in human structures, when, for instance, in architecture, the same external combinations are retained for the sake of symmetry and harmony of proportion, even when they have no practical object.

I disclaim every intention of introducing in this work any evidence irrelevant to my subject or of supporting any conclusions not immediately flowing from it; but I cannot overlook nor disregard here the close connection there is between the facts ascertained by scientific investigations and the discussions now carried on respecting the origin of organized beings. And though I know those who hold it to be very unscientific to believe that thinking is not something inherent in matter, and that there is an essential difference between inorganic and living and thinking beings, I shall not be prevented by any such pretensions of a false philosophy from expressing my conviction that as long as it cannot be shown that matter or physical forces do actually reason, I shall consider any manifestation of thought as evidence of the existence of a thinking being as the author of such thought, and shall look upon an intelligent and intelligible connection between the facts of nature as direct proof of the existence of a thinking God,[11] as certainly as man exhibits the power of thinking when he recognizes their natural relations.

As I am not writing a didactic work, I will not enter here into a detailed illustration of the facts relating to the various subjects submitted to the consideration of my reader beyond what is absolutely necessary to follow the argument, nor dwell at any length upon the conclusions to which they lead; but simply recall the leading features of the evidence, assuming in the argument a full acquaintance with the whole range of data upon which it is founded, whether derived from the affinities or the anatomical structure of animals, or from their habits and their geographical distribution, from their embryology, or from their succession in past

---

[9][Named for Francis Henry Egerton, 8th Earl of Bridgewater, who left £8,000 for the writing of treatises on the "Power, Wisdom and Goodness of God, as Manifested in the Creation." They included the first eight titles in the following Agassiz note, and the fragment by Babbage.]

Thomas Chalmers, *The Adaptation of External Nature to the Moral and Intellectual Constitution of Man* (2 vols., Glasgow, 1839); John Kidd, *The Adaptation of External Nature to the Physical Condition of Man* (London, 1833); William Whewell, *Astronomy and General Physics Considered with Reference to Natural Theology* (London, 1839); Charles Bell, *The Hand, its Mechanism and Vital Endowments, as Evincing Design* (London, 1833); Peter M. Roget, *Animal and Vegetable Physiology Considered with Reference to Natural Theology* (2 vols., London, 1834); William Buckland, *Geology and Mineralogy Considered with Reference to Natural Theology* (2 vols., London, 1836; 2d ed., 1837); William Kirby, *The History, Habits, and Instincts of Animals . . .* (2 vols., London, 1835); William Prout, *Chemistry, Meteorology, and the Function of Digestion Considered with Reference to Natural Theology* (London, 1834). Compare also, Hercule Strauss-Durkheim, *Théologie de la Nature* (3 vols., Paris, 1852); Hugh Miller, *Footprints of the Creator* (Edinburgh, 1849; 3d ed., with a Memoir of the Author by Louis Agassiz, Boston, 1853); Charles Babbage, *The Ninth Bridgewater Treatise, a Fragment* (2d ed., London, 1838).

[10]The unity of structure of the limbs of club-footed or pinnated animals, in which the fingers are never moved, with those which enjoy the most perfect articulations and freedom of motion exhibits this reference most fully.

[11]I am well aware that even the most eminent investigators consider the task of science at an end, as soon as the most general relations of natural phenomena have been ascertained. To many the inquiry into the primitive cause of their existence seems either beyond the reach of man, or as belonging rather to philosophy than to physics. To these the name of God appears out of place in a scientific work, as if the knowledge of secondary agencies constituted alone a worthy subject for their investigations, and as if nature could teach nothing about its Author. Many, again, are no doubt prevented from expressing their conviction that the world was called into existence and is regulated by an intelligent God, either by the fear of being supposed to share clerical or sectarian prejudices; or because it may be dangerous for them to discuss freely such questions without acknowledging at the same time the obligation of taking the Old Testament as the standard by which the validity of their results is to be measured. Science, however, can only prosper when confining itself within its legitimate sphere; and nothing can be more detrimental to its true dignity than discussions like those which took place at the last [1856] meeting of the German association of naturalists, in Göttingen, and which have since then been carried on in several pamphlets in which bigotry vies with personality and invective.

geological ages, and the peculiarities they have exhibited during each,[12] believing as I do that isolated and disconnected facts are of little consequence in the contemplation of the whole plan of creation; and that without a consideration of all the facts furnished by the study of the habits of animals, by their anatomy, their embryology, and the history of the past ages of our globe, we shall never arrive at the knowledge of the natural system of animals.

Let us now consider some of these topics more specially.

SIMULTANEOUS EXISTENCE OF THE MOST DIVERSIFIED TYPES UNDER IDENTICAL CIRCUMSTANCES

It is a fact which seems to be entirely overlooked by those who assume an extensive influence of physical causes upon the very existence of organized beings that the most diversified types of animals and plants are everywhere found under identical circumstances. The smallest sheet of fresh water, every point upon the seashore, every acre of dry land teems with a variety of animals and plants. The narrower the boundaries are which may be assigned as the primitive home of all these beings, the more uniform must be the conditions under which they are assumed to have originated; so uniform, indeed, that in the end the inference would be that the same physical causes could produce the most diversified effects.[13] To concede,

on the contrary, that these organisms may have appeared in the beginning over a wide area, is to grant, at the same time, that the physical influences under which they existed at first were not so specific as to justify the assumption that these could be the cause of their appearance. In whatever connection, then, the first appearance of organized beings upon earth is viewed, whether it is assumed that they originated within the most limited areas, or over the widest range of their present natural geographical distribution, animals and plants being everywhere diversified to the most extraordinary extent, it is plain that the physical influences under which they subsist cannot logically be considered as the cause of that diversity. In this, as in every other respect, when considering the relations of animals and plants to the conditions under which they live, or to one another, we are inevitably led to look beyond the material facts of the case for an explanation of their existence. Those who have taken another view of this subject, have mistaken the action and reaction which exist everywhere between organized beings, and the physical influences under which they live[14] for a causal or genetic connection, and carried their mistake so far as to assert that these manifold influences could really extend to the production of these beings; not considering how inadequate such a cause would be, and that even the action of physical agents upon organized beings presupposes the very existence of those be-

---

[12]Many points little investigated thus far by most naturalists, but to which I have of late years paid particular attention, are here presented only in an aphoristic form, as results established by extensive investigations, though unpublished, most of which will be fully illustrated in my following volumes, or in a special work upon the plan of the creation. (See Agassiz, "On the Difference between Progressive, Embryonic, and Prophetic Types in the Succession of Organized Beings," *Proceedings*, American Association for the Advancement of Science, II (1850), 432–438.

[13]In order fully to appreciate the difficulty alluded to here, it is only necessary to remember how complicated and at the same time how localized the conditions are under which animals multiply. The egg originates in a special organ, the ovary; it grows there to a certain size, until it requires fecundation, that is, the influence of another living being, or at least of the product of another organ, the spermary, to determine the further development of the germ, which, under the most diversified conditions, in different species, passes successively through all those changes which lead to the formation of a new perfect being. I then would ask, is it probable that the circumstances under which animals and plants originated for the first time can be much simpler, or even as simple, as the conditions necessary for their reproduction only, after they have once been created? Preliminary, then, to their first appearance, the conditions necessary for their

growth must have been provided for, if, as I believe, they were created as eggs, which conditions must have been conformable to those in which the living representatives of the types first produced now reproduce themselves. If it were assumed that they originated in a more advanced stage of life, the difficulties would be still greater, as a moment's consideration cannot fail to show, especially if it is remembered how complicated the structure of some of the animals was which are known to have been among the first inhabitants of our globe. When investigating this subject it is of course necessary to consider the first appearance of animals and plants upon the basis of probabilities only, or even simply upon that of possibilities; as with reference to these first-born, at least, the transmutation theory furnishes no explanation of their existence.

For every species belonging to the first fauna and the first flora which have existed upon earth, special relations, special contrivances must, therefore, have been provided. Now, what would be appropriate for the one would not suit the other, so that, excluding one another in this way, they cannot have originated upon the same point; while within a wider area physical agents are too uniform in their mode of action to have laid the foundation for so many such specific differences as existed between the first inhabitants of our globe.

[14]See below, Sect. XVI.

ings.[15] The simple fact that there has been a period in the history of our earth, now well known to geologists,[16] when none of these organized beings as yet existed, and when, nevertheless, the material constitution of our globe, and the physical forces acting upon it, were essentially the same as they are now,[17] shows that these influences are insufficient to call into existence any living being.

Physicists know, indeed, these physical agents more accurately than the naturalists, who ascribe to them the origin of organized beings; let us then ask them, whether the nature of these agents is not specific, whether their mode of action is not specific? They will all answer that they are. Let us further inquire of them, what evidence there is, in the present state of our knowledge, that at any time these physical agents have produced anything they no longer do produce, and what probability there is that they may ever have produced any organized being? If I am not greatly mistaken, the masters in that department of science will, one and all, answer, none whatever.

But the character of the connections between organized beings and the physical conditions under which they live is such as to display thought;[18] these connections are therefore to be considered as established, determined, and regulated by a thinking being. They must have been fixed for each species at its beginning, while the fact of their permanency through successive generations[19] is further evidence that with their natural relations to the surrounding world were also determined the relations of individuals to one another;[20] their generic as well as their family relations, and every higher grade of affinity;[21] showing, therefore, not only thought, in reference to the physical conditions of existence, but such comprehensive thoughts as would embrace simultaneously every characteristic of each species.

Every fact relating to the geographical distribution of animals and plants might be alluded to in confirmation of this argument, but especially the character of every fauna and every flora upon the surface of the globe. How great the diversity of animals and plants living together in the same region may be can be ascertained by the perusal of special works upon the Zoology and Botany of different countries, or from special treatises upon the geographical distribution of animals and plants.[22] I need, therefore, not enter into further details upon this subject, especially since it is discussed more fully below.[23]

It might perhaps be urged that animals living together in exceptional conditions and exhibiting

---

[15]A critical examination of this point may dispel much of the confusion which prevails in the discussions relating to the influence of physical causes upon organized beings. That there exist definite relations between animals as well as plants and the mediums in which they live, no one at all familiar with the phenomena of the organic world can doubt; that these mediums and all physical agents at work in nature have a certain influence upon organized beings is equally plain. But before any such action can take place and be felt, organized beings must exist. The problem before us involves, therefore, two questions, the influence of physical agents upon animals and plants already in existence, and the origin of these beings. Granting the influence of these agents upon organized beings to the fullest extent to which it may be traced (see Sect. XVI), there remains still the question of their origin upon which neither argument nor observation has yet thrown any light. But according to some, they originated spontaneously by the immediate agency of physical forces and have become successively more and more diversified by changes produced gradually upon them, by these same forces. Others believe that there exist laws in nature which were established by the Deity in the beginning, to the action of which the origin of organized beings may be ascribed; while according to others, they owe their existence to the immediate intervention of an intelligent Creator. It is the object of the following paragraphs to show that there are neither agents nor laws in nature known to physicists under the influence and by the action of which these beings could have originated; that, on the contrary, the very nature of these beings and their relations to one another and to the world in which they live exhibit thought and can therefore be referred only to the immediate action of a thinking being, even though the manner in which they were called into existence remains for the present a mystery.

[16]Few geologists only may now be inclined to believe that the lowest strata known to contain fossils are not the lowest deposits formed since the existence of organized beings upon earth. But even those who would assume that still lower fossiliferous beds may yet be discovered or may have entirely disappeared by the influence of plutonic agencies (POWELL, *Essays*, p. 424) must acknowledge the fact that everywhere in the lowest rocks known to contain fossils at all there is a variety of them found together. (See Sect. VII.) Moreover, the similarity in the character of the oldest fossils found in different parts of the world goes far, in my opinion, to prove that we actually do know the earliest types of the animal kingdom which have inhabited our globe. This conclusion seems fully sustained by the fact that we find everywhere below this oldest set of fossiliferous beds other stratified rocks in which no trace of organized beings can be found.

[17]See below, Sect. XXI.

[18]See below, Sect. XVI.

[19]See below, Sect. XV.

[20]See below, Sect. XVII.

[21]See below, Sect. VI.

[22]L. K. Schmarda, *Die geographische Verbreitung der Thiere* (3 vols., Vienna, 1853); William Swainson, *A Treatise on the Geography and Classification of Animals* (London, 1835); E. A. G. Zimmerman, *Specimen Zoologiæ geographicæ, Quadrupedum domiccilia et migrationes sistens* (Leiden, 1777); Alander von Humboldt, *Essai sur la géographie des plantes* (Paris, 1805) and *Ansichten der Natur* (3d ed., Stuttgart and Tübingen, 1849); Robert Brown, *General Remarks on the Botany of Terra Australis* (London, 1814); Joachim F. Schouw, *Grundzüge einer allgemeinen Pflanzengeographie* (Berlin, 1823); Alphonse de Candolle, *Géographie botanique raisonnée* (2 vols., Paris, 1855).

[23]See below, Sect. IX.

structural peculiarities apparently resulting from these conditions, such as the blind fish,[24] the blind crawfish, and the blind insects of the Mammoth Cave in Kentucky, furnish uncontrovertible evidence of the immediate influence of those exceptional conditions upon the organs of vision. If this, however, were the case, how does it happen that that remarkable fish, the *Amblyopsis spelæus,* has only such remote affinities to other fishes? Or were, perhaps, the sum of influences at work to make that fish blind capable also of devising such a combination of structural characters as that fish has in common with all other fishes, with those peculiarities which at the same time distinguish it? Does not, rather, the existence of a rudimentary eye discovered by Dr. J. Wyman in the blind fish show that these animals, like all others, were created with all their peculiarities by the fiat of the Almighty, and this rudiment of eyes left them as a remembrance of the general plan of structure of the great type to which they belong? Or will, perhaps, some one of those naturalists who know so much better than the physicists what physical forces may produce, and that they may produce, and have produced every living being known, explain also to us why subterraneous caves in America produce blind fishes, blind crustacea, and blind insects, while in Europe they produce nearly blind reptiles? If there is no thought in the case, why is it then that this very reptile, the *Proteus anguinus,* forms, with a number of other reptiles living in North America and in Japan, one of the most natural series known in the animal kingdom, every member of which exhibits a distinct grade[25] in the scale?[26]

After we have freed ourselves from the mistaken impression that there may be some genetic connection between physical forces and organized beings, there remains a vast field of investigation to ascertain the true relations between both, to their full extent, and within their natural limits.[27] A mere reference to the mode of breathing of different types of animals and to their organs of locomotion, which are more particularly concerned in these relations, will remind every naturalist of how great importance in Classification is the structure of these parts and how much better they might be understood in this point of view, were the different structures of these organs more extensively studied in their direct reference to the world in which animals live. If this had been done, we should no longer call by the same common name of legs and wings organs so different as the locomotive appendages of the insects and those of the birds! We should no longer call lungs the breathing cavity of snails, as well as the air pipes of mammalia, birds, and reptiles! A great reform is indeed needed in this part of our science, and no study can prepare us better for it than the investigation of the mutual dependence of the structure of animals and the conditions in which they live.

[24]Jeffries Wyman, "Description of a Blind Fish, from a Cave in Kentucky," *American Journal of Science,* XLV (1843), 94–96, and XVII (2d ser., 1854), 258–261; Agassiz, "Observations on the Blind Fish of the Mammoth Cave," in *ibid.,* XI (2d ser., 1851), 127–128.

[25]See below, Sect. XII.

[26][Darwin in Chapter V of the *Origin of Species* was very specific in disputing Agassiz on this evidence, employing the example of the eyeless fish as proof of the influence of natural selection through the use and disuse of parts.]

[27]See below, Sect. XVI.

Name: _____ **Date:** _____

1. Does Agassiz believe that classification systems are "real" or "invented." Why?

2. What objections does Agassiz list toward the argument for the existence of an intelligent Creator based on adaptations? Describe three of them in your own words.

   1.

   2.

   3.

3. Aggasiz concludes by calling for a "great reform." What does Agassiz want to see reformed?

Robert Chambers

Vestiges of the Natural History of Creation, 1844

Chambers (1802-1871) was Scottish publisher and amateur geologist, who throughout his life had been active in politics at both ends of the political spectrum. Drawing from his interest in natural history, Chamber anonymously published *Vestiges of the Natural History of Creation* in 1844, which ultimately argued that in society, as in nature, progress was natural and inevitable. His book was met with wide public discussion and considerable interest. Geologists and biologists, however, disliked the book and openly attacked it. The manner in which Chamber mingled his depiction of nature with a justification for social progress angered many scientists because, they believed, Chambers' goal was not an accurate explanation of nature, but rather was to use nature to justify a particular political position.

HYPOTHESIS OF THE DEVELOPMENT OF THE VEGETABLE AND ANIMAL KINGDOMS

It has been already intimated, as a general fact, that there is an obvious gradation amongst the families of both the vegetable and animal kingdoms, from the simple lichen and animalcule respectively up to the highest order of dicotyledonous trees and the mammalia. Confining our attention, in the meantime, to the animal kingdom—it does not appear that this gradation passes along one line, on which every form of animal life can be, as it were, strung; there may be branching or double lines at some places; or the whole may be in a circle composed of minor circles, as has been recently suggested. But still it is incontestable that there are general appearances of a scale beginning with the simple and advancing to the complicated. The animal kingdom was divided by Cuvier into four sub-kingdoms, or divisions, and these exhibit an unequivocal gradation in the order in which they are here enumerated:—Radiata, (polypes, &c.;) mollusca, (pulpy animals;) articulata, (jointed animals;) vertebrata, (animals with internal skeleton.) The gradation can, in like manner, be clearly traced in the *classes* into which the sub-kingdoms are subdivided, as, for instance, when we take those of the vertebrata in this order—reptiles, fishes, birds, mammals.

While the external forms of all these various animals are so different, it is very remarkable that the whole are, after all, variations of a fundamental plan, which can be traced as a basis throughout the whole, the variations being merely modification of that plan to suit the particular conditions in which each particular animal has been designed to live. Starting from the primeval germ, which, as we have seen, is the representative of a particular order of full-grown animals, we find all others to be merely advances from that type, with the extension of endowments and modification of forms which are required in each particular case; each form, also, retaining a strong affinity to that which precedes it, and tending to impress its own features on that which succeeds. This unity of structure, as it is called, becomes the more remarkable, when we observe that the organs, while preserving a resemblance, are often put to different uses. For example: the ribs become, in the serpent, organs of locomotion, and the snout is extended, in the elephant, into a prehensile instrument.

It is equally remarkable that analogous purposes are served in different animals by organs essentially different. Thus, the mammalia breathe by lungs; the fishes, by gills. These are not modifications of one organ, but distinct organs. In mammifers, the gills exist and act at an early stage of the foetal state, but afterwards go back and appear no more; while the lungs are developed. In fishes, again, the gills only are fully developed; while the lung structure either

Originally published in London, 1844.

makes no advance at all, or only appears in the rudimentary form of an air-bladder. So, also, the baleen of the whale and the teeth of the land mammalia are different organs. The whale, in embryo, shews the rudiments of teeth; but these, not being wanted, are not developed, and the baleen is brought forward instead. The land animals, we may also be sure, have the rudiments of baleen in their organization. In many instances, a particular structure is found advanced to a certain point in a particular set of animals, (for instance, feet in the serpent tribe,) although it is not there required in any degree; but the peculiarity, being carried a little farther forward, is perhaps useful in the next set of animals in the scale. Such are called rudimentary organs. With this class of phenomena are to be ranked the useless mammæ of the male human being, and the unrequired process of bone in the male opossum, which is needed in the female for supporting her pouch. Such curious features are most conspicuous in animals which form links between various classes.

As formerly stated, the marsupials, standing at the bottom of the mammalia, shew their affinity to the oviparous vertebrata, by the rudiments of two canals passing from near the anus to the external surfaces of the viscera, which are fully developed in fishes, being required by them for the respiration of aerated waters, but which are not needed by the atmosphere-breathing marsupials. We have also the peculiar form of the sternum and rib-bones of the lizards *represented* in the mammalia in certain white cartilaginous lines traceable among their abdominal muscles. The struphionidæ (birds of the ostrich type) form a link between birds and mammalia, and in them we find the wings imperfectly or not at all developed, a diaphragm and urinary sac, (organs wanting in other birds,) and feathers approaching the nature of hair. Again, the ornithorynchus belongs to a class at the bottom of the mammalia, and approximating to birds, and in it behold the bill and web-feet of that order!

For further illustration, it is obvious that, various as may be the lengths of the upper part of the vertebral column in the mammalia, it always consists of the same parts. The giraffe has in its tall neck the same number of bones with the pig, which scarcely appears to have a neck at all.[1] Man, again, has no tail; but the notion of a much-ridiculed philosopher of the last century is not altogether, as it happens, without foundation, for the bones of a caudal extremity exist in an undeveloped state in the *os coccygis* of the human subject. The limbs of all the vertebrate animals are, in like manner, on one plan, however various they may appear. In the hind-leg of a horse, for example, the angle called the hock is the same part which in us forms the heel; and the horse, and all other quadrupeds, with almost the solitary exception of the bear, walk, in reality, upon what answers to the toes of a human being. In this and many other quadrupeds the fore part of the extremities is shrunk up in a hoof, as the tail of the human being is shrunk up in the bony mass at the bottom of the back. The bat, on the other hand, has these parts largely developed. The membrane, commonly called its wing, is framed chiefly upon bones answering precisely to those of the human hand; its extinct congener, the pterodactyle, had the same membrane extended upon the fore-finger only, which in that animal was prolonged to an extraordinary extent. In the paddles of the whale and other animals of its order, we see the same bones as in the more highly developed extremities of the land mammifers; and even the serpent tribes, which present no external appearance of such extremities, possess them in reality, but in an undeveloped or rudimental state.

The same law of development presides over the vegetable kingdom. Amongst phanerogamous plants, a certain number of organs appear to be always present, either in a developed or rudimentary state; and those which are rudimentary can be developed by cultivation. The flowers which bear stamens on one stalk and pistils on another, can be caused to produce both, or to become perfect flowers, by having a sufficiency of nourishment supplied to them. So also, where a special function is required for particular circumstances, nature has provided for it, not by a new organ, but by a modification of a common one, which she has effected in development. Thus, for instance, some plants destined to live in arid situations, require to have a store of water which they may slowly absorb. The need is arranged for by a cup-like expansion round the stalk, in which water remains after a shower. Now the *pitcher*, as this is called, is not a new organ, but simply a metamorphose of a leaf.

These facts clearly shew how all the various organic forms of our world are bound up in one—how a fundamental unity pervades and embraces them all, collecting them, from the humblest lichen up to the highest mammifer, in one system, the whole creation of which must have depended upon one law or decree of the Almighty, though it did not all come forth at one time. After what we have seen, the idea of a separate exertion for each must appear totally inadmissible. The single fact of abortive or rudimentary organs condemns it; for these, on such a supposition, could be regarded in no other light than as blemishes or blunders—

---

[1]Daubenton established the rule, that all the viviparous quadrupeds have seven vertebræ in the neck.

the thing of all others most irreconcilable with that idea of Almighty Perfection which a general view of nature so irresistibly conveys. On the other hand, when the organic creation is admitted to have been effected by a general law, we see nothing in these abortive parts but harmless peculiarities of development, and interesting evidences of the manner in which the Divine Author has been pleased to work.

We have yet to advert to the most interesting class of facts connected with the laws of organic development. It is only in recent times that physiologists have observed that each animal passes in the course of its germinal history, through a series of changes resembling the *permanent forms* of the various orders of animals inferior to it in the scale. Thus, for instance, an insect, standing at the head of the articulated animals, is, in the larva state, a true annelid, or worm, the annelida being the lowest in the same class. The embryo of a crab resembles the perfect animal of the inferior order myriapoda, and passes through all the forms of transition which characterize the intermediate tribes of crustacea. The frog, for some time after its birth, is a fish with external gills, and other organs fitting it for an aquatic life, all of which are changed as it advances to maturity, and becomes a land animal. The mammifer only passes through still more stages, according to its higher place in the scale. Nor is man himself exempt from this law. His first form is that which is permanent in the animalcule. His organization gradually passes through conditions generally resembling a fish, a reptile, a bird, and the lower mammalia, before it attains its specific maturity. At one of the last stages of his fœtal career, he exhibits an intermaxillary bone, which is characteristic of the perfect ape; this is suppressed, and he may then be said to take leave of the simial type, and become a true human creature. Even, as we shall see, the varieties of his race are represented in the progressive development of an individual of the highest, before we see the adult Caucasian, the highest point yet attained in the animal scale.

To come to particular points of the organization. The brain of man, which exceeds that of all other animals in complexity of organization and fulness of development, is, at one early period, only "a simple fold of nervous matter, with difficulty distinguishable into three parts, while a little tail-like prolongation towards the hinder parts, and which had been the first to appear, is the only representation of a spinal marrow. Now, in the state it perfectly resembles the brain of an adult fish, thus assuming *in transitu* the form that in the fish is permanent. In a short time, however, the structure is become more

complex, the parts more distinct, the spinal marrow better marked; it is now the brain of a reptile. The change continues; by a singular motion, certain parts *(corpora quadragemina)* which had hitherto appeared on the upper surface, now pass towards the lower; the former is their permanent situation in fishes and reptiles, the latter in birds and mammalia. This is another advance in the scale, but more remains yet to be done. The complication of the organ increases; cavities termed *ventricles* are formed, which do not exist in fishes, reptiles, or birds; curiously organized parts, such as the corpora striata, are added; it is now the brain of the mammalia. Its last and final change alone seems wanting, that which shall render it the brain of MAN."[2] And this change in time takes place.

So also with the heart. This organ, in the mammalia, consists of four cavities, but in the reptiles of only three, and in fishes of two only, while in the articulated animals it is merely a prolonged tube. Now in the mammal fœtus, at a certain early stage, the organ has the form of a prolonged tube; and a human being may be said to have then the heart of an insect. Subsequently it is shortened and widened, and becomes divided by a contraction into two parts, a ventricle and an auricle; it is now the heart of a fish. A subdivision of the auricle afterwards makes a triple-chambered form, as in the heart of the reptile tribes; lastly, the ventricle being also subdivided, it becomes a full mammal heart.

Another illustration here presents itself with the force of the most powerful and interesting analogy. Some of the earliest fishes of our globe, those of the Old Red Sandstone, present, as we have seen, certain peculiarities, as the one-sided tail and an inferior position of the mouth. No fishes of the present day, in a mature state, are so characterized; but some, at a certain stage of their existence, have such peculiarities. It occurred to a geologist to inquire if the fish which existed before the Old Red Sandstone had any peculiarities assimilating them to the fœtal condition of existing fish, and particularly if they were small. The first which occur before the time of the Old Red Sandstone, are those described by Mr. Murchison, as belonging to the Upper Ludlow Rocks; *they are all rather small.* Still older are those detected by Mr. Philips, in the Aymestry Limestone, being the most ancient of the class which have as yet been discovered; *these are so extremely minute as only to be distinguishable by the microscope.* Here we apparently have very clear demonstrations of a parity, or rather identity, of laws presiding over the de-

---

[2]Lord's Popular Physiology. It is to Tiedemann that we chiefly owe these curious observations; but ground was first broken in this branch of physiological science by Dr. John Hunter.

velopment of the animated tribes on the face of the earth, and that of the individual in embryo.

The tendency of all these illustrations is to make us look to *development* as the principle which has been immediately concerned in the peopling of this globe, a process extending over a vast space of time, but which is nevertheless connected in character with the briefer process by which an individual being is evoked from a simple germ. What mystery is there here—and how shall I proceed to enunciate the conception which I have ventured to form of what may prove to be its proper solution! It is an idea by no means calculated to impress by its greatness, or to puzzle by its profoundness. It is an idea more marked by simplicity than perhaps any other of those which have explained the great secrets of nature. But in this lies, perhaps, one of its strongest claims to the faith of mankind.

The whole train of animated beings, from the simplest and oldest up to the highest and most recent, are, then, to be regarded as a series of *advances of the principle of development*, which have depended upon external physical circumstances, to which the resulting animals are appropriate. I contemplate the whole phenomena as having been in the first place arranged in the counsels of Divine Wisdom, to take place, not only upon this sphere, but upon all the others in space, under necessary modifications, and as being carried on, from first to last, here and elsewhere, under immediate favour of the creative will or energy.[3] The nucleated vesicle, the fundamental form of all organization, we must regard as the meeting-point between the inorganic and the organic— the end of the mineral and beginning of the vegetable and animal kingdoms, which thence start in different directions, but in perfect parallelism and analogy. We have already seen that this nucleated vesicle is itself a type of mature and independent being in the infusory animalcules, as well as the starting point of the fœtal progress of every higher individual in creation, both animal and vegetable. We have seen that it is a form of being which electric agency will produce—though not perhaps usher into full life—in albumen, one of those compound elements of animal bodies, of which another (urea) has been made by artificial means. Remembering these things, we are drawn on to the supposition, that the first step in the creation of life upon this planet was *a chemico-electric operation, by which simple germinal vesicles were produced.* This is so much,

but what were the next steps? Let a common vegetable infusion help us to an answer. There, as we have seen, simple forms are produced at first, but afterwards they become more complicated, until at length the life-producing powers of the infusion are exhausted. Are we to presume that, in this case, the simple engender the complicated? Undoubtedly, this would not be more wonderful as a natural process than one which we never think of wondering at, because familiar to us—namely, that in the gestation of the mammals, the animalcule-like ovum of a few days is the parent, in a sense, of the chick-like form of a few weeks, and that in all the subsequent stages—fish, reptile, &c.—the one may, with scarcely a metaphor, be said to be the progenitor of the other. I suggest, then, as an hypothesis already countenanced by much that is ascertained, and likely to be further sanctioned by much that remains to be known, that the first step was *an advance under favour of peculiar conditions, from the simplest forms of being, to the next more complicated, and this through the medium of the ordinary process of generation.*

Unquestionably, what we ordinarily see of nature is calculated to impress a conviction that each species invariably produces its like. But I would here call attention to a remarkable illustration of natural law which has been brought forward by Mr. Babbage, in his *Ninth Bridgewater Treatise.* The reader is requested to suppose himself seated before the calculating machine, and observing it. It is moved by a weight, and there is a wheel which revolves through a small angle round its axis, at short intervals, presenting to his eye successively, a series of numbers engraved on its divided circumference.

Let the figures thus seen be the series, 1, 2, 3, 4, 5, &c., of natural numbers, each of which exceeds its immediate antecedent by unity.

"Now, reader," says Mr. Babbage, "let me ask you how long you will have counted before you are firmly convinced that the engine has been so adjusted, that it will continue, while its motion is maintained, to produce the same series of natural numbers? Some minds are so constituted, that, after passing the first hundred terms, they will be satisfied that they are acquainted with the law. After seeing five hundred terms few will doubt, and after the fifty thousandth term the propensity to believe that the succeeding term will be fifty thousand and one, will be almost irresistible. That term *will* be fifty thousand and one; and the same regular succession will continue; the five millionth and the fifty millionth term will still appear in their expected order, and one unbroken chain of natural numbers will pass before your eyes, from *one* up to *one hundred million.*

"True to the vast induction which has been made, the next succeeding term will be one hundred million and one; but the next number pre-

---

[3]When I formed this idea, I was not aware of one which seems faintly to foreshadow it—namely, Socrates's doctrine, afterwards dilated on by Plato, that "previous to the existence of the world, and beyond its present limits, there existed certain archetypes, the embodiment (if we may use such a word) of general ideas; and that these archetypes were models, in imitation of which all particular beings were created."

sented by the rim of the wheel, instead of being one hundred million and two, is one hundred million *ten thousand* and two. The whole series from the commencement being thus,—

1

2

3

4

5

. . . .

. . . . .

. . . . .

. . . .

99,999,999

100,000,000

regularly as far as 100,000,001

100,010,002 the law changes.

100,030,003

100,060,004

100,100,005

100,150,006

100,210,007

100,280,008

. . . .

. . . .

"The law which seemed at first to govern this series failed at the hundred million and second term. This term is larger than we expected by 10,000. The next term is larger than was anticipated by 30,000, and the excess of each term above what we had expected forms the following table:—

10,000

30,000

60,000

100,000

150,000

. . . . . .

. . . . . .

being, in fact, the series of *triangular numbers,*[4] each multiplied by 10,000.

---

[4]The numbers 1, 3, 6, 10, 15, 21, 28, &c. are formed by adding the successive terms of the series of natural numbers thus:

$1 = 1$

$1 + 2 = 3$

$1 + 2 + 3 = 6$

$1 + 2 + 3 + 4 = 10$, &c.

They are called triangular numbers, because a number of points corresponding to any term can always be placed in the form of a triangle; for instance—

.

. .

. . .

. . . .

1   3   6   10

"If we now continue to observe the numbers presented by the wheel, we shall find, that for a hundred, or even for a thousand terms, they continue to follow the new law relating to the triangular numbers; but after watching them for 2761 terms, we find that this law fails in the case of the 2762d term.

"If we continue to observe, we shall discover another law then coming into action, which also is dependent, but in a different manner, on triangular numbers. This will continue through about 1430 terms, when a new law is again introduced which extends over about 950 terms, and this, too, like all its predecessors, fails, and gives place to other laws, which appear at different intervals.

"Now it must be observed that *the law that each number presented by the engine is greater by unity than the preceding number,* which law the observer had deduced from an induction of a hundred million instances, *was not the true law that regulated its action,* and that the occurrence of the number 100,010,002 at the 100,000,002nd term was *as necessary a consequence of the original adjustment, and might have been as fully foreknown at the commencement, as was the regular succession of any one of the intermediate numbers to its immediate antecedent.* The same remark applies to the next apparent deviation from the new law, which was founded on an induction of 2761 terms, and also to the succeeding law, with this limitation only—that, whilst their consecutive introduction at various definite intervals, is a necessary consequence of the mechanical structure of the engine, our knowledge of analysis does not enable us to predict the periods themselves at which the more distant laws will be introduced."

It is not difficult to apply the philosophy of this passage to the question under consideration. It must be borne in mind that the gestation of a single organism is the work of but a few days, weeks, or months; but the gestation (so to speak) of a whole creation is a matter probably involving enormous spaces of time. Suppose that an ephemeron, hovering over a pool for its one April day of life, were capable of observing the fry of the frog in the water below. In its aged afternoon, having seen no change upon them for such a long time, it would be little qualified to conceive that the external branchiæ of these creatures were to decay, and be replaced by internal lungs, that feet were to be developed, the tail erased, and the animal then to become a denizen of the land. Precisely such may be our difficulty in conceiving that any of the species which people our earth is capable of advancing by generation to a higher type of being. During the whole time which we call the historical era, the limits of species have been, to ordinary observation, rigidly adhered to. But the historical era is, we know, only a small portion of the entire age of our globe. We do not know what may have happened during the ages which preceded its commencement, as we do not know what may happen in ages yet in the distant future. All, therefore, that we can properly infer from the apparently invariable production of like by like is, that such is the ordinary procedure of nature in the time immediately passing before our eyes. Mr. Babbage's illustration powerfully suggests that this ordinary procedure may be subordinate to a higher law which only *permits* it for a time, and in proper season interrupts and changes it. We shall soon see some philosophical evidence for this very conclusion.

It has been seen that, in the reproduction of the higher animals, the new being passes through stages in which it is successively fish-like and reptile-like. But the resemblance is not to the adult fish or the adult reptile, but to the fish and reptile at a certain point in their fœtal progress; this holds true with regard to the vascular, nervous, and other systems alike. It may be illustrated by a simple diagram. The fœtus of all the four classes may be supposed to advance in an identical condition to the point A. The fish there diverges and passes along a line apart, and peculiar to itself, to its mature state at F. The reptile, bird, and mammal, go on together to C, where the reptile diverges in like manner, and advances by itself to R. The bird diverges at D, and goes on to B. The mammal then goes forward in a straight line to the highest 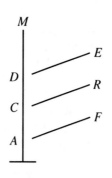 point of organization at M. This diagram shews only the main ramifications; but the reader must suppose minor ones, representing the subordinate differences of orders, tribes, families, genera, &c., if he wishes to extend his views to the whole varieties of being in the animal kingdom. Limiting ourselves at present to the outline afforded by this diagram, it is apparent that the only thing required for an advance from one type to another in the generative process is that, for example, the fish embryo should not diverge at A, but go on to C before it diverges, in which case the progeny will be, not a fish, but a reptile. To protract the *straightforward part of the gestation over a small space*—and from species to species the space would be small indeed—is all that is necessary.

This might be done by the force of certain external conditions operating upon the parturient system. The nature of these conditions we can only conjecture, for their operation, which in the geological eras was so powerful, has in its main strength been long interrupted, and is now perhaps only allowed to work in some of the lowest departments of the organic world, or under extraordinary casualties in some of the higher, and to these points the attention of science has as yet been little directed. But though this knowledge were never to be clearly attained, it need not much affect the present argument, provided it be satisfactorily shewn that there must be some such influence within the range of natural things.

To this conclusion it must be greatly conducive that the law of organic development is still daily seen at work to certain effects, only somewhat short of a transition from species to species. Sex we have seen to be a matter of development. There is an instance, in a humble department of the animal world, of arrangements being made by the animals themselves for adjusting this law to the production of a particular sex. Amongst bees, as amongst several other insect tribes, there is in each community but one true female, the queen bee, the workers being false females or neuters; that is to say, sex is carried on in them to a point where it is attended by sterility. The preparatory states of the queen bee occupy sixteen days; those of the neuters, twenty; and those of males, twenty-four. Now it is a fact, settled by innumerable observations and experiments, that the bees can so modify a worker in the larva state, that, when it emerges from the pupa, it is found to be a queen or true female. For this purpose they enlarge its cell, make a pyramidal hollow to allow of its assuming a vertical instead of a horizontal position, keep it warmer than other larvæ are kept, and feed it with a peculiar kind of food. From these simple circumstances, leading to a shortening of the embryotic condition, results a creature different in form, and also in dispositions, from what would have otherwise been produced. Some of the organs possessed by the worker are here altogether wanting. We have a creature "destined to enjoy love, to burn with jealousy and anger, to be incited to vengeance, and to pass her time without labour," instead of one "zealous for the good of the community, a defender of the public rights, enjoying an immunity from the stimulus of sexual appetite and the pains of parturition; laborious, industrious, patient, ingenious, skilful; incessantly engaged in the nurture of the young, in collecting honey and pollen, in elaborating wax, in constructing cells and the like!—paying the most respectful and assiduous attention to objects which, had its ovaries been developed, it would have hated and pursued with the most vindictive fury till it had destroyed them!"[5] All these changes may be produced by a mere modification of the embryotic progress, which it is within the power of the adult

---

[5]Kirby and Spence.

animals to effect. But it is important to observe that this modification is different from working a direct change upon the embryo. It is not the different food which effects a metamorphosis. All that is done is merely to accelerate the period of the insect's perfection. By the arrangements made and the food given, the embryo becomes sooner fit for being ushered forth in its imago or perfect state. Development may be said to be thus arrested at a particular stage—that early one at which the female sex is complete. In the other circumstances, it is allowed to go on four days longer, and a stage is then reached between the two sexes, which in this species is designed to be the perfect condition of a large portion of the community. Four days more make it a perfect male. It is at the same time to be observed that there is, from the period of oviposition, a destined distinction between the sexes of the young bees. The queen lays the whole of the eggs which are designed to become workers, before she begins to lay those which become males. But probably the condition of her reproductive system governs the matter of sex, for it is remarked that when her impregnation is delayed beyond the twenty-eighth day of her entire existence, she lays only eggs which become males.

We have here, it will be admitted, a most remarkable illustration of the principle of development, although in an operation limited to the production of sex only. Let it not be said that the phenomena concerned in the generation of bees may be very different from those concerned in the reproduction of the higher animals. There is a unity throughout nature which makes the one case an instructive reflection of the other.

We shall now see an instance of development operating within the production of what approaches to the character of variety of species. It is fully established that a human family, tribe, or nation, is liable, in the course of generations, to be either advanced from a mean form to a higher one, or degraded from a higher to a lower, by the influence of the physical conditions in which it lives. The course features, and other structural peculiarities of the negro race only continue while these people live amidst the circumstances usually associated with barbarism. In a more temperature clime, and higher social state, the face and figure become greatly refined. The few African nations which possess any civilization also exhibit forms approaching the European; and when the same people in the United States of America have enjoyed a within-door life for several generations, they assimilate to the whites amongst whom they live. On the other hand, there are authentic instances of a people originally well-formed and good-looking, being brought, by imperfect diet and a variety of physical

hardships, to a meaner form. It is remarkable that prominence of the jaws, a recession and diminution of the cranium, and an elongation and attenuation of the limbs, are peculiarities always produced by these miserable conditions, for they indicate an unequivocal retrogression towards the type of the lower animals. Thus we see nature alike willing to go back and to go forward. Both effects are simply the result of the operation of the law of development in the generative system. Give good conditions, it advances; bad ones, it recedes. Now, perhaps, it is only because there is no longer a possibility, in the higher types of being, of giving sufficiently favourable conditions to carry on species to species, that we see the operation of the law so far limited.

Let us trace this law also in the production of certain classes of monstrosities. A human fœtus is often left with one of the most important parts of its frame imperfectly developed: the heart, for instance, goes no farther than the three-chambered form, so that it is the heart of a reptile. There are even instances of this organ being left in the two-chambered or fish form. Such defects are the result of nothing more than a failure of the power of development in the system of the mother, occasioned by weak health or misery. Here we have apparently a realization of the converse of those conditions which carry on species to species, so far, at least, as one organ is concerned. Seeing a complete specific retrogression in this one point, how easy it is to imagine an access of favourable conditions sufficient to reverse the phenomenon, and make a fish mother develop a reptile heart, or a reptile mother develop a mammal one. It is no great boldness to surmise that a super-adequacy in the measure of this under-adequacy (and the one thing seems as natural an occurrence as the other) would suffice in a goose to give its progeny the body of a rat, and produce the ornithorynchus, or might give the progeny of an ornithorynchus the mouth and feet of a true rodent, and thus complete at two stages the passage from the aves to the mammalia.

Perhaps even the transition from species to species does still take place in some of the obscurer fields of creation, or under extraordinary casualties, though science professes to have no such facts on record. It is here to be remarked, that such facts might often happen, and yet no record be taken of them, for so strong is the prepossession for the doctrine of invariable like-production, that such circumstances, on occurring, would be almost sure to be explained away on some other supposition, or, if presented, would be disbelieved and neglected. Science, therefore, has no such facts, for the very same reason that some small sects are said to have no discreditable members—namely, that they do not receive such persons, and extrude all who begin to verge upon the character. There are, nevertheless, some facts which have chanced to be reported without any reference to this hypothesis, and which it seems extremely difficult to explain satisfactorily upon any other. One of these has already been mentioned—a progression in the forms of the animalcules in a vegetable infusion from the simpler to the more complicated, a sort of microcosm, representing the whole history of the progress of animal creation as displayed by geology. Another is given in the history of the Acarus Crossii, which may be only the ultimate stage of a series of similar transformations effected by electric agency in the solution subjected to it. There is, however, one direct case of a translation of species, which has been presented with a respectable amount of authority.[6] It appears that, whenever oats sown at the usual time are kept cropped down during summer and autumn, and allowed to remain over the winter, a thin crop of rye is the harvest presented at the close of the ensuing summer. This experiment has been tried repeatedly, with but one result; invariably the *secale cereale* is the crop reaped where the *avena sativa,* a recognised different species, was sown. Now it will not satisfy a strict inquirer to be told that the seeds of the rye were latent in the ground and only superseded the dead product of the oats; for if any such fact were in the case, why should the usurping grain be always rye? Perhaps those curious facts which have been stated with regard to forests of one kind of trees, when burnt down, being succeeded (without planting) by other kinds, may yet be found most explicable, as this is, upon the hypothesis of a progression of species which takes place under certain favouring conditions, now apparently of comparatively rare occurrence. The case of the oats is the more valuable, as bearing upon the suggestion as to a protraction of the gestation at a particular part of its course. Here, the generative process is, by the simple mode of cropping down, kept up for a whole year beyond its usual term. The type is thus allowed to advance, and what was oats becomes rye.

The idea, then, which I form of the progress of organic life upon the globe—and the hypothesis is applicable to all similar theatres of vital being—is, *that the simplest and most primitive type, under a law to which that of like-production is subordinate, gave birth to the type next above it, that this again produced the next higher, and so on to the very highest,* the stages of advance being in all cases very small—namely, from one species only to another; so that the phenomenon has always been of a simple and modest character. Whether the whole of any species was at once translated forward, or only a few parents were employed to give birth to the new type, must remain undetermined; but, supposing that the former was the case, we must presume that the moves along the line or lines were simultaneous, so that the place vacated by one species was immediately taken by the next in succession, and so on back to the first, for the supply of which the formation of a new germinal vesicle out of inorganic matter was alone necessary. Thus, the production of new forms, as shewn in the pages of the geological record, has never been anything more than a new stage of progress in gestation, an event as simply natural, and attended as little by any circumstances of a wonderful or startling kind, as the silent advance of an ordinary mother from one week to another of her pregnancy. Yet, be it remembered, the whole phenomena are, in another point of view, wonders of the highest kind, for in each of them we have to trace the effect of an Almighty Will which had arranged the whole in such harmony with external physical circumstances, that both were developed in parallel steps—and probably this development upon our planet is but a sample of what has taken place, through the same cause, in all the other countless theatres of being which are suspended in space.

This may be the proper place at which to introduce the preceding illustrations in a form calculated to bring them more forcibly before the mind of the reader. The following table was suggested to me, in consequence of seeing the scale of animated nature presented in Dr. Fletcher's Rudiments of Physiology. Taking that scale as its basis, it shews the wonderful parity observed in the progress of creation, as presented to our observation in the succession of fossils, and also in the fœtal progress of one of the principal human organs.[7] This scale, it may be remarked, was not made up with a view to support such an hypothesis as the present, nor with any ap-

---

[6]See an article by Dr. Weissenborn, in the New Series of "Magazine of Natural History," vol. i. p. 574.

[7]"It is a fact of the highest interest and moment that as the brain of every tribe of animals appears to pass, during its development, in succession through the types of all those below it, so the brain of man passes through the types of those of every tribe in the creation. It represents, accordingly, before the second month of utero-gestation, that of an avertebrated animal; at the second month, that of an osseous fish; at the third, that of a turtle; at the fourth, that of a bird; at the fifth, that of one of the rodentia; at the sixth, that of one of the ruminantia; at the seventh, that of one of the digitigrada; at the eighth, that of one of the quadrumana; till at length, at the ninth, it compasses the brain of Man! It is hardly necessary to say, that all this is only an approximation to the truth; since neither is the brain of all osseous fishes, of all turtles, of all birds, nor of all the species of any one of the above order of mammals, by any means precisely the same, nor does the brain of the human fœtus at any time precisely resemble, perhaps, that of any individual whatever among the lower

parent regard to the history of fossils, but merely to express the appearance of advancement in the orders of the Cuvierian system, assuming, as the criterion of that advancement, "an increase in the number and extent of the manifestations of life, or of the relations which an organized being bears to the external world." Excepting in the relative situation of the annelida and a few of the mammal orders, the parity is perfect; nor may even these small discrepancies appear when the order of fossils shall have been further investigated, or a more correct scale shall have been formed. Meanwhile, it is a wonderful evidence in favour of our hypothesis, that a scale formed so arbitrarily should coincide to such a nearness with our present knowledge of the succession of animal forms upon earth, and also that both of these series should harmonize so well with the view given by modern physiologists of the embryotic progress of one of the organs of the highest order of animals.

The reader has seen physical conditions several times referred to, as to be presumed to have in some way governed the progress of the development of the zoological circle. This language may seem vague, and, it may be asked,—can any particular physical condition be adduced as likely to have affected development? To this it may be answered, that air and light are probably amongst the principal agencies of this kind which operated in educing the various forms of being. Light is found to be essential to the development of the individual embryo. When tadpoles were placed in a perforated box, and that box sunk in the Seine, light being the only condition thus abstracted, they grew to a great size in their original form, but did not pass through the usual metamorphose which brings them to their mature state as frogs. The proteus, an animal of the frog kind, inhabiting the subterrane-

ous waters of Carniola, and which never acquires perfect lungs so as to become a land animal, is presumed to be an example of arrested development, from the same cause. When, in connexion with these facts, we learn that human mothers living in dark and close cells under ground,—that is to say, with an inadequate provision of air and light,—are found to produce an unusual proportion of defective children,[8] we can appreciate the important effects of both these physical conditions in ordinary reproduction. Now there is nothing to forbid the supposition that the earth has been at different stages of its career under different conditions, as to both air and light. On the contrary, we have seen reason for supposing that the proportion of carbonic acid gas (the element fatal to animal life) was larger at the time of the carboniferous formation than it afterwards became. We have also seen that astronomers regard the zodiacal light as a residuum of matter enveloping the sun, and which was probably at one time denser than it is now. Here we have the indications of causes for a progress in the purification of the atmosphere and in the diffusion of light during the earlier ages of the earth's history, with which the progress of organic life may have been conformable. An accession to the proportion of oxygen, and the effulgence of the central luminary, may have been the immediate prompting cause of all those advances from species to species which we have seen, upon other grounds, to be necessarily supposed as having taken place. And causes of the like nature may well be supposed to operate on other spheres of being, as well as on this. I do not indeed present these ideas as furnishing the true explanation of the progress of organic creation; they are merely thrown out as hints towards the formation of a just hypothesis, the completion of which is only to be looked for when some considerable advances shall have been made in the amount and character of our stock of knowledge.

Early in this century, M. Lamarck, a naturalist of the highest character, suggested an hypothesis of organic progress which deservedly incurred much ridicule, although it contained a glimmer of the truth. He surmised, and endeavoured, with a great deal of ingenuity, to prove, that one being advanced in the course of generations to another, in consequence merely of its experience of wants calling for the exercise of its faculties in a particular direction, by which exercise new developments of organs took

animals. Nevertheless, it may be said to represent, at each of the above-mentioned periods, the aggregate, as it were, of the brains of each of the tribes stated; consisting as it does, about the second month, chiefly of the mesial parts of the cerebellum, the corpora quadrigemina, thalami optici, rudiments of the hemispheres of the cerebrum and corpora striata; and receiving in succession, at the third, the rudiments of the lobes of the cerebrum; at the fourth, those of the fornix, corpus callosum, and septum lucidum; at the fifth, the tubor annulare, and so forth; the posterior lobes of the cerebrum increasing from before to behind, so as to cover the thalami optici about the fourth month, the corpora quadrigemina about the sixth, and the cerebellum about the seventh. This, then, is another example of an increase in the complexity of an organ succeeding its centralization; as if Nature, having first piled up her materials in one spot, delighted afterwards to employ her abundance, not so much in enlarging old parts as in forming new ones upon the old foundations, and thus adding to the complexity of a fabric, the rudimental structure of which is in all animals equally simple."—*Fletcher's Rudiments of Physiology.*

[8]Some poor people having taken up their abode in the cells under the fortifications of Lisle, the proportion of defective infants produced by them became so great, that it was deemed necessary to issue an order commanding these cells to be shut up.

SCALE OF ANIMAL KINGDOM. (The numbers indicate orders:)	ORDER OF ANIMALS IN	ASCENDING SERIES OF ROCKS.	FŒTAL HUMAN BRAIN RESEMBLES, IN
RADIATA (1, 2, 3, 4, 5)	Zoophyta / Polypiaria	1 Gneiss and Mica Slate system	
MOLLUSCA (6, 7, 8, 9, 10, 11)	Conchifera / Double-shelled Mollusks	2 Clay Slate and Grawacke system	1st month, that of an avertebrated animal;
ARTICULATA: Annelida (12, 13, 14); Crustacea (15, 16, 17, 18, 19, 20); Arachnida & Insecta (21–31)	Crustacea / Annelida / Crustaceous Fishes	3 Silurian system	
Pisces (32, 33, 34, 35, 36)	True Fishes	4 Old Red Sandstone	
	Piscine Saurians (ichthyosaurus, &c.) / Pterodactyles	5 Carboniferous formation	2nd month, that of a fish;
Reptilia (37, 38, 39, 40)	Crocodiles / Tortoises / Batrachians	6 New Red Sandstone	3rd month, that of a turtle;
Aves (41, 42, 43, 44, 45, 46)	Birds	7 Oolite / 8 Cretaceous formation	4th month, that of a bird;
VERTEBRATA: Mammalia: 47 Cetacea	(Bone of a marsupial animal)		
48 Ruminantia	Pachydermata (tapirs, horses, &c.)		
49 Pachydermata			
50 Edentata		9 Lower Eocene	5th month, that of a rodent;
51 Rodentia	Rodentia (dormouse, squirrel, &c.)		6th month, that of a ruminant;
52 Marsupialia	Marsupialia (racoon, opossum, &c.)		
53 Amphibia			
54 Digitigrada	Digitigrada (genette, fox, wolf, &c.)	10 Miocene	7th month, that of a digitigrade animal;
55 Plantigrada	Plantigrada (bear)		
56 Insectivora	Cetacea (lamantins, seals, whales) / Edentata (sloths, &c.) / Ruminantia (oxen, deer, &c.)	11 Pliocene	
57 Cheiroptera			
58 Quadrumana	Quadrumana (monkeys)	12 Superficial deposits	8th month, that of the quadrumana;
59 Bimana	Bimana (man)		9th month, attains full human character.

place, ending in variations sufficient to constitute a new species. Thus he thought that a bird would be driven by necessity to seek its food in the water, and that, in its efforts to swim, the outstretching of its claws would lead to the expansion of the intermediate membranes, and it would thus become web-footed. Now it is possible that wants and the exercise of faculties have entered in some manner into the production of the phenomena which we have been considering; but certainly not in the way suggested by Lamarck, whose whole notion is obviously so inadequate to account for the rise of the organic kingdoms, that we only can place it with pity among the follies of the wise. Had the laws of organic development been known in his time, his theory might have been of a more imposing kind. It is upon these that the present hypothesis is mainly founded. I take existing natural means, and shew them to have been capable of producing all the existing organisms, with the simple and easily conceivable aid of a higher generative law, which we perhaps still see operating upon a limited scale. I also go beyond the French philosopher to a very important point, the original Divine conception of all the forms of being which these natural laws were only instruments in working out and realizing. The actuality of such a conception I hold to be strikingly demonstrated by the discoveries of Macleay, Vigors, and Swainson, with respect to the affinities and analogies of animal (and by implication vegetable) organisms. Such a regularity in the *structure,* as we may call it, of the *classification of animals,* as is shewn in their systems, is totally irreconcilable with the idea of form going on to form merely as needs and wishes in the animals themselves dictated. Had such been the case, all would have been irregular, as things arbitrary necessarily are. But, lo, the whole plan of being is as symmetrical as the plan of a house, or the laying out of an old-fashioned garden! This must needs have been devised and arranged for beforehand. And what a preconception or forethought have we here! Let us only for a moment consider how various are the external physical conditions in which animals live—climate, soil, temperature, land, water, air—the peculiarities of food, and the various ways in which it is to be sought; the peculiar circumstances in which the business of reproduction and the care-taking of the young are to be attended to—all these required to be taken into account, and thousands of animals were to be formed suitable in organization and mental character for the concerns they were to have with these various conditions and circumstances—here a tooth fitted for crushing nuts; there a claw fitted to serve as a hook for suspension; here to repress teeth and develop a bony net-work instead; there to arrange for a bronchial apparatus, to last only for a

certain brief time; and all these animals were to be schemed out, each as a part of a great range, which was on the whole to be rigidly regular: let us, I say, only consider these things, and we shall see that the decreeing of laws to bring the whole about was an act involving such a degree of wisdom and device as we only can attribute, adoringly, to the one Eternal and Unchangeable. It may be asked, how does this reflection comport with that timid philosophy which would have us to draw back from the investigation of God's works, lest the knowledge of them should make us undervalue his greatness and forget his paternal character? Does it not rather appear that our ideas of the Deity can only be worthy of him in the ratio in which we advance in a knowledge of his works and ways; and that the acquisition of this knowledge is consequently an available means of our growing in a genuine reverence for him!

But the idea that any of the lower animals have been concerned in any way with the origin of man—is not this degrading? Degrading is a term, expressive of a notion of the human mind, and the human mind is liable to prejudices which prevent its notions from being invariably correct. Were we acquainted for the first time with the circumstances attending the production of an individual of our race, we might equally think them degrading, and be eager to deny them, and exclude them from the admitted truths of nature. Knowing this fact familiarly and beyond contradiction, a healthy and natural mind finds no difficulty in regarding it complacently. Creative Providence has been pleased to order that it should be so, and it must therefore be submitted to. Now the idea as to the progress of organic creation, if we become satisfied of its truth, ought to be received precisely in this spirit. It has pleased Providence to arrange that one species should give birth to another, until the second highest gave birth to man, who is the very highest: be it so, it is our part to admire and to submit. The very faintest notion of there being anything ridiculous or degrading in the theory—how absurd does it appear, when we remember that every individual amongst us actually passes through the characters of the insect, the fish, and reptile, (to speak nothing of others,) before he is permitted to breathe the breath of life! But such notions are mere emanations of false pride and ignorant prejudice. He who conceives them little reflects that they, in reality, involve the principle of a contempt for the works and ways of God, For it may be asked, if He, as appears, has chosen to employ inferior organisms as a generative medium for the production of higher ones, even including ourselves, what right have we, his humble creatures, to find fault? There is, also, in this prejudice, an element of unkindliness towards the lower animals, which is utterly out of place. These creatures are all of them part products of the Almighty Conception, as well as ourselves. All of them display wondrous evidences of his wisdom and benevolence. All of them have had assigned to them by their Great Father a part in the drama of the organic world, as well as ourselves. Why should they be held in such contempt? Let us regard them in a proper spirit, as parts of the grand plan, instead of contemplating them in the light of frivolous prejudices, and we shall be altogether at a loss to see how there should be any degradation in the idea of our race having been genealogically connected with them.

Name: _____ **Date:** _____

1. Chambers presents a number of examples of different organs in different animals being used for the same basic purpose? Describe two examples of this in your own words.

1.

2.

2. Based on this reading, do you think Chambers was an atheist? Why or why not?

3. What is the "principle of development" as Chambers uses the term?

4. How does Chambers, using Babbage's work in the *Ninth Bridgewater Treatise* explain how species could be "programmed" to change?

5. Does Chambers think the idea that humans developed from lower creatures is degrading to human life? Why or why not?

Adam Sedgwick

"Review of *Vestiges of the Natural History of Creation*," 1845

Sedgwick (1785-1873) was an English mathematician and geologist who was one of Darwin's favorite teachers at Cambridge. An Anglican and ardent supporter of natural theology, Sedgwick believed that God had personally and directly created the natural world and that studying nature was a way to study and glorify God. Despite his close relationship to and significant influence on Darwin, Sedgwick never accepted Darwin's theory of evolution by natural selection. In his review of *Vestiges of the Natural History of Creation*, Sedgwick demonstrated his belief that science and Christianity were inherently harmonious, and he attacked the book on theological, philosophical, and scientific grounds.

This is a remarkable book, and has had a sudden run of public favour. A fourth edition has just appeared; but our last perusal having been bestowed upon the third, we shall refer to it in all our extracts, except where the first may demand some passing notice. The book treats of Cosmogonies in the largest sense in which that high-sounding word was ever used by man; and the author, after soaring with us among the clouds, and giving us a bold outline of the 'Nebular hypothesis,' comes down to the lower world, and tells us of the wonders of the earth, and of the marvellous organic forms, in successive generations, which geologists have brought up from regions of darkness, and put before us in the light of day. He then unfolds his theory of Animal Development, in which we learn that the humblest organic structures began first, and were produced by Electricity, or some like power of common nature—That to begin living structures any other way, 'would be an inconceivably paltry exercise 'of creative power'—That nature having thus made a start, all difficulties are over; for, by progressive breeding, the first monads will work their way, without any external help, through all the ascending scale of things, up to Monkeys; and that Monkeys will, in like manner, become at length the parents of Men. He then appeals, in confirmation of his views, to the successive organic forms

From *Edinburgh Review,* July, 1845.

found in the old strata of the earth, and to the fœtal forms of men and beasts; and so builds up a scale of nature which is to be an index of a universal creative law.

The work is systematic and well got up for its purpose, so far as regards its outer form; and in the latter part of this article we mean to track the vestiges in their own natural order. But in the concluding chapters of the work, many subjects (such as the circular system of natural history, phrenology, animal instincts in comparison with human reason, the origin of language, and the diffusion of the various families of the human race) pass under review. All of them we cannot notice, but some we are compelled to glance at; and we do so in the first instance, that our more general views may be less interrupted, and hoping in this introductory matter to make our readers comprehend the peculiar qualities of our author's mind, and his mode of dealing with great physical questions.

It follows of necessity, that in the progress of such a work, subjects must be brought under review which bear upon almost every question belonging to natural science; and we find that every thing is touched upon, while nothing is firmly grasped. We have not the strong master-hand of an independent labourer, either in the field or closet, shown for a single instant. All in the book is shallow; and all is at second-hand. The surface may be beautiful; but it is the glitter of gold-leaf without the solidity of the precious metal. The style is agreeable—sometimes charming; and noble sentiments are scattered here and there; but these harmonies are never lasting. Sober truth and solemn nonsense, strangely blended, and offered to us in a new material jargon, break discordantly on our ears, and hurt our better feelings.

The author is intensely hypothetical, and builds his castles in the air, misconceiving the principles of science, or misunderstanding the facts with which it has to deal; or, what is worse still, distorting them to serve his purpose. He does all this, apparently, without having any just conception of the methods by which men, after the toil of many generations, have ascended, step by step, to the higher elevations of physical knowledge—without any even glimmering conception of what men mean when they tell us of Inductive Science and its sober truths.

But if this be so, how, it may be asked, are we to account for the popularity of the work, and the sudden sale of edition after edition? Men who are fed on nothing better than the trash of literature, and who have never waded beyond the surface of the things they pretend to know, must needs delight in the trashy skimmings of philosophy; and we venture to affirm that no man who has any name in science, properly so called, whether derived from profound study, or original labour in the field, has spoken well of the book, or regarded it with any feelings but those of deep aversion. We say this advisedly, after exchanging thoughts with some of the best informed men in Britain. The public who are not able to judge from their own knowledge, must therefore be plainly told, that the philosophy of the author is borrowed from a false and shallow School; and that the consequences he dares to draw from it, so far as they are new in the scientific literature of our country, are nothing better than mischievous, and sometimes antisocial, nonsense.

The book tells us of things new to many of us—and all of us delight in novelties. It lifts up the curtain of the dissecting-room, and publishes its secrets in rounded sentences of seeming reverence, and in the conventional language of good society. Things useful, and good, and excellent in one place, may be foul and mischievous in another. The world cannot bear to be turned upside down; and we are ready to wage an internecine war with any violation of our modest principles and social manners. Hercules, when he took the distaff in hand, made only a sorry thread; and we presume that Omphalè found her hero's club but a clumsy spindle. It is our maxim, that things must keep their proper places if they are to work together for any good. If our glorious maidens and matrons may not soil their fingers with the dirty knife of the anatomist, neither may they poison the springs of joyous thought and modest feeling, by listening to the seductions of this author; who comes before them with a bright, polished, and many-coloured surface, and the serpent coils of a false philosophy, and asks them again to stretch out their hands and pluck forbidden fruit—to talk familiarly with him of things which cannot be so much as named without raising a blush upon a modest cheek;—who tells them—that their Bible is a fable when it teaches them that they were made in the image of God—that they are the children of apes and the breeders of monsters—that he has *annulled all distinction between physical and moral,*—and that all the phenomena of the universe, dead and living, are to be put before the mind in a new jargon, and as the progression and development of a rank, unbending, and degrading materialism.

But who is the author? We thought, when we began to 'The Vestiges,' that we could trace therein the markings of a woman's foot. We now confess our error; and for having entertained it, we crave pardon of the sex. We were led to this delusion by certain charms of writing—by the popularity of the work—by its ready boundings over the fences of the tree of knowledge, and its utter neglect of the narrow and thorny entrance by which we may lawfully approach it; above all, by the sincerity of faith and love with which the author devotes himself to any system he has taken to his bosom. We thought that no *man* could write so much about natural science without having dipped below the surface, at least in some department of it. In thinking this, we now believe we were mistaken.

But let us not be misunderstood. Within all the becoming bounds of homage, we would do honour to the softer sex little short of adoration. In taste, and sentiment, and instinctive knowledge of what is right and good—in discrimination of human character, and what is most befitting in all the moral duties of common life—in every thing which forms, not merely the grace and ornament, but is the cementing principle and bond of all that is most exalted and delightful in society, we would place our highest trust in woman. But we know, by long experience, that the ascent up the hill of science is rugged and thorny, and ill-fitted for the drapery of a petticoat; and ways must be passed over which are toilsome to the body, and sometimes loathsome to the senses. And every one who has ventured on these ways, has learned a lesson of humility from his own repeated failures. He has learned to appreciate the enormous and continued labour by which every new position has been won; and, above all, he has learned the immeasurable depth of his own ignorance, when he applies his faculties to any higher order of material causation beyond the known truths he derives from others, or from his own observations and experiments. No man living, who has not partaken of this kind of labour, or, to say the least, who has not thoroughly mastered the knowledge put before his senses by the labours of other men, has any right to toss out his fantastical crudities before the public, and give himself the airs of a legislator over the material world.

If we know not the author personally, we may well rejoice in our ignorance; for our criticisms have not the semblance of personal hostility. It is an imperious sense of duty, and an unflinching love of truth, which dictate the language of this article; and in writing it we are moved by ill-will to no one. We may, however, dissect the author's mind from the character of his book; and we believe him to be an accomplished, and, in a certain sense, a well-informed but superficial person. He exhibits a not uncommon union of scepticism and credulity. The combination is not by any means unnatural; for it often requires good and long training to cure a man of subtle doubts, and the first advances of knowledge often lead men of ardent minds into rash and incongruous conclusions. Again, the author is a man of imagination, and delights in resemblances—sometimes real, and sometimes (strange to tell) only to be found in the similarity of sounds, by which, from the natural imperfection of language, things entirely different are confounded under common terms. He hardly seems to know that in the veriest child the perception of resemblances far outstrips the realities of knowledge. It is the part of science to anatomize external things, and to follow out their *differences;* and then, and not till then, to arrange them in their proper places and speculate on their mutual bearings.

He is so enamoured of resemblances, that he will cheat his senses by mere similitudes of sound. Every one has heard of the quickness of thought—of 'glancing from heaven to earth, from earth to heaven,'—and who has not heard of the velocity of the galvanic fluid? Therefore, the speed of thought may be reduced to numbers, and a man may think at the rate of 192,000 miles a second! We know well that the author may shelter himself under the juggle of his own words, and tell us that he speaks only of the transmission of our will through the organs of the body. Let him, then, write in more becoming language. But he closes with his own hands his only door of escape. 'Electricity is almost as metaphysical as ever mind was supposed to be' . . . 'and yet electricity is a real thing, an actual existence,' or, in

other words, a material existence, 'So mental action may be imponderable and intangible, and yet a real existence'—that is, a material existence. In the same passage he tells us, 'that the brain is absolutely identical with a galvanic battery!' As well might he say that the human will and the point of a needle are identical, because each of them can produce the contraction of a muscle. Allowing that some of the functions of the brain resemble galvanism, are we to conclude that all its functions are galvanic? We repudiate the rash conclusion. It may be true that galvanic influence transmitted through a nervous chord, soon after death, will produce muscular contraction; and it may be true that, after sudden death, electric action may be transmitted from the hollow of the cranium, down the nerves which supply the stomach, so as to continue for a short time the operations of digestion. But what is all this for the author's purpose, unless he can re-animate a dead body, and continue the higher functions of life, sensation, and volition? When he has done this, we will listen to his materialism; but not till then. There is an immeasurable difference between the material organic combinations of a body, and its associated phenomena of life, sensation, and volition; and there is not the shadow of a reason why things so different in kind should cease together at the very moment of death. The doctrine of a 'vital principle' may have been pushed too far, and brought to the explanation of phenomena which are resolvable on the more vulgar principles of ordinary chemical combination; but this is not our present question. It is said that hair will continue to grow for several days after death. It is said also, in cases of sudden death, when life is arrested while every organ is in a healthy state, that organic action may for a while go on; and that the dead stomach may, in such a case, be dissolved by the very digestive juice which it has just elaborated. We therefore receive with doubt the digestive experiment of our author. If it be true, we willingly receive its evidence, while we reject the beggarly conclusion he dares to draw from it.

Again, all things living, whether vegetable or animal, may be traced back to some elementary germ, which admits not even of microscopic analysis. Therefore, the author tells us, all things living have one common fundamental and material germ. In tracing backwards the organic structure of different species, we can mark a difference at every step, so long as the things before us are within the ken of sense, and we can aid our senses by instruments of great power; but we lose ourselves at last among the ultimate germs of organic life. Are we then to say that these ultimate and unknown germs are all one and the same; while the phenomena springing from them, by stern unbending physical laws, are all different? One who, like this author, can snatch at the conclusion, has a mind incapable of Inductive reasoning, and cheats himself, at every turn of thought, by nothing better than empty sounds.

◼ ◼ ◼ ◼

We have now done with our author's reasonings, and let us come to his facts. The first question we ask is this—Is there in the mechanism of nature (we now speak figuratively) any apparent contrivance, to produce a shifting from one species to another, on an ascending scale? Our author, of course, says yes, and we most positively say no. His argument professes to be based on some very obscure facts of living nature; and secondly, to be helped out by the still obscurer phenomena presented by the fœtal forms of animals, while in their mother's womb. We will begin with the obscure facts, for we do not wish to blink them; and we profess to know nothing of nature but from reasonings bottomed on observation. We dare not, like our author, go at once to the great First Cause and tell our readers what he MUST have done: and what was, and what was not, a *paltry exercise of his creative power*. We study the laws of nature as the docile children of nature, and we slowly rise to the comprehension of certain laws. We can rise to a conception of a great First Cause co-ordinate with all we see. We see him, dimly it may be, in his works, but we form no conception of his essence; and, strain our souls as we will, we have not the atom of any natural conception of his power beyond the suggestion of the things which form the natural materials of our thoughts. Hence, in reasoning of creation, we dare not, we repeat, tell beforehand of what God must have done. This is rashly and irreverently 'to anthropomorphize God;' and thus our author's weapon is turned against himself. He accuses us of this great folly; but we can bear the charge, while we only seek the truth by listening to the accents of nature's teaching. Let us come, then, to our author's array of facts, and our answers shall be as short as possible.

1. He tells us that oats, if cropped before maturity, and then allowed to remain in the ground over winter, will spring up next year in the form of rye—(p. 226.) This is an old story, and we believe a fable. Let the pretended fact be tried, and should it prove true, it makes nothing (as he himself indeed allows) for his general argument.
2. When lime is laid on waste ground, we are told that white clover will spring up spontaneously; and in situations where no clover seed could have been left dormant in the soil—(p. 181.)

But how is this to be proved? It is certain that many seeds will remain dormant in the soil, perhaps for centuries, and then spring up the first year the soil is turned by the plough. Some seeds have retained their vitality for thousands of years in the old tombs of Egypt. And is it not well-known that such seeds as have a perfect capsule, and have not been crushed by the gizzard of birds or the teeth of beasts, will pass through them, and fall upon the ground with undiminished vitality? The author's case is well-known, and does not throw in our way the shadow of a difficulty.

3. He next contends that the lower animals cannot first spring from an *ovum*, because they increase by 'fissiparous 'generation'—by a splitting up of their bodies. But he destroys his own argument; for, on his own showing, animals which do spring from *ova*, undergo in the first instance this very process. The process is afterwards carried further, but that does not change the first condition of fœtal existence, or separate the cases so as to give the shadow of colour to the author's argument.
4. He tells us that wild pigs never have the measles—a disease produced by a *Hyatid*—that there is a *Tinea* (we believe there are two) only found in dressed wool—and that the larva of the *Oinopota cellaris* only lives in wine and beer—(p. 186.) Hence he concludes, that the *Hyatid*, the *Tinea*, and the *Larva*, must have been created (of course by means purely natural) since we began to eat bacon, to wear woollen coats, and to make wine and beer. Negative arguments have often two edges, and they are odd-tempered weapons, which will sometimes turn their points towards the breast of the man who fences with them clumsily. Has our author a clean bill of health for all the primeval pigs, and well attested by good medical naturalists in all ages before pork was eaten? Wild animals of the genus *Canis* seldom have the mange; but they sometimes have it, as the gentlemen of Melton Mowbray will tell him. Has he peered into every nook and corner of the whole world for the Larvæ? Does he not know (and he ought to know) that the Tinea is quite as injurious to the fleece as it is to the prepared and manufactured wool? If his account be true, it only shows that the creatures are rather nice, and love a clean pasture.
5. He next brings before us the *Pimelodes cyclopum* of the Andes. They are little fishes which swarm in some high lakes, filling up old volcanic craters, and other hollows of the great chain, and they are also found in the

streams gushing from these high lakes. They are not more difficult to account for than the trout and other fishes found in the mountain lakes of Europe. When the pent-up fires rekindle, (perhaps after centuries of repose,) the lakes and all their contents are belched out of the old craters, and fill the neighbouring valleys with pestilence and ruin. These phenomena are most instructive; but our author gains nothing by fishing in such troubled waters.

6. He mentions the *Entozoa*—creatures living in the interior of other animals. The tape-worm which infests the human species, is a well-known and melancholy instance. We allow that they throw some real difficulties in our way; but we deny that they give us the shadow of an argument for the transmutation theory. Difficulties are inevitable while we are among the obscurest parts of nature's workmanship. How came these creatures where we sometimes find them? We are certain that our author blunders (as he so often does when he touches on a point of exact physics)—when he tells us that their ova could not pass through the air, because they are too heavy for the transit. Does he not know that the dust which floats through the air on a windy day, is specifically as heavy as the rock from which it has been ground, and that the distance to which a particle will drift depends far more on its minuteness than on its specific weight? There is no difficulty whatsoever in supposing certain ova to drift through the air, and to settle and grow when they find a proper *nidus*. In some cases we can trace the whole history of these animals—often considered so mysterious. The eggs are dropped by an insect on the skin—the animal licks them off, and so they pass into the stomach, where they find a proper *nidus*, and then pass through their first changes. Speaking generally of the *Entozoa*, we may ask, if these creatures spring spontaneously without ova, how comes it to pass, (as anatomists have proved,) that nature has provided a means for the continuance of the species, and that some of them are almost incredibly prolific? One single individual of the human *Entozoa (Ascaris lumbricoides)* may have within its ovary many million eggs.[1]

Again, many of these eggs, and many of the perfect Entozoa, have such an astonishing vitality, that they will resist both the effects of boiling water, and of the hardest polar frost, without losing the powers of life. We cannot pursue these intricate and obscure subjects any further; but we conclude, partly on direct proof, and partly on analogy, that the *Entozoa* were produced in the common way. And, reviewing all that has been advanced under the six preceding heads, we venture to affirm that our author has not brought before us the semblance of any new fact; and that all his specific instances are worthless for his general argument.

■ ■ ■ ■

Spontaneous generation in the very humblest animal type, and a gradual transmutation from one species to another, in a regularly ascending scale, are the two great principles of our author's borrowed scheme. We have shown to demonstration that they derive no support from the phenomena of the old world; and he has failed to give us so much as a single instance, either of one principle or of the other, drawn from the undoubted facts of living nature. He offers nothing deserving the name of theory; for theory is but a reasonable interpretation of allowed facts; but he offers us instead a well connected scheme of gratuitous hypotheses. As a matter of fact, species do not change, and the fixed organic laws of nature are the first principles of physiology; in the same way that the fixed laws of atomic combination are the first principles of philosophical chemistry. Were nature changeable, there could be no philosophy. The fœtal changes within the womb are matters of the deepest interest; but, whatsoever they may be, they affect not our author's argument one jot; unless he can show some want of fixity in the phenomena which flow from them. But this he has not done, and cannot do. Parents produce an offspring like themselves. Eagles do not hatch owls; geese do not hatch rats, (whatsoever our author may dream;) and no tropical heat can ever bring a beast from the eggs of a reptile. Hence no fœtal changes, we repeat, can affect the general question. And here we might perhaps leave our author and our readers, who may think we have said enough; but we will not yet leave him; and through a few pages we will discuss his wild speculations (all borrowed from a bad school,) and his strange misconceptions on almost every fact he pretends to put before us.

He assumes, not only that the organic germs of all creatures are alike, but that they are identical; and that the higher animals (of course, including men)

---

[1]See Professor Owen's lectures on the invertebrate animals, read before the College of Surgeons, (Vol. i, 8vo, p. 76, 1843.) Many of the Entozoa have a most complicated organic structure; and in our minds it would be as mad to suppose them to spring from any natural or fortuitous concourse of inorganic atoms, as it would be to refer the bodily frame of a horse or a man to such an origin.

pass, while in the womb, through all the successive conditions which are permanent in the animals on the lower grades of the general organic scale; or, in other words, that the fœtus of a man is, during the successive periods of gestation, a monad, a polype, a cephalopod, or an insect; a fish, a reptile, a bird, a beast, ending with a monkey; and, lastly, a man with a permanent organic form. This is the theory: and how does he use this marvellous organic apparatus? He sends off the spokes of his organic wheel from different points of the ascending axle. The monads breed on (for example) till they have become like fishes; and the class of fishes then begins to branch off according to law. But the fishes also improve by breeding; and some one more favoured than the rest, and by a longer gestation, produces the reptile type; and from that type is given off a second spoke, representing, in due time, the class of reptiles. In like manner the other classes are sent off, higher on the axle, till we reach a spoke of the great organic wheel at the end of which are monkeys and men, (p. 217.) Nor is nature ever to stand still; for if our matrons will (as our author tells them) be more patient, they may yet send off another, and a higher spoke, to be 'the crowning type of man!' We fearlessly affirm that this monstrous scheme, is, from first to last, nothing but a pile of wildly gratuitous hypotheses. He stumbles on the threshold of his argument (a bad omen,) and each step he takes is false to the gradations of real nature. We wish with all our hearts we could pass this subject over; for it is fit only for professional books, and it requires illustrations which we cannot give here. But the subject is woven into our author's system, and he has contrived to do so in a popular manner: touch on it, then, we must; and we accordingly proceed to give a sketch of some of the leading changes in the fœtal forms, from their first organic germs up to a perfect mammal.

■ ■ ■ ■

There are strange facts in the metamorphoses of the lower, invertebrate animals; but all of them are governed by an undeviating cycle of organic laws; and none of them gives so much as the shadow of an argument for the hypothesis of transmutation from one species to another. As a general rule, these changes (like the gradual changes in the fœtus of a mammal) are from a lower to a more perfect organic structure. But there are some striking exceptions, or apparent exceptions, to the rule. For example, the myriapods have, at first, three pairs of feet, and in that respect conform to the type of the higher insects; but afterwards the feet increase in number. So that we have here a creature of a lower grade passing during its early stages through the type which is permanent in the higher. Again, the larvæ of some creatures are locomotive, and have eyes; but, in the more fully developed state, when they reach the condition of perfect animals, they become fixed to one spot, and lose the sense of sight. Facts like these are of the deepest interest; but they make nothing for our general argument, and we must leave them. No vertebrate animal, after the first rudiments of its structure are laid down, conforms to the type of an invertebrate. In the beginnings of life, we find a general similitude; but the fundamental rudiments of organic structure are laid down upon an entirely separate plan. The whole animal existence of a vertebrate and invertebrate creature does, however, admit of a general comparison. In each case we have the ovum, the embryo, the larva, and the perfect animal with the power of continuing its species. But by no contrivance or fostering can we make a larva fruitful, or obtain from it a new animal of some lower type:— the attempt must fail, because it involves a physical impossibility. Neither can we, by any artifice of breeding, push the perfect organic form of the complete animal beyond the limits of its species. Numberless attempts of this kind have been made, but they have all failed, and must ever fail, because they are contrary to nature's laws. There is, therefore, a grand unity in the works of nature proving a unity of creative will; but there is no confusion or mixture of species, when species are well ascertained: neither have the natural laws of atomic action in dead matter ever produced so much as one undoubted case, even of the lowest condition of organic structure, endowed with life. All nature, then, at whatever point we meet her, and during whatever age in the past history of the earth, tells us, with one unhesitating voice, that she has not enacted any law of spontaneous generation, and that she will not allow any power inferior to herself to mar her vestiges, or blot out her fixed organic types.[2]

We have now done with the author of the 'Vestiges of Creation.' We have examined fairly, and on common natural ground, every material point of his argument. He fails from his first beginnings—he understands not the present condition of the Nebular Hypothesis—and, admitting the truth of the hypothesis, he has drawn from it the most unwar-

---

[2]We contend that many cases of ambiguous generation are readily explained, by supposing the *ova* to have passed into a properly prepared infusion through the air. From some recent experiments we learn, that when the air, which has access to such an infusion, is made in the first instance to pass through sulphuric acid, no *infusoria* are produced, the floating *ova* having been destroyed during their passage through the acid. Connected with the subjects discussed in the preceding pages, we refer to an elaborate Report by Dr Clark, Professor of Anatomy in the University of Cambridge, read to the British Association in 1834, and published in their third volume.

rantable conclusions. He understands not the present condition of Geology, and he has strangely, and to all appearance unfairly, distorted such facts as were before him, to serve the purposes of his hypothesis. He has not brought one allowed fact from actual nature to bear upon his theory. He seems not to have consulted one good authority on the Fœtal Question; and he has, consequently, misconceived it, or misrepresented it at every turn of his professed argument. 'Men, like von Bäer and Valentin, far from favouring the cry of some eager followers, (now feebly re-echoed in this country)—that the higher animals pass through stages of development, which are permanent in the lower—expressly tell us that such views are one-sided and insufficient. The views they offer towards a system of nature are not made up of materialism, but are the offspring of that grand (but sometimes mistaken) idealism which pervades the philosophy of their country.'—(Dr Clark.)

We conclude, then, that our author's work is not merely shallow and superficial, but utterly false throughout to all the principles of sound philosophy. Of all the books we ever read, it puts before us the largest congeries of positive mistatements, and positively false conclusions. But it is pleasantly written, it is systematic, and it has been prepared for the press with no common care; so that its errors are not the mere errors of inadvertency; and its language (with one or two gross exceptions which we have pointed out) is so reverent, and so like the solemnity of truth, that we are compelled (almost against our senses) to believe that the author is actually labouring under some strange delusion, whereby he cheats himself, while he is doing his best to cheat others; by turning upside down every rule of sound Induction, and by affirming, again and again, and in every solemn form of language, that which is at direct variance with the plainest acknowledged facts of nature.

For our own parts we trust, in all good hope, that human knowledge will go on in the right road of sober Inductive truth; and if that be its direction, we can look for no consequences but such as will tend to the good of the human race. But woe to the world if our knowledge is to be made up of idle speculations, like those we have been reviewing—'as endless as a spider's thread, and of no substance or profit.' Instead of this, we must seek knowledge at the fountain head—in the order of nature—and in an humble contemplation of her works; so may we rise, step by step, to a more lofty knowledge; which, if we be right minded, 'will not be a tower of state for a proud mind to raise itself upon—or a fort or commanding ground for strife and contention—or a shop for profit or sale—but a rich storehouse for the glory of the Creator and the relief of man's estate.'[3]

---

[3]Lord Bacon.—Connected with this part of the article, we earnestly recommend to our readers, a small volume by Dr Whewell, Master of Trinity College, Cambridge, entitled *Indications of the Creator*, very recently published. Though, with the exception of the preface, it consists of Extracts from works published some time before the appearance of the 'Vestiges of Creation,' it meets the author's argument at many of its most important points.

Name: _____ **Date:** _____

1. Why, according to Sedgwick, is *Vestiges* bad science?

2. Why does Sedgwick think that the book may have been written by a woman?

3. Sedgwick lists six facts that the author of *Vestiges* offers in support of his claim that there exists in natural a figurative mechanism by which species change. List and describe these six facts in your own words:

1.

2.

3.

4.

5.

6.

4. Throughout the essay, Sedgwick claims that *Vestiges* does not adhere to the "inductive truth." Look up the word "inductive" and write its definition in your own words.

William Whewell

The Philosophy of the Inductive Sciences, 1840

Whewell (1794-1866) is one of the most influential figures in all of modern science. The son of a English carpenter, Whewell was recognized by a parish priest as a superb mathematician and arrangements were made for him to receive additional education. By virtue of public support and a scholarship he earned from a poetry contest, Whewell attended Cambridge and later took positions there as Professor of Mineralogy and Professor of Moral Philosophy. He was a close friend of many nineteenth-century scientists, including Darwin and Lyell, and is well known for the many valuable scientific terms he coined, including "ion," "cathode," "anode" and most importantly "scientist." His greatest contribution to modern science were his works on the philosophy of science. In this piece, Whewell explained how scientists could use the inductive method to extrapolate knowledge from collections of data. Induction, the act generating conclusions from assorted and often seemingly unconnected bits of information, was vital to Darwin's development of his theory of natural selection.

OF CERTAIN CHARACTERISTICS OF SCIENTIFIC INDUCTION

The two operations spoken of in the preceding chapters,—the Explication of the Conceptions of our own minds, and the Colligation of observed Facts by the aid of such Conceptions,—are, as we have just said, inseparably connected with each other. When united, and employed in collecting knowledge from the phenomena which the world presents to us, they constitute the mental process of *Induction;* which is usually and justly spoken of as the genuine source of all our *real general knowledge* respecting the external world. And we see, from the preceding analysis of this process into its two constituents, from what origin it derives each of its characters. It is *real*, because it arises from the combination of real facts, but it is *general*, because it implies the possession of general ideas. Without the former, it would not be knowledge of the external world; without the latter, it would not be knowledge at all. When Ideas and Facts are separated from each other, the neglect of facts gives rise to empty speculations, idle subtleties, visionary inventions, false opinions concerning the laws of phenomena,

From *The Philosophy of the Inductive Sciences, Founded Upon Their History,* London: John W. Parker, 1840.

disregard of the true aspect of nature: while the want of ideas leaves the mind overwhelmed, bewildered, and stupified by particular sensations, with no means of connecting the past with the future, the absent with the present, the example with the rule; open to the impression of all appearances, but capable of appropriating none. Ideas are the *Form,* facts the *Material,* of our structure. Knowledge does not consist in the empty mould, or in the brute mass of matter, but in the rightly-moulded substance. Induction gathers general truths from particular facts;—and in her harvest, the corn and the reaper, the solid ears and the binding band, are alike requisite. All our knowledge of nature is obtained by Induction; the term being understood according to the explanation we have now given. And our knowledge is then most complete, then most truly deserves the name of Science, when both its elements are most perfect;—when the Ideas which have been concerned in its formation have, at every step, been clear and consistent;—and when they have, at every step also, been employed in binding together real and certain Facts. Of such Induction I have already given so many examples and illustrations in the two preceding chapters, that I need not now dwell further upon the subject.

Induction is familiarly spoken of as the process by which we collect a *general proposition* from a number of *particular cases:* and it appears to be frequently imagined that the general proposition results from a mere juxtaposition of the cases, or at most, from merely conjoining and extending them. But if we consider the process more closely, as exhibited in the cases lately spoken of, we shall perceive that this is an inadequate account of the matter. The particular facts are not merely brought together, but there is a new element added to the combination by the very act of thought by which they are combined. There is a conception of the mind introduced in the general proposition, which did not exist in any of the observed facts. When the Greeks, after long observing the motions of the planets, saw that these motions might be rightly considered as produced by the motion of one wheel revolving in the inside of another wheel, these wheels were creations of their minds, added to the facts which they perceived by sense. And even if the wheels were no longer supposed to be material, but were reduced to mere geometrical spheres or circles, they were not the less products of the mind alone,—something additional to the facts observed. The same is the case in all other discoveries. The facts are known, but they are insulated and unconnected, till the discoverer supplies from his own stores a principle of connexion. The pearls are there, but they will not hang together till some one provides the string. The distances and periods of the planets were all so many separate facts; by Kepler's Third Law they are connected into a single truth: but the conceptions which this law involves were supplied by Kepler's mind, and without these, the facts were of no avail. The planets described ellipses round the sun, in the contemplation of others as well as of Newton; but Newton conceived the deflection from the tangent in these elliptical motions in a new light,—as the effect of a central force following a certain law; and then it was that such a force was discovered truly to exist.

Thus in each inference made by Induction, there is introduced some general conception, which is given, not by the phenomena, but by the mind. The conclusion is not contained in the premises, but includes them by the introduction of a new generality. In order to obtain our inference, we travel beyond the cases which we have before us; we consider them as more exemplifications of some ideal case in which the relations are complete and intelligible. We take a standard, and measure the facts by it; and this standard is constructed by us, not offered by Nature. We assert, for example, that a body left to itself will move on with unaltered velocity; not because our senses ever disclosed to us a body doing this, but because (taking this as our ideal case) we find that all actual cases are intelligible and explicable by means

of the Conception of *Forces,* causing change and motion, and exerted by surrounding bodies. In like manner, we see bodies striking each other, and thus moving and stopping, accelerating and retarding each other: but in all this, we do not perceive by our senses that abstract quantity *Momentum,* which is always lost by one body as it is gained by another. This Momentum is a creation of the mind, brought in among the facts, in order to convert their apparent confusion into order, their seeming chance into certainty, their perplexing variety into simplicity. This the Conception of *Momentum gained and lost* does: and in like manner, in any other case in which a truth is established by Induction, some Conception is introduced, some Idea is applied, as the means of binding together the facts, and thus producing the truth.

Hence in every inference by Induction there is some Conception *superinduced* upon the Facts: and we may henceforth conceive this to be the peculiar import of the term *Induction.* I am not to be understood as asserting that the term was originally or anciently employed with this notion of its meaning; for the peculiar feature just pointed out in Induction has generally been overlooked. This appears by the accounts generally given of Induction. "Induction," says Aristotle, "is when by means of one extreme term[1] we infer the other extreme term to be true of the middle term." Thus, (to take such exemplifications as belong to our subject,) from knowing that Mercury, Venus, Mars, describe ellipses about the Sun, we infer that all Planets describe ellipses about the Sun. In making this inference syllogistically, we assume that the evident proposition, "Mercury, Venus, Mars, do what all Planets do," may be taken *conversely,* "All Planets do what Mercury, Venus, Mars, do." But we remark that, in this passage, Aristotle (as was natural in his line of discussion) turns his attention entirely to the *evidence* of the inference; and overlooks a step which is of far more importance to our knowledge, namely, the *invention* of the second extreme term. In the above instance, the particular luminaries, Mercury, Venus, Mars, are one logical *extreme;* the general designation Planets is the *middle term;* but having these before us, how do we come to think of *description of ellipses,* which is the other extreme of the syllogism? When we have once invented this "second extreme term," we may, or may not, be satisfied with the evidence of the syllogism; we may, or may not, be convinced that, so far as this property goes, the extremes are co-extensive with the middle

---

[1]The syllogism here alluded to would be this:—Mercury, Venus, Mars, describe ellipses about the Sun; All Planets do what Mercury, Venus, Mars, do; Therefore all Planets describe ellipses about the Sun.

term; but the *statement* of the syllogism is the important step in science. We know how long Kepler laboured, how hard he fought, how many devices he tried, before he hit upon this *term,* the elliptical motion. He rejected, as we know, many other "second extreme terms," for example, various combinations of epicyclical constructions, because they did not represent with sufficient accuracy the special facts of observation. When he had established his premiss, that "Mars does describe an ellipse about the Sun," he does not hesitate to *guess* at least that, in this respect, he might *convert* the other premiss, and assert that "All the Planets do what Mars does." But the main business was, the inventing and verifying the proposition respecting the ellipse. The Invention of the Conception was the great step in the *discovery;* the Verification of the Proposition was the great step in the *proof* of the discovery. If Logic consists in pointing out the conditions of proof, the Logic of Induction must consist in showing what are the conditions of proof in such inferences as this: but this subject must be pursued in the next chapter; I now speak principally of the act of *invention* which is requisite in every inductive inference.

Although in every inductive inference an act of invention is requisite, the act soon slips out of notice. Although we bind together facts by superinducing upon them a new conception, this conception, once introduced and applied, is looked upon as inseparably connected with the facts, and necessarily implied in them. Having once had the phenomena bound together in their minds in virtue of the conception, men can no longer easily restore them back to the detached and incoherent condition in which they were before they were thus combined. The pearls once strung, they seem to form a chain by their nature. Induction has given them a unity which it is so far from costing us an effort to preserve, that it requires an effort to imagine it dissolved. For instance, we usually represent to ourselves the earth as round, the earth and the planets as revolving about the sun, and as drawn to the sun by a central force; we can hardly understand how it could cost the Greeks, and Copernicus, and Newton so much pains and trouble to arrive at a view which is to us so familiar. These are no longer to us conceptions caught hold of and kept hold of by a severe struggle; they are the simplest modes of conceiving the facts: they are really facts. We are willing to *own* our obligation to those discoverers, but we hardly *feel* it: for in what other manner (we ask in our thoughts,) could we represent the facts to ourselves?

Thus we see why it is that this step of which we now speak, the invention of a new Conception in every inductive inference, is so generally overlooked

that it has hardly been noticed by preceding philosophers. When once performed by the discoverer, it takes a fixed and permanent place in the understanding of every one. It is a thought which, once breathed forth, permeates all men's minds. All fancy they nearly or quite knew it before. It oft was thought, or almost thought, though never till now expressed. Men accept it and retain it, and know it cannot be taken from them, and look upon it as their own. They will not and cannot part with it, even though they may deem it trivial and obvious. It is a secret, which once uttered, cannot be recalled, even though it be despised by those to whom it is imparted. As soon as the leading term of a new theory has been pronounced and understood, all the phenomena change their aspect. There is a standard to which we cannot help referring them. We cannot fall back into the helpless and bewildered state in which we gazed at them when we possessed no principle which gave them unity. Eclipses arrive in mysterious confusion: the notion of a *Cycle* dispels the mystery. The Planets perform a tangled and mazy dance; but *Epicycles* reduce the maze to order. The Epicycles themselves run into confusion; the conception of an *Ellipse* makes all clear and simple. And thus from stage to stage, new elements of intelligible order are introduced. But this intelligible order is so completely adopted by the human understanding, as to seem part of its texture. Men ask whether Eclipses follow a Cycle; whether the Planets describe Ellipses; and they imagine that so long as they do not *answer* such questions rashly, they take nothing for granted. They do not recollect how much they assume in *asking* the question:—how far the conceptions of Cycles and of Ellipses are beyond the visible surface of the celestial phenomena:—how many ages elapsed, how much thought, how much observation, were needed, before men's thoughts were fashioned into the words which they now so familiarly use. And thus they treat the subject, as we have seen Aristotle treating it; as if it were a question, not of invention, but of proof; not of substance, but of form: as if the main thing were not *what* we assert, but *how* we assert it. But for our purpose it is requisite to bear in mind the feature which we have thus attempted to mark; and to recollect that in every inference by induction, there is a Conception supplied by the mind and superinduced upon the Facts.

In collecting scientific truths by Induction we often find (as has already been observed,) a Definition and a Proposition established at the same time,—introduced together and mutually dependent on each other. The combination of the two constitutes the Inductive act; and we may consider the Definition as representing the superinduced Conception, and the Proposition as exhibiting the Colligation of Facts.

To discover a conception of the mind which will justly represent a train of observed facts is, in some measure, a process of conjecture, as I have stated already; and as I then observed, the business of conjecture is commonly conducted by calling up before our minds several suppositions, and selecting that one which most agrees with what we know of the observed facts. Hence he who has to discover the laws of nature may have to invent many suppositions before he hits upon the right one; and among the endowments which lead to his success, we must reckon that fertility of invention which ministers to him such imaginary schemes, till at last he finds the one which conforms to the true order of nature. A facility in devising hypotheses, therefore, is so far from being a fault in the intellectual character of a discoverer, that it is, in truth, a faculty indispensable to his task. It is, for his purposes, much better that he should be too ready in contriving, too eager in pursuing systems which promise to introduce law and order among a mass of unarranged facts, than that he should be barren of such inventions and hopeless of such success. Accordingly, as we have already noticed, great discoverers have often invented hypotheses which would not answer to all the facts, as well as those which would; and have fancied themselves to have discovered laws, which a more careful examination of the facts overturned.

The tendencies of our speculative nature, carrying us onwards in pursuit of symmetry and rule, and thus producing all true theories, perpetually show their vigour by overshooting the mark. They obtain something, by aiming at much more. They detect the order and connexion which exist, by conceiving imaginary relations of order and connexion which have no existence. Real discoveries are thus mixed with baseless assumptions; profound sagacity is combined with fanciful conjecture; not rarely, or in peculiar instances, but commonly, and in most cases; probably in all, if we could read the thoughts of discoverers as we read the books of Kepler. To try wrong guesses is, with most persons, the only way to hit upon right ones. The character of the true philosopher is, not that he never conjectures hazardously, but that his conjectures are clearly conceived, and brought into rigid contact with facts. He sees and compares distinctly the ideas and the things;—the relations of his notions to each other and to phenomena. Under these conditions it is not only excusable, but necessary for him, to snatch at every semblance of general rule,—to try all promising forms of simplicity and symmetry.

Hence advances in knowledge are not commonly made without the previous exercise of some boldness and license in guessing. The discovery of new truths requires, undoubtedly, minds careful and scrupulous in examining what is suggested; but it requires, no less, such as are quick and fertile in suggesting. What is invention, except the talent of rapidly calling before us the many possibilities, and selecting the appropriate one? It is true that when we have rejected all the inadmissible suppositions, they are often quickly forgotten; and few think it necessary to dwell on these discarded hypotheses, and on the process by which they were condemned. But all who discover truths must have reasoned upon many errors to obtain each truth; every accepted doctrine must have been one chosen out of many candidates. If many of the guesses of philosophers of bygone times now appear fanciful and absurd because time and observation have refuted them, others, which were at the time equally gratuitous, have been confirmed in a manner which makes them appear marvellously sagacious. To form hypotheses, and then to employ much labour and skill in refuting, if they do not succeed in establishing them, is a part of the usual process of inventive minds. Such a proceeding belongs to the *rule* of the genius of discovery, rather than (as has often been taught in modern times) to the *exception*.

But if it be an advantage for the discoverer of truth that he be ingenious and fertile in inventing hypotheses which may connect the phenomena of nature, it is indispensably requisite that he be diligent and careful in comparing his hypotheses with the facts, and ready to abandon his invention as soon as it appears that it does not agree with the course of actual occurrences. This constant comparison of his own conceptions and supposition with observed facts under all aspects, forms the leading employment of the discoverer: this candid and simple love of truth, which makes him willing to suppress the most favourite production of his own ingenuity as soon as it appears to be at variance with realities, constitutes the first characteristic of his temper. He must have neither the blindness which cannot, nor the obstinacy which will not, perceive the discrepancy of his fancies and his facts. He must allow no indolence, or partial views, or self-complacency, or delight in seeming demonstration, to make him tenacious of the schemes which he devises, any further than they are confirmed by their accordance with nature. The framing of hypotheses is, for the inquirer after truth, not the end, but the beginning of his work. Each of his systems is invented, not that he may admire it and follow it into all its consistent consequences, but that he may make it the occasion of a course of active experiment and observation. And if the results of his process contradict his fundamental assumptions, however ingenious, however symmetrical, however elegant his system may be, he rejects it without hesitation. He allows no natural yearning for the offspring of his own mind to draw him aside from the higher duty of loyalty to his sovereign, Truth: to her he not only gives his affections and his wishes, but strenuous labour and scrupulous minuteness of attention.

We may refer to what we have said of Kepler, Newton, and other eminent philosophers, for illustrations of this character. In Kepler we have remarked the courage and perseverance with which he undertook and executed the task of computing his own hypotheses: and, as a still more admirable characteristic, that he never allowed the labour he had spent upon any conjecture to produce any reluctance in abandoning the hypothesis, as soon as he had evidence of its inaccuracy. And in the history of Newton's discovery that the moon is retained in her orbit by the force of gravity, we have noticed the same moderation in maintaining the hypothesis, after it had once occurred to the author's mind. The hypothesis required that the moon should fall from the tangent of her orbit every second through a space of sixteen feet; but according to his first calculations it appeared that in fact she only fell through a space of thirteen feet in that time. The difference seems small, the approximation encouraging, the theory plausible; a man in love with his own fancies would readily have discovered or invented some probable cause of the difference. But Newton acquiesced in it as a disproof of his conjecture, and "laid aside at that time any further thoughts of this matter."

It has often happened that those who have undertaken to instruct mankind have not possessed this pure love of truth and comparative indifference to the maintenance of their own inventions. Men have frequently adhered with great tenacity and vehemence to the hypotheses which they have once framed; and in their affection for these, have been prone to overlook, to distort, and to misinterpret facts. In this manner hypotheses have so often been prejudicial to the genuine pursuit of truth, that they have fallen into a kind of obloquy; and have been considered as dangerous temptations and fallacious guides. Many warnings have been uttered against the fabrication of hypotheses by those who profess to teach philosophy; many disclaimers of such a course by those who cultivate science.

Thus we shall find Bacon frequently discommending this habit under the name of "anticipation of the mind," and Newton thinks it necessary to say emphatically "hypotheses non fingo." It has been constantly urged that the inductions by which

sciences are formed must be *cautious* and *rigorous;* and the various imaginations which passed through Kepler's brain, and to which he has given utterance, have been blamed or pitied as lamentable instances of an unphilosophical frame of mind. Yet it has appeared in the preceding remarks that hypotheses rightly used are among the helps, far more than the dangers, of science;—that scientific induction is not a "cautious" or a "rigorous" process in the sense of *abstaining from* such suppositions, but in *not adhering to* them till they are confirmed by fact, and in carefully seeking from facts confirmation or refutation. Kepler's character was, not that he was peculiarly given to the construction of hypotheses, but that he narrated with extraordinary copiousness and candour the course of his thoughts, his labours, and his feelings. In the minds of most persons, as we have said, the inadmissible suppositions, when rejected, are soon forgotten: and thus the trace of them vanishes from the thoughts, and the successful hypothesis alone holds its place in our memory. But in reality, many other transient suppositions must have been made by all discoverers;—hypotheses which are not afterwards asserted as true systems, but entertained for an instant;—"tentative hypotheses," as they have been called. Each of these hypotheses is followed by its corresponding train of observations, from which it derives its power of leading to truth. The hypothesis is like the captain, and the observations like the soldiers of an army: while he appears to command them, and in this way to work his own will, he does in fact derive all his power of conquest from their obedience, and becomes helpless and useless if they mutiny.

Since the discoverer has thus constantly to work his way onwards by means of hypotheses, false and true, it is highly important for him to possess talents and means for rapidly *testing* each supposition as it offers itself. In this as in other parts of the work of discovery, success has in general been mainly owing to the native ingenuity and sagacity of the discoverer's mind. Yet some rules tending to further this object have been delivered by eminent philosophers, and some others may perhaps be suggested. Of these we shall here notice only some of the most general, leaving for a future chapter the consideration of some more limited and detailed processes by which, in certain cases, the discovery of the laws of nature may be materially assisted.

A maxim which it may be useful to recollect is this;—that hypotheses may often be of service to science, when they involve a certain portion of incompleteness, and even of error. The object of such inventions is to bind together facts which without them are loose and detached; and if they do this, they may lead the way to a perception of the true rule by which the phenomena are associated together, even if they themselves somewhat misstate the matter. The imagined arrangement enables us to contemplate as a whole a collection of special cases which perplex and overload our minds when they are considered in succession; and if our scheme has so much of truth in it as to conjòin what is really connected, we may afterwards duly correct or limit the mechanism of this connexion. If our hypothesis renders a reason for the agreement of cases really similar, we may afterwards find this reason to be false, but we shall be able to translate it into the language of truth.

A conspicuous example of such an hypothesis, one which was of the highest value to science, though very incomplete, and as a representation of nature altogether false, is seen in the *doctrine of epicycles* by which the ancient astronomers explained the motions of the sun, moon, and planets. This doctrine connected the places and velocities of these bodies at particular times in a manner which was, in its general features, agreeable to nature. Yet this doctrine was erroneous in its assertion of the circular nature of all the celestial motions, and in making the heavenly bodies revolve round the earth. It was, however, of immense value to the progress of astronomical science; for it enabled men to express and reason upon many important truths which they discovered respecting the motion of the stars, up to the time of Kepler. Indeed we can hardly imagine that astronomy could, in its outset, have made so great a progress under any other form, as it did in consequence of being cultivated in this shape of the incomplete and false epicyclical hypothesis.

We may notice another instance of an exploded hypothesis, which is generally mentioned only to be ridiculed, and which undoubtedly is both false in the extent of its assertion, and unphilosophical in its expression; but which still, in its day, was not without merit. I mean the doctrine of *Nature's horror of a vacuum (fuga vacui,)* by which the action of siphons and pumps and many other phenomena were explained, till Mersenne and Pascal taught a truer doctrine. This hypothesis was of real service; for it brought together many facts which really belong to the same class, although they are very different in their first aspect. A scientific writer of modern times appears to wonder that men did not at once divine the weight of the air from which the phenomena formerly ascribed to the *fuga vacui* really result. "Loaded, compressed by the atmosphere," he says, "they did not recognize its action. In vain all nature testified that air was elastic and heavy; they shut their eyes to her testimony. The water rose in pumps and flowed in siphons at that time as it does at this

day. They could not separate the boards of a pair of bellows of which the holes were stopped; and they could not bring together the same boards without difficulty if they were at first separated. Infants sucked the milk of their mothers; air entered rapidly into the lungs of animals at every inspiration; cupping-glasses produced tumours on the skin; and in spite of all these striking proofs of the weight and elasticity of the air, the ancient philosophers maintained resolutely that air was light, and explained all these phenomena by the horror which they said nature had for a vacuum." It is curious that it should not have occurred to the author while writing this, that if these facts, so numerous and various, can all be accounted for by *one* principle, there is a strong presumption that the principle is not altogether baseless. And in reality is it not true that nature *does* abhor a vacuum, and do all she can to avoid it? No doubt this power is not unlimited; and we can trace it to a mechanical cause, the pressure of the circumambient air. But the tendency, arising from this pressure, which the bodies surrounding a space void of air have to rush into it, may be expressed, in no extravagant or unintelligible manner, by saying that nature has a repugnance to a vacuum.

That imperfect and false hypotheses, though they may thus explain *some* phenomena, and may be useful in the progress of science, cannot explain *all* phenomena;—and that we are never to rest in our labours or acquiesce in our results, till we have found some view of the subject which *is* consistent with *all* the observed facts:—will of course be understood. We shall afterwards have to speak of the other steps of such a progress.

The hypotheses which we accept ought to explain phenomena which we have observed. But they ought to do more than this: they ought to *foretel* phenomena which have not yet been observed;—at least all of the same kind as those which the hypothesis was invented to explain. For our assent to the hypothesis implies that it is held to be true of all particular instances. That these cases belong to past or to future times, that they have or have not already occurred, makes no difference in the applicability of the rule to them. Because the rule prevails, it includes all cases; and will determine them all, if we can only calculate its real consequences. Hence it will predict the results of new combinations, as well as explain the appearances which have occurred in old ones. And that it does this with certainty and correctness, is one mode in which the hypothesis is to be verified as right and useful.

The scientific doctrines which have at various periods been established have been verified in this manner. For example, the Epicyclical Theory of the heavens was confirmed by its *predicting* truly eclipses of the sun and moon, configurations of the planets, and other celestial phenomena; and by its leading to the construction of Tables by which the places of the heavenly bodies were given at every moment of time. The truth and accuracy of these predictions were a proof that the hypothesis was valuable and, at least to a great extent, true; although, as was afterwards found, it involved a false representation of the structure of the heavens. In like manner, the discovery of the Laws of Refraction enabled mathematicians to *predict,* by calculation, what would be the effect of any new form or combination of transparent lenses. Newton's hypothesis of Fits of Easy Transmission and Easy Reflection in the particles of light, although not confirmed by other kinds of facts, involved a true statement of the law of the phenomena which it was framed to include and served to *predict* the forms and colours of thin plates for a wide range of given cases. The hypothesis that Light operates by Undulations and Interferences, afforded the means of *predicting* results under a still larger extent of conditions. In like manner in the progress of chemical knowledge, the doctrine of Phlogistou supplied the means of *foreseeing* the consequence of many combinations of elements, even before they were tried; but the Oxygen Theory, besides affording predictions, at least equally exact, with regard to the general results of chemical operations, included all the facts concerning the relations of weight of the elements and their compounds, and enabled chemists to *foresee* such facts in untried cases. And the Theory of Electromagnetic Forces, as soon as it was rightly understood, enabled those who had mastered it to *predict* motions such as had not been before observed, which were accordingly found to take place.

Men cannot help believing that the laws laid down by discoverers must be in a great measure identical with the real laws of nature, when the discoverers thus determine effects beforehand in the same manner in which nature herself determines them when the occasion occurs. Those who can do this, must, to a considerable extent, have detected nature's secret;—must have fixed upon the conditions to which she attends, and must have seized the rules by which she applies them. Such a coincidence of untried facts with speculative assertions cannot be the work of chance, but implies some large portion of truth in the principles on which the reasoning is founded. To trace order and law in that which has been observed, may be considered as interpreting what nature has written down for us, and will commonly prove that we understand her alphabet. But to predict what has not been observed, is to attempt ourselves to use the legislative phrases of nature; and when she responds plainly and precisely to that which we thus utter, we cannot but suppose that we have in a great measure made ourselves masters of the meaning and structure of her language. The prediction of results, even of the same kind as those which have been observed, in new cases, is a proof of real success in our inductive processes.

We have here spoken of the prediction of facts *of the same kind* as those from which our rule was collected. But the evidence in favour of our induction is of a much higher and more forcible character when it enables us to explain and determine cases of a *kind different* from those which were contemplated in the formation of our hypothesis. The instances in which this has occurred, indeed, impress us with a conviction that the truth of our hypothesis is certain. No accident could give rise to such an extraordinary coincidence. No false supposition could, after being adjusted to one class of phenomena, so exactly represent a different class, when the agreement was unforeseen and uncontemplated. That rules springing from remote and unconnected quarters should thus leap to the same point, can only arise from *that* being the point where truth resides.

Accordingly the cases in which inductions from classes of facts altogether different have thus *jumped together,* belong only to the best established theories which the history of science contains. And as I shall have occasion to refer to this peculiar feature in their evidence, I will take the liberty of describing it by a particular phrase; and will term it the *Consilience of Inductions.*

It is exemplified principally in some of the greatest discoveries. Thus it was found by Newton that the doctrine of the attraction of the sun varying according to the inverse square of this distance, which explained Kepler's *third law* of the proportionality of the cubes of the distances to the squares of the periodic times of the planets, explained also his *first* and *second laws* of the elliptical motion of each planet; although no connexion of these laws had been visible before. Again, it appeared that the force of universal gravitation, which had been inferred from the *perturbations* of the moon and planets by the sun and by each other, also accounted for the fact, apparently altogether dissimilar and remote, of the *precession of the equinoxes.* Here was a most striking and surprising coincidence, which gave to the theory a stamp of truth beyond the power of ingenuity to counterfeit. In like manner in optics; the hypothesis of alternate fits of easy transmission and reflection would explain the colours of thin plates, and indeed was devised and adjusted for that very purpose; but it could give no account of the phenomena of the fringes of shadows. But the doctrine of interferences, constructed at first with reference to phenomena of the nature of the *fringes,* explained also the *colours of thin plates* better than the supposition of the fits invented for that very purpose. And we have in physical optics another example of the same kind, which is quite as striking as the explanation of precession by inferences from the facts of perturbation. The doctrine of undulations propagated in a spheroidal form was contrived at first by Huyghens, with a view to explain the laws of *double refraction* in calc-spar; and was pursued with the same view by Fresnel. But in the course of the investigation it appeared, in a most unexpected and wonderful manner, that this same doctrine of spheroidal undulations, when it was so modified as to account for the directions of the two refracted rays, accounted also for the positions of their *planes of polarization;* a phenomenon which, taken by itself, it had perplexed previous mathematicians, even to represent.

The theory of universal gravitation, and of the undulatory theory of light, are, indeed, full of examples of this Consilience of Inductions. With regard to the latter, it has been justly asserted by Herschel, that the history of the undulatory theory was a succession of *felicities.* And it is precisely the unexpected coincidences of results drawn from distant parts of the subject which are properly thus described. Thus the laws of the *modification of polarization* to which Fresnel was led by his general views, accounted for the rule respecting the *angle at which light is polarized,* discovered by Brewster. The conceptions of the theory pointed out peculiar *modifications* of the phenomena when *Newton's rings* were produced by polarized light, which were ascertained to take place in fact, by Arago and Airy. When the beautiful phenomena of *dipolarized light* were discovered by Arago and Biot, Young was able to declare that they were reducible to the general laws of *interference* which he had already established. And what was no less striking a confirmation of the truth of the theory, *measures* of the same element deduced from various classes of facts were found to coincide. Thus the *length* of a luminiferous undulation, calculated by Young from the measurement of *fringes* of shadows, was found to agree very nearly with the previous calculation from the colours of *thin plates.*

No example can be pointed out, in the whole history of science, so far as I am aware, in which this Consilience of Inductions has given testimony in favour of an hypothesis afterwards discovered to be false. If we take one class of facts only, knowing the law which they follow, we may construct an hypotheses, or perhaps several, which may represent them: and as new circumstances are discovered, we may often adjust the hypothesis so as to correspond

to these also. But when the hypothesis, of itself and without adjustment for the purpose, gives us the rule and reason of a class of facts not contemplated in its construction, we have a criterion of its reality, which has never yet been produced in favour of falsehood.

In the preceding section I have spoken of the hypothesis with which we compare our facts as being framed *all at once,* each of its parts being included in the original scheme. In reality, however, it often happens that the various suppositions which our system contains are *added* upon occasion of different researches. Thus in the Ptolemaic doctrine of the heavens, new epicycles and eccentrics were added as new inequalities of the motions of the heavenly bodies were discovered; and in the Newtonian doctrine of material rays of light, the supposition that these rays had "fits," was added to explain the colours of thin plates; and the supposition that they had "sides" was introduced on occasion of the phenomena of polarization. In like manner other theories have been built up of parts devised at different times.

This being the mode in which theories are often framed, we have to notice a distinction which is found to prevail in the progress of true and of false theories. In the former class all the additional suppositions *tend to simplicity* and harmony; the new suppositions resolve themselves into the old ones, or at least require only some easy modification of the hypothesis first assumed: the system becomes more coherent as it is further extended. The elements which we require for explaining a new class of facts are already contained in our system. Different members of the theory run together, and we have thus a constant convergence to unity. In false theories, the contrary is the case. The new suppositions are something altogether additional;—not suggested by the original scheme; perhaps difficult to reconcile with it. Every such addition adds to the complexity of the hypothetical system, which at last becomes unmanageable, and is compelled to surrender its place to some simpler explanation.

Such a false theory, for example, was the ancient doctrine of eccentrics and epicycles. It explained the general succession of the places of the Sun, Moon, and Planets; it would not have explained the proportion of their magnitudes at different times, if these could have been accurately observed; but this the ancient astronomers were unable to do. When, however, Tycho and other astronomers came to be able to observe the planets accurately in all positions, it was found that *no* combination of *equable* circular motions would exactly represent all the observations. We may see, in Kepler's works, the many new modifications of the epicyclical hypothesis which offered themselves to him; some of which would have agreed with the phenomena with a certain degree of accuracy, but not so great a degree as Kepler, fortunately for the progress of science, insisted upon obtaining. After these epicycles had been thus accumulated, they all disappeared and gave way to the simpler conception of an *elliptical* motion. In like manner, the discovery of new inequalities in the moon's motions encumbered her system more and more with new machinery, which was at last rejected all at once in favour of the *elliptical* theory. Astronomers could not but suppose themselves in a wrong path when the prospect grew darker and more entangled at every step.

Again; the Cartesian system of vortices might be said to explain the primary phenomena of the revolutions of plants about the sun, and satellites about planets. But the elliptical form of the orbits required new suppositions. Bernoulli ascribed this curve to the shape of the planet, operating on the stream of the vortex in a manner similar to the rudder of a boat. But then the motions of the aphelia, and of the nodes,—the perturbations,—even the action of gravity to the earth,—could not be accounted for without new and independent suppositions. Here as none of the simplicity of truth. The theory of gravitation on the other hand became more simple as the facts to be explained became more numerous. The attraction of the sun accounted for the motions of the planets; the attraction of the planets was the cause of the motion of the satellites. But this being assumed, the perturbations, the motions of the nodes and aphelia, only made it requisite to extend the attraction of the sun to the satellites, and that of the planets to each other:—the tides, the spheroidal form of the earth, the precession, still required nothing more than that the moon and sun should attract the parts of the earth, and that these should attract each other;—so that all the suppositions resolved themselves into the single one, of the universal gravitation of all matter. It is difficult to imagine a more convincing manifestation of simplicity and unity.

Again, to take an example from another science;—the doctrine of phlogiston, brought together many facts in a very plausible manner,—combustion, acidification, and others,—and very naturally prevailed for a while. But the balance came to be used in chemical operations, and the facts of weight as well as of combination were to be accounted for. On the phlogistic theory, it appeared that this could not be done without a new supposition, and *that* a very strange one;—that phlogiston was an element not only not heavy, but absolutely light, so that it diminished the weight of the compounds into which it entered. Some chemists for a time adopted this extravagant view; but the wiser of them saw, in the necessity of such a supposition to the defence of the theory, an evidence that the hypothesis of an element *phlogiston* was erroneous. And the opposite hypothesis, which taught that oxygen was subtracted, and not phlogiston added, was accepted because it required no such novel and inadmissible assumption.

Again, we find the same evidence of truth in the progress of the undulatory theory of light, in the course of its application from one class of facts to another. Thus we explain reflection and refraction by undulations; when we come to thin plates, the requisite "fits" are already involved in our fundamental hypothesis, for they are the length of an undulation: the phenomena of diffraction also require such intervals; and the intervals thus required agree exactly with the others in magnitude, so that no new property is needed. Polarization for a moment appears to require some new hypothesis; yet this is hardly the case; for the direction of our vibrations is hitherto arbitrary:—we allow polarization to decide it, and we suppose the undulations to be transverse. Having done this for the sake of polarization, we turn to the phenomena of double refraction, and inquire what new hypothesis they require. But the answer is, that they require none: the supposition of transverse vibrations, which we have made in order to explain polarization, gives us also the law of double refraction. Truth may give rise to such a coincidence; falsehood cannot. Again, the facts of dipolarization come into view. But they hardly require any new assumption; for the difference of optical elasticity of crystals in different directions, which is already assumed in uniaxal crystals, is extended to biaxal exactly according to the law of symmetry; and this being done, the laws of the phenomena, curious and complex as they are, are fully explained. The phenomena of circular polarization by internal reflection, instead of requiring a new hypothesis, are found to be given by an interpretation of an apparently inexplicable result of an old hypothesis. The circular polarization of quartz and its double refraction does indeed appear to require a new assumption, but still not one which at all disturbs the form of the theory; and in short, the whole history of this theory is a progress, constant and steady, often striking and startling, from one degree of evidence and consistence to another of higher order.

In the emission theory, on the other hand, as in the theory of solid epicycles, we see what we may consider as the natural course of things in the career of a false theory. Such a theory may, to a certain extent, explain the phenomena which it was at first contrived to meet; but every new class of facts requires a new supposition—an addition to the machinery: and as observation goes on, these incoherent appendages accumulate, till they overwhelm and upset the original frame-work. Such has been the hypothesis of the material emission of light. In its original form it explained reflection and refraction: but the colours of thin plates added to it the fits of easy transmission and reflection; the phenomena of diffraction further invested the emitted particles with complex laws of attraction and repulsion; polarization gave them sides: double refraction subjected them to peculiar forces emanating from the axes of the crystal: finally, dipolarization loaded them with the complex and unconnected contrivance of moveable polarization: and even when all this had been done, additional mechanism was wanting. There is here no unexpected success, no happy coincidence, no convergence of principles from remote quarters. The philosopher builds the machine, but its parts do not fit. They hold together only while he presses them. This is not the character of truth.

As another example of the application of the maxim now under consideration, I may perhaps be allowed to refer to the judgment which, in the History of Thermotics, I have ventured to give respecting Laplace's Theory of Gases. I have stated, that we cannot help forming an unfavourable judgment of this theory, by looking for that great characteristic of true theory; namely, that the hypotheses which were assumed to account for *one class* of facts are found to explain *another class* of a different nature. Thus Laplace's first suppositions explain the connexion of compression with density, (the law of Boyle and Mariotte,) and the connexion of elasticity with heat, (the law of Dalton and Gay Lussac.) But the theory requires other assumptions when we come to latent heat; and yet these new assumptions produce no effect upon the calculations in any application of the theory. When the hypothesis, constructed with reference to the elasticity and temperature, is applied to another class of facts, those of latent heat, we have no Simplification of the Hy-

pothesis, and therefore no evidence of the truth of the theory.

The two last sections of this chapter direct our attention to two circumstances, which tend to prove, in a manner which we may term irresistible, the truth of the theories which they characterize:—the *Consilience of Inductions* from different and separate classes of facts;—and the progressive *Simplification of the Theory* as it is extended to new cases. These two Characters are, in fact, hardly different; they are exemplified by the same cases. For if these Inductions, collected from one class of facts, supply an unexpected explanation of a new class, which is the case first spoken of, there will be no need for new machinery in the hypothesis to apply it to the newly-contemplated facts; and thus we have a case in which the system does not become more complex when its application is extended to a wider field, which was the character of true theory in its second aspect. The Consiliences of our Inductions give rise to a constant Convergence of our Theory towards Simplicity and Unity.

But, moreover, both these cases of the extension of the theory, without difficulty or new suppositions, to a wider range and to new classes of phenomena, may be conveniently considered in yet another point of view; namely, as successive steps by which we gradually ascend in our speculative views to a higher and higher point of generality. For when the theory, either by the concurrence of two indications, or by an extension without complication, has included a new range of phenomena, we have, in fact, a new induction of a more general kind, to which the inductions formerly obtained are subordinate, as particular cases to a general proposition. We have in such examples, in short, an instance of *successive generalization*. This is a subject of great importance, and deserving of being well illustrated; it will come under our notice in the next chapter.

Name: _____ **Date:** _____

1. Why, according to Whewell, is knowledge generated from induction real?

2. Why, according to Whewell, is knowledge generated from induction necessarily general?

3. What does Whewell mean when he claims that every inductive inference is an invention?

4. What is required, according to Whewell, in order to generate advances in knowledge?

5. What purposes do false theories and hypotheses serve in the advance of knowledge?

Thomas Malthus

An Essay on the Principle of Population, 1826 Edition

Malthus (1766-1834) was an English political economist and Anglican priest who reacted against the French Revolution. In this piece, originally published in 1798 and revised throughout the first decades of the nineteenth century, Malthus condemned the French revolutionaries for attempting to subvert nature and legislate progress and equality. He argued that because resources grew arithmetically and population increased geometrically, there would inevitably be competition for scarce resources and thus misery. Why would God allow this? It was a mechanism, Malthus argued, for keeping humans from becoming lazy and for compelling them to improve themselves and their civilizations. Without such compulsion, Malthus claimed, "The savage would slumber forever under his tree unless he were roused from his torpor by the cravings of hunger or the pinchings of cold, and the exertions that he makes to avoid these evils, by procuring food, and building himself a covering, are the exercises which form and keep in motion his faculties, which otherwise would sink into listless inactivity." The divinely ordained system that compelled humans toward progress powerfully influenced Darwin, who found in it the raw materials for his theory of natural selection.

RATIOS OF THE INCREASE OF POPULATION AND FOOD

In an inquiry concerning the improvement of society, the mode of conducting the subject which naturally presents itself, is:

1. To investigate the causes that have hitherto impeded the progress of mankind towards happiness; and,
2. To examine the probability of the total or partial removal of these causes in future.

To enter fully into this question, and to enumerate all the causes that have hitherto influenced human improvement, would be much beyond the power of an individual. The principal object of the present essay is to examine the effects of one great cause intimately united with the very nature of man; which, though it has been constantly and powerfully operating since the commencement of society, has been little noticed by the writers who have treated this subject. The facts which establish the existence of this cause have, indeed, been repeatedly stated and acknowledged; but its natural and necessary effects have been almost totally overlooked; though probably among these effects may be reckoned a very considerable portion of that vice and misery, and of that unequal distribution of the bounties of nature, which it has been the unceasing object of the enlightened philanthropist in all ages to correct.

The cause to which I allude, is the constant tendency in all animated life to increase beyond the nourishment prepared for it.

It is observed by Dr Franklin, that there is no bound to the prolific nature of plants or animals, but what is made by their crowding and interfering with each other's means of subsistence. Were the face of the earth, he says, vacant of other plants, it might be gradually sowed and overspread with one kind only, as for instance with fennel: and were it empty of other inhabitants, it might in a few ages be replenished from one nation only, as for instance with Englishmen.[1]

This edition was originally published in 1826.

[1] B. Franklin, *Political, miscellaneous and philosophical pieces* (1779), p. 9.

This is incontrovertibly true. Through the animal and vegetable kingdoms nature has scattered the seeds of life abroad with the most profuse and liberal hand; but has been comparatively sparing in the room and the nourishment necessary to rear them. The germs of existence contained in this earth, if they could freely develop themselves, would fill millions of worlds in the course of a few thousand years. Necessity, that imperious, all-pervading law of nature, restrains them within the prescribed bounds. The race of plants and the race of animals shrink under this great restrictive law; and man cannot by any efforts of reason escape from it.

In plants and irrational animals, the view of the subject is simple. They are all impelled by a powerful instinct to the increase of their species; and this instinct is interrupted by no doubts about providing for their offspring. Wherever therefore there is liberty, the power of increase is exerted; and the superabundant effects are repressed afterwards by want of room and nourishment.

The effects of this check on man are more complicated. Impelled to the increase of his species by an equally powerful instinct, reason interrupts his career, and asks him whether he may not bring beings into the world, for whom he cannot provide the means of support. If he attend to this natural suggestion, the restriction too frequently produces vice. If he hear it not, the human race will be constantly endeavouring to increase beyond the means of subsistence. But as, by that law of our nature which makes food necessary to the life of man, population can never actually increase beyond the lowest nourishment capable of supporting it, a strong check on population, from the difficulty of acquiring food, must be constantly in operation. This difficulty must fall somewhere, and must necessarily be severely felt in some or other of the various forms of misery, or the fear of misery, by a large portion of mankind.

That population has this constant tendency to increase beyond the means of subsistence, and that it is kept to its necessary level by these causes, will sufficiently appear from a review of the different states of society in which man has existed. But, before we proceed to this review, the subject will, perhaps, be seen in a clearer light, if we endeavour to ascertain what would be the natural increase of population, if left to exert itself with perfect freedom; and what might be expected to be the rate of increase in the productions of the earth, under the most favourable circumstances of human industry.

It will be allowed that no country has hitherto been known, where the manners were so pure and simple, and the means of subsistence so abundant, that no check whatever has existed to early marriages from the difficulty of providing for a family,

and that no waste of the human species has been occasioned by vicious customs, by towns, by unhealthy occupations, or too severe labour. Consequently in no state that we have yet known, has the power of population been left to exert itself with perfect freedom.

Whether the law of marriage be instituted, or not, the dictate of nature and virtue seems to be an early attachment to one woman; and where there were no impediments of any kind in the way of an union to which such an attachment would lead, and no causes of depopulation afterwards, the increase of the human species would be evidently much greater than any increase which has been hitherto known.

In the northern states of America, where the means of subsistence have been more ample, the manners of the people more pure, and the checks to early marriages fewer, than in any of the modern states of Europe, the population has been found to double itself, for above a century and a half successively, in less than twenty five years.[2] Yet, even during these periods, in some of the towns, the deaths exceeded the births,[3] a circumstance which clearly proves that, in those parts of the country which supplied this deficiency, the increase must have been much more rapid than the general average.

In the back settlements, where the sole employment is agriculture, and vicious customs and unwholesome occupations are little known, the population has been found to double itself in fifteen years.[4] Even this extraordinary rate of increase is probably short of the utmost power of population. Very severe labour is requisite to clear a fresh country; such situations are not in general considered as particularly healthy; and the inhabitants, probably, are occasionally subject to the incursions of the Indians, which may destroy some lives, or at any rate diminish the fruits of industry.

According to a table of Euler, calculated on a mortality of 1 in 36, if the births be to the deaths in the proportion of 3 to 1, the period of doubling will be only 12⅘ years. And this proportion is not only a possible supposition, but has actually occurred for short periods in more countries than one.

Sir William Petty supposes a doubling possible in so short a time as ten years.[5]

---

[2] It appears, from some recent calculations and estimates, that from the first settlement of America, to the year 1800, the periods of doubling have been but very little above twenty years. See a note on the increase of American population in bk ii, ch. xi.

[3] R. Price, *Observations on reversionary payments, on schemes for providing annuities for widows, and for persons in old age*, 4th ed., 2 vols (1783), i, p. 274.

[4] Price, *Observations*, i, p. 282.

[5] W. Petty, *Several essays in political arithmetic*, 4th ed. (1775), p. 14.

But, to be perfectly sure that we are far within the truth, we will take the slowest of these rates of increase, a rate in which all concurring testimonies agree, and which has been repeatedly ascertained to be from procreation only.

It may safely be pronounced, therefore, that population, when unchecked, goes on doubling itself every twenty five years, or increases in a geometrical ratio.

The rate according to which the productions of the earth may be supposed to increase, it will not be so easy to determine. Of this, however, we may be perfectly certain, that the ratio of their increase in a limited territory must be of a totally different nature from the ratio of the increase of population. A thousand millions are just as easily doubled every twenty five years by the power of population as a thousand. But the food to support the increase from the greater number will by no means be obtained with the same facility. Man is necessarily confined in room. When acre has been added to acre till all the fertile land is occupied, the yearly increase of food must depend upon the melioration of the land already in possession. This is a fund, which, from the nature of all soils, instead of increasing, must be gradually diminishing. But population, could it be supplied with food, would go on with unexhausted vigour; and the increase of one period would furnish the power of a greater increase the next, and this without any limit.

From the accounts we have of China and Japan, it may be fairly doubted, whether the best directed efforts of human industry could double the produce of these countries even once in any number of years. There are many parts of the globe, indeed, hitherto uncultivated, and almost unoccupied; but the right of exterminating, or driving into a corner where they must starve, even the inhabitants of these thinly peopled regions, will be questioned in a moral view. The process of improving their minds and directing their industry would necessarily be slow; and during this time, as population would regularly keep pace with the increasing produce, it would rarely happen that a great degree of knowledge and industry would have to operate at once upon rich unappropriated soil. Even where this might take place, as it does sometimes in new colonies, a geometrical ratio increases with such extraordinary rapidity, that the advantage could not last long. If the United States of America continue increasing, which they certainly will do, though not with the same rapidity as formerly, the Indians will be driven further and further back into the country, till the whole race is ultimately exterminated, and the territory is incapable of further extension.

These observations are, in a degree, applicable to all the parts of the earth, where the soil is imperfectly cultivated. To exterminate the inhabitants of the greatest part of Asia and Africa, is a thought that could not be admitted for a moment. To civilize and direct the industry of the various tribes of Tartars and negroes, would certainly be a work of considerable time, and of variable and uncertain success.

Europe is by no means so fully peopled as it might be. In Europe there is the fairest chance that human industry may receive its best direction. The science of agriculture has been much studied in England and Scotland; and there is still a great portion of uncultivated land in these countries. Let us consider at what rate the produce of this island might be supposed to increase under circumstances the most favourable to improvement.

If it be allowed that by the best possible policy, and great encouragements to agriculture, the average produce of the island could be doubled in the first twenty five years, it will be allowing, probably, a greater increase than could with reason be expected.

In the next twenty five years, it is impossible to suppose that the produce could be quadrupled. It would be contrary to all our knowledge of the properties of land. The improvement of the barren parts would be a work of time and labours and it must be evident to those who have the slightest acquaintance with agricultural subjects, that in proportion as cultivation extended, the additions that could yearly be made to the former average produce must be gradually and regularly diminishing. That we may be the better able to compare the increase of population and food, let us make a supposition, which, without pretending to accuracy, is clearly more favourable to the power of production in the earth, than any experience we have had of its qualities will warrant.

Let us suppose that the yearly additions which might be made to the former average produce, instead of decreasing, which they certainly would do, were to remain the same; and that the produce of this island might be increased every twenty five years, by a quantity equal to what it at present produces. The most enthusiastic speculator cannot suppose a greater increase than this. In a few centuries it would make every acre of land in the island like a garden.

If this supposition be applied to the whole earth, and if it be allowed that the subsistence for man which the earth affords might be increased every twenty five years by a quantity equal to what it at present produces, this will be supposing a rate of increase much greater than we can imagine that any possible exertions of mankind could make it.

It may be fairly pronounced, therefore, that, considering the present average state of the earth, the means of subsistence, under circumstances the most favourable to human industry, could not possibly be made to increase faster than in an arithmetical ratio.

The necessary effects of these two different rates of increase, when brought together, will be very striking. Let us call the population of this island 11 millions; and suppose the present produce equal to the easy support of such a number. In the first twenty five years the population would be 22 millions, and the food being also doubled, the means of subsistence would be equal to this increase. In the next twenty five years, the population would be 44 millions, and the means of subsistence only equal to the support of 33 millions. In the next period the population would be 88 millions, and the means of subsistence just equal to the support of half that number. And, at the conclusion of the first century, the population would be 176 millions, and the means of subsistence only equal to the support of 55 millions, leaving a population of 121 millions totally unprovided for.

Taking the whole earth, instead of this island, emigration would of course be excluded; and, supposing the present population equal to a thousand millions, the human species would increase as the numbers, 1, 2, 4, 8, 16, 32, 64, 128, 256, and subsistence as 1, 2, 3, 4, 5, 6, 7, 8, 9. In two centuries the population would be to the means of subsistence as 256 to 9; in three centuries as 4096 to 13, and in two thousand years the difference would be almost incalculable.

In this supposition no limits whatever are placed to the produce of the earth. It may increase for ever and be greater than any assignable quantity; yet still the power of population being in every period so much superior, the increase of the human species can only be kept down to the level of the means of subsistence by the constant operation of the strong law of necessity, acting as a check upon the greater power.

OF THE GENERAL CHECKS TO POPULATION, AND THE MODE OF THEIR OPERATION

The ultimate check to population appears then to be a want of food, arising necessarily from the different ratios according to which population and food increase. But this ultimate check is never the immediate check, except in cases of actual famine.

The immediate check may be stated to consist in all those customs, and all those diseases, which seem to be generated by a scarcity of the means of subsistence; and all those causes, independent of this scarcity, whether of a moral or physical nature, which tend prematurely to weaken and destroy the human frame.

These checks to population, which are constantly operating with more or less force in every society, and keep down the number to the level of the means of subsistence, may be classed under two general heads—the preventive, and the positive checks.

The preventive check, as far as it is voluntary, is peculiar to man, and arises from that distinctive superiority in his reasoning faculties, which enables him to calculate distant consequences. The checks to the indefinite increase of plants and irrational animals are all either positive, or, if preventive, involuntary. But man cannot look around him, and see the distress which frequently presses upon those who have large families; he cannot contemplate his present possessions or earnings, which he now nearly consumes himself, and calculate the amount of each share, when with very little addition they must be divided, perhaps, among seven or eight, without feeling a doubt whether, if he follow the bent of his inclinations, he may be able to support the offspring which he will probably bring into the world. In a state of equality, if such can exist, this would be the simple question. In the present state of society other considerations occur. Will he not lower his rank in life, and be obliged to give up in great measure his former habits? Does any mode of employment present itself by which he may reasonably hope to maintain a family? Will he not at any rate subject himself to greater difficulties, and more severe labour, than in his single state? Will he not be unable to transmit to his children the same advantages of education and improvement that he had himself possessed? Does he even feel secure that, should he have a large family, his utmost exertions can save them from rags and squalid poverty, and their consequent degradation in the community? And may he not be reduced to the grating necessity of forfeiting his independence, and of being obliged to the sparing hand of charity for support?

These considerations are calculated to prevent, and certainly do prevent, a great number of persons in all civilized nations from pursuing the dictate of nature in an early attachment to one woman.

If this restraint do not produce vice, it is undoubtedly the least evil that can arise from the principle of population. Considered as a restraint on a strong natural inclination, it must be allowed to produce a certain degree of temporary unhappiness; but evidently slight, compared with the evils which result from any of the other checks to population; and merely of the same nature as many other sacrifices of temporary to permanent gratification, which it is the business of a moral agent continually to make.

When this restraint produces vice, the evils which follow are but too conspicuous. A promiscuous intercourse to such a degree as to prevent the birth of children, seems to lower, in the most marked manner, the dignity of human nature. It cannot be without its effect on men, and nothing can be more obvious than its tendency to degrade the female character, and to destroy all its most amiable and distinguishing characteristics. Add to which, that among those unfortunate females, with which all great towns abound, more real distress and aggravated misery are, perhaps, to be found, than in any other department of human life.

When a general corruption of morals, with regard to the sex, pervades all the classes of society, its effects must necessarily be, to poison the springs of domestic happiness, to weaken conjugal and parental affection, and to lessen the united exertions and ardour of parents in the care and education of their children; effects which cannot take place without a decided diminution of the general happiness and virtue of the society; particularly as the necessity of art in the accomplishment and conduct of intrigues, and in the concealment of their consequences necessarily leads to many other vices.

The positive checks to population are extremely various, and include every cause, whether arising from vice or misery, which in any degree contributes to shorten the natural duration of human life. Under this head, therefore, may be enumerated all unwholesome occupations, severe labour and exposure to the seasons, extreme poverty, bad nursing of children, great towns, excesses of all kinds, the whole train of common diseases and epidemics, wars, plague, and famine.

On examining these obstacles to the increase of population which I have classed under the heads of preventive and positive checks, it will appear that they are all resolvable into moral restraint, vice, and misery.

Of the preventive checks, the restraint from marriage which is not followed by irregular gratifications may properly be termed moral restraint.[1]

Promiscuous intercourse, unnatural passions, violations of the marriage bed, and improper arts to conceal the consequences of irregular connections, are preventive checks that] clearly come under the head of vice.

Of the positive checks, those which appear to arise unavoidably from the laws of nature, may be called exclusively misery; and those which we obviously bring upon ourselves, such as wars, excesses, and many others which it would be in our power to avoid, are of a mixed nature. They are brought upon us by vice, and their consequences are misery.[2]

[The sum of all these preventive and positive checks, taken together, forms the immediate check to population; and it is evident that, in every country where the whole of the procreative power cannot be called into action, the preventive and the positive checks must vary inversely as each other; that is, in countries either naturally unhealthy, or subject to a great mortality, from whatever cause it may arise, the preventive check will prevail very little. In those countries, on the contrary, which are naturally healthy, and where the preventive check is found to prevail with considerable force, the positive check will prevail very little, or the mortality be very small.]

In every country some of these checks are, with more or less force, in constant operation; yet, notwithstanding their general prevalence, there are few states in which there is not a constant effort in the population to increase beyond the means of subsistence. This constant effort as constantly tends to subject the lower classes of society to distress, and to prevent any great permanent [melioration] of their condition.

---

[1]It will be observed, that I here use the term *moral* in its most confined sense. By moral restraint I would be understood to mean a restraint from marriage, from prudential motives, with a conduct strictly moral during the period of this restraint; and I have never, intentionally deviated from this sense. When I have wished to consider the restraint from marriage unconnected with its consequences, I have either called it prudential restraint, or a part of the preventive check, of which indeed it forms the principal branch.

In my review of the different stages of society, I have been accused of not allowing sufficient weight in the prevention of population to moral restraint; but when the confined sense of the term, which I have here explained, is adverted to, I am fearful that I shall not be found to have erred much in this respect. I should be very glad to believe myself mistaken.

[2]As the general consequence of vice is misery, and as this consequence is the precise reason why an action is termed vicious, it may appear that the term misery alone would be here sufficient, and that it is superfluous to use both. But the rejection of the term vice would introduce a considerable confusion into our language and ideas. We want it particularly to distinguish those actions, the general tendency of which is to produce misery, [16][and which are therefore prohibited by the commands of the Creator, and the precepts of the moralist, although,] in their immediate or individual effects, they may produce perhaps exactly the contrary. The gratification of all our passions in its immediate effect is happiness, not misery; and, in individual instances, even the remote consequences (at least in this life) may possibly come under the same denomination. There may have been some irregular connections with women, which have added to the happiness of both parties, and have injured no one. These individual actions, therefore, cannot come under the head of misery. But they are still evidently vicious, because an action is so denominated, which violates an express precept, founded upon its general tendency to produce misery, whatever may be its individual effect; and no person can doubt the general tendency of an illicit intercourse between the sexes, to injure the happiness of society.

These effects, in the present state of society, seem to be produced in the following manner. We will suppose the means of subsistence in any country just equal to the easy support of its inhabitants. The constant effort towards population, which is found to act even in the most vicious societies, increases the number of people before the means of subsistence are increased. The food, therefore, which before supported eleven millions, must now be divided among eleven millions and a half. The poor consequently must live much worse, and many of them be reduced to severe distress. The number of labourers also being above the proportion of work in the market, the price of labour must tend to fall, while the price of provisions would at the same time tend to rise. The labourer therefore must do more work, to earn the same as he did before. During this season of distress, the discouragements to marriage and the difficulty of rearing a family are so great, that [the progress of population is retarded.] In the meantime, the cheapness of labour, the plenty of labourers, and the necessity of an increased industry among them, encourage cultivators to employ more labour upon their land, to turn up fresh soil, and to manure and improve more completely what is already in tillage, till ultimately the means of subsistence may become in the same proportion to the population, as at the period from which we set out. The situation of the labourer being then again tolerably comfortable, the restraints to population are in some degree loosened; and, after a short period, the same retrograde and progressive movements, with respect to happiness, are repeated.

This sort of oscillation will not probably be obvious to common view; and it may be difficult even for the most attentive observer to calculate its periods. Yet that, in the generality of old states, some alternation of this kind does exist though in a much less marked, and in a much more irregular manner, than I have described it, no reflecting man, who considers the subject deeply, can well doubt.

One principal reason why this oscillation has been less remarked, and less decidedly confirmed by experience than might naturally be expected, is, that the histories of mankind which we possess are, in general, histories only of the higher classes. We have not many accounts that can be depended upon, of the manners and customs of that part of mankind, where these retrograde and progressive movements chiefly take place. A satisfactory history of this kind, of one people and of one period, would require the constant and minute attention of many observing minds in local and general remarks on the state of the lower classes of society, and the causes that influenced it; and, to draw accurate inferences upon this subject, a succession of such historians for some centuries would be necessary. This branch of statistical knowledge has, of late years, been attended to in some countries,[3] and we may promise ourselves a clearer insight into the internal structure of human society from the progress of these inquiries. But the science may be said yet to be in its infancy, and many of the objects, on which it would be desirable to have information, have been either omitted or not stated with sufficient accuracy. Among these, perhaps, may be reckoned the proportion of the number of adults to the number of marriages; the extent to which vicious customs have prevailed in consequence of the restraints upon matrimony; the comparative mortality among the children of the most distressed part of the community, and of those who live rather more at their ease; the variations in the real price of labour; the observable differences in the state of the lower classes of society, with respect to ease and happiness, at different times during a certain period; and very accurate registers of births, deaths, and marriages, which are of the utmost importance in this subject.

A faithful history, including such particulars, would tend greatly to elucidate the manner in which the constant check upon population acts; and would probably prove the existence of the retrograde and progressive movements that have been mentioned; though the times of their vibration must necessarily be rendered irregular from the op-

---

[3]The judicious questions which Sir John Sinclair circulated in Scotland, and the valuable accounts which he has collected in that part of the island, do him the highest honour; and these accounts will ever remain an extraordinary monument of the learning, good sense, and general information of the clergy of Scotland. It is to be regretted that the adjoining parishes are not put together in the work, which would have assisted the memory both in attaining and recollecting the state of particular districts. The repetitions and contradictory opinions which occur are not in my opinion so objectionable; as, to the result of such testimony, more faith may be given than we could possibly give to the testimony of any individual. Even were this result drawn for us by some master hand, though much valuable time would undoubtedly be saved, the information would not be so satisfactory. If, with a few subordinate improvements, this work had contained accurate and complete registers for the last 150 years, it would have been inestimable, and would have exhibited a better picture of the internal state of a country than has yet been presented to the world. But this last most essential improvement no diligence could have effects. J. Sinclair, *The statistical account of Scotland. Drawn up from the communications of the ministers of the different parishes,* 21 vols (Edinburgh, 1791-9) [hereafter, *Statistical account*].

eration of many interrupting causes; such as, the introduction or failure of certain manufactures; a greater or less prevalent spirit of agricultural enterprise; years of plenty, or years of scarcity; wars, sickly seasons, poor laws, emigrations and other causes of a similar nature.

A circumstance which has, perhaps, more than any other, contributed to conceal this oscillation from common view, is the difference between the nominal and real price of labour. It very rarely happens that the nominal price of labour universally falls; but we well know that it frequently remains the same, while the nominal price of provisions has been gradually rising. This, indeed, will generally be the case, if the increase of manufactures and commerce be sufficient to employ the new labourers that are thrown into the market, and to prevent the increased supply from lowering the money price.[4] But an increased number of labourers receiving the same money wages will necessarily, by their competition, increase the money price of corn. This is, in fact, a real fall in the price of labour; and, during this period, the condition of the lower classes of the community must be gradually growing worse. But the farmers and capitalists are growing rich from the real cheapness of labour. Their increasing capitals enable them to employ a greater number of men; and, as the population had probably suffered some check from the greater difficulty of supporting a family, the demand for labour, after a certain period, would be great in proportion to the supply, and its price would of course rise, if left to find its natural level; and thus the wages of labour, and consequently the condition of the lower classes of society, might have progressive and retrograde movements, though the price of labour might never nominally fall.

In savage life, where there is no regular price of labour, it is little to be doubted that similar oscillations took place. When population has increased nearly to the utmost limits of the food, all the preventive and the positive checks will naturally operate with increased force. Vicious habits with respect to the sex will be more general, the exposing of children more frequent, and both the

probability and fatality of wars and epidemics will be considerably greater; and these causes will probably continue their operation till the population is sunk below the level of the food; and then the return to comparative plenty will again produce an increase, and, after a certain period, its further progress will again be checked by the same causes.[5]

But without attempting to establish these progressive and retrograde movements in different countries, which would evidently require more minute histories than we possess, and which the progress of civilization naturally tends to counteract, the following propositions are intended to be proved:

1. Population is necessarily limited by the means of subsistence.
2. Population invariably increases where the means of subsistence increase, unless prevented by some very powerful and obvious checks.[6]
3. These checks, and the checks which repress the superior power of population, and keep its effects on a level with the means of subsistence, are all resolvable into moral restraint, vice and misery.

   The first of these propositions scarcely needs illustration. The second and third will be sufficiently established by a review of the immediate checks to population in the past and present state of society.

   This review will be the subject of the following chapters.

---

[4]If the new labourers thrown yearly into the market should find no employment but in agriculture, their competition might so lower the money price of labour, as to prevent the increase of population from occasioning an effective demand for more corn; or, in other words, if the landlords and farmers could get nothing but an additional quantity of agricultural labour in exchange for any additional produce which they could raise, they might not be tempted to raise it.

[5]Sir James Steuart very justly compares the generative faculty to a spring loaded with a variable weight *(An inquiry into the principles of political economy,* 2 vols (1767), i, p. 20) which would of course produce exactly that kind of oscillation which has been mentioned. In the first book of his *Political economy,* he has explained many parts of the subject of population very ably.

[6]I have expressed myself in this cautious manner, because I believe there are some instances, where population does not keep up to the level of the means of subsistence. But these are extreme cases; and, generally speaking, it might be said, that:

2. Population always increases where the means of subsistence increase.
3. The checks which repress the superior power of population, and keep its effects on a level with the means of subsistence, are all resolvable into moral restraint, vice and misery.

It should be observed, that, by an increase in the means of subsistence, is here meant such an increase as will enable the mass of the society to command more food. An increase might certainly take place, which in the actual state of a particular society would not be distributed to the lower classes, and consequently would give no stimulus to population.

OF THE CHECKS TO POPULATION IN THE LOWEST STAGE OF HUMAN SOCIETY

The wretched inhabitants of Tierra del Fuego have been placed, by the general consent of voyagers, at the bottom of the scale of human beings.[1] Of their domestic habits and manners, however, we have few accounts. Their barren country, and the miserable state in which they live, have prevented any intercourse with them that might give such information; but we cannot be at a loss to conceive the checks to population among a race of savages, whose very appearance indicates them to be half starved, and who, shivering with cold, and covered with filth and vermin, live in one of the most inhospitable climates in the world, without having sagacity enough to provide themselves with such conveniences as might mitigate its severities, and render life in some measure more comfortable.[2]

Next to these, and almost as low in genius and resources, have been placed the natives of Van Diemen's land;[3] but some late accounts have represented the islands of Andaman is the east as inhabited by a race of savages still lower in wretchedness even than these. Everything that voyagers have related of savage life is said to fall short of the barbarism of this people. Their whole time is spent in search of food: and as their woods yield them few or no supplies of animals, and but little vegetable diet, their principal occupation is that of climbing the rocks, or roving along the margin of the sea, in search of a precarious meal of fish, which, during the tempestuous season, they often seek for in vain. Their stature seldom exceeds five feet; their bellies are protuberant, with high shoulders, large heads, and limbs disproportionably slender. Their countenances exhibit the extreme of wretchedness, a horrid mixture of famine and ferocity; and their extenuated and diseased figures plainly indicate the want of wholesome nourishment. Some of these unhappy beings have been found on the shores in the last stage of famine.[4]

In the next scale of human beings we may place the inhabitants of New Holland, of a part of whom we have some accounts that may be depended upon, from a person who resided a considerable time at Port Jackson, and had frequent opportunities of being a witness to their habits and manners. The narrator of Captain Cook's first voyage having mentioned the very small number of inhabitants that was seen on the eastern coast of New Holland, and the apparent inability of the country, from its desolate state, to support many more, observes, 'By what means the inhabitants of this country are reduced to such a number as it can subsist, is not perhaps very easy to guess; whether, like the inhabitants of New Zealand, they are destroyed by the hands of each other in contests for food; whether they are swept off by accidental famine; or whether there is any cause that prevents the increase of the species, must be left for future adventurers to determine.'[5]

The account which Mr Collins has given of these savages will, I hope, afford in some degree a satisfactory answer. They are described as, in general, neither tall nor well made. Their arms, legs, and thighs, are thin, which is ascribed to the poorness of their mode of living. Those who inhabit the sea coast depend almost entirely on fish for their sustenance, relieved occasionally by a repast on some large grubs which are found in the body of the dwarf gum tree. The very scanty stock of animals in the woods, and the very great labour necessary to take them, keep the inland natives in as poor a condition as their brethren on the coast. They are compelled to climb the tallest trees after honey and the smaller animals, such as the flying squirrel and the opossum. When the stems are of great height, and without branches, which is generally the case in thick forests, this is a process of great labour, and is effected by cutting a notch with their stone hatchets for each foot successively, while their left arm embraces the tree. Trees were observed notched in this manner to the height of eighty feet before the first branch, where the hungry savage could hope to meet with any reward for so much toil.[6]

---

[1]J. Cook, *An account of the voyages undertaken . . . for making discoveries in the southern hemisphere, and successfully performed by Commodore Byron, Capt. Wallis, Capt. Cartaret and Capt. Cook*, 2nd ed., 3 vols (1773), ii, p. 59. [Hereafter *First voyage.*]

[2]J. Cook, *A voyage towards the South Pole, and round the world. Performed in His Majesty's Ships the Resolution and Adventure in the years 1772, 1773, 1774 and 1775*, 2 vols (London, 1777), ii, p. 187. [Hereafter *Second voyage.*]

[3]G. Vancouver, *A voyage of discovery to the north Pacific Ocean, and round the world, in the years 1790–95*, 3 vols (1798), ii, p. 13.

[4]M. Symes, *An account of an embassy to the Kingdom of Ava, sent by the Governor-General of India in the year 1795* (1800), p. 129; W. Dunkin, 'Extract from a diary of a journey over the Great Desert from Aleppo to Bussola, in April 1782', *Asiatic Researches; or, Transactions of the Society instituted in Bengal, for inquiring into the history and antiquities of Asia*, iv (1799), pp. 401–4.

[5]Cook, *First voyage*, iii, p. 240.

[6]D. Collins, *An account of the English colony of New South Wales from its first settlement in January 1788 to August 1801*, 2 vols (1798, 1802), appendix, p. 549.

The woods, exclusive of the animals occasionally found in them, afford but little sustenance. A few berries, the yam, the fern root, and the flowers of the different banksias, make up the whole of the vegetable catalogue.[7]

A native with his child, surprised on the banks of the Hawksbury river by some of our colonists, launched his canoe in a hurry, and left behind him a specimen of his food, and of the delicacy of his stomach. From a piece of water-soaked wood, full of holes, he had been extracting and eating a large worm. The smell both of the worm and its habitation was in the highest degree offensive. These worms, in the language of the country, are called cah-bro; and a tribe of natives dwelling inland, from the circumstance of eating these loathsome worms, is named Cah-brogal. The wood natives also make a paste formed of the fern root and the large and small ants, bruised together; and, in the season, add the eggs of this insect.[8]

In a country, the inhabitants of which are driven to such resources for subsistence, where the supply of animal and vegetable food is so extremely scanty, and the labour necessary to procure it is so severe, it is evident, that the population must be very thinly scattered in proportion to the territory. Its utmost bounds must be very narrow. But when we advert to the strange and barbarous customs of these people, the cruel treatment of their women, and the difficulty of rearing children; instead of being surprised that it does not more frequently press to pass these bounds, we shall be rather inclined to consider even these scanty resources as more than sufficient to support all the population that could grow up under such circumstances.

The prelude to love in this country is violence, and of the most brutal nature. The savage selects his intended wife from the women of a different tribe, generally one at enmity with his own. He steals upon her in the absence of her protectors, and having first stupefied her with blows of a club, or wooden sword, on the head, back, and shoulders, every one of which is followed by a stream of blood, he drags her through the woods by one arm, regardless of the stones and broken pieces of trees that may lie in his route, and anxious only to convey his prize in safety to his own party. The woman thus treated becomes his wife, is incorporated into the tribe to which he belongs, and but seldom quits him for another. The outrage is not resented by the relations of the female, who only retaliate by a similar outrage when it is in their power.[9]

The union of the sexes takes place at an early age; and instances were known to our colonists of very young girls having been much and shamefully abused by the males.[10]

The conduct of the husband to his wife or wives, seems to be nearly in character with this strange and barbarous mode of courtship. The females bear on their heads the traces of the superiority of the males, which is exercised almost as soon as they find strength in their arms to inflict a blow. Some of these unfortunate beings have been observed with more scars on their shorn heads, cut in every direction, than could well be counted. Mr Collins feelingly says, 'The condition of these women is so wretched, that I have often, on seeing a female child borne on its mother's shoulders, anticipated the miseries to which it was born, and thought it would be a mercy to destroy it.'[11] In another place, speaking of Bennilong's wife being delivered of a child, he says, 'I here find in my papers a note, that for some offence Bennilong had severely beaten this woman in the morning, a short time before she was delivered.'[12]

Women treated in this brutal manner must necessarily be subject to frequent miscarriages, and it is probable that the abuse of very young girls, mentioned above as common, and the too early union of the sexes in general, would tend to prevent the females from being prolific. Instances of a plurality of wives were found more frequent than of a single wife; but what is extraordinary, Mr Collins did not recollect ever to have noticed children by more than one. He had heard from some of the natives, that the first wife claimed an exclusive right to the conjugal embrace, while the second was merely the slave and drudge of both.[13]

An absolutely exclusive right in the first wife to the conjugal embrace seems to be hardly probable; but it is possible that the second wife may not be allowed to rear her offspring. At any rate, if the observation be generally true, it proves that many of the women are without children, which can only be accounted for from the very severe hardships which they undergo, or from some particular customs which may not have come to the knowledge of Mr Collins.

---

[7]Collins, *New South Wales*, appendix, p. 557.

[8]Collins, *New South Wales*, appendix, p. 558.

[9]Collins, *New South Wales*, appendix, p. 559.

[10]Collins, *New South Wales*, appendix, p. 563.

[11]Collins, *New South Wales*, appendix, p. 583.

[12]Collins, *New South Wales*, appendix, p. 562n.

[13]Collins, *New South Wales*, appendix, p. 560.

If the mother of a sucking child die, the helpless infant is buried alive in the same grave with its mother. The father himself places his living child on the body of his dead wife, and having thrown a large stone upon it, the grave is instantly filled by the other natives. This dreadful act was performed by Co-le-be, a native well known to our colonists, and who, on being talked to on the subject, justified the proceeding, by declaring that no woman could be found who would undertake to nurse the child, and that therefore it must have died a much worse death than that which he had given it. Mr Collins had reason to believe that this custom was generally prevalent, and observes, that it may in some measure account for the thinness of the population.[14]

Such a custom, though in itself perhaps it might not much affect the population of a country, places in a strong point of view the difficulty of rearing children in savage life. Women obliged by their habits of living to a constant change of place, and compelled to an unremitting drudgery for their husbands, appear to be absolutely incapable of bringing up two or three children nearly of the same age. If another child be born before the one above it can shift for itself, and follow its mother on foot, one of the two must almost necessarily perish for want of care. The task of rearing even one infant, in such a wandering and laborious life, must be so troublesome and painful, that we are not to be surprised that no woman can be found to undertake it who is not prompted by the powerful feelings of a mother.

To these causes, which forcibly repress the rising generation, must be added those which contribute subsequently to destroy it; such as the frequent wars of these savages with different tribes, and their perpetual contests with each other; their strange spirit of retaliation and revenge, which prompts the midnight murder, and the frequent shedding of innocent blood; the smoke and filth of their miserable habitations, and their poor mode of living, productive of loathsome cutaneous disorders; and, above all, a dreadful epidemic like the smallpox, which sweeps off great numbers.[15]

In the year 1789 they were visited by this epidemic, which raged among them with all the appearance and virulence of the smallpox. The desolation, which it occasioned, was almost incredible. Not a living person was to be found in the bays and harbours that were before the most frequented. Not a vestige of a human foot was to be traced on the sands. They had left the dead to bury the dead. The excavations in the rocks were filled with putrid bodies, and in many places the paths were covered with skeletons.[16]

Mr Collins was informed, that the tribe of Co-le-be, the native mentioned before, had been reduced by the effects of this dreadful disorder to three persons, who found themselves obliged to unite with some other tribe, to prevent their utter extinction.[17]

Under such powerful causes of depopulation, we should naturally be inclined to suppose that the animal and vegetable produce of the country would be increasing upon the thinly scattered inhabitants, and, added to the supply of fish from their shores, would be more than sufficient for their consumption; yet it appears, upon the whole, that the population is in general so nearly on a level with the average supply of food, that every little deficiency from unfavourable weather or other causes, occasions distress. Particular times, when the inhabitants seemed to be in great want, are mentioned as not uncommon, and, at these periods, some of the natives were found reduced to skeletons, and almost starved to death.[18]

---

[14]Collins, *New South Wales,* appendix, p. 607.

[15]See generally, the appendix to Collins, *New South Wales.*

[16]Collins, *New South Wales,* appendix, p. 597.

[17]Collins, *New South Wales,* appendix, p. 598.

[18]Collins, *New South Wales,* p. 34, appendix, p. 551.

Name: _____ **Date:** _____

1. Explain in your own words Malthus's two goals in writing this work:
1.

2.

2. Describe in your own words three different checks on population that Malthus offers.
1.

2.

3.

3. Malthus offers a "scale of human beings." List the members of this scale from "lowest" to "highest."

4. What attributes do the "lowest" members of Malthus's scale share that helps identify them as the "lowest" members?

5. What attributes to the "higher" members of Malthus's scale share that helps identify them as the "highest" members?

William Paley

Natural Theology, 1800

Paley (1743-1805) was an English mathematician, theologian, and Anglican priest, who borrowed from ancient and medieval philosophers to fully develop the concept of natural theology. In this piece, which was mastered by every nineteenth-century English university student, Paley described how the order, complexity, and purpose apparent in all of nature compels the careful observer to conclude that the universe and everything in it was the product of a omnipotent designer.

STATE OF THE ARGUMENT

In crossing a heath, suppose I pitched my foot against a *stone* and were asked how the stone came to be there, I might possibly answer that for anything I knew to the contrary it had lain there forever; nor would it, perhaps, be very easy to show the absurdity of this answer. But suppose I had found a *watch* upon the ground, and it should be inquired how the watch happened to be in that place, I should hardly think of the answer which I had before given, that for anything I knew the watch might have always been there. Yet why should not this answer serve for the watch as well as for the stone? Why is it not as admissible in the second case as in the first? For this reason, and for no other, namely, that when we come to inspect the watch, we perceive—what we could not discover in the stone—that its several parts are framed and put together for a purpose, e.g., that they are so formed and adjusted as to produce motion, and that motion so regulated as to point out the hour of the day; that if the different parts had been differently shaped from what they are, of a different size from what they are, or placed after any other manner or in any other order than that in which they are placed, either no motion at all would have been carried on in the machine, or none which would have answered the use that is now served by it. To reckon up a few of the plainest of these parts and of their offices, all tending to one result; we see a cylindrical

box containing a coiled elastic spring, which, by its endeavour to relax itself, turns round the box. We next observe a flexible chain—artificially wrought for the sake of flexure—communicating the action of the spring from the box to the fusee. We then find a series of wheels, the teeth of which catch in and apply to each other, conducting the motion from the fusee to the balance and from the balance to the pointer, and at the same time, by the size and shape of those wheels, so regulating that motion as to terminate in causing an index, by an equable and measured progression, to pass over a given space in a given time. We take notice that the wheels are made of brass, in order to keep them from rust; the springs of steel, no other metal being so elastic; that over the face of the watch there is placed a glass, a material employed in no other part of the work, but in the room of which, if there had been any other than a transparent substance, the hour could not be seen without opening the case. This mechanism being observed—it requires indeed an examination of the instrument, and perhaps some previous knowledge of the subject, to perceive and understand it; but being once, as we have said, observed and understood—the inference we think is inevitable, that the watch must have had a maker-that there must have existed, at some time and at some place or other, an artificer or artificers who formed it for the purpose which we find it actually to answer, who comprehended its construction and designed its use.

1. Nor would it, I apprehend, weaken the conclusion, that we had never seen a watch made—

From *Natural Theology*, 1800.

that we had never known an artist capable of making one—that we were altogether incapable of executing such a piece of workmanship ourselves, or of understanding in what manner it was performed; all this being no more than what is true of some exquisite remains of ancient art, of some lost arts, and, to the generality of mankind, of the more curious productions of modern manufacture. Does one man in a million know how oval frames are turned? Ignorance of this kind exalts our opinion of the unseen and unknown artist's skiff, if he be unseen and unknown, but raises no doubt in our minds of the existence and agency of such an artist, at some former time and in some place or other. . . .

2. Neither, secondly, would it invalidate our conclusion, that the watch sometimes went wrong or that it seldom went exactly right. The purpose of the machinery, the design, and the designer might be evident, and in the case supposed, would be evident, in whatever way we accounted for the irregularity of the movement, or whether we could account for it or not. It is not necessary that a machine be perfect in order to show with what design it was made: still less necessary, where the only question is whether it were made with any design at all.

Suppose, in the next place, that the person who found the watch should after some time discover that, in addition to all the properties which he had hitherto observed in it, it possessed the unexpected property of producing in the course of its movement another watch like itself—the thing is conceivable; that it contained within it a mechanism, a system of parts—a mold, for instance, or a complex adjustment of lathes, baffles, and other tools—evidently and separately calculated for this purpose; let us inquire what effect ought such a discovery to have upon his former conclusion.

1. The first effect would be to increase his admiration of the contrivance, and his conviction of the consummate skill of the contriver. Whether he regarded the object of the contrivance, the distinct apparatus, the intricate, yet in many parts intelligible mechanism by which it was carried on, he would perceive in this new observation nothing but an additional reason for doing what he had already done—for referring the construction of the watch to design and to supreme art. If that construction *without* this property, or, which is the same thing, before this property had

been noticed, proved intention and art to have been employed about it, still more strong would the proof appear when he came to the knowledge of this further property, the crown and perfection of all the rest.

2. He would reflect, that though the watch before him were, *in some sense,* the maker of the watch, which, was fabricated in the course of its movements, yet it was in a very different sense from that in which a carpenter, for instance, is the maker of a chair—the author of its contrivance, the cause of the relation of its parts to their use. With respect to these, the first watch was no cause at all to the second; in no such sense as this was it the author of the constitution and order, either of the arts which the new watch contained, or of the parts by the aid and instrumentality of which it was produced. We might possibly say, but with great latitude of expression, that a stream of water ground corn; but no latitude of expression would allow us to say, no stretch of conjecture could lead us to think that the stream of water built the mill, though it were too ancient for us to know who the builder was. What the stream of water does in the affair is neither more nor less than this: by the application of an unintelligent impulse to a mechanism previously arranged, arranged independently of it and arranged by intelligence, an effect is produced, namely, the corn is ground. But the effect results from the arrangement. The force of the stream cannot be said to be the cause or author of the effect, still less of the arrangement. Understanding and plan in the formation of the mill were not the less necessary for any share which the water has in grinding the corn; yet is this share the same as that which the watch would have contributed to the production of the new watch, upon the supposition assumed in the last section. Therefore,

3. Though it be now no longer probable that the individual watch which our observer had found was made immediately by the hand of an artificer, yet does not this alteration in anyway affect the inference that an artificer had been originally employed and concerned in the production. The argument from design remains as it was. Marks of design and contrivance are no more accounted for now than they were before. In the same thing, we may ask for the cause of different properties. We may ask for the cause of the color of a body, of its hardness, of its heat; and these causes may be all different. We are now asking for the

cause of that subserviency to a use, that relation to an end, which we have remarked in the watch before us. No answer is given to this question by telling us that a preceding watch produced it. There cannot be design without a designer; contrivance without a contriver; order without choice; arrangement without anything capable of arranging; subserviency and relation to a purpose without that which could intend a purpose; means suitable to an end, and executing their office in accomplishing that end, without the end ever having been contemplated or the means accommodated to it. Arrangement, disposition of parts, subserviency of means to an end, relation of instruments to a use imply the presence of intelligence and mind. No one, therefore, can rationally believe that the insensible, inanimate watch, from which the watch before us issued, was the proper cause of the mechanism we so much admire in it—could be truly said to have constructed the instrument, disposed its parts, assigned their office, determined their order, action, and mutual dependency, combined their several motions into one result, and that also a result connected with the utilities of other beings. All these properties, therefore, are as much unaccounted for as they were before.

4. Nor is anything gained by running the difficulty farther back, that is, by supposing the watch before us to have been produced from another watch, that from a former, and so on indefinitely. Our going back ever so far brings us no nearer to the least degree of satisfaction upon the subject. Contrivance is still unaccounted for. We still want a contriver. A designing mind is neither supplied by this supposition nor dispensed with. If the difficulty were diminished the farther we went back, by going back indefinitely we might exhaust it. And this is the only case to which this sort of reasoning applies. Where there is a tendency, or, as we increase the number of terms, a continual approach toward a limit, *there* by supposing the number of terms to be what is called infinite, we may conceive the limit to be attained; but where there is no such tendency or approach, nothing is effected by lengthening the series. There is no difference as to the point in question, whatever there may be as to many points, between one series and another—between a series which is finite and a series which is infinite. A chain composed of an infinite number of links, can no more support itself, than a chain composed of a finite number of links. And of this we are assured, though we never *can* have tried the experiment; because, by increasing the number of links, from ten, for instance, to a hundred, from a hundred to a thousand, etc., we make not the smallest approach, we observe not the smallest tendency toward self support. There is no difference in this respect—yet there may be a great difference in several respects—between a chain of a greater or less length, between one chain and another, between one that is finite and one that is infinite. This very much resembles the case before us. The machine which we are inspecting demonstrates, by its construction, contrivance and design. Contrivance must have had a contriver, design a designer, whether the machine immediately proceeded from another machine or not. That circumstance alters not the case. That other machine may, in like manner, have proceeded from a former machine: nor does that alter the case; contrivance must have had a contriver. That former one from one preceding it: no alteration still; a contriver is still necessary. No tendency is perceived, no approach toward a diminution of this necessity. It is the same with any and every succession of these machines—a succession of ten, of a hundred, of a thousand; with one series, as with another—a series which is finite, as with a series which is infinite. In whatever other respects they may differ, in this they do not. In all equally, contrivance and design are unaccounted for.

The question is not simply, How came the first watch into existence? which question, it may be pretended, is done away by supposing the series of watches thus produced from one another to have been infinite, and consequently to have had no such *first* for which it was necessary to provide a cause. This, perhaps, would have been nearly the state of the question, if nothing had been before us but an unorganized, unmechanized substance, without mark or indication of contrivance. It might be difficult to show that such substance could not have existed from eternity, either in succession—if it were possible, which I think it is not, for unorganized bodies to spring from one another—or by individual perpetuity. But that is not the question now. To suppose it to be so is to suppose that it made no difference whether he had found a watch or a stone. As it is, the metaphysics of that question have no place; for, in the watch which we are examining are seen contrivance, design, an end, a purpose, means for the end, adaptation to the purpose. And the question which irresistibly presses upon our thoughts is, whence this contrivance and design? The thing required is the intending mind, the adapting hand, the intelligence by which that hand was directed. This question, this demand is not shaken off by increasing a number or succession of substances destitute of these properties; nor the more, by increasing that number to infinity. If it be said that, upon the supposition of one watch being produced from another in the course of that other's movements and by means of the mechanism within it, we have a cause for the watch in my hand, namely, the watch from which it proceeded; I deny that for the design, the contrivance, the suitableness of means to an end, the adaptation of instruments to a use, all of which we discover in the watch, we have any cause whatever. It is in vain, therefore, to assign a series of such causes or to allege that a series may be carried back to infinity; for I do not admit that we have yet any cause at all for the phenomena, still less any series of causes either finite or infinite. Here is contrivance but no contriver; proofs of design, but no designer.

5. Our observer would further also reflect that the maker of the watch before him was in truth and reality the maker of every watch produced from it: there being no difference, except that the latter manifests a more exquisite skill, between the making of another watch with his own hands, by the mediation of ffles, lathes, chisels, etc., and the disposing, fixing, and inserting of these instruments, or of others equivalent to them, in the body of the watch already made, in such a manner as to form a new watch in the course of the movements which he had given to the old one. It is only working by one set of tools instead of another.

The conclusion which the *first* examination of the watch, of its works, construction, and movement, suggested, was that it must have had, for cause and author of that construction, an artificer who understood its mechanism and designed its use. This conclusion is invincible. A *second* examination presents us with a new discovery. The watch is found, in the course of its movement, to produce another watch similar to itself; and not only so, but we perceive in it a system of organization separately calculated for that purpose. What effect would this discovery have or ought it to have upon our former inference?

What, as has already been said, but to increase beyond measure our admiration of the skill which had been employed in the formation of such a machine? Or shall it, instead of this, all at once turn us round to an opposite conclusion, namely, that no art or skill whatever has been concerned in the business, although all other evidences of art and skill remain as they were, and this last and supreme piece of art be now added to the rest? Can this be maintained without absurdity? Yet this is atheism. . . .

APPLICATION OF THE ARGUMENT

Every observation which was made in our first chapter concerning the watch may be repeated with strict propriety concerning the eye, concerning animals, concerning plants, concerning, indeed, all the organized parts of the works of nature. As,

1. When we are inquiring simply after the *existence* of an intelligent Creator, imperfection, inaccuracy, liability to disorder, occasional irregularities may subsist in a considerable degree without inducing any doubt into the question; just as a watch may frequently go wrong, seldom perhaps exactly right, may be faulty in some parts, defective in some, without the smallest ground of suspicion from thence arising that it was not a watch, not made, or not made for the purpose ascribed to it. When faults are pointed out, and when a question is started concerning the skill of the artist or dexterity with which the work is executed, then, indeed, in order to defend these qualities from accusation, we must be able either to expose some intractableness and imperfection in the materials or point out some invincible difficulty in the execution, into which imperfection and difficulty the matter of complaint may be resolved; or, if we cannot do this, we must adduce such specimens of consummate art and contrivance proceeding from the same hand as may convince the inquirer of the existence, in the case before him, of impediments like those which we have mentioned, although, what from the nature of the case is very likely to happen, they be unknown and unperceived by him. This we must do in order to vindicate the artist's skill, or at least the perfection of it; as we must also judge of his intention and of the provisions employed in fulfilling that intention, not from an instance in which they fail but from the great plurality of instances in which they succeed. But, after all, these are different questions from the question of the artist's exis-

tence; or, which is the same, whether the thing before us be a work of art or not; and the questions ought always to be kept separate in the mind. So likewise it is in the works of nature. Irregularities and imperfections are of little or no weight in the consideration when that consideration relates simply to the existence of a Creator. When the argument respects His attributes, they are of weight; but are then to be taken in conjunction-the attention is not to rest upon them, but they are to be taken in conjunction with the unexceptionable evidence which we possess of skill, power, and benevolence displayed in other instances; which evidences may, in strength, number, and variety, be such and may so overpower apparent blemishes as to induce us, upon the most reasonable ground, to believe that these last ought to be referred to some cause, though we be ignorant of it, other than defect of knowledge or of benevolence in the author. . . .

Name: _____ **Date:** _____

1. What is an "artificer?" Look up the word and describe it in your own terms.

2. Describe in your own words three different aspects of a watch that Paley claimed suggest that it was created by a artificer.

   1.

   2.

   3.

3. Why, according to Paley, might one mistakenly believe that a watch was not created by an artificer? List and describe two different reasons.

4. What, according to Paley, would an atheist believe about the existence of an artificer?

Section II

Darwin

Charles Darwin

Voyage of the Beagle, 1836

Between the end of 1831 and October of 1836, Charles Darwin (1809-1882) sailed aboard the *H.M.S. Beagle* as the captain's companion. His voyage took him from England, around South America, through New Zealand and Australia, across the Indian Ocean and around the southern tip of Africa. When he left he was a twenty-two year old gentleman with a general university training and aspirations to be an Anglican priest. Five years later, he returned to England a minor celebrity for the many unique plant, animal, and geological specimens he had shipped to the nation's museums. Following the well-established tradition of European explorers, Darwin assembled his notes from the trip and published *Voyage of the Beagle* in 1836. As he wrote it, he was just beginning to piece together his theory of natural selection, so his book contains nothing about evolution, but the tremendous detail and careful observations form the foundation for his later works on natural selection.

ST. JAGO—CAPE DE VERD ISLANDS

After having been twice driven back by heavy southwestern gales, Her Majesty's ship Beagle, a ten-gun brig, under the command of Captain Fitz Roy, R. N., sailed from Devonport on the 27th of December, 1831. The object of the expedition was to complete the survey of Patagonia and Tierra del Fuego, commenced under Captain King in 1826 to 1830—to survey the shores of Chile, Peru, and of some islands in the Pacific—and to carry a chain of chronometrical measurements round the World. On the 6th of January we reached Teneriffe, but were prevented landing, by fears of our bringing the cholera: the next morning we saw the sun rise behind the rugged outline of the Grand Canary island, and suddenly illuminate the Peak of Teneriffe, whilst the lower parts were veiled in fleecy clouds. This was the first of many delightful days never to be forgotten. On the 16th of January, 1832, we anchored at Porto Praya, in St. Jago, the chief island of the Cape de Verd archipelago.

The neighbourhood of Porto Praya, viewed from the sea, wears a desolate aspect. The volcanic fires of a past age, and the scorching heat of a tropical sun, have in most places rendered the soil unfit for vegetation. The country rises in successive steps of tableland, interspersed with some truncate conical hills, and the horizon is bounded by an irregular chain of more lofty mountains. The scene, as beheld through the hazy atmosphere of this climate, is one of great interest; if, indeed, a person, fresh from sea, and who has just walked, for the first time, in a grove of cocoa-nut trees, can be a judge of anything but his own happiness. The island would generally be considered as very uninteresting; but to anyone accustomed only to an English landscape, the novel aspect of an utterly sterile land possesses a grandeur which more vegetation might spoil. A single green leaf can scarcely be discovered over wide tracts of the lava plains; yet flocks of goats, together with a few cows, contrive to exist. It rains very seldom, but during a short portion of the year heavy torrents fall, and immediately afterwards a light vegetation springs out of every crevice. This soon withers; and upon such naturally formed hay the animals live. It had not now rained for an entire year. When the island was discovered, the immediate neighbourhood of Porto Praya was clothed with trees,[1] the reckless destruction of which has caused here, as at St. Helena, and at some of the Canary islands, almost entire sterility. The broad, flat-bottomed valleys, many

From *Voyage of the Beagle*, New York: P.F. Collier & Son, 1909.

[1] I state this on the authority of Dr. E. Dieffenbach, in his German translation of the first edition of this Journal.

of which serve during a few days only in the season as water-courses, are clothed with thickets of leafless bushes. Few living creatures inhabit these valleys. The commonest bird is a kingfisher (Dacelo Iagoensis), which tamely sits on the branches of the castor-oil plant, and thence darts on grasshoppers and lizards. It is brightly coloured, but not so beautiful as the European species: in its flight, manners, and place of habitation, which is generally in the driest valley, there is also a wide difference.

One day, two of the officers and myself rode to Ribeira Grande, a village a few miles eastward of Porto Praya. Until we reached the valley of St. Martin, the country presented its usual dull brown appearance; but here, a very small rill of water produces a most refreshing margin of luxuriant vegetation. In the course of an hour we arrived at Ribeira Grande, and were surprised at the sight of a large ruined fort and cathedral. This little town, before its harbour was filled up, was the principal place in the island: it now presents a melancholy, but very picturesque appearance. Having procured a black Padre for a guide, and a Spaniard who had served in the Peninsular war as an interpreter, we visited a collection of buildings, of which an ancient church formed the principal part. It is here the governors and captain-generals of the islands have been buried. Some of the tombstones recorded dates of the sixteenth century.[2] The heraldic ornaments were the only things in this retired place that reminded us of Europe. The church or chapel formed one side of a quadrangle, in the middle of which a large clump of bananas were growing. On another side was a hospital, containing about a dozen miserable-looking inmates.

We returned to the Vênda to eat our dinners. A considerable number of men, women, and children, all as black as jet, collected to watch us. Our companions were extremely merry; and everything we said or did was followed by their hearty laughter. Before leaving the town we visited the cathedral. It does not appear so rich as the smaller church, but boasts of a little organ, which sent forth singularly inharmonious cries. We presented the black priest with a few shillings, and the Spaniard, patting him on the head, said, with much candour, he thought his colour made no great difference. We then returned, as fast as the ponies would go, to Porto Praya.

Another day we rode to the village of St. Domingo, situated near the centre of the island. On a small plain which we crossed, a few stunted acacias were growing; their tops had been bent by the steady

trade-wind, in a singular manner—some of them even at right angles to their trunks. The direction of the branches was exactly N. E. by N., and S. W. by S., and these natural vanes must indicate the prevailing direction of the force of the trade-wind. The travelling had made so little impression on the barren soil, that we here missed our track, and took that to Fuentes. This we did not find out till we arrived there; and we were afterwards glad of our mistake. Fuentes is a pretty village, with a small stream; and everything appeared to prosper well, excepting, indeed, that which ought to do so most—its inhabitants. The black children, completely naked, and looking very wretched, were carrying bundles of firewood half as big as their own bodies.

Near Fuentes we saw a large flock of guinea-fowl—probably fifty or sixty in number. They were extremely wary, and could not be approached. They avoided us, like partridges on a rainy day in September, running with their heads cocked up; and if pursued, they readily took to the wing.

The scenery of St. Domingo possesses a beauty totally unexpected, from the prevalent gloomy character of the rest of the island. The village is situated at the bottom of a valley, bounded by lofty and jagged walls of stratified lava. The black rocks afford a most striking contrast with the bright green vegetation, which follows the banks of a little stream of clear water. It happened to be a grand feast-day, and the village was full of people. On our return we overtook a party of about twenty young black girls, dressed in excellent taste; their black skins and snow-white linen being set off by coloured turbans and large shawls. As soon as we approached near, they suddenly all turned round, and covering the path with their shawls, sung with great energy a wild song, beating time with their hands upon their legs. We threw them some vintéms, which were received with screams of laughter, and we left them redoubling the noise of their song.

One morning the view was singularly clear; the distant mountains being projected with the sharpest outline on a heavy bank of dark blue clouds. Judging from the appearance, and from similar cases in England, I supposed that the air was saturated with moisture. The fact, however, turned out quite the contrary. The hygrometer gave a difference of 29.6 degrees, between the temperature of the air, and the point at which dew was precipitated. This difference was nearly doubled that which I had observed on the previous mornings. This unusual degree of atmospheric dryness was accompanied by continual flashes of lightning. Is it not an uncommon case, thus to find a remarkable degree of aerial transparency with such a state of weather?

Generally the atmosphere is hazy; and this is caused by the falling of impalpably fine dust, which

---

[2]The Cape de Verd Islands were discovered in 1449. There was a tombstone of a bishop with the date of 1571; and a crest of a hand and dagger, dated 1497.

was found to have slightly injured the astronomical instruments. The morning before we anchored at Porto Praya, I collected a little packet of this brown-coloured fine dust, which appeared to have been filtered from the wind by the gauze of the vane at the masthead. Mr. Lyell has also given me four packets of dust which fell on a vessel a few hundred miles northward of these islands. Professor Ehrenberg[3] finds that this dust consists in great part of infusoria with siliceous shields, and of the siliceous tissue of plants. In five little packets which I sent him, he has ascertained no less than sixty-seven different organic forms! The infusoria, with the exception of two marine species, are all inhabitants of freshwater. I have found no less than fifteen different accounts of dust having fallen on vessels when far out in the Atlantic. From the direction of the wind whenever it has fallen, and from its having always fallen during those months when the harmattan is known to raise clouds of dust high into the atmosphere, we may feel sure that it all comes from Africa. It is, however, a very singular fact, that, although Professor Ehrenberg knows many species of infusoria peculiar to Africa, he finds none of these in the dust which I sent him. On the other hand, he finds in it two species which hitherto he knows as living only in South America. The dust falls in such quantities as to dirty everything on board, and to hurt people's eyes; vessels even have run on shore owing to the obscurity of the atmosphere. It has often fallen on ships when several hundred, and even more than a thousand miles from the coast of Africa, and at points sixteen hundred miles distant in a north and south direction. In some dust which was collected on a vessel three hundred miles from the land, I was much surprised to find particles of stone above the thousandth of an inch square, mixed with finer matter. After this fact one need not be surprised at the diffusion of the far lighter and smaller sporules of cryptogamic plants.

The geology of this island is the most interesting part of its natural history. On entering the harbour, a perfectly horizontal white band in the face of the sea cliff, may be seen running for some miles along the coast, and at the height of about forty-five feet above the water. Upon examination, this white stratum is found to consist of calcareous matter, with numerous shells embedded, most or all of which now exist on the neighbouring coast. It rests on ancient volcanic rocks, and has been covered by a stream of basalt, which must have entered the sea when the white shelly bed was lying at the bottom.

It is interesting to trace the changes, produced by the heat of the overlying lava, on the friable mass, which in parts has been converted into a crystalline limestone, and in other parts into a compact spotted stone. Where the lime has been caught up by the scoriaceous fragments of the lower surface of the stream, it is converted into groups of beautifully radiated fibres resembling arragonite. The beds of lava rise in successive gently-sloping plains, towards the interior, whence the deluges of melted stone have originally proceeded. Within historical times, no signs of volcanic activity have, I believe, been manifested in any part of St. Jago. Even the form of a crater can but rarely be discovered on the summits of the many red cindery hills; yet the more recent streams can be distinguished on the coast, forming lines of cliffs of less height, but stretching out in advance of those belonging to an older series: the height of the cliffs thus affording a rude measure of the age of the streams.

During our stay, I observed the habits of some marine animals. A large Aplysia is very common. This sea-slug is about five inches long; and is of a dirty yellowish colour, veined with purple. On each side of the lower surface, or foot, there is a broad membrane, which appears sometimes to act as a ventilator, in causing a current of water to flow over the dorsal branchiæ or lungs. It feeds on the delicate sea-weeds which grow among the stones in muddy and shallow water; and I found in its stomach several small pebbles, as in the gizzard of a bird. This slug, when disturbed, emits a very fine purplish-red fluid, which stains the water for the space of a foot around. Besides this means of defence, an acrid secretion, which is spread over its body, causes a sharp, stinging sensation, similar to that produced by the Physalia, or Portuguese man-of-war.

I was much interested, on several occasions, by watching the habits of an Octopus, or cuttle-fish. Although common in the pools of water left by the retiring tide, these animals were not easily caught. By means of their long arms and suckers, they could drag their bodies into very narrow crevices; and when thus fixed, it required great force to remove them. At other times they darted tail first, with the rapidity of an arrow, from one side of the pool to the other, at the same instant discolouring the water with a dark chestnut-brown ink. These animals also escape detection by a very extraordinary, chameleon-like power of changing their colour. They appear to vary their tints according to the nature of the ground over which they pass: when in deep water, their general shade was brownish purple, but when placed on the land, or in shallow water, this dark tint changed into one of a yellowish green. The colour, examined more carefully, was a French grey, with numerous minute spots of bright

[3]I must take this opportunity of acknowledging the great kindness with which this illustrious naturalist has examined many of my specimens. I have sent (June, 1845) a full account of the falling of this dust to the Geological Society.

yellow: the former of these varied in intensity; the latter entirely disappeared and appeared again by turns. These changes were effected in such a manner, that clouds, varying in tint between a hyacinth red and a chestnut-brown,[4] were continually passing over the body. Any part, being subjected to a slight shock of galvanism, became almost black: a similar effect, but in a less degree, was produced by scratching the skin with a needle. These clouds, or blushes as they may be called, are said to be produced by the alternate expansion and contraction of minute vesicles containing variously coloured fluids.[5]

This cuttle-fish displayed its chameleon-like power both during the act of swimming and whilst remaining stationary at the bottom. I was much amused by the various arts to escape detection used by one individual, which seemed fully aware that I was watching it. Remaining for a time motionless, it would then stealthily advance an inch or two, like a cat after a mouse; sometimes changing its colour: it thus proceeded, till having gained a deeper part, it darted away, leaving a dusky train of ink to hide the hole into which it had crawled.

While looking for marine animals, with my head about two feet above the rocky shore, I was more than once saluted by a jet of water, accompanied by a slight grating noise. At first I could not think what it was, but afterwards I found out that it was this cuttle-fish, which, though concealed in a hole, thus often led me to its discovery. That it possesses the power of ejecting water there is no doubt, and it appeared to me that it could certainly take good aim by directing the tube or siphon on the under side of its body. From the difficulty which these animals have in carrying their heads, they cannot crawl with ease when placed on the ground. I observed that one which I kept in the cabin was slightly phosphorescent in the dark.

ST. PAUL'S ROCKS

In crossing the Atlantic we hove-to, during the morning of February 16th, close to the island of St. Paul's. This cluster of rocks is situated in 0° 58′ north latitude, and 29° 15′ west longitude. It is 540 miles distant from the coast of America, and 350 from the island of Fernando Noronha. The highest point is only fifty feet above the level of the sea, and the entire circumference is under three-quarters of a mile. This small point rises abruptly out of the depths of the ocean. Its mineralogical constitution is not simple; in some parts the rock is of a cherty, in others of a felspathic nature, including thin veins of serpentine. It is a remarkable fact, that all the many small islands, lying far from any continent, in the Pacific, Indian, and Atlantic Oceans, with the exception of the Seychelles and this little point of rock, are, I believe, composed either of coral or of erupted matter. The volcanic nature of these oceanic islands is evidently an extension of that law, and the effect of those same causes, whether chemical or mechanical, from which it results that a vast majority of the volcanoes now in action stand either near sea-coasts or as islands in the midst of the sea.

The rocks of St. Paul appear from a distance of a brilliantly white colour. This is partly owing to the dung of a vast multitude of seafowl, and partly to a coating of a hard glossy substance with a pearly lustre, which is intimately united to the surface of the rocks. This, when examined with a lens, is found to consist of numerous exceedingly thin layers, its total thickness being about the tenth of an inch. It contains much animal matter, and its origin, no doubt, is due to the action of the rain or spray on the birds' dung. Below some small masses of guano at Ascension, and on the Abrolhos Islets, I found certain stalactitic branching bodies, formed apparently in the same manner as the thin white coating on these rocks. The branching bodies so closely resembled in general appearance certain nulliporæ (a family of hard calcareous sea-plants), that in lately looking hastily over my collection I did not perceive the difference. The globular extremities of the branches are of a pearly texture, like the enamel of teeth, but so hard as just to scratch plate-glass. I may here mention, that on a part of the coast of Ascension, where there is a vast accumulation of shelly sand, an incrustation is deposited on the tidal rocks by the water of the sea, resembling, as represented in the woodcut, certain cryptogamic plants (Marchantiæ) often seen on damp walls. The surface of the fronds is beautifully glossy; and those parts formed where fully exposed to the light are of a jet black colour, but those shaded under ledges are only grey. I have shown specimens of this incrustation to several geologists, and they all thought that they were of volcanic or igneous origin! In its hardness and translucency—in its polish, equal to that of the finest oliva-shell—in the bad smell given out, and loss of colour under the blowpipe—it shows a close similarity with living sea-shells. Moreover, in sea-shells, it is known that the parts habitually covered and shaded by the mantle of the animal, are of a paler colour than those fully exposed to the light, just as is the case with this incrustation. When we remember that lime, either as a phosphate or carbonate, enters into the composition of the hard

---

[4]So named according to Patrick Symes's nomenclature.
[5]See Encyclop. of Anat. and Physiol., article *Cephalopoda*.

parts, such as bones and shells, of all living animals, it is an interesting physiological fact[6] to find substances harder than the enamel of teeth, and coloured surfaces as well polished as those of a fresh shell, reformed through inorganic means from dead organic matter—mocking, also, in shape, some of the lower vegetable productions.

We found on St. Paul's only two kinds of birds—the booby and the noddy. The former is a species of gannet, and the latter a tern. Both are of a tame and stupid disposition, and are so unaccustomed to visitors, that I could have killed any number of them with my geological hammer. The booby lays her eggs on the bare rock; but the tern makes a very simple nest with seaweed. By the side of many of these nests a small flying-fish was placed; which, I suppose, had been brought by the male bird for its partner. It was amusing to watch how quickly a large and active crab (Graspus), which inhabits the crevices of the rock, stole the fish from the side of the nest, as soon as we had disturbed the parent birds. Sir W. Symonds, one of the few persons who have landed here, informs me that he saw the crabs dragging even the young birds out of their nests, and devouring them. Not a single plant, not even a lichen, grows on this islet; yet it is inhabited by several insects and spiders. The following list completes, I believe, the terrestrial fauna: a fly (Olfersia) living on the booby, and a tick which must have come here as a parasite on the birds; a small brown moth, belonging to a genus that feeds on feathers; a beetle (Quedius) and a woodlouse from beneath the dung; and lastly, numerous spiders, which I suppose prey on these small attendants and scavengers of the water-fowl. The often repeated description of the stately palm and other noble tropical plants, then birds, and lastly man, taking possession of the coral islets as soon as formed, in the Pacific, is probably not correct; I fear it destroys the poetry of this story, that feather and dirt-feeding and parasitic insects and spiders should be the first inhabitants of newly formed oceanic land.

The smallest rock in the tropical seas, by giving a foundation for the growth of innumerable kinds of seaweed and compound animals, supports likewise a large number of fish. The sharks and the seamen in the boats maintained a constant struggle which should secure the greater share of the prey caught by the fishing-lines. I have heard that a rock near the Bermudas, lying many miles out at sea, and at a considerable depth, was first discovered by the circumstance of fish having been observed in the neighbourhood.

FERNANDO NORONHA, FEB. 20TH

As far as I was enabled to observe, during the few hours we stayed at this place, the constitution of the island is volcanic, but probably not of a recent date. The most remarkable feature is a conical hill, about one thousand feet high, the upper part of which is exceedingly steep, and on one side overhangs its base. The rock is phonolite, and is divided into irregular columns. On viewing one of these isolated masses, at first one is inclined to believe that it has been suddenly pushed up in a semi-fluid state. At St. Helena, however, I ascertained that some pinnacles, of a nearly similar figure and constitution, had been formed by the injection of melted rock into yielding strata, which thus had formed the moulds for these gigantic obelisks. The whole island is covered with wood; but from the dryness of the climate there is no appearance of luxuriance. Half-way up the mountain, some great masses of the columnar rock, shaded by laurel-like trees, and ornamented by others covered with fine pink flowers but without a single leaf, gave a pleasing effect to the nearer parts of the scenery.

BAHIA, OR SAN SALVADOR BRAZIL, FEB. 29TH

The day has passed delightfully. Delight itself, however, is a weak term to express the feelings of a naturalist who, for the first time, has wandered by himself in a Brazilian forest. The elegance of the grasses, the novelty of the parasitical plants, the beauty of the flowers, the glossy green of the foliage, but above all the general luxuriance of the vegetation, filled me with admiration. A most paradoxical mixture of sound and silence pervades the shady parts of the wood. The noise from the insects is so loud, that it may be heard even in a vessel anchored several hundred yards from the shore; yet within the recesses of the forest a universal silence appears to reign. To a person fond of natural history, such a day as this brings with it a deeper pleasure than he can ever hope to experience again. After wandering about for some hours, I returned to the landing-place; but, before reaching it, I was overtaken by a tropical storm. I tried to find shelter under a tree, which was so thick that it would never have been

---

[6]Mr. Horner and Sir David Brewster have described (Philosophical Transactions, 1836, p. 65) a singular "artificial substance resembling shell." It is deposited in fine, transparent, highly polished, brown-coloured laminæ, possessing peculiar optical properties, on the inside of a vessel, in which cloth, first prepared with glue and then with lime, is made to revolve rapidly in water. It is much softer, more transparent, and contains more animal matter, than the natural incrustation at Ascension; but we here again see the strong tendency which carbonate of lime and animal matter evince to form a solid substance allied to shell.

penetrated by common English rain; but here, in a couple of minutes, a little torrent flowed down the trunk. It is to this violence of the rain that we must attribute the verdure at the bottom of the thickest woods: if the showers were like those of a colder climate, the greater part would be absorbed or evaporated before it reached the ground. I will not at present attempt to describe the gaudy scenery of this noble bay, because, in our homeward voyage, we called here a second time, and I shall then have occasion to remark on it.

Along the whole coast of Brazil, for a length of at least 2000 miles, and certainly for a considerable space inland, wherever solid rock occurs, it belongs to a granitic formation. The circumstance of this enormous area being constituted of materials which most geologists believe to have been crystallized when heated under pressure, gives rise to many curious reflections. Was this effect produced beneath the depths of a profound ocean? or did a covering of strata formerly extend over it, which has since been removed? Can we believe that any power, acting for a time short of infinity, could have denuded the granite over so many thousand square leagues?

On a point not far from the city, where a rivulet entered the sea, I observed a fact connected with a subject discussed by Humboldt.[7] At the cataracts of the great rivers Orinoco, Nile, and Congo, the syenitic rocks are coated by a black substance, appearing as if they had been polished with plumbago. The layer is of extreme thinness; and on analysis by Berzelius it was found to consist of the oxides of manganese and iron. In the Orinoco it occurs on the rocks periodically washed by the floods, and in those parts alone where the stream is rapid; or, as the Indians say, "the rocks are black where the waters are white." Here the coating is of a rich brown instead of a black colour, and seems to be composed of ferruginous matter alone. Hand specimens fail to give a just idea of these brown burnished stones which glitter in the sun's rays. They occur only within the limits of the tidal waves; and as the rivulet slowly trickles down, the surf must supply the polishing power of the cataracts in the great rivers. In like manner, the rise and fall of the tide probably answer to the periodical inundations; and thus the same effects are produced under apparently different but really similar circumstances. The origin, however, of these coatings of metallic oxides, which seem as if cemented to the rocks, is not understood; and no reason, I believe, can be assigned for their thickness remaining the same.

One day I was amused by watching the habits of the Diodon antennatus, which was caught swimming near the shore. This fish, with its flabby skin, is well

known to possess the singular power of distending itself into a nearly spherical form. After having been taken out of water for a short time, and then again immersed in it, a considerable quantity both of water and air is absorbed by the mouth, and perhaps likewise by the branchial orifices. This process is effected by two methods: the air is swallowed, and is then forced into the cavity of the body, its return being prevented by a muscular contraction which is externally visible: but the water enters in a gentle stream through the mouth, which is kept wide open and motionless; this latter action must, therefore, depend on suction. The skin about the abdomen is much looser than that on the back; hence, during the inflation, the lower surface becomes far more distended than the upper; and the fish, in consequence, floats with its back downwards. Cuvier doubts whether the Diodon in this position is able to swim; but not only can it thus move forward in a straight line, but it can turn round to either side. This latter movement is effected solely by the aid of the pectoral fins; the tail being collapsed, and not used. From the body being buoyed up with so much air, the branchial openings are out of water, but a stream drawn in by the mouth constantly flows through them.

The fish, having remained in this distended state for a short time, generally expelled the air and water with considerable force from the branchial apertures and mouth. It could emit, at will, a certain portion of the water; and it appears, therefore, probable that this fluid is taken in partly for the sake of regulating its specific gravity. This Diodon possessed several means of defence. It could give a severe bite, and could eject water from its mouth to some distance, at the same time making a curious noise by the movement of its jaws. By the inflation of its body, the papillæ, with which the skin is covered, become erect and pointed. But the most curious circumstance is, that it secretes from the skin of its belly, when handled, a most beautiful carmine-red fibrous matter, which stains ivory and paper in so permanent a manner that the tint is retained with all its brightness to the present day: I am quite ignorant of the nature and use of this secretion. I have heard from Dr. Allan of Forres, that he has frequently found a Diodon, floating alive and distended, in the stomach of the shark; and that on several occasions he has known it eat its way, not only through the coats of the stomach, but through the sides of the monster, which has thus been killed. Who would ever have imagined that a little soft fish could have destroyed the great and savage shark?

▪ March 18th

We sailed from Bahia. A few days afterwards, when not far distant from the Abrolhos Islets, my atten-

---

[7]Pers. Narr., vol. v., pt. 1., p. 18.

tion was called to a reddish-brown appearance in the sea. The whole surface of the water, as it appeared under a weak lens, seemed as if covered by chopped bits of hay, with their ends jagged. These are minute cylindrical confervæ, in bundles or rafts of from twenty to sixty in each. Mr. Berkeley informs me that they are the same species (Trichodesmium erythræum) with that found over large spaces in the Red Sea, and whence its name of Red Sea is derived.[8] Their numbers must be infinite: the ship passed through several bands of them, one of which was about ten yards wide, and, judging from the mid-like colour of the water, at least two and a half miles long. In almost every long voyage some account is given of these confervæ. They appear especially common in the sea near Australia; and off Cape Leeuwin I found an allied but smaller and apparently different species. Captain Cook, in his third voyage, remarks, that the sailors gave to this appearance the name of sea-sawdust.

Near Keeling Atoll, in the Indian Ocean, I observed many little masses of confervæ a few inches square, consisting of long cylindrical threads of excessive thinness, so as to be barely visible to the naked eye, mingled with other rather larger bodies, finely conical at both ends. Two of these are shown in the woodcut united together. They vary in length from .04 to .06, and even to .08 of an inch in length; and in diameter from .006 to .008 of an inch. Near one extremity of the cylindrical part, a green septum, formed of granular matter, and thickest in the middle, may generally be seen. This, I believe, is the bottom of a most delicate, colourless sac, composed of a pulpy substance, which lines the exterior case, but does not extend within the extreme conical points. In some specimens, small but perfect spheres of brownish granular matter supplied the places of the septa; and I observed the curious process by which they were produced. The pulpy matter of the internal coating suddenly grouped itself into lines, some of which assumed a form radiating from a common centre; it then continued, with an irregular and rapid movement, to contract itself, so that in the course of a second the whole was united into a perfect little sphere, which occupied the position of the septum at one end of the now quite hollow case. The formation of the granular sphere was hastened by any accidental injury. I may add, that frequently a pair of these bodies were attached to each other, as represented above, cone beside cone, at that end where the septum occurs.

I will add here a few other observations connected with the discoloration of the sea from organic causes. On the coast of Chile, a few leagues north of Concepcion, the Beagle one day passed through great bands of muddy water, exactly like that of a swollen river; and again, a degree south of Valparaiso, when fifty miles from the land, the same appearance was still more extensive. Some of the water placed in a glass was of a pale reddish tint; and, examined under a microscope, was seen to swarm with minute animalcula darting about, and often exploding. Their shape is oval, and contracted in the middle by a ring of vibrating curved ciliæ. It was, however, very difficult to examine them with care, for almost the instant motion ceased, even while crossing the field of vision, their bodies burst. Sometimes both ends burst at once, sometimes only one, and a quantity of coarse, brownish, granular matter was ejected. The animal an instant before bursting expanded to half again its natural size; and the explosion took place about fifteen seconds after the rapid progressive motion had ceased: in a few cases it was preceded for a short interval by a rotatory movement on the longer axis. About two minutes after any number were isolated in a drop of water, they thus perished. The animals move with the narrow apex forwards, by the aid of their vibratory cilliæ, and generally by rapid starts. They are exceedingly minute, and quite invisible to the naked eye, only covering a space equal to the square of the thousandth of an inch. Their numbers were infinite; for the smallest drop of water which I could remove contained very many. In one day we passed through two spaces of water thus stained, one of which alone must have extended over several square miles. What incalculable numbers of these microscopical animals! The colour of the water, as seen at some distance, was like that of a river which has flowed through a red clay district; but under the shade of the vessel's side it was quite as dark as chocolate. The line where the red and blue water joined was distinctly defined. The weather for some days previously had been calm, and the ocean abounded, to an unusual degree, with living creatures.[9]

---

[8]M. Montagne, in Comptes Rendus, etc., Juillet, 1844; and Annal. des Scienc. Nat., Dec. 1844.

---

[9]M. Lesson (Voyage de la Coquille, tom. i., p. 255) mentions red water off Lima, apparently produced by the same cause. Peron, the distinguished naturalist, in the Voyage aux Terres Australes, gives no less than twelve references to voyagers who have alluded to the discoloured waters of the sea (vol. ii. p. 239). To the references given by Peron may be added, Humboldt's Pers. Narr., vol. vi. p. 804; Flinders' Voyage, vol. i. p. 92; Labillardière, vol. i. p. 287; Ulloa's Voyage; Voyage of the Astrolabe and of the Coquille; Captain King's Survey of Australia, etc.

In the sea around Tierra del Fuego, and at no great distance from the land, I have seen narrow lines of water of a bright red colour, from the number of crustacea, which somewhat resemble in form large prawns. The sealers call them whale-food. Whether whales feed on them I do not know; but terns, cormorants, and immense herds of great unwieldy seals derive, on some parts of the coast, their chief sustenance from these swimming crabs. Seamen invariably attribute the discoloration of the water to spawn; but I found this to be the case only on one occasion. At the distance of several leagues from the Archipelago of the Galapagos, the ship sailed through three strips of a dark yellowish, or mudlike water; these strips were some miles long, but only a few yards wide, and they were separated from the surrounding water by a sinuous yet distinct margin. The colour was caused by little gelatinous balls, about the fifth of an inch in diameter, in which numerous minute spherical ovules were imbedded: they were of two distinct kinds, one being of a reddish colour and of a different shape from the other. I cannot form a conjecture as to what two kinds of animals these belonged. Captain Colnett remarks, that this appearance is very common among the Galapagos Islands, and that the directions of the bands indicate that of the currents; in the described case, however, the line was caused by the wind. The only other appearance which I have to notice, is a thin oily coat on the water which displays iridescent colours. I saw a considerable tract of the ocean thus covered on the coast of Brazil; the seamen attributed it to the putrefying carcase of some whale, which probably was floating at no great distance. I do not here mention the minute gelatinous particles, hereafter to be referred to, which are frequently dispersed throughout the water, for they are not sufficiently abundant to create any change of colour.

There are two circumstances in the above accounts which appear remarkable: first, how do the various bodies which form the bands with defined edges keep together? In the case of the prawn-like crabs, their movements were as coinstantaneous as in a regiment of soldiers; but this cannot happen from anything like voluntary action with the ovules, or the confervæ, nor is it probable among the infusoria. Secondly, what causes the length and narrowness of the bands? The appearance so much resembles that which may be seen in every torrent, where the stream uncoils into long streaks the froth collected in the eddies, that I must attribute the effect to a similar action either of the currents of the air or sea. Under this supposition we must believe that the various organized bodies are produced in certain

favourable places, and are thence removed by the set of either wind or water. I confess, however, there is a very great difficulty in imagining any one spot to be the birthplace of the millions of millions of animalcula and confervæ: for whence come the germs at such points?—the parent bodies having been distributed by the winds and waves over the immense ocean. But on no other hypothesis can I understand their linear grouping. I may add that Scoresby remarks that green water abounding with pelagic animals is invariably found in a certain part of the Arctic Sea.

GALAPAGOS ARCHIPELAGO

■ September 15th

This archipelago consists of ten principal islands, of which five exceed the others in size. They are situated under the Equator, and between five and six hundred miles westward of the coast of America. They are all formed of volcanic rocks; a few fragments of granite curiously glazed and altered by the heat, can hardly be considered as an exception. Some of the craters, surmounting the larger islands, are of immense size, and they rise to a height of between three and four thousand feet. Their flanks are studded by innumerable smaller orifices. I scarcely hesitate to affirm, that there must be in the whole archipelago at least two thousand craters. These consist either of lava or scoriæ, or of finely-stratified, sandstone-like tuff. Most of the latter are beautifully symmetrical; they owe their origin to eruptions of volcanic mud without any lava: it is a remarkable circumstance that every one of the twenty-eight tuff-craters which were examined, had their southern sides either much lower than the other sides, or quite broken down and removed. As all these craters apparently have been formed when standing in the sea, and as the waves from the trade wind and the swell from the open Pacific here unite their forces on the southern coasts of all the islands, this singular uniformity in the broken state of the craters, composed of the soft and yielding tuff, is easily explained.

Considering that these islands are placed directly under the equator, the climate is far from being excessively hot; this seems chiefly caused by the singularly low temperature of the surrounding water, brought here by the great southern Polar current. Excepting during one short season, very little rain falls, and even then it is irregular; but the clouds generally hang low. Hence, whilst the lower parts of the islands are very sterile, the upper parts, at a height of a thousand feet and upwards, possess a damp climate and a tolerably luxuriant vegetation. This is especially the case on the windward sides of the islands, which first receive and condense the moisture from the atmosphere.

In the morning (17th) we landed on Chatham Island, which, like the others, rises with a tame and rounded outline, broken here and there by scattered hillocks, the remains of former craters. Nothing could be less inviting than the first appearance. A broken field of black basaltic lava, thrown into the most rugged waves, and crossed by great fissures, is everywhere covered by stunted, sun-burnt brushwood, which shows little signs of life. The dry and parched surface, being heated by the noon-day sun, gave to the air a close and sultry feeling, like that from a stove: we fancied even that the bushes smelt unpleasantly. Although I diligently tried to collect as many plants as possible, I succeeded in getting very few; and such wretched-looking little weeds would have better become an arctic than an equatorial Flora. The brushwood appears, from a short distance, as leafless as our trees during winter; and it was some time before I discovered that not only almost every plant was now in full leaf, but that the greater number were in flower. The commonest bush is one of the Euphorbiaceæ: an acacia and a great odd-looking cactus are the only trees which afford any shade. After the season of heavy rains, the islands are said to appear for a short time partially green. The volcanic island of Fernando Noronha, placed in many respects under nearly similar conditions, is the only other country where I have seen a vegetation at all like this of the Galapagos Islands.

The Beagle sailed round Chatham Island, and anchored in several bays. One night I slept on shore on a part of the island, where black truncated cones were extraordinarily numerous: from one small eminence I counted sixty of them, all surmounted by craters more or less perfect. The greater number consisted merely of a ring of red scoriæ or slags, cemented together: and their height above the plain of lava was not more than from fifty to a hundred feet; none had been very lately active. The entire surface of this part of the island seems to have been permeated, like a sieve, by the subterranean vapours: here and there the lava, whilst soft, has been blown into great bubbles; and in other parts, the tops of caverns similarly formed have fallen in, leaving circular pits with steep sides. From the regular form of the many craters, they gave to the country an artificial appearance, which vividly reminded me of those parts of Stafford-shire, where the great iron-foundries are most numerous. The day was glowing hot, and the scrambling over the rough surface and through the intricate thickets, was very fatiguing; but I was well repaid by the strange Cyclopean scene. As I was walking along I met two large tortoises, each of which must have weighed at least two hundred

pounds: one was eating a piece of cactus, and as I approached, it stared at me and slowly walked away; the other gave a deep hiss, and drew in its head. These huge reptiles, surrounded by the black lava, the leafless shrubs, and large cacti, seemed to my fancy like some antediluvian animals. The few dull-coloured birds cared no more for me than they did for the great tortoises.

■ September 23rd

The Beagle proceeded to Charles Island. This archipelago has long been frequented, first by the bucaniers, and latterly by whalers, but it is only within the last six years, that a small colony has been established here. The inhabitants are between two and three hundred in number; they are nearly all people of colour, who have been banished for political crimes from the Republic of the Equator, of which Quito is the capital. The settlement is placed about four and a half miles island, and at a height probably of a thousand feet. In the first part of the road we passed through leafless thickets, as in Chatham Island. Higher up, the woods gradually became greener; and as soon as we crossed the ridge of the island, we were cooled by a fine southerly breeze, and our sight refreshed by a green and thriving vegetation. In this upper region coarse grasses and ferns abound; but there are no tree-ferns: I saw nowhere any member of the palm family, which is the more singular, as 360 miles northward, Cocos Island takes its name from the number of cocoa-nuts. The houses are irregularly scattered over a flat space of ground, which is cultivated with sweet potatoes and bananas. It will not easily be imagined how pleasant the sight of black mud was to us, after having been so long accustomed to the parched soil of Peru and northern Chile. The inhabitants, although complaining of poverty, obtain, without much trouble, the means of subsistence. In the woods there are many wild pigs and goats; but the staple article of animal food is supplied by the tortoises. Their numbers have of course been greatly reduced in this island, but the people yet count on two days' hunting giving them food for the rest of the week. It is said that formerly single vessels have taken away as many as seven hundred, and that the ship's company of a frigate some years since brought down in one day two hundred tortoises to the beach.

■ September 29th

We doubled the south-west extremity of Albemarle Island, and the next day were nearly becalmed between it and Narborough Island. Both are covered with immense deluges of black naked lava, which have flowed either over the rims of the great caldrons, like pitch over the rim of a pot in which it has been boiled, or have burst forth from smaller orifices on the flanks; in their descent they have spread over miles of the sea-coast. On both of these islands, eruptions are known to have taken place; and in Albemarle, we saw a small jet of smoke curling from the summit of one of the great craters. In the evening we anchored in Bank's Cove, in Albemarle Island. The next morning I went out walking. To the south of the broken tuff-crater, in which the Beagle was anchored, there was another beautifully symmetrical one of an elliptic form; its longer axis was a little less than a mile, and its depth about 500 feet. At its bottom there was a shallow lake, in the middle of which a tiny crater formed an islet. The day was overpoweringly hot, and the lake looked clear and blue: I hurried down the cindery slope, and, choked with dust, eagerly tasted the water—but, to my sorrow, I found it salt as brine.

The rocks on the coast abounded with great black lizards, between three and four feet long; and on the hills, an ugly yellowish-brown species was equally common. We saw many of this latter kind, some clumsily running out of the way, and others shuffling into their burrows. I shall presently describe in more detail the habits of both these reptiles. The whole of this northern part of Albemarle Island is miserably sterile.

▮ October 8th

We arrived at James Island: this island, as well as Charles Island, were long since thus named after our kings of the Stuart line. Mr. Bynoe, myself, and our servants were left here for a week, with provisions and a tent, whilst the Beagle went for water. We found here a party of Spaniards, who had been sent from Charles Island to dry fish, and to salt tortoise-meat. About six miles inland, and at the height of nearly 2000 feet, a hovel had been built in which two men lived, who were employed in catching tortoises, whilst the others were fishing on the coast. I paid this party two visits, and slept there one night. As in the other islands, the lower region was covered by nearly leafless bushes, but the trees were here of a larger growth than elsewhere, several being two feet and some even two feet nine inches in diameter. The upper region being kept damp by the clouds, supports a green and flourishing vegetation. So damp was the ground, that there were large beds of a coarse cyperus, in which great numbers of a very small water-rail lived and bred. While staying in this upper region, we lived entirely upon tortoise-meat: the breast-plate roasted (as the Gauchos do *carne con cuero*), with the flesh on it, is very good; and the young tortoises make excellent soup; but otherwise the meat to my taste is indifferent.

One day we accompanied a party of the Spaniards in their whale-boat to a salina, or lake from which salt is procured. After landing, we had a very rough walk over a rugged field of recent lava, which has almost surrounded a tuff-crater, at the bottom of which the sale-lake lies. The water is only three or four inches deep, and rests on a layer of beautifully crystallized, white salt. The lake is quite circular, and is fringed with a border of bright green succulent plants; the almost precipitous walls of the crater are clothed with wood, so that the scene was altogether both picturesque and curious. A few years since, the sailors belonging to a sealing-vessel murdered their captain in this quiet spot; and we saw his skull lying among the bushes.

During the greater part of our stay of a week, the sky was cloudless, and if the trade-wind failed for an hour, the heat became very oppressive. On two days, the thermometer within the tent stood for some hours at 93°; but in the open air, in the wind and sun, at only 85°. The sand was extremely hot; the thermometer placed in some of a brown colour immediately rose to 137°, and how much above that it would have risen, I do not know, for it was not graduated any higher. The black sand felt much hotter, so that even in thick boots it was quite disagreeable to walk over it.

GALAPAGOS ARCHIPELAGO

I have not as yet noticed by far the most remarkable feature in the natural history of this archipelago; it is, that the different islands to a considerable extent are inhabited by a different set of beings. My attention was first called to this fact by the Vice-Governor, Mr. Lawson, declaring that the tortoises differed from the different islands, and that he could with certainty tell from which island any one was brought. I did not for some time pay sufficient attention to this statement, and I had already partially mingled together the collections from two of the islands. I never dreamed that islands, about 50 or 60 miles apart, and most of them in sight of each other, formed of precisely the same rocks, placed under a quite similar climate, rising to a nearly equal height, would have been differently tenanted; but we shall soon see that this is the case. It is the fate of most voyagers, no sooner to discover what is most interesting in any locality, than they are hurried from it; but I ought, perhaps, to be thankful that I obtained sufficient materials to establish this most remarkable fact in the distribution of organic beings.

The inhabitants, as I have said, state that they can distinguish the tortoises from the different islands; and that they differ not only in size, but in other characters. Captain Porter has described those from Charles and from the nearest island to it, namely, Hood Island, as having their shells in front thick and turned up like a Spanish saddle, whilst the tortoises from James Island are rounder, blacker, and have a better taste when cooked. M. Bibron, moreover, informs me that he has seen what he considers two distinct species of tortoise from the Galapagos, but he does not know from which islands. The specimens that I brought from three islands were young ones: and probably owing to this cause neither Mr. Gray nor myself could find in them any specific differences. I have remarked that the marine Amblyrhynchus was larger at Albemarle Island than elsewhere; and M. Bibron informs me that he has seen two distinct aquatic species of this genus; so that the different islands probably have their representative species or races of the Amblyrhynchus, as well as of the tortoise. My attention was first thoroughly aroused, by comparing together the numerous specimens, shot by myself and several other parties on board, of the mocking-thrushes, when, to my astonishment, I discovered that all those from Charles Island belonged to one species (Mimus trifasciatus); all from Albemarle Island to M. parvulus; and all from James and Chatham Islands (between which two other islands are situated, as connecting links) belonged to M. melanotis. These two latter species are closely allied, and would by some ornithologists be considered as only well-marked races or varieties; but the Mimus trifasciatus is very distinct. Unfortunately most of the specimens of the finch tribe were mingled together; but I have strong reasons to suspect that some of the species of the sub-group Geospiza are confined to separate islands. If the different islands have their representatives of Geospiza, it may help to explain the singularly large number of the species of this sub-group in this one small archipelago, and as a probable consequence of their numbers, the perfectly graduated series in the size of their beaks. Two species of the sub-group Cactornis, and two of the Camarhynchus, were procured in the archipelago; and of the numerous specimens of these two sub-groups shot by four collectors at James Island, all were found to belong to one species of each; whereas the numerous specimens shot either on Chatham or Charles Island (for the two sets were mingled together) all belonged to the two other species: hence we may feel almost sure that these islands possess their respective species of these two sub-groups. In land-shells this law of distribution does not appear to hold good. In my very small collection of insects, Mr. Waterhouse remarks, that of those which were ticketed with their locality, not one was common to any two of the islands.

Name of Island.	Total No. of Species	No. of Species Found in Other Parts of the World.	No. of Species Confined to the Galapagos Archipelago.	No. Confined to the One Island.	No. of Species Confined to the Galapagos Archipelago, but Found on More Than the One Island.
James Island	71	33	38	30	8
Albemarle Island	46	18	26	22	4
Chatham Island	32	16	16	12	8
Charles Island	68	39 (or 29, if the probably imported plants be subtracted)	29	21	8

If we now turn to the Flora, we shall find the aboriginal plants of the different islands wonderfully different. I give all the following results on the high authority of my friend Dr. J. Hooker. I may premise that I indiscriminately collected everything in flower on the different islands, and fortunately kept my collections separate. Too much confidence, however, must not be placed in the proportional results, as the small collections brought home by some other naturalists, though in some respects confirming the results, plainly show that much remains to be done in the botany of this group: the Leguminosæ, moreover, has as yet been only approximately worked out:—

Hence we have the truly wonderful fact, that in James Island, of the thirty-eight Galapageian plants, or those found in no other part of the world, thirty are exclusively confined to this one island; and in Albemarle Island, of the twenty-six aboriginal Galapageian plants, twenty-two are confined to this one island, that is, only four are at present known to grow in the other islands of the archipelago; and so on, as shown in the table above, with the plants from Chatham and Charles Islands. This fact will, perhaps, be rendered even more striking, by giving a few illustrations:—thus, Scalesia, a remarkable arborescent genus of the Compositæ, is confined to the archipelago: it has six species: one from Chatham, one from Albemarle, one from Charles Island, two from James Island, and the sixth from one of the three latter islands, but it is not known from which: not one of these six species grows on any two islands. Again, Euphorbia, a mundane or widely distributed genus, has here eight species, of which seven are confined to the archipelago, and not one found on any two islands: Acalypha and Borreria, both mundane genera, have respectively six and seven species, none of which have the same species on two islands, with the exception of one Borreria, which does occur on two islands. The species of the Compositæ are particularly local; and Dr. Hooker has furnished me with several other most striking illustrations of the difference of the species on the different islands. He remarks that this law of distribution holds good both with those genera confined to the archipelago, and those distributed in other quarters of the world: in like manner we have seen that the different islands have their proper species of the mundane genus of tortoise, and of the widely distributed American genus of the mocking-thrush, as well as of two of the Galapageian sub-groups of finches, and almost certainly of the Galapageian genus Amblyrhynchus.

The distribution of the tenants of this archipelago would not be nearly so wonderful, if, for instance, one island had a mocking-thrush, and a second island some other quite distinct genus;—if one island had its genus of lizard, and a second island another distinct genus, or none whatever;—or if the different islands were inhabited, not by representative species of the same genera of plants, but by totally different genera, as does to a certain extent hold good: for, to give one instance, a large berry-bearing tree at James Island has no representative species in Charles Island. But it is the circumstance, that several of the islands possess their own species of the tortoise, mocking-thrush, finches, and numerous plants, these species having the same general habits, occupying analogous situations, and obviously filling the same place in the natural economy of this archipelago, that strikes me with wonder. It may be suspected that some of these representative species, at least in the case of the tortoise and of some of the birds, may hereafter prove to be only well-marked races; but this would be of equally great interest to the philosophical naturalist. I have said that most of the islands are in sight of each other: I may specify that Charles Island is fifty miles from the nearest part of Chatham Island, and thirty-three miles from the nearest part of Albe-marle Island. Chatham Island is sixty miles from the nearest part of James Island, but there are two intermediate islands between them which were not visited by me. James Island is only ten miles from the nearest part of Albemarle Island, but the two points where the collections were made are thirty-two miles apart. I must repeat, that neither the nature of the soil, nor height of the land, nor the climate, nor the general character of the associated beings, and therefore their action one on another, can differ much in the different islands. If there be any sensible difference in their climates, it must be between the Windward group (namely, Charles and Chatham Islands), and that to leeward; but there seems to be no corresponding difference in the productions of these two halves of the archipelago.

The only light which I can throw on this remarkable difference in the inhabitants of the different islands, is, that very strong currents of the sea running in a westerly and W.N.W. direction must separate, as far as transportal by the sea is concerned, the southern islands from the northern ones; and between these northern islands a strong N.W. current was observed, which must effectually separate James and Albemarle Islands. As the archipelago is free to a most remarkable degree from gales of wind, neither the birds, insects, nor lighter seeds, would be blown from island to island. And lastly, the profound depth of the ocean between the islands, and their apparently recent (in a geological sense) volcanic origin, render it highly unlikely that they were ever united; and this, probably, is a far more important consideration than any other, with respect to the geographical distribution of their inhabitants. Reviewing the facts here given, one is astonished at the amount of creative force, if such an expression may be used, displayed on these small, barren, and rocky islands; and still more so, at its diverse yet analogous action on points so near each other. I have said that the Galapagos Archipelago might be called a satellite attached to America, but it should rather be called a group of satellites, physically similar, organically distinct, yet intimately related to each other, and all related in a marked, though much lesser degree, to the great American continent.

Name: _____ **Date:** _____

1. Using Darwin's descriptions from Chapter I, describe the path that he and his shipmates followed as they left England. Be sure to include the locations, the length of time it took to sail from one place to another, and the amount of time they spent at each location.

2. What, according to Darwin, was the most remarkable future in the natural history of the Galapagos Islands? Explain fully how Darwin learned this fact and what evidence he offered that it was true.

Charles Darwin

On the Origin of Species, 1859

Darwin (1809-1882) had formulated the basic outline for his theory of natural selection as early as 1838, but he waited over two decades to publish it. Anxieties about the accuracy of his conclusions, concerns about both scientific and public reactions, and the uproar over the 1844 *Vestiges of the Natural History of Creation* combined to keep Darwin silent about his ideas. By the mid-1850s, convinced that he was correct and both financially and professionally secure, Darwin began discussing his ideas with colleagues, including Charles Lyell and Joseph Hooker. This selection from *Origin* is the final chapter, in which Darwin summarized his argument and explained the shortcomings he identifies with his theory of natural selection.

RECAPITULATION AND CONCLUSION

As this whole volume is one long argument, it may be convenient to the reader to have the leading facts and inferences briefly recapitulated.

That many and grave objections may be advanced against the theory of descent with modification through natural selection, I do not deny. I have endeavoured to give to them their full force. Nothing at first can appear more difficult to believe than that the more complex organs and instincts should have been perfected, not by means superior to, though analogous with, human reason, but by the accumulation of innumerable slight variations, each good for the individual possessor. Nevertheless, this difficulty, though appearing to our imagination insuperably great, cannot be considered real if we admit the following propositions, namely,— that gradations in the perfection of any organ or instinct, which we may consider, either do now exist or could have existed, each good of its kind,— that all organs and instincts are, in ever so slight a degree, variable,—and, lastly, that there is a struggle for existence leading to the preservation of each profitable deviation of structure or instinct. The truth of these propositions cannot, I think, be disputed.

From *On the Origin of Species by Means of Natural Selection, or the Preservation of Favoured Races in the Struggle for Life*, originally published in 1859

It is, no doubt, extremely difficult even to conjecture by what gradations many structures have been perfected, more especially amongst broken and failing groups of organic beings; but we see so many strange gradations in nature, as is proclaimed by the canon, 'Natura non facit saltum,' that we ought to be extremely cautious in saying that any organ or instinct, or any whole being, could not have arrived at its present state by many graduated steps. There are, it must be admitted, cases of special difficulty on the theory of natural selection; and one of the most curious of these is the existence of two or three defined castes of workers or sterile females in the same community of ants; but I have attempted to show how this difficulty can be mastered.

With respect to the almost universal sterility of species when first crossed, which forms so remarkable a contrast with the almost universal fertility of varieties when crossed, I must refer the reader to the recapitulation of the facts given at the end of the eighth chapter, which seem to me conclusively to show that this sterility is no more a special endowment than is the incapacity of two trees to be grafted together; but that it is incidental on constitutional differences in the reproductive systems of the intercrossed species. We see the truth of this conclusion in the vast difference in the result, when the same two species are crossed reciprocally; that is, when one species is first used as the father and then as the mother.

The fertility of varieties when intercrossed and of their mongrel offspring cannot be considered as universal; nor is their very general fertility surprising when we remember that it is not likely that either their constitutions or their reproductive systems should have been profoundly modified. Moreover, most of the varieties which have been experimentised on have been produced under domestication; and as domestication apparently tends to eliminate sterility, we ought not to expect it also to produce sterility.

The sterility of hybrids is a very different case from that of first crosses, for their reproductive organs are more or less functionally impotent; whereas in first crosses the organs on both sides are in a perfect condition. As we continually see that organisms of all kinds are rendered in some degree sterile from their constitutions having been disturbed by slightly different and new conditions of life, we need not feel surprise at hybrids being in some degree sterile, for their constitutions can hardly fail to have been disturbed from being compounded of two distinct organisations. This parallelism is supported by another parallel, but directly opposite, class of facts; namely, that the vigour and fertility of all organic beings are increased by slight changes in their conditions of life, and that the offspring of slightly modified forms or varieties acquire from being crossed increased vigour and fertility. So that, on the one hand, considerable changes in the conditions of life and crosses between greatly modified forms, lessen fertility; and on the other hand, lesser changes in the conditions of life and crosses between less modified forms, increase fertility.

Turning to geographical distribution, the difficulties encountered on the theory of descent with modification are grave enough. All the individuals of the same species, and all the species of the same genus, or even higher group, must have descended from common parents; and therefore, in however distant and isolated parts of the world they are now found, they must in the course of successive generations have passed from some one part to the others. We are often wholly unable even to conjecture how this could have been effected. Yet, as we have reason to believe that some species have retained the same specific form for very long periods, enormously long as measured by years, too much stress ought not to be laid on the occasional wide diffusion of the same species; for during very long periods of time there will always be a good chance for wide migration by many means. A broken or interrupted range may often be accounted for by the extinction of the species in the intermediate regions. It cannot be denied that we are as yet very ignorant of the full extent of the various climatal and geographical changes which have affected the earth during modern periods; and such changes will obviously have greatly facilitated migration. As an example, I have attempted to show

how potent has been the influence of the Glacial period on the distribution both of the same and of representative species throughout the world. We are as yet profoundly ignorant of the many occasional means of transport. With respect to distinct species of the same genus inhabiting very distant and isolated regions, as the process of modification has necessarily been slow, all the means of migration will have been possible during a very long period; and consequently the difficulty of the wide diffusion of species of the same genus is in some degree lessened.

As on the theory of natural selection an interminable number of intermediate forms must have existed, linking together all the species in each group by gradations as fine as our present varieties, it may be asked, Why do we not see these linking forms all around us? Why are not all organic beings blended together in an inextricable chaos? With respect to existing forms, we should remember that we have no right to expect (excepting in rare cases) to discover *directly* connecting links between them, but only between each and some extinct and supplanted form. Even on a wide area, which has during a long period remained continuous, and of which the climate and other conditions of life change insensibly in going from a district occupied by one species into another district occupied by a closely allied species, we have no just right to expect often to find intermediate varieties in the intermediate zone. For we have reason to believe that only a few species are undergoing change at any one period; and all changes are slowly effected. I have also shown that the intermediate varieties which will at first probably exist in the intermediate zones, will be liable to be supplanted by the allied forms on either hand; and the latter, from existing in greater numbers, will generally be modified and improved at a quicker rate than the intermediate varieties, which exist in lesser numbers; so that the intermediate varieties will, in the long run, be supplanted and exterminated.

On this doctrine of the extermination of an infinitude of connecting links, between the living and extinct inhabitants of the world, and at each successive period between the extinct and still older species, why is not every geological formation charged with such links? Why does not every collection of fossil remains afford plain evidence of the gradation and mutation of the forms of life? We meet with no such evidence, and this is the most obvious and forcible of the many objections which may be urged against my theory. Why, again, do whole groups of allied species appear, though certainly they often falsely appear, to have come in suddenly on the several geological stages? Why do we not find great piles of strata beneath the Silurian system, stored with the remains of the progenitors of the Silurian groups of fossils? For certainly on my theory such strata must somewhere have been deposited at these ancient and utterly unknown epochs in the world's history.

I can answer these questions and grave objections only on the supposition that the geological record is far more imperfect than most geologists believe. It cannot be objected that there has not been time sufficient for any amount of organic change; for the lapse of time has been so great as to be utterly inappreciable by the human intellect. The number of specimens in all our museums is absolutely as nothing compared with the countless generations of countless species which certainly have existed. We should not be able to recognise a species as the parent of any one or more species if we were to examine them ever so closely, unless we likewise possessed many of the intermediate links between their past or parent and present states; and these many links we could hardly ever expect to discover, owing to the imperfection of the geological record. Numerous existing doubtful forms could be named which are probably varieties; but who will pretend that in future ages so many fossil links will be discovered, that naturalists will be able to decide, on the common view, whether or not these doubtful forms are varieties? As long as most of the links between any two species are unknown, if any one link or intermediate variety be discovered, it will simply be classed as another and distinct species. Only a small portion of the world has been geologically explored. Only organic beings of certain classes can be preserved in a fossil condition, at least in any great number. Widely ranging species vary most, and varieties are often at first local,—both causes rendering the discovery of intermediate links less likely. Local varieties will not spread into other and distant regions until they are considerably modified and improved; and when they do spread, if discovered in a geological formation, they will appear as if suddenly created there, and will be simply classed as new species. Most formations have been intermittent in their accumulation; and their duration, I am inclined to believe, has been shorter than the average duration of specific forms. Successive formations are separated from each other by enormous blank intervals of time; for fossiliferous formations, thick enough to resist future degradation, can be accumulated only where much sediment is deposited on the subsiding bed of the sea. During the alternate periods of elevation and of stationary level the record will be blank. During these latter periods there will probably be more variability in the forms of life; during periods of subsidence, more extinction.

With respect to the absence of fossiliferous formations beneath the lowest Silurian strata, I can only recur to the hypothesis given in the ninth chapter. That the geological record is imperfect all will admit; but that it is imperfect to the degree which I require, few will be inclined to admit. If we look to long enough intervals of time, geology plainly declares that all species have changed; and they have changed in the manner which my theory requires, for they have changed slowly and in a graduated manner. We clearly see this in the fossil remains from consecutive formations invariably being much more closely related to each other, than are the fossils from formations distant from each other in time.

Such is the sum of the several chief objections and difficulties which may justly be urged against my theory; and I have now briefly recapitulated the answers and explanations which can be given to them. I have felt these difficulties far too heavily during many years to doubt their weight. But it deserves especial notice that the more important objections relate to questions on which we are confessedly ignorant; nor do we know how ignorant we are. We do not know all the possible transitional gradations between the simplest and the most perfect organs; it cannot be pretended that we know all the varied means of Distribution during the long lapse of years, or that we know how imperfect the Geological Record is. Grave as these several difficulties are, in my judgment they do not overthrow the theory of descent with modification.

Now let us turn to the other side of the argument. Under domestication we see much variability. This seems to be mainly due to the reproductive system being eminently susceptible to changes in the conditions of life; so that this system, when not rendered impotent, fails to reproduce offspring exactly like the parent-form. Variability is governed by many complex laws,—by correlation of growth, by use and disuse, and by the direct action of the physical conditions of life. There is much difficulty in ascertaining how much modification our domestic productions have undergone; but we may safely infer that the amount has been large, and that modifications can be inherited for long periods. As long as the conditions of life remain the same, we have reason to believe that a modification, which has already been inherited for many generations, may continue to be inherited for an almost infinite number of generations. On the other hand we have evidence that variability, when it has once come into play, does not wholly cease; for new varieties are still occasionally produced by our most anciently domesticated productions.

Man does not actually produce variability; he only unintentionally exposes organic beings to new conditions of life, and then nature acts on the organisation, and causes variability. But man can and does select the variations given to him by nature, and thus accumulate them in any desired manner. He thus adapts animals and plants for his own benefit or pleasure. He may do this methodically, or he may do it unconsciously by preserving the individuals most useful to him at the time, without any thought of altering the breed. It is certain that he can largely influence the character of a breed by selecting, in each successive generation, individual differences so slight as to be quite inappreciable by an uneducated eye. This process of selection has been the great agency in the production of the most distinct and useful domestic breeds. That many of the breeds produced by man have to a large extent the character of natural species, is shown by the inextricable doubts whether very many of them are varieties or aboriginal species.

There is no obvious reason why the principles which have acted so efficiently under domestication should not have acted under nature. In the preservation of favoured individuals and races, during the constantly-recurrent Struggle for Existence, we see the most powerful and ever-acting means of selection. The struggle for existence inevitably follows from the high geometrical ratio of increase which is common to all organic beings. This high rate of increase is proved by calculation, by the effects of a succession of peculiar seasons, and by the results of naturalisation, as explained in the third chapter. More individuals are born than can possibly survive. A grain in the balance will determine which individual shall live and which shall die,— which variety or species shall increase in number, and which shall decrease, or finally become extinct. As the individuals of the same species come in all respects into the closest competition with each other, the struggle will generally be most severe between them; it will be almost equally severe between the varieties of the same species, and next in severity between the species of the same genus. But the struggle will often be very severe between beings most remote in the scale of nature. The slightest advantage in one being, at any age or during any season, over those with which it comes into competition, or better adaptation in however slight a degree to the surrounding physical conditions, will turn the balance.

With animals having separated sexes there will in most cases be a struggle between the males for possession of the females. The most vigorous individuals, or those which have most successfully struggled with their conditions of life, will generally leave most progeny. But success will often depend on having special weapons or means of defence, or on the charms of the males; and the slightest advantage will lead to victory.

As geology plainly proclaims that each land has undergone great physical changes, we might have expected that organic beings would have varied under nature, in the same way as they generally have varied under the changed conditions of domestication. And if there be any variability under nature, it would be an unaccountable fact if natural selection had not come into play. It has often been asserted, but the assertion is quite incapable of proof, that the amount of variation under nature is a strictly limited quantity. Man, though acting on external characters alone and often capriciously, can produce within a short period a great result by adding up mere individual differences in his domestic productions; and every one admits that there are at least individual differences in species under nature. But, besides such differences, all naturalists have admitted the existence of varieties, which they think sufficiently distinct to be worthy of record in systematic works. No one can draw any clear distinction between individual differences and slight varieties; or between more plainly marked varieties and subspecies, and species. Let it be observed how naturalists differ in the rank which they assign to the many representative forms in Europe and North America.

If then we have under nature variability and a powerful agent always ready to act and select, why should we doubt that variations in any way useful to beings, under their excessively complex relations of life, would be preserved, accumulated, and inherited? Why, if man can by patience select variations most useful to himself, should nature fail in selecting variations useful, under changing conditions of life, to her living products? What limit can be put to this power, acting during long ages and rigidly scrutinising the whole constitution, structure, and habits of each creature,—favouring the good and rejecting the bad? I can see no limit to this power, in slowly and beautifully adapting each form to the most complex relations of life. The theory of natural selection, even if we looked no further than this, seems to me to be in itself probable. I have already recapitulated, as fairly as I could, the opposed difficulties and objections: now let us turn to the special facts and arguments in favour of the theory.

On the view that species are only strongly marked and permanent varieties, and that each species first existed as a variety, we can see why it is that no line of demarcation can be drawn between species, commonly supposed to have been produced by special acts of creation, and varieties which are acknowledged to have been produced by secondary laws. On this same view we can understand how it is that in each region where many species of a genus have been produced, and where they now flourish, these same species should present many varieties; for where the manufactory of species has been active, we might expect, as a general rule, to find it still in action; and this is the case if varieties be incipient species. Moreover, the species of the large genera, which afford the greater number of varieties or incipient species, retain to a certain degree the character of varieties; for they differ from each other by a less amount of difference than do the species of smaller genera. The closely allied species also of the larger genera apparently have restricted ranges, and they are clustered in little groups round other species—in which respects they resemble varieties. These are strange relations on the view of each species having been independently created, but are intelligible if all species first existed as varieties.

As each species tends by its geometrical ratio of reproduction to increase inordinately in number; and as the modified descendants of each species will be enabled to increase by so much the more as they become more diversified in habits and structure, so as to be enabled to seize on many and widely different places in the economy of nature, there will be a constant tendency in natural selection to preserve the most divergent offspring of any one species. Hence during a long-continued course of modification, the slight differences, characteristic of varieties of the same species, tend to be augmented into the greater differences characteristic of species of the same genus. New and improved varieties will inevitably supplant and exterminate the older, less improved and intermediate varieties; and thus species are rendered to a large extent defined and distinct objects. Dominant species belonging to the larger groups tend to give birth to new and dominant forms; so that each large group tends to become still larger, and at the same time more divergent in character. But as all groups cannot thus succeed in increasing in size, for the world would not hold them, the more dominant groups beat the less dominant. This tendency in the large groups to go on increasing in size and diverging in character, together with the almost inevitable contingency of much extinction, explains the arrangement of all the forms of life, in groups subordinate to groups, all within a few great classes, which we now see everywhere around us, and which has prevailed throughout all time. This grand fact of the grouping of all organic beings seems to me utterly inexplicable on the theory of creation.

As natural selection acts solely by accumulating slight, successive, favourable variations, it can produce no great or sudden modification; it can act only by very short and slow steps. Hence the canon of 'Natura non facit saltum,' which every fresh addition to our knowledge tends to make more strictly correct, is on this theory simply intelligible. We can plainly see why nature is prodigal in variety, though niggard in innovation. But why this should be a law

of nature if each species has been independently created, no man can explain.

Many other facts are, as it seems to me, explicable on this theory. How strange it is that a bird, under the form of woodpecker, should have been created to prey on insects on the ground; that upland geese, which never or rarely swim, should have been created with webbed feet; that a thrush should have been created to dive and feed on sub-aquatic insects; and that a petrel should have been created with habits and structure fitting it for the life of an auk or grebe! and so on in endless other cases. But on the view of each species constantly trying to increase in number, with natural selection always ready to adapt the slowly varying descendants of each to any unoccupied or ill-occupied place in nature, these facts cease to be strange, or perhaps might even have been anticipated.

As natural selection acts by competition, it adapts the inhabitants of each country only in relation to the degree of perfection of their associates; so that we need feel no surprise at the inhabitants of any one country, although on the ordinary view supposed to have been specially created and adapted for that country, being beaten and supplanted by the naturalised productions from another land. Nor ought we to marvel if all the contrivances in nature be not, as far as we can judge, absolutely perfect; and if some of them be abhorrent to our ideas of fitness. We need not marvel at the sting of the bee causing the bee's own death; at drones being produced in such vast numbers for one single act, and being then slaughtered by their sterile sisters; at the astonishing waste of pollen by our fir-trees; at the instinctive hatred of the queen bee for her own fertile daughters; at ichneumonidae feeding within the live bodies of caterpillars; and at other such cases. The wonder indeed is, on the theory of natural selection, that more cases of the want of absolute perfection have not been observed.

The complex and little known laws governing variation are the same, as far as we can see, with the laws which have governed the production of so-called specific forms. In both cases physical conditions seem to have produced but little direct effect; yet when varieties enter any zone, they occasionally assume some of the characters of the species proper to that zone. In both varieties and species, use and disuse seem to have produced some effect; for it is difficult to resist this conclusion when we look, for instance, at the logger-headed duck, which has wings incapable of flight, in nearly the same condition as in the domestic duck; or when we look at the burrowing tucutucu, which is occasionally blind, and then at certain moles, which are habitually blind and have their eyes covered with skin; or when we look at the blind animals inhabiting the dark caves of America and Europe. In both varieties and species correction of growth seems to have placed a most important part, so that when one part has been modified other parts are necessarily modified. In both varieties and species reversions to long-lost characters occur. How inexplicable on the theory of creation is the occasional appearance of stripes on the shoulder and legs of the several species of the horse-genus and in their hybrids! How simply is this fact explained if we believe that these species have descended from a striped progenitor, in the same manner as the several domestic breeds of pigeon have descended from the blue and barred rock-pigeon!

On the ordinary view of each species having been independently created, why should the specific characters, or those by which the species of the same genus differ from each other, be more variable than the generic characters in which they all agree? Why, for instance, should the colour of a flower be more likely to vary in any one species of a genus, if the other species, supposed to have been created independently, have differently coloured flowers, than if all the species of the genus have the same coloured flowers? If species are only well-marked varieties, of which the characters have become in a high degree permanent, we can understand this fact; for they have already varied since they branched off from a common progenitor in certain characters, by which they have come to be specifically distinct from each other; and therefore these same characters would be more likely still to be variable than the generic characters which have been inherited without change for an enormous period. It is inexplicable on the theory of creation why a part developed in a very unusual manner in any one species of a genus, and therefore, as we may naturally infer, of great importance to the species, should be eminently liable to variation; but, on my view, this part has undergone, since the several species branched off from a common progenitor, an unusual amount of variability and modification, and therefore we might expect this part generally to be still variable. But a part may be developed in the most unusual manner, like the wing of a bat, and yet not be more variable than any other structure, if the part be common to many subordinate forms, that is, if it has been inherited for a very long period; for in this case it will have been rendered constant by long-continued natural selection.

Glancing at instincts, marvellous as some are, they offer no greater difficulty than does corporeal structure on the theory of the natural selection of successive, slight, but profitable modifications. We can thus understand why nature moves by graduated steps in endowing different animals of the same class with their several instincts. I have attempted to show how much light the principle of gradation throws on the admirable architectural powers of the hive-bee. Habit no doubt sometimes comes into play in modifying instincts; but it certainly is not indispensable, as we see, in the case of neuter insects, which leave no progeny to inherit the effects of long-continued habit. On the view of all the species of the same genus having descended from a common parent, and having inherited much in common, we can understand how it is that allied species, when placed under considerably different conditions of life, yet should follow nearly the same instincts; why the thrush of South America, for instance, lines her nest with mud like our British species. On the view of instincts having been slowly acquired through natural selection we need not marvel at some instincts being apparently not perfect and liable to mistakes, and at many instincts causing other animals to suffer.

If species be only well-marked and permanent varieties, we can at once see why their crossed offspring should follow the same complex laws in their degrees and kinds of resemblance to their parents,—in being absorbed into each other by successive crosses, and in other such points,—as do the crossed offspring of acknowledged varieties. On the other hand, these would be strange facts if species have been independently created, and varieties have been produced by secondary laws.

If we admit that the geological record is imperfect in an extreme degree, then such facts as the record gives, support the theory of descent with modification. New species have come on the stage slowly and at successive intervals; and the amount of change, after equal intervals of time, is widely different in different groups. The extinction of species and of whole groups of species, which has played so conspicuous a part in the history of the organic world, almost inevitably follows on the principle of natural selection; for old forms will be supplanted by new and improved forms. Neither single species nor groups of species reappear when the chain of ordinary generation has once been broken. The gradual diffusion of dominant forms, with the slow modification of their descendants, causes the forms of life, after long intervals of time, to appear as if they had changed simultaneously throughout the world. The fact of the fossil remains of each formation being in some degree intermediate in character between the fossils in the formations above and below, is simply explained by their intermediate position in the chain of descent. The grand fact that all extinct organic beings belong to the same system with recent beings, falling either into the same or into intermediate groups, follows from the living and the extinct being the offspring of common parents. As the groups which have descended from an ancient progenitor have generally diverged in character, the progenitor with its early descendants will often be intermediate in character in comparison with its later descendants; and thus we can see why the more ancient a fossil is, the oftener it stands in some degree intermediate between existing and allied groups. Recent forms are generally looked at as being, in some vague sense, higher than ancient and extinct forms; and they are in so far higher as the later and more improved forms have conquered the older and less improved organic beings in the struggle for life. Lastly, the law of the long endurance of allied forms on the same continent,—of marsupials in Australia, of edentata in America, and other such cases,—is intelligible, for within a confined country, the recent and the extinct will naturally be allied by descent.

Looking to geographical distribution, if we admit that there has been during the long course of ages much migration from one part of the world to another, owing to former climatal and geographical changes and to the many occasional and unknown means of dispersal, then we can understand, on the theory of descent with modification, most of the great leading facts in Distribution. We can see why there should be so striking a parallelism in the distribution of organic beings throughout space, and in their geological succession throughout time; for in both cases the beings have been connected by the bond of ordinary generation, and the means of modification have been the same. We see the full meaning of the wonderful fact, which must have struck every traveller, namely, that on the same continent, under the most diverse conditions, under heat and cold, on mountain and lowland, on deserts and marshes, most of the inhabitants within each great class are plainly related; for they will generally be descendants of the same progenitors and early colonists. On this same principle of former migration, combined in most cases with modification, we can understand, by the aid of the Glacial period, the identity of some few plants, and the close alliance of many others, on the most distant mountains, under the most different climates; and likewise the close alliance of some of the inhabitants of the sea in the northern and southern temperate zones, though separated by the whole intertropical ocean. Although two areas may present the same physical conditions of life, we need feel no surprise at their inhabitants being widely different, if they have been for a long period completely separated from each other; for as the relation of organism to organism is the most important of all relations, and as the two areas will have received colonists from some third source or from each other, at various periods and in different proportions, the course of modification in the two areas will inevitably be different.

On this view of migration, with subsequent modification, we can see why oceanic islands should be inhabited by few species, but of these, that many should be peculiar. We can clearly see why those animals which cannot cross wide spaces of ocean, as frogs and terrestrial mammals, should not inhabit oceanic islands; and why, on the other hand, new and peculiar species of bats, which can traverse the ocean, should so often be found on islands far distant from any continent. Such facts as the presence of peculiar species of bats, and the absence of all other mammals, an oceanic islands, are utterly inexplicable on the theory of independent acts of creation.

The existence of closely allied or representative species in any two areas, implies, on the theory of descent with modification, that the same parents formerly inhabited both areas; and we almost invariably find that whenever many closely allied species inhabit two areas, some identical species common to both still exist. Wherever many closely allied yet distinct species occur, many doubtful forms and varieties of the same species likewise occur. It is a rule of high generality that the inhabitants of each area are related to the inhabitants of the nearest source whence immigrants might have been derived. We see this in nearly all the plants and animals of the Galapagos archipelago, of Juan Fernandez, and of the other American islands being related in the most striking manner to the plants and animals of the neighbouring American mainland; and those of the Cape de Verde archipelago and other African islands to the African mainland. It must be admitted that these facts receive no explanation on the theory of creation.

The fact, as we have seen, that all past and present organic beings constitute one grand natural system, with group subordinate to group, and with extinct groups often falling in between recent groups, is intelligible on the theory of natural selection with its contingencies of extinction and divergence of character. On these same principles we see how it is, that the mutual affinities of the species and genera within each class are so complex and circuitous. We see why certain characters are far more serviceable than others for classification;—why adaptive characters, though of paramount importance to the being, are of hardly any importance in classification; why characters derived from rudimentary parts, though of no service to the being, are often of high classificatory value; and why embryological characters are the most valuable of all. The real affinities of all organic beings are due to inheritance or community of descent. The natural system is a genealogical arrangement, in which we have to discover the lines of descent by the most permanent characters, however slight their vital importance may be.

The framework of bones being the same in the hand of a man, wing of a bat, fin of the porpoise, and leg of the horse,—the same number of vertebrae forming the neck of the giraffe and of the elephant,—and innumerable other such facts, at once explain themselves on the theory of descent with slow and slight successive modifications. The similarity of pattern in the wing and leg of a bat, though used for such different purposes,—in the jaws and legs of a crab,—in the petals, stamens, and pistils of a flower, is likewise intelligible on the view of the gradual modification of parts or organs, which were alike in the early progenitor of each class. On the principle of successive variations not always supervening at an early age, and being inherited at a corresponding not early period of life, we can clearly see why the embryos of mammals, birds, reptiles, and fishes should be so closely alike, and should be so unlike the adult forms. We may cease marvelling at the embryo of an air-breathing mammal or bird having branchial slits and arteries running in loops, like those in a fish which has to breathe the air dissolved in water, by the aid of well-developed branchiae.

Disuse, aided sometimes by natural selection, will often tend to reduce an organ, when it has become useless by changed habits or under changed conditions of life; and we can clearly understand on this view the meaning of rudimentary organs. But disuse and selection will generally act on each creature, when it has come to maturity and has to play its full part in the struggle for existence, and will thus have little power of acting on an organ during early life; hence the organ will not be much reduced or rendered rudimentary at this early age. The calf, for instance, has inherited teeth, which never cut through the gums of the upper jaw, from an early progenitor having well-developed teeth; and we may believe, that the teeth in the mature animal were reduced, during successive generations, by disuse or by the tongue and palate having been fitted by natural selection to browse without their aid; whereas in the calf, the teeth have been left untouched by selection or disuse, and on the principle of inheritance at corresponding ages have been inherited from a remote period to the present day. On the view of each organic being and each separate organ having been specially created, how utterly inexplicable it is that parts, like the teeth in the embryonic calf or like the shrivelled wings under the soldered wing-covers of some beetles, should thus so

frequently bear the plain stamp of inutility! Nature may be said to have taken pains to reveal, by rudimentary organs and by homologous structures, her scheme of modifications, which it seems that we wilfully will not understand.

I have now recapitulated the chief facts and onsiderations which have thoroughly convinced me that species have changed, and are still slowly changing by the preservation and accumulation of successive slight favourable variations. Why, it may be asked, have all the most eminent living naturalists and geologists rejected this view of the mutability of species? It cannot be asserted that organic beings in a state of nature are subject to no variation; it cannot be proved that the amount of variation in the course of long ages is a limited quantity; no clear distinction has been, or can be, drawn between species and well-marked varieties. It cannot be maintained that species when intercrossed are invariably sterile, and varieties invariably fertile; or that sterility is a special endowment and sign of creation. The belief that species were immutable productions was almost unavoidable as long as the history of the world was thought to be of short duration; and now that we have acquired some idea of the lapse of time, we are too apt to assume, without proof, that the geological record is so perfect that it would have afforded us plain evidence of the mutation of species, if they had undergone mutation.

But the chief cause of our natural unwillingness to admit that one species has given birth to other and distinct species, is that we are always slow in admitting any great change of which we do not see the intermediate steps. The difficulty is the same as that felt by so many geologists, when Lyell first insisted that long lines of inland cliffs had been formed, and great valleys excavated, by the slow action of the coast-waves. The mind cannot possibly grasp the full meaning of the term of a hundred million years; it cannot add up and perceive the full effects of many slight variations, accumulated during an almost infinite number of generations.

Although I am fully convinced of the truth of the views given in this volume under the form of an abstract, I by no means expect to convince experienced naturalists whose minds are stocked with a multitude of facts all viewed, during a long course of years, from a point of view directly opposite to mine. It is so easy to hide our ignorance under such expressions as the 'plan of creation,' 'unity of design,' &c., and to think that we give an explanation when we only restate a fact. Any one whose disposition leads him to attach more weight to unexplained difficulties than to the explanation of a certain number of facts will certainly reject my theory. A few naturalists, endowed with much flexibility of mind, and who have already begun to doubt on the immutability of species, may be influenced by this volume; but I look with confidence to the future, to young and rising naturalists, who will be able to view both sides of the question with impartiality. Whoever is led to believe that species are mutable will do good service by conscientiously expressing his conviction; for only thus can the load of prejudice by which this subject is overwhelmed be removed.

Several eminent naturalists have of late published their belief that a multitude of reputed species in each genus are not real species; but that other species are real, that is, have been independently created. This seems to me a strange conclusion to arrive at. They admit that a multitude of forms, which till lately they themselves thought were special creations, and which are still thus looked at by the majority of naturalists, and which consequently have every external characteristic feature of true species,—they admit that these have been produced by variation, but they refuse to extend the same view to other and very slightly different forms. Nevertheless they do not pretend that they can define, or even conjecture, which are the created forms of life, and which are those produced by secondary laws. They admit variation as a *vera causa* in one case, they arbitrarily reject it in another, without assigning any distinction in the two cases. The day will come when this will be given as a curious illustration of the blindness of preconceived opinion. These authors seem no more startled at a miraculous act of creation than at an ordinary birth. But do they really believe that at innumerable periods in the earth's history certain elemental atoms have been commanded suddenly to flash into living tissues? Do they believe that at each supposed act of creation one individual or many were produced? Were all the infinitely numerous kinds of animals and plants created as eggs or seed, or as full grown? and in the case of mammals, were they created bearing the false marks of nourishment from the mother's womb? Although naturalists very properly demand a full explanation of every difficulty from those who believe in the mutability of species, on their own side they ignore the whole subject of the first appearance of species in what they consider reverent silence.

It may be asked how far I extend the doctrine of the modification of species. The question is difficult to answer, because the more distinct the forms are which we may consider, by so much the arguments fall away in force. But some arguments of the greatest weight extend very far. All the members of whole classes can be connected together by chains of affinities, and all can be classified on the same principle, in groups subordinate to groups. Fossil remains sometimes tend to fill up very wide intervals between existing orders. Organs in a rudimentary condition plainly show that an early progenitor had the organ in a fully developed state; and this in some instances necessarily implies an enormous amount of modification in the descendants. Throughout whole classes various structures are formed on the same pattern, and at an embryonic age the species closely resemble each other. Therefore I cannot doubt that the theory of descent with modification embraces all the members of the same class. I believe that animals have descended from at most only four or five progenitors, and plants from an equal or lesser number.

Analogy would lead me one step further, namely, to the belief that all animals and plants have descended from some one prototype. But analogy may be a deceitful guide. Nevertheless all living things have much in common, in their chemical composition, their germinal vesicles, their cellular structure, and their laws of growth and reproduction. We see this even in so trifling a circumstance as that the same poison often similarly affects plants and animals; or that the poison secreted by the gall-fly produces monstrous growths on the wild rose or oak-tree. Therefore I should infer from analogy that probably all the organic beings which have ever lived on this earth have descended from some one primordial form, into which life was first breathed.

When the views entertained in this volume on the origin of species, or when analogous views are generally admitted, we can dimly foresee that there will be a considerable revolution in natural history. Systematists will be able to pursue their labours as at present; but they will not be incessantly haunted by the shadowy doubt whether this or that form be in essence a species. This I feel sure, and I speak after experience, will be no slight relief. The endless disputes whether or not some fifty species of British brambles are true species will cease. Systematists will have only to decide (not that this will be easy) whether any form be sufficiently constant and distinct from other forms, to be capable of definition; and if definable, whether the differences be sufficiently important to deserve a specific name. This latter point will become a far more essential consideration than it is at present; for differences, however slight, between any two forms, if not blended by intermediate gradations, are looked at by most naturalists as sufficient to raise both forms to the rank of species. Hereafter we shall be compelled to acknowledge that the only distinction between species and well-marked varieties is, that the latter are known, or believed, to be connected at the present day by intermediate gradations, whereas species were formerly thus connected. Hence, without quite rejecting the consideration of the present existence of intermediate gradations between any two forms, we shall be led to weigh more carefully and to value higher the actual amount of difference between them. It is quite possible that forms now generally acknowledged to be merely varieties may hereafter be thought worthy of specific names, as with the primrose and cowslip; and in this case scientific and common language will come into accordance. In short, we shall have to treat species in the same manner as those naturalists treat genera, who admit that genera are merely artificial combinations made for convenience. This may not be a cheering prospect; but we shall at least be freed from the vain search for the undiscovered and undiscoverable essence of the term species.

The other and more general departments of natural history will rise greatly in interest. The terms used by naturalists of affinity, relationship, community of type, paternity, morphology, adaptive characters, rudimentary and aborted organs, &c., will cease to be metaphorical, and will have a plain signification. When we no longer look at an organic being as a savage looks at a ship, as at something wholly beyond his comprehension; when we regard every production of nature as one which has had a history; when we contemplate every complex structure and instinct as the summing up of many contrivances, each useful to the possessor, nearly in the same way as when we look at any great mechanical invention as the summing up of the labour, the experience, the reason, and even the blunders of numerous workmen; when we thus view each organic being, how far more interesting, I speak from experience, will the study of natural history become!

A grand and almost untrodden field of inquiry will be opened, on the causes and laws of variation, on correlation of growth, on the effects of use and disuse, on the direct action of external conditions, and so forth. The study of domestic productions will rise immensely in value. A new variety raised by man will be a far more important and interesting subject for study than one more species added to the infinitude of already recorded species. Our classifications will come to be, as far as they can be so made, genealogies; and will then truly give what may be called the plan of creation. The rules for classifying will no doubt become simpler when we have a definite object in view. We possess no pedigrees or armorial bearings; and we have to discover and trace the many diverging lines of descent in our natural genealogies, by characters of any kind which have long been inherited. Rudimentary organs will speak infallibly with respect to the nature of long-lost structures. Species and groups of species, which are called

aberrant, and which may fancifully be called living fossils, will aid us in forming a picture of the ancient forms of life. Embryology will reveal to use the structure, in some degree obscured, of the prototypes of each great class.

When we can feel assured that all the individuals of the same species, and all the closely allied species of most genera, have within a not very remote period descended from one parent, and have migrated from some one birthplace; and when we better know the many means of migration, then, by the light which geology now throws, and will continue to throw, on former changes of climate and of the level of the land, we shall surely be enabled to trace in an admirable manner the former migrations of the inhabitants of the whole world. Even at present, by comparing the differences of the inhabitants of the sea on the opposite sides of a continent, and the nature of the various inhabitants of that continent in relation to their apparent means of immigration, some light can be thrown on ancient geography.

The noble science of Geology loses glory from the extreme imperfection of the record. The crust of the earth with its embedded remains must not be looked at as a well-filled museum, but as a poor collection made at hazard and at rare intervals. The accumulation of each great fossiliferous formation will be recognised as having depended on an unusual concurrence of circumstances, and the blank intervals between the successive stages as having been of vast duration. But we shall be able to gauge with some security the duration of these intervals by a comparison of the preceding and succeeding organic forms. We must be cautious in attempting to correlate as strictly contemporaneous two formations, which include few identical species, by the general succession of their forms of life. As species are produced and exterminated by slowly acting and still existing causes, and not by miraculous acts of creation and by catastrophes; and as the most important of all causes of organic change is one which is almost independent of altered and perhaps suddenly altered physical conditions, namely, the mutual relation of organism to organism,—the improvement of one being entailing the improvement or the extermination of others; it follows, that the amount of organic change in the fossils of consecutive formations probably serves as a fair measure of the lapse of actual time. A number of species, however, keeping in a body might remain for a long period unchanged, whilst within this same period, several of these species, by migrating into new countries and coming into competition with foreign associates, might become modified; so that we must not overrate the accuracy of organic change as a measure of time. During early periods of the earth's history, when the forms of life were probably fewer and simpler, the rate of change was probably slower; and at the first dawn of life, when very few forms of the simplest structure existed, the rate of change may have been slow in an extreme degree. The whole history of the world, as at present, known, although of a length quite incomprehensible by us, will hereafter be recognised as a mere fragment of time, compared with the ages which have elapsed since the first creature, the progenitor of innumerable extinct and living descendants, was created.

In the distant future I see open fields for far more important researches. Psychology will be based on a new foundation, that of the necessary acquirement of each mental power and capacity by gradation. Light will be thrown on the origin of man and his history.

Authors of the highest eminence seem to be fully satisfied with the view that each species has been independently created. To my mind it accords better with what we know of the laws impressed on matter by the Creator, that the production and extinction of the past and present inhabitants of the world should have been due to secondary causes, like those determining the birth and death of the individual. When I view all beings not as special creations, but as the lineal descendants of some few beings which lived long before the first bed of the Silurian system was deposited, they seem to me to become ennobled. Judging from the past, we may safely infer that not one living species will transmit its unaltered likeness to a distant futurity. And of the species now living very few will transmit progeny of any kind to a far distant futurity; for the manner in which all organic beings are grouped, shows that the greater number of species of each genus, and all the species of many genera, have left no descendants, but have become utterly extinct. We can so far take a prophetic glance into futurity as to fortell that it will be the common and widely-spread species, belonging to the larger and dominant groups, which will ultimately prevail and procreate new and dominant species. As all the living forms of life are the lineal descendants of those which lived long before the Silurian epoch, we may feel certain that the ordinary succession by generation has never once been broken, and that no cataclysm has desolated the whole world. Hence we may look with some confidence to a secure future of equally inappreciable length. And as natural selection works solely by and for the good of each being, all corporeal and mental endowments will tend to progress towards perfection.

It is interesting to contemplate an entangled bank, clothed with many plants of many kinds, with birds singing on the bushes, with various insects flitting about, and with worms crawling through the damp earth, and to reflect that these elaborately constructed forms, so different from each other, and dependent on each other in so complex a manner, have all been produced by laws acting around us. These laws, taken in the largest sense, being Growth with Reproduction; Inheritance which is almost implied by reproduction; Variability from the indirect and direct action of the external conditions of life, and from use and disuse; a Ratio of Increase so high as to lead to a Struggle for Life, and as a consequence to Natural Selection, entailing Divergence of Character and the Extinction of less-improved forms. Thus, from the war of nature, from famine and death, the most exalted object which we are capable of conceiving, namely, the production of the higher animals, directly follows. There is grandeur in this view of life, with its several powers, having been originally breathed into a few forms or into one; and that, whilst this planet has gone cycling on according to the fixed law of gravity, from so simple a beginning endless forms most beautiful and most wonderful have been, and are being, evolved.

Name: _____ **Date:** _____

1. What is Darwin's answer to the argument that, if his theory is correct, we should find a great deal more evidence in the geological record than we do.

2. What factors does Darwin claim influence the production of variations in living creatures?

3. Why is it important for Darwin to stress that variations in domesticated animals are not produced through human interference?

4. What evidence does Darwin offer to suggest similaries (and thus common descent) among humans and animals?

5. Look at the last sentence in this reading. According to Darwin, who or what created life?

Charles Darwin

Descent of Man & Selection in Relation to Sex, 1871

Twelve years after Darwin (1809-1822) published *On the Origin of Species,* he wrote *Descent of Man,* which focused entirely on the evolution of humans. In it he offered another type of selection, sexual selection, and claimed that species could be shaped by the selective powers of females in choosing mates that possessed the attributes they most admired.

THE EVIDENCE OF THE DESCENT OF MAN FROM SOME LOWER FORM

He who wishes to decide whether man is the modified descendant of some pre-existing form, would probably first enquire whether man varies, however slightly, in bodily structure and in mental faculties; and if so, whether the variations are transmitted to his offspring in accordance with the laws which prevail with the lower animals. Again, are the variations the result, as far as our ignorance permits us to judge, of the same general causes, and are they governed by the same general laws, as in the case of other organisms; for instance, by correlation, the inherited effects of use and disuse, &c.? Is man subject to similar malconformations, the result of arrested development, of reduplication of parts, &c., and does he display in any of his anomalies reversion to some former and ancient type of structure? It might also naturally be enquired whether man, like so many other animals, has given rise to varieties and sub-races, differing but slightly from each other, or to races differing so much that they must be classed as doubtful species? How are such races distributed over the world; and how, when crossed, do they react on each other in the first and succeeding generations? And so with many other points.

The enquirer would next come to the important point, whether man tends to increase at so rapid a rate, as to lead to occasional severe struggles for existence; and consequently to beneficial variations, whether in body or mind, being preserved, and injurious ones eliminated. Do the races or species of men, whichever term may be applied, encroach on the replace one another, so that some finally become extinct? We shall see that all these questions, as indeed is obvious in respect to most of them, must be answered in the affirmative, in the same manner as with the lower animals. But the several considerations just referred to may be conveniently deferred for a time: and we will first see how far the bodily structure of man shows traces, more or less plain, of his descent from some lower form. In succeeding chapters the mental powers of man, in comparison with those of the lower animals, will be considered.

THE BODILY STRUCTURE OF MAN

It is notorious that man is constructed on the same general type or model as other mammals. All the bones in his skeleton can be compared with corresponding bones in a monkey, bat, or seal. So it is with his muscles, nerves, blood-vessels and internal viscera. The brain, the most important of all the organs, follows the same law, as shewn by Huxley and other anatomists. Bischoff,[1] who is a hostile witness, admits that every chief fissure and fold in the brain of man has its analogy in that of the orang; but he adds that at no period of development do their brains perfectly agree; nor could perfect agreement be expected, for otherwise their mental powers would have been the same. Vulpian[2] remarks: "Les

---

From *Descent of Man and Selection in Relation to Sex,* New York: D. Appleton and Company, 1898.

[1]'Grosshirnwindungen des Menschen,' 1868, s. 96. The conclusions of this author, as well as those of Gratiolet and Aeby, concerning the brain, will be discussed by Prof. Huxley in the Appendix alluded to in the Preface to this edition.

[2]'Leç. sur la Phys.' 1866, p. 890, as quoted by M. Dally, 'L'Ordre des Primates et le Transformisme,' 1868, p. 29.

différences réelles qui existent entre l'encéphale de l'homme et celui des singes supérieurs, sont bien minimes. Il ne faut pas se faire d'illusions à cet égard. L'homme est bien plus près des singes anthropomorphes par les caractères anatomiques de son cerveau que ceux-ci ne le sont non seulement des autres mammifères, mais même de certains quadrumanes, des guenons et des macaques." But it would be superfluous here to give further details on the correspondence between man and the higher mammals in the structure of the brain and all other parts of the body.

It may, however, be worth while to specify a few points, not directly or obviously connected with structure, by which this correspondence or relationship is well shewn.

Man is liable to receive from the lower animals, and to communicate to them, certain diseases, as hydrophobia, variola, the glanders, syphilis, cholera, herpes, &c.;[3] and this fact proves the close similarity[4] of their tissues and blood, both in minute structure and composition, far more plainly than does their comparison under the best microscope, or by the aid of the best chemical analysis. Monkeys are liable to many of the same non-contagious diseases as we are; thus Rengger,[5] who carefully observed for a long time the *Cebus Azaræ* in its native land, found it liable to catarrh, with the usual symptoms, and which, when often recurrent, led to consumption. These monkeys suffered also from apoplexy, inflammation of the bowels, and cataract in the eye. The younger ones when shedding their milk-teeth often died from fever. Medicines produced the same effect on them as on us. Many kinds of monkeys have a strong taste for tea, coffee, and spirituous liquors: they will also, as I have myself seen, smoke tobacco with pleasure.[6] Brehm asserts that the natives of north-eastern Africa catch the wild baboons by exposing vessels with strong beer, by which they are made drunk. He has seen some of these animals, which he kept in confinement, in this state; and he

gives a laughable account of their behaviour and strange grimaces. On the following morning they were very cross and dismal; they held their aching heads with both hands, and wore a most pitiable expression: when beer or wine was offered them, they turned away with disgust, but relished the juice of lemons.[7] An American monkey, an Ateles, after getting drunk on brandy, would never touch it again, and thus was wiser than many men. These trifling facts prove how similar the nerves of taste must be in monkeys and man, and how similarly their whole nervous system is affected.

Man is infested with internal parasites, sometimes causing fatal effects; and is plagued by external parasites, all of which belong to the same genera or families as those infesting other mammals, and in the case of scabies to the same species.[8] Man is subject, like other mammals, birds, and even insects,[9] to that mysterious law, which causes certain normal processes, such as gestation, as well as the maturation and duration of various diseases, to follow lunar periods. His wounds are repaired by the same process of healing; and the stumps left after the amputation of his limbs, especially during an early embryonic period, occasionally possess some power of regeneration, as in the lowest animals.[10]

■ ■ ■ ■

GENERAL SUMMARY AND CONCLUSION

A brief summary will be sufficient to recall to the reader's mind the more salient points in this work. Many of the views which have been advanced are highly speculative, and some no doubt will prove erroneous; but I have in every case given the reasons which have led me to one view rather than to another. It seemed worth while to try how far the principle of evolution would throw light on some of the more complex problems in the natural history of man. False facts are highly injurious to the progress of science, for they often endure long; but false views, if supported by some evidence, do little harm, for every one takes a salutary pleasure in

---

[3]Dr. W. Lauder Lindsay has treated this subject at some length in the 'Journal of Mental Science,' July 1871; and in the 'Edinburgh Veterinary Review,' July 1858.

[4]A Reviewer has criticised ('British Quarterly Review,' Oct. 1st, 1871, p. 472) what I have here said with much severity and contempt; but as I do not use the term identity, I cannot see that I am greatly in error. There appears to me a strong analogy between the same infection or contagion producing the same result, or one closely similar, in two distinct animals, and the testing of two distinct fluids by the same chemical reagent.

[5]'Naturgeschichte der Säugethiere von Paraguay,' 1830, s. 50.

[6]The same tastes are common to some animals much lower in the scale. Mr. A. Nicols informs me that he kept in Queensland, in Australia, three individuals of the *Phaseolarctus cinereus;* and that, without having been taught in any way, they acquired a strong taste for rum, and for smoking tobacco.

[7]Brehm, 'Thierleben,' B. i. 1864, s. 75, 86. On the Ateles, s. 105. For other analogous statements, see s. 25, 107.

[8]Dr. W. Lauder Lindsay, 'Edinburgh Vet. Review,' July 1858, p. 13.

[9]With respect to insects see Dr. Laycock, "On a General Law of Vital Periodicity," 'British Association,' 1842. Dr. Macculloch, 'Sulliman's North American Journal of Science,' vol. xvii. p. 305, has seen a dog suffering from tertian ague. Hereafter I shall return to this subject.

[10]I have given the evidence on this head in my 'Variation of Animals and Plants under Domestication,' vol. ii. p. 15, and more could be added.

proving their falseness: and when this is done, one path towards error is closed and the road to truth is often at the same time opened.

The main conclusion here arrived at, and now held by many naturalists who are well competent to form a sound judgment, is that man is descended from some less highly organised form. The grounds upon which is conclusion rests will never be shaken, for the close similarity between man and the lower animals in embryonic development, as well as in innumerable points of structure and constitution, both of high and of the most trifling importance,— the rudiments which he retains, and the abnormal reversions to which he is occasionally liable,—are facts which cannot be disputed. They have long been known, but until recently they told us nothing with respect to the origin of man. Now when viewed by the light of our knowledge of the whole organic world, their meaning is unmistakable. The great principle of evolution stands up clear and firm, when these groups or facts are considered in connection with others, such as the mutual affinities of the members of the same group, their geographical distribution in past and present times, and their geological succession. It is incredible that all these facts should speak falsely. He who is not content to look, like a savage, at the phenomena of nature as disconnected, cannot any longer believe that man is the work of a separate act of creation. He will be forced to admit that the close resemblance of the embryo of man to that, for instance, of a dog—the construction of his skull, limbs and whole frame on the same plan with that of other mammals, independently of the uses to which the parts may be put—the occasional re-appearance of various structures, for instance of several muscles, which man does not normally possess, but which are common to the Quadrumana— and a crowd of analogous facts—all point in the plainest manner to the conclusion that man is the co-descendant with other mammals of a common progenitor.

We have seen that man incessantly presents individual differences in all parts of his body and in his mental faculties. These differences or variations seem to be induced by the same general causes, and to obey the same laws as with the lower animals. In both cases similar laws of inheritance prevail. Man tends to increase at a greater rate than his means of subsistence; consequently he is occasionally subjected to a severe struggle for existence, and natural selection will have effected whatever lies within its scope. A succession of strongly-marked variations of a similar nature is by no means requisite; slight fluctuating differences in the individual suffice for the work of natural selection; not that we have any reason to suppose that in the same species, all parts of the organisation tend to vary to the same degree.

We may feel assured that the inherited effects of the long-continued use or disuse of parts will have done much in the same direction with natural selection. Modifications formerly of importance, though no longer of any special use, are long-inherited. When one part is modified, other parts change through the principle of correlation, of which we have instances in many curious cases of correlated monstrosities. Something may be attributed to the direct and definite action of the surrounding conditions of life, such as abundant food, heat or moisture; and lastly, many characters of slight physiological importance, some indeed of considerable importance, have been gained through sexual selection.

No doubt man, as well as every other animal, presents structures, which seem to our limited knowledge, not to be now of any service to him, nor to have been so formerly, either for the general conditions of life, or in the relations of one sex to the other. Such structures cannot be accounted for by any form of selection, or by the inherited effects of the use and disuse of parts. We know, however, that many strange and strongly-marked peculiarities of structure occasionally appear in our domesticated productions, and if their unknown causes were to act more uniformly, they would probably become common to all the individuals of the species. We may hope hereafter to understand something about the causes of such occasional modifications, especially through the study of monstrosities: hence the labours of experimentalists, such as those of M. Camille Dareste, are full of promise for the future. In general we can only say that the cause of each slight variation and of each monstrosity lies much more in the constitution of the organism, than in the nature of the surrounding conditions; though new and changed conditions certainly play an important part in exciting organic changes of many kinds.

Through the means just specified, aided perhaps by others as yet undiscovered, man has been raised to his present state. But since he attained to the rank of manhood, he has diverged into distinct races, or as they may be more fitly called, sub-species. Some of these, such as the Negro and European, are so distinct that, if specimens had been brought to a naturalist without any further information, they would undoubtedly have been considered by him as good and true species. Nevertheless all the races agree in so many unimportant details of structure and in so many mental peculiarities, that these can be accounted for only by inheritance from a common progenitor; and a progenitor thus characterised would probably deserve to rank as man.

It must not be supposed that the divergence of each race from the other races, and of all from a common stock, can be traced back to any one pair of progenitors. On the contrary, at every stage in the process of modification, all the individuals which were in any way better fitted for their conditions of life, though in different degrees, would have survived in greater numbers than the less well-fitted. The process would have been like that followed by man, when he does not intentionally select particular individuals, but breeds from all the superior individuals, and neglects the inferior. He thus slowly but surely modifies his stock, and unconsciously forms a new strain. So with respect to modifications acquired independently of selection, and due to variations arising from the nature of the organism and the action of the surrounding conditions, or from changed habits of life, no single pair will have been modified much more than the other pairs inhabiting the same country, for all will have been continually blended through free intercrossing.

By considering the embryological structure of man,—the homologies which he presents with the lower animals,—the rudiments which he retains,—and the reversions to which he is liable, we can partly recall in imagination the former condition of our early progenitors; and can approximately place them in their proper place in the zoological series. We thus learn that man is descended from a hairy, tailed quadruped, probably arboreal in its habits, and an inhabitant of the Old World. This creature, if its whole structure had been examined by a naturalist, would have been classed amongst the Quadrumana, as surely as the still more ancient progenitor of the Old and New World monkeys. The Quadrumana and all the higher mammals are probably derived from an ancient marsupial animal, and this through a long line of diversified forms, from some amphibian-like creature, and this again from some fish-like animal. In the dim obscurity of the past we can see that the early progenitor of all the Vertebrata must have been an aquatic animal, provided with branchiæ, with the two sexes united in the same individual, and with the most important organs of the body (such as the brain and heart) imperfectly or not at all developed. This animal seems to have been more like the larvæ of the existing marine Ascidians than any other known form.

The high standard of our intellectual powers and moral disposition is the greatest difficulty which presents itself, after we have been driven to this conclusion on the origin of man. But every one who admits the principle of evolution, must see that the mental powers of the higher animals, which are the same in kind with those of man, though so different in degree, are capable of advancement. Thus the interval between the mental powers of one of the higher apes and of a fish, or between those of an ant and scale-insect, is immense; yet their development does not offer any special difficulty; for with our domesticated animals, the mental faculties are certainly variable, and the variations are inherited. No one doubts that they are of the utmost importance to animals in a state of nature. Therefore the conditions are favourable for their development through natural selection. The same conclusion may be extended to man; the intellect must have been allimportant to him, even at a very remote period, as enabling him to invent and use language, to make weapons, tools, traps, &c., whereby with the aid of his social habits, he long ago became the most dominant of all living creatures.

A great stride in the development of the intellect will have followed, as soon as the half-art and half-instinct of language came into use; for the continued use of language will have reacted on the brain and produced an inherited effect; and this again will have reacted on the improvement of language. As Mr. Chauncey Wright[11] has well remarked, the largeness of the brain in man relatively to his body, compared with the lower animals, may be attributed in chief part to the early use of some simple form of language,—that wonderful engine which affixes signs to all sorts of objects and qualities, and excites trains of thought which would never arise from the mere impression of the senses, or if they did arise could not be followed out. The higher intellectual powers of man, such as those of ratiocination, abstraction, self-consciousness, &c., probably follow from the continued improvement and exercise of the other mental faculties.

The development of the moral qualities is a more interesting problem. The foundation lies in the social instincts, including under this term the family ties. These instincts are highly complex, and in the case of the lower animals give special tendencies towards certain definite actions; but the more important elements are love, and the distinct emotion of sympathy. Animals endowed with the social instincts take pleasure in one another's company, warn one another of danger, defend and aid one another in many ways. These instincts do not extend to all the individuals of the species, but only to those of the same community. As they are highly beneficial to the species, they have in all probability been acquired through natural selection.

A moral being is one who is capable of reflecting on his past actions and their motives—of approving

---

[11]'On the Limits of Natural Selection,' in the 'North American Review,' Oct. 1870, p. 295.

of some and disapproving of others; and the fact that man is the one being who certainly deserves this designation, is the greatest of all distinctions between him and the lower animals. But in the fourth chapter I have endeavoured to shew that the moral sense follows, firstly, from the enduring and ever-present nature of the social instincts; secondly, from man's appreciation of the approbation and disapprobation of his fellows; and thirdly, from the high activity of his mental faculties, with past impressions extremely vivid; and in these latter respects he differs from the lower animals. Owing to this condition of mind, man cannot avoid looking both backwards and forwards, and comparing past impressions. Hence after some temporary desire or passion has mastered his social instincts, he reflects and compares the now weakened impression of such past impulses with the ever-present social instincts; and he then feels that sense of dissatisfaction which all unsatisfied instincts leave behind them, he therefore resolves to act differently for the future,—and this is conscience. Any instinct, permanently stronger or more enduring than another, gives rise to a feeling which we express by saying that it ought to be obeyed. A pointer dog, if able to reflect on his past conduct, would say to himself, I ought (as indeed we say of him) to have pointed at that hare and not have yielded to the passing temptation of hunting it.

Social animals are impelled partly by a wish to aid the members of their community in a general manner, but more commonly to perform certain definite actions. Man is impelled by the same general wish to aid his fellows; but has few or no special instincts. He differs also from the lower animals in the power of expressing his desires by words, which thus become a guide to the aid required and bestowed. The motive to give aid is likewise much modified in man: it no longer consists solely of a blind instinctive impulse, but is much influenced by the praise or blame of his fellows. The appreciation and the bestowal of praise and blame both rest on sympathy; and this emotion, as we have seen, is one of the most important elements of the social instincts. Sympathy, though gained as an instinct, is also much strengthened by exercise or habit. As all men desire their own happiness, praise or blame is bestowed on actions and motives, according as they lead to this end; and as happiness is an essential part of the general good, the greatest-happiness principle indirectly serves as a nearly safe standard of right and wrong. As the reasoning powers advance and experience is gained, the remoter effects of certain lines of conduct on the character of the individual, and on the general good, are perceived; and then the self-regarding virtues come within the scope of public opinion, and receive praise, and

their opposites blame. But with the less civilised nations reason often errs, and many bad customs and base superstitions come within the same scope, and are then esteemed as high virtues, and their breach as heavy crimes.

The moral faculties are generally and justly esteemed as of higher value than the intellectual powers. But we should bear in mind that the activity of the mind in vividly recalling past impressions is one of the fundamental though secondary bases of conscience. This affords the strongest argument for educating and stimulating in all possible ways the intellectual faculties of every human being. No doubt a man with a torpid mind, if his social affections and sympathies are well developed, will be led to good actions, and may have a fairly sensitive conscience. But whatever renders the imagination more vivid and strengthens the habit of recalling and comparing past impressions, will make the conscience more sensitive, and may even somewhat compensate for weak social affections and sympathies.

The moral nature of man has reached its present standard, partly through the advancement of his reasoning powers and consequently of a just public opinion, but especially from his sympathies having been rendered more tender and widely diffused through the effects of habit, example, instruction, and reflection. It is not improbable that after long practice virtuous tendencies may be inherited. With the more civilised races, the conviction of the existence of an all-seeing Deity has had a potent influence on the advance of morality. Ultimately man does not accept the praise or blame of his fellows as his sole guide, though few escape this influence, but his habitual convictions, controlled by reason, afford him the safest rule. His conscience then becomes the supreme judge and monitor. Nevertheless the first foundation or origin of the moral sense lies in the social instincts, including sympathy; and these instincts no doubt were primarily gained, as in the case of the lower animals, through natural selection.

The belief in God has often been advanced as not only the greatest, but the most complete of all the distinctions between man and the lower animals. It is however impossible, as we have seen, to maintain that this belief is innate or instinctive in man. On the other hand a belief in all-pervading spiritual agencies seems to be universal; and apparently follows from a considerable advance in man's reason, and from a still greater advance in his faculties of imagination, curiosity and wonder. I am aware that the assumed instinctive belief in God has been used by many persons as an argument for His existence. But this is a rash argument, as we should thus be compelled to believe in the existence of many cruel and malignant spirits, only a little more powerful than man; for the belief in them is far more general than in a beneficent Deity. The idea of a universal and beneficent Creator does not seem to arise in the mind of man, until he has been elevated by long-continued culture.

He who believes in the advancement of man from some low organised form, will naturally ask how does this bear on the belief in the immortality of the soul. The barbarous races of man, as Sir J. Lubbock has shewn, possess no clear belief of this kind; but arguments derived from the primeval beliefs of savages are, as we have just seen, of little or no avail. Few persons feel any anxiety from the impossibility of determining at what precise period in the development of the individual, from the first trace of a minute germinal vesicle, man becomes an immortal being; and there is no greater cause for anxiety because the period cannot possibly be determined in the gradually ascending organic scale.[12]

I am aware that the conclusions arrived at in this work will be denounced by some as highly irreligious; but he who denounces them is bound to shew why it is more irreligious to explain the origin of man as a distinct species by descent from some lower form, through the laws of variation and natural selection, than to explain the birth of the individual through the laws of ordinary reproduction. The birth both of the species and of the individual are equally parts of that grand sequence of events, which our minds refuse to accept as the result of blind chance. The understanding revolts at such a conclusion, whether or not we are able to believe that every slight variation of structure,—the union of each pair in marriage,—the dissemination of each seed,—and other such events, have all been ordained for some special purpose.

Sexual selection has been treated at great length in this work; for, as I have attempted to shew, it has played an important part in the history of the organic world. I am aware that much remains doubtful, but I have endeavoured to give a fair view of the whole case. In the lower divisions of the animal kingdom, sexual selection seems to have done nothing: such animals are often affixed for life to the same spot, or have the sexes combined in the same individual, or what is still more important, their perceptive and intellectual faculties are not sufficiently advanced to allow of the feelings of love and jealousy, or of the exertion of choice. When, however, we come to the Arthropoda and Vertebrata, even to the lowest classes in these two great Sub-Kingdoms, sexual selection has effected much.

In the several great classes of the animal kingdom,—in mammals, birds, reptiles, fishes, insects, and even crustaceans,—the differences between the sexes follow nearly the same rules. The males are almost always the wooers; and they alone are armed with special weapons for fighting with their rivals. They are generally stronger and larger than the females, and are endowed with the requisite qualities of courage and pugnacity. They are provided, either exclusively or in a much higher degree than the females, with organs for vocal or instrumental music, and with odoriferous glands. They are ornamented with infinitely diversified appendages, and with the most brilliant or conspicuous colours, often arranged in elegant patterns, whilst the females are unadorned. When the sexes differ in more important structures, it is the male which is provided with special sense-organs for discovering the female, with locomotive organs for reaching her, and often with prehensile organs for holding her. These various structures for charming or securing the female are often developed in the male during only part of the year, namely the breeding-season. They have in many cases been more or less transferred to the females; and in the latter case they often appear in her as mere rudiments. They are lost or never gained by the males after emasculation. Generally they are not developed in the male during early youth, but appear a short time before the age for reproduction. Hence in most cases the young of both sexes resemble each other; and the female somewhat resembles her young offspring throughout life. In almost every great class a few anomalous cases occur, where there has been an almost complete transposition of the characters proper to the two sexes; the females assuming characters which properly belong to the males. This surprising uniformity in the laws regulating the differences between the sexes in so many and such widely separated classes, is intelligible if we admit the action of one common cause, namely sexual selection.

Sexual selection depends on the success of certain individuals over others of the same sex, in relation to the propagation of the species; whilst natural selection depends on the success of both sexes, at all ages, in relation to the general conditions of life. The sexual struggle is of two kinds; in the one it is between the individuals of the same sex, generally the males, in order to drive away or kill their rivals, the females remaining passive; whilst in the other, the struggle is likewise between the individuals of the same sex, in order to excite or charm those of the opposite sex, generally the females, which no longer remain passive, but select the more agreeable partners. This latter kind of selection is closely analogous to that which man unin-

---

[12]The Rev. J. A. Picton gives a discussion to this effect in his 'New Theories and the Old Faith,' 1870.

tentionally, yet effectually, brings to bear on his domesticated productions, when he preserves during a long period the most pleasing or useful individuals, without any wish to modify the breed.

The laws of inheritance determine whether characters gained through sexual selection by either sex shall be transmitted to the same sex, or to both; as well as the age at which they shall be developed. It appears that variations arising late in life are commonly transmitted to one and the same sex. Variability is the necessary basis for the action of selection, and is wholly independent of it. It follows from this, that variations of the same general nature have often been taken advantage of and accumulated through sexual selection in relation to the propagation of the species, as well as through natural selection in relation to the general purposes of life. Hence secondary sexual characters, when equally transmitted to both sexes can be distinguished from ordinary specific characters only by the light of analogy. The modifications acquired through sexual selection are often so strongly pronounced that the two sexes have frequently been ranked as distinct species, or even as distinct genera. Such strongly-marked differences must be in some manner highly important; and we know that they have been acquired in some instances at the cost not only of inconvenience, but of exposure to actual danger.

The belief in the power of sexual selection rests chiefly on the following considerations. Certain characters are confined to one sex; and this alone renders it probable that in most cases they are connected with the act of reproduction. In innumerable instances these characters are fully developed only at maturity, and often during only a part of the year, which is always the breeding-season. The males (passing over a few exceptional cases) are the more active in courtship; they are the better armed, and are rendered the more attractive in various ways. It is to be especially observed that the males display their attractions with elaborate care in the presence of the females; and that they rarely or never display them excepting during the season of love. It is incredible that all this should be purposeless. Lastly we have distinct evidence with some quadrupeds and birds, that the individuals of one sex are capable of feeling a strong antipathy or preference for certain individuals of the other sex.

Bearing in mind these facts, and the marked results of man's unconscious selection, when applied to domesticated animals and cultivated plants, it seems to me almost certain that if the individuals of one sex were during a long series of generations to prefer pairing with certain individuals of the other sex, characterised in some peculiar manner, the off-spring would slowly but surely become modified in this same manner. I have not attempted to conceal that, excepting when the males are more numerous than the females, or when polygamy prevails, it is doubtful how the more attractive males succeed in leaving a larger number of offspring to inherit their superiority in ornaments or other charms than the less attractive males; but I have shewn that this would probably follow from the females,—especially the more vigorous ones, which would be the first to breed,—preferring not only the more attractive but at the same time the more vigorous and victorious males.

Although we have some positive evidence that birds appreciate bright and beautiful objects, as with the bowerbirds of Australia, and although they certainly appreciate the power of song, yet I fully admit that it is astonishing that the females of many birds and some mammals should be endowed with sufficient taste to appreciate ornaments, which we have reason to attribute to sexual selection; and this is even more astonishing in the case of reptiles, fish, and insects. But we really know little about the minds of the lower animals. It cannot be supposed, for instance, that male birds of paradise or peacocks should take such pains in erecting, spreading, and vibrating their beautiful plumes before the females for no purpose. We should remember the fact given on excellent authority in a former chapter, that several peahens, when debarred from an admired male, remained widows during a whole season rather than pair with another bird.

Nevertheless I know of no fact in natural history more wonderful than that of the female Argus pheasant should appreciate the exquisite shading of the ball-and-socket ornaments and the elegant patterns on the wing-feathers of the male. He who thinks that the male was created as he now exists must admit that the great plumes, which prevent the wings from being used for flight, and which are displayed during courtship and at no other time in a manner quite peculiar to this one species, were given to him as an ornament. If so, he must likewise admit that the female was created and endowed with the capacity of appreciating such ornaments. I differ only in the conviction that the male Argus pheasant acquired his beauty gradually, through the preference of the females during many generations for the more highly ornamented males; the æsthetic capacity of the females having been advanced through exercise or habit, just as our own taste is gradually improved. In the male through the fortunate chance of a few feathers being left unchanged, we can distinctly trace how simple spots with a little fulvous shading on one side may have been developed by small steps into the wonderful ball-and-socket ornaments; and it is probable that they were actually thus developed.

Everyone who admits the principle of evolution, and yet feels great difficulty in admitting that female mammals, birds, reptiles, and fish, could have acquired the high taste implied by the beauty of the males, and which generally coincides with our own standard, should reflect that the nerve-cells of the brain in the highest as well as in the lowest members of the Vertebrate series, are derived from those of the common progenitor of this great Kingdom. For we can thus see how it has come to pass that certain mental faculties, in various and widely distinct groups of animals, have been developed in nearly the same manner and to nearly the same degree.

The reader who has taken the trouble to go through the several chapters devoted to sexual selection, will be able to judge how far the conclusions at which I have arrived are supported by sufficient evidence. If he accepts these conclusions he may, I think, safely extend them to mankind; but it would be superfluous here to repeat what I have so lately said on the manner in which sexual selection apparently has acted on man, both on the male and female side, causing the two sexes to differ in body and mind, and the several races to differ from each other in various characters, as well as from their ancient and lowly-organised progenitors.

He who admits the principle of sexual selection will be led to the remarkable conclusion that the nervous system not only regulates most of the existing functions of the body, but has indirectly influenced the progressive development of various bodily structures and of certain mental qualities. Courage, pugnacity, perseverance, strength and size of body, weapons of all kinds, musical organs, both vocal and instrumental, bright colours and ornamental appendages, have all been indirectly gained by the one sex or the other, through the exertion of choice, the influence of love and jealousy, and the appreciation of the beautiful in sound, colour or form; and these powers of the mind manifestly depend on the development of the brain.

Man scans with scrupulous care the character and pedigree of his horses, cattle, and dogs before he matches them; but when he comes to his own marriage he rarely, or never, takes any such care. He is impelled by nearly the same motives as the lower animals, when they are left to their own free choice, though he is in so far superior to them that he highly values mental charms and virtues. On the other hand he is strongly attracted by mere wealth or rank. Yet he might by selection do something not only for the bodily constitution and frame of his offspring, but for their intellectual and moral qualities. Both sexes ought to refrain from marriage if they are in

any marked degree inferior in body or mind; but such hopes are Utopian and will never be even partially realised until the laws of inheritance are thoroughly known. Everyone does good service, who aids towards this end. When the principles of breeding and inheritance are better understood, we shall not hear ignorant members of our legislature rejecting with scorn a plan for ascertaining whether or not consanguineous marriages are injurious to man.

The advancement of the welfare of mankind is a most intricate problem: all ought to refrain from marriage who cannot avoid abject poverty for their children; for poverty is not only a great evil, but tends to its own increase by leading to recklessness in marriage. On the other hand, as Mr. Galton has remarked, if the prudent avoid marriage, whilst the reckless marry, the inferior members tend to supplant the better members of society. Man, like every other animal, has no doubt advanced to his present high condition through a struggle for existence consequent on his rapid multiplication; and if he is to advance still higher, it is to be feared that he must remain subject to a severe struggle. Otherwise he would sink into indolence, and the more gifted men would not be more successful in the battle of life than the less gifted. Hence our natural rate of increase, though leading to many and obvious evils, must not be greatly diminished by any means. There should be open competition of all men; and the most able should not be prevented by laws or customs from succeeding best and rearing the largest number of offspring. Important as the struggle for existence has been and even still is, yet as far as the highest part of man's nature is concerned there are other agencies more important. For the moral qualities are advanced, either directly or indirectly, much more through the effects of habit, the reasoning powers, instruction, religion, &c., than through natural selection; though to this latter agency may be safely attributed the social instincts, which afforded the basis for the development of the moral sense.

The main conclusion arrived at in this work, namely that man is descended from some lowly organised form, will, I regret to think, be highly distasteful to many. But there can hardly be a doubt that we are descended from barbarians. The astonishment which I felt on first seeing a party of Fuegians on a wild and broken shore will never be forgotten by me, for the reflection at once rushed into my mind—such were our ancestors. These men were absolutely naked and bedaubed with paint, their long hair was tangled, their mouths frothed with excitement, and their expression was wild, startled, and distrustful. They possessed hardly any arts, and like wild animals lived on what they could catch;

they had no government, and were merciless to every one not of their own small tribe. He who has seen a savage in his native land will not feel much shame, if forced to acknowledge that the blood of some more humble creature flows in his veins. For my own part I would as soon be descended from that heroic little monkey, who braved his dreaded enemy in order to save the life of his keeper, or from that old baboon, who descending from the mountains, carried away in triumph his young comrade from a crowd of astonished dogs—as from a savage who delights to torture his enemies, offers up bloody sacrifices, practises infanticide without remorse, treats his wives like slaves, knows no decency, and is haunted by the grossest superstitions.

Man may be excused for feeling some pride at having risen, though not through his own exertions, to the very summit of the organic scale; and the fact of his having thus risen, instead of having been aboriginally placed there, may give him hope for a still higher destiny in the distant future. But we are not here concerned with hopes or fears, only with the truth as far as our reason permits us to discover it; and I have given the evidence to the best of my ability. We must, however, acknowledge, as it seems to me, that man with all his noble qualities, with sympathy which feels for the most debased, with benevolence which extends not only to other men but to the humblest living creature, with his god-like intellect which has penetrated into the movements and constitution of the solar system—with all these exalted powers—Man still bears in his bodily frame the indelible stamp of his lowly origin.

Name: _____ **Date:** _____

1. How does Darwin suggest we begin to answer the question, are humans a descendant of pre-existing forms?

2. What sorts of examples does Darwin offer in support of his claim that humans and animals share a great many similarities?

3. How, according to Darwin, did humans develop moral qualities?

4. What evidence does Darwin give in support of his theory of sexual selection?

5. Darwin concludes by explaining his understanding that many people will find the notion that humans are descended from lower forms distasteful. What examples of does Darwin provide to help bridge the gaps between humans and animals?

Section III

The Reception of Darwin

Samuel Wilberforce

Review of Darwin's *Origin of Species,* 1860

Wilberforce (1805-1873) is best known for his heated exchange with T. H. Huxley over the validity of Darwin's theory of natural selection. An excellent mathematician, dedicated liberal, skilled debater, and an accomplished athlete, he chose a career in the Anglican church where he reorganized and reinvigorated his diocese. Wilberforce is often caricatured as a hard-line biblical literalist, which as this selection demonstrates, is unfair. Nonetheless, he rejected Darwin's theory of natural selection on both philosophical and theological grounds, believing that it was an interesting but inaccurate depiction of nature.

Any contribution to our Natural History literature from the pen of Mr. C. Darwin is certain to command attention. His scientific attainments, his insight and carefulness as an observer, blended with no scanty measure of imaginative sagacity, and his clear and lively style, make all his writings unusually attractive. His present volume on the 'Origin of Species' is the result of many years of observation, thought, and speculation; and is manifestly regarded by him as the 'opus' upon which his future fame is to rest. It is true that he announces it modestly enough as the mere precursor of a mightier volume. But that volume is only intended to supply the facts which are to support the completed argument of the present essay. In this we have a specimen-collection of the vast accumulation; and, working from these as the high analytical mathematician may work from the admitted results of his conic sections, he proceeds to deduce all the conclusions to which he wishes to conduct his readers.

The essay is full of Mr. Darwin's characteristic excellences. It is a most readable book; full of facts in natural history, old and new, of his collecting and of his observing; and all of these are told in his own perspicuous language, and all thrown into picturesque combinations, and all sparkle with the colours of fancy and the lights of imagination. It assumes, too, the grave proportions of a sustained argument upon a matter of the deepest interest, not to naturalists only, or even to men of science exclusively, but to every one who is interested in the history of man and of the relations of nature around him to the history and plan of creation.

■ ■ ■ ■

Now, the main propositions by which Mr. Darwin's conclusion is attained are these:

1. That observed and admitted variations spring up in the course of descents from a common progenitor.
2. That many of these variations tend to an improvement upon the parent stock.
3. That, by a continued selection of these improved specimens as the progenitors of future stock, its powers may be unlimitedly increased.
4. And, lastly, that there is in nature a power continually and universally working out this selection, and so fixing and augmenting these improvements.

Mr. Darwin's whole theory rests upon the truth of these propositions, and crumbles utterly away if only one of them fail him. These therefore we must closely scrutinise. We will begin with the last in our series, both because we think it the newest and the most ingenious part of Mr. Darwin's whole argument, and also because, whilst we absolutely deny the mode in which he seeks to apply the existence of the power to help him in his argument, yet we think that he throws great and very interesting light upon the fact that such a self-acting power does actively and continuously work in all creation around us.

■ ■ ■ ■

From *Quarterly Review,* 108, 1860.

Mr. Darwin begins by endeavouring to prove that such variations are produced under the selecting power of man amongst domestic animals. Now here we demur *in limine*. Mr. Darwin himself allows that there is a plastic habit amongst domesticated animals which is not found amongst them when in a state of nature. 'Under domestication, it may be truly said that the whole organization becomes in some degree plastic.' If so, it is not fair to argue, from the variations of the plastic nature, as to what he himself admits is the far more rigid nature of the undomesticated animal. But we are ready to give Mr. Darwin this point, and to join issue with him on the variations which he is able to adduce, as having been produced under circumstances the most favourable to change. He takes for this purpose the domestic pigeon, the most favourable specimen no doubt, for many reasons, which he could select, as being a race eminently subject to variation, the variations of which have been most carefully observed by breeders, and which, having been for some 4000 years domesticated, affords the longest possible period for the accumulation of variations. But with all this in his favour, what is he able to show? He writes a delightful chapter upon pigeons. Runts and fantails, short-faced tumblers and long-faced tumblers, long-beaked carriers and pouters, black barbs, jacobins, and turbits, coo and tumble, inflate their œsophagi, and pout and spread out their tails before us. We learn that 'pigeons have been watched and tended with the utmost care, and loved by many people.' They have been domesticated for thousands of years in several quarters of the world. The earliest known record of pigeons is in the fifth Egyptian dynasty, about 3000 B.C., though 'pigeons are given in a bill of fare' (what an autograph would be that of the chef-de-cuisine of the day!) 'in the previous dynasty' and so we follow pigeons on down to the days of 'that most skilful breeder Sir John Sebright,' who 'used to say, with respect to pigeons, that "he would produce any given feather in three years, but it would take him six years to produce beak and head."'

Now all this is very pleasant writing, especially for pigeon-fanciers; but what step do we really gain in it at all towards establishing the alleged fact that variations are but species in the act of formation, or in establishing Mr. Darwin's position that a well-marked variety may be called an incipient species? We affirm positively that no single *fact* tending even in that direction is brought forward. On the contrary, every one points distinctly towards the opposite conclusion; for with all the change wrought in appearance, with all the apparent variation in manners, there is not the faintest beginning of any such change in what that great comparative anatomist, Professor Owen, calls 'the characteristics of the skeleton or other parts of the frame upon which specific differences are founded.' There is no tendency to that great law of sterility which, in spite of Mr. Darwin, we affirm ever to mark the hybrid; for every variety of pigeon, and the descendants of every such mixture, breed as freely, and with as great fertility, as the original pair; nor is there the very first appearance of that power of accumulating variations until they grow into specific differences, which is essential to the argument for the transmutation of species; for, as Mr. Darwin allows, sudden returns in colour, and other most altered appearances, to the parent stock continually attest the tendency of variations not to become fixed, but to vanish, and manifest the perpetual presence of a principle which leads not to the accumulation of minute variations into well-marked species, but to a return from the abnormal to the original type. So clear is this, that it is well known that any relaxation in the breeder's care effaces all the established points of difference, and the fancy-pigeon reverts again to the character of its simplest ancestor.

The same relapse may moreover be traced in still wider instances. There are many testimonies to the fact that domesticated animals, removed from the care and tending of man, lose rapidly the peculiar variations which domestication had introduced amongst them, and relapse into their old untamed condition. 'Plus,' says M. P. S. Pallas, 'je réfléchis, plus je suis disposé à croire que la race des chevaux sauvages que l'on trouve dans les landes baignées par le Jaik et le Don, et dans celles de Baraba, ne provient que de chevaux Kirguis et Kalmouks devenus sauvages,' &c.; and he proceeds to show how far they have relapsed from the type of tame into that of wild horses. Prichard, in his 'Natural History of Man,' remarks that the present state of the escaped domesticated animals, which, since the discovery of the Western Continent by the Spaniards, have been transported from Europe to America, gives us an opportunity of seeing how soon the relapse may become almost complete. 'Many of these races have multiplied (he says) exceedingly on a soil and under a climate congenial to their nature. Several of them have run wild in the vast forests of America, and have lost all the most obvious appearances of domestication.'[1] This he proceeds to prove to be more or less the case as to the hog, the horse, the ass, the sheep, the goat, the cow, the dog, the cat, and gallinaceous fowls.

Now, in all these instances we have the result of the power of selection exercised on the most favourable species for a very long period of time, in

---

[1] 'Natural History of Man,' pp. 27, 28.

a race of that peculiarly plastic habit which is the result of long domestication; and that result is, to prove that there has been no commencement of any such mutation as could, if it was infinitely prolonged, become really a specific change.

■ ■ ■ ■

We come then to these conclusions. All the facts presented to us in the natural world tend to show that none of the variations produced in the fixed forms of animal life, when seen in its most plastic condition under domestication, give any promise of a true transmutation of species; first, from the difficulty of accumulating and fixing variations within the same species; secondly, from the fact that these variations, though most serviceable for man, have no tendency to improve the individual beyond the standard of his own specific type, and so to afford matter, even if they were infinitely produced, for the supposed power of natural selection on which to work; whilst all variations from the mixture of species are barred by the inexorable law of hybrid sterility. Further, the embalmed records of 3000 years show that there has been no beginning of transmutation in the species of our most familiar domesticated animals; and beyond this, that in the countless tribes of animal life around us, down to its lowest and most variable species, no one has ever discovered a single instance of such transmutation being now in prospect; no new organ has ever been known to be developed—no new natural instinct to be formed—whilst, finally, in the vast museum of departed animal life which the strata of the earth imbed for our examination, whilst they contain far too complete a representation of the past to be set aside as a mere imperfect record, yet afford no one instance of any such change as having ever been in progress, or give us anywhere the missing links of the assumed chain, or the remains which would enable now existing variations, by gradual approximations, to shade off into unity.

■ ■ ■ ■

There are no parts of Mr. Darwin's ingenious book in which he gives the reins more completely to his fancy than where he deals with the improvement of instinct by his principle of natural selection. We need but instance his assumption, without a fact on which to build it, that the marvellous skill of the honey-bee in constructing its cells is thus obtained, and the slave-making habits of the Formica Polyerges thus formed. There seems to be no limit here to the exuberance of his fancy, and we cannot but think that we detect one of those hints by which Mr. Darwin indicates the application of his system from the lower animals to man himself, when he

dwells so pointedly upon the fact that it is always the *black* ant which is enslaved by his other coloured and more fortunate brethren. 'The slaves are black!' We believe that, if we had Mr. Darwin in the witness-box, and could subject him to a moderate cross-examination, we should find that he believed that the tendency of the lighter-coloured races of mankind to prosecute the negro slave-trade was really a remains, in their more favoured condition, of the 'extraordinary and odious instinct' which had possessed them before they had been 'improved by natural selection' from Formica Polyerges into Homo. This at least is very much the way in which he slips in quite incidentally the true identity of man with the horse, the bat, and the porpoise:—

'The framework of bones being the same in the hand of a man, wing of a bat, fin of a porpoise, and leg of the horse, the same number of vertebræ forming the neck of the giraffe and of the elephant, and innumerable other such facts, at once explain themselves on the theory of descent with slow and slight successive modifications.'

Such assumptions as these, we once more repeat, are most dishonourable and injurious to science; and though, out of respect to Mr. Darwin's high character and to the tone of his work, we have felt it right to weigh the 'argument' again set by him before us in the simple scales of logical examination, yet we must remind him that the view is not a new one, and that it has already been treated with admirable humour when propounded by another of his name and of his lineage. We do not think that, with all his matchless ingenuity, Mr. Darwin has found any instance which so well illustrates his own theory of the improved descendant under the elevating influences of natural selection exterminating the progenitor whose specialities he has exaggerated as he himself affords us in this work. For if we go back two generations we find the ingenious grandsire of the author of the 'Origin of Species' speculating on the same subject, and almost in the same manner with his more daring descendant.

■ ■ ■ ■

Our readers will not have failed to notice that we have objected to the views with which we have been dealing solely on scientific grounds. We have done so from our fixed conviction that it is thus that the truth or falsehood of such arguments should be tried. We have no sympathy with those who object to any facts or alleged facts in nature, or to any inference logically deduced from them, because they believe them to contradict what it appears to them is taught by Revelation. We think that all such objections savour of a timidity which is really inconsistent with a firm and well-instructed faith:—

'Let us for a moment,' profoundly remarks Professor Sedgwick, 'suppose that there are some religious difficulties in the conclusions of geology. How, then, are we to solve them? Not by making a world after a pattern of our own—not by shifting and shuffling the solid strata of the earth, and then dealing them out in such a way as to play the game of an ignorant or dishonest hypothesis—not by shutting our eyes to facts, or denying the evidence of our senses—but by patient investigation, carried on in the sincere love of truth, and by learning to reject every consequence not warranted by physical evidence.

He who is as sure as he is of his own existence that the God of Truth is at once the God of Nature and the God of Revelation, cannot believe it to be possible that His voice in either, rightly understood, can differ, or deceive His creatures. To oppose facts in the natural world because they seem to oppose Revelation, or to humour them so as to compel them to speak its voice, is, he knows, but another form of the ever-ready feebleminded dishonesty of lying for God, and trying by fraud or falsehood to do the work of the God of truth. It is with another and a nobler spirit that the true believer walks amongst the works of nature. The words graven on the everlasting rocks are the words of God, and they are graven by His hand. No more can they contradict His Word written in His book, than could the words of the old covenant graven by His hand on the stony tables contradict the writings of His hand in the volume of the new dispensation. There may be to man difficulty in reconciling all the utterances of the two voices. But what of that? He has learned already that here he knows only in part, and that the day of reconciling all apparent contradictions between what must agree is nigh at hand. He rests his mind in perfect quietness on this assurance, and rejoices in the gift of light without a misgiving as to what it may discover:—

'A man of deep thought and great practical wisdom,' says Sedgwick,[2] 'one whose piety and benevolence have for many years been shining before the world, and of whose sincerity no scoffer (of whatever school) will dare to start a doubt, recorded his opinion in the great assembly of the men of science who during the past year were gathered from every corner of the Empire within the walls of this University, "that Christianity had everything to hope and nothing to fear from the advancement of philosophy."'[3]

This is as truly the spirit of Christianity as it is that of philosophy. Few things have more deeply injured the cause of religion than the busy fussy energy with which men, narrow and feeble alike in

faith and in science, have bustled forth to reconcile all new discoveries in physics with the word of inspiration. For it continually happens that some larger collection of facts, or some wider view of the phenomena of nature, alter the whole philosophic scheme; whilst Revelation has been committed to declare an absolute agreement with what turns out after all to have been a misconception or an error. We cannot, therefore, consent to test the truth of natural science by the Word of Revelation. But this does not make it the less important to point out on scientific grounds scientific errors, when those errors tend to limit God's glory in creation, or to gainsay the revealed relations of that creation to Himself. To both these classes of error, though, we doubt not, quite unintentionally on his part, we think that Mr. Darwin's speculations directly tend.

Mr. Darwin writes as a Christian, and we doubt not that he is one. We do not for a moment believe him to be one of those who retain in some corner of their hearts a secret unbelief which they dare not vent; and we therefore pray him to consider well the grounds on which we brand his speculations with the charge of such a tendency. First, then, he not obscurely declares that he applies his scheme of the action of the principle of natural selection to MAN himself, as well as to the animals around him. Now, we must say at once, and openly, that such a notion is absolutely incompatible not only with single expressions in the word of God on that subject of natural science with which it is not immediate concerned, but, which in our judgment is of far more importance, with the whole representation of that moral and spiritual condition of man which is its proper subject-matter. Man's derived supremacy over the earth; man's power of articulate speech; man's gift of reason; man's free-will and responsibility; man's fall and man's redemption; the incarnation of the Eternal Son; the indwelling of the Eternal Spirit,—all are equally and utterly irreconcilable with the degrading notion of the brute origin of him who was created in the image of God, and redeemed by the Eternal Son assuming to himself his nature. Equally inconsistent, too, not with any passing expressions, but with the whole scheme of God's dealings with man as recorded in His word, is Mr. Darwin's daring notion of man's further development into some unknown extent of powers, and shape, and size, through natural selection acting through that long vista of ages which he casts mistily over the earth upon the most favoured individuals of his species. We care not in these pages to push the argument further. We have done enough for our purpose in thus succinctly intimating its course. If any of our readers doubt what must be the result of such speculations carried to their logical and legitimate conclusion, let them turn to

[2]'A Discourse on the Studies of the University,' p. 153.

[3]Speech of Dr. Chalmers at the Meeting of the British Association for the Advancement of Science, June, 1833.

the pages of Oken, and see for themselves the end of that path the opening of which is decked out in these pages with the bright hues and seemingly innocent deductions of the transmutation-theory.

Nor can we doubt, secondly, that this view, which thus contradicts the revealed relation of creation to its Creator, is equally inconsistent with the fulness of His glory. It is, in truth, an ingenious theory for diffusing throughout creation the working and so the personality of the Creator. And thus, however unconsciously to him who holds them, such views really tend inevitably to banish from the mind most of the peculiar attributes of the Almighty.

How, asks Mr. Darwin, can we possibly account for the manifest plan, order, and arrangement which pervade creation, except we allow to it this self-developing power through modified descent?

As Milne-Edwards has well expressed it, Nature is prodigal in variety, but niggard in innovation. Why, on the theory of creation, should this be so? Why should all the parts and organs of many independent beings, each supposed to have been separately created for its proper place in nature, be so commonly linked together by graduated steps? Why should not Nature have taken a leap from structure to structure?

And again:—

'It is a truly wonderful fact—the wonder of which we are apt to overlook from familiarity—that all animals and plants throughout all time and space should be related to each other in group subordinate to group, in the manner which we everywhere behold, namely, varieties of the same species most closely related together, species of the same genus less closely and unequally related together, forming sections and sub-genera, species of distinct genera much less closely related, and genera related in different degrees, forming sub-families, families, orders, sub-classes, and classes.'—pp. 128–9.

How can we account for all this? By the simplest and yet the most comprehensive answer. By declaring the stupendous fact that all creation is the transcript in matter of ideas eternally existing in the mind of the Most High—that order in the utmost perfectness of its relation pervades His works, because it exists as in its centre and highest fountainhead in Him the Lord of all. Here is the true account of the fact which has so utterly misled shallow observers, that Man himself, the Prince and Head of this creation, passes in the earlier stages of his being through phases of existence closely analogous, so far as his earthly tabernacle is concerned, to those in which the lower animals ever remain. At that point of being the development of the protozoa is arrested. Through it the embryo of their chief passes to the perfection of his earthly frame. But the types of those lower forms of being must be found in the ani-

mals which never advance beyond them—not in man for whom they are but the foundation for an after-development; whilst he too, Creation's crown and perfection, thus bears witness in his own frame to the law of order which pervades the universe.

In like manner, could we answer every other question as to which Mr. Darwin thinks all oracles are dumb unless they speak his speculation. He is, for instance, more than once troubled by what he considers imperfections in Nature's work. 'If,' he says, 'our reason leads us to admire with enthusiasm a multitude of inimitable contrivances in Nature, this same reason tells us that some other contrivances are less perfect.'

'Nor ought we to marvel if all the contrivances in nature be not, as far as we can judge, absolutely perfect; and if some of them be abhorrent to our idea of fitness. We need not marvel at the sting of the bee causing the bee's own death; at drones being produced in such vast numbers for one single act, with the great majority slaughtered by their sterile sisters; at the astonishing waste of pollen by our fir-trees; at the instinctive hatred of the queen-bee for her own fertile daughters; at ichneumonidæ feeding within the live bodies of caterpillars; and at other such cases. The wonder indeed is, on the theory of natural selection, that more cases of the want of absolute perfection have not been observed.'

We think that the real temper of this whole speculation as to nature itself may be read in these few lines. It is a dishonouring view of nature.

That reverence for the work of God's hands with which a true belief in the All-wise Worker fills the believer's heart is at the root of all great physical discovery; it is the basis of philosophy. He who would see the venerable features of Nature must not seek with the rudeness of a licensed roysterer violently to unmask her countenance; but must wait as a learner for her willing unveiling. There was more of the true temper of philosophy in the poetic fiction of the Pan-ic shriek, than in the atheistic speculations of Lucretius. But this temper must beset those who do in effect banish God from nature. And so Mr. Darwin not only finds in it these bungling contrivances which his own greater skill could amend, but he stands aghast before its mightier phenomena. The presence of death and famine seems to him inconceivable on the ordinary idea of creation; and he looks almost aghast at them until reconciled to their presence by his own theory that 'a ratio of increase so high as to lead to a struggle for life, and as a consequence to natural selection entailing divergence of character and the extinction of less improved forms, as decidedly followed by the most exalted object which we are capable of conceiving, namely, the production of the higher animals'. But we can give him a simpler solution still for the presence of these strange forms of imperfection and suffering amongst the works of God.

■ ■ ■ ■

It is by our deep conviction of the truth and importance of this view for the scientific mind of England that we have been led to treat at so much length Mr. Darwin's speculation. The contrast between the sober, patient, philosophical courage of our home philosophy, and the writings of Lamarck and his followers and predecessors, of M.M. Demailet, Bory de Saint Vincent, Virey, and Oken, is indeed most wonderful; and it is greatly owing to the noble tone which has been given by those great men whose words we have quoted to the school of British science. That Mr. Darwin should have wandered from this broad highway of nature's works into the jungle of fanciful assumption is no small evil. We trust that he is mistaken in believing that he may count Sir C. Lyell as one of his converts. We know indeed the strength of the temptations which he can bring to bear upon his geological brother. The Lyellian hypothesis, itself not free from some of Mr. Darwin's faults, stands eminently in need for its own support of some such new scheme of physical life as that propounded here. Yet no man has been more distinct and more logical in the denial of the transmutation of species than Sir C. Lyell, and that not in the infancy of his scientific life, but in its full vigour and maturity.

Sir C. Lyell devotes the 33rd to the 36th chapter of his 'Principles of Geology' to an examination of this question. He gives a clear account of the mode in which Lamarck supported his belief of the transmutation of species; he 'interrupts the author's argument to observe that no positive fact is cited to exemplify the substitution of some *entirely new* sense, faculty, or organ—because no examples were to be found; and remarks that when Lamarck talks' of 'the effects of internal sentiment,' &c., as causes whereby animals and plants may acquire *new organs,* he substitutes names for things, and with a disregard to the strict rules of induction resorts to fictions.

He shows the fallacy of Lamarck's reasoning, and by anticipation confutes the whole theory of Mr. Darwin, when gathering clearly up into a few heads the recapitulation of the whole argument in favour of the reality of species in nature. He urges:—

1. That there is a capacity in all species to accommodate themselves to a certain extent to a change of external circumstances.
2. The entire variation from the original type . . . may usually be effected in a brief period of time, after which no further deviation can be obtained.
3. The intermixing distinct species is guarded against by the sterility of the mule offspring.
4. It appears that species have a real existence in nature, and that each was endowed at the time of its creation with the attributes and organization by which it is now distinguished.[4]

We trust that Sir. C. Lyell abides still by these truly philosophical principles; and that with his help and with that of his brethren this flimsy speculation may be as completely put down as was what in spite of all denials we must venture to call its twin though less-instructed brother, the 'Vestiges of Creation.' In so doing they will assuredly provide for the strength and continually growing progress of British science.

Indeed, not only do all laws for the study of nature vanish when the great principle of order pervading and regulating all her processes is given up, but all that imparts the deepest interest in the investigation of her wonders will have departed too. Under such influences man soon goes back to the marvelling stare of childhood at the centaurs and hippogriffs of fancy, or if he is of a philosophic turn, he comes like Oken to write a scheme of creation under 'a sort of inspiration;' but it is the frenzied inspiration of the inhaler of mephitic gas. The whole world of nature is laid for such a man under a fantastic law of glamour, and he becomes capable of believing anything: to him it is just as probable that Dr. Livingstone will find the next tribe of negroes with their heads growing under their arms as fixed on the summit of the cervical vertebræ; and he is able, with a continually growing neglect of all the facts around him, with equal confidence and equal delusion, to look back to any past and to look on to any future.

---

[4]Principles of Geology, edit. 1853.

Name: _____ **Date:** _____

1. According to Wilberforce, what was Darwin's reputation before the publication of *Origin of Species?*

2. Restate in your own words Wilberforce's summary of Darwin's four main propositions:

1.

2.

3.

4.

3. What, according to Wilberforce, happens to Darwin's theory if any one of these four propositions can be proven false?

4. What are Wilberforce's claims about Darwin's religious views?

5. Does Wilberforce believe that Darwin's theory is compatible with Christianity? Why or why not?

Richard Owen

"Darwin on the Origin of Species," 1860

Owen (1804-1892) was an English medical doctor and anatomist who, in the 1830s, became an ardent follower of Cuvier's comparative anatomy. Through the 1840s and '50s his scientific reputation grew as he served as a government representative on all matters relating to natural science. In 1856, just as Darwin began discussing his theory of natural selection with close colleagues, Owen was appointed Superintendent of the natural history collections at the British Museum. As an anatomist, Owen was particularly influential in synthesizing the approaches of French and German anatomists, and he contributed much to modern biology, including the concept of homology, which is when similar organs serve fundamentally different functions in two different species of animals. When Darwin published *Origin*, Owen was quick to attack it, but in later years his statements on evolution were confusing and often contradictory.

Mr. Charles Darwin has long been favourably known, not merely to the Zoological but to the Literary World, by the charming style in which his original observations on a variety of natural phenomena are recorded in the volume assigned to him in the narrative of the circumnavigatory voyage of H.M.S. Beagle, by Capt. (now Admiral) Fitz Roy, F.R.S. Mr. Darwin earned the good opinion of geologists by the happy applications of his observations on coral reefs,[1] made during that voyage, to the explanation of some of the phenomena of the changes of level of the earth's crust. He took high rank amongst the original explorers of the minute organisation of the invertebrate animals, upon the appearance of his monographs, in the publications by the Ray Society, on the Cirripedia, Sub-Classes Lepadidæ (1851), and Balanidæ (1854). Of independent means, he has full command of his time for the prosecution of original research: his tastes have led him to devote himself to Natural History; and those who enjoy his friendship and confidence are aware that the favourite subject of his observations and experiments for some years past has been the nature and origin of the so-called *species* of plants and animals.

Mr. Darwin claims another convert in an older name of scientific note: in reference to the immutability of species, he tells us, 'I have reason to believe that one great authority, Sir Charles Lyell, from further reflection, entertains grave doubts on this subject.' For our own part, governed by the motto of the parent society for the promotion of natural knowledge, 'nullius in verba' our attention was principally directed, in the first perusal of Mr. Darwin's work, to the direct observation of nature which seemed to be novel and original, and to the additional grounds, based on facts, on which a more lasting superstructure of the theory of the mutability of species might be raised.

■ ■ ■ ■

The scientific world has looked forward with great interest to the facts which Mr. Darwin might finally deem adequate to the support of his theory on this supreme question in biology, and to the course of inductive original research which might issue in throwing light on 'that mystery of mysteries.' But having now cited the chief, if not the whole, of the original observations adduced by its author in the volume now before us, our disappointment may be conceived. Failing the adequacy of such observations, not merely to carry conviction, but to give a colour to the hypothesis, we were then left to confide in the superior grasp of mind,

---

[1] On the Structure and Distribution of Coral Reefs, 8vo. 1842.

From *Edinburgh Review,* April 1860.

strength of intellect, clearness and precision of thought and expression, which might raise one man so far above his contemporaries, as to enable him to discern in the common stock of facts, of coincidences, correlations and analogies in Natural History, deeper and truer conclusions than his fellow-labourers had been able to reach.

These expectations, we must confess, received a check on perusing the first sentence in the book.

'When on board H.M.S. "Beagle," as naturalist, I was much struck with certain facts in the distribution of the inhabitants of South America, and in the geological relations of the present to the past inhabitants of that continent. These facts seemed to me to throw some light on the origin of species—that mystery of mysteries, as it has been called by some of our greatest philosophers.'

What is there, we asked ourselves, as we closed the volume to ponder on this paragraph,—what can there possibly be in the inhabitants, we suppose he means aboriginal inhabitants, of South America, or in their distribution on that continent, to have suggested to any mind that man might be a transmuted ape, or to throw any light on the origin of the human or other species? Mr. Darwin must be aware of what is commonly understood by an 'uninhabited island;' he may, however, mean by the inhabitants of South America, not the human kind only, whether aboriginal or otherwise, but all the lower animals. Yet again, why are the fresh-water polypes or sponges to be called 'inhabitants' more than the plants? Perhaps what was meant might be, that the distribution and geological relations of the organised beings generally in South America, had suggested transmutational views. They have commonly suggested ideas as to the independent origin of such localized kinds of plants and animals. But what the 'certain facts' were, and what may be the nature of the light which they threw upon the mysterious beginning of species, is not mentioned or further alluded to in the present work.

The origin of species is the question of questions in Zoology; the supreme problem which the most untiring of our original labourers, the clearest zoological thinkers, and the most successful generalizers, have never lost sight of, whilst they have approached it with due reverence. We have a right to expect that the mind proposing to treat of, and assuming to have solved, the problem, should show its equality to the task. The signs of such intellectual power we look for in a clearness of expression, and in the absence of all ambiguous or unmeaning terms. Now, the present work is occupied by arguments, beliefs, and speculations on the origin of species, in which, as it seems to us, the fundamental mistake is committed, of confounding the questions, of species

being the result of a secondary cause of law, and of the nature of that creative law. Various have been the ideas promulgated respecting its mode of operation; such as the reciprocal action of an impulse from within, and an influence from without, upon the organisation (Demaillet, Lamarck); premature birth of an embryo at a phase of development, so distinct from that of the parent, as, with the power of life and growth, under that abortive phase, to manifest differences equivalent to specific (Vestiges of Creation); the hereditary transmission of what are called 'accidental monstrosities;' the principle of gradual transmutation by 'degeneration' (Buffon) as contrasted with the 'progressional' view.

Lamarck,[2] in 1809, cited, as the most exact, that of 'a collection of like (semblables) individuals produced by other individuals equally like them (pareils à eux). But the progress of discovery, especially, perhaps, in palæontology, led him to affirm that species were not as ancient as Nature herself, nor all of the same antiquity; that this alleged constancy was relative to the circumstances and influences to which every individual was subject, and that as certain individuals, subjected to certain influences, varied so as to constitute races, such variations might and do graduate (s'avancent) towards the assumption of characters which the naturalist would arbitrarily regard, some as varieties, others as species. He comments in almost the words of Mr. Darwin, on the embarrassment and confusion which the different interpretation of the nature and value of such observed differences, in the works of different naturalists, had occasioned. The true method of surveying the diversities of organisation is from the simple to the compound forms, which course Lamarck affirms to be graduated and regularly progressive, save where local circumstances, and others influencing the mode of life, have occasioned anomalous diversities.

Cuvier had preceded Lamarck in specifying the kinds and degrees of variation, which his own observations and critical judgment of the reports of others led him to admit. 'Although organisms produce only bodies similar to themselves, there are circumstances which, in the succession of generations, alter to a certain point their primitive form. Here it may be remarked, that the whole question at issue hinges upon the proof of the determination of that limit of variety. Cuvier gives no proof that the alteration stops 'at a certain point.' It merely appears from what follows, that his means of knowing by his own and others' observations had not carried him beyond the point in question, and he was not the man to draw conclusions beyond his premises.

---

[2]Philosophie Zoologique, 8vo. 1809, vol. i. p. 54.

'Less abundant food,' he goes on to say, 'makes the young acquire less size and force. Climate more or less cold, air more or less moist, exposure to light more or less continuous, produce analogous effects; but, above all, the pains bestowed by man on the animal and vegetable productions which he raises for his uses, the consecutive attention with which he restricts them in regard to exercise, or to certain kinds of food, or to influences other than those to which they would be subject in a state of nature, all tend to alter more quickly and sensibly their properties.'

Cuvier admits that the determination by experiment of these variable properties, of the precise causes to which they are due, of the degree of variability and of the powers of the modifying influences, is still very imperfect ('mais ce travail est encore très-imparfait.') The most variable properties in organisms are, according to Cuvier, *size* and *colour*.

'The first mainly depends on abundance of food; the second on light and many other causes so obscure that it seems to vary by chance. The length and strength of the hairs are very variable. A villous plant, for example, transported to a moist place, becomes smooth. Beasts lose hair in hot countries, but gain hair in cold. Certain external parts, such as stamens, thorns, digits, teeth, spines, are subject to variations of number both in the more and the less; parts of minor importance, such as barbs of wheat, &c., vary as to their proportions; homologous parts ('des parties de nature analogue') change one into another, *i.e.*, stamens into petals as in double flowers, wings into fins, feet into jaws, and we might add, adhesive into breathing organs [as in the case of the barnacles cited by Mr. Darwin].'

As to the alleged test of difference between a species and a variety by the infecundity of the hybrid of two parents which may differ in a doubtful degree, Cuvier, in reference to this being the case when the parents are of distinct species, and not mere varieties, empathically affirms, 'Cette assertion ne repose sur aucune preuve' it is at least constant that individuals of the same species, however different, produce together; 'quel-que différens qu'ils soient, peuvent toujours produire ensemble.' But Cuvier warns us not to conclude, when individuals of two different races produce an intermediate and fecund offspring, that they must be of the same species, and that they have not been originally distinct.

'"The number of varieties, or amount of variation," says Cuvier, "relates to geographical circumstances." At the present day, many such varieties appear to have been confined around their primitive centre, either by seas which they could neither traverse by swimming or by flight, or by tempera-

tures which they were not able to support, or by mountains which they could not cross, &c.'*

◼ ◼ ◼

All who have brought the transmutative speculations to the test of observed facts and ascertained powers in organic life, and have published the results, usually adverse to such speculations, are set down by Mr. Darwin as 'curiously illustrating the blindness of preconceived opinion;' and whosoever may withhold assent to his own or other transmutationists' views, is described as 'really believing that at innumerable periods of the earth's history certain elemental atoms suddenly flashed into living tissues.'

Which, by the way, is but another notion of the mode of becoming of a species as little in harmony with observation as the hypothesis of natural selection by external influence, or of exceptional birth or development. Nay, Mr. Darwin goes so far as to affirm—

'All the most eminent palæontologists, namely, Cuvier, Owen, Agassiz, Barrande, Falconer, E. Forbes, &c., and all our greatest geologists, as Lyell, Murchison, Sedgwick, &c., have unanimously, often vehemently, maintained the immutability of species.'

But if by this is meant that they as unanimously reject the evidences of a constantly operative secondary cause or law in the production of the succession of specifically differing organisms, made known by Palæontology, it betrays not only the confusion of ideas as to the fact and the nature of the law, but an ignorance or indifference to the matured thoughts, and expressions of some of those eminent authorities on this supreme question in Biology.

One of the disciples would seem to be as shortsighted as the master in regard to this distinction.

'It has been urged,' writes Dr. Hooker, 'against the theory that existing species have arisen through the variation of pre-existing ones and the destruction of intermediate varieties, that it is a hasty inference from a few facts in the life of a few variable plants, and is therefore unworthy of confidence; but it appears to me that the opposite theory, which demands an independent creative act for each species, is an equally hasty inference.'

Here it is assumed, as by Mr. Darwin, that no other mode of operation of a secondary law in the foundation of a form with distinct specific characters, can have been adopted by the Author of all creative laws than the one which the transmutationists have imagined. Any physiologist who may find the Lamarckian, or the more diffused and attenu-

---

*'Les variétés de chacune ont dû être d'autaut

ated Darwinian, exposition of the law inapplicable to a species, such as the gorilla, considered as a step in the transmutative production of man, is forthwith clamoured against as one who swallows up every fact and every phenomenon regarding the origin and continuance of species 'in the gigantic conception of a power intermittently exercised in the development, out of inorganic elements, of organisms the most bulky and complex as well as the most minute and simple.' Significantly characteristic of the partial view of organic phenomena taken by the transmutationists, and of their inadequacy to grapple with the working out and discovery of a great natural law, is their incompetency to discern the indications of any other origin of one specific form out of another preceding it, save by their way of gradual change through a series of varieties assumed to have become extinct.

But has the free-swimming medusa, which bursts its way out of the ovicapsule of a campanularia, been developed out of inorganic particles? Or have certain elemental atoms suddenly flushed up into acalephal form? Has the polype-parent of the acalephe necessarily become extinct by virtue of such anomalous birth? May it not, and does it not proceed to propagate its own lower species, in regard to form and organisation, notwithstanding its occasional production of another very different and higher kind. Is the fact of one animal giving birth to another not merely specifically, but generally and ordinally, distinct, a solitary one? Has not Cuvier, in a score or more of instances, placed the parent in one class, and the fruitful offspring in another class, of animals? Are the entire series of parthenogenetic phenomena to be of no account in the consideration of the supreme problem of the introduction of fresh specific forms into this planet? Are the transmutationists to monopolise the privilege of conceiving the possibility of the occurrence of unknown phenomena, to be the exclusive propounders of beliefs and surmises, to cry down every kindred barren speculation, and to allow no indulgence in any mere hypothesis save their own? Is it to be endured that every observer who points out a case to which transmutation, under whatever term disguised, is inapplicable, is to be set down by the refuted theorist as a believer in a mode of manufacturing a species, which he never did believe in, and which may be inconceivable?

We would ask Mr. Darwin and Dr. Hooker to give some thought to these queries, and if they should see the smallest meaning in them, to reconsider their future awards of the alternative which they may be pleased to grant to a fellow-labourer, hesitating to accept the proposition, either that life commenced under other than actually operating laws, or that 'all the beings that ever lived on this earth have descended,' by the way of 'natural selection,' from a hypothetical unique instance of a miraculously created primordial form.

We are aware that Professor Owen and others, who have more especially studied the recently discovered astounding phenomena of generation summed up under the terms Parthenogenesis and Alternation of Generations, have pronounced against those phenomena having, as yet, helped us 'to penetrate the mystery of the origin of different species of animals,' and have affirmed, at least so far as observation has yet extended, that 'the cycle of changes is definitely closed;' that is, that when the ciliated 'monad' has given birth to the 'gregarina,' and this to the 'cercaria,' and the 'cercaria' to the 'distoma'— that the ferilised egg of the fluke-worm again excludes the progeny under the infusorial or monadic form, and the cycle again recommences. But circumstances are conceivable,—changes of surrounding influences, the operation of some intermittent law at long intervals, like that of the calculating-machine quoted by the author of 'Vestiges,'—under which the monad might go on splitting up into monads, the gregarina might go on breeding gregarinæ, the cercaria cercariæ, &c., and thus four or five not merely different specific, but different generic, and ordinal forms, zoologically viewed, might all diverge from an antecedent quite distinct form. For how many years, and by how many generations, did the captive polypeprogeny of the *Medusa aurita* go on breeding polypes of their species (*Hydra tuba*), without resolving themselves into any higher form, in Sir John Dalyell's aquarium! The natural phenomena already possessed by science are far from being exhausted on which hypotheses, other than transmutative, of the production of species by law might be based, and on a foundation at least as broad as that which Mr. Darwin has exposed in this essay.

We do not advocate any of these hypotheses in preference to the one of 'natural selection,' we merely affirm that this at present rests on as purely a conjectural basis. The exceptions to that and earlier forms of transmutationism which rise up in the mind of the working naturalist and original observer, are so many and so strong, as to have left the promulgation and advocacy of the hypothesis, under any modification, at all times to individuals of more imaginative temperament; such as Demaillet in the last century, Lamarck in the first half of the present, Darwin in the second half. The great names to which the steady inductive advance of zoology has been due during those periods, have kept aloof from any hypothesis on the origin of species. One only, in connexion, with his palæontological discoveries, with his development of the law of irrelative repetition and of homologies, including the relation of the latter to an archetype, has pronounced in favour of the view of the origin of species by a continuously operative creational law; but he, at the same time, has set forth some of the strongest objections or exceptions to the hypothesis of the nature of that law as a progressively and gradually transmutational one.

Mr. Darwin rarely refers to the writings of his predecessors, from whom, rather than from the phenomena of the distribution of the inhabitants of South America, he might be supposed to have derived his ideas as to the origin of species. When he does allude to them, their expositions on the subject are inadequately represented. Every one studying the pages of Lamarck's original chapters (iii. vi. vii., vol. i., and the supplemental chapter of 'additions' to vol. ii. of the 'Philosophie Zoologique'), will see how much weight he gives to inherent constitutional adaptability, to hereditary influences, and to the operation of long lapses of time on successive generations, in the course of transmuting a species. The common notion of Lamarck's philosophy, drawn from the tirades which a too figurative style of illustrating the reciprocal influence of innate tendencies and outward influences have drawn upon the blind philosopher, is incorrect and unjust. Darwin writes:—

> 'Naturalists continually refer to external conditions, such as climate, food, &c., as the only possible cause of variation. In one very limited sense, as we shall hereafter see, this may be true; but it is preposterous to attribute to mere external conditions, the structure, for instance, of the woodpecker, with its feet, tail, beak, and tongue, so admirably adapted to catch insects under the bark of trees. In the case of the misseltoe, which draws its nourishment from certain trees, which has seeds that must be transported by certain birds, and which has flowers with separate sexes absolutely requiring the agency of certain insects to bring pollen from one flower to the other; it is equally preposterous to account for the structure of this parasite, with its relations to several distinct organic beings, by the effects of external conditions, or of habit, or of the volition of the plant itself.
>
> 'The author of the "Vestiges of Creation" would, I presume, say that, after a certain unknown number of generations, some bird had given birth to a woodpecker, and some plant to the misseltoe, and that these had been produced perfect as we now see them; but this assumption seems to me to be no explanation, for it leaves the case of the coadaptations of organic beings to each other and to their physical conditions of life untouched and unexplained.'

The last cited ingenious writer came to the task of attempting to unravel the 'mystery of mysteries,' when a grand series of embryological researches had brought to light the extreme phases of form that the higher animals passed through in the course of fœtal development, and the striking analogies which transitory embryonal phases of a higher species presented to series of lower species in their premanent or completely developed state. He also instances the abrupt departure from the specific type manifested by a malformed or monstrous offspring, and called to mind the cases in which such malformations had lived and propagated the deviating structure. The author of 'Vestiges,' therefore, speculates—and we think not more rashly or unlawfully than his critic has done—on other possibilities, other conditions of change, than the Lamarckian ones; as, for example, on the influence of permature birth and of prolonged fœtation in establishing the beginning of a specific form different from that of the parent. And does not the known history of certain varieties, such as that of M. Graux's cachemir-wooled sheep, which began suddenly by malformation, show the feasibility of this view?[3] 'The whole train of animated beings,' writes the author of 'Vestiges of Creation,' 'are the results *first,* of an inherent impulse in the forms of life to advance, in definite times, through grades of organisation terminating in the highest dicotyledons and mammals; *second,* of external physical circumstances, operating reactively upon the central impulse to produce the requisite peculiarities of exterior organisation,—the adaptation of the natural theologian.' But he, likewise, requires the same additional element which Mr. Darwin so freely invokes. 'The gestation of a single organism is the work of but a few days, weeks, or months; but the gestation (so to speak) of a whole creation is a matter involving enormous spaces of time.' . . . . 'Though distinctions admitted as specific are not now, to ordinary observation, superable, time may have a power over these.' . . . . 'Geology shows successions of forms, and grants enormous spaces of time within which we may believe them to have changed from each other by the means which we see producing varieties. Brief spaces of time admittedly sufficing to produce these so-called varieties, is it unreasonable to suppose that large spaces of time would effect mutations somewhat more decided, but of the same character?[4]

Unquestionably not, replies Mr. Darwin:—

> 'To give an imaginary example from changes in progress on an island: let the organisation of a canine animal which preyed chiefly on rabbits, but sometimes on hares, become slightly plastic; let these same changes cause the number of rabbits very

---

[3]Reports of the Juries Exhibition of the Works of All Nations, 8vo., 1852, p. 70.

[4]Vestiges of Creation, 8vo., 1846, p. 231.

slowly to decrease, and the number of hares to increase; the effect of this would be that the fox or dog would be driven to try to catch more hares; his organisation, however, being slightly plastic, those individuals with the lightest forms, longest limbs, and best eyesight, let the difference be ever so small, would be slightly favoured, and would tend to live longer, and to survive during that time of the year when food was scarcest; they would also rear more young, which would tend to inherit these slight peculiarities. The less fleet ones would be rigidly destroyed. I can see no more reason to doubt that these causes in a thousand generations would produce a marked effect, and adapt the form of the fox or dog to the catching of hares instead of rabbits, than that greyhounds can be improved by selection and careful breeding.'

◼ ◼ ◼ ◼

Mr. Darwin, availing himself of the more exact ideas of the affinities and relationships of animal groups obtained by subsequent induction, says: 'I believe that animals have descended from at most only four or five progenitors,' [evidently meaning, or answering to, the type-forms of the four or five 'sub-kingdoms' in modern zoology], 'and plants from an equal or lesser number.'

But if the means which produce varieties have operated 'through the enormous species of time, within which species are changed,' the minor modifications which produce, under our brief scope of observation, so called varieties, might well amount to differences equivalent to those now separating sub-kingdoms; and, accordingly, 'analogy,' Mr. Darwin logically admits, 'would lead us one step further, namely, to the belief that all animals and plants have descended from some one prototype;' and, summing up the conditions which all living things have in common, this writer infers from that analogy, 'that probably all the organic beings which have ever lived on this earth, have descended from some one primordial form, into which life was first breathed.'

By the latter scriptural phrase, it may be inferred that Mr. Darwin formally recognises, in the so-limited beginning, a direct creative act, something like that supernatural or miraculous one which, in the preceding page, he defines, as 'certain elemental atoms which have been commanded suddenly to flash into living tissues.' He has, doubtless, framed in his imagination some ideas of the common organic prototype; but he refrains from submitting it to criticism. He leaves us to imagine our globe, void, but so advanced as to be under the conditions which render life possible; and he then restricts the Divine power of breathing life into organic form to its minimum of direct operation. All subsequent organisms henceforward result from properties imparted to the organic elements at the moment of their creation, pre-adapting them to the infinity of complications and their morphological results, which now try to the utmost the naturalist's faculties to comprehend and classify. And we admit, with Buckland, that such an aboriginal constitution, 'far from superseding an intelligent agent, would only exalt our conceptions of the consummate skill and power, that could comprehend such an infinity of future uses, under future systems, in the original groundwork of his creation.' We would accordingly assure Professor Owen that he 'may conceive the existence of such ministers, personified as Nature, without derogation of the Divine power;' and that he, with other inductive naturalists, may confidently advance in the investigation of those 'natural laws or secondary causes, to which the orderly succession and progression of organic phenomena have been committed.'[5] We have no sympathy whatever with Biblical objectors to creation by law, or with the sacerdotal revilers of those who would explain such law. Literal scripturalism in the time of Lactantius, opposed and reviled the demonstrations of the shape of the earth; in the time of Galileo it reviled and persecuted the demonstrations of the movements of the earth; in the time of Dean Cockburn of York, it anathematised the demonstrations of the antiquity of the earth; and the eminent geologist who then personified the alleged antiscriptural heresy, has been hardly less emphatic than his theological assailant, in his denunciations of some of the upholders of the 'becoming and succession of species by natural law,' or by 'a continuously operating creative force.' What we have here to do, is to express our views of the hypothesis as to the nature and mode of operation of the creative law, which has been promulgated by Messrs. Wallace and Darwin.

The author of the volume 'On the Origin of Species,' starts from a single supernaturally created form. He does not define it; it may have been beyond his power of conception. It is, however, eminently plastic, is modified by the influence of external circumstances, and propagates such modifications by generation. Where such modified descendants find favourable conditions of existence, there they thrive; where otherwise they perish. In the first state of things, the result is so analogous to that which man brings about, in establishing a breed of domestic animals from a selected stock, that is suggested the phrase of 'Natural Selection;' and we are appealed to, or at least 'the young and rising naturalists with plastic minds',[6] are adjured, to believe that the

---

[5]On the Nature of Limbs, p. 86.
[6]On the Nature of the Limbs, p. 482.

reciprocal influences so defined have operated, through divergence of character and extinction, on the descendants of a common parent, so as to produce all the organic beings that live, or have ever lived, on our planet.

Now we may suppose that the primeval prototype began by producing, in the legal generative way, creatures like itself, or so slightly affected by external influences, as at first to be scarcely distinguishable from their parent. When, as the progeny multiplied and diverged, they came more and more under the influence of 'Natural Selection,' so, through countless ages of this law's operation, then finally rose to man. But, we may ask, could any of the prototype's descendants utterly escape the surrounding influences? To us such immunity, in the illimitable period during which the hypothesis of Natural Selection requires it to have operated, is inconceivable. No living being, therefore, can now manifest the mysterious primeval form to which Darwin restricts the direct creative act; and we may presume that this inevitable consequence of his hypothesis, became to him an insuperable bar to the definition of that form.

But do the facts of actual organic nature square with the Darwinian hypothesis? Are all the recognised organic forms of the present data, so differentiated, so complex, so superior to conceivable primordial simplicity of form and structure, as to testify to the effects of Natural Selection continuously operating through untold time? Unquestionably not. The most numerous living beings now on the globe are precisely those which offer such a simplicity of form and structure, as best agrees, and we take leave to affirm can only agree, with that ideal prototype from which, by any hypothesis of natural law, the series of vegetable and animal life might have diverged.

If by the patient and honest study and comparison of plants and animals, under their manifold diversities of matured form, and under every step of development by which such form is attained, any idea may be gained of a hypothetical primitive organism,—if its nature is not to be left wholly to the unregulated fancies of dreamy speculation—we should say that the form and condition of life which are common, at one period of existence, to every known kind and grade of organism, would be the only conceivable form and condition of the one primordial being from which 'Natural Selection' infers that all the organisms which have ever lived on this earth have descended.

■ ■ ■ ■

The essential element in the complex idea of species, as it has been variously framed and defined by naturalists, viz., the blood-relationship between all the individuals of such species, is annihilated on the hypothesis of 'natural selection.' According to this view a genus, a family, an order, a class, a sub-kingdom,—the individuals severally representing these grades of difference or relationship,—now differ from individuals of the same species only in degree: the species, like every other group, is a mere creature of the brain; it is no longer from nature. With the present evidence from form, structure, and procreative phenomena, of the truth of the opposite proposition, that 'classification is the task of science, but species the work of nature,' we believe that this aphorism will endure; we are certain that it has not yet been refuted; and we repeat in the words of Linnæus, '*Classis et Ordo* est sapientiæ, *Species* naturæ opus.'

Name: _____ **Date:** _____

1. What, according to Owen, was Darwin's reputation before he published *Origin of Species?*

2. Owen places Darwin's work within the context of earlier proponents of transmutationism. Who does he include among these earlier proponents?

3. Does Owen support the claims made by those who offered Biblical opposition to evolution? Why or why not?

4. List and describe in your own words Owen's principal objections to Darwin's claims.

Fleeming Jenkin

"The Origin of Species [Review Article]," 1867

Jenkin (1833-1885) was a Scottish engineer and an economist. In 1867 he published this review of Darwin's theory of natural selection in which he argued that Darwin's mechanism for evolution, the slow accumulation of beneficial traits that arose in new generations of organisms, could not work to change a species. His argument centered on the concept of blending inheritance, which posited that individual organisms were the product of its two parents' traits blended together. Given this notion, any new trait that arose in a given population would be quickly swamped out of existence by the mass of previously existing traits, even if the new trait was far superior. In the years before the rediscovery of Mendel's work, biologists lacked a working theory of inheritance. How could traits be passed intact from one generation to another unless both parents possessed that trait? In the last decades of the nineteenth century, Jenkin's critique of Darwin's theory of natural selection weighed heavily on Darwinists. It was not until 1900, when researchers rediscovered Mendel's work, that Jenkin's criticism was overcome.

The theory proposed by Mr. Darwin as sufficient to account for the origin of species has been received as probably, and even as certainly true, by many who from their knowledge of physiology, natural history, and geology, are competent to form an intelligent opinion. The facts, they think, are consistent with the theory. Small differences are observed between animals and their offspring. Greater differences are observed between varieties known to be sprung form a common stock. The differences between what have been termed species are sometimes hardly greater in appearance than those between varieties owning a common origin. Even when species differ more widely, the difference they say, is one of degree only, not of kind. They can see no clear, definite distinction by which to decide in all cases, whether two animals have sprung from a common ancestor or not. They feel warranted in concluding, that for aught the structure of animals shows to the contrary, they may be descended from a few ancestors only,—nay, even from a single pair.

The most marked differences between varieties known to have sprung from one source have been obtained by artificial breeding. Men have selected, during many generations, those individuals possessing the desired attributes in the highest degree. They have thus been able to add, as it were, small successive differences, till they have at last produced marked varieties. Darwin shows that by a process, which he calls natural selection, animals more favourably constituted than their fellows will survive in the struggle for life, will produce descendants resembling themselves, of which the strong will live, the weak will die; and so, generation after generation, nature, by a metaphor, may be said to choose certain animals, even as man does when he desires to raise a special breed. The device of nature is based on the attributes most useful to the animal; the device of man on the attributes useful to man, or admired by him. All must agree that the process termed natural selection is in universal operation. The followers of Darwin believe that by that process differences might be added even as they are added by man's selection, though more slowly, and that this addition might in time be carried to so great an extent as to produce every known species of animal from one or two pairs, perhaps from organisms of the lowest type.

A very long time would be required to produce in this way the great differences observed between ex-

From *The North British Review*, 46, June 1867.

isting beings. Geologists say their science shows no ground for doubting that the habitable world has existed for countless ages. Drift and inundation, proceeding at the rate we now observe, would require cycles of ages to distribute the materials of the surface of the globe in their present form and order; and they add, for aught we know, countless ages of rest may at many places have intervened between the ages of action.

But if all beings are thus descended from a common ancestry, a complete historical record would show an unbroken chain of creatures, reaching from each one now known back to the first type, with each link differing from its neighbour by no more than the several offspring of a single pair of animals now differ. We have no such record; but geology can produce vestiges which may be looked upon as a few out of the innumerable links of the whole conceivable chain, and what, say the followers of Darwin, is more certain than that the record of geology must necessarily be imperfect? The records we have show a certain family likeness between the beings living at each epoch, and this is at least consistent with our views.

There are minor arguments in favour of the Darwinian hypothesis, but the main course of the argument has, we hope, been fairly stated. It bases large conclusions as to what has happened upon the observation of comparatively small facts now to be seen. The cardinal facts are the production of varieties by man, and the similarity of all existing animals. About the truth and extent of those facts none but men possessing a special knowledge of physiology and natural history have any right to an opinion; but the superstructure based on those facts enters the region of pure reason, and may be discussed apart from all doubt as to the fundamental facts.

Can natural selection choose special qualities, and so breed special varieties, as man does? Does it appear that man has the power indefinitely to magnify the peculiarities which distinguish his breeds from the original stock? Is there no other evidence than that of geology as to the age of the habitable earth? and what is the value of the geological evidence? How far, in the absence of other knowledge, does the mere difficulty in classifying organized beings justify us in expecting that they have had a common ancestor? And finally, what value is to be attached to certain minor facts supposed to corroborate the new theory? These are the main questions to be debated in the present essay, written with the belief that some of them have been unduly overlooked. The opponents of Darwin have been chiefly men having special knowledge similar to his own, and they have therefore naturally directed their attention to the cardinal facts of his theory. They have asserted that animals are not so similar but that specific differences can be detected, and that man can produce no varieties differing from the parent stock, as one species differs from another. They naturally neglect the deductions drawn from facts which they deny. If your facts were true, they say, perhaps nature would select varieties, and in endless time, all you claim might happen; but we deny the facts. You produce no direct evidence that your selection took place, claiming only that your hypothesis is not inconsistent with the teaching of geology. Perhaps not, but you only claim a 'may be,' and we attack the direct evidence you think you possess.

To an impartial looker-on the Darwinians seem rather to have had the best of the argument on this ground, and it is at any rate worth while to consider the question from the other point of view; admit the facts, and examine the reasoning. This we now propose to do, and for clearness will divide the subject into heads corresponding to the questions asked above, as to the extent of variability, the efficiency of natural selection, the lapse of time, the difficulty of classification, and the value of minor facts adduced in support of Darwin.

Some persons seem to have thought his theory dangerous to religion, morality, and what not. Others have tried to laugh it out of court. We can share neither the fears of the former nor the merriment of the latter; and, on the contrary, own to feeling the greatest admiration both for the ingenuity of the doctrine and for the temper in which it was broached, although, from a consideration of the following arguments, our opinion is adverse to its truth.

EFFICIENCY OF NATURAL SELECTION

Those individual of any species which are most adapted to the life they lead, live on an average longer than those which are less adapted to the circumstances in which the species is placed. The individuals which live the longest will have the most numerous offspring, and as the offspring on the whole resemble their parents, the descendants from any given generation will on the whole resemble the more favoured rather than the less favoured individuals of the species. So much of the theory of natural selection will hardly be denied; but it will be worth while to consider how far this process can tend to cause a variation in some one direction. It is clear that it will frequently, and indeed generally, tend to prevent any deviation from the common type. The mere existence of a species is a proof that it is tolerably well adapted to the life it must lead; many of the variations which may occur will be variations for the worse, and natural selection will assuredly stamp these out. A white grouse in the heather, or a white hare on a fallow would be sooner detected by its enemies than one of the usual plumage or colour. Even so, any favourable deviation must, according to the very terms of the statement, give its fortunate possessor a better chance of life; but this conclusion differs widely from the supposed consequence that a whole species may or will gradually acquire some one new quality, or wholly change in one direction and in the same manner. In arguing this point, two distinct kinds of possible variation must be separately considered: *first,* that kind of common variation which must be conceived as not only possible, but inevitable, in each individual of the species, such as longer and shorter legs, better or worse hearing, etc.; and, *secondly,* that kind of variation which only occurs rarely, and may be called a sport of nature, or more briefly a 'sport,' as when a child is born with six fingers on each hand. The common variation is not limited to one part of any animal, but occurs in all; and when we say that on the whole the stronger live longer than the weaker, we mean that in some cases long life will have been due to good lungs, in others to good ears, in others to good legs. There are few cases in which one faculty is preeminently useful to an animal beyond all other faculties, and where that is not so, the effect of natural selection will simply be to kill the weakly, and insure a sound, healthy, well-developed breed. If we could admit the principle of a gradual accumulation of improvements, natural selection would gradually improve the breed of everything, making the hare of the present generation run faster, hear better, digest better, than his ancestors; his enemies, the weasels, greyhounds, etc., would have improved likewise, so that perhaps the hare would not be really better off; but at any rate the direction of the change would be from a war of pigmies to a war of Titans. Opinions may differ as to the evidence of this gradual perfectibility of all things, but it is beside the question to argue this point, as the origin of species requires not the gradual improvement of animals retaining the same habits and structure, but such modification of those habits and structure as will actually lead to the appearance of new organs. We freely admit, that if an accumulation of slight improvements be possible, natural selection might improve hares as hares, and weasels as weasels, that is to say, it might produce animals having every useful faculty and every useful organ of their ancestors developed to a higher degree; more than this, it may obliterate some once useful organs when circumstances have so changed that they are no longer useful, for since that organ will

weigh for nothing in the struggle of life, the average animal must be calculated as though it did not exist.

We will even go further: if, owing to a change of circumstances some organ becomes pre-eminently useful, natural selection will undoubtedly produce a gradual improvement in that organ, precisely as man's selection can improve a special organ. In all cases the animals above the average live longer, those below the average die sooner, but in estimating the chance of life of a particular animal, one special organ may count much higher or lower according to circumstances, and will accordingly be improved or degraded. Thus it must apparently be conceded that natural selection is a true cause or agency whereby in some cases variations of special organs may be perpetuated and accumulated, but the importance of this admission is much limited by a consideration of the cases where it applies: first of all we have required that it should apply to variations which must occur in every individual, so that enormous numbers of individuals will exist, all having a little improvement in the same direction; as, for instance, each generation of hares will include an enormous number which have longer legs than the average of their parents although there may be an equally enormous number who have shorter legs; secondly, we require that the variation shall occur in an organ already useful owing to the habits of the animal. Such a process of improvement as is described could certainly never give organs of sight, smell or hearings to organisms which had never possessed them. It could not add a few legs to a hare, or produce a new organ, or even cultivate any rudimentary organ which was not immediately useful to any enormous majority of hares. No doubt half the hares which are born have longer tails than the average of their ancestors; but as no large number of hares hang by their tails, it is inconceivable that any change of circumstances should breed hares with prehensile tails; or, to take an instance less shocking in its absurdity, half the hares which are born may be presumed to be more like their cousins the rabbits in their burrowing organs than the average hare ancestor was; but this peculiarity cannot be improved by natural selection as described above, until a considerable number of hares begin to burrow, which we have as yet seen no likelihood of their doing. Admitting, therefore, that natural selection may improve organs already useful to great numbers of a species, does not imply an admission that it can create or develop new organs, and so original species.

But it may be urged, although many hares do not burrow, one may, or least may hide in a hole, and a little scratching may just turn the balance in his favour in the struggle for life. So it may, and this brings us straight to the consideration of 'sports,' the second kind of variation above alluded to. A hare which saved its life by burrowing would come under this head; let us here consider whether a few hares in a century saving themselves by this process could, in some indefinite time, make a burrowing species of hare. It is very difficult to see how this can be accomplished, even when the sport is very eminently favourable indeed; and still more difficult when the advantage gained is very lights, as must generally be the case. The advantage, whatever it may be, is utterly outbalanced by numerical inferiority. A million creatures are born; ten thousand survive to produce offspring. One of the million has twice as good a chance as any other of surviving, but the chances are fifty to one against the gifted individuals being one of the hundred survivors. No doubt, the chances are twice as great against any one other individual, but this does not prevent their being enormously in favour of *some* average individual. However slight the advantage may be, if it is shared by half the individuals produced, it will probably be present in at least fifty-one of the survivors, and in a larger proportion of their offspring; but the chances are against the preservation of any one 'sport' in a numerous tribe. The vague use of an imperfectly understood doctrine of chance has led Darwinian supporters, first, to confuse the two cases above distinguished; and, secondly to imagine that a very slight balance in favour of some individual sport must lead to its perpetuation. All that can be said, is that in the above example the favoured sport would be preserved once in fifty times. Let us consider what will be its influence on the main stock when preserved. It will breed and have a progeny of say 100; now this progeny will, on the whole, be intermediate between the average individual and the sport. The odds in favour of one of this generation of the new breed will be, say 1 to 1, as compared with the average individual; the odds in their favour will therefore be less than that of their parent; but owing to their greater number, the chances are that about 1 of them would survive. Unless these breed together, a most improbable event, their progeny would again approach the average individual; there would be 150 of them, and their superiority would be say in the ratio of 1 to 1; the probability would now be that nearly two of them would survive, and have 200 children, with an eighth superiority. Rather more than two of these would survive; but the superiority would again dwindle, until after a few generations it would no longer be observed and would count for no more in the struggle for life, than any of the hundred trifling advantages which occur in the ordinary organs. An illustration will bring this conception home. Suppose a white man to have been wrecked on an island inhabited by negroes, and to have established himself in friendly relations with a powerful tribe, whose customs he has learnt. Suppose him to possess the physical strength, energy, and ability of a dominant white race, and let the food and climate of the island suit his constitution; grant him every advantage which we can conceive a white to possess over the native; concede that in the struggle for existence his chance of a long life will be much superior to that of the native chiefs; yet from all these admissions, there does not follow the conclusion that, after a limited or unlimited number of generations, the inhabitants of the island will be white. Our shipwrecked hero would probably become king; he would kill a great many blacks in the struggle for existence; he would have a great many wives and children, while many of his subjects would live and die as bachelors; an insurance company would accept his life at perhaps one-tenth of the premium which they would exact from the most favoured of the negroes. Our white's qualities would certainly tend very much to preserve him to good old age, and yet he would not suffice in any number of generations to turn his subjects' descendants white. It may be said that the white colour is not the cause of the superiority. True, but it may be used simply to bring before the senses the way in which qualities belonging to one individual in a large number must be gradually obliterated. In the first generation there will be some dozens of intelligent young mulattoes, much superior in average intelligence to the negroes. We might expect the throne for some generations to be occupied by a more or less yellow king; but can any one believe that the whole island will gradually acquire a white, or even a yellow population, or that the islanders would acquire the energy, courage, ingenuity, patience, self-control, endurance, in virtue of which qualities our hero killed so many of their ancestors, and begot so many children; those qualities, in fact, which the struggle for existence would select, if it could select anything?

Here is a case in which a variety was introduced, with far greater advantages than any sport every heard of, advantages tending to its preservation, and yet powerless to perpetuate the new variety.

Darwin says that in the struggle for life a grain may turn the balance in favour of a given structure, which will then be preserved. But one of the weights in the scale of nature is due to the number of a given tribe. Let there be 7000 A's and 7000 B's, representing two varieties of a given animal, and let all the B's, in virtue of a slight difference of structure, have the better chance of life by 1/7000th part. We must allow that there is a slight probability that the descendants of B will supplant the descendants of A; but let there be only 7001 A's against 7000 B's at first, and the chances are once more equal, while if there be 7002 A's to start, the odds would be said on the A's. True, they stand a greater chance of being killed; but then they can better afford to be killed. The grain will only turn the scales when these are very nicely balanced, and an advantage in numbers counts for weight, even as an advantage in structure. As the numbers of the favoured variety diminish, so must its relative advantage increase, if the chance of its existence is to surpass the chance of its extinction, until hardly any conceivable advantage would enable the descendants of a single pair to exterminate the descendants of many thousands if they and their descendants are supposed to breed freely with the inferior variety, and so gradually lose their ascendancy. If it is impossible that any sport or accidental variation in a single individual, however favourable to life, should be preserved and transmitted by natural selection, still less can slight an imperceptible variations, occurring in single individuals be garnered up and transmitted to continually increasing numbers; for if a very highly-favoured white cannot blanch a nation of negroes, it will hardly be contended that a comparatively very dull mulatto has a good chance of producing a tawny tribe; the idea, which seems almost absurd when presented in connexion with a practical case, rests on a fallacy of exceedingly common occurrence in mechanics and physics generally. When a man shows that a tendency to produce a given effect exists he often thinks he has proved that the effect must follow. He does not take into account for opposing tendencies, much less does he measure the various forces, with a view to calculate the result. For instance, there is a tendency on the part of a submarine cable to assume a catenary curve, and very high authorities once said it would; but, in fact, forces neglected by them utterly alter the curve from the catenary. There is a tendency on the part of the same cables, as usually made, to untwist entirely, luckily there are opposing forces, and they untwist very little. These cases will hardly seem obvious; but what should we say to a man who asserted that the centrifugal tendency of the earth must send it off in a tangent? One tendency is balanced or outbalanced by others; the advantage of structure possessed by an isolated specimen is enormously outbalanced by the advantage of numbers possessed by the others.

■ ■ ■ ■

Let us now consider what direct evidence Darwin brings forward to prove that animals really are descended from a common ancestor. As direct evidence we may admit the possession of webbed feet by unplumed birds; the stripes observed on some kinds of horses and hybrids of horses, resembling not their parents, but other species of the genus; the generative variability of abnormal organs; the greater tendency to vary of widely diffused and widely ranging species, certain peculiarities of distribution. All these facts are consistent with Darwin's theory, and if it could be shown that they could not possibly have occurred except in consequence of natural selection, they would prove the truth of this theory. It would, however, clearly be impossible to prove that in no other way could these phenomena have been produced, and Darwin makes no attempt to prove this. He only says he cannot imagine why unplumed birds should have webbed feet, unless in consequence of their direct descent from web-footed ancestors who lived in the water; that he thinks it would in some way be derogatory to the Cretaor to let hybrids have stripes on their legs, unless some ancestors of theirs had stripes on his leg. He cannot imagine why abnormal organs and widely diffused genera should vary more than others, unless his views be true; and he says he cannot account for the peculiarities of distribution in any way but one. It is perhaps hardly necessary to combat these arguments, and to show that our inability to account for certain phenomena, in any way but one, is no proof of the truth of the explanation given, but simply is a confession of our ignorance. When a man says a glowworm must be on fire, and in answer to our doubts challenges us to say how it can give out light unless it be on fire, we do not admit his challenge as any proof of his assertion, and indeed we allow it no weight whatever as against positive proof we have that the glowworm is not on fire. We conceive Darwin's theory to be in exactly the same case; its untruth can, as we think, be proved, and his or our own inability to explain a few isolated facts consistent with his views would simply prove his and our ignorance of the true explanation. But although unable to give any certainly true explanations of the above phenomena, it is possible to suggest explanations perhaps as plausible as the Darwinian theory, and though the fresh suggestions may very probably not be correct, they may serve to show that at least more than one conceivable explanation may be given.

It is a familiar fact that certain complexions go with certain temperaments, that roughly something of a man's character may be told from the shape of his head, his nose, or perhaps from most parts of his body. We find certain colours almost always accompanying certain forms and tempers of horses. There is a connexion between the shape of the hand and the foot, and so forth. No horse has the head of a cart-horse and the hind-quarters of a racer; so that, in general, if we know the shape of most parts of a man or horse, we can make a good guess at the probable shape of the remainder. All this shows that there is a certain correlation of parts, leading us to expect that when the heads of two birds are very much alike, their feet will not be very different. From the assumption of a limited number of possible combinations or animals, it would naturally follow that the combination of elements producing a bird having a head very similar to that of a goose, could not fail to produce a foot also somewhat similar. According to this view, we might expect most animals to have a good many superfluities of a minor kind, resulting necessarily from the combination required to produce the essential or important organs. Surely, then, it is not very strange than an animal intermediate by birth between a horse and ass should resemble a quagga, which results from a combination intermediate between the horse and ass combination. The quagga is in general appearance intermediate between the horse and ass, therefore, *a priori,* we may expect that in general appearance a hybrid between the horse and the ass will resemble the quagga, and if in general it does resemble a quagga, we may expect that owing to the correlation of parts it will resemble the quagga in some special particulars. It is difficult to suppose that every stripe on a zebra or quagga, or cross down a donkey's back, is useful to it. It seems possible, even probable, that these things are the unavoidable consequences of the elementary combination which will produce the quagga, or a beast like it. Darwin himself appears to admit that correlation will or may produce results which are not themselves useful to the animal; thus how can we suppose that the beauty of feathers which are either never uncovered, or very rarely so, can be of any advantage to a bird? Nevertheless those concealed parts are often very beautiful, and the beauty of the markings on these parts must be supposed due to correlation. The exposed end of a peacock's feather could not be so gloriously coloured without beautiful colours even in the unexposed parts. According to the view already explained, the combination producing the one was impossible unless it included the other. The same idea may perhaps furnish the clue to the variability of abnormal organs and widely diffused species, the abnormal organ may with some plausibility be looked upon as the rare combination difficult to effect, and only possible under very special circumstances. There is little difficulty in believing that it would more probably vary with varying circumstances than a simple and ordinary combination. It is easy to produce two common wine-glasses which differ in no apparent manner; two Venice goblets could hardly be blown

alike. It is not meant here to predicate ease of difficulty of the action of omnipotence; but just as mechanical laws allow one form to be reproduced with certainty, so the occult laws of reproduction may allow certain simpler combinations to be produced with much greater certainty than the more complex combinations. The variability of widely diffused species might be explained in a similar way. These may be looked on as the simple combinations of which many may exist similar one to the other, whereas the complex combinations may only be possible within comparatively narrow limits, inside which one organ may indeed be variable, though the main combination is the only possible one of its kind.

We by no means wish to assert that we know the above suggestions to be the true explanation of the facts. We merely wish to show that other explanation than those given by Darwin are conceivable, although this is indeed not required by our argument, since, if his main assumptions can be proved false, his theory will derive no benefit from the few facts which may be allowed to be consistent with its truth.

The peculiarities of geographic distribution seem very difficult of explanation on any theory. Darwin calls in alternately winds, tides, birds, beasts, all animated nature, as the diffusers of species, and then a good many of the same agencies as impenetrable barriers. There are some impenetrable barriers between the Galapagos Islands, but not between New Zealand and South America. Continents are created to join Australia and the Cape of Good Hope, while a sea as broad as the British Channel is elsewhere a valid line of demarcation. With these facilities of hypothesis there seems to be no particular reason why many theories should not be true. However an animal may have been produced, it must have been produced somewhere, and it must either have spread very widely, or not have spread, and Darwin can give good reason for both results. If produced according to any law at all, it would seem probable that groups of similar animals would be produced in given places. Or we might suppose that all animals having been created anywhere, those have been extinguished which were not suited to such climate; nor would it be an answer to say that the climate, for instance, of Australia, is less suitable now to marsupials than to other animals introduced from Europe, because we may suppose that this was not so when the race began; but in truth it is hard to believe any of the suppositions, nor can we just now invent any better, and this peculiarity of distribution, namely, that all the products of a given continent have a kind of family resemblance, is the sole argument brought forward by Darwin which seems to us to lend any countenance to the theory of a common origin and the transmutation of species.

Our main arguments are now completed. Something might be said as to the alleged imperfection of the geological records. It is certain that, when compared with the total number of animals which have lived, they must be very imperfect; but still we observe that of many species of beings thousands and even millions of specimens have been preserved. If Darwin's theory be true, the number of varieties differing one from another a very little must have been indefinitely great, so great indeed as probably far to exceed the number of individual which have existed of any one variety. If this be true, it would be more probable that no two specimens preserved as fossils should be of one variety than that we should find a great many specimens collected from a very few varieties, provided, of course, the chances of preservation are equal for all individuals. But this assumption may be denied, and some may think it probable that the conditions favourable to preservation only recur rarely, at remote periods, and never last long enough to show a gradual unbroken change. It would rather seem probable that fragments, at lest, of perfect series would be preserved of those beings which lead similar lives favourable to their preservation as fossils. Have any fragments of these Darwinian series been found where the individuals merge from one variety insensibly to another?

It is really strange that vast numbers of perfectly similar specimens should be found, the chances against their perpetuation as fossils are so great; but it is also very strange that the specimens should be so exactly alike as they are, if, in fact, they came and vanished by a gradual change. It is, however, not worth while to insist much on this argument, which by suitable hypotheses might be answered, as by saying, that the changes were often quick, taking only a few myriad ages, and that then a species was permanent for a vastly longer time, and that if we have not anywhere a gradual change clearly recorded, the steps from variety to variety are gradually being diminished as more specimens are discovered. These answers do not seem sufficient, but the point is hardly worth contesting, when other arguments directly disproving the possibility of the assumed change have been advanced.

These arguments are cumulative. If it be true that no species can vary beyond defined limits, it matters little whether natural selection would be efficient in producing definite variations. If natural selection, though it does select the stronger average animals, and under peculiar circumstances may de-

velop special organs already useful, can never select new imperfect organs such as are produced in sports, then, even though eternity were granted, and no limit assigned to the possible changes of animals, Darwin's cannot be the true explanation of the manner in which change has been brought about. Lastly, even if no limit be drawn to the possible difference between offspring and their progenitors, and if natural selection were admitted to be an efficient cause capable of building up even new senses, even then, unless time, vast time, be granted, the changes which might have been produced by the gradual selection of peculiar offspring have not really been so produced. Any one of the main pleas of our argument, if established, is fatal to Darwin's theory. When then shall we say if we believe that experiment has shown a sharp limit to the variation of every species, that natural selection is powerless to perpetuate new organs even should they appear, that countless ages of a habitable globe are rigidly proven impossible by the physical laws which forbid the assumption of infinite power in a finite mass? What can we believe but that Darwin's theory is an ingenious and plausible speculation, to which future physiologists will look back with the kind of admiration we bestow on the atoms of Lucretius, or the crystal spheres of Eudoxus, containing like these some faint half-truths, marking at once the ignorance of the age and the ability of the philosopher. Surely the time is past when a theory unsupported by evidence is received as probable, because in our ignorance we know not why it should be false, though we cannot show it to be true. Yet we have heard grave men gravely urge, that because Darwin's theory was the most plausible known, it should be believed. Others seriously allege that it is more consonant with a lofty idea of the Creator's action to suppose that he produced beings by natural selection, rather than by the finikin process of making each separate little race by the exercise of Almighty power. The argument such as it is, means simply that the user of it thinks that this is how he personally would act if possessed of almighty power and knowledge, but this speculations as to his probable feelings and actions, after such a great change of circumstances, are not worth much. If we are told that our experience shows that God works by laws, then we answer, 'Why the special Darwinian law?' A plausible theory should not be accepted while unproven; and if the arguments of this essay be admitted, Darwin's theory of the origin of species is not only without sufficient support from evidence, but is proved false by a cumulative proof.

Name: _____ **Date:** _____

1. According to Jenkin, if Darwin is correct, what should the paleontological record show?

2. Jenkins uses the analogy of a white man shipwrecked on an island to make a point. What is that point?

3. What does Jenkins assume is included in the term "white?"

Louis Agassiz

"Evolution and Permanence of Type," 1874

Agassiz (1807-1873), the last great hold-out against the idea of evolution and one of the most aggressive opponents of Darwin's theory of natural selection, offered this critique of evolution at the end of his life. In it, he offers examples to undermine the notion that species are mutable in an attempt to demonstrate that, however convincing Darwin's argument may be, it was ultimately wrong because species were fixed entities.

In connection with modern views of science we hear so much of evolution and evolutionists that it is worth our while to ask if there is any such process as evolution in nature. Unquestionably, yes. But all that is actually known of this process we owe to the great embryologists of our century, Döllinger and his pupils K. E. vou Baer, Pander, and others,—the men in short who have founded the science of Embryology. It is true there are younger men who have done since, and are doing now, noble work in this field of research; but the glory must, after all, be given to those who opened the way in which more recent students are pressing forward.

The pioneers in the science of Embryology, by a series of investigations which will challenge admiration as long as patience and accuracy of research are valued, have proved that all living beings produce eggs, and that these eggs contain a yolk-substance out of which new beings, identical with their parents, are evolved by a succession of gradual changes. These successive stages of growth constitute evolution, as understood by embryologists, and within these limits all naturalists who know anything of Zoölogy may be said to be evolutionists. The law of evolution, however, so far as its working is understood, is a law controlling development and keeping types within appointed cycles of growth, which revolve forever upon themselves, returning at appointed intervals to the same starting-point and repeating through a succession of phases the same course. These cycles have never been known to oscillate or to pass into each other; indeed, the only struc-

tural differences known between individuals of the same stock are monstrosities or peculiarities pertaining to sex, and the latter are as abiding and permanent as type itself. Taken together the relations of sex constitute one of the most obscure and wonderful features of the whole organic world, all the more impressive for its universality.

Under the recent and novel application of the terms "evolution" and "evolutionist," we are in danger of forgetting the only process of the kind in the growth of animals which has actually been demonstrated, as well as the men to whom we owe that demonstration. Indeed, the science of Zoölogy, including everything pertaining to the past and present life and history of animals, has furnished, since the beginning of the nineteenth century, an amount of startling and exciting information in which men have lost sight of the old landmarks. In the present ferment of theories respecting the relations of animals to one another, their origin, growth, and diversity, those broader principles of our science—upon which the whole animal kingdom has been divided into a few grand comprehensive types, each one a structural unit in itself—are completely overlooked.

It is not very long since, with the exception of Insects, all the lower animals were grouped together in one division as Worms, on account of their simple structure. A century ago this classification, established by Linnæus, was still unquestioned. Cuvier was the first to introduce a classification based not merely upon a more or less complicated organization but upon ideas or plans of structure. He recognized four of these plans in the whole animal kingdom, neither more nor less. However, when this

From *Atlantic Monthly*, XXXIII, January 1874.

principle was first announced, the incompleteness of our knowledge made it impossible to apply it correctly in every case, and Cuvier himself placed certain animals of obscure or intricate structure under the wrong head. Nevertheless the law was sanctioned, and gave at once a new aim and impulse to investigation. This idea of structural plans, as the foundation of a natural classification, dates only from the year 1812, and was first presented by Cuvier in the Annals of the Museum in Paris.

About the same time another great investigator, Karl Ernst von Baer, then a young naturalist, Döllinger's favorite and most original pupil, was studying in Germany the growth of the chicken in the egg. In a different branch of research, though bearing equally on the structural relations of organized beings, he, without knowing of Cuvier's investigations, arrived at a like conclusion, namely, that there are four different modes of growth among animals. This result has only been confirmed by later investigators. Every living creature is formed in an egg and grows up according to a pattern and a mode of development common to its type, and of these embryonic norms there are but four. Here, then, was a double confirmation of the distinct circumscription of types, as based upon structure, announced almost simultaneously by two independent investigators, ignorant of each other's work, and arriving at the same result by different methods. The one, building up from the first dawn of life in the embryonic germs of various animals, worked out the four great types of organic life from the beginning; while his co-worker reached the same end through a study of their perfected structure in adult forms. Starting from diametrically opposite points, they met at last on the higher ground to which they were both led by their respective studies.

For a quarter of a century following, the aim of all naturalists was to determine the relations of these groups to one another with greater precision, and to trace the affinities between the minor divisions of the whole animal kingdom. It was natural to suppose that all living beings were in some way or other connected; and, indeed, the discoveries in Geology, with its buried remains of extinct life, following fast upon those of Cuvier in structure and of Vou Baer in Embryology, seemed to reveal, however dimly and in broken outlines, a consistent history carried on coherently through all times and extending gradually over the whole surface of the earth, until it culminated in the animal kingdom as it at present exists, with man at its head.

The next step, though a natural result of the flood of facts poured in upon us under the new stimulus to research, led men away from the simple and, as I believe, sound principles of classification established by the two great masters of zoölogical science. The announcement of four typical divisions in the animal kingdom stirred investigators to a closer comparison of their structure. The science of Comparative Anatomy made rapid strides; and since the ability of combining facts is a much rarer gift than that of discerning them, many students lost sight of the unity of structural design in the multiplicity of structural detail. The natural result of this was a breaking up of the four great groups of Radiates, Mollusks, Articulates and Vertebrates into a larger number of primary divisions. Classifications were multiplied with astonishing rapidity, and each writer had his own system of nomenclature, until our science was perplexingly burdened with synonymes. I may mention, as a sample, one or two of the more prominent changes introduced at this time into the general classification of animals.

The Radiates had been divided by Cuvier into three classes, to which, on imperfect data, he erroneously added the Intestinal Worms and the Infusoria. These classes, as they now stand according to his classification, with some recent improvements, are Polyps (corals, sea-anemones, and the like), Acalephs (jelly-fishes), and Echinderms (star-fishes, sea-urchins, and holothurians, better known, perhaps, as Beche-de-mer). Of these three classes the two first, Polyps and Acalephs, were set apart by Leuckart and other naturalists as "Cœlenterata," while the Echinoderms by themselves were elevated into a primary division. There is, however, no valid ground for this. The plan of structure is the same in all three classes, the only difference being that various organs which in the Polyps and Acalephs are, as it were, simply hollowed out of the substance of the body, have in the Echinoderms walls of their own. This is a special complication of structural execution, but makes no difference in the structural plan. The organs and the whole structural combination are the same in the two divisions. In the same way Cephalopods, squids and cuttlefishes, which form the highest class among Mollusks, were separated from the Gasteropods and Acephala, and set apart as a distinct type, because their eggs undergo only a surface segmentation instead of being segmented through and through, as is the case with the members of the two other classes. But this surface segmentation leads ultimately to a structure which has the same essential features as that of the other Mollusks. Indeed, we find also in other branches of the animal kingdom, the Vertebrates for instance, partial or total segmentation, in different classes; but it does not lead to any typical differences there, any more than among Mollusks. Another instance is that of the Bryozoa and Tunicata, which were separated from the Mollusks on account of the greater simplicity of their structure and associated with those simpler Worms in which articulated limbs are wanting. In short, the numerous types admitted nowadays by most zoölogists are founded only upon structural complication, without special regard to the plan of their structure; and the comprehensive principle of structural conception or plan, as determining the primary types, so impressive when first announced, has gradually lost its hold upon naturalists through their very familiarity with special complications of structure. But since we are still in doubt as to the true nature of many organisms, such as the sponges and the Protozoa so-called, it is too early to affirm positively that all the primary divisions of the animal kingdom are included in Cuvier's four types. Yet it is safe to say that no primary division will stand which does not bear the test he applied to the four great groups, Radiates, Mollusks, Articulates, and Vertebrates, namely, that of a distinct plan of structure for each.

The time has, perhaps, not come for an impartial appreciation of the views of Darwin, and the task is the more difficult because it involves an equally impartial review of the modifications his theory has undergone at the hands of his followers. The aim of his first work on The Origin of Species was to show that neither vegetable nor animal forms are so distinct from one another or so independent in their origin and structural relations as most naturalists believed. This idea was not new. Under different aspects it had been urged repeatedly for more than a century by DeMaillet, by Lamarck, by E. Geoffroy St. Hilaire and others; nor was it wholly original even with them, for the study of the relations of animals and plants has at all times been one of the principal aims of all the more advanced students of Natural History; they have differed only in their methods and appreciations. But Darwin has placed the subject on a different basis from that of all his predecessors, and has brought to the discussion a vast amount of well-arranged information, a convincing cogency of argument, and a captivating charm of presentation. His doctrine appealed the more powerfully to the scientific world because he maintained it at first not upon metaphysical ground but upon observation. Indeed it might be said that he treated his subject according to the best scientific methods, had he not frequently overstepped the boundaries of actual knowledge and allowed his imagination to supply the links which science does not furnish.

The excitement produced by the publication of The Origin of Species may be fairly compared to that which followed the appearance of Oken's Natur-Philosophie, over fifty years ago, in which it was claimed that the key had been found to the whole system of organic life. According to Oken, the animal kingdom, in all its diversity, is but the presentation in detail of the organization of man. The Infusoria are the primordial material of life scattered broadcast everywhere, and man himself but a complex of such Infusoria. The Vertebrates represent what Oken calls flesh, that is, bones, muscles, nerves, and the senses, in various combinations; the Fishes are Bone-animals (Knochen-Thiere); the Reptiles, Muscle-animals (Muskel-Thiere); the Birds, Nerve-animals (Nerven-Thiere); the Mammals—with man, combining in his higher structure the whole scheme of organic life, at their head—are Sense-animals (Sinnen-Thiere). The parallelism was drawn with admirable skill and carried into the secondary divisions, down to the families and even the genera. The Articulates were likened to the systems of respiration and circulation; the Mollusks to those of reproduction; the Radiates to those of digestion. The comprehensiveness and grandeur of these views, in which the scattered elements of organic life, serving distinct purposes in the lower animals, are gathered into one structural combination in the highest living being appealed powerfully to the imagination. In Germany they were welcomed with an enthusiasm such as is shown there for Darwinism. England was lukewarm, and France turned a cold shoulder, as she at present does to the theory of the great English naturalist. The influence of Cuvier and the Jussieux was deeply felt in Western Europe, and perhaps saved French naturalists from falling into a fanciful but attractive doctrine, numbered now among the exploded theories of the past.

Darwin's first work, though it did not immediately meet with the universal acceptance since accorded to it, excited, nevertheless, intense and general interest. The circumstance that almost identical views were simultaneously expressed by Wallace, and that several prominent investigators hailed them as the solution of the great problem, gave them double strength; for it seemed improbable that so many able students of nature should agree in their interpretation of facts, unless that interpretation were the true one. The Origin of Species was followed by a second work, The Variation of Animals and Plants under Domestication, to which a third soon succeeded, The Descent of Man. The last phase of the doctrine is its identification with metaphysics in Darwin's latest work on The Expression of the Emotions in Man and Animals. I can only rejoice that the discussion has taken this turn, much as I dissent from the treatment of the subject. It cannot be too soon understood that science is one, and that whether we investigate language, philosophy, theology, history, or physics, we are dealing with the same problem, culminating in the knowledge of ourselves. Speech is known only in connection with the organs of man, thought in connection with his brain, religion as the expression of his aspirations, history as the record of his deeds, and physical sciences as the laws under which he lives. Philosophers and theologians have yet to learn that a physical fact is as sacred as a moral principle. Our own nature demands from us this double allegiance.

It is hardly necessary to give here an analysis of the theory contained in these works of Darwin. Its watchwords, "natural selection," "struggle for existence," "survival of the fittest," are equally familiar to those who do and to those who do not understand them; as well known, indeed, to the amateur in science as to the professional naturalist. It is supported by a startling array of facts respecting the changes animals undergo under domestication, respecting the formation of breeds and varieties, respecting metamorphoses, respecting the dangers to life among all animals and the way in which nature meets them, respecting the influence of climate and external conditions upon superficial structural features, and respecting natural preferences and proclivities between animals as influencing the final results of interbreeding. In the Variation of Animals and Plants under Domestication all that experiments in breeding or fancy horticulture could teach, whether as recorded in the literature and traditions of the subject or gathered from the practical farmers, stock-breeders, and gardeners, was brought together and presented with equal erudition and clearness. No fact was omitted showing the pliability of plants and animals under the fostering care of man. The final conclusion of the author is summed up in his theory of Pangenesis. And yet this book does but prove more conclusively what was already known, namely, that all domesticated animals and cultivated plants are traceable to distinct species, and that the domesticated pigeons which furnish so large a portion of the illustration are, notwithstanding their great diversity under special treatment, no exception to this rule. The truth is, our domesticated animals, with all their breeds and varieties, have never been traced back to anything but their own species, nor have artificial varieties, so far as we know, failed to revert to the wild stock when left to themselves. Darwin's works and those of his followers have added nothing new to our previous knowledge concerning the origin of man and his associates in domestic life, the horse, the cow, the sheep, the dog, or, indeed, of any animal. The facts upon which Darwin, Wallace, Hæckel, and others base their views are in the possession of every well-educated naturalist. It is only a question of interpretation,

not of discovery or of new and unlooked-for information.

Darwin's third book, The Descent of Man, treats a more difficult part of the subject. In this book the question of genealogy is the prominent topic. It had been treated already, it is true, in The Origin of Species, but with no special allusion to mankind. The structure was as yet a torso, a trunk without a head. In these two volumes the whole ground of heredity, of qualities transmitted to the new individual by his progenitors, and that of resemblance—whether physical, intellectual, or moral, between mankind and the higher mammalia, and especially between ourselves and our nearest relations, the anthropoid monkeys,—are brought out with the fulness of material and the skill of treatment so characteristic of the author. But here again the reader seeks in vain for any evidence of a transition between man and his fellow-creatures. Indeed, both with Darwin and his followers, a great part of the argument is purely negative. It rests partly upon the assumption that, in the succession of ages, just those transition types have dropped out from the geological record which would have proved the Darwinian conclusions had these types been preserved, and that in the living animal the process of transition is too subtle for detection. Darwin and his followers thus throw off the responsibility of proof with respect both to embryonic growth and geological succession.

Within the last three or four years, however, it has seemed as if new light were about to be thrown at least upon one of these problems. Two prominent naturalists announced that they had found indications of a direct structural connection between primary types: in the one case between Mollusks and Vertebrates, in the other between Radiates and Articulates. The first of these views was published by a Russian investigator of great skill and eminence, Kowalevsky. He stated that the Ascidians (the so-called soft-shelled clams) showed, in the course of their growth, a string of cells corresponding to the dorsal cord in Vertebrates. For the uninitiated I must explain that, at one stage of its development, in the upper layer of cells of which the Vertebrate germ consists, there arise two folds which, curving upward and inward, form first a longitudinal furrow and finally a cavity for the nervous centres, the brain and spinal cord, while the lower layer of these cells folds downward to enclose the organs of digestion, circulation, and reproduction. Between these two folds, but on the dorsal side, that is, along the back, under the spinal marrow, arises a solid string of more condensed substance, which develops into the dorsal cord, the basis of the backbone. Kowalevsky describes, in the Ascidians, a formation of longitudinally arranged cells as representing an incipient backbone, running from the middle of the body into the tail, along a furrow of the germ of these animals in which the main nervous swelling is situated. This was hailed as a great discovery by the friends of the transmutation theory. At last the transition point was found between the lower and higher animals, and man himself was traced back to the Ascidians. One could hardly open a scientific journal or any popular essay on Natural History, without meeting some allusion to the Ascidians as our ancestors. Not only was it seized upon by the many amateur contributors to the literature of this subject, but Darwin himself, and his ardent followers, welcomed this first direct evidence of structural affinity between the Vertebrates and the lower animals.

The existence of these cells, though never thought of in this light before, was not unknown to naturalists. I have myself seen and examined them, and had intended to say something in this article of their nature and position; but while I was preparing it for the press the subject was taken from me and treated by the hand of a master whom all naturalists venerate. I have received very recently from the aged Nestor of the science of Embryology, K. E. von Baer, to whose early investigations I have already alluded, a pamphlet upon the development of the Ascidians as compared to that of the Vertebrates. There is something touching in the conditions under which he enters the lists with the younger men who have set aside the great laws of typical structure, to the interpretation of which his whole life has been given. He is now very feeble and nearly blind; but the keen, far-reaching, internal sight is undimmed by age. With the precision and ease which only a complete familiarity with all the facts can give, he shows that the actual development of the Ascidians has no true homology with that of the Vertebrates; that the string of cells in the former— compared to the dorsal cord of the latter—does not run along the back at all, but is placed on the ventral side of the body. To say that the first Vertebrates or their progenitors carried their backbones in this fashion is about as reasonable as to say that they walked on their heads. It is reversing their whole structure, and putting their vertebral column where the abdominal cavity should be. Von Baer closes his paper in these words: "It will readily be granted that I have written for zoölogists and anatomists; but I may perhaps be blamed for being frequently very circumstantial where a brief allusion would have been sufficient. In so doing, I had the many dilletanti in view, who believe in complete transmutations, and who might be disposed to consider it mere conceit not to recognize the Ascidians as the ancestors of Man. I beg to apologize for some repetitions arising from this consideration for the dilletanti."

The other so-called discovery is that of Haeckel, that star-fishes are compound animals, made up, as it were, of worm-like beings united like rays in one organism. A similar opinion had already been entertained by Duvernoy, and in a measure also by Oken, who described the Echinoderms as Radiate-worms. This doctrine, if true, would at once establish a transition from Radiates to Articulates. There is, in the first place, not the slightest foundation for this assumption in the structure of the star-fish. The arms of these animals are made up of the same parts as the vertical zones of a sea-urchin and of all the Radiates, and have no resemblance whatever to the structure of the Worms. Each ambulacral zone of a star-fish or a sea-urchin is strictly homological to a structural segment of an Acaleph or to a radiating chamber of a Polyp. Moreover, the homology between a sea-urchin and a star-fish is complete; if one is an organic unit the other must be so also, and no one ever suggested that the sea-urchin was anything but a single organism. In comparing the Radiates with other animals, it is essential to place them in the same attitude, so that we compare like with like; otherwise, we make the mistake of the Russian naturalist, and compare the front side of one animal with the dorsal side of another, or the upper side of one with the lower side of another; thus taking mere superficial resemblance between totally distinct parts for true homologies. In all Mollusks, Articulates, and Vertebrates the parts are arranged along a longitudinal axis; in Radiates alone they are disposed around a vertical axis, like spherical wedges, comparable in some instances to the segments of an orange. This organic formula, for so we may call it, is differently expressed and more or less distinct in different Radiates. It may be built up in a sphere, as in the sea-urchins, or opened out into a star, like the five-finger; it may be in the form of a sac divided internally, as in the sea-anemones, or in that of a disk, channelled or furrowed so as to divide it into equal segments, like the jelly-fish; but upon comparison the same structural elements are found in all. These structural elements bear an identical relation to the vertical axis of the animals. To compare any Radiate with any Articulate is therefore to compare the vertical axis of one animal with the horizontal axis of the other. The parallelism will not bear examination any more than that between the Mollusks and Vertebrates. Even in those holothurians and sea-urchins in which one side of the body is flattened, the structure exhibits the same plan and the parts are arranged in the same way as in all other Radiates, whatever be their natural attitude in the element in which they live; whether they stand upright with the mouth turned upward, or hang down in the reverse position, or crawl about horizontally. In like manner the vertical position of man in no way invalidates the homology of his organization with that of the fishes, reptiles, birds, and mammalia. These two cases are thus far the only instances which have been brought forward to prove actual structural affinity between distinct primary divisions of the animal kingdom.

It is not my intention to take up categorically all the different points on which the modern theory of transmutation is based. Metamorphosis plays a large part in it, and is treated as an evidence of transition from one animal into another. The truth is that metamorphosis, like all embryonic growth, is a normal process of development, moving in regular cycles, returning always to the same starting-point, and leading always to the same end; such are the alternative generations in the lower animals and the metamorphoses in higher ones, as in the butterflies and other insects, or in certain reptiles, frogs and toads, salamanders, and the like. In some of these types the development lasts for a long time and the stages of embryonic growth are often so distinct that, until the connection between them is traced, each phase may seem like a separate existence, whereas they are only chapters in one and the same life. I have myself watched carefully all the successive changes of development in the North American Axolotl, whose recently discovered metamorphoses have led to much discussion in connection with the modern doctrine of evolution. I can see no difference between this and other instances of metamorphosis. Certain organs, conspicuous in one phase of the animal's life, are resorbed and disappear in a succeeding phase. But this does not differ at all from like processes in the toads and frogs, for instance; nor does it even differ essentially from like processes in the ordinary growth of all animals. The higher Vertebrates, including man himself, breathe through gill-like organs in the early part of their life. These gills disappear and give place to lungs only in a later phase of their existence. Metamorphoses have all the constancy and invariability of other modes of embryonic growth, and have never been known to lead to any transition of one species into another.

Another fertile topic in connection with this theory is that of heredity. No one can deny that inheritance is a powerful factor in the maintenance of race and in the improvement of breeds and varieties. But it has never been known that acquired qualities, even though retained through successive generations, have led to the production of new species. Darwin's attractive style is never more alluring than in connection with this subject. His concise and effective phrases have the weight of aphorisms and pass current for principles, when they may be only unfounded assertions. Such is "the survival of the fittest." After reading some chapters of The Descent of Man, could any one doubt, unless indeed he happened to be familiar with the facts, that animals, possessing certain advantages over others, are necessarily winners in the race for life? And yet it is not true that, outside of the influence of man, there are, in nature, privileged individuals among animals capable of holding on to a positive gain, generation after generation, and of transmitting successfully their peculiarities until they become the starting point for another step; the descendants losing at last, through this cumulative process, all close resemblance to their progenitors. It is not true that a slight variation, among the successive offspring of the same stock, goes on increasing until the difference amounts to a specific distinction. On the contrary, it is a matter of fact that extreme variations finally degenerate or become sterile; like monstrosities they die out, or return to their type.

The whole subject of inheritance is exceedingly intricate, working often in a seemingly capricious and fitful way. Qualities, both good and bad, are dropped as well as acquired, and the process ends sometimes in the degradation of the type and the survival of the unfit rather than the fittest. The most trifling and fantastic tricks of inheritance are quoted in support of the transmutation theory; but little is said of the sudden apparition of powerful original qualities which almost always rise like pure creations and are gone with their day and generation. The noblest gifts are exceptional, and are rarely inherited; this very fact seems to me an evidence of something more and higher than mere evolution and transmission concerned in the problem of life.

In the same way, the matter of natural and sexual selection is susceptible of very various interpretations. No doubt, on the whole, Nature protects her best. But it would not be difficult to bring together an array of facts as striking as those produced by the evolutionists in favor of their theory, to show that sexual selection is by no means always favorable to the elimination of the chaff and the preservation of the wheat. A natural attraction, independent of strength or beauty, is an unquestionable element in this problem, and its action is seen among animals as well as among men. The fact that fine progeny are not infrequently the offspring of weak parents and *vice versa* points perhaps to some innate power of redress by which the caprices of choice are counterbalanced. But there can be no doubt that types are as often endangered as protected by the so-called law of sexual selection.

As to the influence of climate and physical conditions, we all know their power for evil and for good upon living beings. But there is, nevertheless, nothing more striking in the whole book of nature than the power shown by types and species to resist physical conditions. Endless evidence may be brought from the whole expanse of land and air and water, showing that identical physical conditions will do nothing toward the merging of species into one another, neither will variety of conditions do anything toward their multiplication. One thing only we know absolutely, and in this treacherous, marshy ground of hypothesis and assumption, it is pleasant to plant one's foot occasionally upon a solid fact here and there. Whatever be the means of preserving and transmitting properties, the primitive types have remained permanent and unchanged—in the long succession of ages amid all the appearance and disappearance of kinds, the fading away of one species and the coming in of another—from the earliest geological periods of the present day. How these types were first introduced, how the species which have successively represented them have replaced one another,—these are the vital questions to which no answer has been given. We are as far from any satisfactory solution of this problem as if development theories had never been discussed.

This brings us to the geological side of the question. As a palæontologist I have from the beginning stood aloof from this new theory of transmutation, now so widely admitted by the scientific world. Its doctrines, in fact, contradict what the animal forms buried in the rocky strata of our earth tell us of their own introduction and succession upon the surface of the globe. Let us therefore hear them;—for, after all, their testimony is that of the eye-witness and the actor in the scene. Take first the type to which we ourselves belong. If it be true that there has been a progressive transmutation of the whole type of Vertebrates, beginning with the lowest and culminating in the highest, the earlier should of course be structurally inferior to the later ones. What then is the lowest living Vertebrate? Every zoölogist will answer, The Amphioxus, that elongated, worm-like Vertebrate whose organization is nothing more than a dorsal cord, with a nervous thread above, and a respiratory and digestive cavity below, containing also the reproductive organs, the whole being clothed in flesh. Yet low as it is in the scale of life, the Amphioxus is, by virtue of its vertebral column, a member of the same type as ourselves. Next to the Amphioxus come the Myxinoids, structurally but little above them, and the Lamper-eels. These are the ani-

mals which Hæckel places at the base of his zoölogical tree, rooting the whole Vertebrate branch of the animal kingdom in the Amphioxus as the forefather (Stamm-Vater) of the type. Let us look now at the earliest Vertebrates, as known and recorded in geological surveys. They should of course, if there is any truth in the transmutation theory, correspond with the lowest in rank or standing. What then are the earliest known Vertebrates? They are Selachians (sharks and their allies) and Ganoids (garpikes and the like), the highest of all living fishes, structurally speaking. I shall be answered that these belong to the Silurian and Devonian periods, and that it is believed that Vertebrates may have existed before that time. It will also be argued that Myzonts, namely Amphioxus, Myxinoids, and Lamper-eels, have no hard parts and could not have been preserved on that account. I will grant both these points, though the fact is that the Myzonts do possess solid parts, in the jaws, as capable of preservation as any bone, and that these solid parts, if ever found, even singly, would be as significant, for a zoölogist, as the whole skeleton. Granting also that Amphioxus-like fishes may have lived and may have disappeared before the Silurian period; the Silurian deposits follow immediately upon those in which life first appeared, and should therefore contain not the highest fishes, but the fishes next in order to the Myzonts, and these are certainly neither the Ganoids not the Selachians. The presence of the Selachians at the dawn of life upon earth is in direct contradiction to the idea of a gradual progressive development. They are nevertheless exceedingly abundant in the Palæozoic beds, and these fossil forms are so similar to the living representatives of the same group that what is true of the organization and development of the latter is unquestionably equally true of the former. In all their features the Selachians, more than any other fishes, resemble the higher animals. They lay few eggs, the higher kinds giving birth only to three, four, or five at a brood, whereas the common fishes lay myriads of eggs, hundreds of thousands in some instances, and these are for the greater part cast into the water to be developed at random. The limitation of the young is unquestionably a mark of superiority. The higher we rise in the scale of animal life the more restricted is the number of offspring. In proportion to this reduction in number, the connection of the offspring with the parent is drawn closer, organically and morally, till this relation becomes finally the foundation of all social organization, of all human civilization. In some Selachians there is an actual organic connection between parent and progeny, resembling the placental connection which marks the embryonic development of the higher Vertebrates. This feature is in harmony with the sexual relations among them; for it is of all facts in their organic history the most curious, that, among Vertebrates, the Selachians are the only ones with whom the connection of the sexes recalls that of the human family. Now, these higher fishes being the first representatives of the Vertebrates on earth, or at least those next following their earliest representatives, where do we find the Myzonts, fishes which are structurally inferior to all others, and of which the Amphioxus is the lowest member? They come in during the latest period of our world's history, with what is called the present period, to which we ourselves belong. This certainly does not look like a connected series beginning with the lowest and ending with the highest, for the highest fishes come first and the lowest come last.

The companions of the Selachians in the earlier geological periods, the Ganoids, belong also to the higher representatives of the class of fishes. Some of them have the ball-and-socket vertebral joint of the reptiles and birds, enabling the head to move upon the neck with greater freedom than in the lower fishes. I am aware that these synthetic and prophetic types, which I have myself been the first to point out, and in which features of higher and later groups are combined or hinted at in lower and earlier ones, have been interpreted as transition types. It has even been said that I have myself furnished the strongest evidence of the transmutation theory. This might perhaps be so, did these types follow, instead of preceding, the lower fishes. But the whole history of geological succession shows us that the lowest in structure is by no means necessarily the earliest in time, either in the Vertebrate type or any other. Synthetic and prophetic types have accompanied the introduction of all the primary divisions of the animal kingdom. With these may be found what I have called embryonic types, which never rise, even in their adult state, above those conditions which in higher structures are but the prelude to the adult state. It may, therefore, truly be said that a great diversity of types has existed from the beginning.

The most advanced Darwinians seem reluctant to acknowledge the intervention of an intellectual power in the diversity which obtains in nature, under the plea that such an admission implies distinct creative acts for every species. What of it, if it were true? Have those who object to repeated acts of creation ever considered that no progress can be made in knowledge without repeated acts of thinking? And what are thoughts but specific acts of the mind? Why should it then be unscientific to infer that the facts of nature are the result of a similar process, since there is no evidence of any other cause? The world has arisen in some way or other. How it originated is the great question, and Darwin's theory, like all other attempts to explain the origin of life, is thus far merely conjectural. I believe he has not even made the best conjecture possible in the present state of our knowledge.

The more I look at the great complex of the animal world, the more sure do I feel that we have not yet reached its hidden meaning, and the more do I regret that the young and ardent spirits of our day give themselves to speculation rather than to close and accurate investigation.

I hope in future articles to show, first, that, however broken the geological record may be, there is a complete sequence in many parts of it, from which the character of the succession may be ascertained; secondly, that, since the most exquisitely delicate structures, as well as embryonic phases of growth of the most perishable nature, have been preserved from very early deposits, we have no right to infer the disappearance of types because their absence disproves some favorite theory; and, lastly, that there is no evidence of a direct descent of later from earlier species in the geological succession of animals.

Name: _____ **Date:** _____

1. Agassiz claims that there is only one instance in which researchers have demonstrated development in animals. What is that instance and how does it differ from evolution?

2. Despite his antagonism toward Darwin's theory of natural selection, Agassiz said he was pleased that Darwin published *The Expression of Emotions in Man and Animal.* Why was he happy about its publication?

3. How novel does Agassiz think Darwin's work was?

Name: _____ **Date:** _____

4. Agassiz describes a number of problems about which biological researchers know very little. List and describe in your own words two of these problems:

1.

2.

Thomas H. Huxley

"The Darwinian Hypothesis," 1859

Huxley (1825-1895), widely known as "Darwin's bulldog" for his aggressive promotion of Darwin's work, published this piece within weeks of the release of the first edition of *On the Origin of Species*. Fourteen years younger than Darwin and much more eager to enter into public debates over evolution, Huxley quickly became Darwin's representative to public and professional audiences. In this piece, Huxley sets out to support Darwin's argument in *Origin* by demonstrating the problems that exist for natural theology and for those who believe that species are not mutable.

The hypothesis of which the present work of Mr. Darwin is but the preliminary outline, may be stated in his own language as follows:—"Species originated by means of natural selection, or through the preservation of the favoured races in the struggle for life." To render this thesis intelligible, it is necessary to interpret its terms. In the first place, what is a species? The question is a simple one, but the right answer to it is hard to find, even if we appeal to those who should know most about it. It is all those animals or plants which have descended from a single pair of parents; it is the smallest distinctly definable group of living organisms; it is an eternal and immutable entity; it is a mere abstraction of the human intellect having no existence in nature. Such are a few of the significations attached to this simple word which may be culled from authoritative sources; and if, leaving terms and theoretical subtleties aside, we turn to facts and endeavour to gather a meaning for ourselves, by studying the things to which, in practice, the name of species is applied, it profits us little. For practice varies as much as theory. Let two botanists or two zoologists examine and describe the productions of a country, and one will pretty certainly disagree with the other as to the number, limits, and definitions of the species into which he groups the very same things. In these islands, we are in the habit of regarding mankind as of one species, but a fortnight's steam will land us in a country where divines and savants, for once in agreement, vie with one another in loudness of assertion, if not in cogency of proof, that men are of different species; and, more particularly, that the species negro is so distinct from our own that the Ten Commandments have actually no reference to him. Even in the calm region of entomology, where, if anywhere in this sinful world, passion and prejudice should fail to stir the mind, one learned coleopterist will fill ten attractive volumes with descriptions of species of beetles, nine-tenths of which are immediately declared by his brother beetle-mongers to be no species at all.

The truth is that the number of distinguishable living creatures almost surpasses imagination. At least 100,000 such kinds of insects alone have been described and may be identified in collections, and the number of separable kinds of living things is under-estimated at half a million. Seeing that most of these obvious kinds have their accidental varieties, and that they often shade into others by imperceptible degrees, it may well be imagined that the task of distinguishing between what is permanent and what fleeting, what is a species and what a mere variety, is sufficiently formidable.

But is it not possible to apply a test whereby a true species may be known from a mere variety? Is there no criterion of species? Great authorities affirm that there is—that the unions of members of the same species are always fertile, while those of distinct species are either sterile, or their offspring, called hybrids, are so. It is affirmed not only that this is an experimental fact, but that it is a provision

From *The Times*, 12/26/1859.

for the preservation of the purity of species. Such a criterion as this would be invaluable; but, unfortunately, not only is it not obvious how to apply it in the great majority of cases in which its aid is needed, but its general validity is stoutly denied. The Hon. and Rev. Mr. Herbert, a most trustworthy authority, not only asserts as the result of his own observations and experiments that many hybrids are quite as fertile as the parent species, but he goes so far as to assert that the particular plant *Crinum capense* is much more fertile when crossed by a distinct species than when fertilised by its proper pollen! On the other hand, the famous Gaertner, though he took the greatest pains to cross the Primrose and the Cowslip, succeeded only once or twice in several years; and yet it is a well-established fact that the Primrose and the Cowslip are only varieties of the same kind of plant. Again, such cases as the following are well established. The female of species A, if crossed with the male of species B, is fertile; but, if the female of B is crossed with the male of A, she remains barren. Facts of this kind destroy the value of the supposed criterion.

If, weary of the endless difficulties involved in the determination of species, the investigator, contenting himself with the rough practical distinction of separable kinds, endeavours to study them as they occur in nature—to ascertain their relations to the conditions which surround them, their mutual harmonies and discordancies of structure, the bond of union of their present and their past history, he finds himself, according to the received notions, in a mighty maze, and with, at most, the dimmest adumbration of a plan. If he starts with any one clear conviction, it is that every part of a living creature is cunningly adapted to some special use in its life. Has not his Paley told him that that seemingly useless organ, the spleen, is beautifully adjusted as so much packing between the other organs? And yet, at the outset of his studies, he finds that no adaptive reason whatsoever can be given for one-half of the peculiarities of vegetable structure. He also discovers rudimentary teeth, which are never used, in the gums of the young calf and in those of the fœtal whale; insects which never bite have rudimental jaws, and others which never fly have rudimental wings; naturally blind creatures have rudimental eyes; and the halt have rudimentary limbs. So, again, no animal or plant puts on its perfect form at once, but all have to start from the same point, however various the course which each has to pursue. Not only men and horses, and cats and dogs, lobsters and beetles, periwinkles an mussels, but even the very sponges and animalcules commence their existence under forms which are essentially undistinguishable; and this is true of all the infinite variety of plants. Nay,

more, all living beings march, side by side, along the high road of development, and separate the later the more like they are; like people leaving church, who all go down the aisle, but having reached the door, some turn into the parsonage, others go down the village, and others part only in the next parish. A man in his development runs for a little while parallel with, though never passing through, the form of the meanest worm, then travels for a space beside the fish, then journeys along with the bird and the reptile for his fellow travellers; and only at last, after a brief companionship with the highest of the four-footed and four-handed world, rises into the dignity of pure manhood. No competent thinker of the present day dreams of explaining these indubitable facts by the notion of the existence of unknown and undiscoverable adaptations to purpose. And we would remind those who, ignorant of the facts, must be moved by authority, that no one has asserted the incompetence of the doctrine of final causes, in its application to physiology and anatomy, more strongly than our own eminent anatomist, Professor Owen, who, speaking of such cases, says ("On the Nature of Limbs," pp. 39, 40)—"I think it will be obvious that the principle of final adaptations fails to satisfy all the conditions of the problem."

But, if the doctrine of final causes will not help us to comprehend the anomalies of living structure, the principle of adaptation must surely lead us to understand why certain living beings are found in certain regions of the world and not in others. The Palm, as we know, will not grow in our climate, nor the Oak in Greenland. The white bear cannot live where the tiger thrives, nor *vice versâ,* and the more the natural habits of animal and vegetable species are examined, the more do they seem, on the whole, limited to particular provinces. But when we look into the facts established by the study of the geographical distribution of animals and plants it seems utterly hopeless to attempt to understand the strange and apparently capricious relations which they exhibit. One would be inclined to suppose *à priori* that every country must be naturally peopled by those animals that are fittest to live and thrive in it. And yet how, on this hypothesis, are we to account for the absence of cattle in the Pampas of South America, when those parts of the New World were discovered? It is not that they were unfit for cattle, for millions of cattle now run wild there; and the like holds good of Australia and New Zealand. It is a curious circumstance, in fact, that the animals and plants of the Northern Hemisphere are not only as well adapted to live in the Southern Hemisphere as its own autochthones, but are, in many cases, absolutely better adapted, and so overrun and extirpate the aborigines. Clearly, therefore, the species which naturally inhabit a country are not necessarily the best adapted to its climate and other conditions. The inhabitants of islands are often distinct from any other known species of animal or plants (witness our recent examples from the work of Sir Emerson Tennent, on Ceylon), and yet they have almost always a sort of general family resemblance to the animals and plants of the nearest mainland. On the other hand, there is hardly a species of fish, shell, or crab common to the opposite sides of the narrow isthmus of Panama. Wherever we look, then, living nature offers us riddles of difficult solution, if we suppose that what we see is all that can be known of it.

But our knowledge of life is not confined to the existing world. Whatever their minor differences, geologists are agreed as to the vast thickness of the accumulated strata which compose the visible part of our earth, and the inconceivable immensity of the time the lapse of which they are the imperfect but the only accessible witnesses. Now, throughout the greater part of this long series of stratified rocks are scattered, sometimes very abundantly, multitudes of organic remains, the fossilised exuviæ of animals and plants which lived and died while the mud of which the rocks are formed was yet soft ooze, and could receive and bury them. It would be a great error to suppose that these organic remains were fragmentary relics. Our museums exhibit fossil shells of immeasurable antiquity, as perfect as the day they were formed; whole skeletons without a limb disturbed; nay, the changed flesh, the developing embryos, and even the very footsteps of primæval organisms. Thus the naturalist finds in the bowels of the earth species as well defined as, and in some groups of animals more numerous than, those which breathe the upper air. But, singularly enough, the majority of these entombed species are wholly distinct from those that now live. Nor is this unlikeness without its rule and order. As a broad fact, the further we go back in time the less the buried species are like existing forms; and, the further apart the sets of extinct creatures are, the less they are like one another. In other words, there has been a regular succession of living beings, each younger set, being in a very broad and general sense, somewhat more like those which now live.

It was once supposed that this succession had been the result of vast successive catastrophes, destructions, and re-creations *en masse;* but catastrophes are now almost eliminated from geological, or at least palæontological speculation; and it is admitted, on all hands, that the seeming breaks in the chain of being are not absolute, but only relative to our imperfect knowledge; that species have replaced species, not in assemblages, but one by one; and that, if it were possible to have all the phenomena of the past presented to us, the convenient epochs and formations of the geologist, though having a certain distinctness, would fade into one another with limits as undefinable as those of the distinct and yet separable colours of the solar spectrum.

Such is a brief summary of the main truths which have been established concerning species. Are these truths ultimate and irresolvable facts, or are their complexities and perplexities the mere expressions of a higher law?

A large number of persons practically assume the former position to be correct. They believe that the writer of the Pentateuch was empowered and commissioned to teach us scientific as well as other truth, that the account we find there of the creation of living things is simply and literally correct, and that anything which seems to contradict it is, by the nature of the case, false. All the phenomena which have been detailed are, on this view, the immediate product of a creative fiat and, consequently, are out of the domain of science altogether.

Whether this view prove ultimately to be true or false, it is, at any rate, not at present supported by what is commonly regarded as logical proof, even if it be capable of discussion by reason; and hence we consider ourselves at liberty to pass it by, and to turn to those views which profess to rest on a scientific basis only, and therefore admit of being argued to their consequences. And we do this with the less hesitation as it so happens that those persons who are practically conversant with the facts of the case (plainly a considerable advantage) have always thought fit to range themselves under the latter category.

The majority of these competent persons have up to the present time maintained two positions—the first, that every species is, within certain defined limits, fixed and incapable of modification; the second, that every species was originally produced by a distinct creative act. The second position is obviously incapable of proof or disproof, the direct operations of the Creator not being subjects of science; and it must therefore be regarded as a corollary from the first, the truth or falsehood of which is a matter of evidence. Most persons imagine that the arguments in favour of it are overwhelming; but to some few minds, and these, it must be confessed, intellects of no small power and grasp of knowledge, they have not brought conviction. Among these minds, that of the famous naturalist Lamarck, who possessed a greater acquaintance with the lower forms of life than any man of his day, Cuvier not expected, and was a good botanist to boot, occupies a prominent place.

Two facts appear to have strongly affected the course of thought of this remarkable man—the one, that finer or stronger links of affinity connect all living beings with one another, and that thus the highest creature grades by multitudinous steps into the lowest; the other, that an organ may be developed in particular directions by exerting itself in particular ways, and that modifications once induced may be transmitted and become hereditary. Putting these facts together, Lamarck endeavoured to account for the first by the operation of the second. Place an animal in new circumstances, says he, and its needs will be altered; the new needs will create new desires, and the attempt to gratify such desires will result in an appropriate modification of the organs exerted. Make a man a blacksmith, and his brachial muscles will develop in accordance with the demands made upon them, and in like manner, says Lamarck, "the efforts of some short-necked bird to catch fish without wetting himself have, with time and perseverance, given rise to all our herons and long-necked waders."

The Lamarckian hypothesis has long since been justly condemned, and it is the established practice for every tyro to raise his heel against the carcase of the dead lion. But it is rarely either wise or instructive to treat even the errors of a really great man with mere ridicule, and in the present case the logical form of the doctrine stands on a very different footing from its substance.

If species have really arisen by the operation of natural conditions, we ought to be able to find those conditions now at work; we ought to be able to discover in nature some power adequate to modify any given kind of animal or plant in such a manner as to give rise to another kind, which would be admitted by naturalists as a distinct species. Lamarck imagined that he had discovered this *versa causa* in the admitted facts that some organs may be modified by exercise; and that modifications, once produced, are capable of hereditary transmission. It does not seem to have occurred to him to inquire whether there is any reason to believe that there are any limits to the amount of modification producible, or to ask how long an animal is likely to endeavour to gratify an impossible desire. The bird, in our example, would surely have renounced fish dinners long before it had produced the least effect on leg or neck.

Since Lamarck's time, almost all competent naturalists have left speculations on the origin of species to such dreamers as the author of the "Vestiges," by whose well-intentioned efforts the Lamarckian theory received its final condemnation in the minds of all sound thinkers. Notwithstanding this silence, however, the transmutation theory, as it has been called, has been a "skeleton in the closet" to many

an honest zoologist and botanist who had a soul above the mere naming of dried plants and skins. Surely, has such an one thought, nature is a mighty and consistent whole, and the providential order established in the world of life must, if we could only see it rightly, be consistent with that dominant over the multiform shapes of brute matter. But what is the history of astronomy, of all the branches of physics, of chemistry, of medicine, but a narration of the steps by which the human mind has been compelled, often sorely against its will, to recognise the operation of secondary causes in events where ignorance beheld an immediate intervention of a higher power? And when we know that living things are formed of the same elements as the inorganic world, that they act and react upon it, bound by a thousand ties of natural piety, is it probable, nay is it possible, that they, and they alone, should have no order in their seeming disorder, no unity in their seeming multiplicity, should suffer no explanation by the discovery of some central and sublime law of mutual connection?

Questions of this kind have assuredly often arisen, but it might have been long before they received such expression as would have commanded the respect and attention of the scientific world, had it not been for the publication of the work which prompted this article. Its author, Mr. Darwin, inheritor of a once celebrated name, won his spurs in science when most of those now distinguished were young men, and has for the last twenty years held a place in the front ranks of British philosophers. After a circumnavigatory voyage, undertaken solely for the love of his science, Mr. Darwin published a series of researches which at once arrested the attention of naturalists and geologists; his generalisations have since received ample confirmation and now command universal assent, nor is it questionable that they have had the most important influence on the progress of science. More recently Mr. Darwin, with a versatility which is among the rarest of gifts, turned his attention to a most difficult question of zoology and minute anatomy; and no living naturalist and anatomist has published a better monograph than that which resulted from his labours. Such a man, at all events, has not entered the sanctuary with unwashed hands, and when he lays before us the results of twenty years' investigation and reflection we must listen even though we be disposed to strike. But, in reading his work, it must be confessed that the attention which might at first be dutifully, soon becomes willingly, given, so clear is the author's thought, so outspoken his conviction, so honest and fair the candid expression of his doubts. Those who would judge the book must read it: we shall endeavour only to make its line of argument and its philosophical position intelligible to the general reader in our own way.

The Baker Street Bazaar has just been exhibiting its familiar annual spectacle. Straight-backed, small-headed, big-barrelled oxen, as dissimilar from any wild species as can well be imagined, contended for attention and praise with sheep of half-a-dozen different breeds and styes of bloated preposterous pigs, no more like a wild boar or sow than a city alderman is like an ourang-outang. The cattle show has been, and perhaps may again be, succeeded by a poultry show, of whose crowing and clucking prodigies it can only be certainly predicated that they will be very unlike the aboriginal *Phasianus gallus*. If the seeker after animal anomalies is not satisfied, a turn or two in Seven Dials will convince him that the breeds of pigeons are quite as extraordinary and unlike one another and their parent stock, while the Horticultural Society will provide him any number of corresponding vegetable aberrations from nature's types. He will learn with no little surprise, too, in the course of his travels, that the proprietors and producers of these animal and vegetable anomalies regard them as distinct species, with a firm belief, the strength of which is exactly proportioned to their ignorance of scientific biology, and which is the more remarkable as they are all proud of their skill in originating such "species."

On careful inquiry it is found that all these, and the many other artificial breeds or races of animals and plants, have been produced by one method. The breeder—and a skilful one must be a person of much sagacity and natural or acquired perceptive faculty—notes some slight difference, arising he knows not how, in some individuals of his stock. If he wish to perpetuate the difference, to form a breed with the peculiarity in question strongly marked, he selects such male and female individuals as exhibit the desired character, and breeds from them. Their offspring are then carefully examined, and those which exhibit the peculiarity the most distinctly are selected for breeding; and this operation is repeated until the desired amount of divergence from the primitive stock is reached. It is then found that by continuing the process of selection—always breeding, that is, from well-marked forms, and allowing no impure crosses to interfere—a race may be formed, the tendency of which to reproduce itself is exceedingly strong; nor is the limit to the amount of divergence which may be thus produced known; but one thing is certain, that, if certain breeds of dogs, or of pigeons, or of horses, were known only in a fossil state, no naturalist would hesitate in regarding them as distinct species.

But in all these cases we have human interference. Without the breeder there would be no selection, and without the selection no race. Before admitting the possibility of natural species having originated in any similar way, it must be proved that there is in Nature some power which takes the place of man, and performs a selection *suâ sponte*. It is the claim of Mr. Darwin that he professes to have discovered the existence and the *modus operandi* of this "natural selection," as he terms it; and, if he be right, the process is perfectly simple and comprehensible, and irresistibly deducible from very familiar but well nigh forgotten facts.

Who, for instance, has duly reflected upon all the consequences of the marvellous struggle for existence which is daily and hourly going on among living beings? Not only does every animal live at the expense of some other animal or plant, but the very plants are at war. The ground is full of seeds that cannot rise into seedlings; the seedlings rob one another of air, light and water, the strongest robber winning the day, and extinguishing his competitors. Year after year, the wild animals with which man never interferes are, on the average, neither more nor less numerous than they were; and yet we know that the annual produce of every pair is from one to perhaps a million young; so that it is mathematically certain that, on the average, as many are killed by natural causes as are born every year, and those only escape which happen to be a little better fitted to resist destruction than those which die. The individuals of a species are like the crew of a foundered ship, and none but good swimmers have a chance of reaching the land.

Such being unquestionably the necessary conditions under which living creatures exist, Mr. Darwin discovers in them the instrument of natural selection. Suppose that in the midst of this incessant competition some individuals of a species (A) present accidental variations which happen to fit them a little better than their fellows for the struggle in which they are engaged, then the chances are in favour, not only of these individuals being better nourished than the others, but of their predominating over their fellows in other ways, and of having a better chance of leaving offspring, which will of course tend to reproduce the peculiarities of their parents. Their offspring will, by a parity of reasoning, tend to predominate over their contemporaries, and there being (suppose) no room for more than one species such as A, the weaker variety will eventually be destroyed by the new destructive influence which is thrown into the scale, and the stronger will take its place. Surrounding conditions remaining unchanged, the new variety (which we may call B)—supposed, for argument's sake, to be the best adapted for these conditions which can be got out of the original stock—will remain unchanged, all accidental deviations from the type becoming at once extinguished, as less fit for their post than B itself. The tendency of B to persist will grow with its persistence through successive generations, and it will acquire all the characters of a new species.

But, on the other hand, if the conditions of life change in any degree, however slight, B may no longer be that form which is best adapted to withstand their destructive, and profit by their sustaining, influence; in which case if it should give rise to a more competent variety (C), this will take its place and become a new species; and thus, by natural selection, the species B and C will be successively derived from A.

That this most ingenious hypothesis enables us to give a reason for many apparent anomalies in the distribution of living beings in time and space, and that it is not contradicted by the main phenomena of life and organisation appear to us to be unquestionable; and, so far, it must be admitted to have an immense advantage over any of its predecessors. But it is quite another matter to affirm absolutely either the truth or falsehood of Mr. Darwin's views at the present stage of the inquiry. Goethe has an excellent aphorism defining that state of mind which he calls "Thätige Skepsis"—active doubt. It is doubt which so loves truth that it neither dares rest in doubting, nor extinguish itself by unjustified belief; and we commend this state of mind to students of species, with respect to Mr. Darwin's or any other hypothesis, as to their origin. The combined investigations of another twenty years may, perhaps, enable naturalists to say whether the modifying causes and the selective power, which Mr. Darwin has satisfactorily shown to exist in Nature, are competent to produce all the effects he ascribes to them; or whether, on the other hand, he has been led to over-estimate the value of the principle of natural selection, as greatly as Lamarck over-estimated his *vera causa* of modification by exercise.

But there is, at all events, one advantage possessed by the more recent writer over his predecessor. Mr. Darwin abhors mere speculation as nature abhors a vacuum. He is as greedy of cases and precedents as any constitutional lawyer, and all the principles he lays down are capable of being brought to the test of observation and experiment. The path he bids us follow professes to be, not a mere airy track, fabricated of ideal cobwebs, but a solid and broad bridge of facts. If it be so, it will carry us safely over many a chasm in our knowledge, and lead us to a region free from the snares of those fascinating but barren virgins, the Final Causes, against whom a high authority has so justly warned us. "My sons, dig in the vineyard," were the last words of the old man in the fable: and, though the sons found no treasure, they made their fortunes by the grapes.

Name: _____ **Date:** _____

1. What, according to Huxley, is Darwin's argument in *The Origin of Species?* Explain it in your own words.

2. In support of Darwin's work, Huxley provides a number of examples that appear to undermine Paley's design argument. List and describe three of them:

1.

2.

3.

Name: _____ **Date:** _____

3. In addition to the existing world around us, what does Huxley claim can be used to study evolution?

4. Before Darwin, Huxley explains, "competent persons" have made two claims about the nature of living things. What are these two claims?

1.

2.

5. What, according to Huxley, makes Darwin and his work different than the authors and works on evolution that preceded him?

Asa Gray

"Natural Selection Not Inconsistent with Natural Theology," 1860

Gray (1810-1888) was an American botanist and the leading supporter of Darwin's theory of natural selection in the United States. In sharp contrast to those who portrayed evolution as incompatible with natural theology, Gray was convinced that natural selection could be a method by which an omnipotent God brought about new species and perfected pre-existing ones. In this piece he detailed his argument and demonstrated how one could fit Darwin's theory of natural selection into the widely popular idea of deism.

Novelties are enticing to most people; to us they are simply annoying. We cling to a long-accepted theory, just as we cling to an old suit of clothes. A new theory, like a new pair of breeches (the *Atlantic* still affects the older type of nether garment), is sure to have hard-fitting places; or, even when no particular fault can be found with the article, it oppresses with a sense of general discomfort. New notions and new styles worry us, till we get well used to them, which is only by slow degrees.

Wherefore, in Galileo's time, we might have helped to proscribe, or to burn—had he been stubborn enough to warrant cremation—even the great pioneer of inductive research; although, when we had fairly recovered our composure, and had leisurely excogitated the matter, we might have come to conclude that the new doctrine was better than the old one, after all, at least for those who had nothing to unlearn.

Such being our habitual state of mind, it may well be believed that the perusal of the new book "On the Origin of Species by Means of Natural Selection" left an uncomfortable impression, in spite of its plausible and winning ways. We were not wholly unprepared for it, as many of our contemporaries seem to have been. The scientific reading in which we indulge as a relaxation from severer studies had raised dim forebodings. Investigations about the succession of species in time, and their

actual geographical distribution over the earth's surface, were leading up from all sides and in various ways to the question of their origin. Now and then we encountered a sentence, like Prof. Owen's "axiom of the continuous operation of the ordained becoming of living things," which haunted us like an apparition. For, dim as our conception must needs be as to what such oracular and grandiloquent phrases might really mean, we felt confident that they presaged no good to old beliefs. Foreseeing, yet deprecating, the coming time of trouble, we still hoped that, with some repairs and makeshifts, the old views might last out our days. *Après nous le déluge.* Still, not to lag behind the rest of the world, we read the book in which the new theory is promulgated. We took it up, like our neighbors, and, as was natural, in a somewhat captious frame of mind.

Well, we found no cause of quarrel with the first chapter. Here the author takes us directly to the barn-yard and the kitchen-garden. Like an honorable rural member of our General Court, who sat silent until, near the close of a long session, a bill requiring all swine at large to wear pokes was introduced, when he claimed the privilege of addressing the house, on the proper ground that he had been "brought up among the pigs, and knew all about them"—so we were brought up among cows and cabbages; and the lowing of cattle, the cackle of hens, and the cooing of pigeons, were sounds native and pleasant to our ears. So "Variation under Domestication" dealt with familiar subjects in a

From *Atlantic Monthly,* 1860.

natural way, and gently introduced "Variation under Nature," which seemed likely enough. Then follows "Struggle for Existence"—a principle which we experimentally know to be true and cogent—bringing the comfortable assurance, that man, even upon Leviathan Hobbes's theory of society, is no worse than the rest of creation, since all Nature is at war, one species with another, and the nearer kindred the more internecine—bringing in thousandfold confirmation and extension of the Malthusian doctrine that population tends far to outrun means of subsistence throughout the animal and vegetable world, and has to be kept down by sharp preventive checks; so that not more than one of a hundred or a thousand of the individuals whose existence is so wonderfully and so sedulously provided for ever comes to anything, under ordinary circumstances; so the lucky and the strong must prevail, and the weaker and ill-favored must perish; and then follows, as naturally as one sheep follows another, the chapter on "Natural Selection," Darwin's *cheval de bataille,* which is very much the Napoleonic doctrine that Providence favors the strongest battalions—that, since many more individuals are born than can possibly survive, those individuals and those variations which possess any advantage, however slight, over the rest, are in the long-run sure to survive, to propagate, and to occupy the limited field, to the exclusion or destruction of the weaker brethren. All this we pondered, and could not much object to. In fact, we began to contract a liking for a system which at the outset illustrates the advantages of good breeding, and which makes the most "of every creature's best."

Could we "let by-gones be by-gones," and, beginning now, go on improving and diversifying for the future by natural selection, could we even take up the theory at the introduction of the actually existing species, we should be well content; and so, perhaps, would most naturalists be. It is by no means difficult to believe that varieties are incipient or possible species, when we see what trouble naturalists, especially botanists, have to distinguish between them—one regarding as a true species what another regards as a variety; when the progress of knowledge continually increases, rather than diminishes, the number of doubtful instances; and when there is less agreement than ever among naturalists as to what is the basis in Nature upon which our idea of species reposes, or how the word is to be defined. Indeed, when we consider the endless disputes of naturalists and ethnologists over the human races, as to whether they belong to one species or to more, and, if to more, whether to three, or five, or fifty, we can hardly help fancying that both

may be right—or rather, that the uni-humanitarians would have been right many thousand years ago, and the multi-humanitarians will be several thousand years later; while at present the safe thing to say is, that probably there is some truth on both sides.

"Natural selection," Darwin remarks, "leads to divergence of character; for the more living beings can be supported on the same area, the more they diverge in structure, habits, and constitution" (a principle which, by-the-way, is paralleled and illustrated by the diversification of human labor); and also leads to much extinction of intermediate or unimproved forms. Now, though this divergence may "steadily tend to increase," yet this is evidently a slow process in Nature, and liable to much counteraction wherever man does not interpose, and so not likely to work much harm for the future. And if natural selection, with artificial to help it, will produce better animals and better men than the present, and fit them better "to the conditions of existence," why, let it work, say we, to the top of its bent. There is still room enough for improvement. Only let us hope that it always works for good: if not, the divergent lines on Darwin's lithographic diagram of "Transmutation made Easy," ominously show what small deviations from the straight path may come to in the end.

The prospect of the future, accordingly, is on the whole pleasant and encouraging. It is only the backward glance, the gaze up the long vista of the past, that reveals anything alarming. Here the lines converge as they recede into the geological ages, and point to conclusions which, upon the theory, are inevitable, but hardly welcome. The very first step backward makes the negro and the Hottentot our blood-relations—not that reason or Scripture objects to that, though pride may. The next suggests a closer association of our ancestors of the olden time with "our poor relations" of the quadrumanous family than we like to acknowledge. Fortunately, however—even if we must account for him scientifically—man with his two feet stands upon a foundation of his own. Intermediate links between the *Bimana* and the *Quadrumana* are lacking altogether; so that, put the genealogy of the brutes upon what footing you will, the four-handed races will not serve for our forerunners—at least, not until some monkey, live or fossil, is producible with great-toes, instead of thumbs, upon his nether extremities; or until some lucky geologist turns up the bones of his ancestor and prototype in France or England, who was so busy "napping the chuckie-stanes" and chipping out flint knives and arrow-heads in the time of the drift, very many ages ago—before the British Channel existed, says Lyell[1]—and until these men of the olden time are shown to have worn their great-toes in the divergent and thumblike fashion. That would be evidence indeed: but, until some testimony of the sort is produced, we must needs believe in the separate and special creation of man, however it may have been with the lower animals and with plants.

No doubt, the full development and symmetry of Darwin's hypothesis strongly suggest the evolution of the human no less than the lower animal races out of some simple primordial animal—that all are equally "lineal descendants of some few beings which lived long before the first bed of the Silurian system was deposited." But, as the author speaks disrespectfully of spontaneous generation, and accepts a supernatural beginning of life on earth, in some form or forms of being which included potentially all that have since existed and are yet to be, he is thereby not warranted to extend his inferences beyond the evidence or the fair probability. There seems as great likelihood that one special origination should be followed by another upon fitting occasion (such as the introduction of man), as that one form should be transmuted into another upon fitting occasion, as, for instance, in the succession of species which differ from each other only in some details. To compare small things with great in a homely illustration: man alters from time to time his instruments or machines, as new circumstances or conditions may require and his wit suggest. Minor alterations and improvements he adds to the machine he possesses; he adapts a new rig or a new rudder to an old boat: this answers to *Variation.* "Like begets like," being the great rule in Nature, if boats could engender, the variations would doubtless be propagated, like those of domestic cattle. In course of time the old ones would be worn out or wrecked; the best sorts would be chosen for each particular use, and further improved upon; and so the primordial boat be developed into the scow, the skiff, the sloop, and other species of water-craft—the very diversification, as well as the successive improvements, entailing the disappearance of intermediate forms, less adapted to any one particular purpose; wherefore these go slowly out of use, and become extinct species: this is *Natural Selection.* Now, let a great and important advance be made, like that of steam navigation: here, though the en-

gine might be added to the old vessel, yet the wiser and therefore the actual way is to make a new vessel on a modified plan: this may answer to *Specific Creation.* Anyhow, the one does not necessarily exclude the other. Variation and natural selection may play their part, and so may specific creation also. Why not?

This leads us to ask for the reasons which call for this new theory of transmutation. The beginning of things must needs lie in obscurity, beyond the bounds of proof, though within those of conjecture or of analogical inference. Why not hold fast to the customary view, that all species were directly, instead of indirectly, created after their respective kinds, as we now behold them—and that in a manner which, passing our comprehension, we intuitively refer to the supernatural? Why this continual striving after "the unattained and dim?" why these anxious endeavors, especially of late years, by naturalists and philosophers of various schools and different tendencies, to penetrate what one of them calls "that mystery of mysteries," the origin of species?

To this, in general, sufficient answer may be found in the activity of the human intellect, "the delirious yet divine desire to know," stimulated as it has been by its own success in unveiling the laws and processes of inorganic Nature; in the fact that the principal triumphs of our age in physical science have consisted in tracing connections where none were known before, in reducing heterogeneous phenomena to a common cause or origin, in a manner quite analogous to that of the reduction of supposed independently originated species to a common ultimate origin—thus, and in various other ways, largely and legitimately extending the domain of secondary causes. Surely the scientific mind of an age which contemplates the solar system as evolved from a common revolving fluid mass—which, through experimental research, has come to regard light, heat, electricity, magnetism, chemical affinity, and mechanical power as varieties or derivative and convertible forms of one force, instead of independent species—which has brought the so-called elementary kinds of matter, such as the metals, into kindred groups, and pertinently raised the question, whether the members of each group may not be mere varieties of one species—and which speculates steadily in the direction of the ultimate unity of matter, of a sort of prototype or simple element which may be to the ordinary species of matter what the *Protozoa* or what the component cells of an organism are to the higher sorts of animals and plants—the mind of such an age cannot be expected to let the old belief about species pass unquestioned. It will raise the question,

---

[1]*Vide* "Proceedings of the British Association for the Advancement of Science," 1859, and London *Athenæum, passim.* It appears to be conceded that these "celts" or stone knives are artificial productions, and apparently of the age of the mammoth, the fossil rhinoceros, etc.

how the diverse sorts of plants and animals came to be as they are and where they are, and will allow that the whole inquiry transcends its powers only when all endeavors have failed. Granting the origin to be supernatural, or miraculous even, will not arrest the inquiry. All real origination, the philosophers will say, is supernatural; their very question is, whether we have yet gone back to the origin, and can affirm that the present forms of plants and animals are the primordial, the miraculously created ones. And, even if they admit that, they will still inquire into the order of the phenomena, into the form of the miracle. You might as well expect the child to grow up content with what it is told about the advent of its infant brother. Indeed, to learn that the new-comer is the gift of God, far from lulling inquiry, only stimulates speculation as to how the precious gift was bestowed. That questioning child is father to the man—is philosopher in short-clothes.

Since, then, questions about the origin of species will be raised, and have been raised—and since the theorizings, however different in particulars, all proceed upon the notion that one species of plant or animal is somehow derived from another, that the different sorts which now flourish are lineal (or unlineal) descendants of other and earlier sorts—it now concerns us to ask, What are the grounds in Nature, the admitted facts, which suggest hypotheses of derivation in some shape or other? Reasons there must be, and plausible ones, for the persistent recurrence of theories upon this genetic basis. A study of Darwin's book, and a general glance at the present state of the natural sciences, enable us to gather the following as among the most suggestive and influential. We can only enumerate them here, without much indication of their particular bearing. There is—

1. The general fact of variability, and the general tendency of the variety to propagate its like—the patent facts that all species vary more or less; that domesticated plants and animals, being in conditions favorable to the production and preservation of varieties, are apt to vary widely; and that, by interbreeding, any variety may be fixed into a race, that is, into a variety which comes true from seed. Many such races, it is allowed, differ from each other in structure and appearance as widely as do many admitted species; and it is practically very difficult, even impossible, to draw a clear line between races and species. Witness the human races, for instance. Wild species also vary, perhaps about as widely as those of domestica-

tion, though in different ways. Some of them apparently vary little, others moderately, others immoderately to the great bewilderment of systematic botanists and zoölogists, and increasing disagreement as to whether various forms shall be held to be original species or strong varieties. Moreover, the degree to which the descendants of the same stock, varying in different directions, may at length diverge, is unknown. All we know is, that varieties are themselves variable, and that very diverse forms have been educed from one stock.

2. Species of the same genus are not distinguished from each other by equal amounts of difference. There is diversity in this respect analogous to that of the varieties of a polymorphous species, some of them slight, others extreme. And in large genera the unequal resemblance shows itself in the clustering of the species around several types or central species, like satellites around their respective planets. Obviously suggestive this of the hypothesis that they were satellites, not thrown off by revolution, like the moons of Jupiter, Saturn, and our own solitary moon, but gradually and peacefully detached by divergent variation. That such closely-related species may be only varieties of higher grade, earlier origin, or more favored evolution, is not a very violent supposition. Anyhow, it was a supposition sure to be made.

3. The actual geographical distribution of species upon the earth's surface tends to suggest the same notion. For, as a general thing, all or most of the species of a peculiar genus or other type are grouped in the same country, or occupy continuous, proximate, or accessible areas. So well does this rule hold, so general is the implication that kindred species are or were associated geographically, that most trustworthy naturalists, quite free from hypotheses of transmutation, are constantly inferring former geographical continuity between parts of the world now widely disjoined, in order to account thereby for certain generic similarities among their inhabitants; just as philologists infer former connection of races, and a parent language, to account for generic similarities among existing languages. Yet no scientific explanation has been offered to account for the geographical association of kindred species, except the hypothesis of a common origin.

4. Here the fact of the antiquity of creation, and in particular of the present kinds of the

earth's inhabitants, or of a large part of them, comes in to rebut the objection that there has not been time enough for any marked diversification of living things through divergent variation—not time enough for varieties to have diverged into what we call species.

So long as the existing species of plants and animals were thought to have originated a few thousand years ago, and without predecessors, there was no room for a theory of derivation of one sort from another, nor time enough even to account for the establishment of the races which are generally believed to have diverged from a common stock. Not so much that five or six thousand years was a short allowance for this; but because some of our familiar domesticated varieties of grain, of fowls, and of other animals, were pictured and mummified by the old Egyptians more than half that number of years ago, if not earlier. Indeed, perhaps the strongest argument for the original plurality of human species was drawn from the identification of some of the present races of men upon these early historical monuments and records.

But this very extension of the current chronology, if we may rely upon the archæologists, removes the difficulty by opening up a longer vista. So does the discovery in Europe of remains and implements of prehistoric races of men, to whom the use of metals was unknown—men of the *stone age,* as the Scandinavian archæologists designate them. And now, "axes and knives of flint, evidently wrought by human skill, are found in beds of the drift at Amiens (also in other places, both in France and England), associated with the bones of extinct species of animals." These implements, indeed, were noticed twenty years ago; at a place in Suffolk they have been exhumed from time to time for more than a century; but the full confirmation, the recognition of the age of the deposit in which the implements occur, their abundance, and the appreciation of their bearings upon most interesting questions, belong to the present time. To complete the connection of these primitive people with the fossil ages, the French geologists, we are told, have now "found these axes in Picardy associated with remains of *Elephas primigenius, Rhinoceros tichorhinus, Equus fossilis,* and an extinct species of *Bos.*"[2] In plain language, these workers in flint lived in the time of the mammoth, of a rhinoceros now extinct, and along with horses and cattle unlike any now

existing—specifically different, as naturalists say, from those with which man is now associated. Their connection with existing human races may perhaps be traced through the intervening people of the stone age, who were succeeded by the people of the bronze age, and these by workers in iron.[3] Now, various evidence carries back the existence of many of the present lower species of animals, and probably of a larger number of plants, to the same drift period. All agree that this was very many thousand years ago. Agassiz tells us that the same species of polyps which are now building coral walls around the present peninsula of Florida actually made that peninsula, and have been building there for many thousand centuries.

5. The overlapping of existing and extinct species, and the seemingly gradual transition of the life of the drift period into that of the present, may be turned to the same account. Mammoths, mastodons, and Irish elks, now extinct, must have lived down to human, if not almost to historic times. Perhaps the last dodo did not long outlive his huge New Zealand kindred. The auroch, once the companion of mammoths, still survives, but owes his present and precarious existence to man's care. Now, nothing that we know of forbids the hypothesis that some new species have been independently and supernaturally created within the period which other species have survived. Some may even believe that man was created in the days of the mammoth, became extinct, and was recreated at a later date. But why not say the same of the auroch, contemporary both of the old man and of the new? Still it is more natural, if not inevitable, to infer that, if the aurochs of that olden time were the ancestors of the aurochs of the Lithuanian forests, so likewise were the men of that age the ancestors of the present human races. Then, whoever concludes that these primitive makers of rude flint axes and knives were the ancestors of the better workmen of the succeeding stone age, and these again of the succeeding artificers in brass and iron, will also be likely to suppose that the *Equus* and *Bos* of that time, different though they be, were the remote progenitors of our own horses and cattle. In all candor we must at

---

[2]*See* "Correspondence of M. Nicklès," in *American Journal of Science and Arts,* for March, 1860.

[3]*See* Morlot, "Some General Views on Archæology," in *American Journal of Science and Arts,* for January, 1860, translated from "Bulletin de la Société Vaudoise," 1859.

least concede that such considerations suggest a genetic descent from the drift period down to the present, and allow time enough—if time is of any account—for variation and natural selection to work out some appreciable results in the way of divergence into races, or even into so-called species. Whatever might have been thought, when geological time was supposed to be separated from the present era by a clear line, it is now certain that a gradual replacement of old forms by new ones is strongly suggestive of some mode of origination which may still be operative. When species, like individuals, were found to die out one by one, and apparently to come in one by one, a theory for what Owen sonorously calls "the continuous operation of the ordained becoming of living things" could not be far off.

That all such theories should take the form of a derivation of the new from the old seems to be inevitable, perhaps from our inability to conceive of any other line of secondary causes in this connection. Owen himself is apparently in travail with some transmutation theory of his own conceiving, which may yet see the light, although Darwin's came first to the birth. Different as the two theories will probably be, they cannot fail to exhibit that fundamental resemblance in this respect which betokens a community of origin, a common foundation on the general facts and the obvious suggestions of modern science. Indeed—to turn the point of a pungent simile directed against Darwin—the difference between the Darwinian and the Owenian hypotheses may, after all, be only that between homœopathic and heroic doses of the same drug.

If theories of derivation could only stop here, content with explaining the diversification and succession of species between the teritiary period and the present time, through natural agencies or secondary causes still in operation, we fancy they would not be generally or violently objected to by the *savants* of the present day. But it is hard, if not impossible, to find a stopping-place. Some of the facts or accepted conclusions already referred to, and several others, of a more general character, which must be taken into the account, impel the theory onward with accumulated force. *Vires* (not to say *virus*) *acquirit eundo*. The theory hitches on wonderfully well to Lyell's uniformitarian theory in geology—that the thing that has been is the thing that is and shall be—that the natural operations now going on will account for all geological changes in a quiet and easy way, only give them time enough, so connecting the present and the proximate with the farthest past by almost imperceptible gradations—a view which finds large and increasing, if not general, acceptance in physical geology, and of which Darwin's theory is the natural complement.

■ ■ ■ ■

. . . [It] is undeniable that Mr. Darwin has purposely been silent upon the philosophical and theological applications of his theory. This reticence, under the circumstances, argues design, and raises inquiry as to the final cause or reason why. Here, as in higher instances, confident as we are that there is a final cause, we must not be overconfident that we can infer the particular or true one. Perhaps the author is more familiar with natural-historical than with philosophical inquiries, and, not having decided which particular theory about efficient cause is best founded, he meanwhile argues the scientific questions concerned—all that relates to secondary causes—upon purely scientific grounds, as he must do in any case. Perhaps, confident, as he evidently is, that his view will finally be adopted, he may enjoy a sort of satisfaction in hearing it denounced as sheer atheism by the inconsiderate, and afterward, when it takes its place with the nebular hypothesis and the like, see this judgment reversed, as we suppose it would be in such event.

Whatever Mr. Darwin's philosophy may be, or whether he has any, is a matter of no consequence at all, compared with the important questions, whether a theory to account for the origination and diversification of animal and vegetable forms through the operation of secondary causes does or does not exclude design; and whether the establishment by adequate evidence of Darwin's particular theory of diversification through variation and natural selection would essentially alter the present scientific and philosophical grounds for theistic views of Nature. The unqualified affirmative judgment rendered by the two Boston reviewers, evidently able and practised reasoners, "must give us pause." We hesitate to advance our conclusions in opposition to theirs. But, after full and serious consideration, we are constrained to say that, in our opinion, the adoption of a derivative hypothesis, and of Darwin's particular hypothesis, if we understand it, would leave the doctrines of final causes, utility, and special design, just where they were before. We do not pretend that the subject is not environed with difficulties. Every view is so environed; and every shifting of the view is likely, if it removes some difficulties, to bring others into prominence. But we cannot perceive that Darwin's theory brings in any new kind of scientific difficulty, that is, any with which philosophical naturalists were not already familiar.

Since natural science deals only with secondary or natural causes, the scientific terms of a theory of derivation of species—no less than of a theory of dynamics—must needs be the same to the theist as to the atheist. The difference appears only when the inquiry is carried up to the question of primary cause—a question which belongs to philosophy. Wherefore, Darwin's reticence about efficient cause does not disturb us. He considers only the scientific questions. As already stated, we think that a theistic view of Nature is implied in his book, and we must charitably refrain from suggesting the contrary until the contrary is logically deduced from his premises. If, however, he anywhere maintains that the natural causes through which species are diversified operate without an ordaining and directing intelligence, and that the orderly arrangements and admirable adaptations we see all around us are fortuitous or blind, undesigned results—that the eye, though it came to see, was not designed for seeing, nor the hand for handling—then, we suppose, he is justly chargeable with denying, and very needlessly denying, all design in organic Nature; otherwise, we suppose not. Why, if Darwin's well-known passage about the eye—equivocal though some of the language be—does not imply ordaining and directing intelligence, then he refutes his own theory as effectually as any of his opponents are likely to do. He asks:

"May we not believe that [under variation proceeding long enough, generation multiplying the better variations times enough, and natural selection securing the improvements] a living optical instrument might be thus formed as superior to one of glass as the works of the Creator are to those of man?"

This must mean one of two things: either that the living instrument was made and perfected under (which is the same thing as by) an intelligent First Cause, or that it was not. If it was, then theism is asserted; and as to the mode of operation, how do we know, and why must we believe, that, fitting precedent forms being in existence, a living instrument (so different from a lifeless manufacture) would be originated and perfected in any other way, or that this is not the fitting way? If it means that it was not, if he so misuses words that by the Creator he intends an unintelligent power, undirected force, or necessity, then he has put his case so as to invite disbelief in it. For then blind forces have produced not only manifest adaptions of means to specific ends—which is absurd enough—but better adjusted and more perfect instruments or machines than intellect (that is, human intellect) can contrive and human skill execute—which no sane person will believe.

On the other hand, if Darwin even admits—we will not say adopts—the theistic view, he may save himself much needless trouble in the endeavor to account for the absence of every sort of intermediate form. Those in the line between one species and another supposed to be derived from it he may be bound to provide; but as to "an infinite number of other varieties not intermediate, gross, rude, and purposeless, the unmeaning creations of an unconscious cause," born only to perish, which a relentless reviewer has imposed upon his theory—rightly enough upon the atheistic alternative—the theistic view rids him at once of this "scum of creation." For, as species do not now vary at all times and places and in all directions, nor produce crude, vague, imperfect, and useless forms, there is no reason for supposing that they ever did. Good-for-nothing monstrosities, failures of purpose rather than purposeless, indeed, sometimes occur; but these are just as anomalous and unlikely upon Darwin's theory as upon any other. For his particular theory is based, and even overstrictly insists, upon the most universal of physiological laws, namely, that successive generations shall differ only slightly, if at all, from their parents; and this effectively excludes crude and impotent forms. Wherefore, if we believe that the species were designed, and that natural propagation was designed, how can we say that the actual varieties of the species were not equally designed? Have we not similar grounds for inferring design in the supposed varieties of species, that we have in the case of the supposed species of a genus? When a naturalist comes to regard as three closely-related species what he before took to be so many varieties of one species, how has he thereby strengthened our conviction that the three forms are designed to have the differences which they actually exhibit? Wherefore, so long as gradatory, orderly, and adapted forms in Nature argue design, and at least while the physical cause of variation is utterly unknown and mysterious, we should advise Mr. Darwin to assume, in the philosophy of his hypothesis, that variation has been led along certain beneficial lines. Streams flowing over a sloping plain by gravitation (here the counterpart of natural selection) may have worn their actual channels as they flowed; yet their particular courses may have been assigned; and where we see them forming definite and useful lines of irrigation, after a manner unaccountable on the laws of gravitation and dynamics, we should believe that the distribution was designed.

To insist, therefore, that the new hypothesis of the derivative origin of the actual species is incompatible with final causes and design, is to take a position which we must consider philosophically untenable.

We must also regard it as highly unwise and danger-ous, in the present state and present prospects of physical and physiological science. We should ex-pect the philosophical atheist or skeptic to take this ground; also, until better informed, the unlearned and unphilosophical believer; but we should think that the thoughtful theistic philosopher would take the other side. Not to do so seems to concede that only supernatural events can be shown to be de-signed, which no theist can admit—seems also to misconceive the scope and meaning of all ordinary arguments for design in Nature. This misconception is shared both by the reviewers and the reviewed. At least, Mr. Darwin uses expressions which imply that the natural forms which surround us, because they have a history or natural sequence, could have been only generally, but not particularly designed—a view at once superficial and contradictory; whereas his true line should be, that his hypothesis concerns the *order* and not the *cause,* the *how* and not the *why* of the phenomena, and so leaves the question of de-sign just where it was before.

To illustrate this from the theist's point of view: Transfer the question for a moment from the origi-nation of species to the origination of individuals, which occurs, as we say, naturally. Because natural, that is, "stated, fixed, or settled," is it any the less designed on that account? We acknowledge that God is our maker—not merely the originator of the race, but *our* maker as individuals—and none the less so because it pleased him to make us in the way of ordinary generation. If any of us were born un-like our parents and grandparents, in a slight de-gree, or in whatever degree, would the case be al-tered in this regard?

The whole argument in natural theology pro-ceeds upon the ground that the inference for a final cause of the structure of the hand and of the valves in the veins is just as valid now, in individuals pro-duced through natural generation, as it would have been in the case of the first man, supernaturally cre-ated. Why not, then, just as good even on the sup-position of the descent of men from chimpanzees and gorillas, since those animals possess these same contrivances? Or, to take a more supposable case: If the argument from structure to design is convinc-ing when drawn from a particular animal, say a Newfoundland dog, and is not weakened by the knowledge that this dog came from similar parents, would it be at all weakened if, in tracing his geneal-ogy, it were ascertained that he was a remote de-scendant of the mastiff or some other breed, or that both these and other breeds came (as is suspected) from some wolf? If not, how is the argument for de-sign in the structure of our particular dog affected by the supposition that his wolfish progenitor came

from a post-tertiary wolf, perhaps less unlike an ex-isting one than the dog in question is to some other of the numerous existing races of dogs, and that this post-tertiary came from an equally or more dif-ferent tertiary wolf? And if the argument from structure to design is not invalidated by our present knowledge that our individual dog was developed from a single organic cell, how is it invalidated by the supposition of an analogous natural descent, through a long line of connected forms, from such a cell, or from some simple animal, existing ages be-fore there were any dogs?

Again, suppose we have two well-known and ap-parently most decidedly different animals or plants, A and D, both presenting, in their structure and in their adaptations to the conditions of existence, as valid and clear evidence of design as any animal or plant ever presented: suppose we have now discov-ered two intermediate species, B and C, which make up a series with equable differences from A to D. Is the proof of design or final cause in A and D, what-ever it amounted to, at all weakened by the discov-ery of the intermediate forms? Rather does not the proof extend to the intermediate species, and go to show that all four were equally designed? Suppose, now, the number of intermediate forms to be much increased, and therefore the gradations to be closer yet—as close as those between the various sorts of dogs, or races of men, or of horned cattle: would the evidence of design, as shown in the structure of any of the members of the series, be any weaker than it was in the case of A and D? Whoever contends that it would be, should likewise maintain that the orig-ination of individuals by generation is incompati-ble with design, or an impossibility in Nature. We might all have confidently thought the latter, an-tecedently to experience of the fact of reproduction. Let our experience teach us wisdom.

These illustrations make it clear that the evidence of design from structure and adaptation is fur-nished *complete* by the individual animal or plant it-self, and that our knowledge or our ignorance of the history of its formation or mode of production adds nothing to it and takes nothing away. We infer de-sign from certain arrangements and results; and we have no other way of ascertaining it. Testimony, un-less infallible, cannot prove it, and is out of the question here. *Testimony is not the appropriate proof of design: adaptation to purpose is.* Some arrange-ments in Nature appear to be contrivances, but may leave us in doubt. Many others, of which the eye and the hand are notable examples, compel belief with a force not appreciably short of demonstra-tion. Clearly to settle that such as these must have been designed goes far toward proving that other organs and other seemingly less explicit adaptations in Nature must also have been designed, and clinches our belief, from manifold considerations, that all Nature is a preconcerted arrangement, a manifested design. A strange contradiction would it be to insist that the shape and markings of certain rude pieces of flint, lately found in drift-deposits, prove design, but that nicer and thousand-fold more complex adaptations to use in animals and vegetables do not *a fortiori* argue design.

We could not affirm that the arguments for design in Nature are conclusive to all minds. But we may insist, upon grounds already intimated, that, whatever they were good for before Darwin's book appeared, they are good for now. To our minds the argument from design always appeared conclusive of the being and continued operation of an intelligent First Cause, the Ordainer of Nature; and we do not see that the grounds of such belief would be disturbed or shifted by the adoption of Darwin's hypothesis. We are not blind to the philosophical difficulties which the thoroughgoing implication of design in Nature has to encounter, nor is it our vocation to obviate them. It suffices us to know that they are not new nor peculiar difficulties—that, as Darwin's theory and our reasonings upon it did not raise these perturbing spirits, they are not bound to lay them. Meanwhile, that the doctrine of design encounters the very same difficulties in the material that it does in the moral world is just what ought to be expected.

So the issue between the skeptic and the theist is only the old one, long ago argued out—namely, whether organic Nature is a result of design or of chance. Variation and natural selection open no third alternative; they concern only the question how the results, whether fortuitous or designed, may have been brought about. Organic Nature abounds with unmistakable and irresistible indications of design, and, being a connected and consistent system, this evidence carries the implication of design throughout the whole. On the other hand, chance carries no probabilities with it, can never be developed into a consistent system, but, when applied to the explanation of orderly or beneficial results, heaps up improbabilities at every step beyond all computation. To us, a fortuitous Cosmos is simply inconceivable. The alternative is a designed Cosmos.

It is very easy to assume that, because events in Nature are in one sense accidental, and the operative forces which bring them to pass are themselves blind and unintelligent (physically considered, all forces are), therefore they are undirected, or that he who describes these events as the results of such forces thereby assumes that they are undirected. This is the assumption of the Boston reviewers, and

of Mr. Agassiz, who insists that the only alternative to the doctrine, that all organized beings were supernaturally created just as they are, is, that they have arisen *spontaneously* through the *omnipotence of matter.*[4]

As to all this, nothing is easier than to bring out in the conclusion what you introduce in the premises. If you import atheism into your conception of variation and natural selection, you can readily exhibit it in the result. If you do not put it in, perhaps there need be none to come out. While the mechanician is considering a steamboat or locomotive-engine as a material organism, and contemplating the fuel, water, and steam, the source of the mechanical forces, and how they operate, he may not have occasion to mention the engineer. But, the orderly and special results accomplished, the *why* the movements are in this or that particular direction, etc., is inexplicable without him. If Mr. Darwin believes that the events which he supposes to have occurred and the results we behold were undirected and undesigned, or if the physicist believes that the natural forces to which he refers phenomena are uncaused and undirected, no argument is needed to show that such belief is atheism. But the admission of the phenomena and of these natural processes and forces does not necessitate any such belief, nor even render it one whit less improbable than before.

Surely, too, the accidental element may play its part in Nature without negativing design in the theist's view. He believes that the earth's surface has been very gradually prepared for man and the existing animal races, that vegetable matter has through a long series of generations imparted fertility to the soil in order that it may support its present occupants, that even beds of coal have been stored up for man's benefit. Yet what is more accidental, and more simply the consequence of physical agencies, than the accumulation of vegetable matter in a peat-bog, and its transformation into coal? No scientific person at this day doubts that our solar system is a progressive development, whether in his conception he begins with molten masses, or aëriform or nebulous masses, or with a fluid revolving mass of vast extent, from which the specific existing worlds have been developed one by one. What theist doubts that the actual results of the development in the inorganic worlds are not merely compatible with design, but are in the truest sense designed results? Not Mr. Agassiz, certainly, who adopts a remarkable illustration of design directly founded on the nebular hypothesis, drawing from the position

---

[4]In *American Journal of Science*, July, 1860, pp. 147–149.

and times of the revolution of the world, so originated, "direct evidence that the physical world has been ordained in conformity with laws which obtain also among living beings." But the reader of the interesting exposition[5] will notice that the designed result has been brought to pass through what, speaking after the manner of men, might be called a chapter of accidents.

A natural corollary of this demonstration would seem to be, that a material connection between a series of created things—such as the development of one of them from another, or of all from a common stock—is highly compatible with their intellectual connection, namely, with their being designed and directed by one mind. Yet upon some ground which is not explained, and which we are unable to conjecture, Mr. Agassiz concludes to the contrary in the organic kingdoms, and insists that, *because* the members of such a series have an intellectual connection, "they cannot be the result of a material differentiation of the objects themselves,"[6] that is, they cannot have had a genealogical connection. But is there not as much intellectual connection between the successive generations of any species as there is between the several species of a genus, or the several genera of an order? As the intellectual connection here is realized through the material connection, why may it not be so in the case of species and genera? On all sides, therefore, the implication seems to be quite the other way.

Returning to the accidental element, it is evident that the strongest point against the compatibility of Darwin's hypothesis with design in Nature is made when natural selection is referred to as picking out those variations which are improvements from a vast number which are not improvements, but perhaps the contrary, and therefore useless or purposeless, and born to perish. But even here the difficulty is not peculiar; for Nature abounds with analogous instances. Some of our race are useless, or worse, as regards the improvement of mankind; yet the race may be designed to improve, and may be actually improving. Or, to avoid the complication with free agency—the whole animate life of a country depends absolutely upon the vegetation, the vegetation upon the rain. The moisture is furnished by the ocean, is raised by the sun's heat from the ocean's surface, and is wafted inland by the winds. But what multitudes of raindrops fall back into the ocean—are as much without a final cause as the incipient varieties which come to nothing! Does it therefore follow that the rains which are bestowed upon the soil with such rule and average regularity were not designed to support vegetable and animal life? Consider, likewise, the vast proportion of seeds and pollen, of ova and young—a thousand or more to one—which come to nothing, and are therefore purposeless in the same sense, and only in the same sense, as are Darwin's unimproved and unused slight variations. The world is full of such cases; and these must answer the argument—for we cannot, except by thus showing that it proves too much.

Finally, it is worth noticing that, though natural selection is scientifically explicable, variation is not. Thus far the cause of variation, or the reason why the offspring is sometimes unlike the parents, is just as mysterious as the reason why it is generally like the parents. It is now as inexplicable as any other origination; and, if ever explained, the explanation will only carry up the sequence of secondary causes one step farther, and bring us in face of a somewhat different problem, but which will have the same element of mystery that the problem of variation has now. Circumstances may preserve or may destroy the variations; man may use or direct them; but selection, whether artificial or natural, no more originates them than man originates the power which turns a wheel, when he dams a stream and lets the water fall upon it. The origination of this power is a question about efficient cause. The tendency of science in respect to this obviously is not toward the omnipotence of matter, as some suppose, but toward the omnipotence of spirit.

So the real question we come to is as to the way in which we are to conceive intelligent and efficient cause to be exerted, and upon what exerted. Are we bound to suppose efficient cause in all cases exerted upon nothing to evoke something into existence—and this thousands of times repeated, when a slight chance in the details would make all the difference between successive species? Why may not the new species, or some of them, be designed diversifications of the old?

There are, perhaps, only three views of efficient cause which may claim to be both philosophical and theistic:

1. The view of its exertion at the beginning of time, endowing matter and created things with forces which do the work and produce the phenomena.

2. This same view, with the theory of insulated interpositions, or occasional direct action, engrafted upon it—the view that events and operations in general go on in virtue simply of

---

[5]In "Contributions to the Natural History of the United States," vol. i., pp. 128, 129. [JHL pp. 127–130.]

[6]"Contributions to the Natural History of the United States," vol. i., p. 130 [JHL p. 130]; and *American Journal of Science*, July, 1860, p. 143.

forces communicated at the first, but that now and then, and only now and then, the Deity puts his hand directly to the work.

3. The theory of the immediate, orderly, and constant, however infinitely diversified, action of the intelligent efficient Cause.

It must be allowed that, while the third is preëminently the Christian view, all three are philosophically compatible with design in Nature. The second is probably the popular conception. Perhaps most thoughtful people oscillate from the middle view toward the first or the third—adopting the first on some occasions, the third on others. Those philosophers who like and expect to settle all mooted questions will take one or the other extreme. The *Examiner* inclines toward, the *North American* reviewer fully adopts, the third view, to the logical extent of maintaining that "*the origin of an individual,* as well as the origin of a species or a genus, can be explained only by the *direct* action of an intelligent creative cause." To silence his critics, that is the line for Mr. Darwin to take; for it at once and completely relieves his scientific theory from every theological objection which his reviewers have urged against it.

At present we suspect that our author prefers the first conception, though he might contend that his hypothesis is compatible with either of the three. That it is also compatible with an atheistic or pantheistic conception of the universe, is an objection which, being shared by all physical, and some ethical or moral science, cannot specially be urged against Darwin's system. As he rejects spontaneous generation, and admits of intervention at the beginning of organic life, and probably in more than one instance, he is not wholly excluded from adopting the middle view, although the interventions he would allow are few and far back. Yet one interposition admits the principle as well as more. Interposition presupposes particular necessity or reason for it, and raises the question, when and how often it may have been necessary. It might be the natural supposition, if we had only one set of species to account for, or if the successive inhabitants of the earth had no other connections or resemblances than those which adaptation to similar conditions, which final causes in the narrower sense, might explain. But if this explanation of organic Nature requires one to "believe that, at innumerable periods in the earth's history, certain elemental atoms have been commanded suddenly to flash into living tissues," and this when the results are seen to be strictly connected and systematic, we cannot wonder that such interventions should at length be considered, not as interpositions or interferences, but rather—to use

the reviewer's own language—as "exertions so frequent and beneficent that we come to regard them as the ordinary action of Him who laid the foundation of the earth, and without whom not a sparrow falleth to the ground."[7]

What does the difference between Mr. Darwin and his reviewer now amount to? If we say that according to one view the origination of species is *natural*, according to the other *miraculous*, Mr. Darwin agrees that "what is natural as much requires and presupposes an intelligent mind to render it so—that is, to effect it continually or at stated times—as what is supernatural does to effect it for once."[8] He merely inquires into the form of the miracle, may remind us that all recorded miracles (except the primal creation of matter) were transformations or actions in and upon natural things, and will ask how many times and how frequently may the origination of successive species be repeated before the supernatural merges in the natural.

In short, Darwin maintains that the origination of a species, no less than that of an individual, is natural; the reviewer, that the natural origination of an individual, no less than the origination of a species, requires and presupposes Divine power. *A fortiori,* then, the origination of a variety requires and presupposes Divine power. And so between the scientific hypothesis of the one and the philosophical conception of the other no contrariety remains. And so, concludes the *North American* reviewer, "a proper view of the nature of causation places the vital doctrine of the being and the providence of a God on ground that can never be shaken."[9] A worthy conclusion, and a sufficient answer to the denunciations and arguments of the rest of the article, so far as philosophy and natural theology are concerned. If a writer must needs use his own favorite dogma as a weapon with which to give *coup de grace* to a pernicious theory, he should be careful to seize his edge-tool by the handle, and not by the blade.

■ ■ ■ ■

We must close here. We meant to review some of the more general scientific objections which we thought not altogether tenable. But, after all, we are not so anxious just now to know whether the new theory is well founded on facts, as whether it would be harmless if it were. Besides, we feel quite unable to answer some of these objections, and it is pleasanter to take up those which one thinks he can.

---

[7]*North American Review* for April, 1860, p. 506.

[8]*Vide* motto from Butler, prefixed to the second edition of Darwin's work.

[9]*North American Review, loc. cit.,* p. 504.

Among the unanswerable, perhaps the weightiest of the objections, is that of the absence, in geological deposits, of vestiges of the intermediate forms which the theory requires to have existed. Here all that Mr. Darwin can do is to insist upon the extreme imperfection of the geological record and the uncertainty of negative evidence. But, withal, he allows the force of the objection almost as much as his opponents urge it—so much so, indeed, that two of his English critics turn the concession unfairly upon him, and charge him with actually basing his hypothesis upon these and similar difficulties—as if he held it because of the difficulties, and not in spite of them; a handsome return for his candor!

As to this imperfection of the geological record, perhaps we should get a fair and intelligible illustration of it by imagining the existing animals and plants of New England, with all their remains and products since the arrival of the Mayflower, to be annihilated; and that, in the coming time, the geologists of a new colony, dropped by the New Zealand fleet on its way to explore the ruins of London, undertake, after fifty years of examination, to reconstruct in a catalogue the flora and fauna of our day, that is, from the close of the glacial period to the present time. With all the advantage of a surface exploration, what a beggarly account it would be! How many of the land animals and plants which are enumerated in the Massachusetts official reports would it be likely to contain?

Another unanswerable question asked by the Boston reviewers is, Why, when structure and instinct or habit vary—as they must have varied, on Darwin's hypothesis—they vary together and harmoniously, instead of vaguely? We cannot tell, because we cannot tell why either varies at all. Yet, as they both do vary in successive generations—as is seen under domestication—and are correlated, we can only adduce the fact. Darwin may be precluded from our answer, but we may say that they vary together because designed to do so. A reviewer says that the chance of their varying together is inconceivably small; yet, if they do not, the variant individuals must all perish. Then it is well that it is not left to chance. To refer to a parallel case: before we were born, nourishment and the equivalent to respiration took place in a certain way. But the moment we were ushered into this breathing world, our actions promptly conformed, both as to respiration and nourishment, to the before unused structure and to the new surroundings.

"Now," says the *Examiner*, "suppose, for instance, the gills of an aquatic animal converted into lungs, while instinct still compelled a continuance under water, would not drowning ensue?" No doubt. But—simply contemplating the facts, instead of theorizing—we notice that young frogs do not keep their heads under water after ceasing to be tadpoles. The instinct promptly changes with the structure, without supernatural interposition—just as Darwin would have it, if the development of a variety of incipient species, though rare, were as natural as a metamorphosis.

"Or if a quadruped, not yet furnished with wings, were suddenly inspired with the instinct of a bird, and precipitated itself from a cliff, would not the descent be hazardously rapid?" Doubtless the animal would be no better supported than the objection. But Darwin makes very little indeed of voluntary efforts as a cause of change, and even poor Lamarck need not be caricatured. He never supposed that an elephant would take such a notion into his wise head, or that a squirrel would begin with other than short and easy leaps; yet might not the length of the leap be increased by practice?

The *North American* reviewer's position, that the higher brute animals have comparatively little instinct and no intelligence, is a heavy blow and great discouragement to dogs, horses, elephants, and monkeys. Thus stripped of their all, and left to shift for themselves as they may in this hard world, their pursuit and seeming attainment of knowledge under such peculiar difficulties are interesting to contemplate. However, we are not so sure as is the critic that instinct regularly increases downward and decreases upward in the scale of being. Now that the case of the bee is reduced to moderate proportions,[10] we know of nothing in instinct surpassing that of an animal so high as a bird, the talegal, the male of which plumes himself upon making a hotbed in which to hatch his partner's eggs—which he tends and regulates the heat of about as carefully and skillfully as the unplumed biped does an eccaleobion.

As to the real intelligence of the higher brutes, it has been ably defended by a far more competent observer, Mr. Agassiz, to whose conclusions we yield

---

[10]The role of instinct in the mathematical accomplishments of the bee in making a geometrically perfect comb was a live subject in Cambridge. The reference here is one more evidence that the philosopher Chauncey Wright participated in the Darwinian debate in Cambridge in cooperation with Gray. Chauncey Wright, "The Economy and Symmetry of the Honey-Bees' Cells," *Mathematical Monthly* 2 (June 1860), 304–319. Jeffries Wyman was also in on the discussion. Jeffries Wyman, "Notes on the Cells of the Bee," American Academy of Arts and Sciences, *Proceedings,* 7 (1865–1868), 68–83. A. Hunter Dupree, ed., "Some Letters from Charles Darwin to Jeffries Wyman," *Isis,* 42 (1951), 104–110.

a general assent, although we cannot quite place the best of dogs "in that respect upon a level with a considerable proportion of poor humanity," nor indulge the hope, or indeed the desire, of a renewed acquaintance with the whole animal kingdom in a future life.

The assertion that acquired habitudes or instincts, and acquired structures, are not heritable, any breeder or good observer can refute.[11]

That "the human mind has become what it is out of a developed instinct,"[12] is a statement which Mr. Darwin nowhere makes, and, we presume, would not accept.[13] That he would have us believe that individual animals acquire their instincts gradually,[14] is a statement which must have been penned in inadvertence both of the very definition of instinct, and of everything we know of in Mr. Darwin's book.

---

[11]Still stronger assertions have recently been hazarded—even that heritability is of species only, not of individual characteristics—strangely overlooking the fundamental peculiarity of plants and animals, which is that they *reproduce,* and that the species is continued as such only because individuals reproduce their like.

• • • • • • • •

It has also been urged that variation is never cumulative. If this means that varieties are not capable of further variation, it is not borne out by observation. For cultivators and breeders well know that the main difficulty is to initiate a variation, and that new varieties are particularly prone to vary more.

[12]*North American Review,* April, 1860, p. 475.

[13]No doubt he would equally distinguish in kind between *instinct* (which physiologically is best conceived of as *congenital habit,* so that habits when inherited become instincts, just as varieties become fixed into races) and intelligence; but would maintain that both are endowments of the higher brutes and of man, however vastly and unequal their degree, and with whatever superaddition to simple intelligence in the latter

(Prof. Joseph Le Conte, in *Popular Science Monthly,* September, 1875, refers to his definition of instinct as "inherited experience," published in April, 1871, as having been anticipated by that of Hering, as "inherited memory," in February of the same year. Doubtless the idea has been expressed by others long before us.)

To allow that "brutes have certain mental endowments in common with men," . . . desires, affections, memory, simple imagination or the power of reproducing the sensible past in mental pictures, and even judgment of the simple or intuitive kind"—that "they compare and judge" ("Memoirs of American Academy," vol. viii., p. 118)—is to concede that the intellect of brutes really acts, so far as we know, like human intellect, as far it goes; for the philosophical logicians tell us all reasoning is reducible to a series of simple judgments. And Aristotle declares that even reminiscence—which is, we suppose, "reproducing the sensible past in mental pictures"—is a sort of reasoning.

On the other hand, Mr. Darwin's expectation that "psychology will be based on a new foundation, that of the *necessary* acquirement of each mental power and capacity by gradation," seems to come from a school of philosophy with which we have no sympathy.

[14]*American Journal of Science,* July, 1860, p. 146.

It has been attempted to destroy the very foundation of Darwin's hypothesis by denying that there are any wild varieties, to speak of, for natural selection to operate upon. We cannot gravely sit down to prove that wild varieties abound. We should think it just as necessary to prove that snow falls in winter. That variation among plants cannot be largely due to hybridism, and that their variation in Nature is not essentially different from much that occurs in domestication, and, in the long-run, probably hardly less in amount, we could show if our space permitted.

As to the sterility of hybrids, that can no longer be insisted upon as absolutely true, nor be practically used as a test between species and varieties, unless we allow that hares and rabbits are of one species. That such sterility, whether total or partial, subserves a purpose in keeping species apart, and was so designed, we do not doubt. But the critics fail to perceive that this sterility proves nothing whatever against the derivative origin of the actual species; for it may as well have been intended to keep separate those forms which have reached a certain amount of divergence, as those which were always thus distinct.

The argument for the permanence of species, drawn from the identity with those now living of cats, birds, and other animals preserved in Egyptian catacombs, was good enough as used by Cuvier against St.-Hilaire, that is, against the supposition that time brings about a gradual alteration of whole species; but it goes for little against Darwin, unless it be proved that species never vary, or that the perpetuation of a variety necessitates the extinction of the parent breed. For Darwin clearly maintains—what the facts warrant—that the mass of a species remains fixed so long as it exists at all, though it may set off a variety now and then. The variety may finally supersede the parent form, or it may coexist with it; yet it does not in the least hinder the unvaried stock from continuing true to the breed, unless it crosses with it. The common law of inheritance may be expected to keep both the original and the variety mainly true as long as they last, and none the less so because they have given rise to occasional varieties. The tailless Manx cats, like the curtailed fox in the fable, have not induced the normal breeds to dispense with their tails, nor have the Dorkings (apparently known to Pliny) affected the permanence of the common sort of fowl.

As to the objection that the lower forms of life ought, on Darwin's theory, to have been long ago improved out of existence, and replaced by higher forms, the objectors forget what a vacuum that would leave below, and what a vast field there is to which a simple organization is best adapted, and where an advance would be no improvement, but the contrary. To accumulate the greatest amount of being upon a given space, and to provide as much enjoyment of life as can be under the conditions, is what Nature seems to aim at; and this is effected by diversification.

Finally, we advise nobody to accept Darwin's or any other derivative theory as true. The time has not come for that, and perhaps never will. We also advise against a similar credulity on the other side, in a blind faith that species—that the manifold sorts and forms of existing animals and vegetables—"have no secondary cause." The contrary is already not unlikely, and we suppose will hereafter become more and more probable. But we are confident that, if a derivative hypothesis ever is established, it will be so on a solid theistic ground.

Meanwhile an inevitable and legitimate hypothesis is on trial—an hypothesis thus far not untenable—a trial just now very useful to science, and, we conclude, not harmful to religion, unless injudicious assailants temporarily make it so.

One good effect is already manifest; its enabling the advocates of the hypothesis of a multiplicity of human species to perceive the double insecurity of their ground. When the races of men are admitted to be of one *species,* the corollary, that they are of one *origin,* may be expected to follow. Those who allow them to be of one species must admit an actual diversification into strongly-marked and persistent varieties, and so admit the basis of fact upon which the Darwinian hypothesis is built; while those, on the other hand, who recognize several or numerous human species, will hardly be able to maintain that such species were primordial and supernatural in the ordinary sense of the word.

The English mind is prone to positivism and kindred forms of materialistic philosophy, and we must expect the derivative theory to be taken up in that interest. We have no predilection for that school, but the contrary. If we had, we might have looked complacently upon a line of criticism which would indirectly, but effectively, play into the hands of positivists and materialistic atheists generally. The wiser and stronger ground to take is, that the derivative hypothesis leaves the argument for design, and therefore for a designer, as valid as it ever was; that to do any work by an instrument must require, and therefore presuppose, the exertion rather of more than of less power than to do it directly; that whoever would be a consistent theist should believe that Design in the natural world is coextensive with Providence, and hold as firmly to the one as he does to the other, in spite of the wholly similar and apparently insuperable difficulties which the mind encounters whenever it endeavors to develop the idea into a system, either in the material and organic, or in the moral world. It is enough, in the way of obviating objections, to show that the philosophical difficulties of the one are the same, and only the same, as of the other.

Name: _____ **Date:** _____

1. Based on the contents of this article, what do you think was Gray's purpose in writing it?

2. What argument does Gray make for challenging old ways of thinking about the origin and nature of species?

3. What reasons does Gray offer in his speculation for Darwin's apparent silence on the philosophical and theological issues surrounding his work?

Name: _____ **Date:** _____

4. List and describe in your own words three of the objections that Gray raises to Darwin's theory of natural selection
    1.

    2.

    3.

Charles Darwin

Letter: Charles Darwin to Asa Gray, 1860

This letter from Darwin (1809-1882) to Gray (1810-188), written only a few months after the publication of On the Origin of Species, *demonstrated both Gray's financial support for Darwin as well as Darwin's theological views on the question of evolution. Far from being an atheist, Darwin revealed in this letter that he accepted a deistic view of God and believed that his theory of natural selection in no way undermines the existence of God.*

To Asa Gray 22 May [1860]

Down Bromley Kent
May 22d

My dear Gray,

   Again I have to thank you for one of your very pleasant letters (of May 7th), enclosing a very pleasant remittance of 22£.—I am in simple truth astonished at all the kind trouble you have taken for me. I return Appleton's account.—For the chance of your wishing for a formal acknowledgment, I send one.—If you have any further communication to the Appletons pray express my acknowledgment for his generosity; for it is generosity in my opinion. I am not at all surprised at sale diminishing: my extreme surprise is at greatness of sale. No doubt the public has been *shamefully* imposed on! for they bought the book, thinking that it would be nice easy reading. I expect the sale to stop soon in England: yet Lyell wrote to me the other day that calling at Murrays he heard that 50 copies had gone in previous 48 hours.—I am extremely glad that you will notice in Silliman additions in the Origin. Judging from letters (& I have just seen one from Thwaites to Hooker) & from remarks, the most serious omission in my book was not explaining how it is, as I believe, that all forms do not necessarily advance,—how there can now be *simple* organisms still existing.—The article in Med. & Chirurg. Review is by Carpenter.—I would send Pictet's, if you cannot see it, but I sh^d require it back.—Sedgwick has been firing broadsides into me, but exclusively on geological grounds.—Prof. Clarke of Cambridge says publickly that the chief characteristic of such books as mine is their "consummate impudence".—

   I hear there is **very** severe review on me in North British by a Revd Mr Dunns, a free-Kirk minister & dabbler in Nat. Hist^y I sh^d be very glad to see any good American Reviews,—as they are all more or less useful.— You say that you shall touch on other Reviews.—Huxley told me some time ago that after a time he would write review on all Reviews, whether he will I know not.—If you allude to Edinburgh, pray notice *some* of the points which I will point out on separate slip. In "Saturday Review" (one of our cleverest periodicals) of May 5th p. 573 there is a nice article on Owen's Review, defending Huxley, but not Hooker; & the latter I think Owen treats most ungenerously.—But surely you will get sick unto death of me & my Reviewers.—

   With respect to the theological view of the question; this is always painful to me.—I am bewildered.—I had no intention to write atheistically. But I own that I cannot see, as plainly as others do, & as I sh^d wish to do, evidence of design & beneficence on all sides of us. There seems to me too much misery in the world. I cannot persuade myself that a beneficent & omnipotent God would have designedly created the Ichneumonidæ with the express intention of their feeding within the living bodies of caterpillars, or that a cat should play with mice. Not believing this, I see no necessity in the belief that the eye was expressly designed.

From *The Correspondence of Charles Darwin*, Volume 8, 1860.

On the other hand I cannot anyhow be contented to view this wonderful universe & especially the nature of man, & to conclude that everything is the result of brute force. I am inclined to look at everything as resulting from designed laws, with the details, whether good or bad, left to the working out of what we may call chance. Not that this notion *at all* satisfies me. I feel most deeply that the whole subject is too profound for the human intellect. A dog might as well speculate on the mind of Newton.—Let each man hope & believe what he can.—

Certainly I agree with you that my views are not at all necessarily atheistical. The lightning kills a man, whether a good one or bad one, owing to the excessively complex action of natural laws,—a child (who may turn out an idiot) is born by action of even more complex laws,—and I can see no reason, why a man, or other animal, may not have been aboriginally produced by other laws; & that all these laws may have been expressly designed by an omniscient Creator, who foresaw every future event & consequence. But the more I think the more bewildered I become; as indeed I have probably shown by this letter.

Most deeply do I feel your generous kindness & interest.—

Yours sincerely & cordially | Charles Darwin

[Enclosure 1]

Asa Gray for M.ʳ Darwin

Statement of the Sale of Darwin's "Origin of Species" to May 1st, 1860

On hand last account,		—	*On hand this date,*	250	
Printed since	Jany/60	1500	*In hands of Booksellers,*	300	550
	Feby—/60	500	*Given away,*		200
	Mch/60	500	*Sold to date,*		1750
		2500			2500

1750 *Sold,* at 5% on $1.25 *Copyright amounting to* $109.37

Name: _____ **Date:** _____

1. Based on what you read in the letter, what help did Gray provide Darwin?

2. Considering Darwin's statements to Gray, do you think that Darwin hoped his work would convince people of the fallacy of religious belief?

3. In your own words, describe why did not Darwin believe in the argument from design.

4. Do you think Darwin felt confident about his beliefs in religion and evolution? Why or why not?

Edward Drinker Cope

The Origin of the Fittest, 1886

Cope (1840-1897) was an American paleontologist and an advocate of evolution. He was not, however, a Darwinian; rather, he believed that changes in the timing of and addition of stages to an individual's development was the root cause of evolutionary change. He believed that more advanced organisms passed through additional stages of development and that parts of the body that were most often used instigated further stages of development in successive generations. In this way, he was one of the founders of the neo-Lamarckian school of evolutionary thought that developed in the late nineteenth century. In this selection he demonstrated how a biologist could be an evolutionist, but oppose Darwinism.

EVOLUTION AND ITS CONSEQUENCES

The broad theory of evolution includes the theories of development of the solar system and its members, as expressed by the nebular hypothesis; the theory of development of life by molecular movements consequent upon certain combinations of non-living matter; and, lastly, the theory of development of the species of animals and plants by descent, the later from the earlier, with accompanying change of form and character. It attempts nothing less than a history of the process of creation of the universe, so far as we can behold it; and is, therefore, an attempt to formulate the plans and thoughts of the Author of that universe. Hence, it is not surprising that it excites the interest of the best of men, especially as it is one of the results of the efforts of a class of these, crowning many centuries of labor and thought.

The object of the present essay is to discuss familiarly the latter of these theories of evolution, viz., that respecting the species of animals and plants. As all are aware, this mode of accounting for the creation of organized beings has attained especial prominence at the present time, and possesses more of interest to most readers because of its explanation of our own origin. Moreover, it rests on more indubitable evidence than the two other theories.

From *The Origin of the Fittest: Essays on Evolution,* D. Appleton & Company, 1887.

The constitution and arrangement of the members of the solar system point to their origin by derivation from primal masses of vaporous matter through the mutual operation of the ordinary laws of attraction and motion. The *positioning* is precisely as it should be had such process taken place, but the process itself, that is, the change from type to type of celestial body, has not been observed.

The case is far different with the theory as regards organized or living beings. Not only are the mutual relations of animals and plants to each other such as should have resulted from a descent or development, but the changes from type to type have been actually observed, and in sufficient number to place the hypothesis on the basis of ascertained fact, as referring to a certain range of objects—say, in the case of the animal kingdom, to individuals distinguished by structural characters within the range of each of the three to six great primary divisions or "branches."

There are two totally distinct propositions involved in this question, which are confounded by the general public, and not unfrequently by students and writers on it. These are, first, the evidence which seems to prove that this evolution has taken place; secondly, the evidence as to the nature of the laws of its progress. A want of constant distinction between these views of the case has greatly obscured it and injured the evidence on one side or the other.

The evidence in favor of evolution is abundant, and is cited in fragments by various contemporary writers, foremost among whom, both in time and abundance of writings, comes Charles Darwin.

Much less has been done in explanation of the laws of evolution. Darwin and his immediate followers have brought out the law of "natural selection"; Spencer has endeavored to express them in terms of force; while Hyatt, Cope, Packard, and others have advanced the law of "acceleration and retardation."

In earlier days, when information was distributed slowly and books were few, it was long before any new truth or doctrine reached the majority of people, still less was adopted by the ruling classes. But the modern theory of evolution has been spread everywhere with unexampled rapidity, thanks to our means of printing and transportation. It has met with remarkably rapid acceptance by those best qualified to judge of its merits, viz., the zoölogists and botanists, while probably a majority of the public, in this region at least, profess to reject it. This inconsistency is due to two principal causes. In the first place, Darwin's demonstration contained in the "Origin of Species" extends little further than as stated in the title of his work. He proves little more than that species of the same genus or other restricted groups have had a common origin; and, further, his theory of natural selection is to the plainest understanding incomplete as an explanation of their "origin," as its author indeed freely allows. Besides, the unscientific world is particularly unreasonable on one point. Little knowing the slow steps and laborious effort by which any general truth is reached, they find in incompleteness ground of condemnation of the whole. Science is glad if she can prove that the earth stands on an elephant, and gladder if she can demonstrate that the elephant stands on a turtle; but, if she can not show the support of the turtle, she is not discouraged, but labors patiently, trusting that the future of discovery will justify the experience of the past.

If, then, some of the people find Mr. Darwin's argument incomplete, or in some points weak, it may be answered, so do the student classes, who, nevertheless, believe it. This is largely because Darwin's facts and thoughts repeat a vast multiplicity of experiences of every student, which are of as much significance as those cited by him, and which only required a courageous officer to marshal them into line, a mighty host, conquering and to conquer. These will slowly find their way into print, some in one country and some in another.

THE FACT OF EVOLUTION

As to the truth of the theory, the proof has been stated in more than one form. The first and simplest, and essentially the central argument of Darwin, is as follows:

In every family or larger group of animals and plants there exists one or more genera in which the species present an aggregation of specific intensity of form; that is, that species become more and more closely related, and finally varieties of single species have to be admitted for the sake of obtaining a systematic definition or "diagnosis," which will apply to all the individuals. These varieties are frequently as well marked as the nearly-related species, so far as *amount* of difference is concerned, the distinction between the two cases being that in the varieties there is a gradation from one to the other; in the species, none. Nevertheless, between some of the varieties transitions may be of rare occurrence, and in the case of the "species" an intermediate individual or two may occasionally be found. Thus it is that differences, called varietal and specific, are distinguished by degree only, and not in kind, and are, therefore, the results of the operation of uniform laws. Yet, according to the old theory, the varieties have a common origin, and the species an independent one! To find examples of what is asserted, it is only necessary to refer to the diagnostic tables and keys of the best and most honest zoölogists and botanists. It is true that these diagnoses are dry reading to the non-professional, yet they embrace nearly all that is of value in this part of biological science, and must be mastered in some department before the student is in possession of the means of forming an opinion. The neglect to do this explains why it is that, after all that has been written and said about *protean* species, etc., the subject should be so little understood.

It is true that in but few of these cases have the varieties been seen to be bred from common parents, a circumstance entirely owing to the difficulties of observation. The reasoning derived from the relations of differences appears to be conclusive as to their common origin, unless we are prepared to adopt the opposite view, that the varieties have originated separately. As these avowedly grade into individual variations, we must at once be led to believe that individuals have been created independently— a manifest absurdity.

But variations in the same brood have been found among wild animals; for example, both the red and gray varieties of the little horned owl *(Scops asio)* have been taken from the same nest.

As further examples of gradation between species and variety, found in nature, I only have to select those genera most numerous in species, and *best studied*. Among birds, *Corvus, Empidonax, Buteo, Falco,* etc. Reptiles, *Eutaenia, Anolis, Lycodon, Naja, Caudisona, Elaps, Oxyhrropus,* etc. Batrachia, *Rana, Hyla, Chorophilus, Borborocoetes, Amblystoma, Spelerpes,* etc. Fishes, *Ptychostomus, Plecostomus, Amiurus, Salmo, Perca,* and many others.

In all these groups of species, or "genera," it is impossible in some cases to determine what is variety and what species. This is notoriously the case with the salmon and trout *(Salmo)*, for one of the greatest opponents of close division of species, Dr. Günther, of London, thought himself necessitated, a very few years ago, to name and describe half a dozen new species of trout from the lakes of the British Islands, and, from being a stanch supporter of the old view of distinct creations, was completely converted to evolutionism.

Such is one of the views which has forced conviction on the minds of thoroughly honest men who were not only desirous of knowing the truth, but were in many cases brought over from a position of strong opposition. But the earnest objector says, you have not after all shown me any real transitions from species to species; until that is done your development is but a supposition.

The all-sufficient answer to this statement is to be found in the imperfection of our system of classification. Thus, if we first assume, with the anti-developmentalist, that varieties have a common parentage, and species distinct ones, when intermediate forms connecting so-called species are discovered, we must confess ourselves in error, and admit that the forms supposed to have had a different origin really had a common one. Such intermediate forms really establish the connection between species, but the question is begged at once by asserting unity of species, and, therefore, of origin, so soon as the intermediate form is found; for, as before observed, it is not degree, but constancy of distinction, which establishes the species of the zoölogical systems. Transitions between species are constantly discovered in existing animals; when numerous in individuals, the more diverse forms are regarded as "aberrant"; when few, the extremes become "varieties," and it is only necessary to destroy the annectant forms altogether to leave two or more species. As the whole of a variable species generally has wide geographical range, the varieties coinciding with sub-areas, the submergence, or other change in the intervening surface, would destroy connecting forms, and naturally produce the isolated species.

Formerly naturalists sometimes did this in their studies. A zoölogist known to fame once pointed out to me some troublesome specimens which set his attempts at definition of certain species at defiance. "These," said he, "are the kind that I throw out of the window." Naturalists having abandoned throwing puzzling forms out of the window, the result of more honest study is a belief in evolution by nine tenths of them.

But, says the inquirer again, your variations and transitions are but a drop in the ocean of well-distinguished species, classes, etc. The permanent distinction of species is matter of every-day observation; your examples of changes are few and far between, and utterly insufficient for your purpose.

It is true that the cases of transition, intermediate forms, or diversity in the brood, observed and cited by naturalists in proof of evolution, are few compared with the number of well-defined, isolated species, genera, etc., known; though far more numerous than the book-student of natural history is apt to discover. But although the origin of most species by descent has not been observed, every one knows the worthlessness of argument based on a negative. Unless these cases exhibit opposing evidence of a positive character, they are absolutely silent witnesses.

He who cites them against evolution commits the error of the native of the Green Isle who testified at a murder trial. "Although the prosecuting attorney brought three witnesses to swear positively that they saw the murder committed, I could produce *thirty* who swore they did not see it done!"

By the inductive process of reasoning we transfer the unknown in the known, for it is the key of knowledge. It rests upon the invariability of Nature's operations under identical circumstances, and for its application merely demands that analysis and comparison shall fix that the nature of that of which something is unknown is identical with that of which the same thing is known. We then with certainty refer that which is known as an attribute of that object of which the same quality had been previously unknown. The following form exhibits its application to the question of evolution. As preliminary facts it may be assumed that:

1. Many species are composed of identical elemental parts which present minor differences.
2. Some of these differences have been seen to originate spontaneously from parents which did not possess them, or, what is the same thing, are known to exist in individuals whose parentage is identical with others which do not possess them.
3. The gradation of differences of the same elemental parts is one of degree only, and not of kind.
4. *Induction.*—Therefore all such differences have originated by a modification in growth, or have made their appearance without transmission in descent.

THE MANNER OF EVOLUTION

In discussing this point, new evidence in favor of development must be produced, and some statements of the history of the opinion made.

The laws which are expressed by all that we find of structure in animals are four, viz.:

1. *Homology.*—This means that animals are composed of corresponding parts; that the variations of an original and fixed number of elements constitute their only differences. A part large in one animal may be small in another, or *vice versa;* or complex in one and simple in another. The analysis of animals with skeletons or vertebrata has yielded several hundred original elements, out of which the 28,000 included species are constructed. Different this from the inorganic world, which can only claim about sixty-two elemental substances. The study of homologies is thus an extended one, and is far from complete at the present day.

2. *Successional Relation.*—This expresses the fact that species naturally arrange themselves into series in consequence of a mathematical order of excess and deficiency in some feature or features. Thus species with three toes naturally intervene between those with one and four toes. So with the number of chambers of the heart, of segments of the body, the skeleton, etc. There are greater series and lesser series, and mistakes are easily made by taking the one for the other.

3. *Parallelism.*—This states that while all animals in their embryonic and later growth pass through a number of stages and conditions, some traverse more and others traverse fewer stages; and that, as the stages are nearly the same for both, those which accomplish less resemble or are *parallel* with the young of those which accomplish more. This is the broad statement, and is qualified by the details.

4. *Teleology.*—This is the law of adaptation so much dwelt upon by the old writers, and admired in its exhibitions by men generally. It includes the many cases of fitness of a structure for its special use, and expresses broadly the general adaptations of an animal to its home and habits.

Of course, these laws must be all laws of evolution, if evolution be true. And such they are; but this is far from being perceived by some students, for some of them were in abeyance or neglect prior to the stimulus to thought caused by the appearance of the "Origin of Species."

Forty or fifty years ago Germany had been flooded with the writings of the "physiophilosophs." Oken and Goethe had obtained glimpses of the wonderful "unity in variety" expressed by the laws of homology. The latter saw vertebræ in the segments of the skull, and leaves in the floral organs of plants. He had found the magic wand, and many were the harmonious visions that delighted the laborious toilers among old bones and dusty skins; the patient haruspices saw omens in the intestines of birds and snakes, and he whose hours were spent over his lens ceased to be a mere wondermonger. But fashion is fashion, and always ends in absurdity and stagnation. The physiophilosophs became extravagant, and mistook superficial appearances for realities. They did not dream how misleading some of the resemblances between different elements, for example, of the skeleton may be, and for once German students did not analyze exhaustively. Cuvier laughed at these seekers for beauty, and confounded the true and the nature in one condemnation. But the best men labored forward; errors began to be exposed, and soon a reaction set in. Another extreme followed, and the school of Müller, at Berlin, denied the meaning of these resemblances and ceased to see anything but differences. Minute and thorough investigation flourished in their hands, and the modern school of German anatomists has seen no superiors. So the theory of evolution found Berlin. The disfavor in which physiophilosophy was held secured to evolution a cold welcome, and it has been for Jena and other universities to give it its true impetus in Germany.

So it has been with the law of parallelism. Some of the physiophilosophs declared it, stating that the inferior animals were merely the repressed conditions of the higher. This view was taught by some men in high position in France. Their statements were, however, too broad and uncritical. The father of embryology, von Baer, of Koenigsberg, declared there was *"keine Rede"* of such theory, and Lereboullet stated "that it is founded on false and deceptive appearances." Even Professor Agassiz in our day has asserted that no embryonic animal is ever the same as the adult of another, though he also once informed the writer that the embryology of two nearly related species had never been studied and compared. This was subsequently done by Professor Hyatt, of Salem, for the nautilus and ammonite division of mollusks, and at about the same time by the writer, for many species of our native frogs and salamanders, and the result has been a complete clearing up of the confusion about parallelism, and the clear establishment of the law.

The results attained are these: The smaller the number of structural characters which separate the two species when adult, the more nearly will the less complete of the series be identical with an incomplete stage of the higher species. As we compare species which are more and more different, the more necessarily must we confine the assertion of parallelism to single parts of the animals, and less to the whole animal. When we reach species as far removed as man and a shark, which are separated by the extent of the series of vertebrated animals, we can only say that the infant man is identical in its numerous origins of the arteries from the heart, and in the cartilaginous skeletal tissue, with the class of sharks, and in but few other respects. But the importance of this consideration must be seen from the fact that it is *on single characters of this kind that the divisions of the zoölogist depend.* Hence we can say truly that one order is identical with an incomplete stage of another order, though the species of the one may never at the present time bear the same relation in their entirety to the species of the other. Still more frequently can we say that such a genus is the same in character as a stage passed by the next higher genus; but when we can say this of species, then their distinction is almost gone. It will then depend on the opinion of the naturalist as to whether the repressed characters are permanent or not. Parallelism is then reduced to this definition: that each separate character of every kind, which we find in a species, represents a more or less complete stage of the fullest growth of which the character appears to be capable. In proportion as those characters in one species are contrasted with those of another by reason of their number, by so much must we confine our comparison to the characters alone, and the divisions they represent; but when the contrast is reduced by reason of the fewness of differing characters, so much the more truly can we say that the one species is really a suppressed or incomplete form of the other. The denial of this principle by the authorities cited has been in consequence of this relation having been assigned to orders and classes, when the statement should have been confined *to single characters;* and divisions characterized by them. There seems, however, to have been a want of exercise of the classifying quality or power of "abstraction" of the mind on the part of the objectors. This faculty seems to be by no means so common as one would expect, judging from the systematic ideas of many.

To explain by a few examples selected at random: First, of species characters, I may cite the fact that all deer are spotted when young, and that some of the species of eastern and southern Asia retain the spotted coloration throughout life. All salamanders are uniform, often olive during a larval stage; some species, and some individuals of other species, retain the color in maturity. To take a genus character: all the deer in the second year develop their first horn, which is unbranched and small, or a "spike." A genus of deer inhabiting South America never develops anything else. To take a character of higher grade: the exogenous plants usually present net-veined leaves, but the first pair, or those of the plumule, are of much simpler structure, being often parallel-veined; for example, the cucumbers and squashes. Now, the endogens usually produce nothing else than parallel-veined leaves, and no case is known where a plant bearing this type of leaf exhibits the net-veined type as its earliest growth.

But what do these facts mean? As in growth the genus characters usually appear last, I will suppose a case where one genus represents truly, or is identical with, the incomplete stage of another one.

In *A* we have four species whose growth attains a given point, a certain number of stages having been passed prior to its termination, or maturity. In *B* we have another series of four (the number a matter of no importance), which, during the period of growth, can not be distinguished by any common, i.e., generic character, from the individuals

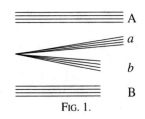

FIG. 1.

of group *A*, but whose growth has only attained to a point short of that reached by those of group *A* at maturity. Here we have a parallelism, but no true evidence of descent. But if we now find a set of individuals belonging to one species (or, still better, the individuals of a single brood), and therefore held to have had a common origin or parentage, which present differences among themselves of the character in question, we have gained a point. We know in this case that the individuals, *a*, have attained to the completeness of character presented by group *A*, while others, *b*, of the same parentage have only attained to the structure of those of group *B*. It is perfectly obvious that the individuals of the first part of the family have grown further, and, therefore, in one sense faster, than those of group *b*. If the parents were like the individuals of the more completely grown, then the offspring which did not attain that completeness may be said to have been *retarded* in their development. If, on the other hand, the parents were like those less fully grown, then the offspring which have added something have been *accelerated* in their development. I claim that a consideration of the uniformity of nature's processes, or inductive reasoning, requires me to believe that the groups of species, that is, groups *A* and *B*, are also derived from common parents, and the more advanced have been *accelerated* or the less advanced *retarded,* as the case may have been with regard to the parents.

This is not an imaginary case, but a true representation of many cases which have come under notice. I can not repeat them here, but refer to the original memoirs, where they may be found.[1]

This is a simple statement of the law of "acceleration and retardation" of some American naturalists, which probably expresses better than any other the "manner of evolution," the proposition with which we started.

Hyatt thus defines it as seen in a group of ammonites which he studied: "The young of higher species are thus constantly accelerating their development, and reducing to a more and more embryonic condition the stages of growth corresponding to the adult periods of preceding or lower species."[2]

This form of demonstration of evolution is of far wider application than that which I first brought forward.[3] In the latter case the induction may be limited to a certain range of variation, but the present law is as extensive as the organic world; that is, the "positioning" essential to it is found everywhere, from the lowest to the highest, and in characters from the least to the greatest in import.

Let an application be made to the origin of the human species. It is scarcely necessary to point out at the start the fact, universally admitted by anatomists, that man and monkeys belong to the same order of Mammalia, and differ in those minor characters, generally used to define a "family" in zoölogy.

Now, these differences are as follows: In man we have the large head with prominent forehead and short jaws; short canine teeth without interruption behind (above); short arms, and thumb of hind foot not opposable. In monkeys we have the reverse of all these characters. But what do we see in young monkeys? A head and brain as large relatively to the body as in man; a facial angle quite as large as in many men, with jaws not more prominent than in some races; the arms not longer than in the long-armed races of men, that is, a little beyond half way along the femur. These observations are made on a half-grown *Cebus apella,* from Brazil, a member of a group more remote from men than are the Old World apes, yet with an unusually large facial angle. At this age of the individual the distinctive characters are therefore those of *homo,* with the exception of the opposable thumb of the hind foot, and the longer canine tooth; nevertheless, the canine tooth is shorter in the young than in the adult.

Now, in the light of various cases observed, where members of the same species or brood are found at adult age to differ in the number of immature characters they possess, we may conclude that man originated in the following way: that is, by a delay or retardation in growth of the body and fore limbs as compared with the head; retardation of the jaws as compared with the brain case, and retardation in the protrusion of the canine teeth. The precise process as regards the hinder thumb remains obscure, but it is probably a very simple matter. The proportions of the young *Cebus apella* enable it to walk on the hind limbs with great facility, and it does so much more frequently than an adult *C. capucinus* with which it is confined.[4]

The "retardation" in the growth of the jaws still progresses. Some of our dentists have observed that the last (3d) molar teeth (wisdom teeth) are in natives of the United States very liable to imperfect growth or suppression, and to a degree entirely unknown among savage or even many civilized races. The same suppression has been observed in the outer pair of superior incisors. This is not only owing to a reduction in the size of the arches of the jaws, but to successively prolonged delay in the appearance of the teeth. In the same way men, and the man-like apes, have fewer teeth than the lower monkeys, and these again fewer than the ordinary Mammalia, and this reduction has proceeded in relation to an enlargement of the upper part of the head and of the brain.

The *cause* of development may be next considered, and under this head may be discussed the natural selection of Wallace and Darwin and other propositions of similar import.

"Retardation" continued terminates in extinction. Examples of this result are common; among the best known are those of the atrophy of the organs of sight in animals inhabiting caves. It is asserted that the young of both the blind crawfish *(Orconectes pellucidus)* and the lesser blind fish *(Typhlichthys subterraneus)* of the Mammoth Cave possess eyes. If these statements be accurate, we have here an example of what is known to occur else-

---

[1]See "Origin of Genera, and Method of Creation," Naturalists' Agency, Salem, Massachusetts; or McCalla & Stavely, 237 Dock Street, Philadelphia.

[2]"On the Parallelism between Stages in the Individual and those in the Group of the Tetrabranchiata." "Boston Society of Natural History," 4to, 1866, p. 203.

[3]It is quite misunderstood by Darwin, as will be sufficiently evident from the following quotation from the last edition of his "Origin of Species," 1872, p. 149: "There is another possible mode of transition, namely, through the acceleration or retardation of the period of reproduction. This has lately been insisted on by Prof. Cope and others in the United States." This has only been dwelt on as accounting for a very minor grade of differences seen in race and sex.

[4]The same relations of man to the anthropoid apes have been dwelt upon by Prof. C. Vogt.

where, for instance, in the whalebone whales. In a foetal stage these animals possess rudimental teeth like those of many other Cetacea when adult, which are subsequently absorbed. So also with the foetal ox; the upper incisor teeth appear in a rudimental condition, but are very early removed. The disappearance of the eyes is regarded by Dr. Packard, with reason, as evidence of the descent of the blind forms from those with visual organs. I would suggest that the process of reduction illustrates the law of "retardation" accompanied by another phenomenon. Where characters which appear latest in embryonic history are lost, we have simple retardation, that is, the animal in successive generations fails to grow up to the highest point of completion, falling farther and farther back, thus presenting an increasingly slower growth in the special direction in question. Where, as in the presence of eyes, we have a character early assumed in embryonic life, retardation presents a somewhat different phase. Each successive generation, it is true, fails to come up to the completeness of its predecessor at maturity, and thus exhibits "retardation," but this process of reduction of rate of growth is followed by its termination in the part long before growth has ceased in other organs. This is an exaggeration of retardation, and means the early termination of the process of force-conversion, which has been previously diminishing steadily in activity.

Thus the eyes of the *Orconectes* probably exhibited for a time at maturity the incomplete character now found in the young, a retarded growth continuing to adult age, before the termination of growth was withdrawn by degrees to earlier stages. With this early termination of growth came the phase of atrophy, the incomplete organ being removed and its materials transferred to other parts through the greater activity of "growth-force." Thus, for the reduction of organs, we have "retardation"; but for their extinction, "retardation and atrophy."

Name: _____   **Date:** _____

1. According to Cope, what does the theory of evolution include and what does it attempt to do?

2. How does Cope answer critics who claim that, until scientists have actually witnessed the transition of one species into another, evolution is merely superstition?

3. Based on your reading of this article and in your own words, define each of the following terms:
    Homology:

    Successional Relation:

Name: _____   **Date:** _____

Parallelism:

Teleology:

4. What is "retardation" as Cope uses the term?

Evolution in the Interphase

Hugo de Vries

"The Origin of Species by Mutation," 1902

de Vries (1848-1935), a Dutch physiologist, was one of three separate biologists who in 1900 each simultaneously rediscovered Mendel's 1865 research on inheritance. Later Mendel's work was integrated with Darwin's theory of natural selection and today the two men's contributions are considered vital to our understanding of evolution, but in the first decades of the twentieth century many biologists believed that Mendel's work contradicted Darwin's notions of inheritance and evolutionary change. This was due largely to de Vries' argument that evolution occurred in jumps, as opposed to Darwin's belief that evolution happened through slow, continuous change. Mutations, de Vries claimed, appeared regularly and were acted upon by natural selection. The result was that evolution, he believed, occurred in fits and starts as new mutations appeared and were either preserved or destroyed through natural selection, which acted as a filtering mechanism for the new mutations.

Forty years ago Darwin's 'Origin of Species' was given to the world. The number of those who witnessed its appearance gradually diminishes year by year. Few are left to remember the condition of things at that period, and the shock which its publication caused. We had grown up firmly convinced of the invariability of species. The precepts and commands of Linnæus reigned supreme over our thoughts and deeds alike. To take the last specimen from a locality, no one would have dared, not even in the seclusion of the forest primeval. Far less would any one have had the temerity to give even a single thought to those phenomena whose study he had forbidden. Many an interesting variation did I meet with on my walks when a student, but, obedient disciple that I was, left uncollected.

With the appearance of Darwin's book came the complete overthrow of the old doctrine. What formerly had been *the* science now became merely its primer. New demands were made upon investigation, interest was not directed into entirely new channels. An endless field was opened for thoughts, for observation, or comparison and the drawing of conclusions. The result was a hard-fought war, openly carried on against Darwin, and ending in his complete victory. But before we were able to declare ourselves advocates of the new doctrine, the bonds which held us were to be severed, and we had to break loose from the old prejudices.

Of the present generation none have known this internal struggle. They have been brought up in the new doctrine. The common descent of species and genera is for them a dogma, as much as the creation of species was for their fathers. With different eyes they watch the progress of science in this new territory. They neither feel the pride of the victor, nor have they the personal example of Darwin's untiring labor. It is much to be regretted that everywhere, in the manner of both working and thinking, we find evidence of this. Deductive treatment has taken the place of observation and investigation. An immense superstructure of speculative science has risen on the foundation of Darwin's selection theory. The possible influence of selection in past times has been discussed for numerous cases, but its actual influence at the present time was left uninvestigated. Thought, instead—of Nature, became the source of theory, and the latter consequently became farther and farther removed from the truth.

At last the tide is turning. Conn, in a recent book on evolution, exclaims: 'Let us leave our books and return to Nature,' adding, 'leave speculation and turn to observation.' The necessity of this is making

From *Science*, 15, No. 384, May 9, 1902.

itself felt everywhere. The time of contemplation is past. We no longer ask how things *might be;* how things *are* is the question of the hour.

De Varigny, the well-known French translator of Wallace's book on 'Darwinism,' formulates as the first requisite, viz., that we should see species originate. It is no longer sufficient to be convinced that it is so, we must know it from experience. During the last decade a few investigators have sought the paths which lead to this goal. It is but recently that the results they obtained have been published. And though the paths followed are very divergent, and the results differ greatly, yet for all the initial point was Darwin's book; none were influenced by subsequent speculations. Darwin's theory of adaptation led to the investigations on the origin of species in the Alps by Kerner and von Wettstein; Darwin's selection theory to the statistical investigations of variability by Galton and Weldon, and to the mathematical studies of Karl Pearson. And likewise finding its origin in Darwin's great work, stands the study of discontinuous variability, the study of the single variations or mutations,[1] and the question whether in these must be sought the origin of species.

Only a single case has been discovered in which it is possible to actually see species originate; and this not accidentally, but experimentally, so that one can watch and carefully follow the manner of their origin.

Three kinds of evening primroses occur in Holland, all three introduced from America about a century ago, but since escaped from cultivation. The youngest of the three, or rather the one most recently introduced, and at the same time the most rare, is the large-flowered evening primrose, described at the beginning of the nineteenth century by Lamarck, and named after him *Oenothera Lamarckiana.* It is a beautiful, freely branching plant, often attaining a height of five feet or more. The branches are placed at a sharp angle with the erect stem and in their turn bear numerous side branches. Nearly all branches and side branches are crowned with flowers, which, because of their size and bright yellow color, attract immediate attention, even from a distance. The flowers, as the name indicates, open towards evening, shortly before sunset, and this so suddenly that it seems as if a magic wand had touched the land and covered it

with a golden sheet. Bumble bees and moths, especially those of *Plusia gamma* and of *Agrotis segetum,* are the principal visitors. During the hot weather the flowering period is limited to the evening hours. In daytime often nothing is to be seen but faded and half-faded flowers and closed buds. Each flower bears a long style with four or more stigmas, which protrude at some distance above the eight anthers, and would therefore, as a rule, not be fertilized without the help of insects. When the flowers, including their apparent stem, the calyx tube, drop off, there remains behind a perigynous ovary, which finally becomes a capsule. At first green, it becomes brown on ripening and finally opens with four valves, setting free the seeds. A stem with ten to twenty, or even thirty or forty, capsules is not rare, nor consequently a plant with a hundred or more fruits. And since each fruit contains more than a hundred seeds it would be quite possible for a plant of this species to reproduce itself several thousandfold, provided all seeds could germinate and grow.

It is this plant, *Oenothera Lamarckiana,* which exhibits the long-sought peculiarity of producing each year a number of new species, and this not only in my experimental garden, but also when growing wild. But in the latter case the new species have as a rule but a very short lease of life; they are took weak and too few in number to survive in the struggle for existence with the hundreds and thousands of their fellows. In the experimental garden, however, they can be recognized at an early stage, and with especial care may be isolated and cultivated. It is thus that in the experimental garden we are readily able to see that which, among wild-growing plants, is lost to observation.

The new species vary but little from the old. An inexperienced eye detects no difference. Only a careful comparison shows that here we have to deal with a new type. There are some, for instance a dwarf species, and species with a peculiar close crown (*O. nanella* and *O. lata*), which at once attract our attention, because they are short of stature. Again, some are more slender and delicate, others low and unbranched, or robust and tall. A difference may be detected in the shape of the leaves, their color and their surface. The fruits vary in the same manner; sometimes they are long, sometimes short, sometimes slender, sometimes stout. The more one observes these plants, the more differences one sees. Gradually it becomes apparent that here we have to deal, not with a chaos of new forms, but rather with a series of sharply defined types. Each of these types originated from a seed produced by the parent species, growing wild, and fertilized in the usual

---

[1]Sudden variability, comprising the deviations from the rules of heredity in the wider sense, as opposed to fluctuating variability, *e.g.,* the degree of variability peculiar to each character of a species. Hugo de Vries, 'Die Mutationstheorie.' Leipzig, Veit & Co. 1901.

manner, or growing in the experimental garden, and fertilized artificially, with its own pollen.

Here then we have our first result. The new species originate suddenly, without preparation or intermediate forms. But they do not differ from the old species like an apple from a pear, a pine from a spruce, or a horse from a donkey. The deviations are far smaller. But every one knows how difficult it is to distinguish the common oak from *Quercus sessiliflora,* or the lime tree from *Tilia grandifolia.* Yet these are forms which by the disciples of Linnæus are recognized as true species. And what botanist has not been entangled in the species of *Hieracium,* or who is able to recognize at first sight the closely related forms of *Cochlearia?*

Because of the dying out of intermediate forms, more ancient species may be widely separated. On the other hand, more recent species, whose ancestors are still alive, may form narrow groups because of and with these surviving ancestors. Good illustrations of the latter are yielded by roses, willows and brambles, as shown by the facility with which the closely related forms can be cross-fertilized, as well as by the great trouble the numerous bastards cause in determination. Such genera are found everywhere in the plant kingdom; the gentians of the Alps, for instance, or the *Helianthemums,* which with us seem to be composed of fairly distinct types. Everything indicates that in these cases the species are of more recent date, and that only through the dying out of intermediate forms the differences between the remaining ones have attained that degree of distinctness which so greatly facilitates the separation of the other groups.

In this regard the *Oenotheras* agree exactly with what may be observed in nature. Recent forms group themselves around the mother form with minute, hardly perceptible gradations.

Once formed, the new species are as a rule at once constant. No series of generations, no selection, no struggle for existence are needed. Each time a new form has made its appearance in my garden, I have fertilized the flowers with their own pollen and have collected and sown the seed separately. The dwarf forms produce nothing but dwarfs (*O. nanella*), the white ones nothing but white ones (*O. albida*), the *O. gigas* nothing but *O. gigas,* the red-nerved ones nothing but corresponding specimens. But a single form made an exception. This was the small *O. scintillans,* the seeds of which produced but a percentage of *scintillans* plants, but here this inconstancy is and was as much the rule as the constancy of the other species.

As an example I may cite *O. gigas.* The plant is as tall as *O. Lamarckiana* but has a more robust stem,

denser foliage, a broader crown of large, widely opening flowers and stouter flowering-buds. The fruits attain but one half the length of those of plants of the mother species and consequently contain fewer seeds. But the individual seeds, on the other hand, are rounder, fuller and heavier. This type originated in my cultures of 1895 as a solitary specimen, which at first was overlooked. At that time I desired to hibernate some plants, and in the latter part of the autumn chose for that purpose twelve of the strongest and best developed. It was only in the following summer, when the plants began to flower, that I noticed that one plant showed differences, the importance of which I did not fully realize until the fruits, on ripening, became much shorter and stouter than ordinarily was the case. It was only then that I placed the raceme in a bag so as to prevent fertilization with other pollen. Afterwards this seed was collected separately and in the spring of 1897 sown in a flower bed between other beds sown with seeds of the normal *Oenothera Lamarckiana.* Immediately subsequent to germination no difference was apparent, but when the third and fourth leaves unfolded it suddenly became evident that a new species had originated. All plants differed from their neighbors, were more robust and bore broader, darker leaves. Though two to three hundred in number, all evidently belonged to one distinct type. Not having, at the time, paid special attention to the mother plant, I was unfortunately unable to compare the latter with the type at this age. But when, during the summer, first the stems and afterwards the flowers and the fruits, made their appearance, the agreement became perfect. All specimens closely resembled the mother, and together they formed the new species, *Oenothera gigas.* This species therefore was at once constant, even though it found its origin in but a single specimen. Evolved with a sudden leap from the mother species, differing from it in general appearance as well as in the character of its various organs, it remained unchanged. It was no rough cast which selection had to correct and polish before it could represent a distinct form; the new type was at once perfect and needed no smoothing, no correction.

My other species originated in the same manner, suddenly and without transitions. We may therefore assume that species, when growing wild, do not appear gradually, slowly adapting themselves to existing conditions, but suddenly, entirely independent of their surroundings. Species are not arbitrary groups, as Bailey, and with him many others, believed should be deduced from the theory of descent, but sharply defined types, unmistakable, for one who has once seen them.

Each species is an individual, says Gillot, having a birth, a lease of life, and an inevitable death. From the moment of birth until the time of death, it remains the same. Only when taking this point of view can we reconcile our daily experience of the constancy of species with the theory of descent. This is fully confirmed by the results of my experiments.

If species originated gradually, in the course of centuries, their birth could never be observed. Were it so, this most interesting phenomenon would forever remain hidden from us. Happily it is not so. Each species as soon as born takes its place as peer in the ranks of the older species. This birth may be directly observed. One can even collect the seeds in which the new types are hidden, and one can observe the first steps in the development of these types. Literally the new species originates at the time of the formation of the seed, but it is born only at the time of germination. But at this period it is not recognizable as such; this only becomes possible after the first leaves have unfolded. The plant can then be photographed, and in this manner we may preserve the type as soon as it becomes discernible and recognizable. In fact, one can study the birth of a species as readily as that of any individual, be it plant or animal.

Yet it shows one important difference. It is not at all necessary that a species should originate in but a single specimen as we saw in the case of O. gigas. The same leap, the same mutation may occur again, and actually did so in my experiments, where, in fact, it seemed to be the rule. All that is required is that the cultures consist of some thousands instead of some hundreds of specimens. Two

things then become apparent: First, that in each lot several specimens of O. nanella, O. lata, O. oblonga and of certain other new species appear; secondly, that it is only a few types (and no others) which make their appearance. The number of new forms is far from unlimited. On the contrary, but few types make their appearance annually, and this among a large number of specimens. There are some that are more rare, as for instance O. gigas and a most graceful, small-flowered mutation which put in an appearance during the past year. In the latter, unfortunately, the seeds did not ripen, and therefore, for the present at least, it has disappeared, leaving no trace, with the exception of a plate, a few photographs and some alcoholic material.

To give a general view of the whole course of my experiments on mutation in this genus, I might combine them in the form of a

O. Lamarckiana forms the main stem; all other species originated from its seeds. Descendants of the mutations are not included in the scheme, so as not to make it too intricate.

The first two generations showed but comparatively few types. The reason for this may be sought in the fact that at the time I did not know how to trace them. Hence the fourth generation shows a marked improvement, which continued after the sowing had undergone a great numerical reduction.

O. oblonga appeared by hundreds. All of these plants closely resembled each other. They could be recognized as rosettes of root leaves by the narrow leaves with broad veins, and later on by their delicate, stiff, nearly unbranched, seemingly naked

Genealogical Tree of Oenothera Lamarckiana.

Generations:	gigas	albida	oblonga	rubrinervis	Oenothera, Lamarckiana	nanella	lata	scintillans
8th Generation, 1899 Annual.		5	1		1700	21	1	
7th Generation, 1898 Annual.			9		3000	11		
6th Generation, 1897 Annual.		11	29	3	1800	9	5	1
5th Generation, 1896 Annual.		25	135	20	8000	49	142	6
4th Generation, 1895 Annual.	41	15	176	8	14000	60	63	1
3d Generation, 1890–1891 Biennial.				1	10000	3	3	
2d Generation, 1888–1889 Biennial.					15000	5	5	
1st Generation, 1886–1887 Biennial.					9			

stems. The same is true for the dwarf forms. Our genealogical tree shows of these about 150; in other experiments I have met with even larger numbers. These plants again form a distinct type, which could readily be recognized whatever the age of the specimens. *O. rubrinervis, O. albida* and *O. scintillans* were far rarer, but as a rule appeared each year, always bearing exactly the same character.

A species therefore is not born only a single time, but repeatedly, in a large number of individuals and during a series of consecutive years.

It is clear that this fact, so apparent in my experiments, must be of enormous importance in the case of wild-growing plants. How small is the chance of a single plant to triumph in the struggle for existence! Only when a number, or rather a large number, of similar individuals do battle together for the same cause is it that this chance acquires a value. *O. gigas* would have been nipped in the bud were it not for my aid. I have never found it growing wild, as I did some specimens of the less rare *O. lata,* and *O. nanella.* But these also meet with too many hardships. Only once have I found a single specimen in flower.

But next to the question of the more or less frequent appearance of a new species stands another which has as potent an influence upon its life. It is of course a matter of pure chance whether a mutation is or is not better adapted to the environment than the parent species. Sometimes it will go one way, sometimes the other, or both may be equally well adapted. Our *O. gigas* and *O. rubrinervis* are, during the flowering period, as robust as the mother species. Perhaps the first is, because of its broader leaves and stouter stem, a little better adapted. Probably both would survive in the struggle for existence if the early stages were not detrimental. *O. albida* and *O. oblonga,* on the other hand, are extremely weak, and it is with great difficulty that they can be persuaded to produce flowers and fruit. When growing wild they could never survive, in fact, they are never met with, though in the garden experiments they made their appearance in large numbers. For *O. nanella* the form is an objection, at least, under existing conditions, though were these different, it might prove an advantage. In regard to *O. lata,* which until now I have hardly mentioned, the plants are low, with a limp stem, bent tips and side branches, all very brittle, but with dense foliage and luxuriant growth. But unlike its relations, it possesses no pollen. It is true there are apparently robust anthers, but they are dry, wrinkled and devoid of contents. Only by cross-fertilization can *O. lata* produce seeds, and so it is unfit to found a wild type. Certain structural characters of this plant are therefore detrimental, or at least useless, and 'useless characters,' as every one knows, were among the earliest objections to the doctrine of

the gradual origin of species by selection. For this theory can explain none but useful characters.

These observations are also important from another point of view. They teach us that the variability of species is independent of environment. This hypothesis, already formulated by Darwin, and which for him was the basis of a simple, logical explanation, is fully confirmed by the results of our experiments. Before Darwin published his 'Origin of Species,' it was generally believed to be otherwise; it was thought that environment had a direct influence on species. Changes in environment would call forth various needs and these in their turn would cause gradual changes in various organs. Use would have a strengthening, disuse a weakening, effect; a functioning in a certain direction would fit the organ better for that function. The changes would take place gradually and imperceptibly, but if only the influence continued long enough in one direction, specific differences would finally appear. On this theory are based the attempts already mentioned to make new species by transporting lowland plants to the highlands and *vice versa.* When this is done, great modifications may be observed, even during the first year. In the Alps the plants assume the compact, woody, small-leaved form which we meet with there so frequently; in the plains they are tall, with slender stems and ample but delicate foliage. At first it appears as if these experiments bore out the general opinion, but Bonnier has shown the opposite. He has proved that it is nothing but adaptation, something which any plant can show and which stands in no relation to heredity and the origin of species.

In my experiments the mother species mutates in all directions, in nearly all organs and characters as well as for better or worse. These changes occur, as far as could be learned, on a poor sandy soil as well as on heavily manured garden soil, with careful treatment and plenty of room between the plants. The mutation therefore is independent of environment, its direction is not governed by circumstances. Numerous species originate at the same time, forming a group in the same manner as the above-mentioned genera. The question which of these will persist in the wild state, which, as legitimate species, will some time form part of our flora, does not concern us at present. This can only be decided when the new forms have lived next to the others for a prolonged period, as some of them have done for the last fifteen years. For sooner or later must begin the struggle for existence, and the species which is best adapted will come out triumphant. But it is not a struggle between individuals, as is commonly believed, but war between species. The question is whether *O. gigas* or *O. rubrinervis,* or perhaps *O. nanella* or some other species will be best adapted to the new environment. Only then will be decided which shall remain and which shall go.

Here we have elimination of the weak, selection of the strong. 'Many are called but few are chosen.' In Nature this is true of species as well as of individuals.

The development of the entire plant kingdom points to a gradual progress. Nature passes from simple to complex, from generalities to particulars, from the lower to the more highly organized, from species with few characters to those which possess a countless number. Are our mutations a step forward in this direction? I believe I am able to answer this question in the affirmative, if we except perhaps *O. lata*, which possesses feminine characters only, and the dwarf forms, whose type is too common.

It is exactly because of this peculiarity that I arrive at this conclusion. Dwarfs constitute the only type which is also met with among other species, a type which is found among a large number of plants, such as dahlias, chrysanthemums, ageratums and a long list of species belonging to the most widely divergent families. A dwarf form is therefore nothing new, it is but an old principle under a new guise. The same is true for so many other forms which is horticultural and systematic botany are dignified by the name of variety. White varieties are found among most red- or blue-flowered species; with hirsute or thorny species occur nearly as many glabrous or thornless forms. Such repetitions are evidently no progress. They contribute largely to the great variety of Nature, but are usually retrogressive and not progressive changes. And ordinarily they deviate from the species in but a single character, something indicated as a rule by the name.

Quite different from this are the mutations of *Oenothera*. Recognizable as seedlings, as rosettes differing in shape, edge and color of the root-leaves, and later with stems differing in structure and mode of branching, agreeing in the flowers, varying in the fruits, they possess a type entirely their own, a type quite novel. Neither in other species of this genus nor in other genera belonging to the same family, nor anywhere else in the plant kingdom, do we find a *rubrinervis* or an *albida* with all their distinctive characters. Here we have something absolutely new, something entirely original.

My observations constitute but a first step in a new direction. But that direction is the one demanded by the times.

Any advance in our knowledge depends on the possibility of seeing species originate. Of course this does not refer to present species. Such a thing would be as impossible, as absurd, as expecting to witness the birth of an individual already inhabiting the earth. The species living at present are too old. But they may give rise to new ones. There seems to be sufficient reason for suspecting that this is happening at this very moment, and in our immediate surroundings, only we are not aware of it. Such cases must therefore be searched for with great care and patience. Once found, they must be carefully and extensively studied. The one case which I have mentioned here shows sufficiently the great treasure of new facts which lies within our reach. All that is necessary is to overcome the first difficulties.

Not only would such studies aid the theories of science, but they would also be of great advantage to the practical side of life. Our improved agricultural plants may serve as an illustration. According to Hays the produce of entire districts may be increased ten per cent. by the careful and repeated selection of seed. And these results were reached by the aid of old methods, applied during a few years only. How great is the promise of the new methods, with their larger prospects and greater chances.

Next to new races are new species. Let this be the motto of science and practice alike, for the welfare of agriculture as well as for the welfare of man.

Name: _____   **Date:** _____

1. List and describe three different ways in which Darwin's *Origin of Species* changed the way naturalists thought or worked.

1.

2.

3.

2. What is de Vries' definition of "mutation?"

3. What is the only, according to de Vries, instance in which scientists have witnessed the production of a new species? How did this new species originate?

4. The author claims that new species originate suddenly and without transitions. What is the significance of this fact to Darwin's theory of natural selection?

Jacques Loeb

"The Recent Development of Biology," 1904

Loeb (1859-1924) was German immigrant to the United States and was sharply critical of the speculative nature of American biology. Believing that physicists and chemists were capable of much more certain conclusions about their subject matters, Loeb argued that for biology to become a true science, it would have to discard notions like instincts and adopt physical and chemical explanations for all animal behaviors. In this selection, Loeb called for the creation of "technical biology," which would eschew antiquated notions of the meaning of life and replace them with chemical and physical causes.

The task allotted to me on this occasion is a review of the development of biology during the last century. The limited time at our disposal will necessitate many omissions and will force me to confine myself to the discussion of a few of the departures in biology which have led or promise to lead to fertile discoveries.

The problem of a scientific investigator can always be reduced to two tasks; the first, to determine the independent variables of the phenomena which he has under investigation, and secondly, to find the formula which allows him to calculate the value of the function for every value of the variable. In physics and chemistry the independent variables are in many cases so evident that the investigation may begin directly with the quantitative determination of the relation between the change of the essential variable and the function. In biology, however, the variables, as a rule, can not be recognized so easily and a great part of the mental energy of the investigators must be spent in the search for these variables. To give an example, we know that in many eggs the development only begins after the entrance of a spermatozoon into the egg. The spermatozoon must produce some kind of a change in the egg, which is responsible for the development. But we do not know which variable in the egg is changed by the spermatozoon, whether the latter produces a chemical or an osmotic change, or whether it brings about

a change of phase or some other effect. It goes without saying that a theory of sexual fertilization is impossible until the independent variable in the process of sexual fertilization is known.

But the investigations of the biologist differ from those of the chemist and physicist in that the biologist deals with the analysis of the mechanism of a special class of machines. Living organisms are chemical machines, made of essentially colloidal material which possess the peculiarity of developing, preserving and reproducing themselves automatically. The machines which have thus far been produced artificially lack the peculiarity of developing, growing, preserving and reproducing themselves, though no one can say with certainty that such machines might not one day be constructed artificially.

The specific and main work of the biologist will, therefore, be directed toward the analysis of the automatic mechanisms of development of self-preservation and reproduction.

THE DYNAMICS OF THE CHEMICAL PROCESSES IN LIVING ORGANISMS

The progress made by chemistry, especially physical chemistry, has definitely put an end to the idea that the chemistry of living matter is different from the chemistry of inanimate matter. The presence of catalyzers in all living tissues makes it intelligible that in spite of the comparatively low temperature at which life phenomena occur the reaction velocities

From *Science*, 20, No. 519, December 9, 1904.

for the essential processes in living organisms are comparatively high. It has been shown, moreover, that the action of the catalyzers found in living organisms can be imitated by certain metals or other inorganic catalyzers. We may, therefore, say that it is now proved beyond all doubt that the variables in the chemical processes in living organisms are identical with those with which the chemist has to deal in the laboratory. As a consequence of this result chemical biology has during the last years entered into the series of those sciences which are capable of predicting their results quantitatively. The application of the theory of chemical equilibrium to life phenomena has led biological chemists to look for reversible chemical processes in living organisms and the result is the discovery of the reversible enzyme actions, which we owe to A. C. Hill. I think it marks the beginning of a new epoch of the physiology of metabolism that we now know that the same enzymes not only accelerate the hydrolysis, but also in some cases, if not generally, the synthesis of the products of cleavage. It is not impossible that the results thus obtained in the field of biology will ultimately in return benefit chemistry, inasmuch as they may enable chemistry to accomplish syntheses with the help of enzymes found in living organisms which could otherwise not be so easily obtained.

A very beautiful example of the conquest of biological chemistry through chemical dynamics is offered by the work of Arrhenius and Madsen. These authors have successfully applied the laws of chemical equilibrium to toxins and anti-toxins so that it is possible to calculate the degree of saturation between toxins and antitoxins for any concentration with the same ease and certainty as for any other chemical reaction.

We know as yet but little concerning the method by which enzymes produce their accelerating effects. It seems that the facts recently gathered speak in favor of the idea of intermediary reactions. According to this idea the catalyzers participate in the reaction, but form combinations that are again rapidly decomposed. This makes it intelligible that at the end of the reaction the enzymes and catalyzers are generally in the same condition as at the beginning of the reaction, and that a comparatively small quantity of the catalyzer is sufficient for the transformation of large quantities of the reacting substances.

This chapter should not be concluded without mentioning the discovery of zymase by Buchner. It had long been argued that only certain of the fermentative actions of yeast depended on the presence of enzymes which could be separated from the living cells, but that the alcoholic fermentation of sugar by yeast was inseparably linked together with the life of the cell. Buchner showed that the enzyme which accelerates the alcoholic fermentation of sugar can also be separated from the living cell, with this purely technical difference only, that it requires a much higher pressure to extract zymase than any other enzymes from the yeast cell.

PHYSICAL STRUCTURE OF LIVING MATTER

We have stated that living organisms are chemical machines whose framework is formed by colloidal material consisting of proteins, fatty compounds, and carbohydrates. These colloids possess physical qualities which are believed to play a great rôle in life phenomena. Among these qualities are the slow rate of diffusion, the existence of a double layer of electricity at the surface of the dissolved or suspended colloidal particles, and the production of definite structures when they are precipitated. We may consider it as probable that the cytological and histological structures of living matter will be reduced to the physical qualities of the colloids. But, inasmuch as the physics of the colloids is still in its beginning, we must not be surprised that the biological application of its results is still in the stage of mere suggestions. The most important result which has thus far been accomplished through the application of the physics of colloids to biology is Traube's invention of the semipermeable membranes. To Traube we owe the discovery that every living cell behaves as if it were surrounded with a surface film which does not possess equal permeability for water and the substances dissolved in it. Salts which are dissolved in water, as a rule, migrate much more slowly into the living cells than water. This discovery of the semi-permeability of the surface films of living protoplasm made, it possible to recognize the variable which determines the exchange of liquids between protoplasm and the liquid medium by which it is surrounded, namely, the osmotic pressure. Inasmuch as the osmotic pressure is measurable, this field of biology has entered upon a stage where every hypothesis can be tested exactly and biology is no longer compelled to carry a ballast of shallow phrases. We are now able to analyze quantitatively such functions as lymph formation and the secretion of glands.

Recent investigations have thrown some light on the nature of the conditions which seem to determine the semi-permeability of living matter. Quincke had already mentioned that a film of oil acts like a semipermeable membrane. From certain considerations of surface tension and surface energy it follows that every particle of protoplasm which is surrounded by a watery liquid must form an extremely thin film of oil at its surface. Overton has recently shown that of all dissolved substances those which possess a high solubility in fat, *e.g.,* alcohol, ether, chloroform, diffuse most easily into living cells. Overton concludes that lipoid substances such as lecithin and cholesterin which are found in every cell determine the phenomenon of the semi-permeability of living matter.

DEVELOPMENT AND HEREDITY

We now come to the discussion of those phenomena which constitute the specific difference between living machines and the machines which we have thus far been able to make artificially. Living organisms show the phenomena of development. During the last century it was ascertained that the development of an animal egg, in general, does not occur until a spermatozoon has entered it, but, as already stated, we do not know which variable in the egg is changed by the spermatozoon. An attempt has been made to fill the gap by causing unfertilized eggs to develop with the aid of physico-chemical means. The decisive variable by which such an artificial parthenogenesis can be best produced is the osmotic pressure. It has been possible to cause the unfertilized eggs of echinoderms, annelids and mollusks to develop into swimming larvæ by increasing transitorily the osmotic pressure of the surrounding solution. Even in vertebrates (the frog and petromyzon), Bataillon has succeeded in calling forth the first processes of development in this way. In other forms specific chemical influences cause the development, *e.g.,* in the eggs of star-fish diluted acids and, best of all, as Delage has shown, carbon dioxide. In the eggs of *Chœtotopterus* potassium salts produce this result and in the case of *Amphitrite,* calcium salts.

From a sexual cell only a definite organism can arise whose properties can be predicted if we know from which organism the sexual cell originates. The foundations of the theory of heredity were laid by Gregory Mendel in his treatise on the 'Hybrids of Plants,' one of the most prominent papers ever published in biology. Mendel showed in his experiments that certain simple characteristics, as, for example, the round or angular shape of the seeds of peas or the color of their endosperm is already determined in the germ by definite determinants. He showed, moreover, that in the case of the hybridization of certain forms one half of the sexual cells of each child contains the determinants of the one parent, the other half contains the determinants of the other parent. In thus showing that the results of hybridization can be predicted numerically not only for one but for a series of generations, according to the laws of the calculus of probability, he gave not a hypothesis, but an exact theory of heredity. Mendel's experiments remained unnoticed until Hugo de Vries discovered the same facts anew, and at the same time became aware of Mendel's treatise.

The theory of heredity of Mendel and de Vries is in full harmony with the idea of evolution. The modern idea of evolution originated, as is well known, with Lamarck, and it is the great merit of Darwin to have revived this idea. It is, however, remarkable that none of the Darwinian authors seemed to consider it necessary that the transformation of species should be the object of direct observation. It is generally understood in the natural sciences either that direct observation should form the foundation of our conclusions or mathematical laws which are derived from direct observations. This rule was evidently considered superfluous by those writing on the hypothesis of evolution. Their scientific conscience was quieted by the assumption that processes like that of evolution could not be directly observed, as they occurred too slowly, and that for this reason indirect observations must suffice. I believe that this lack of direct observation explains the polemical character of this literature, for wherever we can base our conclusions upon direct observations polemics become superfluous. It was, therefore, a decided progress when de Vries was able to show that the hereditary changes of forms, so-called 'mutations,' can be directly observed, at least in certain groups of organisms, and secondly, that these changes take place in harmony with the idea that for definite hereditary characteristics definite determinants, possibly in the form of chemical compounds, must be present in the sexual cells. It seems to me that the work of Mendel and de Vries and their successors marks the beginning of a real theory of heredity and evolution. If it is at all possible to produce new species artificially I think that the discoveries of Mendel and de Vries must be the starting point.

It is at present entirely unknown how it happens that in living organisms, as a rule, larger quantities of sexual cells begin to form at a definite period in their existence. Miescher attempted to solve this problem in his researches on the salmon. But it seems that Miescher laid too much emphasis upon a more secondary feature of this phenomenon, namely, that the sexual cells in the salmon apparently develop at the expense of the muscular substance of the animal. According to our present knowledge of the chemical dynamics of the animal body it seems rather immaterial whether the proteins and other constituents of the sexual cell come from the body of the animal or from the food taken up. The causes which determine the formation of large masses of sexual cells in an organism at a certain period of its existence are entirely unknown.

A little more progress has been made in regard to another problem which belongs to this group of phenomena, namely how it happens that in many species one individual forms sperm, the other eggs. It has been known for more than a century that it is possible to produce at desire either females exclusively or both sexes in plant lice. In bees and related forms, as a rule at least, only males originate from the unfertilized eggs; from the fertilized eggs only females. It is, moreover, known that in higher vertebrates those twins which originate from one egg have the same sex, while the sex of twins originating from different eggs may be different. All facts which are thus far known in regard to the determination of sex seem to indicate that the sex of the embryo is already determined in the unfertilized egg, or at least immediately after fertilization. I consider it possible that in regard to the determination of sex, just as in the case of artificial parthenogenesis, a general variable will be found by which we can determine whether an egg cell will assume male or female character.

INSTINCT AND CONSCIOUSNESS

The difference between our artificial machines and the living organisms appears, perhaps; most striking when we compare the many automatic devices by which the preservation of individuals and species is guaranteed. Where separate sexes exist we find automatic arrangements by which the sexual cells of the two sexes are brought together. Wherever the development of the eggs and larvæ occurs outside of the body of the mother or the nest we often find automatic mechanisms whereby the eggs are deposited in such places as contain food on which the young larva can exist and grow. We have to raise the question how far has the analysis of these automatic mechanisms been pushed. Metaphysics has supplied us with the terms 'instinct' and 'will' for these phenomena. We speak of instinct wherever an animal performs, without foresight of the ends, those acts by which the preservation of the individual or the species is secured. The term 'will' is reserved for those cases where these processes form constituents of consciousness. The words 'instinct' and 'will' do, however, not give us the variables by which we can analyze or control the mechanism of these actions. Scientific analysis has shown that the motions of animals which are directed towards a definite aim depend upon a mechanism which is essentially a function of the symmetrical structure and the symmetrical distribution of irritability. Symmetrical points of the surface of an animal, as a rule, have the same irritability, which means that, when stimulated equally, they produce the same

quantity of motion. The points at the oral pole as a rule possess a qualitatively different or greater irritability than those at the aboral pole. If rays of light or current curves, or lines of diffusion or gravitation, start from one point and strike an organism, which is sensitive for the form of energy involved, on one side only, the tension of the symmetrical muscles or contractile elements does not remain the same on both sides of the body, and a tendency for rotation will result. This will continue until the symmetrical points of the animal are struck equally. As soon as this occurs there is no more reason why the animal should deviate to the right or left from the direction of its plane or axis of symmetry. These phenomena of automatic orientation of animals in a field of energy have been designated as tropisms. It has been possible to dissolve a series of mysterious instincts into cases of simple tropisms. The investigation of the various cases of tropism has shown their great variety and there can be no doubt that further researches will increase the variety of tropisms and tropism-like phenomena. I am inclined to believe that we possess in the tropisms and tropism-like mechanisms the independent variable of such functions as the instinctive selection of food and similar regulatory phenomena.

As far as the mechanism of consciousness is concerned no scientific fact has thus far been found that promises an unraveling of this mechanism in the near future. It may be said, however, that at least the nature of the biological problem here involved can be stated. From a scientific point of view we may say that what we call consciousness is the function of a definite machine which we will call the machine of associative memory. Whatever the nature of this machine in living beings may be, it has an essential feature in common with the phonograph, namely, that it is capable of reproducing impressions in the same chronological order in which they come to us. Even simultaneous impressions of a different physical character, such as, for instance, optical and acoustical, easily fuse in memory and form an inseparable complex. The mechanism upon which associative memory depends seems to be located, in higher vertebrates at least, in the cerebral hemispheres, as the experiments of Goltz have shown. The same author has shown, moreover, that one of the two hemispheres suffices for the efficiency of this mechanism and for the full action of consciousness. As far, however, as the physical or chemical character of the mechanism of memory is concerned, we possess only a few starting points. We know that the nerve cells are especially rich in fatty constituents and Overton and Hans Meyer have shown that substances which are easily soluble in fat also act as very powerful anesthetics, for instance, chloroform, ether and alcohol, and so on. It may be possible that the mechanism of associative memory depends in some way upon the constitution or action of the fatty compounds in our nerve cells. Another fact which may prove of importance is the observation made by Speck that if the partial pressure of oxygen in the air falls below one third of its normal value, mental activity very soon becomes impaired and consciousness is lost. Undoubtedly the unraveling of the mechanism of associated memory is one of the greatest discoveries which biology has still in store.

ELEMENTARY PHYSIOLOGICAL PROCESSES

It is, perhaps, possible that an advance in the analysis of the mechanism of memory will be made when we shall know more about the processes that occur in nerve cells in general. The most elementary mechanisms of self preservation in higher animals are the respiratory motions and the action of the heart. The impulse for the respiratory action starts from the nerve cells. As far as the impulses for the activity of the heart are concerned we can say that in one form at least they start from nerve cells, and in all cases from those regions where nerve cells are situated. But as far as the nature of these impulses is concerned we know as little about the cause of the rhythmical phenomena of respiration and heart beat as we know concerning the mechanism of associative memory. It is rather surprising, but nevertheless a fact, that physiology has not progressed beyond the stage of mere suggestions and hypotheses in the analysis of such elementary phenomena as nerve action, muscular contractility and cell division. Among the suggestions concerning the nature of contractility those seem most promising which take into consideration the phenomena of surface tension. The same lack of definite knowledge is found in regard to the changes in the sense organs which give rise to sensations. It is obvious that the most striking gaps in biology are found in that field of biology which has been cultivated by the physiologists. The reason for this is in part, that the analysis of the elementary protoplasmic processes is especially difficult, but I believe that there are other reasons. Medical physiologists have confined themselves to the study of a few organisms, and this has had the effect that for the last fifty years the same work has been repeated with slight modifications over and over again.

TECHNICAL BIOLOGY

I think the creation of technical biology must be considered the most significant turn biology has taken during the last century. This turn is connected with a number of names, among which Liebig and Pasteur are the most prominent. Agriculture may be considered as an industry for the transformation of radiating into chemical energy. It was known for a long time that the green plants were able to build up, with the help of the light, the carbohydrates from the carbon dioxide of the air. Liebig showed that for the growth of the plant definite salts are necessary, that these salts are withdrawn from the soil by the plants, and that in order to produce crops these salts must be given back to the soil. One important point had not been cleared up by the work of Liebig, namely, the source of nitrates in the soil which the plants need for the manufacture of their proteins. This gap was filled by Hellriegel, who found that the tubercles of the leguminosæ, or rather the bacteria contained in these tubercles, are capable of transforming the inert nitrogen of the air into a form in which the plant can utilize it for the synthesis of its proteins. Winogradski subsequently discovered that not only the tubercle bacteria of leguminosæ are capable of fixing the nitrogen of the air in the soil in a form in which it can be utilized by the plant, but that the same can be done by certain other bacteria, for instance, *Chlostridium pasteurianum*. These facts have a bearing which goes beyond the interests of agriculture. The question of obtaining nitrates from the nitrogen of the air is of importance also for chemical industry, and it is not impossible that chemists may one day utilize the experience obtained in nitrifying bacteria.

With the discovery of the culture of nitrifying bacteria we have already entered the field of Pasteur's work. Yeast had been used for the purposes of fermentation before Pasteur, but Pasteur freed this field of biology just as much from the influence of chance as Liebig did in the case of agriculture. The chemist Pasteur taught biologists how to discriminate between the useful and harmful forms of yeast and bacteria, and thus rendered it possible to put the industry of fermentation upon a safe basis.

In recent times the fact has often been mentioned that the coal fields will be exhausted sooner or later. If this is true every source of available energy which is neglected to-day may one day become of importance. Professor Hensen has recognized the importance of the surface of the ocean for the production of crops. The surface of the ocean is inhabited by endless masses of microscopic organisms which contain chlorophyl and which are capable of transforming the radiating energy of the sun into chemical energy.

Not only through the industry of fermentation and agriculture has technical biology asserted its place side by side with physical and chemical technology, but also in the conquest of new regions for civilization. As long as tropical countries are continually threatened by epidemics no steady industrial development is possible. Biology has begun to remove this danger. It is due to Koch if epidemics of cholera can be suppressed to-day and to Yersin if the spreading of plague can now be prevented. Theobald Smith discovered that the organisms of Texas fever are carried by a certain insect, and this discovery has had the effect of reducing and possibly in the near future destroying two dreaded diseases, namely, malaria and yellow fever.

It is natural that the rapid development of technical biology has reacted beneficially upon the development of theoretical biology. Just as physics and chemistry are receiving steadily new impulses from technology, the same is true for biology. The working out of the problems of immunity has created new fields for theoretical biology. Ehrlich has shown that in the case of immunity toxins are rendered harmless by their being bound by certain bodies, the so-called anti-toxins. The investigation of the nature and the origin of toxins in the case of acquired immunity is a new problem which technical biology has given to theoretical biology. The same may be said in regard to the experiments of Pfeifer and Bordet on bacteriolysis and hemolysis. Bordet's work has led to the development of methods which have been utilized for the determination of the blood relationship of animals.

The representatives of the mental sciences often reproach the natural sciences that the latter only develop the material but not the mental or moral interests of humanity. It seems to me, however, that this statement is wrong. The struggle against superstition is entirely carried on by the natural sciences, and especially by the applied sciences. The nature of superstition consists in a gross misunderstanding of the causes of natural phenomena. I have not gained the impression that the mental sciences have been able to reduce the amount of superstition. Lourdes and Mecca are in no danger from the side of the representatives of the mental sciences, but only from the side of scientific medicine. Superstition disappears so slowly for the reason that the masses as a rule are not taught any sciences. If the day comes in our universities neither by chairs nor by laboratories. We have laboratories for physiology, but to show how little interest physiologists take in general biology I may mention the fact that the editor of a physiological annual review excludes papers on the development and fertilization from his report, as in his opinion, this belongs to anatomy. On the other hand, anatomists and zoologists must give their full energy to their morphological investigations and have, as a rule, neither the time for experimental work nor very often the training necessary for that kind of work. Only the botanists have kept up their interest in general biology, but they of course pay no attention to animal biology. In working out this short review of the development of biology during the last century I have been impressed with the necessity of our making better provisions for that side of biology where, in my opinion, the chances for the great discoveries seem to lie, namely, *general* or *experimental* biology.

Name: _____ **Date:** _____

1. According to Loeb, in what ways is the task of a biologist different from the job of chemists and physicists?

2. How does Loeb define or describe life? That is, when he thinks of a living thing, what does he think of?

3. How, according to Loeb, are living things different from non-living things?

4. What does Loeb believe is the cause of animals' instincts?

5. What is "technical biology" according to Loeb?

William Bateson

"Evolutionary Faith and Modern Doubts," 1922

Bateson (1861-1926) was an English biologist, advocate of Mendelism, and founder of the science of genetics. In this piece he presented the problems that biologists confronted in explaining precisely how evolution occurred and admitted, "I have put before you very frankly the considerations which have made us agnostic as to the actual mode and processes of evolution." Bateson wrote the piece believing that evolution occurred, and most other biologists viewed the article as a research agenda and a call to duty, but religious critics of evolutionary theory used to attack the reality of evolutionary change.

I visit Canada for the first time in delightful circumstances. After a period of dangerous isolation, intercourse between the centres of scientific development is once more beginning, and I am grateful to the American Association for this splendid opportunity of renewing friendship with my western colleagues in genetics, and of coming into even a temporary partnership in the great enterprise which they have carried through with such extraordinary success.

In all that relates to the theme which I am about to consider we have been passing through a period of amazing activity and fruitful research. Coming here after a week in close communion with the wonders of Columbia University, I may seem behind the times in asking you to devote an hour to the old topic of evolution. But though that subject is no longer in the forefront of debate, I believe it is never very far from the threshold of our minds, and it was with pleasure that I found it appearing in conspicuous places in several parts of the program of this meeting.

Standing before the American Association, it is not unfit that I should begin with a personal reminiscence. In 1883 I first came to the United States to study the development of Balanoglossus at the Johns Hopkins summer laboratory, then at Hampton, Va. This creature had lately been found there in an easily accessible place. With a magnanimity, that on looking back I realize was superb, Professor W. K.

From *Science*, 55, No. 1412, January 20, 1922.

Brooks had given me permission to investigate it, thereby handing over to a young stranger one of the prizes which in this age of more highly developed patriotism, most teachers would keep for themselves and their own students. At that time one morphological laboratory was in purpose and aim very much like another. Morphology was studied because it was the material believed to be most favorable for the elucidation of the problems of evolution, and we all thought that in embryology the quintessence of morphological truth was most palpably presented. Therefore every aspiring zoologist was an embryologist, and the one topic of professional conversation was evolution. It had been so in our Cambridge school, and it was so at Hampton.

I wonder if there is now a single place where the academic problems of morphology which we discussed with such avidity can now arouse a moment's concern. There were of course men who saw a little further, notably Brooks himself. He was at that time writing a book on heredity, and, to me at least, the notion on which he used to expatiate, that there was a special physiology of heredity capable of independent study, came as a new idea. But no organized attack on that problem was begun, nor had any one an inkling of how to set about it. So we went on talking about evolution. That is basely 40 years ago; to-day we feel silence to be the safer course.

Systematists still discuss the limits of specific distinction in a spirit, which I fear is often rather scholastic than progressive, but in the other centers of biological research a score of concrete and immediate problems have replaced evolution.

Discussions of evolution came to an end primarily because it was obvious that no progress was being made. Morphology having been explored in its minutest corners, we turned elsewhere. Variation and heredity, the two components of the evolutionary path, were next tried. The geneticist is the successor of the morphologist. We became geneticists in the conviction that there at least must evolutionary wisdom be found. We got on fast. So soon as a critical study of variation was undertaken, evidence came in as to the way in which varieties do actually arise in descent. The unacceptable doctrine of the secular transformation of masses by the accumulation of impalpable changes became not only unlikely but gratuitous. An examination in the field of the interrelations of pairs of well characterized but closely allied "species" next proved, almost wherever such an inquiry could be instituted, that neither could both have been gradually evolved by natural selection from a common intermediate progenitor, nor either from the other by such a process. Scarcely ever where such pairs co-exist in nature, or occupy conterminous areas do we find an intermediate normal population as the theory demands. The ignorance of common facts bearing on this part of the inquiry which prevailed among evolutionists, was, as one looks back, astonishing and inexplicable. It had been decreed that when varieties of a species co-exist in nature, they must be connected by all intergradations, and it was an article of faith of almost equal validity that the intermediate form must be statistically the majority, and the extremes comparatively rare. The plant breeder might declare that he had varieties of Primula or some other plant, lately constituted, uniform in every varietal character breeding strictly true in those respects, or the entomologist might state that a polymorphic species of a beetle or of a moth fell obviously into definite types, but the evolutionary philosopher knew better. To him such statements merely showed that the reporter was a bad observer, and not improbably a destroyer of inconvenient material. Systematists had sound information but no one consulted them on such matters or cared to hear what they might have to say. The evolutionist of the eighties was perfectly certain that species were a figment of the systematist's mind, not worthy of enlightened attention.

Then came the Mendalian clue. We saw the varieties arising. Segregation maintained their identity. The discontinuity of variation was recognized in abundance. Plenty of the Mendelian combinations would in nature pass the scrutiny of even an exacting systematist and be given "specific rank." In the light of such facts the origin of species was no doubt a similar phenomenon. All was clear ahead. But soon, though knowledge advanced at a great rate, and though whole ranges of phenomena which had seemed capricious and disorderly fell rapidly into a co-ordinated system, less and less was heard about evolution in genetical circles, and now the topic is dropped. When students of other sciences ask us what is now currently believed about the origin of species we have no clear answer to give. Faith has given place to agnosticism for reasons which on such an occasion as this we may profitably consider.

Where precisely has the difficulty arisen? Though the reasons for our reticence are many and present themselves in various forms, they are in essence one; that as we have come to know more of living things and their properties, we have become more and more impressed with the inapplicability of the evidence to these questions of origin. There is no apparatus which can be brought to bear on them which promises any immediate solution.

In the period I am thinking of it was in the characteristics and behavior of animals and plants in their more familiar phases, namely, the Zygotic phases that attention centered. Genetical research has revealed the world of gametes from which the zygotes—the products of fertilization are constructed. What has been there witnessed is of such extraordinary novelty and so entirely unexpected that in presence of the new discoveries we would fain desist from speculation for a while. We see long courses of analysis to be traveled through and for some time to come that will be a sufficient occupation. The evolutionary systems of the eighteenth and nineteenth centuries were attempts to elucidate the order seen prevailing in this world of zygotes and to explain it in simpler terms of cause and affect: we now perceive that that order rests on and is determined by another equally significant and equally in need of "explanation." But if we for the present drop evolutionary speculation it is in no spirit of despair. What has been learned about the gametes and their natural history constitutes progress upon which we shall never have to go back. The analysis has gone deeper than the most sanguine could have hoped.

We have turned still another bend in the track and behind the gametes we see the chromosomes. For the doubts—which I trust may be pardoned in one who had never seen the marvels of cytology, save as through a glass darkly—can not as regards the main thesis of the Drosophila workers, be any longer maintained. The arguments of Morgan and his colleagues, and especially the demonstrations of Bridges, must allay all scepticism as to the direct association of particular chromosomes with particular features of the zygote. The transferable characters borne by the gametes have been successfully referred to the visible details of nuclear configuration.

The traces of order in variation and heredity which so lately seemed paradoxical curiosities have led step by step to this beautiful discovery. I come at this Christmas Season to lay my respectful homage before the stars that have arisen in the west. What wonder if we hold our breath? When we knew nothing of all this the words came freely. How easy it all used to look! What glorious assumptions went without rebuke. Regardless of the obvious consideration that "modification by descent" must be a chemical process, and that of the principles governing that chemistry science had neither hint, nor surmise, nor even an empirical observation of its working, professed men of science offered very confidently positive opinions on these nebulous topics which would now scarcely pass muster in a newspaper or a sermon. It is a wholesome sign of return to sense that these debates have been suspended.

Biological science has returned to its rightful place, investigation of the structure and properties of the concrete and visible world. We cannot see how the differentiation into species came about. Variation of many kinds, often considerable, we daily witness, but no origin of species. Distinguishing what is known from what may be believed we have absolute certainty that new forms of life, new orders and new species have arisen on the earth. That is proved by the paleontological record. In a spirit of paradox even this has been questioned. It has been asked how do you *know* for instance that there were no mammals in palæozoic times? May there not have been mammals somewhere on the earth though no vestige of them has come down to us? We may feel confident there were no mammals then, but are we sure? In very ancient rocks most of the great orders of animals are represented. The absence of the others might by no great stress of imagination be ascribed to accidental circumstances.

Happily however there is one example of which we can be sure. There were no Angiosperms—that is to say "higher plants" with protected seeds—in the carboniferous epoch. Of that age we have abundant remains of a world wide and rich flora. The Angiosperms are cosmopolitan. By their means of dispersal they must immediately have become so. Their remains are very readily preserved. If they had been in existence on the earth in carboniferous times they must have been present with the carboniferous plants, and must have been preserved with them. Hence we may be sure that they did appear on the earth since those times. We are not certain, using certain in the strict sense, that the Angiosperms are the lineal descendants of the carboniferous plants,

but it is very much easier to believe that they are than that they are not.

Where is the difficulty? If the Angiosperms came from the carboniferous flora why may we not believe the old comfortable theory in the old way? Well so we may if by belief we mean faith, the substance, the foundation of things hoped for, the evidence of things not seen. In dim outline evolution is evident enough. From the facts it is a conclusion which inevitably follows. But that particular and essential bit of the theory of evolution which is concerned with the origin and nature of *species* remains utterly mysterious. We no longer feel as we used to do, that the process of variation, now contemporaneously occurring, is the beginning of a work which needs merely the element of time for its completion; for even time can not complete that which has not yet begun. The conclusion in which we were brought up, that species are a product of a summation of variations ignored the chief attribute of species first pointed out by John Ray that the product of their crosses is frequently sterile in greater or less degree. Huxley, very early in the debate pointed out this grave defect in the evidence, but before breeding researches had been made on a large scale no one felt the objection to be serious. Extended work might be trusted to supply the deficiency. It has not done so, and the significance of the negative evidence can no longer be denied.

When Darwin discussed the problem of inter-specific sterility in the "Origin of Species" this aspect of the matter seems to have escaped him. He is at great pains to prove that inter-specific crosses are *not always* sterile, and he shows that crosses between forms which pass for distinct species may produce hybrids which range from complete fertility to complete sterility. The fertile hybrids he claims in support of his argument. If species arose from a common origin, clearly they should not always give sterile hybrids. So Darwin is concerned to prove that such hybrids are by no means always sterile, which to us is a commonplace of everyday experience. If species have a common origin, where did they pick up the ingredients which produce this sexual incompatibility? Almost certainly it is a variation in which something has been added. We have come to see that variations can very commonly— I do not say always—be distinguished as positive and negative. The validity of this distinction has been doubted, especially by the *Drosophila* workers. Nevertheless in application to a very large range of characters, I am satisfied that the distinction holds, and that in analysis it is a useful aid. Now we have no difficulty in finding evidence of variation by loss. Examples abound, but variation by addition are rarities, even if there are any which must be so accounted. The variations to which inter-specific sterility is due are obviously variations in which something is apparently added to the stock of ingredients. It is one of the common experiences of the breeder that when a hybrid is partially sterile, and from it any fertile offspring can be obtained, the sterility, once lost, disappears. This has been the history of many, perhaps most of our cultivated plants of hybrid origin.

The production of an indubitably sterile hybrid from completely fertile parents which have arisen under critical observation from a single common origin is the event for which we wait. Until this event is witnessed, our knowledge of evolution is incomplete in a vital respect. From time to time a record of such an observation is published, but none has yet survived criticism. Meanwhile, though our faith in evolution stands unshaken, we have no acceptable account of the origin of "species."

Curiously enough, it is at the same point that the validity of the claim of natural selection as the main directing force was most questionable. The survival of the fittest was a plausible account of evolution in broad outline, but failed in application to specific difference. The Darwinian philosophy convinced us that every species must "make good" in nature if it is to survive, but no one could tell how the differences—often very sharply fixed—which we recognize as specific, do in fact enable the species to make good. The claims of natural selection as the chief factor in the determination of species have consequently been discredited.

I pass to another part of the problem, where again, though extraordinary progress in knowledge has been made, a new and formidable difficulty has been encountered. Of variations we know a great deal more than we did. Almost all that we have seen are variations in which we recognize that elements have been lost. In addressing the British Association in 1914 I dwelt on evidence of this class. The developments of the last seven years, which are memorable as having provided in regard to one animal, the fly Drosophila, the most comprehensive mass of genetic observation yet collected, serve rather to emphasize than to weaken the considerations which I then referred. Even in Drosophila, where hundreds of genetically distinct factors have been identified, very few new dominants, that is to say positive additions, have been seen, and I am assured that none of them are of a class which could be expected to be viable under natural conditions. I understand even that none are certainly viable in the homozygous state.

If we try to trace back the origin of our domesticated animals and plants, we can scarcely ever point to a single wild species as the probable progenitor.

Almost every naturalist who has dealt with these questions in recent years has had recourse to theories of multiple origin, because our modern races have positive characteristics which we cannot find in any existing species, and which combination of the existing species seem unable to provide. To produce our domesticated races it seems that ingredients must have been added. To invoke the hypothetical existence of lost species provides a poor escape from this difficulty, and we are left with the conviction that some part of the chain of reasoning is missing. The weight of this objection will be most felt by those who have most experience in practical breeding. I can not, for instance, imagine a round seed being found on a wrinkled variety of pea except by crossing. Such seeds, which look round, sometimes appear, but this is a superficial appearance, and either these seeds are seen to have the starch of wrinkled seeds or can be proved to be the produce of stray pollen. Nor can I imagine a fern-leaved Primula producing a palm-leaf, or a star-shaped flower producing the old type of *sinensis* flower. And so on through long series of forms which we have watched for twenty years.

Analysis has revealed hosts of transferable characters. Their combinations suffice to supply in abundance series of types which might pass for new species, and certainly would be so classed if they were met with in nature. Yet critically tested, we find that they are not distinct species and we have no reason to suppose that any accumulations of characters of the same order would culminate in the production of distinct species. Specific difference therefore must be regarded as probably attaching to the base upon which these transferables are implanted, of which we know absolutely nothing at all. Nothing that we have witnessed in the contemporary world can colorably be interpreted as providing the sort of evidence required.

Twenty years ago, de Vries made what looked like a promising attempt to supply this so far as *Oenothera* was concerned. In the light of modern experiments, especially those of Renner, the interest attaching to the polymorphism of *Oenothera* has greatly developed, but in application to that phenomenon the theory of mutation falls. We see novel forms appearing, but they are no new species of *Oenothera*, nor are the parents which produce them pure or homozygous forms. Renner's identification of the several complexes allocated to the male and female sides of the several types is a wonderful and significant piece of analysis introducing us to new genetical conceptions. The Oenotheras illustrate in the most striking fashion how crude and inadequate are the suppositions which we entertained before the world of gametes was revealed.

The appearance of the plant tells us little or nothing of these things. In Mendelism, we learnt to appreciate the implication of the fact that the organism is a double structure, containing ingredients derived from the mother and from the father respectively. We have now to admit the further conception that between the male and female sides of the same plant these ingredients may be quite differently apportioned, and that the genetical composition of each may be so distinct that the systematist might without extravagance recognize them as distinct specifically. If then our plant may by appropriate treatment be made to give off two distinct forms, why is not that phenomenon a true instance of Darwin's origin of species? In Darwin's time it must have been acclaimed as exactly supplying all and more than he ever hoped to see. We know that that is not the true interpretation. For that which comes out is no new creation.

Only those who are keeping up with these new developments can fully appreciate their vast significance or anticipate the next step. That is the province of the geneticist. Nevertheless, I am convinced that biology would greatly gain by some cooperation among workers in the several branches. I had expected that genetics would provide at once common ground for the systematist and the laboratory worker. This hope has been disappointed. Each still keeps apart. Systematic literature grows precisely as if the genetical discoveries had never been made and the geneticists more and more withdraw each into his special "claim"—a most lamentable result. Both are to blame. If we cannot persuade the systematists to come to us, at least we can go to them. They too have built up a vast edifice of knowledge which they are willing to share with us, and which we greatly need. They too have never lost that longing for the truth about evolution which to men of my date is the salt of biology, the impulse which made us biologists. It is from them that the raw materials for our researches are to be drawn, which alone can give catholicity and breadth to our studies. We and the systematists have to devise a common language.

Both we and the systematists have everything to gain by a closer alliance. Of course we must specialize, but I suggest to educationists that in biology at least specialization begins too early. In England certainly harm is done by a system of examinations discouraging to that taste for field natural history and collecting, spontaneous in so many young people. How it may be on this side, I can not say, but with us attainments of that kind are seldom rewarded, and are too often despised as trivial in comparison with the stereotyped biology which can be learnt from text-books. Nevertheless, given the aptitude, a very wide acquaintance with nature and the diversity of living things may be acquired before the age at which more intensive study must be begun, the best preparation for research in any of the branches of biology.

The separation between the laboratory men and the systematists already imperils the work, I might almost say the sanity, of both. The systematists will feel the ground fall from beneath their feet, when they learn and realize what genetics has accomplished, and we, close students of specially chosen examples, may find our eyes dazzled and blinded when we look up from our work-tables to contemplate the brilliant vision of the natural world in its boundless complexity.

I have put before you very frankly the considerations which have made us agnostic as to the actual mode and processes of evolution. When such confessions are made the enemies of science see their chance. If we cannot declare here and now how species arose, they will obligingly offer us the solutions with which obscurantism is satisfied. Let us then proclaim in precise and unmistakable language that our faith in evolution is unshaken. Every available line of argument converges on this inevitable conclusion. The obscurantist has nothing to suggest which is worth a moment's attention. The difficulties which weigh upon the professional biologist need not trouble the layman. Our doubts are not as to the reality or truth of evolution, but as to the origin of *species,* a technical, almost domestic, problem. Any day that mystery may be solved. The discoveries of the last twenty-five years enable us for the first time to discuss these questions intelligently and on a basis of fact. That synthesis will follow on an analysis, we do not and cannot doubt.

Name: _____ **Date:** _____

1. Why did Bateson and his colleagues stop talking about evolution during the 1880s and 1890s?

2. How did the rediscovery of Mendel's work reinvigorate Bateson's interest in evolution?

3. What is a systemicist?

4. How, according to Bateson, does the lack of communication between systemicists and laboratory biologists harm the development of biology?

5. Bateson concludes by explaining what he confidently believes and what he is confident biologists do not know. What does Bateson include in each of these categories?

What biologists know:

What biologists do not know:

David Starr Jordan

"A Plea for Old Fashioned Natural History," 1916

Jordan (1851-1931) was an ichthyologist, the first President of Stanford University, and prominent Darwinist. In this piece, which is a speech he gave at the opening of the Scripps Institution of Oceanography in 1916, Jordan sought to undermine efforts of biologists who studied living organisms as through they were merely machines consisting of chemical and physical reactions.

In this talk I shall have three purposes. The first is to express my appreciation of the kindly and intelligent interest in biological research shown by the founders of this Institution. Second, I would congratulate my old friend, Dr. Ritter, and his colleagues on their continuing and increasing opportunity to add to the sum of our knowledge of the life of the sea. Finally, with Dr. Ritter's permission and approval, I would say a word for old-fashioned Natural History, as a method of study and a means of grace.

Biology in its various forms ranks among the inexact sciences. It is inexact because it leaves always more to learn. The more we know, the more remains to know. Exact science, strictly speaking, is not science at all. It is a form of logic. Pure mathematics, in so far as it is pure, not contaminated by observation or experiment, is a process of thinking. Its conclusions are all involved in its definitions or premises. It deals as readily with a world in four dimensions or two or possibly ten, as with the world we know, which is satisfied with three. It takes observation or experiment to show that this is a world of three dimensions, and that neither line nor surface can exist except as mental concepts framed for the purpose. In treating of either we must ignore for the moment breath or thickness or both although neither can ever be absent in any material object. A line without depth or width was never encountered in human experience and there was never an actual surface without some sort of backing, however thin the veneer.

By "old-fashioned" Natural History I mean to recognition or study of animals and plants as completed organisms, each greater than the sum of all the parts. It involves a knowledge of names and of some degree of classification. It leads up to the problem of the origin of the species, the affinities of forms, the complex relations we call habits, the problems of geological and geographical distribution, the details of evolution and a balanced knowledge of things as they are, as actual though temporary stages in a universe of change. It is at once the beginning and the end of biological study. The beginning, because almost everyone who has left an impress in biological research has been drawn to these studies by contact with nature and by the love of first-hand knowledge,—the end, because all forms of biological experiment and observation lead finally towards the greater problems the aggregate of which we call Life. And its final end or purpose is interpretation, not of a narrow world of specialized experiment, a universe of chromosomes, unit characters, tropisms, synonymy, but of the whole great world of Life as it is, as it was, and through all its protean changes, must forever be. These are the questions which meet us first and which thereafter lead us on. What is it? What is it to me? And the fascinating problem as to what it will do for mankind intellectually or morally, is the one which grips us finally. Observation comes first and then experiment and both lead from the gathering of facts to the contemplation of causes. Experiment is not necessarily nobler than observation because it comes later. Observation is the co-ordination of world experiments. All nature is one huge category of relations of cause and effect on every side and

From *Biological Bulletins* 1, 1916

covering every phase of life. Our experiments detach a fragment of nature to be viewed in intensive detail; we succeed in isolating two or three of her minor problems, asking her to solve these for us without interference from the rest. We are not sure in these minor sections of nature that we have include enough or that we have not taken too much to make the answers we receive intelligible or capable of rising to the rank of truths. An experiment is often the easiest line to attack, but it may also be the most deceptive.

Those sciences like physics and chemistry, often called exact, are the ones in which experiment can most completely segregate and simplify the phenomena of nature. Physical substance and chemical composition may run comparatively uniform. One mass behaves like another mass and like reagents yields like results. The sciences concerned with masses, force and reactions may be relatively exact. They may freely use mathematics as an instrument of precision applied to tested and unvarying premises, by the elucidation of which we may deduce unvarying truth. But by mathematics alone we may not gather any of the crude material from which Truth can be crystallized. In biology facts are individual. No two objects are ever exactly alike, hence the relative futility of biometric versions of its problems. The effort may be roughly though not quite justly compared to genus and species into Physics. The naturalist Rafinesque once described some twenty new species of thunder and lightning observed by him at the Falls of Ohio, but his taxonomy can have no genetic basis and therefore no real kinship with classification of animals and plants.

Yet even Physics, Astronomy, and Chemistry, however stable their basal concepts, can never be exact sciences. If they were we could learn nothing more about them. The most that can be claimed is that they are exact in spots, and moreover the unquestioned data no longer compel our first interest. But Zoology and Botany are not complete, even in spots. For though the great framework on which these groups are built up is becoming relatively stable, no part of it is finished. Science is human experience tested and set in order. The greater the accumulation of tested results, the more extended the outlook for further human contact with its further accretion of facts and relations.

What we call law in nature is merely as Darwin asserted "the ascertained sequence of events." Every relation of cause to effect involves some sort of law and every slightest fact in natural history has some history of causation behind it. The flowers of the scarlet Ixia before us have a peculiarly bent corolla,—all the Amaryllis family have it more or

less. Behind this fact lies a cause if only we could find it. A curious fatality there is in plant as in animal life. The Amaryllis corolla would not be bent if it, under all conditions of its past history, it could have been anything else. There is philosophy behind the old explanation of why a crab runs sideways. Such is the meanness of the crab that it would run some other way, backwards or forwards, if it possibly could! Yet every crab varies the method a bit, each in his own way. All the rest of us animals and "our brother organisms, the plants," are like the crab in this regard. We run our race in our own way, but with the limitation that we could run in some other way if we possibly could.

A word as to tolerance in science may not be out of place. Many new lines of observation and especially of experiment have opened in the last twenty-five years. Many more will open in the quarter century to come. These involve additions to knowledge, not a sweeping away of old, nor relegation to dust heap of the methods of Humboldt, Carl Ritter, Cuvier, Linnaeus, Agassiz or Baird. We stand on their shoulders, dwarfs on the shoulders of the giants. They strove to glance at the whole majestic Cosmos. Such a vision is as glorious now as in the days before the microscope and microtome had ranged the infinitely small along with the infinitely great. No one of us can compass the whole, but every man may look beyond his bit of field out over the broader vision of the whole, each meanwhile devoting himself to that part which he can work best and enjoy most heartily. We should not ask which is most "popular," most repaying, most up-to-date. It is discouraging to see the young biologists in Dr. Coulter's words, "all paddling in the same pool," however alluring the pool may be.

Some thirty years ago I was at Johns Hopkins University, when the collections of a Maryland Natural History Society were turned over to the institution. Two or three advanced students were picking out the fishes. The bowfin, the gar pike and some small sharks were regarded as treasures. These species bore some relation to problems in the morphology of the higher vertebrates. Every specimen that did not make some such appeal was thrown away, regardless of the other problems it might help to answer, and regardless of the fact that even the bony fishes, humble as they are, have a morphology, an embryology and an evolution of their own. The pool we paddled in those days was morphology. Then came embryology, the second of the "ancestral documents" of Haeckel, the third being paleontology. But the results of embryology were unexpectedly indecisive. In other words, its problems, like others, are very complex. Next came the movements towards histology, a field which proved amazingly rich. In our day similar wealth is found in genetics, and in physiology, while in ecology as a modern subject we come back close to old-fashioned natural history with which we started. I should not in the slightest degree depreciate any of these lines of research. Each of them has helped to illuminate our whole intellectual field. Each is clearing and strengthening our conception of evolution, though sometimes they interfere with the simplicity of our formula.

With all this we have not destroyed the old charm of the study of nature in detail, nor have we reduced the need of it. Through our ignorance of species and of the methods of taxonomy some of us have made systematic study unfashionable. In the contemplation of organisms in the closet or the garden, we sometimes overlook the fact that species exist out of doors, each one as a different kind of living being. It should be no disgrace to know an animal or plant by its scientific name. It has no other name, and if we know it, we must speak of it. The confusion into which systematic biology has been sometimes thrown comes mainly from those who do not understand that accuracy is as important in this field as in any other. An exact nomenclature is as important as in systematic science as sharp knives in anatomy. Those who wish to know animals without getting the names right should be recommended to the popular text books "How to Know the Birds, the Insects, the Plants" without knowing anything about them. In no field can accurate knowledge come from casual survey.

Exact determination of genera and species lies at the bottom of all real study of geographical distribution and of geological succession as well. There is all the difference in science between the actual truth and "something equally good," which is said to obtain in Pharmacy. In an address before the Association for the Advancement of Science some years ago on "The Making of Darwin" I tried to show that three elements were vital. First and greatest the raw material, the germ plasm-the stuff of heredity, which determined the original Darwin. To build up Darwin these potentialities must first exist. Next they must be aroused by contact with Nature, her facts and her problems, to "fanaticism for veracity," to borrow one of Huxley's finest phrases. Lastly, contact with inspired and inspiring teachers, those by whom from generation to generation the "Higher Heredity" of naturalists has been vivified and kept alive. Darwin tells us that at Cambridge he "walked with Henslow," eager teacher and learned botanist, even as we of the passing generation have "walked with Agassiz" and as you of the present generation have walked with Agassiz's pupils—with Brooks and Wilder and Morse and William James, with Verrill and Minot, with Packard, Hyatt, Hartt and Snow, and the rest whose torches were kindled at that flame of the same great teacher.

And here I may well close with a sentence I once heard from Agassiz, one of the last words ever spoken to those who were his disciples,—"This is the charm of the study of Nature herself; she brings us back to absolute truth every time we wander."

Name: _____ **Date:** _____

1. What was old-fashioned natural history according to Jordan?

2. What did Jordan believe was the difference between the exact sciences and the inexact sciences? Give specific examples of both kinds of sciences according to Jordan.

3. Jordan described old-fashioned Natural History as a method to study the natural world and a "means of grace." What do you think he means by "means of grace?"

4.   What role did Darwin play in Jordan's conception of the history of biology?

5.   Who do you think Jordan was arguing against in this speech?

Vernon Kellogg

Darwinism To-Day, 1908

Vernon Lyman Kellogg (1867-1937) was a American entomologist and ardent proponent of the scientific study of evolution. Born only a few years after Darwin published *On the Origin of Species*, Kellogg was among the first generation of biologists trained after the widespread acceptance of evolution as a fact. For Kellogg and his colleagues, evolution was a fact; there was, however, considerable argument over precisely how evolution occurred. In *Darwinism To-Day*, Kellogg presented the variety of claims about the mechanisms of evolution, which by the early twentieth century included over two dozed different explanations for how evolution occurred. In this selection, Kellogg struggled to explain to readers that biologists were confident that evolution was a biological fact, while demonstrating the many different claims that biologists had made about how it worked.

THE "DEATH-BED OF DARWINISM"

"Vom Sterbelager des Darwinismus!" [The Death-bed of Darwinism] This is the title of a recent pamphlet[1] lying before me. But ever since there has been Darwinism there have been occasional death-beds of Darwinism on title pages of pamphlets, ad-

---

[1] Dennert, E., "Vom Sterbelager des Darwinismus," Stuttgart, 1903. An intemperate and unconvincing but interesting brief against the Darwinian factors, *i. e.*, the selection theories, in evolution. Author fully accepts the theory of descent, but in no degree the Darwinian causal explanation of this descent. "Was ich in diesen Berichten nachzuweisen suche, ist die Tatsache, dass der Darwinismus nunmehr bald der Vergangenheit, der Geschichte angehört, dass wir an seinem Sterbelager stehen und dass auch seine Freunde sich eben anschicken, ihm wenigstens noch ein anständiges Begräbnis zu sichern" (p. 4). The valuable thing about the paper is that it is largely given to a gathering together of the anti-Darwinian opinions and declarations of numerous, mostly well-known and reputably placed biologists. Some of these declarations are interpreted by Dr. Dennert in a way that would probably hardly be wholly acceptable to the declarers, but for the most part the anti-Darwinian beliefs of these biologists are unmistakably revealed by their own words. Among the biologists and biological philosophers thus agglomerated into the camp of anti-Darwinism are Wigand, Haacke, von Sachs, Goette, Korschinsky, Haberlandt, Steinmann, Eimer, M. Wagner, von Kölliker, Nägeli, Kerner, F. von Wagner, Fleischmann, O. Schultze, O. Hertwig, and others. This list includes reputable botanists, zoölogists, and palæontologists.

From *Darwinism To-Day*, New York: Henry Holt & Company, 1908.

dresses, and sermons. Much more worth consideration than any clerical pamphlets or dissertations, under this title, by *frischgebackenen* German doctors of philosophy—the title alone proving prejudice or lack of judgment or of knowledge—are the numerous books and papers which, with less sensational headlines but infinitely more important contents, are appearing now in such numbers and from such a variety of reputable sources as to reveal the existence among biologists and philosophers of a widespread belief in the marked weakening, at least, if not serious indisposition, of Darwinism. A few of these books and papers from scientific sources even suggest that their writers see shadows of a death-bed.

The present extraordinary activity in biology is two-phased; there is going on a most careful re-examination or scrutiny of the theories connected with organic evolution, resulting in much destructive criticism of certain long-cherished and widely held beliefs, and at the same time there are being developed and almost feverishly driven forward certain fascinating and fundamentally important new lines, employing new methods, of biological investigation. Conspicuous among these new kinds of work are the statistical or quantitative study of variations and that most alluring work variously called developmental mechanics, experimental morphology, experimental physiology of development, or, most suitably of all because most comprehensively, experimental biology.[2] This work includes the controlled modification of conditions attending development and behaviour, and the pedigreed breeding of pure and hybrid generations. Now this combination of destructive critical activity and active constructive experimental investigation has plainly resulted, or is resulting, in the distinct weakening or modifying of certain familiar and long-entrenched theories concerning the causative factors and the mechanism of organic evolution. Most conspicuous among these theories now in the white light of scientific scrutiny are those established by Darwin, and known, collectively, to biologists, as Darwinism.

To too many general readers Darwinism is synonymous with organic evolution or the theory of descent. The word is not to be so used or considered. Darwinism, primarily, is a most ingenious, most plausible, and, according to one's belief, most effective or most inadequate, causo-mechanical explanation of adaptation and species-transforming. It is that factor which, ever since its proposal by Darwin in 1859, has been held by a majority of biologists to be the chief working agent in the descent, that is, the origin, of species. However worthy Darwin is of having his name applied directly to the great theory of descent—for it was only by Darwin's aid that this theory, conceived and more or less clearly announced by numerous pre-Darwinian naturalists and philosophers, came to general and nearly immediate acceptance—the fact is that the name Darwinism has been pretty consistently applied by biologists only to those theories practically original with Darwin which offer a mechanical explanation of the accepted fact of descent. Of these Darwinian theories the primary and all-important one is that of natural selection. Included with this in Darwinism are the now nearly wholly discredited theories of sexual selection and of the pangenesis of gemmules. It may also be fairly said that the theory of the descent of man from the lower animals should be included in Darwinism. For Darwin was practically the first naturalist bold enough to admit the logical and obvious consequences of the general acceptance of the theory of descent, and to include man in the general chain of descending, or ascending, organisms. So that the popular notion that Darwinism is in some way the right word to apply to the doctrine that man has come from the monkeys is rather nearer right than wrong. But biologists do not recognise the descent of man as a special phase of Darwinism, but rather of the whole theory of descent, or organic evolution.

Darwinism, then, is not synonymous with organic evolution, nor with the theory of descent (which two phases are used by the biologist practically synonymously). Therefore when one reads of the "death-bed of Darwinism," it is not of the death-bed of organic evolution or of the theory of descent that one is reading. While many reputable biologists to-day strongly doubt the commonly reputed effectiveness of the Darwinian selection factors to explain descent—some, indeed, holding them to be of absolutely no species-forming value—practically no naturalists[3] of position and recognised attainment doubt the theory of descent.[4] Organic evolution, that is, the descent of species, is looked on by biologists to be as proved a part of their science as gravitation is in the science of physics or chemical affinity in that of chemistry. Doubts of Darwinism are not, then, doubts, of organic evolution. Darwinism might indeed be on its death-bed without shaking in any considerable degree the confidence of biologists and natural philosophers in the theory of descent.

But the educated reader, the scientific layman, the thinker and worker in any line of sociologic, philosophic, or even theologic activity is bound to

---

[2]For a recent account of such work, see Morgan, T. H., "Experimental Zoölogy," 1907.

[3]A. Fleischmann, professor of zoology in the University of Erlangen, is the only biologist of recognised position, of whom I am aware, who publicly declares a disbelief in the theory of descent. He seems to base his disbelief on the fact that the phyletic (genealogic) series in numerous animal groups are as yet unexplained. See his book, "Die Descendenztheorie," Leipzig, 1901. "Allein je mehr ich mich in die vermeintlichen Beweisgründe derselben [the theory of descent] vertiefte und durch Spezialuntersuchungen positive Anhaltspunkte für die Stammesverwandtschaft der Tiere zu gewinnen suchte, um so klarer stellte sich mir die Erkenntniss heraus, dass jene Theorie eben doch mehr nur ein bestrickender, Ergebnisse und Aufklärung vortäuschender Roman sei, als eine auf positiven Grundlagen aufgebaute Lehre." (From the preface of this book).

[4]A curious attempt to formulate a scientific theory explaining the conditions as we know them in the world of life, to replace the theory of descent, is contained in a recent small book called "Die Konvergenz der Organismen" (1904), by Hermann Friedmann. The author assumes that the diversity of organisms is the primary condition, and that their similarity has been brought about through convergence, as opposed to the postulate of the theory of descent to the effect that diversity of life has grown out of primary identity or homogeneity. I quote (p. 12) as follows from Friedmann: "Diese Annahme, die in dem vorliegenden Buch vertreten wird, ist folgendermassen zu erläutern. Wir gehen von dem Hauptsatze aus, dass das Leben immer als ein bestimmter, unwandelbarer Spezialcharakter auftritt. Die spezifisch verschiedenen Lebensformen erscheinen jedoch einander angenähert, bezw. annäherbar, durch drei (Teil-) prinzipien, von denen das Leben beherrscht wird: Das Prinzip, vermöge dessen spezifisch verschiedene Formen sloche Übereinstimmungen aufweisen, die wir als primärgesetzliche betrachten, nennen wir das Prinzip der Homologie; als einen Ausfluss des Prinzips der Analogie bezeichnen wir diejenigen Übereinstimmungen, die unter dem Einflüsse gleichwirkender äusserer (mittelbar oder unmittelbar bewirkender oder selektiver) Bedingungen entstehen; und wir erkennen drittens die Macht und die Tragweite eines Prinzips der direkten Konvergenz, welches das Entstehen von Übereinstimmungen zwischen den Genossen einer Biosphäre aus psychischen Ursachen bewirkt. Die drei Prinzipien bilden die Grundlage der Konvergenztheorie."

be disturbed and unsettled by rumours from the camp of professional biologists of any weakness or mortal illness of Darwinism. We have only just got ourselves and our conceptions of nature, of sociology and philosophy, well oriented and adjusted with regard to Darwinism. And for relentless hands now to come and clutch away our foundations is simply intolerable. *Zum Teufel* with these German professors! For it is precisely the German biologists who are most active in this undermining of the Darwinian theories. But there are others with them; Holland, Russia, Italy, France, and our own country all contribute their quota of disturbing questions and declarations of protest and revolt. The English seem mostly inclined to uphold the glory of their illustrious countryman. But there are rebels even there. Altogether it may be stated with full regard to facts that a major part of the current published output of general biological discussions, theoretical treatises, addresses, and brochures dealing with the great evolutionary problems, is distinctly *anti-Darwinian* in character. This major part of the public discussion of the status of evolution and its causes, its factors and mechanism, by working biologists and thinking natural philosophers, reveals a lack of belief in the effectiveness or capacity of the natural selection theory to serve as a sufficient causo-mechanical explanation of species-forming and evolution. Nor is this preponderance of anti-Darwinian expression in current biological literature to be wholly or even chiefly attributed to a dignified silence on the part of the believers in selection. Answers and defences have appeared and are appearing. But in practically *all these defences two characteristics* are *to be noted,* namely, a tendency to propose supporting hypotheses or theories, and a tendency to make certain distinct concessions to the beleaguering party. The fair truth is that the Darwinian selection theories, considered with regard to their claimed capacity to be an independently sufficient mechanical explanation of descent, *stand to-day seriously discredited in the biological world.* On the other hand, it is also fair truth to say that no replacing hypothesis or theory of species-forming has been offered by the opponents of selection which has met with any general or even considerable acceptance by naturalists. *Mutations* seem to be too few and far between; for *orthogenesis* we can discover no satisfactory mechanism; and the same is true for the *Lamarckian theories* of modification by the cumulation, through inheritance, or acquired or ontogenic characters. *Kurz und gut,* we are immensely unsettled.

Now but little of this philosophic turmoil and wordy strife has found its way as yet into current American literature. Our bookshop windows offer no display, as in Germany, of volumes and pamphlets on the newer evolutionary study; our serious-minded quarterlies, if we have any, and our critical monthlies and weeklies contain no debates or discussions over *"das Sterbelager des Darwinismus."* Our popular magazines keep to the safe and pleasant task of telling sweetly of the joys of making Nature's acquaintance through field-glasses and the attuned ear. But just as certainly as the many material things "made in Germany" have found their way to us so will come soon the echoes and phrases of the present intellectual activity in evolutionary affairs, an activity bound to continue as long as the new lines of biological investigation continue their amazing output of new facts to serve as the bases for new critical attacks on the old notions and for the upbuilding of new hypotheses. If now the first of these echoes to come across the water to us prove to be, as wholly likely, those from the more violent and louder debaters, they may lead to an undue dismay and panic on our part. Things are really in no such desperate way with Darwinism as the polemic vigour of the German and French anti-Darwinians leads them to suggest. Says one of them:[5] "Darwinism now belongs to history, like that other curiosity of our century, the Hegelian philosophy; both are variations on the theme: how one manages to lead a whole generation by the nose." The same writer also speaks of "the softening of the brain of the Darwinians." Another one,[6] in similarly relegating Darwinism to the past, takes much pleasure in explaining that "we [anti-Darwinians] are now standing by the death-bed of Darwinism, and making ready to send the friends of the patient a little money to insure a decent burial of the remains." No less intemperate and indecent is Wolff's[7] reference to the "episode of Darwinism" and his suggestion that our attitude toward Darwin should be "as if he had never existed." Such absurdity of expression might pass unnoticed in the mouth of a violent non-scientific debater—let us say an indignant theologian of Darwin's own days—but in the mouth of a biologist of recognised achievement, of thorough scientific training and unusually keen mind—for this expression came from just such a man—it can only be referred to as a deplorable example of those things that make the judicious to grieve. Such violence blunts or breaks one's own weapons.

While I have said that the coming across the water of the more vigorous anti-Darwinian utterances might cause some dismay and panic in the ranks of the educated reader—really unnecessary panic, as I hope to point out—it will doubtless oc-

[5]Driesch, H., *Biolog. Centralb.,* v. 16, p. 355, 1896.

[6]Dennert, E., "Vom Sterbelager des Darwinismus," p. 4, 1903.

[7]Wolff, G., "Beiträge zur Kritik der Darwin'schen Lehre," p. 54, 1898.

cur to some of my readers to say that this fear of panic is unwarranted. If the first phrases to come are as injudicious and intemperate, hence as unconvincing, as those just cited, the whole anti-Darwinian movement will be discredited and given no attention. Which, I hasten to reply, will be as much of a mistake as panic would be. There is something very seriously to be heeded in the chorus of criticism and protest, and wholly to stop one's ears to these criticisms is to refuse enlightenment and to show prejudice. I have thought it, therefore, worth while to try to anticipate the coming of fragmentary and disturbing extracts from the rapidly increasing mass of recent *anti-Darwinian* literature by presenting in this book a summary account not alone of these modern criticisms, but of the answers to them by the steadfast Darwinians, and of the concessions and supporting hypotheses which the supporters of both sides have been led to offer during the debates. I shall try to give a fair statement of the recent attacks on, and the defence and present scientific standing of, the familiar Darwinian theories, and to give also concise expositions, with some critical comment, of the more important new, or *newly remodelled alternative* and auxiliary theories of species-forming and descent, such as heterogenesis, orthogenesis, isolation, etc., and an estimate of their degree of acceptance by naturalists.

---

[1]One of the most serious and detailed critical analyses of the selection theory, resulting in conclusions totally antagonistic to Darwinism, is that of the Marburg botanist, Prof. Albert Wigand, composing the three volumes entitled "Der Darwinismus und die Naturforschung Newtons und Cuviers" (Vol. I, 1874; Vol. II, 1876; Vol. III, 1877). From the "Announcements" at the beginning of each volume I quote as follows:

From Vol. I. "Die hier dargebotene Kritik der Darwin'schen Lehre weist zunächst durch eingehende Prüfung der hierher gehörigen naturhistorischen Thatsachen nach, dass weder die Voraussetzungen, von denen die Theorie ausgeht, noch ihre Consequenzen mit der wirklichen Natur übereinstimmen, dass sie demnach den Anforderungen an eine wissenschaftliche Hypothese nicht entspricht. Vielmehr erweist sich dieselbe als eine philosophische Speculation, welche nicht nur die unserer Naturerkenntniss vorgezeichneten Grenzen überschreitet, sondern vor Allem die wichtigsten Grundsätze der wahren Forschung, wie sie durch die grossen Meister aufgestellt und in der bisherigen Entwickelung der Naturwissenschaft allgemein anerkannt und unbedingt maassgebend gewesen sind, insbesondere die Principien der Causalität und der organischen Entwickelung, aufs grobste verleugnet. Demnach erkennt das vorliegende Werk seine Hauptaufgabe gerade darin, der bis dahin befolgten Forschungsweise gegenüber jener neuesten Naturphilosophie ihr Recht zu wahren."

From Vol. II. "Vermittelst der hierdurch gewonnenen Kriterien gelangt die Untersuchung in Betreff des Darwinismus zu folgendem Ergebnis: Derselbe geht nicht bloss von falschen Voraussetzungen aus, erweist sich nicht nur unfähig in Beziehung auf die versprochenen Leistungen, ist nicht nur verfehlt durch die principielle Unmöglichkeit seiner Aufgabe, ist nicht nur eine der

DARWINISM'S PRESENT STANDING

A river rises from a perennial spring on the mountain side; gravitation compels the water to keep moving, and rock walls, intervening hills, and soft loam banks determine the course of the stream. The living stream of descent finds its never-failing primal source in ever-appearing variations; the eternal flux of Nature, coupled with this inevitable primal variation, compels the stream to keep always in motion, and selection guides it along the ways of least resistance. Although there can be no modification, no evolution, without variation, yet neither can this variation, whatever its character and extent, whether slight and fluctuating, large and mutational, determinate or fortuitous, long compel descent to go contrary to adaptation. And the guardian of the course is natural selection. Selection will inexorably bar the forward movement, will certainly extinguish the direction of any orthogenetic process, Nägelian, Eimerian, or de Vriesian, which is not fit, that is, not adaptive. Darwinism, then, as the natural selection of the fit, the final arbiter in descent control, stands unscathed, clear and high above the obscuring cloud of battle. At least, so it seems to me. But Darwinism, as the all-sufficient or even most important causo-mechanical factor in species-forming and hence as the sufficient explanation of descent, is discredited and cast down.[1] At least, again, so it seems to me. But Darwin himself claimed no *Allmacht* for selection. Darwin may well cry to be saved from his friends!

Naturforschung fremdartige, rein speculative Operation, sondern indem derselbe das Princip der Causalität und Entwickelung mit dem Zufall und der Teleologie als Erklärungsgrunde vertauscht, erscheint er als eine der Naturforschung in ihrer Fundamentalmaxime widersprechende, darum dieselbe geradezu gefährdende Verirrung, um so mehr als er unter ihrer Maske auftritt. Der Darwinismus ist einer jener Versuche, welche im Namen der Naturforschung die Naturforschung verderben."

From Vol. III. "Der vorliegende dritte Band, mit welchem dieses Werk abschliesst, hat zum Gegenstand nicht die dem Darwinismus zu Grunde liegende Theorie, sondern die concrete Gestalt, in welcher derselbe als eine für unsere Zeit charakteristische culturhistorische Thatsache in die Erscheinung tritt. Insbesondere wird versucht, ein Bild von der Darwin'schen Schule als der Gesammtheit der die Transmutationstheorie vertretenden Auctoren und von der Art und Weise, wie sich die letztere im Lichte ihrer Bekenner darstellt, zu entwerfen. Hierbei ergibt sich, dass der Darwinismus mehr in einer ziellosen Zeitströmung und in einer wissenschaftlich nicht motivirten Stimmung der Geister als in einer bestimmt zu formulirenden Lehre besteht, und dass derselbe bereits in seinem eigenen Lager in allen wesentlichen Punkten wissenschaftlich überwunden ist, und zwar in solcher Weise, dass in den widerstreitenden Ansichten der Darwinianer doch zugleich der Keim für die allein richtige Auffassung der organischen Natur, wenn auch grossentheils unklar und unbewusst, verborgen liegt."

A special answer to this exhaustive pleading of Wigand is offered by H. Spitzer in his "Beiträge zur Descendenztheorie und zur Methodologie der Naturwissenschaft," 1886.

The selection theories do not satisfy present-day biologists[2] as efficient causal explanations of species-transformation. The fluctuating variations are not sufficient handles for natural selection; the hosts of trivial, indifferent species differences are not the result of an adaptively selecting agent. On the other hand the declarations of Korschinsky, Wolff, Driesch, and others that natural selection is nonexistent, is a vagary, a form of speech, or a negligible influence in descent, are unconvincing; they are unproved.

And these bitter antagonists of selection are especially unconvincing when they come to offer a replacing theory, an alternative explanation of transformation and descent. To my mind every theory of heterogenesis, of orthogenesis, or of modification by the transmission of acquired characters, confesses itself ultimately subordinate to the natural selection theory. However independent of selection and Darwinism may be the beginnings of modification, the incipiency of new species and of new lines of descent; even, indeed, however necessary to nat-

ural selection some auxiliary or supporting theory to account for the beginnings of change confessedly is, the working factor or influence postulated by any such auxiliary theory soon finds its independence lost, its influence in evolution dominated and controlled by natural selection. As soon as the new modifications, the new species characters, the new lines of descent, if they may come so far, attain that degree of development where they have to submit to the test of utility, of fitness, just there they are practically delivered over to the tender mercies of selection. No orthogenetic line of descent can persist in a direction not adaptive, that is, not fit, and certainly no present-day biologist is ready to fall back on the long deserted stand-point of teleology and ascribe to heterogenesis or orthogenesis an auto-determination toward adaptiveness and fitness. Modification and development may have been proved to occur along determinate lines without the aid of natural selection. I believe they have. But such development cannot have an aim; it cannot be assumed to be directed toward advance; there is no independent progress upward, *i. e.*, toward higher specialisation. At least, there is no scientific proof of any such capacity in organisms. Natural selection[3]

---

[2]However, there still exist, especially in England, thorough-going Darwinians who see nothing serious in all this criticism of their great compatriot's explanation of the origin of species. Lankester, one of the most prominent of English naturalists, said at York, last August (1906), in his inaugural address as president of the British Association for the Advancement of Science: "Under the title 'Darwinism' it is convenient to designate the various work of biologists tending to establish, develop or modify Mr. Darwin's great theory of the origin of species. In looking back over twenty-five years it seems to me that we must say that the conclusions of Darwin as to the origin of species by the survival of selected races in the struggle for existence are more firmly established than ever. And this because there have been many attempts to gravely tamper with essential parts of the fabric as he left it, and even to substitute conceptions for those which he endeavoured to establish, at variance with his conclusions. These attempts must, I think, be considered as having failed."

[3]"Physiologic facts concerning the origin of species in nature were unknown in the time of Darwin. It was a happy idea to choose the experience of the breeders in the production of new varieties, as a base on which to build an explanation of the processes of nature. In my opinion Darwin was quite right, and he has succeeded in giving the desired proof. But the basis was a frail one, and would not stand too close an examination. Of this Darwin was always well aware. He has been prudent to the utmost, leaving many points undecided, and among them especially the range of validity of his several arguments. Unfortunately this prudence has not been adopted by his followers. Without sufficient warrant they have laid stress on one phase of the problem, quite overlooking the others. Wallace has even gone so far in his zeal and ardent veneration for Darwin, as to describe as Darwinism some things, which, in my opinion, had never been a part of Darwin's conceptions.

"The experience of the breeders was quite inadequate to the use which Darwin made of it. It was neither scientific, nor critically accurate. Laws of variation were barely conjectured; the different types of variability were only imperfectly distinguished. The breeders' conception was fairly sufficient for practical purposes, but science needed a clear understanding of the factors in the general process of variation. Repeatedly Darwin tried to formulate these causes, but the evidence available did not meet his requirements.

"Quetelet's law of variation had not yet been published. Mendel's claim of hereditary units, for the explanation of certain laws of hybrids discovered by him, was not yet made. The clear distinction between spontaneous and sudden changes, as compared with the ever-present fluctuating variations, is only of late coming into recognition by agriculturists. Innumerable minor points which go to elucidate the breeders' experience, were unknown in Darwin's time. No wonder that he made mistakes, and laid stress on modes of descent which have since been proved to be of minor importance or even of doubtful validity.

"Notwithstanding all these apparently unsurmountable difficulties, Darwin discovered the great principle which rules the evolution of organisms. It is the principle of natural selection. It is the sifting out of all organisms of minor worth through the struggle for life. It is only a sieve, and not a force of nature, no direct cause of improvement, as many of Darwin's adversaries, and unfortunately many of his followers also, have so often asserted. It is only a sieve, which decides which is to live, and what is to die. But evolutionary lines are of great length, and the evolution of a flower, or of an insectivorous plant is a way with many side-paths. It is the sieve that keeps evolution on the main line, killing all, or nearly all that try to go in other directions. By this means natural selection is the one directing cause of the broad lines of evolution.

"Of course, with the single steps of evolution it has nothing to do. Only after the step has been taken, the sieve acts, eliminating the unfit. The problem, as to how the individual steps are brought about, is quite another side of the question" (De Vries, "Species and Varieties," pp. 4–7, 1905).

The distinguished French zoölogist (Professor in the University of Paris), Delage, leader among French morphologists and experimenters, voices his position concerning Darwinism in the following concise phrases ("L'Hérédité," 2d ed., p. 397, 1903): "La sélection naturelle est un principe admirable et parfaitement juste. Tout le monde est d'accord aujourd'hui sur ce point. Mais où l'on n'est pas d'accord, c'est sur la limite de sa puissance et sur la question de savoir si elle peut engendrer des formes spécifiques nouvelles. Il semble bien demontrer aujourd'hui qu'elle ne le peut pas."

remains the one causo-mechanical explanation of the large and general progress toward fitness; the movement toward specialisation; that is, descent as we know it.

But what Darwinism does not do is to explain the beginnings of change, the modifications in indifferent characters and in indifferent directions. And all this is tremendously important, for there are among animals and plants hosts of existent indifferent characters, and many apparently indifferent directions of specialisation. As to the obvious necessity of beginnings nothing need be said. What is needed, then, is a satisfactory explanation of the pre-useful and pre-hurtful stages in the modifications of organisms: an explanation to relieve Darwinism of its necessity of asking natural selection to find in the fluctuating individual variations a handle for its action; an explanation of how there ever comes to be a handle of advantage or disadvantage of life-and-death-determining degree. With such an explanation in our possession—and whether any one or more of the various theories proposed to fill this need, such as Eimerian orthogenesis, de Vriesian heterogenesis, Rouxian battle of the parts, or Weismannian germinal selection, etc., give us this explanation, may be left for the moment undebated—with such a satisfactory explanation, I say, once in our hands, we may depend with confidence on natural selection to do the rest of the work called for by the great theory of descent. Among all the divergent lines of development and change, instituted by this agent of beginnings, natural selection will choose those to persist by saying No to those that may not. And the result is organic evolution.

But all this is equivalent to saying that there are other important factors in descent than selection, and that as to the beginnings of descent—and this is species-forming—these other factors are the more important ones. Which I believe is true. The causes of variation and the means of segregation or isolation are the chief factors in actual species-forming. Certainly the mutations theory is not yet ready to offer itself as an explanation of adaptation, however confidently it may claim to be enrolled among species-forming factors. The very same objections that have served to topple down selection from its high seat of honour, can be directed immediately and effectively against this latest claimant for recognition as the Great Cause of descent. Nor can geographical isolation explain modification where adaptation is included. Nor can Lamarck's beautiful explanation of adaptation claim validity, until the actuality of its fundamental postulate, the carrying over of ontogenic acquirements into phylogeny, be proved. And so with Buffon and St. Hilaire's influ-

ence of the ambient medium, and Eimer's modifying factors. Nor can any Nägelian automatic perfecting principle hold our suffrage for a moment unless we stand with theologists on the insecure basis of teleology.

No, let no ambitious student hesitate to take up the search for the truth about evolution from the notion that biology is a read book. The "Origin of Species" was the first opening of the book—that the world recognised at least; poor Lamarck opened the book but could not make the world read in it—and that time when it shall be closed because read through is too far away even to speculate about. With Osborn[4] let us join the believers in the "unknown factors in evolution." Let us begin our motto with *Ignoramus*, but never follow it with *Ignoribimus*.

Now if we do not know, but want to know, and are willing to make an attempt toward knowing, where shall our energy of exploration and discov-

---

[4]"A study of the recent discussion in the *Contemporary Review* between Spencer and Weismann leads to the conclusion that neither of these acknowledged leaders of biological thought supports his position upon inductive evidence. Each displays his main force in destructive criticism of his opponent; neither presents his case constructively in such a manner as to carry conviction either to his opponent or to others. In short, beneath the surface of fine controversial style we discern these leaders respectively maintaining as finally established theories which are less grounded upon fact that upon the logical improbabilities of rival theories. Such a conclusion is deeply significant; to my mind it marks a turning point in the history of speculation, for certainly we shall not arrest research with any evolution factor grounded upon logic rather than upon inductive demonstration. A retrograde chapter in the history of science would open if we should do so and should accept as established laws which rest so largely upon negative reasoning. . . .

"The first step then towards progress is the straightforward confession of the limits of our knowledge and of our present failure to base either Lamarckism or neo-Darwinism as universal principles upon induction. The second is the recognition that all our thinking still centres around the five working hypotheses which have thus far been proposed; namely, those of Buffon, Lamarck, St. Hilaire, Darwin, and Nägeli. Modern criticism has highly differentiated, but not essentially altered these hypothetical factors since they were originally conceived. Darwin's 'survival of the fittest' we may alone regard as absolutely demonstrated as a real factor, without committing ourselves as to the 'origin of fitness.' The third step is to recognise that there may be an unknown factor or factors which will cause quite as great surprise as Darwin's." . . .

"The general conclusion we reach from a survey of the whole field is, that for Buffon's and Lamarck's factors we have no theory of heredity, while the original Darwin factor, or neo-Darwinism, offers an inadequate explanation of evolution. If acquired variations are transmitted, there must be, therefore, some unknown principle in heredity; if they are not transmitted, there must be some unknown factor in evolution." (Osborn, H. F., "The Unknown Factors of Evolution," in Wood's Holl Biological Lectures, pp. 79, 80, 81, 98, and 99, 1894.)

ery be first directed?[5] To what particular points or aspects of the causes-of-evolution problem shall we give our first attention, what fields of study first invade? What, in a word, is the principal desideratum in present-day investigation of evolution? I should answer, the *intensive study of variability*. Not alone of the statics of variation but of its dynamics. Indeed, above all its dynamics. The experimental study of the stimuli, external and internal, the influences, extrinsic and intrinsic, which are the factors and causes of variation,—this is the great desideratum; this the crying call to the evolution student. Experiment in variation study includes controlled modification of ontogeny (experimental development) and controlled modification of phylogeny (pedigreed breeding). In the study of variation statics, biometry is the greatest advance in modern methods, and the essential basis of biometric study, namely, quantitative and statistical data, must have its part in the investigation of variation dynamics. But in entering the realm of the causal study of variability, "we must not," as Roux has clearly pointed out, "conceal from ourselves the fact that the causal investigation of organism is one of the most difficult, if not the most difficult, problem which the human intellect has attempted to solve, and that this investigation, like every causal science, can never reach completeness, since every new cause ascertained only gives rise to fresh questions concerning the cause of this cause."

I believe that the neglect on the part of the selectionists to pay sufficient attention to the origin and causes of the variation which is such an indispensable basis of their theory, has been one of the most obvious reasons for the present strong reaction against the selection theories. Thankfully accepting the bricks and stones handed to them they have built a house of great beauty: but with stones of different shape a house of quite different appearance might have been built. Is it not a cause for wonder that the selection masons have not been more inquisitive concerning the whence and why of this magical supply of just the needed sort of material at just the right time? As a matter of fact, Darwin himself gave serious attention to the origin of his always-ready variations, but his tremendous undertaking was too nearly super-human already to permit him to add to it an ade-

quate attention to the problem of causes. But that same excuse does not attach to his followers. And it is, I repeat, largely this neglect to strive to penetrate the so-far unrent veil of obscurity lying over the beginnings of species change that has contributed to the growing revolt against the *Allmacht* of the selection dogma. Who would in these days have a following for his explanation of species origin must include in his theory some fairly satisfying explanation of the first visible beginnings of modification.

Then, after the explanation of the why and how of variability, comes the necessity of explaining the cumulation of this variability along certain lines, the first visible issuance of these lines being as species, and later becoming more and more pronounced as courses of descent. This explanation has got to begin lower down in phyletic history than natural selection can begin. Before ever there can be utility and advantage there must have come about a certain degree of heaping up, of cumulating, of intensifying variations. What are these factors? They are possibly only two:

1. orthogenetic or determinate variation as the outcome of plasm preformation or of epigenetic influences,
2. the segregation of similar variations by physiologic or topographic conditions.

Hence, next to the cause or origin of variability the great desideratum is a knowledge of the means of cumulating and directing variability. And both these great fundamental needs of a satisfactory understanding of organic evolution seem to me to be wholly unreferred to in the theory of natural selection. To be sure the control and cumulation of such large differences among organisms and species as are positively sufficient to determine the saving or the loss of life are explicable by selection. And this factor is sooner or later in any phyletic history bound to step in and probably be the dominant one. But a species, or a character, will always have a longer or shorter preselective existence and history, and it is precisely these days before the Inquisition of which we demand information. For of one thing we are now certain, and that is, that evolution and the origin of species have both their beginnings and a certain period of history before the day of the coming of the Grand Inquisitor, selection.

Finally there is still another desideratum and one whose seeking will carry us into dangerous country. For while there may be and are selectionists who might allow us to fumble about in the darkness of preselective time for first causes, there is probably

---

[5]Davenport, C. B., "Animal Morphology in its Relation to Other Sciences," *Congress of Arts and Sciences*, Vol. V, pp. 244–257, 1906. In this paper are pointed out in admirable manner the present-moment problems, interests, and points of view of evolution biologists.

none who will allow us to question his right to explain that other element in evolution besides species transformation, namely, adaptation, or, as the Germans untranslatably put it, *Zweckmässigkeit.* But by no means all biologists[6] find in natural selection a sufficient explanation of adaptation.

In the visible expression of organic evolution are two chief elements, one the variety of life kinds, the existence of species, the reality of lines of descent; and the other the adaptedness and adaptiveness of these life kinds. The varieties of organic kinds show themselves adapted in structure and function to the varieties of environment and life-conditions. Hence, the task of an evolution is a double one; it must explain not only diversity or variety in life, but adaptive diversity or variety. And there is no gainsaying to the selection explanation its claim to stand among all proposed explanations of adaptation as that one least shaken by the critical attack of its adversaries. However mightily the

scientific imagination must exert itself to deliver certain difficult cases into the hands of selection, and however sophisticated and lawyer-like the argument from the selection side may be for any single refractory example, the fact remains that the selectionist seems to be able to stretch his explanation to fit all adaptations with less danger of finding it brought up against positive adverse facts than is possible to the champion of any other so far proposed explanation. The explanation of adaptation by natural selection steers wide of teleology on one hand and of unproved assumptions concerning heredity on the other. The protoplasmic consciousness of Cope and the automatic perfecting principle of Nägeli and those of his manner of explanation, are only indirect ways of attributing to natural forces visions and anticipations of what does not yet exist; while the influence of the ambient medium of St. Hilaire and of the extrinsic factors of Eimer, and the impressing photographi-

---

[6]Henry de Varigny, in "La Nature et La Vie," 1905, says that for many adaptations "il n'y a pas à se dissimuler que, dans beaucoup de cas, cette explication [of the adaptation] est purement verbale; nous constatons un résultat, nous l'exprimons en essayant de l'interpréter; mais le mécanisme reste obscur. . . . Dans beaucoup de cas, l'adaptation est un phénomène que l'on constate sans peine mais qui dans l'état actuel de nos connaissances, reste sans explication" (p. 184 and p. 185).

Klebs, Georg, "Willkürliche Entwicklungsänderungen bei Pflanzen," 1903. An interesting, suggestive, and valuable account of experiments, and their significance, on altering the developmental phenomena of plants. Although he is strongly opposed to any vitalistic theory which attributes to life an independence of physico-chemical laws, Klebs does not accept the Darwinian explanation of adaptiveness. Darwin "betrachtet die Zweckmässigkeit selbst als den wesentlichsten Faktor der Artbildung, indem nach seiner Meinung die natürliche Zuchtwahl aus der Menge der richtungslos auftretenden variationen nur die zweckmässigkeiten Merkmale zur Ausbildung und weiteren Entfaltung bringt. *Daher stammt die früher so verbreitete und heute uns sonderbar erscheinende Meinung, dass die Deutung eines Merkmales als eines zweckmässigen schon als eine Erklärung für sein Entstehen und seine Ausbildung angenommen wurde.* Die Geltung der Darwin'schen Theorie muss seit den Arbeiten Nägelis, de Vries, u. a. jedenfalls eingeschränkt werden. Das eigentliche Problem der Artbildung muss, wie wir später sehen werden in anderer Weise, formuliert werden" (p. 3).

Friedländer ("Entdeckung eines 'Atlantischen Palolo,'" etc., *Biol. Centralbl.,* Vol. XXI, pp. 352–366, 1901) refers to the Darwinian explanation of *Zweckmässigkeit* as follows:

"Der ganze Darwinismus im weiteren, also auch vordarwin'schen Sinne der Descendenzhypothese, mit oder ohne Betonung der Selektionstheorie, und samt den allseitig als fertig und sicher festgestellt gedachten Stammbäumen aller Organismen, würde, wenn auch alles damit sonst seine Richtigkeit hätte, unsere Gesamterkenntnis keineswegs in so übermässigem Grade bereichern, wie man früher wähnte und vor allem nicht in dem Masse, als dass es sich lohnte, auf die Herstellung der zudem immer problematischen Stammbäume sonderliche Zeit und Mühe zu verwenden. Zweitens aber haben die neueren Experimentalforschungen Arten der Zweckmässigkeit an den Tag gebracht, welche aus rein logischen Gründen durch die Selektionstheorie

durchaus nicht, auch nicht einmal scheinbar, 'erklärt' werden können. Nun ist aber doch gerade die vermeintliche 'Erklärung' der organischen Zweckmässigkeit oder sogen. 'Anpassungsvollkommenheit' die Hauptstärke des eigenlichen Darwinismus. Wie die Sache jetzt liegt, müssten die Verteidiger des Darwinismus annehmen, dass die organische Zweckmässigkeit zwei vollkommen verschiedene Wurzeln habe. Die eine wäre die alte Darwin'sche oder darwinistische—da nämlich, wo diese logischerweise möglich ist; obwohl ja auch hier die Erklärung die nicht recht befriedigende Form hat, dass gesagt wird, die Zweckmässigkeit rühre daher, dass die weniger zweckmässigen Formen ausgestorben seien. Die zweite Wurzel der organischen Zweckmässigkeit, wie sie sich namentlich in den Selbstregulationserscheinungen äussert und zwar auch unter solchen Bedingungen, die in der freien Natur kaum jemals vorkommen und daher für das 'Bestehender Art' nicht von irgend welcher Bedeutung sein können— diese zweite Wurzel der Zweckmässigkeit ist der eigentliche Stein des Anstosses. Die Thatsachen sind hartnäckig, eine darwinistische Scheinerklärung ist hier unmöglich und die an sich doch so äusserst interessanten Erscheinungen, sowie die ganze experimentelle Forschungsmethode ist bei den eigentlichen Darwinisten nicht in gutem Ansehen; aus dem sehr begreiflichen Grunde, weil jene Thatsachen für die betreffende Richtung unbequem sind. Eine Reihe sicher festgestellter Thatsachen aus dem Gebiete der sogen. Selbstregulation beweist also, dass es organische Zweckmässigkeiten und obendrein typische Beispiele von solchen giebt, welche dem Darwin'schen Erklärungsschema vollkommen trotzen. Nun aber hat die organische Zweckmässigkeit im ganzen ein so einheitliches Gepräge, dass ein doppelter Ursprung von vorn herein äusserst unwahrscheinlich ist. Hieraus folgt dann weiter, dass die darwinistische Betrachtungsweise in der Wirklichkeit wahrscheinlich auch in den Fällen nicht zutrifft, wo sie logisch wenigstens die Möglichkeit einer Erklärung oder Quasierklärung darzubieten scheint. Endlich aber sollten auch diejenigen, denen die Bedenken gegen die darwinistischen Schlussfolgerungen nicht recht eingehen wollen, nachgerade doch wenigstens das einsehen, dass der Teil der Biologie, der sich allenfalls im darwinistischen Sinne behandeln liesse oder doch in Sinne jener Richtung nach Darwin'schen Prinzipien behandelt werden kann,—dass dieser Teil nur ein kleines und vergleichsweise auch unwichtiges Gebiet umfasst."

cally on the species and the carrying over into phylogeny, with approximate identity, of characteristics and modifications acquired ontogenetically by the individual as a result of functional stimulation—all these are assumptions not only apparently unproved, but in the light of our present knowledge of the mechanism of heredity seemingly unprovable.

Yet the explanation of species transformation and of adaptation by the introduction into phylogeny of modifications (reaction effects) arising in the individual during its ontogeny, has to its credit a certain logical proof, or basis, which has great validity in my mind, and yet which has enjoyed little general recognition and almost no emphasis from supporters of Lamarckism or neo-Lamarckism. As the great strength of the natural selection explanation of species-change and adaptation lies precisely in the logical nature of its premises and conclusions rather than on scientific observation and experiment,[7] it certainly is not unfair to emphasise any similar kind of proof tending to support the Lamarckian type of explanation.

The logical proof that I refer to is simply this: It is a universally admitted fact that environment and functional stimulation can and do modify organisms during their lifetime, and that this modifica-

tion is usually plainly adaptive. It is also an admitted fact that species differences or modifications are often identical with these ontogenetic modifications. That is, that under similar environment or life conditions species modification often follows the same lines as ontogenetic or individual modification. Now when we recall the possibilities of the hosts of ways in which the necessities of adaptation to varying environment might be met by selection among nearly infinite fortuitous variations, and yet see that exactly that means or line or kind of adaptive change occurs, which in the case of the individual is plainly and confessedly a direct personal adaptive reaction to varying environment, is it not the logical conclusion that the species change and adaptation is derived, not by the chance appearance of the needed variation, but by the compelled or determined appearance of this variation? In other words when species differences and adaptations are identical with differences and modifications readily directly producible in the individual by varying environment, are we not justified, on the basis of logical deduction, to assume the transmutation of ontogenetic acquirements into phyletic acquirements, even though we are as yet ignorant of the physico-chemical or vital mechanism capable of effecting the carrying over? Has natural selection's claimed capacity to effect species change, unseen by observer, untested by experimenter, any better or even other proof of actuality than that just offered on behalf of species modification as a direct result of the stimulus of varying environment and functional exercise? I cannot see that it has.

And this kind of argument, based half on observed facts and half on deduction, may be extended even farther on behalf of the theory that species change is the direct reaction to environmental conditions. For there are many ontogenetic variations produced directly in response to environment that are not plainly adaptive; many, indeed, between which and the environmental conditions that produce them no *reasonable* relation is apparent; no relation, that is, that would be exactly expected or could be foretold until empirically determined. In other words, many apparently nonsignificant ontogenetic differences or variations appear as direct result of environmental influence or stimulus. For example, individuals of certain species of the Crustacean phyllopod genus Artemia show marked structural differences when grown in salt water of varying density. These differences are in the size and shape of the plate-like lateral gills, the segmentation of the post-abdomen, the length of the caudal flaps (telson) and the hairiness of these flaps. The size of the whole body is also affected, individuals developing in water of higher density

---

[7] Jacques Loeb, in a recent address ("Recent Development of Biology," *Congress of Arts and Sciences*, Vol. V, p. 17, 1906), takes this attitude toward the problem of species-forming: "The theory of heredity of Mendel and de Vries is in full harmony with the idea of evolution. The modern idea of evolution originated, as is well known, with Lamarck, and it is the great merit of Darwin to have revived this idea. It is, however, remarkable that none of the Darwinian authors seemed to consider it necessary that the transformation of species should be the object of direct observation. It is generally understood in the natural sciences either that direct observation should form the foundation of our conclusions or mathematical laws, which are derived from direct observations. This rule was evidently considered superfluous by those writing on the hypothesis of evolution. Their scientific conscience was quieted by the assumption that processes like that of evolution could not be directly observed, as they occurred too slowly, and that for this reason indirect observations must suffice. I believe that this lack of direct observation explains the polemical character of this literature, for wherever we can base our conclusions upon direct observations polemics become superfluous. It was, therefore, a decided progress when de Vries was able to show that the hereditary changes of forms, so-called 'mutations,' can be directly observed, at least in certain groups of organisms, and secondly, that these changes take place in harmony with the idea that for definite hereditary characteristics definite determinants, possibly in the form of chemical compounds, must be present in the sexual cells. It seems to me that the work of Mendel and de Vries and their successors marks the beginning of a real theory of heredity and evolution. If it is at all possible to produce new species artificially, I think that the discoveries of Mendel and de Vries must be the starting point."

being markedly smaller than those which have been grown in less dense water. Now of all these differences only two seem to have what I call a reasonable relation to the environmental differences. The increased proportional size of the gills shown by the Artemias grown in denser water appears to be a regulatory change connected with the smaller amount of oxygen in the water, and the decreased size of the body may similarly be conceived by some to be an expected concomitant of the denser water condition. But what of the extra abdominal segment, the longer telson projections and their increased hairiness, all of which as shown by Schmankewitsch[8] (however mistakenly this investigator may have interpreted his results as examples of actual species modification) and Anikin[9] for *Artemia salina* and by the writer[10] for *Artemia franciscanus*, are the ontogenetic differences that varying density of salt water actually produces in individuals of a single Artemia species. These differences, these variations, are of the sort that I am calling non-significant, non-adaptive, non-reasonable. They would not be prophesied; they seem to have no reasonable correlation with the causes which produce them. But they are actually the results or effects of determined proximate causes which are extrinsic or environmental. If now the logical argument (based on identity of adaptive modification in individuals and in species) for the transmutation of ontogenetic changes into phyletic changes has any validity, then these non-adaptive, indifferent modifications may be transmuted as well as the adaptive ones, and thus hosts of trivial, non-adaptive indifferent species differences be explained on this Lamarcko-Eimerian basis as well as the obviously adaptive modifications. But I am not insisting on this sort of argument too strongly. It is exactly the sort of argument upon which the theory of natural selection chiefly rests, and I have certainly tried to make evident in this book my belief in the danger of the substitution of this sort of logical or metaphysical basis of belief in a theory for a scientific basis of observation and experiment.

Finally, let us ask ourselves why we have adopted the common belief that our search for a cause of variability is a search for some so far unknown, some quite new factor or force in biology? May it not be that the factor is already familiar to us; so familiar indeed perhaps that we are esteeming it too

simple and too obvious to play the rôle of the Great Desideratum, a causal factor of variability.

When one attempts to picture the process of the making of a new individual, and follows the complex phenomena of fecundation, of embryology, and post-embryonic development, is it not impossible to conceive of the production of two identical individuals? In all the course of this development, from the first cleavage of the fertilised egg-cell on, it is practically impossible to repeat processes absolutely identically, hence to produce absolutely identical organs, parts, cells. Now the germ-cells have their very origin in a repeated complex process, mitotic cell division; they are produced as nearly alike as possible, but it is not possible to make them absolutely identical.

Development, whether largely epigenetic or largely evolutionary, depends at least partly (probably largely) on the physical, *i. e.*, structural, character of the germ-cells. Slight differences in the germ-cells then would lead to considerable differences in the fully developed organ. If the differences in the germ-cells happened, as would occasionally or rarely be the case, to be considerable, then the differences in the adults would be very considerable (mutations, sports, monsters, etc.). We know enough of the complex and epigenetic character of ontogeny to see plainly that identity among individuals, even of the same brood, is impossible.

Variation, then, seems the necessary, the absolutely unavoidable outcome of the conditions to which the developing individual is exposed. Indeed, all the individuals of a species might start (as fertilised eggs) exactly alike, and yet I cannot see how any two could come out alike. The inevitable slight differences in position, and hence in nutrition, in the results of the host of dividing and folding, invaginating and evaginating processes, the relations of each individual, whether in the mother's body or out of it, to everything else outside of itself—all these are conditions bound to vary a little between any two individuals. And as we know from the facts of experimental embryology that development is, partly at least, epigenetic in character, *i.e.*, depends on and is influenced by external factors, this inevitable variation in influencing conditions is bound to produce variations in the individuals.

Is there, indeed, any need at all for assuming (1) any mysterious "tendency" of the germ-plasm to vary? and (2) that the individual (continuous) variation depends wholly on germ-plasm structure? Why cannot the simple fluctuating or Darwinian variations be chiefly the result of the inevitable variation in the epigenetic factors, which, when not intruded on by exceptional disturbances, would themselves follow the "law of error" and hence pro-

---

[8]Schmankewitsch, A., *Zeitschr. f. wiss. Zool.*, Vol. XXV, p. 103, 1875; also *Zeitschr. f. wiss. Zool.*, Vol. XXIX, p. 429, 1877.

[9]Adelung, *Zool-Centralbl.*, Vol. VI, p. 757, 1899. (A review of Anikin's paper, which is in Russian.)

[10]Kellogg, V. L., "A New Artemia, and Its Life-Conditions," *Science*, N. S., Vol. XXIV, 594–596, 1906.

duce "law of error" variability? All normal swingings of the variation pendulum in any part or character, between long and short, large and small, round and angular, smooth and rough, etc., etc., would result from the normal variation of the processes; the larger (extremes of range) variations being the fewer because the larger (extremes of range) variations in the ontogenetic processes would be the fewer. Exceptionally large epigenetic variations would produce exceptionally large variations in the individual—sports, mutations.

Klebs,[11] as a result of his masterly experimental studies on modifications of plant development, comes to the conclusion that the only proved causes of variation are extrinsic influences stimulating, working through, or combined with, intrinsic conditions (not vitalistic, but physicochemical). Similarly, Tower,[12] from his protracted studies on the variations in certain insects, concludes that all these variations are caused by external stimuli working on the germ-plasm.

If variation is thus simply the wholly natural and unavoidable effect[13] of this inevitable non-identity of vital process and environmental condition, why does not evolution possess in this state of affairs the much sought for, often postulated, all-necessary, automatic modifying principle antedating and preceding selection which must effect change, determinate though not purposeful? Nägeli's automatic perfecting principle is an impossibility to the thorough-going evolutionist seeking for a causo-mechanical explanation of change. But an automatic modifying principle which results in determinate or purposive change, that is, in the change needed as the indispensable basis for the upbuilding of the great fabric of species diversity and descent; is not that the very thing provided by the simple physical or mechanical impossibility of perfect identity between process and environment in the case of one individual and process and environment in the case of any other? It seems so to me.

But I do not know. Nor in the present state of our knowledge does any one know, nor will any one know until, as Brooks[14] says of another problem, we find out. We are ignorant; terribly, immensely ignorant. And our work is, to learn. To observe, to experiment, to tabulate, to induce, to deduce. Biology was never a clearer or more inviting field for fascinating, joyful, hopeful work. To question life by new methods, from new angles, on closer terms, under more precise conditions of control; this is the requirement and the opportunity of the biologist of to-day. May his generation hear some whisper from the Sphinx!

---

[11]Klebs, G., "Willkürliche Entwickelungsänderungen bei Pflanzen," 1903.

[12]Tower, W. L., "Evolution in Chrysomelid Beetles of the Genus Leptinotarsa," Pub. No. 48, Carnegie Institution of Washington.

"The phenomenon of variation primarily owes its existence to the fact that community of descent and heredity tends to produce the exact counterpart of the parent organisms; the process of development, however, is not carried out under absolutely constant or uniform conditions, but in a world wherein there exist changing environmental states in endless proximity. This results in the turning aside in the line of development from the parental standard, perhaps ever so little or only in one character; but in this we have deviation or variation" (p. 298).

"In the explanation of origin of variation in organisms the only assumption we need make is that the original unit of organic matter was possessed of the attributes which characterise organic matter to-day—motion, sensation, growth, and reproduction. This assumption cannot meet with any serious objection unless we change our ideas and definition of organic units. Granted the existence of one single organic unit endowed as above, there is no reason for introducing further complications by the explanation of phenomena through undemonstrable hypotheses, because the fact of variation in organic units can be explained solely through their existence in a natural world surrounded by varying conditions of existence" (p. 299).

"In the third chapter, where colour characters are used as subjects, it is demonstrated that variation is directly produced by stimuli—that from relatively invariable parents, stimuli produce variable offspring; and again in the fifth chapter it is shown that variations arise in direct response to stimuli" (p. 300).

"I maintain, therefore, that all organic variations are responsive to stimuli, and are not due to inherent tendencies or latencies, or the product of mystic elements" (p. 300).

[13]Montgomery, T. A., in a recent book of much interest ("Analysis of Racial Descent in Animals," 1906), explains clearly his belief in the inevitable production of variation (even that called blastogenic or congenital), and the influence on heredity (through this variation) by the influences of environment.

[14]Brooks, W. K., "The Foundations of Zoology," p. 43, 1899. A most thoughtful and keen discussion of many of the conspicuous problems of "philosophical biology," written in lucid and epigrammatic style. In many ways Brooks stands at the head of American philosophical biologists.

Name: _____ **Date:** _____

1. What claims does Kellogg report some critiques have made about Darwinism's demise?

2. Why should Americans be concerned about the debates over the validity of Darwinism?

3. What elements of evolutionary change, according to Kellogg, is Darwinism capable of explaining?

4. What elements of evolutionary change does Kellogg claim Darwinism is not capable of explaining?

5. Kellogg concludes by declaring that biology in his day was "never a clearer or more inviting field for fascinating, joyful, hopeful work." Why do you think Kellogg was so enthusiastic about biology's promise?

Herbert Spencer

The Social Organism, 1860

Spencer (1820-1903) was an English biologist and social philosopher whose work formed the foundation for much of the modern social sciences. He was an evolutionist even before Darwin published *On the Origin of Species* and developed a belief about evolutionary change that synthesized Darwinian and Lamarckian evolutionary theories. He also coined the expression "survival of the fittest" and thought about both biological and social evolution as part of a broader framework of evolutionary change. For Spencer, evolution was synonymous with progress. In this piece he explained how societies evolved over time, becoming increasingly complex in much the same way as species evolved.

Sir James Macintosh got great credit for the saying, that "constitutions are not made, but grow." In our day, the most significant thing about this saying is, that it was ever thought so significant. As from the surprise displayed by a man at some familiar fact, you may judge of his general culture; so from the admiration which an age accords to a new thought, its average degree of enlightenment may be inferred. That this apophthegm of Macintosh should have been quoted and requoted as it has, shows how profound has been the ignorance of social science. A small ray of truth has seemed brilliant, as a distant rushlight looks like a star in the surrounding darkness.

Such a conception could not, indeed, fail to be startling when left fall in the midst of a system of thought to which it was utterly alien. Universally in Macintosh's day, things were explained on the hypothesis of manufacture, rather than that of growth; as indeed they are, by the majority, in our own day. It was held that the planets were severally projected round the Sun from the Creator's hand, with just the velocity required to balance the Sun's attraction. The formation of the Earth, the separation of sea from land, the production of animals, were mechanical works from which God rested as a labourer rests. Man was supposed to be moulded after a manner somewhat akin to that in which a modeller makes a clay-figure. And of course, in

harmony with such ideas, societies were tacitly assumed to be arranged thus or thus by direct interposition of Providence; or by the regulations of lawmakers; or by both.

Yet that societies are not artificially put together, is a truth so manifest, that it seems wonderful men should ever have overlooked it. Perhaps nothing more clearly shows the small value of historical studies, as they have been commonly pursued. You need but to look at the changes going on around, or observe social organization in its leading traits, to see that these are neither supernatural, nor are determined by the wills of individual men, as by implication the older historians teach; but are consequent on general natural causes. The one case of the division of labour suffices to prove this. It has not been by command of any ruler that some men have become manufacturers, while others have remained cultivators of the soil. In Lancashire, millions have devoted themselves to the making of cotton-fabrics; in Yorkshire, another million lives by producing woollens; and the pottery of Staffordshire, the cutlery of Sheffield, the hardware of Birmingham, severally occupy their hundreds of thousands. These are large facts in the structure of English society; but we can ascribe them neither to miracle, nor to legislation. It is not by "the hero as king," any more than by "collective wisdom," that men have been segregated into producers, wholesale distributors, and retail distributors. Our industrial organization, from its main outlines down to its minutest details, has become what it is, not simply without legisla-

From *The Westminister Review,* 1860.

tive guidance, but, to a considerable extent, in spite of legislative hindrances. It has arisen under the pressure of human wants and resulting activities. While each citizen has been pursuing his individual welfare, and none taking thought about division of labour, or conscious of the need of it, division of labour has yet been ever becoming more complete. It has been doing this slowly and silently: few having observed it until quite modern times. By steps so small, that year after year the industrial arrangements have seemed just what they were before—by changes as insensible as those through which a seed passes into a tree; society has become the complex body of mutually-dependent workers which we now see. And this economic organization, mark, is the all-essential organization. Through the combination thus spontaneously evolved, every citizen is supplied with daily necessaries; while he yields some product or aid to others. That we are severally alive to-day, we owe to the regular working of this combination during the past week; and could it be suddenly abolished, multitudes would be dead before another week ended. If these most conspicuous and vital arrangements of our social structure have arisen not by the devising of any one, but through the individual efforts of citizens to satisfy their own wants; we may be tolerably certain that the less important arrangements have similarly arisen.

"But surely," it will be said, "the social changes directly produced by law, cannot be classed as spontaneous growths. When parliaments or kings order this or that thing to be done, and appoint officials to do it, the process is clearly artificial; and society to this extent becomes a manufacture rather than a growth." No, not even these changes are exceptions, if they be real and permanent changes. The true sources of such changes lie deeper than the acts of legislators. To take first the simplest instance. We all know that the enactments of representative governments ultimately depend on the national will: they may for a time be out of harmony with it, but eventually they must conform to it. And to say that the national will finally determines them, is to say that they result from the average of individual desires; or, in other words—from the average of individual natures. A law so initiated, therefore, really grows out of the popular character. In the case of a Government representing a dominant class, the same thing holds, though not so manifestly. For the very existence of a class monopolizing all power, is due to certain sentiments in the commonalty. Without the feeling of loyalty on the part of retainers, a feudal system could not exist. We see in the protest of the Highlanders against the abolition of heritable jurisdictions, that they preferred that kind of local rule. And if to the popular nature must be

ascribed the growth of an irresponsible ruling class; then to the popular nature must be ascribed the social arrangements which that class creates in the pursuit of its own ends. Even where the Government is despotic, the doctrine still holds. The character of the people is, as before, the original source of this political form; and, as we have abundant proof, other forms suddenly created will not act, but rapidly retrograde to the old form. Moreover, such regulations as a despot makes, if really operative, are so because of their fitness to the social state. His acts being very much swayed by general opinion—by precedent, by the feeling of his nobles, his priesthood, his army—are in part immediate results of the national character; and when they are out of harmony with the national character, they are soon practically abrogated. The failure of Cromwell permanently to establish a new social condition, and the rapid revival of suppressed institutions and practices after his death, show how powerless is a monarch to change the type of the society he governs. He may disturb, he may retard, or he may aid the natural process of organization; but the general course of this process is beyond his control. Nay, more than this is true. Those who regard the histories of societies as the histories of their great men, and think that these great men shape the fates of their societies, overlook the truth that such great men are the products of their societies. Without certain antecedents—without a certain average national character, they neither could have been generated nor could have had the culture which formed them. If their society is to some extent re-moulded by them, they were, both before and after birth, moulded by their society—were the results of all those influences which fostered the ancestral character they inherited, and gave their own early bias, their creed, morals, knowledge, aspirations. So that such social changes as are immediately traceable to individuals of unusual power, are still remotely traceable to the social causes which produced these individuals; and hence, from the highest point of view, such social changes also, are parts of the general developmental process.

Thus that which is so obviously true of the industrial structure of society, is true of its whole structure. The fact that "constitutions are not made, but grow," is simply a fragment of the much larger fact, that under all its aspects and through all its ramifications, society is a growth and not a manufacture.

A perception that there exists some analogy between the body politic and a living individual body, was early reached; and has from time to time re-appeared in literature. But this perception was necessarily vague and more or less fanciful. In the absence of physiological science, and especially of those comprehensive generalizations which it has but lately reached, it was impossible to discern the real parallelisms.

The central idea of Plato's model Republic, is the correspondence between the parts of a society and the faculties of the human mind. Classifying these faculties under the heads of Reason, Will, and Passion, he classifies the members of his ideal society under what he regards as three analogous heads:—councillors, who are to exercise government; military or executive, who are to fulfil their behests; and the commonalty, bent on gain and selfish gratification. In other words, the ruler, the warrior, and the craftsman, are, according to him, the analogues of our reflective, volitional, and emotional powers. Now even were there truth in the implied assumption of a parallelism between the structure of a society and that of a man, this classification would be indefensible. It might more truly be contended that, as the military power obeys the commands of the Government, it is the Government which answers to the Will; while the military power is simply an agency set in motion by it. Or, again, it might be contended that whereas the Will is a product of predominant desires, to which the Reason serves merely as an eye, it is the craftsmen, who, according to the alleged analogy, ought to be the moving power of the warriors.

Hobbes sought to establish a still more definite parallelism: not, however, between a society and the human mind, but between a society and the human body. In the introduction to the work in which he develops this conception, he says—

"For by art is created that great Leviathan called a Commonwealth, or State, in Latin Civitas, which is but an artificial man; though of greater stature and strength than the natural, for whose protection and defence it was intended, and in which the *sovereignty* is an artificial *soul,* as giving life and motion to the whole body; the *magistrates* and other *officers* of judicature and execution, artificial *joints; reward* and *punishment,* by which, fastened to the seat of the sovereignty, every joint and member is moved to perform his duty, are the *nerves,* that do the same in the body natural, the *wealth* and *riches* of all the particular members are the *strength; salus populi,* the *people's safety,* its *business; counsellors,* by whom all things needful for it to know are suggested unto it, are the *memory; equity* and *laws* an artificial *reason* and *will; concord, health; sedition, sickness;* and *civil war, death.*"

And Hobbes carries this comparison so far as actually to give a drawing of the Leviathan—a vast human-shaped figure, whose body and limbs are made up of multitudes of men. Just noting that these different analogies asserted by Plato and Hobbes, serve to cancel each other (being, as they are, so completely at variance), we may say that on the whole those of Hobbes are the more plausible. But they are full of inconsistencies. If the sovereignty is the *soul* of the body-politic, how can it be that magistrates, who are a kind of deputy-sovereigns, should be comparable to *joints?* Or, again, how can the three mental functions, memory, reason, and will, be severally analogous, the first to counsellors, who are a class of public officers, and the other two to equity and laws, which are not classes of officers, but abstractions? Or, once more, if magistrates are the artificial joints of society, how can reward and punishment be its nerves? Its nerves must surely be some class of persons. Reward and punishment must in socreties, as in individuals, be *conditions* of the nerves, and not the nerves themselves.

But the chief errors of these comparisons made by Plato and Hobbes, lie much deeper. Both thinkers assume that the organization of a society is comparable, not simply to the organization of a living body in general, but to the organization of the human body in particular. There is no warrant whatever for assuming this. It is in no way implied by the evidence; and is simply one of those fancies which we commonly find mixed up with the truths of early speculation. Still more erroneous are the two conceptions in this, that they construe a society as an artificial structure. Plato's model republic—his ideal of a healthful body-politic—is to be consciously put together by men, just as a watch might be; and Plato manifestly thinks of societies in general as thus originated. Quite specifically does Hobbes express a like view. "For by *art,*" he says, "is created that great Leviathan called a Commonwealth." And he even goes so far as to compare the supposed social contract, from which a society suddenly originates, to the creation of a man by the divine fiat. Thus they both fall into the extreme inconsistency of considering a community as similar in structure to a human being, and yet as produced in the same way as an artificial mechanism—in nature, an organism; in history, a machine.

■ ■ ■ ■

The lowest animal and vegetal forms—*Protozoa* and *Protophyta*—are chiefly inhabitants of the water. They are minute bodies, most of which are made individually visible only by the microscope. All of them are extremely simple in structure, and some of them, as the *Rhizopods,* almost structureless. Multiplying, as they ordinarily do, by the spontaneous division of their bodies, they produce halves which may either become quite separate and move away in different directions, or may continue attached.

By the repetition of this process of fission, aggregations of various sizes and kinds are formed. Among the *Protophyta* we have some classes, as the *Diatomaceœ* and the Yeast-plant, in which the individuals may be either separate or attached in groups of two, three, four, or more; other classes in which a considerable number of cells are united into a thread (*Conferva, Monilia*); others in which they form a network (*Hydrodictyon*); others in which they form plates (*Ulva*); and others in which they form masses (*Laminaria, Agaricus*): all which vegetal forms, having no distinction of root, stem, or leaf, are called *Thallogens*. Among the *Protozoa* we find parallel facts. Immense numbers of *Amœba*-like creatures, massed together in a framework of horny fibres, constitute Sponge. In the *Foraminifera* we see smaller groups of such creatures arranged into more definite shapes. Not only do these almost structureless *Protozoa* unite into regular or irregular aggregations of various sizes, but among some of the more organized ones, as the *Vorticellœ*, there are also produced clusters of individuals united to a common stem. But these little societies of monads, or cells, or whatever else we may call them, are societies only in the lowest sense: there is no subordination of parts among them—no organization. Each of the component units lives by and for itself; neither giving nor receiving aid. The only mutual dependence is that consequent on mechanical union.

Do we not here discern analogies to the first stages of human societies? Among the lowest races, as the Bushmen, we find but incipient aggregation: sometimes single families, sometimes two or three families wandering about together. The number of associated units is small and variable, and their union inconstant. No division of labour exists except between the sexes, and the only kind of mutual aid is that of joint attack or defence. We see an undifferentiated group of individuals, forming the germ of a society; just as in the homogeneous groups of cells above described, we see the initial stage of animal and vegetal organization.

The comparison may now be carried a step higher. In the vegetal kingdom we pass from the *Thallogens*, consisting of mere masses of similar cells, to the *Acrogens*, in which the cells are not similar throughout the whole mass; but are here aggregated into a structure serving as leaf and there into a structure serving as root; thus forming a whole in which there is a certain subdivision of functions among the units, and therefore a certain mutual dependence. In the animal kingdom we find analogous progress. From mere unorganized groups of cells, or cell-like bodies, we ascend to groups of such cells arranged into parts that have different duties. The common Polype, from the substance of which may be separated cells that exhibit, when detached, appearances and movements like those of a solitary *Amœba*, illustrates this stage. The component units, though still showing great community of character, assume somewhat diverse functions in the skin, in the internal surface, and in the tentacles. There is a certain amount of "physiological division of labour."

Turning to societies, we find these stages paralleled in most aboriginal tribes. When, instead of such small variable groups as are formed by Bushmen, we come to the larger and more permanent groups formed by savages not quite so low, we find traces of social structure. Though industrial organization scarcely shows itself, except in the different occupations of the sexes; yet there is more or less of governmental organization. While all the men are warriors and hunters, only a part of them are included in the council of chiefs; and in this council of chiefs some one has commonly supreme authority. There is thus a certain distinction of classes and powers; and through this slight specialization of functions is effected a rude co-operation among the increasing mass of individuals, whenever the society has to act in its corporate capacity. Beyond this analogy in the slight extent to which organization is carried, there is analogy in the indefiniteness of the organization. In the *Hydra*, the respective parts of the creature's substance have many functions in common. They are all contractile; omitting the tentacles, the whole of the external surface can give origin to young *hydræ*; and, when turned inside out, stomach performs the duties of skin and skin the duties of stomach. In aboriginal societies such differentiations as exist are similarly imperfect. Notwithstanding distinctions of rank, all persons maintain themselves by their own exertions. Not only do the head men of the tribe, in common with the rest, build their own huts, make their own weapons, kill their own food; but the chief does the like. Moreover, such governmental organization as exists is inconstant. It is frequently changed by violence or treachery, and the function of ruling assumed by some other warrior. Thus between the rudest societies and some of the lowest forms of animal life, there is analogy alike in the slight extent to which organization is carried, in the indefiniteness of this organization, and in its want of fixity.

A further complication of the analogy is at hand. From the aggregation of units into organized groups, we pass to the multiplication of such groups, and their coalescence into compound groups. The *Hydra*, when it has reached a certain bulk, puts forth from its surface a bud which, growing and gradually assuming the form of the parent, finally becomes detached; and by this process of gemmation the creature peoples the adjacent water with others like itself. A parallel process is seen in the multiplication of those lowly-organized tribes above described. When one of them has increased to a size that is either too great for co-ordination under so rude a structure, or else that is greater than the surrounding country can supply with game and other wild food, there arises a tendency to divide; and as in such communities there often occur quarrels, jealousies, and other causes of division, there soon comes an occasion on which a part of the tribe separates under the leadership of some subordinate chief and migrates. This process being from time to time repeated, an extensive region is at length occupied by numerous tribes descended from a common ancestry. The analogy by no means ends here. Though in the common *Hydra* the young ones that bud out from the parent soon become detached and independent; yet throughout the rest of the class *Hydrozoa,* to which this creature belongs, the like does not generally happen. The successive individuals thus developed continue attached; give origin to other such individuals which also continue attached; and so there results a compound animal. As in the *Hydra* itself we find an aggregation of units which, considered separately, are akin to the lowest *Protozoa;* so here, in a *Zoophyte,* we find an aggregation of such aggregations. The like is also seen throughout the extensive family of *Polyzoa* or *Molluscoida.* The Ascidian Mollusks, too, in their many forms, show us the same thing: exhibiting, at the same time, various degrees of union among the component individuals. For while in the *Salpœ* the component individuals adhere so slightly that a blow on the vessel of water in which they are floating will separate them; in the *Botryllidœ* there exist vascular connexions among them, and a common circulation. Now in these different stages of aggregation, may we not see paralleled the union of groups of connate tribes into nations? Though, in regions where circumstances permit, the tribes descended from some original tribe migrate in all directions, and become far removed and quite separate; yet, where the territory presents barriers to distant migration, this does not happen: the small kindred communities are held in closer contact, and eventually become more or less united into a nation. The contrast between the tribes of American Indians and the Scottish clans, illustrates this. And a glance at our own early history, or the early histories of continental nations, shows this fusion of small simple communities taking place in various ways and to various extents. As says M. Guizot, in his *History of the Origin of Representative Government,*—

"By degrees, in the midst of the chaos of the rising society, small aggregations are formed which feel the want of alliance and union with each other. . . . Soon inequality of strength is displayed among neighbouring aggregations. The strong tend to subjugate the weak, and usurp at first the rights of taxation and military service. Thus political authority leaves the aggregations which first instituted it, to take a wider range."

That is to say, the small tribes, clans, or feudal groups, sprung mostly from a common stock, and long held in contact as occupants of adjacent lands, gradually get united in other ways than by kinship and proximity.

A further series of changes begins now to take place, to which, as before, we find analogies in individual organisms. Returning to the *Hydrozoa,* we observe that in the simplest of the compound forms the connected individuals are alike in structure, and perform like functions; with the exception that here and there a bud, instead of developing into a stomach, mouth, and tentacles, becomes an egg-sac. But with the oceanic *Hydrozoa* this is by no means the case. In the *Calycophoridœ* some of the polypes growing from the common germ, become developed and modified into large, long, sack-like bodies, which, by their rhythmical contractions, move through the water, dragging the community of polypes after them. In the *Physophoridœ* a variety of organs similarly arise by transformation of the budding polypes; so that in creatures like the *Physalia,* commonly known as the "Portuguese Man-of-war," instead of that tree-like group of similar individuals forming the original type, we have a complex mass of unlike parts fulfilling unlike duties. As an individual *Hydra* may be regarded as a group of *Protozoa* which have become partially metamorphosed into different organs; so a *Physalia* is, morphologically considered, a group of *Hydrœ* of which the individuals have been variously transformed to fit them for various functions.

This differentiation upon differentiation is just what takes place during the evolution of a civilized society. We observed how, in the small communities first formed, there arises a simple political organization: there is a partial separation of classes having different duties. And now we have to observe how, in a nation formed by the fusion of such small communities, the several sections, at first alike in structures and modes of activity, grow unlike in both—gradually become mutually-dependent parts, diverse in their natures and functions.

■ ■ ■ ■

The analogies between the evolution of governmental structures in societies, and the evolution of governmental structures in living bodies, are, however, more strikingly displayed during the formation of nations by coalescence of tribes—a process already shown to be, in several respects, parallel to the development of creatures that primarily consist of many like segments. Among other points of community between the successive rings which make up the body in the lower *Annulosa,* is the possession of similar pairs of ganglia. These pairs of ganglia, though connected by nerves, are very incompletely dependent on any general controlling power. Hence it results that when the body is cut in two, the hinder part continues to move forward under the propulsion of its numerous legs; and that when the chain of ganglia has been divided without severing the body, the hind limbs may be seen trying to propel the body in one direction while the fore limbs are trying to propel it in another. But in the higher *Annulosa,* called *Articulata,* sundry of the anterior pairs of ganglia, besides growing larger, unite in one mass; and this great cephalic ganglion having become the co-ordinator of all the creature's movements, there no longer exists much local independence. Now may we not in the growth of a consolidated kingdom out of petty sovereignties or baronies, observe analogous changes? Like the chiefs and primitive rules above described, feudal lords, exercising supreme power over their respective groups of retainers, discharge functions analogous to those of rudimentary nervous centres. Among these local governing centres there is, in early feudal times, very little subordination. They are in frequent antagonism; they are individually restrained chiefly by the influence of parties in their own class; and they are but irregularly subject to that most powerful member of their order who has gained the position of head-suzerain or king. As the growth and organization of the society progresses, these local directive centres fall more and more under the control of a chief directive centre. Closer commercial union between the several segments is accompanied by closer governmental union; and these minor rulers end in being little more than agents who administer, in their several localities, the laws made by the supreme ruler: just as the local ganglia above described, eventually become agents which enforce, in their respective segments, the orders of the cephalic ganglion. The parallelism holds still further. We remarked above, when speaking of the rise of aboriginal kings, that in proportion as their territories increase, they are obliged not only to perform their executive functions by deputy, but also to gather round themselves advisers to aid in their directive functions; and that thus, in place of a solitary governing unit, there grows up a group of governing units, comparable to a ganglion consisting of many cells. Let us here add that the advisers and chief officers who thus form the rudiment of a ministry, tend from the beginning to exercise some control over the ruler. By the information they give and the opinions they express, they sway his judgment and affect his commands. To this extent he is made a channel through which are communicated the directions originating with them; and in course of time, when the advice of ministers becomes the acknowledged source of his actions, the king assumes the character of an automatic centre, reflecting the impressions made on him from without.

Beyond this complication of governmental structure many societies do not progress; but in some, a further development takes place. Our own case best illustrates this further development and its further analogies. To kings and their ministries have been added, in England, other great directive centres, exercising a control which, at first small, has been gradually becoming predominant: as with the great governing ganglia which especially distinguish the highest classes of living beings. Strange as the assertion will be thought, our Houses of Parliament discharge, in the social economy, functions which are in sundry respects comparable to those discharged by the cerebral masses in a vertebrate animal. As it is in the nature of a single ganglion to be affected only by special stimuli from particular parts of the body; so it is in the nature of a single ruler to be swayed in his acts by exclusive personal or class interests. As it is in the nature of a cluster of ganglia, connected with the primary one, to convey to it a greater variety of influences from more numerous organs, and thus to make its acts conform to more numerous requirements; so it is in the nature of the subsidiary controlling powers surrounding a king to adapt his rule to a greater number of public exigencies. And as it is in the nature of those great and latest-developed ganglia which distinguish the higher animals, to interpret and combine the multiplied and varied impressions conveyed to them from all parts of the system, and to regulate the actions in such way as duly to regard them all; so it is in the nature of those great and latest-developed legislative bodies which distinguish the most advanced societies, to interpret and combine the wishes of all classes and localities, and to make laws in harmony with the general wants. We may describe the office of the brain as that of *averaging* the interests of life, physical, intellectual, moral, and a good brain is one in which the desires answering to these respective interests are so balanced, that the conduct they jointly dictate, sacrifices none of them. Similarly, we may describe the office of a Parliament as that of *averaging* the interests of the various classes in a community; and a good Parliament is one in which the parties answering to these respective interests are so balanced, that their united legislation allows to each class as much as consists with the claims of the rest. Besides being comparable in their duties, these great directive centres, social and individual, are comparable in the processes by which their duties are discharged. The cerebrum is not occupied with direct impressions from without but with the ideas of such impressions. Instead of the actual sensations produced in the body, and directly appreciated by the sensory ganglia, or primitive nervous centres, the cerebrum receives only the representations of these sensations; and its consciousness is called *representative* consciousness, to distinguish it from the original or *presentative* consciousness. Is it not significant that we have hit on the same word to distinguish the function of our House of Commons? We call it a *representative* body, because the interests with which it deals are not directly presented to it, but represented to it by its various members, and a debate is a conflict of representations of the results likely to follow from a proposed course—a description which applies with equal truth to a debate in the individual consciousness. In both cases, too, these great governing masses take no part in the executive functions. As, after a conflict in the cerebrum, those desires which finally predominate act on the subjacent ganglia, and through their instrumentality determine the bodily actions; so the parties which, after a parliamentary struggle, gain the victory, do not themselves carry out their wishes, but get them carried out by the executive divisions of the Government. The fulfilment of all legislative decisions still devolves on the original directive centres: the impulse passing from the Parliament to the Ministers and from the Ministers to the King, in whose name everything is done; just as those smaller, first-developed ganglia, which in the lowest vertebrata are the chief controlling agents, are still, in the brains of the higher vertebrata, the agents through which the dictates of the cerebrum are worked out. Moreover, in both cases these original centres become increasingly automatic. In the developed vertebrate animal, they have little function beyond that of conveying impressions to, and executing the determinations of, the larger centres. In our highly organized government, the monarch has long been lapsing into a passive agent of Parliament; and now, ministries are rapidly falling into the same position. Nay, between the two cases there is a parallelism even in respect of the exceptions to this automatic action. For in the individual creature it happens that under circumstances of sudden alarm, as from a loud sound close at hand, an unexpected object starting up in front, or a slip from insecure footing, the danger is guarded against by some quick involuntary jump, or adjustment of the limbs, which occurs before there is time to consider the impending evil and take deliberate measures to avoid it: the rationale of which is that these violent impressions produced on the senses, are reflected from the sensory ganglia to the spinal cord and muscles, without, as in ordinary cases, first passing through the cerebrum. In like manner on national emergencies calling for prompt action, the King and Ministry, not having time to lay the matter before the great deliberative bodies, themselves issue commands for the requisite movements or precautions: the primitive, and now almost automatic, directive centres, resume for a moment their original uncontrolled power. And then, strangest of all, observe that in either case there is an after-process of approval or disapproval. The individual on recovering from his automatic start, at once contemplates the cause of his fright; and, according to the case, concludes that it was well he moved as he did, or condemns himself for his groundless alarm. In like manner, the deliberative powers of the State discuss, as soon as may be, the unauthorized acts of the executive powers; and, deciding that the reasons were or were not sufficient, grant or withhold a bill of indemnity.

Thus far in comparing the governmental organization of the body-politic with that of an individual body, we have considered only the respective co-ordinating centres. We have yet to consider the channels through which these co-ordinating centres receive information and convey commands. In the simplest societies, as in the simplest organisms, there is no "internuncial apparatus," as Hunter styled the nervous system. Consequently, impressions can be but slowly propagated from unit to unit throughout the whole mass. The same progress, however, which, in animal-organization, shows itself in the establishment of ganglia or directive centres, shows itself also in the establishment of nerve-threads, through which the ganglia receive and convey impressions and so control remote organs. And in societies the like eventually takes place. After a long period during which the directive centres communicate with various parts of the society through other means, there at last comes into existence an "internuncial apparatus," analogous to that found in individual bodies. The comparison of telegraph-wires to nerves is familiar to all. It applies, however, to an extent not commonly supposed. Thus, throughout the vertebrate sub-kingdom, the great nerve-bundles diverge from the vertebrate axis side by side with the great arteries; and similarly, our groups of telegraph-wires are carried along the sides of our railways. The most striking parallelism, however, remains. Into each great bundle of nerves, as it leaves the axis of the body along with an artery, there enters a branch of the sympathetic nerve; which branch, accompanying the artery throughout its ramifications, has the function of regulating its diameter and otherwise controlling the flow of blood through it according to local requirements. Analogously, in the group of telegraph-wires running alongside each railway, there is a wire for the purpose of regulating the traffic—for retarding or expediting the flow of passengers and commodities, as the local conditions demand. Probably, when our now rudimentary telegraph-system is fully developed, other analogies will be traceable.

Such, then, is a general outline of the evidence which justifies the comparison of societies to living organisms. That they gradually increase in mass; that they become little by little more complex; that at the same time their parts grow more mutually dependent; and that they continue to live and grow as wholes, while successive generations of their units appear and disappear; are broad peculiarities which bodies-politic display in common with all living bodies; and in which they and living bodies differ from everything else. And on carrying out the comparison in detail, we find that these major analogies involve many minor analogies, far closer than might have been expected. Others might be added. We had hoped to say something respecting the different types of social organization, and something also on social metamorphoses; but we have reached our assigned limits.

Name: _____ **Date:** _____

1. Where does Spencer claim the notion originates that there is an analogy between the growth of the state and the growth of an individual's body?

2. What, according to Spencer, was Hobbes' contribution to the state-individual analogy?

3. Spencer makes a number of analogies between the evolutionary development of life and the evolutionary development of societies. Describe two of them in your own words.

   1.

   2.

4. Describe an example Spencer offers of the similarities between the evolution of governmental structures in society and the evolution of governing structures in the body.

Andrew Carnegie

"The Gospel of Wealth," 1901

Carnegie (1835-1919) was a Scottish immigrant to the United States and the icon of the American dream. A rags-to-riches story, Carnegie was a weaver's assistant, messenger boy, and telegraph operator who, through careful investments and aggressive business practices, amassed a tremendous fortune. In 1901 he sold his steel business and spent the remainder of his life giving away over $350 million to educational, scientific, and cultural causes. In this selection, Carnegie described his motivations and methods for distributing wealth and argued that "the man who dies thus rich dies disgraced." Despite his incredible philanthropy, Carnegie is considered Social Darwinist because of the manner in which he believed money ought to be distributed by wealthy patrons.

THE PROBLEM OF THE ADMINISTRATION OF WEALTH

The problem of our age is the proper administration of wealth, that the ties of brotherhood may still bind together the rich and poor in harmonious relationship. The conditions of human life have not only been changed, but revolutionized, within the past few hundred years. In former days there was little difference between the dwelling, dress, food, and environment of the chief and those of his retainers. The Indians are to-day where civilized man then was. When visiting the Sioux, I was led to the wigwam of the chief. It was like the others in external appearance, and even within the difference was trifling between it and those of the poorest of his braves. The contrast between the palace of the millionaire and the cottage of the laborer with us to-day measures the change which has come with civilization. This change, however, is not to be deplored, but welcomed as highly beneficial. It is well, nay, essential, for the progress of the race that the houses of some should be homes for all that is highest and best in literature and the arts, and for all the refinements of civilization, rather than that none should be so. Much better this great irregularity than universal squalor. Without wealth there can be

no Mæcenas. The "good old times" were not good old times. Neither master nor servant was as well situated then as to-day. A relapse to old conditions would be disastrous to both—not the least so to him who serves—and would sweep away civilization with it. But whether the change be for good or ill, it is upon us, beyond our power to alter, and, therefore, to be accepted and made the best of. It is a waste of time to criticize the inevitable.

It is easy to see how the change has come. One illustration will serve for almost every phase of the cause. In the manufacture of products we have the whole story. It applies to all combinations of human industry, as stimulated and enlarged by the inventions of this scientific age. Formerly, articles were manufactured at the domestic hearth, or in small shops which formed part of the household. The master and his apprentices worked side by side, the latter living with the master, and therefore subject to the same conditions. When these apprentices rose to be masters, there was little or no change in their mode of life, and they, in turn, educated succeeding apprentices in the same routine. There was, substantially, social equality, and even political equality, for those engaged in industrial pursuits had then little or no voice in the State.

The inevitable result of such a mode of manufacture was crude articles at high prices. To-day the world obtains commodities of excellent quality at prices which even the preceding generation would have deemed incredible. In the commercial world

From *The Gospel of Wealth,* 1901, New York: The Century Company.

similar causes have produced similar results, and the race is benefited thereby. The poor enjoy what the rich could not before afford. What were the luxuries have become the necessaries of life. The laborer has now more comforts than the farmer had a few generations ago. The farmer has more luxuries than the landlord had, and is more richly clad and better housed. The landlord has books and pictures rarer and appointments more artistic than the king could then obtain.

The price we pay for this salutary change is, no doubt, great. We assemble thousands of operatives in the factory, and in the mine, of whom the employer can know little or nothing, and to whom he is little better than a myth. All intercourse between them is at an end. Rigid castes are formed, and, as usual, mutual ignorance breeds mutual distrust. Each caste is without sympathy with the other, and ready to credit anything disparaging in regard to it. Under the law of competition, the employer of thousands is forced into the strictest economies, among which the rates paid to labor figure prominently, and often there is friction between the employer and the employed, between capital and labor, between rich and poor. Human society loses homogeneity.

The price which society pays for the law of competition, like the price it pays for cheap comforts and luxuries, is also great; but the advantages of this law are also greater still than its cost—for it is to this law that we owe our wonderful material development, which brings improved conditions in its train. But, whether the law be benign or not, we must say of it, as we say of the change in the conditions of men to which we have referred: It is here; we cannot evade it; no substitutes for it have been found; and while the law may be sometimes hard for the individual, it is best for the race, because it insures the survival of the fittest in every department. We accept and welcome, therefore, as conditions to which we must accommodate ourselves, great inequality of environment; the concentration of business, industrial and commercial, in the hands of a few; and the law of competition between these, as being not only beneficial, but essential to the future progress of the race. Having accepted these, it follows that there must be great scope for the exercise of special ability in the merchant and in the manufacturer who has to conduct affairs upon a great scale. That this talent for organization and management is rare among men is proved by the fact that it invariably secures enormous rewards for its possessor, no matter where or under what laws or conditions. The experienced in affairs always rate the MAN whose services can be obtained as a partner as not only the first consideration, but

such as render the question of his capital scarcely worth considering: for able men soon create capital; in the hands of those without the special talent required, capital soon takes wings. Such men become interested in firms or corporations using millions; and, estimating only simple interest to be made upon the capital invested, it is inevitable that their income must exceed their expenditure and that they must, therefore, accumulate wealth. Nor is there any middle ground which such men can occupy, because the great manufacturing or commercial concern which does not earn at least interest upon its capital soon becomes bankrupt. It must either go forward or fall behind; to stand still is impossible. It is a condition essential to its successful operation that it should be thus far profitable, and even that, in addition to interest on capital, it should make profit. It is a law, as certain as any of the others named, that men possessed of this peculiar talent for affairs, under the free play of economic forces must, of necessity, soon be in receipt of more revenue than can be judiciously expended upon themselves; and this law is as beneficial for the race as the others.

Objections to the foundations upon which society is based are not in order, because the condition of the race is better with these than it has been with any other which has been tried. Of the effect of any new substitutes proposed we cannot be sure. The Socialist or Anarchist who seeks to overturn present conditions is to be regarded as attacking the foundation upon which civilization itself rests, for civilization took its start from the day when the capable, industrious workman said to his incompetent and lazy fellow, "If thou dost now sow, thou shalt not reap," and thus ended primitive Communism by separating the drones from the bees. One who studies this subject will soon be brought face to face with the conclusion that upon the sacredness of property civilization itself depends—the right of the laborer to his hundred dollars in the savings-bank, and equally the legal right of the millionaire to his millions. Every man must be allowed "to sit under his own vine and fig-tree, with none to make afraid," if human society is to advance, or even to remain so far advanced as it is. To those who propose to substitute Communism for this intense Individualism, the answer therefore is: The race has tried that. All progress from that barbarous day to the present time has resulted from its displacement. Not evil, but good, has come to the race from the accumulation of wealth by those who have had the ability and energy to produce it. But even if we admit for a moment that it might be better for the race to discard its present foundation, Individualism,—that it is a nobler ideal that man should labor, not for himself alone, but in and for a brotherhood of his fellows, and share with them all in common, realizing Swedenborg's idea of heaven, where, as he says, he angels derive their happiness, not from laboring for self, but for each other,—even admit all this, and a sufficient answer is, This is not evolution, but revolution. It necessitates the changing of human nature itself—a work of eons, even if it were good to change it, which we cannot know.

It is not practicable in our day or in our age. Even if desirable theoretically, it belongs to another and long-succeeding sociological stratum. Our duty is with what is practicable now—with the next step possible in our day and generation. It is criminal to waste our energies in endeavoring to uproot, when all we can profitably accomplish is to bend the universal tree of humanity a little in the direction most favorable to the production of good fruit under existing circumstances. We might as well urge the destruction of the highest existing type of man because he failed to reach our ideal as to favor the destruction of Individualism, Private Property, the Law of Accumulation of Wealth, and the Law of Competition; for these are the highest result of human experience, the soil in which society, so far, has produced the best fruit. Unequally or unjustly, perhaps, as these laws sometimes operate, and imperfect as they appear to the Idealist, they are, nevertheless, like the highest type of man, the best and most valuable of all that humanity has yet accomplished.

We start, then, with a condition of affairs under which the best interests of the race are promoted, but which inevitably gives wealth to the few. Thus far, accepting conditions as they exist, the situation can be surveyed and pronounced good. The question then arises,—and if the foregoing be correct, it is the only question with which we have to deal,—What is the proper mode of administering wealth after the laws upon which civilization is founded have thrown it into the hands of the few? And it is of this great question that I believe I offer the true solution. It will be understood that fortunes are here spoken of, not moderate sums saved by many years of effort, the returns from which are required for the comfortable maintenance and education of families. This is not wealth, but only competence, which it should be the aim of all to acquire, and which it is for the best interests of society should be acquired.

There are but three modes in which surplus wealth can be disposed of. It can be left to the families of the decedents; or it can be bequeathed for public purposes; or, finally, it can be administered by its possessors during their lives. Under the first and second modes most of the wealth of the world that has reached the few has hitherto been applied. Let us in turn consider each of these modes. The first is the most injudicious. In monarchical countries, the estates and the greatest portion of the wealth are left to the first son, that the vanity of the parent may be gratified by the thought that his name and title are to descend unimpaired to succeeding generations. The condition of this class in Europe to-day teaches the failure of such hopes or ambitions. The successors have become impoverished through their follies, or from the fall in the value of land. Even in Great Britain the strict law of entail has been found inadequate to maintain an hereditary class. Its soil is rapidly passing into the hands of the stranger. Under republican institutions the division of property among the children is much fairer; but the question which forces itself upon thoughtful men in all lands is, Why should men leave great fortunes to their children? If this is done from affection, is it not misguided affection? Observation teaches that, generally speaking, it is not well for the children that they should be so burdened. Neither is it well for the State. Beyond providing for the wife and daughters moderate sources of income, and very moderate allowances indeed, if any, for the sons, men may well hesitate; for it is no longer questionable that great sums bequeathed often work more for the injury than for the good of the recipients. Wise men will soon conclude that, for the best interests of the members of their families, and of the State, such bequests are an improper use of their means.

It is not suggested that men who have failed to educate their sons to earn a livelihood shall cast them adrift in poverty. If any man has seen fit to rear his sons with a view to their living idle lives, or, what is highly commendable, has instilled in them the sentiment that they are in a position to labor for public ends without reference to pecuniary considerations, then, of course, the duty of the parent is to see that such are provided for in moderation. There are instances of millionaires' sons unspoiled by wealth, who, being rich, still perform great services to the community. Such are the very salt of the earth, as valuable as, unfortunately, they are rare. It is not the exception, however, but the rule, that men must regard; and, looking at the usual result of enormous sums conferred upon legatees, the thoughtful man must shortly say, "I would as soon leave to my son a curse as the almighty dollar," and admit to himself that it is not the welfare of the children, but family pride, which inspires these legacies.

As to the second mode, that of leaving wealth at death for public uses, it may be said that this is only a means for the disposal of wealth, provided a man is content to wait until he is dead before he becomes of much good in the world. Knowledge of the results of legacies bequeathed is not calculated to inspire the brightest hopes of much posthumous good being accomplished by them. The cases are not few in which the real object sought by the testator is not attained, nor are they few in which his real wishes are thwarted. In many cases the bequests are so used as to become only monuments of his folly. It is well to remember that it requires the exercise of not less ability than that which acquires it, to use wealth so as to be really beneficial to the community. Besides this, it may fairly be said that no man is to be extolled for doing what he cannot help doing, nor is he to be thanked by the community to which he only leaves wealth at death. Men who leave vast sums in this way may fairly be thought men who would not have left it at all had they been able to take it with them. The memories of such cannot be held in grateful remembrance, for there is no grace in their gifts. It is not to be wondered at that such bequests seem so generally to lack the blessing.

The growing disposition to tax more and more heavily large estates left at death is a cheering indication of the growth of a salutary change in public opinion. The State of Pennsylvania now takes—subject to some exceptions—one tenth of the property left by its citizens. The budget presented in the British Parliament the other day proposes to increase the death duties; and, most significant of all, the new tax is to be a graduated one. Of all forms of taxation this seems the wisest. Men who continue hoarding great sums all their lives, the proper use of which for public ends would work good to the community from which it chiefly came, should be made to feel that the community, in the form of the State, cannot thus be deprived of its proper share. By taxing estates heavily at death the State marks its condemnation of the selfish millionaire's unworthy life.

It is desirable that nations should go much further in this direction. Indeed, it is difficult to set bounds to the share of a rich man's estate which should go at his death to the public through the agency of the State, and by all means such taxes should be graduated, beginning at nothing upon moderate sums to dependants, and increasing rapidly as the amounts swell, until of the millionaire's hoard, as of Shylock's, at least

> The other half
> Comes to the privy coffer of the State.

This policy would work powerfully to induce the rich man to attend to the administration of wealth during his life, which is the end that society should always have in view, as being by far the most fruit-

ful for the people. Nor need it be feared that this policy would sap the root of enterprise and render men less anxious to accumulate, for, to the class whose ambition it is to leave great fortunes and be talked about after their death, it will attract even more attention, and, indeed, be a somewhat nobler ambition, to have enormous sums paid over to the State from their fortunes.

There remains, then, only one mode of using great fortunes; but in this we have the true antidote for the temporary unequal distribution of wealth, the reconciliation of the rich and the poor—a reign of harmony, another ideal, differing, indeed, from that of the Communist in requiring only the further evolution of existing conditions, not the total overthrow of our civilization. It is founded upon the present most intense Individualism, and the race is prepared to put it in practice by degrees whenever it pleases. Under its sway we shall have an ideal State, in which the surplus wealth of the few will become, in the best sense, the property of the many, because administered for the common good; and this wealth, passing through the hands of the few, can be made a much more potent force for the elevation of our race than if distributed in small sums to the people themselves. Even the poorest can be made to see this, and to agree that great sums gathered by some of their fellow-citizens and spent for public purposes, from which the masses reap the principal benefit, are more valuable to them than if scattered among themselves in trifling amounts through the course of many years.

▪ ▪ ▪ ▪

This, then, is held to be the duty of the man of wealth: To set an example of modest, unostentatious living, shunning display or extravagance; to provide moderately for the legitimate wants of those dependent upon him; and, after doing so, to consider all surplus revenues which come to him simply as trust funds, which he is called upon to administer, and strictly bound as a matter of duty to administer in the manner which, in his judgment, is best calculated to produce the most beneficial results for the community—the man of wealth thus becoming the mere trustee and agent for his poorer brethren, bringing to their service his superior wisdom, experience, and ability to administer, doing for them better than they would or could do for themselves.

▪ ▪ ▪ ▪

The best uses to which surplus wealth can be put have already been indicated. Those who would administer wisely must, indeed, be wise; for one of the serious obstacles to the improvement of our race is indiscriminate charity. It were better for mankind that the millions of the rich were thrown into the sea than so spent as to encourage the slothful, the drunken, the unworthy. Of every thousand dollars spent in so-called charity to-day, it is probable that nine hundred and fifty dollars is unwisely spent—so spent, indeed, as to produce the very evils which it hopes to mitigate or cure. A well-known writer of philosophic books admitted the other day that he had given a quarter of a dollar to a man who approached him as he was coming to visit the house of his friend. He knew nothing of the habits of this beggar, knew not the use that would be made of this money, although he had every reason to suspect that it would be spent improperly. This man professed to be a disciple of Herbert Spencer; yet the quarter-dollar given that night will probably work more injury than all the money will do good which its thoughtless donor will ever be able to give in true charity. He only gratified his own feelings, saved himself from annoyance—and this was probably one of the most selfish and very worst actions of his life, for in all respects he is most worthy.

In bestowing charity, the main consideration should be to help those who will help themselves; to provide part of the means by which those who desire to improve may do so; to give those who desire to rise the aids by which they may rise; to assist, but rarely or never to do all. Neither the individual nor the race is improved by almsgiving. Those worthy of assistance, except in rare cases, seldom require assistance. The really valuable men of the race never do, except in case of accident or sudden change. Every one has, of course, cases of individuals brought to his own knowledge where temporary assistance can do genuine good, and these he will not overlook. But the amount which can be wisely given by the individual for individuals is necessarily limited by his lack of knowledge of the circumstances connected with each. He is the only true reformer who is as careful and as anxious not to aid the unworthy as he is to aid the worthy, and, perhaps, even more so, for in almsgiving more injury is probably done by rewarding vice than by relieving virtue.

The rich man is thus almost restricted to following the examples of Peter Cooper, Enoch Pratt of Baltimore, Mr. Pratt of Brooklyn, Senator Stanford, and others, who know that the best means of benefiting the community is to place within its reach the ladders upon which the aspiring can rise—free libraries, parks, and means of recreation, by which men are helped in body and mind; works of art, certain to give pleasure and improve the public taste; and public institutions of various kinds, which will improve the general condition of the people; in this manner returning their surplus wealth to the mass of their fellows in the forms best calculated to do them lasting good.

Thus is the problem of rich and poor to be solved. The laws of accumulation will be left free, the laws of distribution free. Individualism will continue, but the millionaire will be but a trustee for the poor, intrusted for a season with a great part of the increased wealth of the community, but administering it for the community far better than it could or would have done for itself. The best minds will thus have reached a stage in the development of the race in which it is clearly seen that there is no mode of disposing of surplus wealth creditable to thoughtful and earnest men into whose hands it flows, save by using it year by year for the general good. This day already dawns. Men may die without incurring the pity of their fellows, still sharers in great business enterprises from which their capital cannot be or has not been withdrawn, and which is left chiefly at death for public uses; yet the day is not far distant when the man who dies leaving behind him millions of available wealth, which was free for him to administer during life, will pass away "unwept, unhonored, and unsung," no matter to what uses he leaves the dross which he cannot take with him. Of such as these the public verdict will then be: "The man who dies thus rich dies disgraced."

Such, in my opinion, is the true gospel concerning wealth, obedience to which is destined some day to solve the problem of the rich and the poor, and to bring "Peace on earth, among men good will."

Name: _____ **Date:** _____

1. In your own words, describe the three methods Carnegie explains surplus wealth can be disposed of.

   1.

   2.

   3.

2. Which of these three methods does Carnegie think is best? Why?

3. Why are the other two methods inferior?

4. Why, according to Carnegie, is it true that the man who dies rich dies disgraced?

5. How was Carnegie, despite his advocacy of philanthropy, a social Darwinist?

William Graham Sumner

"The Absurd Effort to Make the World Over," 1894

Sumner (1840-1910), a Yale sociologist and proponent of Social Darwinism, believed that the "laws of evolution" justified *laissez-faire* economic and political policies associated with political conservatives in the United States. In this selection, Sumner argues against reform-minded social and political leaders by claiming that society is too large and powerful to be successfully influenced by liberal reforms. Instead, he claimed, should realize that society, like nature, has inherent mechanisms to insure progress, and they should allow society to take its natural course.

It will not probably be denied that the burden of proof is on those who affirm that our social condition is utterly diseased and in need of radical regeneration. My task at present, therefore, is entirely negative and critical; to examine the allegations of fact and the doctrines which are put forward to prove the correctness of the diagnosis and to warrant the use of the remedies proposed.

The propositions put forward by social reformers nowadays are chiefly of two kinds. There are assertions in historical form, chiefly in regard to the comparison of existing with earlier social states, which are plainly based on defective historical knowledge, or at most on current stock historical dicta which are uncritical and incorrect. Writers very often assert that something never existed before because they do not know that it ever existed before, or that something is worse than ever before because they are not possessed of detailed information about what has existed before. The other class of propositions consists of dogmatic statements, which, whether true or not, are unverifiable. This class of propositions is the pest and bane of current economic and social discussion. Upon a more or less superficial view of some phenomenon a suggestion arises which is embodied in a philosophical proposition and promulgated as a truth. From the form and nature of such propositions they can always be brought under the head of "ethics." This word at least gives them an air of elevated senti-

From *The Forum* 17, 1894.

ment and purpose, which is the only warrant they possess. It is impossible to test or verify them by any investigation or logical process whatsoever. It is therefore very difficult for any one who feels a high responsibility for historical statements, and who absolutely rejects any statement which is unverifiable, to find a common platform for discussion, or to join issue satisfactorily in taking the negative.

When any one asserts that the class of skilled and unskilled manual laborers of the United States are worse off now in respect to diet, clothing, lodgings, furniture, fuel, and lights; in respect to the age at which they can marry; the number of children they can provide for; the start in life which they can give to their children; and their chances of accumulating capital,—than they ever have been at any former time, he makes a reckless assertion for which no facts have been offered in proof. Upon an appeal to facts, the contrary of this assertion would be clearly established. It suffices, therefore, to challenge those who are responsible for the assertion to make it good.

If it is said that the employed class are under much more stringent discipline than they were thirty years ago or earlier, it is true. It is not true that there has been any qualitative change in this respect within thirty years, but it is true that a movement which began at the first settlement of the country has been advancing with constant acceleration, and has become a noticeable feature within our time. This movement is the advance in the industrial organization. The first settlement was made by agriculturists, and for a long time there was scarcely any organization. There were scattered farmers, each working for himself, and some small towns with only rudimentary commerce and handicrafts. As the country has filled up, the arts and professions have been differentiated and the industrial organization has been advancing. This fact and its significance has hardly been noticed at all; but the stage of the industrial organization existing at any time, and the rate of advance in its development, are the absolutely controlling social facts. Nine-tenths of the socialistic and semisocialistic, and sentimental or ethical, suggestions by which we are overwhelmed come from failure to understand the phenomena of the industrial organization and its expansion. It controls us all because we are all in it. It creates the conditions of our existence, sets the limits of our social activity, regulates the bonds of our social relations, determines our conceptions of good and evil, suggests our life philosophy, moulds our inherited political institutions, and reforms the oldest and toughest customs, like marriage and property. I repeat that the turmoil of heterogeneous and antagonistic social whims and speculations in which we live is due to the failure to understand what the industrial organization is, and its all-pervading control over human life, while the traditions of our schools of philosophy lead us always to approach the industrial organization, not from the side of objective study, but from that of philosophical doctrine. Hence it is that we find that the method of measuring what we see happening by what are called ethical standards, and of proposing to attack the phenomena by methods thence deduced, is so popular.

The advance of a new country from the very simplest social coordination up to the highest organization is a most interesting and instructive chance to study the development of the organization. It has of course been attended all the way along by stricter subordination and higher discipline. All organization implies restriction of liberty. The gain of power is won by narrowing individual range. The methods of business in colonial days were loose and slack to an inconceivable degree. The movement of industry has been all the time toward promptitude, punctuality, and reliability. It has been attended all the way by lamentations about the good old times; about the decline of small industries; about the lost spirit of comradeship between employer and employee; about the narrowing of the interests of the workman; about his conversion into a machine or into a "ware"; and about industrial war. These lamentations have all had reference to unquestionable phenomena attendant on advancing organization. In all occupations the same movement is discernible,—in the learned professions, in schools, in trade, commerce, and transportation. It is to go on faster than ever, now that the continent is filled up by the first superficial layer of population over its whole extent, and the intensification of industry has begun. The great inventions both make the intension of the organization possible, and make it inevitable, with all its consequences, whatever they may be. I must expect to be told here, according to the current fashions of thinking, that we ought to control the development of the organization. The first instinct of the modern man is to get a law passed to forbid or prevent what, in his wisdom, he disapproves. A thing which is inevitable, however, is one which we cannot control. We have to make up our minds to it, adjust ourselves to it, and sit down to live with it. Its inevitableness may be disputed, in which case we must re-examine it; but if our analysis is correct, when we reach what is inevitable we reach the end, and our regulations must apply to ourselves, not to the social facts.

Now the intensification of the social organization is what gives us greater social power. It is to it that we owe our increased comfort and abundance. We are none of us ready to sacrifice this. On the contrary, we want more of it. We would not return to the colonial simplicity and the colonial exiguity if we could. If not, then we must pay the price. Our life is bounded on every side by conditions. We can have this, if we will agree to submit to that. In the case of industrial power and product the great condition is combination of force under discipline and strict co-ordination. Hence the wild language about wage-slavery and capitalistic tyranny.

In any state of society no great achievements can be produced without great force. Formerly great force was attainable only by slavery aggregating the power of great numbers of men. Roman civilization was built on this. Ours has been built on steam. It is to be built on electricity. Then we are all forced into an organization around these natural forces and adapted to the methods or their application; and although we indulge in rhetoric about political liberty, nevertheless we find ourselves bound tight in a new set of conditions, which control the modes of our existence and determine the directions in which alone economic and social liberty can go.

If it is said that there are some persons in our time who have become rapidly and in a great degree rich, it is true; if it is said that large aggregations of wealth in the control of individuals is a social danger, it is not true.

The movement of the industrial organization which has just been described has brought out a great demand for men capable of managing great enterprises. Such have been called "captains of industry." The analogy with military leaders suggested by this name is not misleading. The great leaders in the development of the industrial organization need those talents of executive and administrative skill, power to command, courage, and fortitude, which were formerly called for in military affairs and scarcely anywhere else. The industrial army is also as dependent on its captains as a military body is on its generals. One of the worst features of the existing system is that the employees have a constant risk in their employer. If he is not competent to manage the business with success, they suffer with him. Capital also is dependent on the skill of the captain of industry for the certainty and magnitude of its profits. Under these circumstances there has been a great demand for men having the requisite ability for this function. As the organization has advanced, with more impersonal bonds of coherence and wider scope of operations, the value of this functionary has rapidly increased. The possession of the requisite ability is a natural monopoly. Consequently, all the conditions have concurred to give to those who possessed this monopoly excessive and constantly advancing rates of remuneration.

Another social function of the first importance in an intense organization is the solution of those crises in the operation of it which are called the conjuncture of the market. It is through the market that the lines of relation run which preserve the system in harmonious and rhythmical operation. The conjuncture is the momentary sharper misadjustment of supply and demand which indicates that a redistribution of productive effort is called for. The industrial organization needs to be insured against these conjunctures, which, if neglected, produce a crisis and catastrophe; and it needs that they shall be anticipated and guarded against as far as skill and foresight can do it. The rewards of this function for the bankers and capitalists who perform it are very great. The captains of industry and the capitalists who operate on the conjuncture, therefore, if they are successful, win, in these days, great fortunes in a short time. There are no earnings which are more legitimate or for which greater services are rendered to the whole industrial body. The popular notions about this matter really assume that all the wealth accumulated by these classes of persons would be here just the same if they had not existed. They are supposed to have appropriated it out of the common stock. This is so far from being true that, on the contrary, their own wealth would not be but for themselves; and, besides that, millions more, many-fold greater than their own, scattered in the hands of thousands, would not exist but for them.

Within the last two years I have travelled from end to end of the German Empire several times on all kinds of trains. I reached the conviction, looking at the matter from the passenger's standpoint, that, if the Germans could find a Vanderbilt, and put their railroads in his hands for twenty-five years, letting him reorganize the system and make twenty-five million dollars out of it for himself in that period, they would make an excellent bargain.

But it is repeated until it has become a commonplace which people are afraid to question, that there is some social danger in the possession of large amounts of wealth by individuals. I ask, why? I heard a lecture two years ago by a man who holds perhaps the first chair of political economy in the world. He said, among other things, that there was great danger in our day from great accumulations; that this danger ought to be met by taxation, and he referred to the fortunes of the Rothschilds and to the great fortunes made in America, to prove his point. He omitted, however, to state in what the danger consisted, or to specify what harm has ever been done by the Rothschild fortunes or by the great fortunes accumulated in America. It seemed to me that the assertions he was making, and the measures he was recommending, *ex cathedra,* were very serious to be thrown out so recklessly. It is hardly to be expected that novelists, popular magazinists, amateur economists, and politicians will be more responsible. It would be easy, however, to show what good is done by accumulations of capital in a few hands,—that is, under close and direct management, permitting prompt and accurate application; also to tell what harm is done by loose and unfounded denunciations of any social component or any social group. In the recent debates on the income tax, the assumption that great accumulations of wealth are socially harmful and ought to be broken down by taxation was treated as an axiom, and we had direct proof how dangerous it is to fit out the average politician with such unverified and unverifiable dogmas, as his warrant for his modes of handling the direful tool of taxation.

Great figures are set out as to the magnitude of certain fortunes and the proportionate amount of the national wealth held by a fraction of the population, and eloquent exclamation-points are set against them. If the figures were beyond criticism, what would they prove? Where is the rich man who is oppressing anybody? If there was one, the newspapers would ring with it. The facts about the accumulation of wealth do not constitute a plutocracy, as I will show below. Wealth, in itself considered, is only power, like steam, or electricity, or knowledge. The question of its good or ill turns on the question how it will be used. To prove any harm in aggregations of wealth it must be shown that great wealth is, as a rule, in the ordinary course of social affairs, put to a mischievous use. This cannot be shown beyond the very slightest degree, if at all.

Therefore, all the allegations of general mischief, social corruption, wrong, and evil in our society must be referred back to those who make them, for particulars and specifications. As they are offered to us we cannot allow them to stand, because we discern in them faulty observation of facts, or incorrect interpretation of facts, or a construction of facts according to some philosophy, or misunderstanding of phenomena and their relations, or incorrect inferences, or crooked deductions.

Assuming, however, that the charges against the existing "capitalistic"—that is, industrial—order of things are established, it is proposed to remedy the ill by reconstructing the industrial system on the principles of democracy. Once more we must untangle the snarl of half ideas and muddled facts.

Democracy is, of course, a word to conjure with. We have a democratic-republican political system, and we like it so well that we are prone to take any new step which can be recommended as "democratic," or which will round out some "principle" of democracy to a fuller fulfilment. Everything connected with this domain of political thought is crusted over with false historical traditions, cheap philosophy, and undefined terms, but it is useless to try to criticise it. The whole drift of the world for five hundred years has been toward democracy. That drift, produced by great discoveries and inventions, and by the discovery of a new continent, has raised the middle class out of the servile class. In alliance with the crown they crushed the feudal classes. They made the crown absolute in order to do it. Then they turned against the crown, and, with the aid of the handicraftsmen and peasants, conquered it. Now the next conflict which must inevitably come is that between the middle capitalist class and the proletariat, as the word has come to be used. If a certain construction is put on this conflict, it may be called that between democracy and plutocracy, for it seems that industrialism must be developed into plutocracy by the conflict itself. That is the conflict which stands before civilized society to-day. All the signs of the times indicate its commencement, and it is big with fate to mankind and to civilization.

Although we cannot criticise democracy profitably, it may be said of it, with reference to our present subject, that up to this time democracy never has done anything, either in politics, social affairs, or industry, to prove its power to bless mankind. If we confine our attention to the United States, there are three difficulties with regard to its alleged achievements, and they all have the most serious bearing on the proposed democratization of industry.

1. The time during which democracy has been tried in the United States is too short to warrant any inferences. A century or two is a very short time in the life of political institutions, and if the circumstances change rapidly during the period the experiment is vitiated.

2. The greatest question of all about American democracy is whether it is a cause or a consequence. It is popularly assumed to be a cause, and we ascribe to its beneficent action all the political vitality, all the easiness of social relations, all the industrial activity and enterprise which we experience, and which we value and enjoy. I submit, however, that, on a more thorough examination of the matter, we shall find that democracy is a consequence. There are economic and sociological causes for our political vitality and vigor, for the ease and elasticity of our social relations, and for our industrial power and success. Those causes have also produced democracy, given it success, and have made its faults and errors innocuous. Indeed, in any true philosophy, it must be held that in the economic forces which control the material prosperity of a population lie the real causes of its political institutions, its social class-adjustments, its industrial prosperity, its moral code, and its world-philosophy. If democracy and the industrial system are both products of the economic conditions which exist, it is plainly absurd to set democracy to defeat those conditions in the control of industry. If, however, it is not true that democracy is a consequence, and I am well aware that very few people believe it, then we must go back to the view that democracy is a cause. That being so, it is difficult to see how democracy, which has had a clear field here in America, is not responsible for the ills which Mr. Bellamy and his comrades in opinion see in our present social state, and it is difficult to see the grounds of asking us to entrust it also with industry. The first and chief proof of success of political measures and systems is that, under them, society advances in health and vigor, and that industry develops without causing social disease. If this has not been the case in America, American democracy has not succeeded. Neither is it easy to see how the masses, if they have undertaken to rule, can escape the responsibilities of ruling, especially so far as the conse-

quences affect themselves. If, then, they have brought all this distress upon themselves under the present system, what becomes of the argument for extending the system to a direct and complete control of industry?

3. It is by no means certain that democracy in the United States has not, up to this time, been living on a capital inherited from aristocracy and industrialism. We have no pure democracy. Our democracy is limited at every turn by institutions which were developed in England in connection with industrialism and aristocracy, and these institutions are of the essence of our system. While our people are passionately democratic in temper, and will not tolerate a doctrine that one man is not as good as another, they have common sense enough to know that he is not; and it seems that they love and cling to the conservative institutions quite as strongly as they do to the democratic philosophy. They are, therefore, ruled by men who talk the philosophy and govern by the institutions. Now it is open to Mr. Bellamy to say that the reason why democracy in America seems to be open to the charge made in the last paragraph, of responsibility for all the ill which he now finds in our society, is because it has been infected with industrialism (capitalism); but, in that case, he must widen the scope of his proposition and undertake to purify democracy before turning industry over to it. The Socialists generally seem to think that they make their undertakings easier when they widen their scope, and make them easiest when they propose to re-make everything; but in truth social tasks increase in difficulty in an enormous ratio as they are widened in scope.

The question, therefore, arises, if it is proposed to reorganize the social system on the principles of American democracy, whether the institutions of industrialism are to be retained. If so, all the virus of capitalism will be retained. It is forgotten, in many schemes of social reformation in which it is proposed to mix what we like with what we do not like, in order to extirpate the latter, that each must undergo a reaction from the other, and that what we like may be extirpated by what we do not like. We may find that instead of democratizing capitalism we have capitalized democracy,—that is, have brought in plutocracy. Plutocracy is a political system in which the ruling force is wealth. The denunciations of capital which we hear from all the reformers is the most eloquent proof that the great-

est power in the world to-day is capital. They know that it is, and confess it most when they deny it most strenuously. At present the power of capital is social and industrial, and only in a small degree political. So far as capital is political, it is on account of political abuses, such as tariffs and special legislation on the one hand, and legislative strikes on the other. These conditions exist in the democracy to which it is proposed to transfer the industries. What does that mean except bringing all the power of capital once for all into the political arena, and precipitating the conflict of democracy and plutocracy at once? Can any one imagine that the masterfulness, the overbearing disposition, the greed of gain, and the ruthlessness in methods, which are the faults of the master of industry at his worst, would cease when he was a functionary of the State, which had relieved him of risk and endowed him with authority? Can any one imagine that politicians would no longer be corruptly fond of money, intriguing, and crafty, when they were charged, not only with patronage and government contracts, but also with factories, stores, ships, and railroads? Could we expect anything except that, when the politician and the master of industry were joined in one, we should have the vices of both unchecked by the restraints of either? In any socialistic state there will be one set of positions which will offer chances of wealth beyond the wildest dreams of avarice, viz. on the governing committees. Then there will be rich men whose wealth will indeed be a menace to social interests, and instead of industrial peace there will be such war as no one has dreamed of yet: the war between the political ins and outs,—that is, between those who are on the committee and those who want to get on it.

We must not drop the subject of democracy without one word more. The Greeks already had occasion to notice a most serious distinction between two principles of democracy which lie at its roots. Plutarch says that Solon got the archonship in part by promising equality, which some understood of esteem and dignity, others of measure and number. There is one democratic principle which means that each man should be esteemed for his merit and worth for just what he is, without regard to birth, wealth, rank, or other adventitious circumstances. The other principle is that each one of us ought to be equal to all the others in what he gets and enjoys. The first principle is only partially realizable, but, so far as it goes it is elevating and socially progressive and profitable. The second is not capable of an intelligible statement. The first is a principle of industrialism. It proceeds from and is intelligible only in a society built on the industrial virtues, free endeavor, security of property and repression of the baser vices; that is, in a society whose industrial system is built on labor and exchange. The other is only a rule of division for robbers who have to divide plunder, or monks who have to divide gifts. If, therefore, we want to democratize industry in the sense of the first principle, we need only perfect what we have now especially on its political side. If we try to democratize it in the sense of the other principle, we corrupt politics at one stroke; we enter upon an industrial enterprise which will waste capital and bring us all to poverty; and we set loose greed and envy as ruling social passions.

If this poor old world is as bad as they say, one more reflection may check the zeal of the headlong reformer. It is at any rate a though old world. It has taken its trend and curvature and all its twists and tangles from a long course of formation. All its wry and crooked gnarls and knobs are therefore stiff and stubborn. If puny men by our arts can do anything at all to straighten them, will only be by modifying the tendencies of some of the forces work, so that, after a sufficient time, their action may be changed a little, and slowly the lines of movement may be modified. This effort, however, can at most be only slight, and it will take a long time. In the mean time spontaneous forces will be at work, compared with which our efforts are like those of a man trying to deflect a river; and these forces will have changed the whole problem before our interferences have time to make themselves felt. The great stream of time and earthly things will sweep on just the same in spite of us. It bears with it now all the errors and follies of the past, the wreckage of all the philosophies, the fragments of all the civilizations, the wisdom of all the abandoned ethical systems, the débris of all the institutions, and the penalties of all the mistakes. It is only in imagination that we stand by and look at it, and criticise it, and plan to change it. Every one of us is a child of his age and cannot get out of it. He is in the stream and is swept along with it. All his sciences and philosophy come to him out of it. Therefore the tide will not be changed by us. It will swallow up both us and our experiments. It will absorb the efforts at change and take them into itself as new but trivial components, and the great movement of tradition and work will go on unchanged by our fads and schemes. The things which will change it are the great discoveries and inventions, the new reactions inside the social organism, and the changes in the earth itself on account of changes in the cosmical forces. These causes will make of it just what, in fidelity to them, it ought to be. The men will be carried along with it and be made by it. The utmost they can do by their cleverness will be to note and record their course as they are carried along, which is what we do now, and is that which leads us to the vain fancy that we can make or guide the movement. That is why it is the greatest folly of which a man can be capable, to sit down with a slate and pencil to plan out a new social world.

Name: _____ **Date:** _____

1. In your own words describe the two kinds of propositions that Sumner claims reforms offer.

1.

2.

2. Sumner claims that there is no evidence that Democracy has been the cause of American's progress. What three arguments does he offer to support that claim?

1.

2.

3.

3. What forces does Sumner argue are at work that make successful reforms impossible?

Walter Bagehot

Physics and Politics: Thoughts on the Application of the Principles of "Natural Selection" and "Inheritance" to Polital Society, 1916

Bagehot (1826-1877) was an English journalist and editor of *The Economist.* He sought to apply the theory of organic evolution to society by arguing that successful social groups formed into nations, who grew increasingly larger through victories in the inevitable conflict with other groups. Bagehot's writings, along with other Social Darwinists of the late nineteenth century, were part of a school of thought in which Darwin's theory of natural selection was adapted and applied to social organization to justify imperialism and *laissez-faire* economic and political policies.

THE USE OF CONFLICT

'The difference between progression and stationary inaction,' says one of our greatest living writers, 'is one of the great secrets which science has yet to penetrate.' I am sure I do not pretend that I can completely penetrate it; but it undoubtedly seems to me that the problem is on the verge of solution, and that scientific successes in kindred fields by analogy suggest some principles which wholly remove many of its difficulties, and indicate the sort of way in which those which remain may hereafter be removed too.

But what is the problem? Common English, I might perhaps say common civilised thought, ignores it. Our habitual instructors, our ordinary conversation, our inevitable and ineradicable prejudices tend to make us think that 'Progress' is the normal fact in human society, the fact which we should expect to see, the fact which we should be surprised if we did not see. But history refutes this. The ancients had no conception of progress; they did not so much as reject the idea; they did not even entertain the idea. Oriental nations are just the same now. Since history began they have always been what they are. Savages, again, do not improve; they hardly seem to have the basis on which to

From *Physics and Politics,* New York: D. Appleton and Company, 1916.

build, much less the material to put up anything worth having. Only a few nations, and those of European origin, advance; and yet these think—seem irresistibly compelled to think—such advance to be inevitable, natural, and eternal. Why then is this great contrast?

Before we can answer, we must investigate more accurately. No doubt history shows that most nations are stationary now; but it affords reason to think that all nations once advanced. Their progress was arrested at various points; but nowhere, probably not even in the hill tribes of India, not even in the Andaman Islanders, not even in the savages of Terra del Fuego, do we find men who have not got some way. They have made their little progress in a hundred different ways; they have framed with infinite assiduity a hundred curious habits; they have, so to say, *screwed* themselves into the uncomfortable corners of a complex life, which is odd and dreary, but yet is possible. And the corners are never the same in any two parts of the world. Our record begins with a thousand unchanging edifices, but it shows traces of previous building. In historic times there has been little progress; in prehistoric times there must have been much.

In solving, or trying to solve, the question, we must take notice of this remarkable difference, and explain it, too, or else we may be sure our principles are utterly incomplete, and perhaps altogether unsound. But what then is that solution, or what are the principles which tend towards it? Three laws, or approximate laws, may, I think, be laid down, with only one of which I can deal in this paper, but all three of which it will be best to state, that it may be seen what I am aiming at.

First. In every particular state of the world, those nations which are strongest tend to prevail over the others; and in certain marked peculiarities the strongest tend to be the best.

Secondly. Within every particular nation the type or types of character then and there most attractive tend to prevail; and the most attractive, though with exceptions, is what we call the best character.

Thirdly. Neither of these competitions is in most historic conditions intensified by extrinsic forces, but in some conditions, such as those now prevailing in the most influential part of the world, both are so intensified.

These are the sort of doctrines with which, under the name of 'natural selection' in physical science, we have become familiar; and as every great scientific conception tends to advance its boundaries and to be of use in solving problems not thought of when it was started, so here, what was put forward for mere animal history may, with a change of form, but an identical essence, be applied to human history.

At first some objection was raised to the principle of 'natural selection' in physical science upon religious grounds; it was to be expected that so active an idea and so large a shifting of thought would seem to imperil much which men valued. But in this, as in other cases, the objection is, I think, passing away; the new principle is more and more seen to be fatal to mere outworks of religion, not to religion itself. At all events, to the sort of application here made of it, which only amounts to searching out and following up an analogy suggested by it, there is plainly no objection. Everyone now admits that human history is guided by certain laws, and all that is here aimed at is to indicate, in a more or less distinct way, an infinitesimally small portion of such laws.

The discussion of these three principles cannot be kept quite apart except by pedantry; but it is almost exclusively with the first—that of the competition between nation and nation, or tribe and tribe (for I must use these words in their largest sense, and so as to include every cohering aggregate of human beings)—that I can deal now; and even as to that I can but set down a few principal considerations.

The progress of the military art is the most conspicuous, I was about to say the most *showy*, fact in human history. Ancient civilisation may be compared with modern in many respects, and plausible arguments constructed to show that it is better; but you cannot compare the two in military power. Napoleon could indisputably have conquered Alexander; our Indian army would not think much of the Retreat of the Ten Thousand. And I suppose the improvement has been continuous: I have not the slightest pretence to special knowledge; but, looking at the mere surface of the facts, it seems likely that the aggregate battle array, so to say, of mankind, the fighting force of the human race, has constantly and invariably grown. It is true that the ancient civilisation long resisted the 'barbarians,' and was then destroyed by the barbarians. But the barbarians had improved. 'By degrees,' says a most accomplished writer,[1] 'barbarian mercenaries came to form the largest, or at least the most effective, part of the Roman armies. The body-guard of Augustus had been so composed; the prætorians were generally selected from the bravest frontier troops, most of them Germans.' 'Thus,' he continues, 'in many ways was the old antagonism broken down, Romans admitting barbarians to rank and office; barbarians catching something of the manners and culture of their neighbours. And thus, when the final movement came, the Teutonic tribes slowly established themselves through the provinces, knowing something of the system to which they came, and not unwilling to be considered its members.' Taking friend and foe together, it may be doubted whether the fighting capacity of the two armies was not as great at last, when the Empire fell, as ever it was in the long period while the Empire prevailed. During the Middle Ages the combining power of men often failed; in a divided time you cannot collect as many soldiers as in a concentrated time. But this difficulty is political, not military. If you added up the many little hosts of any century of separation, they would perhaps be found equal or greater than the single host, or the fewer hosts, of previous centuries which were more united. Taken as a whole, and allowing for possible exceptions, the aggregate fighting power of mankind has grown immensely, and has been growing continuously since we knew anything about it.

Again, this force has tended to concentrate itself more and more in certain groups which we call 'civilised nations.' The *literati* of the last century were for ever in fear of a new conquest of the barbarians, but only because their imagination was overshadowed and frightened by the old conquests. A very little consideration would have shown them that, since the monopoly of military inventions by cultivated states, real and effective military power

---

[1] Mr. Bryce.

tends to confine itself to those states. The barbarians are no longer so much as vanquished competitors; they have ceased to compete at all.

The military vices, too, of civilisation seem to decline just as its military strength augments. Somehow or other civilisation does not make men effeminate or unwarlike now as it once did. There is an improvement in our fibre—moral, if not physical. In ancient times city people could not be got to fight—seemingly could not fight; they lost their mental courage, perhaps their bodily nerve. But now-a-days in all countries the great cities could pour out multitudes wanting nothing but practice to make good soldiers, and abounding in bravery and vigour. This was so in America; it was so in Prussia; and it would be so in England too. The breed of ancient times was impaired for war by trade and luxury, but the modern breed is not so impaired.

A curious fact indicates the same thing probably, it not certainly. Savages waste away before modern civilisation; they seem to have held their ground before the ancient. There is no lament in any classical writer for the barbarians. The New Zealanders say that the land will depart from their children; the Australians are vanishing; the Tasmanians have vanished. If anything like this had happened in antiquity, the classical moralists would have been sure to muse over it; for it is just the large solemn kind of fact that suited them. On the contrary, in Gaul, in Spain, in Sicily—everywhere that we know of—the barbarian endured the contact of the Roman, and the Roman allied himself to the barbarian. Modern science explains the wasting away of savage men; it says that we have diseases which we can bear, though they cannot, and that they die away before them as our fatted and protected cattle died out before the rinderpest, which is innocuous, in comparison, to the hardy cattle of the Steppes. Savages in the first year of the Christian era were pretty much what they were in the 1800th; and if they stood the contact of ancient civilised men, and cannot stand ours, it follows that our race is presumably tougher than the ancient; for we have to bear, and do bear, the seeds of greater diseases than those the ancients carried with them. We may use, perhaps, the unvarying savage as a metre to gauge the vigour of the constitutions to whose contact he is exposed.

Particular consequences may be dubious, but as to the main fact there is no doubt: the military strength of man has been growing from the earliest time known to our history, straight on till now. And we must not look at times known by written records only; we must travel back to older ages, known to us only by what lawyers call *real* evidence—the evidence of things. Before history began, there was at least as much progress in the military art as there has been since. The Roman legionaries or Homeric Greeks were about as superior to the men of the shell mounds and the flint implements as we are superior to them. There has been a constant acquisition of military strength by man since we know anything of him, either by the documents he has composed or the indications he has left.

The cause of this military growth is very plain. The strongest nation has always been conquering the weaker; sometimes even subduing it, but always prevailing over it. Every intellectual gain, so to speak, that a nation possessed was in the earliest times made use of—was *invested* and taken out—in war; all else perished. Each nation tried constantly to be the stronger, and so made or copied the best weapons; by conscious and unconscious imitation each nation formed a type of character suitable to war and conquest. Conquest improved mankind by the intermixture of strengths; the armed truce, which was then called peace, improved them by the competition of training and the consequent creation of new power. Since the long-headed men first drove the short-headed men out of the best land in Europe, all European history has been the history of the superposition of the more military races over the less military—of the efforts, sometimes successful, sometimes unsuccessful, of each race to get more military; and so the art of war has constantly improved.

But why is one nation stronger than another? In the answer to that, I believe, lies the key to the principal progress of early civilisation, and to some of the progress of all civilisation. The answer is that there are very many advantages—some small and some great—every one of which tends to make the nation which has it superior to the nation which has it not; that many of these advantages can be imparted to subjugated races, or imitated by competing races; and that, though some of these advantages may be perishable or inimitable, yet, on the whole, the energy of civilisation grows by the coalescence of strengths and by the competition of strengths.

Name: _____ **Date:** _____

1. Bagehot begins by positing three "laws." What are they?
1.

2.

3.

2. How, according to Bagehot, has there been progress in science?

3. In ways and why does Bagehot believe the military has progressed?

Theodore Roosevelt

"Biological Analogies in History," 1910

Roosevelt (1858-1919), U.S. president from 1901 to 1909, turned to publishing after he left office. An avid outdoorsman and longtime advocate of a strong American military, Roosevelt believed that nature offered valuable lessons to policy-makers. In this piece, he drew from early twentieth-century concepts of inheritance and evolution to discuss the rise and fall of nations.

An American who, in response to such an invitation as I have received, speaks in this University of ancient renown cannot but feel with peculiar vividness the interest and charm of his surroundings, fraught as they are with a thousand associations. Your great universities, and all the memories that make them great, are living realities in the minds of scores of thousands of men who have never seen them and who dwell across the seas in other lands. Moreover, these associations are no stronger in the men of English stock than in those who are not. My people have been for eight generations in America; but in one thing I am like the Americans of to-morrow rather than like many of the Americans of to-day, for I have in my veins the blood of men who came from many different European races. The ethnic make-up of our people is slowly changing, so that constantly the race tends to become more and more akin to that of those Americans who, like myself, are of the old stock but not mainly of English stock. Yet I think that, as time goes by, mutual respect, understanding, and sympathy among the English-speaking peoples grow greater and not less. Any of my ancestors, Hollander or Huguenot, Scotchman or Irishman, who had come to Oxford in "the spacious days of great Elizabeth" would have felt far more alien that I, their descendant, now feel. Common heirship in the things of the spirit makes a closer bond than common heirship in the things of the body.

More than ever before in the world's history, we of to-day seek to penetrate the causes of the myster-ies that surround not only mankind but all life, both in the present and the past. We search, we peer, we see things dimly; here and there we get a ray of clear vision as we look before and after. We study the tremendous procession of the ages, from the immemorial past when in "cramp elf and saurian forms" the creative forces "swathed their too-much power," down to the yesterday, a few score thousand years distant only, when the history of man became the overwhelming fact in the history of life on this planet; and, studying, we see strange analogies in the phenomena of life and death, of birth, growth, and change, between those physical groups of animal life which we designate as species, forms, races, and the highly complex and composite entities which rise before our minds when we speak of nations and civilizations.

It is this study which has given science its present-day prominence. In the world of intellect, doubtless the most marked features in the history of the past century have been the extraordinary advances in scientific knowledge and investigation and in the position held by the men of science with reference to those engaged in other pursuits. I am not now speaking of applied science—of the science, for instance, which, having revolutionized transportation on the earth and the water, is now on the brink of carrying it into the air; of the science that finds its expression in such extraordinary achievements as the telephone and the telegraph; of the sciences which have so accelerated the velocity of movement in social and industrial conditions—for the changes in the mechanical appliances of ordinary life during the last three generations have been greater than in all the preceding generations since history dawned. I

From *Outlook 95,* 1910.

speak of the science which has no more direct bearing upon the affairs of our every-day life than literature or music, painting or sculpture, poetry or history. A hundred years ago the ordinary man of cultivation had to know something of these last subjects; but the probabilities were rather against his having any but the most superficial scientific knowledge. At present all this has changed, thanks to the interest taken in scientific discoveries, the large circulation of scientific books, and the rapidity with which ideas originating among students of the most advanced and abstruse sciences become, at least partially, domiciled in the popular mind.

Another feature of the change, of the growth in the position of science in the eyes of every one, and of the greatly increased respect naturally resulting for scientific methods, has been a certain tendency among scientific students to encroach on other fields. This is particularly true of the field of historical study. Not only have scientific men insisted upon the necessity of considering the history of man, especially in its early stages, in connection with what biology shows to be the history of life, but, furthermore, there has arisen a demand that history shall itself be treated as a science. Both positions are in their essence right; but as regards each position the more arrogant among the invaders of the new realm of knowledge take an attitude to which it is not necessary to assent. As regards the latter of the two positions, that which would treat history henceforth merely as one branch of scientific study, we must of course cordially agree that accuracy in recording facts and appreciation of their relative worth and interrelationship are just as necessary in historical study as in any other kind of study. The fact that a book, though interesting, is untrue, of course removes it at once from the category of history, however much it may still deserve to retain a place in the always desirable group of volumes which deal with entertaining fiction. But the converse also holds, at least to the extent of permitting us to insist upon what would seem to be the elementary fact that a book which is written to be read should be readable. This rather obvious truth seems to have been forgotten by some of the more zealous scientific historians, who apparently hold that the worth of a historical book is directly in proportion to the impossibility of reading it, save as a painful duty. Now I am willing that history shall be treated as a branch of science, but only on condition that it also remains a branch of literature; and, furthermore, I believe that as the field of science encroaches on the field of literature, there should be a corresponding encroachment of literature upon science; and I hold that one of the great needs, which can only be met by very able men whose culture is broad enough to include literature as well as science, is the need of books for scientific laymen. We need a literature of science which shall be readable. So far from doing away with the school of great historians, the school of Polybius and Tacitus, Gibbon and Macaulay, we need merely that the future writers of history, without losing the qualities which have made those men great, shall also utilize the new facts and new methods which science has put at their disposal. Dryness is not in itself a measure of value. No "scientific" treatise about St. Louis will displace Joinville, for the very reason that Joinville's place is in both history and literature; no minute study of the Napoleonic wars will teach us more than Marbot—and Marbot is as interesting as Walter Scott. Moreover, certain at least of the branches of science should likewise be treated by masters in the art of presentment, so that the layman interested in science, no less than the layman interested in history, shall have on his shelves classics which can be read. Whether this wish be or be not capable of realization, it assuredly remains true that the great historian of the future must essentially represent the ideal striven after by the great historians of the past. The industrious collector of facts occupies an honorable but not an exalted position, and the scientific historian who produces books which are not literature must rest content with the honor, substantial but not of the highest type, that belongs to him who gathers material which some time some great master shall arise to use.

Yet, while freely conceding all that can be said of the masters of literature, we must insist upon the historian of mankind working in the scientific spirit, and using the treasure-houses of science. He who would fully treat of man must know at least something of biology, of the science that treats of living, breathing things; and especially of that science of evolution which is inseparably connected with the great name of Darwin. Of course there is no exact parallelism between the birth, growth, and death of species in the animal world and the birth, growth, and death of societies in the world of man. Yet there is a certain parallelism. There are strange analogies; it may be that there are homologies.

How far the resemblances between the two sets of phenomena are more than accidental, how far biology can be used as an aid in the interpretation of human history, we cannot at present say. The historian should never forget, what the highest type of scientific man is always teaching us to remember, that willingness to admit ignorance is a prime factor in developing wisdom out of knowledge. Wisdom is advanced by research which enables us to add to knowledge; and, moreover, the way for wisdom is made ready when men who record facts of vast but unknown import, when asked to explain their full significance, are willing frankly to answer that they do not know. The research which enables us to add to the sum of complete knowledge stands first; but second only stands the research which, while enabling us clearly to pose the problem, also requires us to say that with our present knowledge we can offer no complete solution.

Let me illustrate what I mean by an instance or two taken from one of the most fascinating branches of world history, the history of the higher forms of life, of mammalian life, on this globe.

Geologists and astronomers are not agreed as to the length of time necessary for the changes that have taken place. At any rate, many hundreds of thousands of years, some millions of years, have passed by since in the eocene, at the beginning of the tertiary period, we find the traces of an abundant, varied, and highly developed mammalian life on the land masses out of which have grown the continents as we see them to-day. The ages swept by, until, with the advent of man substantially in the physical shape in which we now know him, we also find a mammalian fauna not essentially different in kind, though widely differing in distribution, from that of the present day. Throughout this immense period form succeeds form, type succeeds type, in obedience to laws of evolution, of progress and retrogression, of development and death, which we as yet understand only in the most imperfect manner. As knowledge increases, our wisdom is often turned into foolishness, and many of the phenomena of evolution which seemed clearly explicable to the learned master of science who founded these lectures, to us nowadays seem far less satisfactorily explained. The scientific men of most note now differ widely in their estimates of the relative parts played in evolution by natural selection, by mutation, by the inheritance of acquired characteristics; and we study their writings with a growing impression that there are forces at work which our blinded eyes wholly fail to apprehend; and where this is the case, the part of wisdom is to say that we believe we have such and such partial explanations, but that we are not warranted in saying that we have the whole explanation. In tracing the history of the development of faunal life during this period, the age of mammals, there are some facts which are clearly established, some great and sweeping changes for which we can ascribe with certainty a reason. There are other facts as to which we grope in the dark, and vast changes, vast catastrophes, of which we can give no adequate explanation.

Before illustrating these types, let us settle one or two matters of terminology. In the changes, the development and extinction, of species we must remember that such expressions as "a new species," or as "a species becoming extinct," are each commonly and indiscriminately used to express totally different and opposite meanings. Of course the "new" species is not new in the sense that its ancestors appeared later on the globe's surface than those of any old species tottering to extinction. Phylogenetically, each animal now living must necessarily trace its ancestral descent back through countless generations, through æons of time, to the early stages of the appearance of life on the globe. All that we mean by a "new" species is that, from some cause or set of causes, one of these ancestral stems slowly or suddenly develops into a form unlike any that has preceded it: so that while in one form of life the ancestral type is continuously repeated and the old species continues to exist, in another form of life there is a deviation from the ancestral type and a new species appears.

Similarly, "extinction of species" is a term which has two entirely different meanings. The type may become extinct by dying out and leaving no descendants. Or it may die out because, as the generations go by, there is change, slow or swift, until a new form is produced. Thus in one case the line of life comes to an end. In the other case it changes into something different. The huge titanothere and the small three-toed horse both existed at what may roughly be called the same period of the world's history, back in the middle of the mammalian age. Both are extinct in the same sense that each has completely disappeared, and that nothing like either is to be found in the world to-day. But whereas all the individual titanotheres finally died out, leaving no descendants, a number of the three-toed horses did leave descendants, and these descendants, constantly changing as the ages went by, finally developed into the highly specialized one-toed horses, asses, and zebras of to-day.

■ ■ ■ ■

As in biology, so in human history, a new form may result from the specialization of a long-existing and hitherto very slowly changing generalized or non-specialized form; as, for instance, when a barbaric race from a variety of causes suddenly develops a more complex cultivation and civilization. This is what occurred, for instance, in western Europe during the centuries of the Teutonic and later the Scandinavian ethnic overflows from the north. All the modern countries of western Europe are descended from the states created by these northern invaders. When first created they could be called "new" or "young" states in the sense that part or all of the people composing them were descended from races that hitherto had not been civilized at all, and that therefore for the first time entered on the career of civilized communities. In the southern part of western Europe the new states thus formed consisted in bulk of the inhabitants already in the land under the Roman Empire; and it was here that the new kingdoms first took shape. Through a reflex action their influence then extended back into the cold forests from which the invaders had come, and Germany and Scandinavia witnessed the rise of communities with essentially the same civilization as their southern neighbors; though in those communities, unlike the southern communities, there was no infusion of new blood, and in each case the new civilized nation which gradually developed was composed entirely of members of the same race which in the same region had for ages lived the life of a slowly changing barbarism. The same was true of the Slavs and the Slavonized Finns of eastern Europe, when an infiltration of Scandinavian leaders from the north and an infiltration of Byzantine culture from the south joined to produce the changes which have gradually, out of the little Slav communities of the forest and the steppe, formed the mighty Russian Empire of to-day.

Again, the new form may represent merely a splitting off from a long-established, highly developed and specialized nation. In this case the nation is usually spoken of as a "young," and is correctly spoken of as a "new," nation; but the term should always be used with a clear sense of the difference between what is described in such case and what is described by the same term in speaking of a civilized nation just developed from a barbarism. Carthage and Syracuse were new cities compared with Tyre and Corinth; but the Greek or Phœnician race was in every sense of the word as old in the new city as in the old city. So, nowadays, Victoria or Manitoba is a new community compared with England or Scotland; but the ancestral type of civilization and culture is as old in one case as in the other. I of course do not mean for a moment that great changes are not produced by the mere fact that the old civilized race is suddenly placed in surroundings where it has again to go through the work of taming the wilderness, a work finished many centuries before in the original home of the race; I merely mean that the ancestral history is the same in each case. We can rightly use the phrase "a new people" in speaking of Canadians or Australians, Americans or Afrikanders. But we use it in an entirely different sense from that in which we use it when speaking of such communities as those founded by the Northmen and their descendants during that period of astonishing growth which saw the descendants of the Norse sea-thieves conquer and transform Normandy, Sicily, and the British Is-

lands; we use it in an entirely different sense from that in which we use it when speaking of the new states that grew up around Warsaw, Kief, Novgorod, and Moscow, as the wild savages of the steppes and the marshy forests struggled haltingly and stumblingly upward to become builders of cities and to form stable governments. The kingdoms of Charlemagne and Alfred were "new," compared with the empire on the Bosphorus; they were also in every way different; their lines of ancestral descent had nothing in common with those of the polyglot realm which paid tribute to the Cæsars of Byzantium; their social problems and aftertime history were totally different. This is not true of those "new" nations which spring direct from old nations. Brazil, the Argentine, the United States, are all "new" nations, compared with the nations of Europe; but, with whatever changes in detail, their civilization is nevertheless of the general European type, as shown in Portugal, Spain, and England. The differences between these "new" American and these "old" European nations are not as great as those which separate the "new" nations one from another and the "old" nations one from another. There are in each case very real differences between the new and the old nation—differences both for good and for evil; but in each case there is the same ancestral history to reckon with, the same type of civilization, with its attendant benefits and shortcomings; and, after the pioneer stages are passed, the problems to be solved, in spite of superficial differences, are in their essence the same; they are those that confront all civilized peoples, not those that confront peoples struggling from barbarism into civilization.

So, when we speak of the "death" of the tribe, a nation, or a civilization, the term may be used for either one or two totally different processes; the analogy with what occurs in biological history being complete. Certain tribes of savages, the Tasmanians, for instance, and various little clans of American Indians, have within the last century or two completely died out: all of the individuals have perished, leaving no descendants, and the blood has disappeared. Certain other tribes of Indians have as tribes disappeared or are now disappearing: but their blood remains, being absorbed into the veins of the white intruders, or of the black men introduced by these white intruders: so that in reality they are merely being transformed into something absolutely different from what they were. In the United States, in the new State of Oklahoma, the Creeks, Cherokees, Chickasaws, Delawares, and other tribes are in process of absorption into the mass of the white population; when the State was admitted, a couple of years ago, one of the two Senators and three of the five Representatives in Congress were partly of Indian blood. In but a few years these Indian tribes will have disappeared as completely as those that have actually died out; but the disappearance will be by absorption and transformation into the mass of the American population.

■　■　■　■

Every modern civilized nation has many and terrible problems to solve within its own borders, problems that arise not merely from juxtaposition of poverty and riches, but especially from the self-consciousness of both poverty and riches. Each nation must deal with these matters in its own fashion, and yet the spirit in which the problem is approached must ever be fundamentally the same. It must be a spirit of broad humanity; of brotherly kindness; of acceptance of responsibility, one for each and each for all; and at the same time a spirit as remote as the poles from every form of weakness and sentimentality. As in war to pardon the coward is to do cruel wrong to the brave man whose life his cowardice jeopardizes, so in civil affairs it is revolting to every principle of justice to give to the lazy, the vicious, or even the feeble and dull-witted, a reward which is really the robbery of what braver, wiser, abler men have earned. The only effective way to help any man is to help him to help himself; and the worst lesson to teach him is that he can be permanently helped at the expense of some one else. True liberty shows itself to best advantage in protecting the rights of others, and especially of minorities. Privilege should not be tolerated because it is to the advantage of a minority, nor yet because it is to the advantage of a majority. No doctrinaire theories of vested rights or freedom of contract can stand in the way of our cutting out abuses from the body politic. Just as little can we afford to follow the doctrinaires of an impossible—and incidentally of a highly undesirable—social revolution which, in destroying individual rights (including property rights) and the family, would destroy the two chief agents in the advance of mankind, and the two chief reasons why either the advance or the preservation of mankind is worth while. It is an evil and a dreadful thing to be callous to sorrow and suffering, and blind to our duty to do all things possible for the betterment of social conditions. But it is an unspeakably foolish thing to strive for this betterment by means so destructive that they would leave no social conditions to better. In dealing with all these social problems, with the intimate relations of the family, with wealth in private use and business use, with labor, with poverty, the one prime necessity is to remember that, though hardness of heart is

a great evil, it is no greater an evil than softness of head.

But in addition to these problems, the most intimate and important of all, which to a larger or less degree affect all the modern nations somewhat alike, we of the great nations that have expanded, that are now in complicated relations with one another and with alien races, have special problems and special duties of our own. You belong to a nation which possesses the greatest empire upon which the sun has ever shone. I belong to a nation which is trying, on a scale hitherto unexampled, to work out the problems of government for, of, and by the people, while at the same time doing the international duty of a great power. But there are certain problems which both of us have to solve, and as to which our standards should be the same. The Englishman, the man of the British Isles, in his various homes across the seas, and the American, both at home and abroad, are brought into contact with utterly alien peoples, some with a civilization more ancient than our own, others still in, or having but recently arisen from, the barbarism which our people left behind ages ago. The problems that arise are of well-nigh inconceivable difficulty. They cannot be solved by the foolish sentimentality of stay-at-home people, with little patent recipes, and those cut-and-dried theories of the political nursery which have such limited applicability amid the crash of elemental forces. Neither can they be solved by the raw brutality of the men who, whether at home or on the rough frontier of civilization, adopt might as the only standard of right in dealing with other men, and treat alien races only as subjects for exploitation.

No hard and fast rule can be drawn as applying to all alien races, because they differ from one another far more widely than some of them differ from us. But there are one or two rules which must not be forgotten. In the long run, there can be no justification for one race managing or controlling another unless the management and control are exercised in the interest and for the benefit of that other race. This is what our peoples have in the main done, and must continue in the future in even greater degree to do, in India, Egypt, and the Philippines alike. In the next place, as regards every race, everywhere, at home or abroad, we cannot afford to deviate from the great rule of righteousness which bids us treat each man on his worth as a man. He must not be sentimentally favored because he belongs to a given race; he must not be given immunity in wrong-doing, or permitted to cumber the ground, or given other privileges which would be denied to the vicious and unfit among ourselves. On the other hand, where he acts in a way which would entitle him to respect and reward if he were of our own stock, he is just as much entitled to that respect and reward if he comes of another stock, even though that other stock produces a much smaller proportion of men of his type than does our own. This has nothing to do with social intermingling, with what is called social equality. It has to do merely with the question of doing to each man and each woman that elementary justice which will permit him or her to gain from life the reward which should always accompany thrift, sobriety, self-control, respect for the rights of others, and hard and intelligent work to a given end. To more than such just treatment no man is entitled, and less than such just treatment no man should receive.

The other type of duty is the international duty, the duty owed by one nation to another. I hold that the laws of morality which should govern individuals in their dealings one with the other are just as binding concerning nations in their dealings one with the other. The application of the moral law must be different in the two cases, because in one case it has, and in the other it has not, the sanction of a civil law with force behind it. The individual can depend for his rights upon the courts, which themselves derive their force from the police power of the State. The nation can depend upon nothing of the kind; and therefore, as things are now, it is the highest duty of the most advanced and freest peoples to keep themselves in such a state of readiness as to forbid to any barbarism or depotism the hope of arresting the progress of the world by striking down the nations that lead in that progress. It would be foolish indeed to pay heed to the unwise persons who desire disarmament to be begun by the very peoples who, of all others, should not be left helpless before any possible foe. But we must reprobate quite as strongly both the leaders and the peoples who practice, or encourage or condone, aggression and iniquity by the strong at the expense of the weak. We should tolerate lawlessness and wickedness neither by the weak nor by the strong: and both weak and strong we should in return treat with scrupulous fairness. The foreign policy of a great and self-respecting country should be conducted on exactly the same plane of honor, of insistence upon one's own rights and of respect for the rights of others, as when a brave and honorable man is dealing with his fellows. Permit me to support this statement out of my own experience. For nearly eight years I was the head of a great nation and charged especially with the conduct of its foreign policy; and during those years I took no action with reference to any other people on the face of the earth that I would not have felt justified in taking as an individual in dealing with other individuals.

I believe that we of the great civilized nations of to-day have a right to feel that long careers of achievement lie before our several countries. To each of us is vouchsafed the honorable privilege of doing his part, however small, in that work. Let us strive hardily for success even if by so doing we risk failure, spurning the poorer souls of small endeavor who know neither failure nor success. Let us hope that our own blood shall continue in the land, that our children and children's children to endless generations shall arise to take our places and play a mighty and dominant part in the world. But whether this be denied or granted by the years we shall not see, let at least the satisfaction be ours that we have carried onward the lighted torch in our own day and generation. If we do this, then, as our eyes close, and we go out into the darkness, and other hands grasp the torch, at least we can say that our part has been borne well and valiantly.

Name: _____ **Date:** _____

1. What, according to Roosevelt, are some of the successes that science has achieved?

2. How does Roosevelt think can science help us better understand history?

3. Roosevelt distinguishes between two types of extinctions. What are they?

1.

2.

4. When Roosevelt uses the term "blood," what does he mean by it?

Petr Kropotkin

Mutual Aid: A Factor in Evolution, 1902

Kropotkin (1842-1921) was a Russian political philosopher, anarchist, and geologist. He was arrested in 1974 for inciting workers to rebel and escaped to western Europe two years later, where he stayed until the Russian Revolution in 1917. While in exile, Kropotkin wrote several books on rebellion and revolution along with the book from which the below selection is taken, *Mutual Aid*. In it, Kropotkin synthesized the works of a number of Russian and European biologists with his political views to argue that in society and in nature cooperation was common. In stark contrast to Social Darwinists, who asserted that Darwin's descriptions of competition among animals and between species provided a natural justification for *laissez-faire* economic and political policies, Kropotkin's emphasis on cooperation provided a similar justification for pacifism in human society.

When the present war began, involving nearly all Europe in a terrible struggle, and this struggle assumed, in those parts of Belgium and France which were invaded by the Germans, a never yet known character of wholesale destruction of life among the non-combatants and pillage of the means of subsistence of the civil population, "struggle for existence" became a favourite explanation with those who tried to find an excuse for these horrors.

A protest against such an abuse of Darwin's terminology appeared then in a letter published in the *Times*. It was said in this letter that such an explanation was "little more than an application to philosophy and politics of ideas taken from crude popular misconceptions of the Darwinian theory (of 'struggle for existence' and 'will to power,' 'survival of the fittest' and 'superman,' etc.)"; that there was, however, a work in English "which interprets biological and social progress not in terms of overbearing brute force and cunning, but in terms of mutual co-operation." It was suggested, therefore, that a cheap reprint of this book should be published without delay.

Such a reprint is now before the reader. It is a full reprint of the first edition, from which the Appendix only has been omitted as it contains matter of a rather special character.

From *Mutual Aid: A Factor in Evolution* by Petr Kropotkin. Published 1925 Alfred A. Knopf, Inc.

Twelve years have passed since the first edition of this work was published, and it can be said that its fundamental idea—the idea that mutual aid represents in evolution an important *progressive* element—begins to be recognized by biologists. In most of the chief works on evolution which have appeared lately on the Continent, it is already indicated that *two* different aspects of the struggle for life must be distinguished: the *exterior* war of the species against the adverse natural conditions and the rival species, and the *inner* war for the means of existence within the species. It is also admitted that both the extent of the latter and its importance in Evolution have been exaggerated, much to the regret of Darwin himself; while the importance of sociability and social instinct in animals for the well-being of the species, contrarily to Darwin's teaching, was underrated.

However, if the importance of mutual aid and support among animals begins to win recognition among modern thinkers, this is not yet the case for the second part of my thesis—the importance of these two factors in the history of Man, for the growth of his progressive social institutions.

The leaders of contemporary thought are still inclined to maintain that the masses had little concern in the evolution of the sociable institutions of man, and that all the progress made in this direction was due to the intellectual, political, and military leaders of the inert masses.

The present war, having brought the majority of the civilized nations of Europe into a close contact, not only with the realities of war, but also with thousands of its side effects in daily life, surely will contribute to alter the current teachings. It will show how much the creative, constructive genius of the mass of the people is required, whenever a nation has to live through a difficult moment of its history.

It was not the masses of the European nations who prepared the present war-calamity and worked out its barbarous methods: it was their rulers, their intellectual leaders. The masses of the people have nowhere had a voice in the preparation of the present slaughter, and still less so in the working out of the present methods of warfare, which represent an entire disregard of what we considered the best inheritance of civilization.

And if the wreckage of this inheritance will not be complete; if notwithstanding the crimes committed during this "civilized" war, we may still be sure that the teachings and traditions of human solidarity will, after all, emerge intact from the present ordeal, it is because, by the side of the extermination organized from above, we see thousands of those manifestations of spontaneous mutual aid, of which I speak in this book in the chapters devoted to Man.

The peasant women who, on seeing German and Austrian war prisoners wearily trudging through the streets of Kieff, thrust into their hands bread, apples, and occasionally a copper coin; the thousands of women and men who attend the wounded, without making any distinction between friend and foe, officer or soldier; the French and Russian peasants—old men left behind in their villages and women—who decide in their village folkmotes to plough and to sow the fields of those who are "there," under the enemy's fire; the co-operative kitchens and *popottes communistes* which sprang up all over France; the spontaneous aid to the Belgian nation which comes from England and the United States, and to devastated Poland from the Russian people—both these undertakings implying such an immense amount of voluntary, freely organized labour and energy that all character of "charity" is lost in them, and they become mere neighbours' help—all these facts and many more similar ones are the seeds of new forms of life. They will lead to new institutions, just as mutual aid in the earlier ages of mankind gave origin later on to the best progressive institutions of civilized society.

To the chapters of this book which deal with the primitive and mediæval forms of mutual aid I should like especially now to draw the attention of the reader.

I do so in the earnest hope that in the midst of the misery and agony which this war has flung over the world, there is still room for the belief that the constructive forces of men being nevertheless at work, their action will tend to promote a better understanding between men, and eventually among nations.

MUTUAL AID AMONG ANIMALS

Struggle for existence. Mutual Aid, a law of Nature and chief factor of progressive evolution. Invertebrates. Ants and Bees. Birds, hunting and fishing associations. Sociability. Mutual protection among small birds. Cranes, parrots.

The conception of struggle for existence as a factor of evolution, introduced into science by Darwin and Wallace, has permitted us to embrace an immensely-wide range of phenomena in one single generalization, which soon became the very basis of our philosophical, biological, and sociological speculations. An immense variety of facts: adaptations of function and structure of organic beings to their surroundings; physiological and anatomical evolution; intellectual progress, and moral development itself, which we formerly used to explain by so many different causes, were embodied by Darwin in one general conception. We understood them as continued endeavours—as a struggle against adverse circumstances—for such a development of individuals, races, species and societies, as would result in the greatest possible fulness, variety, and intensity of life. It may be that at the outset Darwin himself was not fully aware of the generality of the factor which he first invoked for explaining one series only of facts relative to the accumulation of individual variations in incipient species. But he foresaw that the term which he was introducing into science would lose its philosophical and its only true meaning if it were to be used in its narrow sense only—that of a struggle between separate individuals for the sheer means of existence. And at the very beginning of his memorable work he insisted upon the term being taken in its "large and metaphorical sense including dependence of one being on another, and including (which is more important) not only the life of the individual, but success in leaving progeny."

While he himself was chiefly using the term in its narrow sense for his own special purpose, he warned his followers against committing the error (which he seems once to have committed himself) of overrating its narrow meaning. In *The Descent of Man* he gave some powerful pages to illustrate its proper, wide sense. He pointed out how, in numberless animal societies, the struggle between separate individuals for the means of existence disappears, how *struggle* is replaced by *co-operation,* and how that substitution results in the development of intellectual and moral faculties which secure to the species the best conditions for survival. He intimated that in such cases the fittest are not the physically strongest, nor the cunningest, but those who learn to combine so as mutually to support each other, strong and weak alike, for the welfare of the community. "Those communities," he wrote, "which included the greatest number of the most sympathetic members would flourish best, and rear the greatest number of offspring" (2nd edit., p. 163). The term, which originated from the narrow Malthusian conception of competition between each and all, thus lost its narrowness in the mind of one who knew Nature.

Unhappily, these remarks, which might have become the basis of most fruitful researches, were overshadowed by the masses of facts gathered for the purpose of illustrating the consequences of a real competition for life. Besides, Darwin never attempted to submit to a closer investigation the relative importance of the two aspects under which the struggle for existence appears in the animal world, and he never wrote the work he proposed to write upon the natural checks to over-multiplication, although that work would have been the crucial test for appreciating the real purport of individual struggle. Nay, on the very pages just mentioned, amidst data disproving the narrow Malthusian conception of struggle, the old Malthusian leaven reappeared—namely, in Darwin's remarks as to the alleged inconveniences of maintaining the "weak in mind and body" in our civilized societies (ch. v). As if thousands of weak-bodied and infirm poets, scientists, investors, and reformers, together with other thousands of so-called "fools" and "weak-minded enthusiasts," were not the most precious weapons used by humanity in its struggle for existence by intellectual and moral arms, which Darwin himself emphasized in those same chapters of *Descent of Man*.

It happened with Darwin's theory as it always happens with theories having any bearing upon human relations. Instead of widening it according to his own hints, his followers narrowed it still more. And while Herbert Spencer, starting on independent but closely-allied lines, attempted to widen the inquiry into that great question, "Who are the fittest?" especially in the appendix to the third edition of the *Data of Ethics*, the numberless followers of Darwin reduced the notion of struggle for existence to its narrowest limits. They came to conceive the animal world as a world of perpetual struggle among half-starved individuals, thirsting for one another's blood. They made modern literature resound with the war-cry of *woe to the vanquished*, as if it were the last word of modern biology. They raised the "pitiless" struggle for personal advantages to the height of a biological principle which man must submit to as well, under the menace of otherwise succumbing in a world based upon mutual extermination. Leaving aside the economists who know of natural science but a few words borrowed from second-hand vulgarizers, ,we must recognize that even the most authorized exponents of Darwin's views did their best to maintain those false ideas. In fact, if we take Huxley, who certainly is considered as one of the ablest exponents of the theory of evolution, were we not taught by him, in a paper on the 'Struggle for Existence and its Bearing upon Man,' that,

> "from the point of view of the moralist, the animal world is on about the same level as a gladiator's show. The creatures are fairly well treated, and set to fight; whereby the strongest, the swiftest, and the cunningest live to fight another day. The spectator has no need to turn his thumb down, as no quarter is given."

Or, further down in the same article, did he not tell us that, as among animals, so among primitive men,

> "the weakest and stupidest went to the wall, while the toughest and shrewdest, those who were best fitted to cope with their circumstances, but not the best in another way, survived. Life was a continuous free fight, and beyond the limited and temporary relations of the family, the Hobbesian war of each against all was the normal state of existence."[1]

In how far this view of nature is supported by fact, will be seen from the evidence which will be here submitted to the reader as regards the animal world, and as regards primitive man. But it may be remarked at once that Huxley's view of nature had as little claim to be taken as a scientific deduction as the opposite view of Rousseau, who saw in nature but love, peace, and harmony destroyed by the accession of man. In fact, the first walk in the forest, the first observation upon any animal society, or even the perusal of any serious work dealing with animal life (D'Orbigny's, Audubon's, Le Vaillant's, no matter which), cannot but set the naturalist thinking about the part taken by social life in the life of animals, and prevent him from seeing in Nature nothing but a field of slaughter, just as this would prevent him from seeing in Nature nothing but harmony and peace. Rousseau had committed the error of excluding the beak-and-claw fight from his thoughts; and Huxley committed the opposite error; but neither Rousseau's optimism nor Huxley's pessimism can be accepted as an impartial interpretation of nature.

---

[1] *Nineteenth Century*, Feb. 1888, p. 165.

As soon as we study animals—not in laboratories and museums only, but in the forest and the prairie, in the steppe and the mountains—we at once perceive that though there is an immense amount of warfare and extermination going on amidst various species, and especially amidst various classes of animals, there is, at the same time, as much, or perhaps even more, of mutual support, mutual aid, and mutual defence amidst animals belonging to the same species or, at least, to the same society. Sociability is as much a law of nature as mutual struggle. Of course it would be extremely difficult to estimate, however roughly, the relative numerical importance of both these series of facts. But if we resort to an indirect test, and ask Nature: "Who are the fittest: those who are continually at war with each other, or those who support one another?" we at once see that those animals which acquire habits of mutual aid are undoubtedly the fittest. They have more chances to survive, and they attain, in their respective classes, the highest development of intelligence and bodily organization. If the numberless facts which can be brought forward to support this view are taken into account, we may safely say that mutual aid is as much a law of animal life as mutual struggle, but that, as a factor of evolution, it most probably has a far greater importance, inasmuch as it favours the development of such habits and characters as insure the maintenance and further development of the species, together with the greatest amount of welfare and enjoyment of life for the individual, with the least waste of energy.

Of the scientific followers of Darwin, the first, as far as I know, who understood the full purport of Mutual Aid *as a law of Nature and the chief factor of evolution,* was a well-known Russian zoologist the late Dean of the St. Petersburg University, Professor Kessler. He developed his ideas in an address which he delivered in January 1880, a few months before his death, at a Congress of Russian naturalists; but, like so many good things published in the Russian tongue only, that remarkable address remains almost entirely unknown.[2]

"As a zoologist of old standing," he felt bound to protest against the abuse of a term—the struggle for existence—borrowed from zoology, or, at least, against overrating its importance. Zoology, he said, and those sciences which deal with man, continually insist upon what they call the pitiless law of struggle for existence. But they forget the existence of another law which may be described as the law of mutual aid, which law, at least for the animals, is far more essential than the former. He pointed out how the need of leaving progeny necessarily brings animals together, and, "the more the individuals keep together, the more they mutually support each other, and the more are the chances of the species for surviving, as well as for making further progress in its intellectual development." "All classes of animals," he continued, "and especially the higher ones, practise mutual aid," and he illustrated his idea by examples borrowed from the life of the burying beetles and the social life of birds and some mammalia. The examples were few, as might have been expected in a short opening address, but the chief points were clearly stated; and, after mentioning that in the evolution of mankind mutual aid played a still more prominent part, Professor Kessler concluded as follows:

> "I obviously do not deny the struggle for existence, but I maintain that the progressive development of the animal kingdom, and especially of mankind, is favoured much more by mutual support than by mutual struggle. . . . All organic beings have two essential needs: that of nutrition, and that of propagating the species. The former brings them to a struggle and to mutual extermination, while the needs of maintaining the species bring them to approach one another and to support one another. But I am inclined to think that in the evolution of the organic world—in the progressive modification of organic beings—mutual support among individuals plays a much more important part than their mutual struggle."[3]

The correctness of the above views struck most of the Russian zoologists present, and Syevertsoff,

---

[2]Leaving aside the pre-Darwinian writers, like Toussenel, Fée, and many others, several works containing many striking instances of mutual aid—chiefly, however, illustrating animal intelligence—were issued previously to that date. I may mention those of Houzeau, *Les facultés mentales des animaux,* 2 vols., Brussels, 1872; L. Büchner's *Aus dem Geistesleben der Thiere,* 2nd ed. in 1877: and Maximilian Perty's *Ueber das Seelenleben der Thiere,* Leipzig, 1876. Espinas published his most remarkable work, *Les Sociétés animales,* in 1877, and in that work he pointed out the importance of animal societies, and their bearing upon the preservation of species, and entered upon a most valuable discussion of the origin of societies. In fact, Espinas's book contains all that has been written since upon mutual aid, and many good

things besides. If I nevertheless make a special mention of Kessler's address, it is because he raised mutual aid to the height of a law much more important in evolution than the law of mutual struggle. The same ideas were developed next year (in April 1881) by J. Lanessan in a lecture published in 1882 under this title: *La lutte pour l'existence et l'association pour la lutte.* G. Romanes's capital work, *Animal Intelligence,* was issued in 1882, and followed next year by the *Mental Evolution in Animals.* About the same time (1883), Büchner published another work, *Liebe und Liebes-Leben in der Thierwelt,* a second edition of which was issued in 1885. The idea, as seen, was in the air.

[3]*Memoirs (Trudy) of the St. Petersburg Society of Naturalists,* vol. xi. 1880.

whose work is well known to ornithologists and geographers, supported them and illustrated them by a few more examples. He mentioned some of the species of falcons which have "an almost ideal organization for robbery," and nevertheless are in decay, while other species of falcons, which practise mutual help, do thrive. "Take, on the other side, a sociable bird, the duck," he said; "it is poorly organized on the whole, but it practises mutual support, and it almost invades the earth, as may be judged from its numberless varieties and species."

The readiness of the Russian zoologists to accept Kessler's views seems quite natural, because nearly all of them have had opportunities of studying the animal world in the wide uninhabited regions of Northern Asia and East Russia; and it is impossible to study like regions without being brought to the same ideas. I recollect myself the impression produced upon me by the animal world of Siberia when I explored the Vitim regions in the company of so accomplished a zoologist as my friend Polyakoff was. We both were under the fresh impression of the *Origin of Species,* but we vainly looked for the keen competition between animals of the same species which the reading of Darwin's work had prepared us to expect, even after taking into account the remarks of the third chapter (p. 54). We saw plenty of adaptations for struggling, very often in common, against the adverse circumstances of climate, or against various enemies, and Polyakoff wrote many a good page upon the mutual dependency of carnivores, ruminants, and rodents in their geographical distribution; we witnessed numbers of facts of mutual support, especially during the migrations of birds and ruminants; but even in the Amur and Usuri regions, where animal life swarms in abundance, facts of real competition and struggle between higher animals of the same species came very seldom under my notice, though I eagerly searched for them. The same impression appears in the works of most Russian zoologists, and it probably explains why Kessler's ideas were so welcomed by the Russian Darwinists, whilst like ideas are not in vogue amidst the followers of Darwin in Western Europe.

MUTUAL AID AMONGST OURSELVES

Popular revolts at the beginning of the State-period. Mutual Aid institutions of the present time. The village community, its struggles for resisting its abolition by the State. Habits derived from the village-community life, retained in our modern villages: Switzerland, France, Germany, Russia.

The mutual-aid tendency in man has so remote an origin, and is so deeply interwoven with all the past evolution of the human race, that it has been maintained by mankind up to the present time, notwithstanding all vicissitudes of history. It was chiefly evolved during periods of peace and prosperity; but when even the greatest calamities befell men—when whole countries were laid waste by wars, and whole populations were decimated by misery, or groaned under the yoke of tyranny—the same tendency continued to live in the villages and among the poorer classes in the towns; it still kept them together, and in the long run it reacted even upon those ruling, fighting, and devastating minorities which dismissed it as sentimental nonsense. And whenever mankind had to work out a new social organization, adapted to a new phasis of development, its constructive genius always drew the elements and the inspiration for the new departure from that same ever-living tendency. New economical and social institutions, in so far as they were a creation of the masses, new ethical systems, and new religions, all have originated from the same source, and the ethical progress of our race, viewed in its broad lines, appears as a gradual extension of the mutual-aid principles from the tribe to always larger and larger agglomerations, so as to finally embrace one day the whole of mankind, without respect to its divers creeds, languages, and races.

After having passed through the savage tribe, and next through the village community, the Europeans came to work out in mediæval times a new form of organization, which had the advantage of allowing great latitude for individual initiative, while it largely responded at the same time to man's need of mutual support. A federation of village communities, covered by a network of guilds and fraternities, was called into existence in the mediæval cities. The immense results achieved under this new form of union—in well-being for all, in industries, art, science, and commerce—were discussed at some length in two preceding chapters, and an attempt was also made to show why, towards the end of the fifteenth century, the mediæval republics—surrounded by domains of hostile feudal lords, unable to free the peasants from servitude, and gradually corrupted by ideas of Roman Cæsarism—were doomed to become a prey to the growing military States.

However, before submitting for three centuries to come, to the all-absorbing authority of the State, the masses of the people made a formidable attempt at reconstructing society on the old basis of mutual aid and support. It is well known by this time that the great movement of the reform was not a mere revolt against the abuses of the Catholic Church. It had its constructive ideal as well, and that ideal was life in free, brotherly communities. Those of the early writings and sermons of the period which found most response with the masses were imbued with ideas of the economical and social brotherhood of mankind. The "Twelve Articles" and similar professions of faith, which were circulated among the German and Swiss peasants and artisans, maintained not only every one's right to interpret the Bible according to his own understanding, but also included the demand of communal lands being restored to the village communities and feudal servitudes being abolished, and they always alluded to the "true" faith—a faith of brotherhood. At the same time scores of thousands of men and women joined the communist fraternities of Moravia, giving them all their fortune and living in numerous and prosperous settlements constructed upon the principles of communism.[4] Only wholesale massacres by the thousand could put a stop to this widely-spread popular movement, and it was by the sword, the fire, and the rack that the young States secured their first and decisive victory over the masses of the people.[5]

For the next three centuries the States, both on the Continent and in these islands, systematically weeded out all institutions in which the mutual-aid tendency had formerly found its expression. The village communities were bereft of their folkmotes, their courts and independent administration; their lands were confiscated. The guilds were spoliated of their possessions and liberties, and placed under the control, the fancy, and the bribery of the State's official. The cities were divested of their sovereignty, and the very springs of their inner life—the folkmote, the elected justices and administration, the sovereign parish and the sovereign guild—were annihilated; the State's functionary took possession of

every link of what formerly was an organic whole. Under that fatal policy and the wars it engendered, whole regions, once populous and wealthy, were laid bare; rich cities became insignificant boroughs; the very roads which connected them with other cities became impracticable. Industry, art, and knowledge fell into decay. Political education, science, and law were rendered subservient to the idea of State centralization. It was taught in the Universities and from the pulpit that the institutions in which men formerly used to embody their needs of mutual support could not be tolerated in a properly organized State; that the State alone could represent the bonds of union between its subjects; that federalism and "particularism" were the enemies of progress, and the State was the only proper initiator of further development. By the end of the last century the kings on the Continent, the Parliament in these isles, and the revolutionary Convention in France, although they were at war with each other, agreed in asserting that no separate unions between citizens must exist within the State; that hard labour and death were the only suitable punishments to workers who dared to enter into "coalitions." "No state within the State!" The State alone, and the State's Church, must take care of matters of general interest, while the subjects must represent loose aggregations of individuals, connected by no particular bonds, bound to appeal to the Government each time that they feel a common need. Up to the middle of the nineteenth century this was the theory and practice in Europe. Even commercial and industrial societies were looked at with suspicion. As to the workers, their unions were treated as unlawful almost within our own lifetime in this country and within the last twenty years on the Continent. The whole system of our State education was such that up to the present time, even in this country, a notable portion of society would treat as a revolutionary measure the concession of such rights as every one, freeman or serf, exercised five hundred years ago in the village folkmote, the guild, the parish, and the city.

The absorption of all social functions by the State necessarily favoured the development of an unbridled, narrow-minded individualism. In proportion as the obligations towards the State grew in numbers, the citizens were evidently relieved from their obligations towards each other. In the guild—and in mediæval times every man belonged to some guild or fraternity—two "brothers" were bound to watch in turns a brother who had fallen ill; it would be sufficient now to give one's neighbour the address of the next paupers' hospital. In barbarian society, to assist at a fight between two men, arisen from a quarrel, and not to prevent it from taking a fatal issue, meant to be oneself treated as a mur-

---

[4] A bulky literature, dealing with this formerly much-neglected subject, is now growing in Germany. Keller's works, *Ein Apostel der Wiedertäufer* and *Geschichte der Wiedertäufer*, Cornelius's *Geschichte des münsterischen Aufruhrs*, and Janssen's *Geschichte des deutschen Volkes* may be named as the leading sources. The first attempt at familiarizing English readers with the results of the wide researches made in Germany in this direction has been made in an excellent little work by Richard Heath—"Anabaptism from its Rise at Zwickau to its Fall at Münster, 1521–1536," London, 1895 (*Baptist Manuals*, vol. i.)—where the leading features of the movement are well indicated, and full bibliographical information is given. Also K. Kautsky's *Communism in Central Europe in the Time of the Reformation*, London, 1897.

[5] Few of our contemporaries realize both the extent of this movement and the means by which it was suppressed. But those who wrote immediately after the great peasant war estimated at from 100,000 to 150,000 men the number of peasants slaughtered after their defeat in Germany. See Zimmermann's *Allgemeine Geschichte des grossen Bauernkrieges*. For the measures taken to suppress the movement in the Netherlands see Richard Heath's *Anabaptism*.

derer; but under the theory of the all-protecting State the bystander need not intrude: it is the policeman's business to interfere, or not. And while in a savage land, among the Hottentots, it would be scandalous to eat without having loudly called out thrice whether there is not somebody wanting to share the food, all that a respectable citizen has to do now is to pay the poor tax and to let the starving starve. The result is, that the theory which maintains that men can, and must, seek their own happiness in a disregard of other people's wants is now triumphant all round—in law, in science, in religion. It is the religion of the day, and to doubt of its efficacy is to be a dangerous Utopian. Science loudly proclaims that the struggle of each against all is the leading principle of nature, and of human societies as well. To that struggle Biology ascribes the progressive evolution of the animal world. History takes the same line of argument; and political economists, in their naïve ignorance, trace all progress of modern industry and machinery to the "wonderful" effects of the same principle. The very religion of the pulpit is a religion of individualism, slightly mitigated by more or less charitable relations to one's neighbours, chiefly on Sundays. "Practical" men and theorists, men of science and religious preachers, lawyers and politicians, all agree upon one thing—that individualism may be more or less softened in its harshest effects by charity, but that it is the only secure basis for the maintenance of society and its ulterior progress.

It seems, therefore, hopeless to look for mutual-aid institutions and practices in modern society. What could remain of them? And yet, as soon as we try to ascertain how the millions of human beings live, and begin to study their everyday relations, we are struck with the immense part which the mutual-aid and mutual-support principles play even now-a-days in human life. Although the destruction of mutual-aid institutions has been going on in practice and theory, for full three or four hundred years, hundreds of millions of men continue to live under such institutions; they piously maintain them and endeavour to reconstitute them where they have ceased to exist. In our mutual relations every one of us has his moments of revolt against the fashionable individualistic creed of the day, and actions in which men are guided by their mutual-aid inclinations constitute so great a part of our daily intercourse that if a stop to such actions could be put all further ethical progress would be stopped at once. Human society itself could not be maintained for even so much as the lifetime of one single generation. These facts, mostly neglected by sociologists and yet of the first importance for the life and further elevation of mankind, we are now going to analyze, beginning with the standing institutions of mutual support, and passing next to those acts of mutual aid which have their origin in personal or social sympathies.

When we cast a broad glance on the present constitution of European society we are struck at once with the fact that, although so much has been done to get rid of the village community, this form of union continues to exist to the extent we shall presently see, and that many attempts are now made either to reconstitute it in some shape or another or to find some substitute for it. The current theory as regards the village community is, that in Western Europe it has died out by a natural death, because the communal possession of the soil was found inconsistent with the modern requirements of agriculture. But the truth is that nowhere did the village community disappear of its own accord; everywhere, on the contrary, it took the ruling classes several centuries of persistent but not always successful efforts to abolish it and to confiscate the communal lands.

Name: _____ **Date:** _____

1. In your own words, describe the two types of struggle for life that Kropotkin identifies.

2. What is mutual aid?

3. Describe three different institutions humans have created that embody mutual aid.
 1.

 2.

 3.

David Starr Jordan

"Social Darwinism," 1918

Jordan (1851-1931) was an ichthyologist, the first President of Stanford University, and prominent Darwinist. He wrote this piece during World War I as part of a larger propaganda movement in the United States to demonize the German government and motivate Americans to support the war. Jordan, a long-time pacifist and opponent to those political and social theorists who used Darwinism to justify competition and war, condemned the Germans for "misusing" Darwin's work to rationalize their military aggressions in Europe.

In the last half-century, there has been developed, in Germany, a doctrine called "Social Darwinism." This dogma, based on a vicious and ignorant misinterpretation of Darwin's teachings, involves two conceptions:

1. There is a constant struggle among races and nations whereby the largest, strongest and fiercest survive, and the others go to the wall.
2. It is incumbent on the strong nations—those most populous and enjoying the most complete discipline—to subdue or to exterminate the others.

This call to duty is the justification for international war and racial oppression. And the doctrine of frightfulness points to the swiftest and most effective method of subjugation.

This "biological argument for war" has no scientific validity and no legitimate relation to the teachings of Darwin. In fact, it has been developed, as a form of special pleading, to meet the exigencies of the existing dynastic system.

"Darwinism," as properly understood, is the theory that in the course of evolution, by which man and other organisms have been derived from preexisting forms by natural processes, a leading factor is "Natural Selection"—the elimination of the unadaptable in the "Struggle for Existence."

This struggle is not primarily a life and death rivalry between individuals, or between races. Competition with like as well as struggle against unlike organisms are both features of the larger problem of adaptation to environment.

The philosophy of "Social Darwinism" involves not merely the facts of a struggle, with the elimination of the unadapted so-called "unfit," among humanity. It demands their destruction as a matter of national duty. Its advocates insist that the strong must "get behind" Evolution by obliteration of the weak.

It is claimed that if a strong nation succeeds in "the rigorous and ruthless struggle for existence" its right is thereby vindicated. "This struggle should occur precisely that the various types may be tested, and the best not only preserved, but put into position to impose its kind of social organization, or *Kultur*, on the others, or alternately to destroy and displace them. The menace of this philosophy is that its adherents believe what they say, and they act on this belief, that war is necessary as a test of their portion and claim. Hence they oppose 'all mercy, all compromise with human soft-heartedness.'"

This contention overlooks four vital truths.

1. The "Struggle for Existence" is primarily not a matter of rivalry but the condition of persistence even in the face of adverse conditions.
2. The competition involved is one of the necessity of life, not a demand for a collective or national duty of destruction.
3. The contention totally ignores the "law of mutual aid," and the established fact that Altruism is itself one of the most potent factors in natural selection.

From *The Public* 21, 1918.

4. The qualities of permanence and progress are not those of the forceful and merciless against whom the greater power of the altruistic and cooperative races are sure to combine. "The race is not to the swift, nor the battle to the strong," but to those who can hold together.

Altruism is mutual aid, and in its biological sense represents in general those relations of one organism to others of its own type which are most favorable to the development of both. It is the quality of "neighborliness," of combination in the midst of competition.

Altruism is, by no means, a purely human attribute. There is no part of the animal kingdom in which it is not evident, and traces appear throughout the plant kingdom as well. Wherever life exists, varied conditions of environment are found, and the progress of life consists of adaptations to these conditions. Altruistic social adjustments are powerful factors in the struggle for existence in the life of animals as well as man. Care of the young is an agency far more effective in race preservation than the "tooth and claw" of competitive struggle. The readiness of the parent to die, if need be, for its young is a guarantee of race survival.

Altruism, moreover, is a robust impulse set deep in the breast of living organisms, beyond all danger of extinction. It is as old as selfishness, and as hard to eradicate. It needs coddling no more than hunger does. It asks no external sanction, for individuals deficient in altruism pass away, leaving no descendants. There is a bounty on their heads, whether they be wolves, or hawks, or predatory men.

Altruism expresses itself in all that makes the human life sane, joyous, effective. Science is the consummate fruit of the altruism of the ages. No man's experiences belong to himself alone, but are part of the heritage of those who follow. Human institutions grow out of the social instinct. *They are fossils of past altruism.* Art, literature, music, religion arise, and are developed, through mutual help.

In the very beginnings of life altruism appears. The conjugation of one-celled animals involves the interchange of hereditary cell structures, after which, neither the one nor the other is exactly what it was before. This change modifies the descendants by the law of heredity in accord with the law of variation whereby no organism that exists is ever an exact or slavish copy of any other, not even of parent or sister. From this simple function of the conjugation of primitive cells arises with evolution all the complex relations of love, conjugal, filial and parental. The ultimate purpose of the sex relation, so far as one may speak of ultimate purposes in nature, is to produce and promote variety among organisms.

Altruism appears in another form in the aggregation of cells. A one-celled animal or plant is an organic unit. When the new cells produced by the processes of cell division remain joined to each other, a complex organism is built up. By such means, the sperm-cell in the higher animals develops into the embryo, and the embryo passes through the stages of infancy and youth into the complicated structure of maturity. Specialization, differentiation, organization, sensation, will, intellect, are all resultants of altruistic cell cooperation.

Individual men unite to form societies, as do individual cells to form the human body. But while the individual man is capable of separating himself from society, the individual cell is bound to the fate of its associates.

Among men, the growth of society abridges individual human freedom by making freedom worth having. Mutual aid involves mutual dependence. It gives a security and strength forever impossible under purely individualistic conditions. Altruism can never become outworn or exhausted. No species and "no race ever became extinct through an excess of brotherly love."[1] "This world is not the abode of the Strong alone; it is also the home of the Loving."[2]

---

[1]Amos G. Warner.
[2]J. Arthur Thomson.

Name: _____ **Date:** _____

1. What group of people does Jordan claim are responsible for perpetuating social Darwinism?

2. When was this piece published? What events were occurring that might have encouraged the publication of this article?

3. Why, according to Jordan, is social Darwinism dangerous?

4. In your own words, describe Jordan's four arguments against social Darwinism.
   1.

   2.

3.

4.

5. What is altruism and how is it relevant to social Darwinism?

Vernon Kellogg

Headquarters Nights: A Record of Conversations and Experiences at the Headquarters of the German Army in France and Belgium, 1917

Vernon Kellogg (1867-1937), who also wrote the *Darwinism To-Day* selection found earlier in this volume, was a American entomologist and ardent supporter of evolution. In 1914 Kellogg resigned his position as Professor of Entomology and Bionomics at Stanford University to join his former student, Herbert Hoover, in Europe distributing food and clothing to civilians trapped in German-occupied Belgium and northern-France. When the United States joined the war against Germany in 1917, Kellogg and other humanitarian aid workers were expelled from Europe. He returned to the United States and joined the propaganda effort against Germany by writing *Headquarters Nights*. In it, Kellogg claimed that the Germans perverted evolutionary theory to justify their aggressive militarism. They were, he wrote, misusing Darwinian evolutionary theory to support particular political positions.

We do not hear much now from the German intellectuals. Some of the professors are writing for the German newspapers, but most of them are keeping silent in public. The famous Ninety-three are not issuing any more proclamations. When your armies are moving swiftly and gloriously forward under the banners of sweetness and light, to carry the proper civilization to an improperly educated and improperly thinking world, it is easier to make declarations of what is going to happen, and why it is, than when your armies are struggling for life with their backs to the wall—of a French village they have shot and burned to ruin for a reason that does not seem so good a reason now.

But some of the intellectuals still speak in the old strain in private. It has been my peculiar privilege to talk through long evening hours with a few of these men at Headquarters. Not exactly the place, one would think, for meeting these men, but let us say this for them: some of them fight as well as talk. And they fight, not simply because they are forced to, but because, curiously enough, they believe much of their talk. This is one of the dangers from the Germans to which the world is exposed: they really believe much of what they say.

From *Headquarters Night,* Boston: The Atlantic Monthly Press, 1917.

A word of explanation about the Headquarters, and how I happened to be there. It was—it is no longer, and that is why I can speak more freely about it—not only Headquarters but the Great Headquarters—*Grosses Hauptquartier*—of all the German Armies of the West. Here were big Von Schoeler, *General-Intendant,* and the scholarly-looking Von Freytag, *General-Quartiermeister,* with his unscholarly-looking, burly chief of staff, Von Zoellner. Here also were Von Falkenhayn, the Kaiser's Chief of Staff, and sometimes even the All-Highest himself, who never missed the Sunday morning service in the long low corrugated-iron shed which looked all too little like a royal chapel ever to interest a flitting French bomber.

But not only was this small gray town on the Meuse, just where the water pours out of its beautiful cañon course through the Ardennes, the headquarters of the German General Staff—it was also the station, by arrangement with the staff, of the American Relief Commission's humble ununiformed chief representative for the North of France (occupied French territory). For several months I held this position, living with the German officer detached from the General Quartermaster's staff to protect me—and watch me. Later, too, as director of the Commission at Brussels, I had frequent occasion to visit

Headquarters for conferences with officers of the General Staff. It was thus that I had opportunity for these Headquarters Nights.

Among the officers and officials of Headquarters there were many strong and keen German militaristic brains—that goes without saying—but there were also a few of the professed intellectuals—men who had exchanged, for the moment, the academic robes of the *Aula* for the field-gray uniforms of the army. The second commandant of the Headquarters town was a professor of jurisprudence at the University of Marburg; and an infantry captain, who lived in the house with my guardian officer and me, is the professor of zoölogy in one of the larger German universities, and one of the most brilliant of present-day biologists. I do not wish to indicate his person more particularly, for I shall say some hard things about him—or about him as representative of many—and we are friends. Indeed, he was *Privat-docent* in charge of the laboratory in which I worked years ago at the University of Leipzig, and we have been correspondents and friends ever since. How he came to be at Headquarters, and at precisely the same time that I was there, is a story which has its interest, but cannot be told at present.

Our house was rather a favored centre, for 'my officer,' Graf W.— he always called me 'my American,' but he could no more get away from me than I from him—is a generous entertainer, and our dinners were rarely without guests from other headquarters houses. Officers, from veteran generals down to pink-cheeked lieutenants, came to us and asked us to them. The discussions, begun at dinner, lasted long into the night. They sat late, these German officers, over their abundant wine—French vintages conveniently arranged for. And always we talked and tried to understand one another; to get the other man's point of view, his *Weltanschauung*.

Well, I say it dispassionately but with conviction: if I understand theirs, it is a point of view that will never allow any land or people controlled by it to exist peacefully by the side of a people governed by our point of view. For their point of view does not permit of a live-and-let-live kind of carrying on. It is a point of view that justifies itself by a whole-hearted acceptance of the worst of Neo-Darwinism, the *Allmacht* of natural selection applied rigorously to human life and society and *Kultur*.

Professor von Flussen—that is not his name—is a biologist. So am I. So we talked out the biological argument for war, and especially for this war. The captain-professor has a logically constructed argument why, for the good of the world, there should be this war, and why, for the good of the world, the Germans should win it, win it completely and terribly. Perhaps I can state his argument clearly enough, so that others may see and accept his reasons, too. Unfortunately for the peace of our evenings, I was never convinced. That is, never convinced that for the good of the world the Germans should win this war, completely and terribly. I was convinced, however, that this war, once begun, must be fought to a finish of decision—a finish that will determine whether or not Germany's point of view is to rule the world. And this conviction, thus gained, meant the conversion of a pacifist to an ardent supporter, not of War, but of *this* war; of fighting this war to a definitive end—that end to be Germany's conversion to be a good Germany, or not much of any Germany at all. My 'Headquarters Nights' are the confessions of a converted pacifist.

In talking it out biologically, we agreed that the human race is subject to the influence of the fundamental biologic laws of variation, heredity, selection, and so forth, just as are all other animal—and plant—kinds. The factors of organic evolution, generally, are factors in human natural evolution. Man has risen from his primitive bestial stage of glacial time, a hundred or several hundred thousand years ago, when he was animal among animals, to the stage of to-day, always under the influence of these great evolutionary factors, and partly by virtue of them.

But he does not owe all of his progress to these factors, or, least of all, to any one of them, as natural selection, a thesis Professor von Flussen seemed ready to maintain.

Natural selection depends for its working on a rigorous and ruthless struggle for existence. Yet this struggle has its ameliorations, even as regards the lower animals, let alone man.

There are three general phases of this struggle:—

1. An inter-specific struggle, or the lethal competition among different animal kinds for food, space, and opportunity to increase;
2. An intra-specific struggle, or lethal competition among the individuals of a single species, resultant on the over-production due to natural multiplication by geometric progression; and,
3. The constant struggle of individuals and species against the rigors of climate, the danger of storm, flood, drought, cold, and heat.

Now any animal kind and its individuals may be continually exposed to all of these phases of the struggle for existence, or, on the other hand, any one or more of these phases may be largely ameliorated or even abolished for a given species and its individuals. This amelioration may come about through a happy accident of time or place, or because of the adoption by the species of a habit or mode of life that continually protects it from a certain phase of the struggle.

For example, the voluntary or involuntary migration of representatives of a species hard pressed to exist in its native habitat, may release it from the too severe rigors of a destructive climate, or take it beyond the habitat of its most dangerous enemies, or give it the needed space and food for the support of a numerous progeny. Thus, such a single phenomenon as migration might ameliorate any one or more of the several phases of the struggle for existence.

Again, the adoption by two widely distinct and perhaps antagonistic species of a commensal or symbiotic life, based on the mutual-aid principle—thousands of such cases are familiar to naturalists—would ameliorate or abolish the interspecific struggle between these two species. Even more effective in the modification of the influence due to a bitter struggle for existence, is the adoption by a species of an altruistic or communistic mode of existence so far as its own individuals are concerned. This, of course, would largely ameliorate for that species the intra-specific phase of its struggle for life. Such animal altruism, and the biological success of the species exhibiting it, is familiarly exemplified by the social insects (ants, bees, and wasps).

As a matter of fact, this reliance by animal kinds for success in the world upon a more or less extreme adoption of the mutual-aid principle, as contrasted with the mutual-fight principle, is much more widely spread among the lower animals than familiarly recognized, while in the case of man, it has been the greatest single factor in the achievement of his proud biological position as king of living creatures.

Altruism—or mutual aid, as the biologists prefer to call it, to escape the implication of assuming too much consciousness in it—is just as truly a fundamental biologic factor of evolution as is the cruel, strictly self-regarding, exterminating kind of struggle for existence with which the Neo-Darwinists try to fill our eyes and ears, to the exclusion of the recognition of all other factors.

Professor von Flussen is Neo-Darwinian, as are most German biologists and natural philosophers.

The creed of the *Allmacht* of a natural selection based on violent and fatal competitive struggle is the gospel of the German intellectuals; all else is illusion and anathema. The mutual-aid principle is recognized only as restricted to its application within limited groups. For instance, it may and does exist, and to positive biological benefit, within single ant communities, but the different ant kinds fight desperately with each other, the stronger destroying or enslaving the weaker. Similarly, it may exist to advantage within the limits of organized human groups—as those which are ethnographically, nationally, or otherwise variously delimited. But as with the different ant species, struggle—bitter, ruthless struggle—is the rule among the different human groups.

This struggle not only must go on, for that is the natural law, but it should go on, so that this natural law may work out in its cruel, inevitable way the salvation of the human species. By its salvation is meant its desirable natural evolution. That human group which is in the most advanced evolutionary stage as regards internal organization and form of social relationship is best, and should, for the sake of the species, be preserved at the expense of the less advanced, the less effective. It should win in the struggle for existence, and this struggle should occur precisely that the various types may be tested, and the best not only preserved, but put in position to impose its kind of social organization—its *Kultur*—on the others, or, alternatively, to destroy and replace them.

This is the disheartening kind of argument that I faced at Headquarters; argument logically constructed on premises chosen by the other fellow. Add to these assumed premises of the *Allmacht* of struggle and selection based on it, and the contemplation of mankind as a congeries of different, mutually irreconcilable kinds, like the different ant species, the additional assumption that the Germans are the chosen race, and German social and political organization the chosen type of human community life, and you have a wall of logic and conviction that you can break your head against but can never shatter—by headwork. You long for the muscles of Samson.

Name: _____ **Date:** _____

1. Why was Kellogg in Germany during World War I?

2. Why, according to Kellogg, did his German colleagues believe that the war was both necessary and beneficial to mankind?

3. Describe in your own words the three types of struggle that Kellogg explained the German's believed directed evolution.
   1.

   2.

   3.

4. What is altruism and how did Kellogg believe that it influenced the direction of evolution?

5. What is Kultur?

Section V

Eugenics and the Health
of the Race

Francis Galton

Hereditary Genius, 1869

Galton (1822-1911) was an explorer, anthropologist, pioneer in the study of intelligence, and the man responsible for coining the term "eugenics." As Darwin's cousin, Galton was a prominent member of English society and a well-respected researcher. In *Hereditary Genius*, Galton sought to quantify the relationship between individuals of high reputation, which he used as a measure for an individual's inherent quality, and that person's parents and children. Did, Galton asked, individuals of high reputation have a greater chance of having parents of high reputation than did the average citizen?

I propose to show in this book that a man's natural abilities are derived by inheritance, under exactly the same limitations as are the form and physical features of the whole organic world. Consequently, as it is easy, notwithstanding those limitations, to obtain by careful selection a permanent breed of dogs or horses gifted with peculiar powers of running, or of doing anything else, so it would be quite practicable to produce a highly-gifted race of men by judicious marriages during several consecutive generations. I shall show that social agencies of an ordinary character, whose influences are little suspected, are at this moment working towards the degradation of human nature, and that others are working towards its improvement. I conclude that each generation has enormous power over the natural gifts of those that follow, and maintain that it is a duty we owe to humanity to investigate the range of that power, and to exercise it in a way that, without being unwise towards ourselves, shall be most advantageous to future inhabitants of the earth.

I am aware that my views, which were first published four years ago in *Macmillan's Magazine* (in June and August 1865), are in contradiction to general opinion; but the arguments I then used have been since accepted, to my great gratification, by many of the highest authorities on heredity. In reproducing them, as I now do, in a much more elaborate form, and on a greatly enlarged basis of induc-

tion, I feel assured that, inasmuch as what I then wrote was sufficient to earn the acceptance of Mr. Darwin ("Domestication of Species," ii. 7), the increased amount of evidence submitted in the present volume is not likely to be gainsaid.

The general plan of my argument is to show that high reputation is a pretty accurate test of high ability; next to discuss the relationships of a large body of fairly eminent men—namely, the Judges of England from 1660 to 1868, the Statesmen of the time of George III., and the Premiers during the last 100 years—and to obtain from these a general survey of the laws of heredity in respect to genius. Then I shall examine, in order, the kindred of the most illustrious Commanders, men of Literature and of Science, Poets, Painters, and Musicians, of whom history speaks. I shall also discuss the kindred of a certain selection of Divines and of modern Scholars. Then will follow a short chapter, by way of comparison, on the hereditary transmission of physical gifts, as deduced from the relationships of certain classes of Oarsmen and Wrestlers. Lastly, I shall collate my results, and draw conclusions.

It will be observed that I deal with more than one grade of ability. Those upon whom the greater part of my volume is occupied, and on whose kinships my argument is most securely based, have been generally reputed as endowed by nature with extraordinary genius. There are so few of these men that, although they are scattered throughout the whole historical period of human existence, their number does not amount to more than 400, and yet a considerable proportion of them will be found to be interrelated.

From *Heredity Genius: An Inquiry into Its Laws and Consequences*, 1869.

Another grade of ability with which I deal is that which includes numerous highly eminent, and all the illustrious names of modern English history, whose immediate descendants are living among us, whose histories are popularly known, and whose relationships may readily be traced by the help of biographical dictionaries, peerages, and similar books of reference.

A third and lower grade is that of the English Judges, massed together as a whole, for the purpose of the prefatory statistical inquiry of which I have already spoken. No more doubts that many of the ablest intellects of our race are to be found among the Judges; nevertheless the *average* ability of a Judge cannot be rated as equal to that of the lower of the two grades I have described.

I trust the reader will make allowance for a large and somewhat important class of omissions I have felt myself compelled to make when treating of the eminent men of modern days. I am prevented by a sense of decorum from quoting names of their relations in contemporary life who are not recognised as public characters, although their ability may be highly appreciated in private life. Still less consistent with decorum would it have been, to introduce the names of female relatives that stand in the same category. My case is so overpoweringly strong, that I am perfectly able to prove my point without having recourse to this class of evidence. Nevertheless, the reader should bear in mind that it exists; and I beg he will do me the justice of allowing that I have not overlooked the whole of the evidence that does not appear in my pages. I am deeply conscious of the imperfection of my work, but my sins are those of omission, not of commission. Such errors as I may and must have made, which give a fictitious support to my arguments, are, I am confident, out of all proportion fewer than such omissions of facts as would have helped to establish them.

I have taken little notice in this book of modern men of eminence who are not English, or at least well known to Englishmen. I feared, if I included large classes of foreigners, that I should make glaring errors. It requires a very great deal of labour to hunt out relationships, even with the facilities afforded to a countryman having access to persons acquainted with the various families; much more would it have been difficult to hunt out the kindred of foreigners. I should have especially liked to investigate the biographies of Italians and Jews, both of whom appear to be rich in families of high intellectual breeds. Germany and America are also full of interest. It is a little less so with respect to France, where the Revolution and the guillotine made sad havoc among the progeny of her abler races.

There is one advantage to a candid critic in my having left so large a field untouched; it enables me to propose a test that any well-informed reader may easily adopt who doubts the fairness of my examples. He may most reasonably suspect that I have been unconsciously influenced by my theories to select men whose kindred were most favourable to their support. If so, I beg he will test my impartiality as follows:—Let him take a dozen names of his own selection, as the most eminent in whatever profession and in whatever country he knows most about, and let him trace out for himself their relations. It is necessary, as I find by experience, to take some pains to be sure that none, even of the immediate relatives, on either the male or female side, have been overlooked. If he does what I propose, I am confident he will be astonished at the completeness with which the results will confirm my theory. I venture to speak with assurance, because it has often occurred to me to propose this very test to incredulous friends, and invariably, so far as my memory serves me, as large a proportion of the men who were named were discovered to have eminent relations, as the nature of my views on heredity would have led me to expect.

CLASSIFICATION OF MEN ACCORDING TO THEIR REPUTATION

The arguments by which I endeavour to prove that genius is hereditary, consist in showing how large is the number of instances in which men who are more or less illustrious have eminent kinsfolk. It is necessary to have clear ideas on the two following matters before my arguments can be rightly appreciated. The first is the degree of selection implied by the words "eminent" and "illustrious." Does "eminent" mean the foremost in a hundred, in a thousand, or in what other number of men? The second is the degree to which reputation may be accepted as a test of ability.

It is essential that I, who write, should have a minimum qualification distinctly before my eyes whenever I employ the phrases "eminent" and the like, and that the reader should understand as clearly as myself the value I attach to those qualifications. An explanation of these words will be the subject of the present chapter. A subsequent chapter will be given to the discussion of how far "eminence" may be accepted as a criterion of natural gifts. It is almost needless for me to insist that the subjects of these two chapters' are entirely distinct.

I look upon social and professional life as a continuous examination. All are candidates for the good opinions of others, and for success in their several professions, and they achieve success in proportion as the general estimate is large of their aggregate merits. In ordinary scholastic examinations marks are allotted in stated proportions to various specified subjects—so many for Latin, so many for Greek, so many for English history, and the rest. The world, in the same way, but almost unconsciously, allots marks to men. It gives them for originality of conception, for enterprise, for activity and energy, for administrative skill, for various acquirements, for power of literary expression, for oratory, and much besides of general value, as well as for more specially professional merits. It does not allot these marks according to a proportion that can easily be stated in words, but there is a rough commonsense that governs its practice with a fair approximation to constancy. Those who have gained most of these tacit marks are ranked, by the common judgment of the leaders of opinion, as the foremost men of their day.

The metaphor of an examination may be stretched much further. As there are alternative groups in any one of which a candidate may obtain honours, so it is with reputations—they may be made in law, literature, science, art, and in a host of other pursuits. Again: as the mere attainment of a general fair level will obtain no honours in an examination, no more will it do so in the struggle for eminence. A man must show conspicuous power in at least one subject in order to achieve a high reputation.

Let us see how the world classifies people, after examining each of them, in her patient, persistent manner, during the years of their manhood. How many men of "eminence" are there, and what proportion do they bear to the whole community?

I will begin by analysing a very painstaking biographical handbook, lately published by Routledge and Co., called "Men of the Time." Its intention, which is very fairly and honestly carried out, is to include none but those whom the world honours for their ability. The catalogue of names is 2,500, and a full half of it consists of American and Continental celebrities. It is well I should give in a footnote[1] an analysis of its contents, in order to show the exhaustive character of its range. The numbers I have prefixed to each class are not strictly accurate, for I measured them off rather than counted them, but they are quite close enough. The same name often appears under more than one head.

On looking over the book, I am surprised to find how large a proportion of the "Men of the Time" are past middle age. It appears that in the cases of high (but by no means in that of the highest) merit, a man must outlive the age of fifty to be sure of being widely appreciated. It takes time for an able man, born in the humbler ranks of life, to emerge from them and to take his natural position. It would not, therefore, be just to compare the numbers of Englishmen in the book with that of the whole adult male population of the British isles; but it is necessary to confine our examination to those of the celebrities who are past fifty years of age, and to compare their number with that of the whole male population who are also above fifty years. I estimate, from examining a large part of the book, that there are about 850 of these men, and that 500 of them are decidedly well known to persons familiar with literary and scientific society. Now, there are about two millions of adult males in the British isles above fifty years of age; consequently, the total number of the "Men of the Time" are as 425 to a million, and the more select part of them as 250 to a million.

The qualifications for belonging to what I call the more select part are, in my mind, that a man should have distinguished himself pretty frequently either by purely original work, or as a leader of opinion. I wholly exclude notoriety obtained by a single act. This is a fairly, well-defined line, because there is not room for many men to be eminent. Each interest or idea has its mouthpiece, and a man who has attained and can maintain his position as the representative of a party or an idea, naturally becomes much more conspicuous than his coadjutors who are nearly equal but inferior in ability. This is eminently the case in positions where eminence may be won by official acts. The balance may be turned by a grain that decides whether A, B, or C shall be promoted to a vacant post. The man who obtains it has opportunities of distinction denied to the others. I do not, however, take much note of official rank. People who have left very great names behind them have mostly done so through non-professional labours. I certainly should not include mere officials, except of the highest ranks, and in open professions, among my select list of eminent men.

Another estimate of the proportion of eminent men to the whole population was made on a different basis, and gave much the same result. I took the obituary of the year 1868, published in the *Times* on January 1st, 1869, and found in it about fifty names

---

[1]*Contents of the "Dictionary of Men of the Time," Ed. 1865:*—

62 actors, singers, dancers, &c.; 72 agriculturists; 71 antiquaries, archæologists, numismatists, &c.; 20 architects; 120 artists (painters and designers); 950 authors; 400 divines; 43 engineers and mechanicians; 10 engravers; 140 lawyers, judges, barristers, and legists; 94 medical practitioners, physicians, surgeons, and physiologists; 39 merchants, capitalists, manufacturers, and traders; 168 military officers; 12 miscellaneous; 7 moral and metaphysical philosophers, logicians; 32 musicians and composers; 67 naturalists, botanists, zoologists, &c.; 36 naval officers; 40 philologists and ethnologists; 60 poets (but also included in authors); 60 political and social economists and philanthropists; 154 men of science, astronomers, chemists, geologists, mathematicians, &c.; 29 sculptors; 64 sovereigns, members of royal families, &c.; 376 statesmen, diplomatists, colonial governors, &c.; 76 travellers and geographers.

of men of the more select class. This was in one sense a broader, and in another a more rigorous selection than that which I have just described. It was broader, because I included the names of many whose abilities were high, but who died too young to have earned the wide reputation they deserved; and it was more rigorous, because I excluded old men who had earned distinction in years gone by, but had not shown themselves capable in later times to come again to the front. On the first ground, it was necessary to lower the limit of the age of the population with whom they should be compared. Forty-five years of age seemed to me a fair limit, including, as it was supposed to do, a year or two of broken health preceding decease. Now, 210,000 males die annually in the British isles above the age of forty-five; therefore, the ratio of the more select portion of the "Men of the Time" on these data is as 50 to 210,000, or as 238 to a million.

Thirdly, I consulted obituaries of many years back, when the population of these islands was much smaller, and they appeared to me to lead to similar conclusions, viz. that 250 to a million is an ample estimate.

There would be no difficulty in making a further selection out of these, to any degree of rigour. We could select the 200, the 100, or the 50 best out of the 250, without much uncertainty. But I do not see my way to work downwards. If I were asked to choose the thousand per million best men, I should feel we had descended to a level where there existed no sure data for guidance, where accident and opportunity had undue influence, and where it was impossible to distinguish general eminence from local reputation, or from mere notoriety.

These considerations define the sense in which I propose to employ the word "eminent." When I speak of an eminent man, I mean one who has achieved a position that is attained by only 250 persons in each million of men, or by one person in each 4,000. 4,000 is a very large number—difficult for persons to realize who are not accustomed to deal with great assemblages. On the most brilliant of starlight nights there are never so many as 4,000 stars visible to the naked eye at the same time; yet we feel it to be an extraordinary distinction to a star to be accounted as the brightest in the sky. This, be it remembered, is my narrowest area of selection. I propose to introduce no name whatever into my lists of kinsmen (unless it be marked off from the rest by brackets) that is less distinguished.

The mass of those with whom I deal are far more rigidly selected—many are as one in a million, and not a few as one of many millions. I use the term "illustrious" when speaking of these. They are men whom the whole intelligent part of the nation mourns when they die; who have, or deserve to have, a public funeral; and who rank in future ages as historical characters.

Permit me to add a word upon the meaning of a million, being a number so enormous as to be difficult to conceive. It is well to have a standard by which to realize it. Mine will be understood by many Londoners; it is as follows:—One summer day I passed the afternoon in Bushey Park to see the magnificent spectacle of its avenue of horse-chestnut trees, a mile long, in full flower. As the hours passed by, it occurred to me to try to count the number of spikes of flowers facing the drive on one side of the long avenue—I mean all the spikes that were visible in full sunshine on one side of the road. Accordingly, I fixed upon a tree of average bulk and flower, and drew imaginary lines—first halving the tree, then quartering, and so on, until I arrived at a sub-division that was not too large to allow of my counting the spikes of flowers it included. I did this with three different trees, and arrived as pretty much the same result: as well as I recollect, the three estimates were as nine, ten, and eleven. Then I counted the trees in the avenue, and, multiplying all together, I found the spikes to be just about 100,000 in number. Ever since then, whenever a million is mentioned, I recall the long perspective of the avenue of Bushey Park, with its stately chestnuts clothed from top to bottom with spikes of flowers, bright in the sunshine, and I imagine a similarly continuous floral band, of ten miles in length.

In illustration of the value of the extreme rigour implied by a selection of one in a million, I will take the following instance. The Oxford and Chambridge boat-race excites almost a national enthusiasm, and the men who represent their Universities as competing crews have good reason to be proud of being the selected champions of such large bodies. The crew of each boat consists of eight men, selected out of about 800 students; namely, the available undergraduates of about two successive years. In other words, the selection that is popularly felt to be so strict, is only as one in a hundred. Now, suppose there had been so vast a number of universities that it would have been possible to bring together 800 men, each of whom had pulled in a University crew, and that from this body the eight best were selected to form a special crew of comparatively rare merit: the selection of each of these would be as 1 to 10,000 ordinary men. Let this process be repeated, and then, and not till then, do you arrive at a superlative crew, representing selections of one in a million. This is a perfectly fair deduction, because the youths at the Universities are a hap-hazard collection of men, so far as regards their thews and sinews. No one is sent to a University on account of his powerful muscle. Or, to put the same facts into another form:—it would require a period of no less than 200 years, before either University could furnish eight men, each of whom would have sufficient boating eminence to rank as one of the medium crew. Twenty thousand years must elapse before eight men could be furnished, each of whom would have the rank of the superlative crew.

It is, however, quite another matter with respect to brain power, for, as I shall have occasion to show, the Universities attract to themselves a large proportion of the eminent scholastic talent of all England. There are nearly half a million males in Great Britain who arrive each year at the proper age for going to the University: therefore, if Cambridge, for example, received only one in every five of the ablest scholastic intellects, she would be able, in every period of ten years, to boast of the fresh arrival of an undergraduate, the rank of whose scholastic eminence was that of one in a million.

Name: _____ **Date:** _____

1. What, according to Galton, is the relationship between a person's reputation and that person's natural abilities?

2. List three observations Galton made when he examined "Men of the Time."

3. Approximately how often does an "eminent man" appear?

4. Why, according to Galton, is London a particularly good place to find eminent men?

Charles Benedict Davenport

Heredity in Relation to Eugenics, 1911

Davenport (1866-1944) was an evolutionary biologist who led the American scientific community in supporting both genetic research and the promotion of eugenic solutions to social, political, and economic problems in the United States. In 1902 Davenport, using money secured from the Carnegie Institution of Washington, founded the Station for Experiment Evolution in Cold Spring Harbor, New York, which is today one of the most important biological research stations in the United States. In 1910 he raised money from private donors to create the Eugenics Record Office to promote the research and dissemination of information about eugenics. In this selection, Davenport demonstrated both the scientific basis for eugenics and explained the potential value of the eugenics movement in the United States.

EUGENICS: ITS NATURE, IMPORTANCE AND AIMS

▓ What Eugenics Is

Eugenics is the science of the improvement of the human race by better breeding or, as the late Sir Francis Galton expressed it:—"The science which deals with all influences that improve the inborn qualities of a race." The eugenical standpoint is that of the agriculturalist who, while recognizing the value of culture, believes that permanent advance is to be made only by securing the best "blood." Man is an organism—an animal; and the laws of improvement of corn and of race horses hold true for him also. Unless people accept this simple truth and let it influence marriage selection human progress will cease.

Eugenics has reference to offspring. The success of a marriage from the standpoint of eugenics is measured by the number of disease-resistant, cultivable offspring that come from it. Happiness or unhappiness of the parents, the principal theme of many novels and the proceedings of divorce courts, has little eugenic significance; for eugenics has to do with traits that are in the blood, the protoplasm. The superstition of prenatal influence and the real effects of venereal disease, dire as they are, lie out-

From *Heredity in Relation to Eugenics,* New York: Henry Holt and Company, 1911.

side the pale of eugenics in its strictest sense. But no lover of his race can view with complaisance the ravages of these diseases nor fail to raise his voice in warning against them. The parasite that induces syphilis is not only hard to kill but it frequently works extensive damage to heart, arteries and brain, and may be conveyed from the infected parent to the unborn child. Gonorrhea, like syphilis, is a parasitic disease that is commonly contracted during illicit sexual intercourse. Conveyed by an infected man to his wife it frequently causes her to become sterile. Venereal diseases are disgenic agents of the first magnitude and of growing importance. The danger of acquiring them should be known to all young men. Society might well demand that before a marriage license is issued the man should present a certificate, from a reputable physician, of freedom from them. Fortunately, nature protects most of her best blood from these diseases; for the acts that lead to them are repugnant to strictly normal persons; and the sober-minded young women who have had a fair opportunity to make a selection of a consort are not attracted by the kind of men who are most prone to sex-immorality.

▓ The Need of Eugenics

The human babies born each year constitute the world's most valuable crop. Taking the population of the globe to be one and one-half billion, probably about 50 million children are born each year. In the continental United States with over 90 million souls probably 2½ million children are annually born. When we think of the influence of a single man in this country, of a Harriman, of an Edison, of a William James, the potentiality of these 2½ million annually can be dimly conceived as beyond computation. But for better or worse this potentiality is far from being realized. Nearly half a million of these infants die before they attain the age of one year, and half of all are dead before they reach their 23rd year—before they have had much chance to affect the world one way or another. However, were only one and a quarter million of the children born each year in the United States destined to play an important part for the nation and humanity we could look with equanimity on the result. But alas! only a small part of this army will be fully effective in rendering productive our three million square miles of territory, in otherwise utilizing the unparalleled natural resources of the country, and in forming a united, altruistic, God-serving, law-abiding, effective and productive nation, leading the remaining 93 per cent of the globe's population to higher ideals. On the contrary, of the 1200 thousand who reach full maturity each year 40 thousand will be ineffective through temporary sickness, 4 to 5 thousand will be segregated in the care of institutions, unknown thousands will be kept in poverty through mental deficiency, other thousands will be the cause of social disorder and still other thousands will be required to tend and control the weak and unruly. We may estimate at not far from 100 thousand, or 8 per cent, the number of the non-productive or only slightly productive, and probably this proportion would hold for the 600 thousand males considered by themselves. The great mass of the yearly increment, say 550 thousand males, constitute a body of solid, intelligent workers of one sort and another, engaged in occupations that require, in the different cases, various degrees of intelligence but are none the less valuable in the progress of humanity, Of course, in these gainful occupations the men are assisted by a large number of their sisters, but four-fifths of the women are still engaged in the no less useful work of home-making. The ineffectiveness of 6 to 8 per cent of the males and the probable slow tendency of this proportion to increase is deserving of serious attention.

It is a reproach to our intelligence that we as a people, proud in other respects of our control of nature, should have to support about half a million insane, feeble-minded, epileptic, blind and deaf, 80,000 prisoners and 100,000 paupers at a cost of over 100 million dollars per year. A new plague that rendered four per cent of our population, chiefly at the most productive age, not merely incompetent but a burden costing 100 million dollars yearly to support, would instantly attract universal attention. But we have become so used to crime, disease and degeneracy that we take them as necessary evils. That they were so in the world's ignorance is granted; that they must remain so is denied.

◼ The General Procedure in Applied Eugenics

The general program of the eugenist is clear—it is to improve the race by inducing young people to make a more reasonable selection of marriage mates; to fall in love intelligently. It also includes the control by the state of the propagation of the mentally incompetent. It does not imply destruction of the unfit either before or after birth. It certainly has only disgust for the free love propaganda that some ill-balanced persons have sought to attach to the name. Rather it trusts to that good sense with which the majority of people are possessed and believes that in the life of such there comes a time when they realize that they are drifting toward marriage and stop to consider if the contemplated union will result in healthful, mentally well-endowed offspring. At present there are few facts so generally known that they will help such persons in the inquiry. It is the province of the new science of eugenic to study the laws of inheritance of human traits and, a these laws are ascertained, to make them known. There is no doubt that when such laws are clearly formulated many certainly unfit matings will be avoided and other fit matings that have been shunned through false scruples will be happily contracted.

THE METHOD OF EUGENICS

◼ Unit Characters and Their Combination

When we look among our acquaintances we are struck by their diversity in physical, mental, and moral traits. Some of them have black hair, others brown, yellow, flaxen, or red. The eyes may be either blue, green, or brown; the hair straight or curly; noses long, short, narrow, broad, straight, aquiline, or pug. They may be liable to colds or resistant; with weak digestion or strong. The hearing may be quick or dull, sight keen or poor, mathematical ability great or small. The disposition may be cheerful or mecancholic; they may be selfish or altruistic, conscientious or liable to shirk. It is just the fact of diversity of characteristics of people that gives the basis for the belief in the practicability of improving the qualities of the "human harvest." For these characteristics are inheritable, they are independent of each other, and they may be combined in any desirable mosaic.

The method of inheritance of these characteristics not always so simple as might be anticipated. Extensive studies of heredity have, of late years, led to a more precise knowledge of the facts. The element of inheritance is not the individual as a whole nor even, in many cases, the traits as they are commonly recognized but, on the contrary, certain unit characters. What are, indeed, units inheritance and what are complexes it is not always easy to determine and it can be determined only by the results of breeding. To get at the facts it is necessary to study the progeny of human marriages. Now marriage can be and is looked at from many points of view. In novels, as the climax of human courtship; in law, largely as a union of two lines of property-descent; in society, as fixing a certain status; but in eugenics, which considers its biological aspect, marriage is an experiment in breeding; and the children, in their varied combinations of characters, give the result of the experiment. That marriage should still be only an *experiment* in breeding, while the breeding of many animals and plants has been reduced to a science, is ground for reproach. Surely the human product is superior to that of poultry; and as we may now predict with precision the characters of the offspring of a particular pair of pedigreed poultry so may it sometime be with man. As we now know how to make almost any desired combination of the characters of guinea-pigs, chickens, wheats, and cottons so may we hope to do with man.

At present, matings, even among cultured people, seem to be made at haphazard. Nevertheless there is some evidence of a crude selection in peoples of all stations. Even savages have a strong sense of personal beauty and a selection of marriage mates is influenced by this fact, as Darwin has shown. It is, indeed, for the purpose of adding to their personal attractiveness that savage women or men tattoo the skin, bind up various parts of the body including the feet, and insert ornaments into lips, nose and ears. Among civilized peoples personal beauty still plays a part in selective mating. If, as is sometimes alleged, large hips in the female are an attraction, then such a preference has the eugenic result that it tends to make easy the birth of large, well-developed babies, since there is probably a correlation between the spread of the iliac bones of the pelvis and the size of the space between the pelvic bones through which the child must pass. Even a selection on the ground of social position and wealth has a rough eugenic value since success means the presence of certain effective traits in the stock. The general idea of marrying health, wealth, and wisdom is a rough eugenic ideal. A curious antipathy is that of red haired persons of opposite sex for each other. Among thousands of matings that I have considered I have found only two cases where both husband and wife are red headed, and I am assured by red haired persons that the antipathy exists. If, as is sometimes alleged, red hair is frequently associated with a condition of nervous irritability this is an eugenic antipathy.

In so far as young men and women are left free to select their own marriage mates the widest possible acquaintance with different sorts of people, to increase the amplitude of selection, is evidently desirable. This is the great argument for coeducation of the sexes both at school and college that they may increase the range of their experience with people and gain more discrimination in selection. The custom that prevails in America and England of free selection of mates makes the more necessary the proper instruction of young people in the principles of eugenical matings.

The theory of independent unit characters has an important bearing upon our classifications of human being and shows how essentially vague and even false in conception these classifications are. A large part of the time and expense of maintaining the courts is due to this antiquated classification with its tacit assumption that each class stands as a type of men. Note the extended discussions in courts as to whether A belongs to the white race or to the black race, or whether B is feeble-minded or not. Usually they avoid, as if by intention, the fundamental question of definition, and if experts be called in to give a definition the situation is rendered only worse. Thus one expert will define a feeble-minded person as one incapable of protecting his life against the ordinary hazards of civilization, but this is very vague and the test is constantly changing. For a person may be quick-witted enough to void being run over by a horse and carriage but not quick enough to escape an automobile. A second expert will define a feeble-minded person as one who cannot meet all (save two) of the Binet test for three years below his own; if he fail in one only he is no longer feeble-minded. But this definition seems to me socially insufficient just because there are moral imbeciles who can answer all but the moral question for their proper age. Every attempt to classify persons into a limited number of mental categories ends unsatisfactorily.

The facts seem to be rather that no person possesses all of the thousands of unit traits that are possible and that are known in the species. Some of these traits we are better off without but the lack of others is a serious handicap. If we place in the feeble-minded class every person who lacks any known mental trait we extend it to include practically all persons. If we place there only those who lack some trait desirable in social life, again our class is too inclusive. Perhaps the best definition would be: "deficient in some socially important trait" and then the class would include (as perhaps it should) also the sexually immoral, the criminalistic, those who cannot control their use of narcotics, those who habitually tell lies by preference, and those who run away from school or home. If from the term "feeble-minded" we exclude the sexually immoral, the criminalistic, and the narcotics such a restriction carried out into practice would greatly reduce the population of institutions or that class. Thus one sees that a full and free recognition of the theory of unit characters in its application to man opens up large social, legal and administrative questions and leads us in the interests of truth, to avoid classifying *persons* and to consider rather their *traits*.

▮ The Mechanism of the Inheritance of Characteristics

That traits are inherited has been known since man became a sentient being. That children are dissimilar combinations of characteristics has long been recognized. That characteristics have a development in the child is equally obvious; but the mechanism by which they are transmitted in the germ plasm has become known only in recent years.

We know that the development of the child is started by the union of two small portions of the germ plasm—the egg from the mother's side of the house and the sperm from the father's. We know that the fertilized egg does not contain the organs of the adult and yet it is definitely destined to produce them as though they were there in miniature. The different unit characters, though absent, must be represented in some way; not necessarily each organ by a particle but, in general, the resulting characteristics are determined by chemical substances in the fertilized egg. It is because of certain chemical and physical differences in two fertilized eggs that one develops into an ox and the other into a man. The differences may be called *determiners*.

Determiners are located, then, in the germ cells, and recent studies indicate a considerable probability that they are to be more precisely located in the nucleus and even in the chromatic material of the nucleus. To make this clear a series of diagrams will be necessary.

In the division of a cell into two similar daughter cells the most striking fact is the exact division of the chromatin. We know enough to say that the nucleus is the center of the cell's activity and for reasons that we shall see immediately it is probable that the chromatin is the most active portion of the nucleus.

The fertilization of the egg brings together determiners from two germ plasms and we know that,

on the whole, the two germ cells play an equal rôle in carrying determiners. Now the germ cells are of very different size in the female (egg) and the male (sperm). Even the nuclei are different; but the amount of chromatic substance is the same. Hence it seems probable that the chromatic substance is the carrier of the equal determiners.

But if determiners from the male are added to those from the female in fertilization it would seem necessary that the number of these determiners should double in every succeeding generation. There must be some special mechanism to prevent this result. An appropriate mechanism is, indeed, ready and had been seen and studied long before its significance was understood; this is the elimination from both the immature egg and the immature sperm of half of the chromatic material. Thus if the immature sex-cell contains four chromatic bodies (chromosomes) each mature sex-cell will contain only two chromosomes. Moreover, each of the chromosomes in the immature sex-cell is double; one half having originated long before in its maternal germ plasm and the other half in its paternal germ plasm. The mechanism for maturation is such that either the paternal or maternal component of any chromosome is eliminated in the process, but not both. Beyond the condition that one half of each kind of chromosome must go to each daughter cell it seems to be a matter of chance whether the portion that goes to a particular cell be of paternal or of maternal origin. It is even conceivable that one germ cell should have all of its chromosomes of maternal origin while the other cell has all of a paternal origin.

The important point is that the number of chromosomes in the ripe germ cell has become reduced to half and so it is ready to receive an equal half number from the germ cell with which it unites in fertilization.

▮ The Laws of Heredity

We are now in a position to understand the modern laws of heredity. First of all it will be recognized that nothing is inherited except the determiners in the germ cells; the characters themselves, on the contrary, are not directly inherited. A clear grasp of this fact gives the answer to many questions. Thus the possibility of the transmission of somatic mutilations is seen to depend upon the capacity of such mutilations to modify the determiners in the germ plasm, and such capacity has never been proved. On the other hand, the germ cells receive nutritive and other particles from the blood and they may receive also poisons from it. Hence arises the possibility of depauperization of the germ plasm and of "race poisons;" but these are exceptional and little known phenomena.

To understand the way heredity acts, let us take the case where both germ cells that unite to produce the fertilized egg carry the determiner for a unit character, A. Then in the child that develops out of that fertilized egg there is a *double* stimulus to the development of the unit character A. We say the character is of *duplex* origin. If, on the other hand, only one germ cell, say the egg, has the determiner of a character while the other, the sperm, lacks it, then in the fertilized egg the determiner is *simplex* and the resulting character is of simplex origin. Such a character is often less perfectly developed than the corresponding character of duplex origin. Finally, if neither germ cell carries the determiner of the character A, it will be absent in the embryo and the developed child. A person who shows a character in his body (soma) may or may not have the determiner for that character in all of the ripe germ cells he carries, but a person who lacks a given unit character ordinarily lacks the corresponding determiner in all of his germ cells; for, were the determiner present anywhere in his organization (including his germ cells) the corresponding character would ordinarily show in his soma.

In connection with the so-called Mendelian analysis of heredity a nomenclature has grown up which is somewhat different from that here employed. Thus the absent character is often called *recessive*, the present character *dominant* and the condition in the offspring resulting from a crossing of the two is called *heterozygous*, which is the equivalent of simplex. It is to be kept in mind that in this work "absence" does not always imply absolute but only relative absence. Thus the pigmentation of light brown hair is "absent" to "black," and "tow" is absent to light brown; but pigment is present in all these grades of hair. To avoid the confusion between relative and absolute absence the terms recessive and dominant are often used to advantage, wherever a series of grades of a character is under consideration.

These general principles may be rendered clearer by means of a Table of the different sorts of matings of germ cells. And, to focus attention, let us have in mind a concrete example; that of pigment of the iris of the human eye. In the following table P stands for the determiner of brown pigment and p for its absence. Six sorts of unions are possible.

In the case of an individual who has received the determiner for one of his unit characters from one side of the house only (say from mother), not only is the character simplex, but when the germ cells mature in that person they are of two types, namely, with the determiner and without the determiner; and these two types are equally numerous (Fig. 5). This is the phenomenon known as segregation of presence and absence in the germ cells. If both parents are simplex in a character, so that they produce an equal number of germ cells with and without the character then in a large number of offspring, 1 in 4 will have the character duplex; 2 in 4 simplex, and 1 in 4 will not have the character at all (nulliplex). This gives in the offspring of such a pair the famous 3 to 1 ratio, sometimes called the Mendelian ratio.

Now the foregoing rules, which we have illustrated by the case of eye-color, hold generally for any positive determiner or its unit character.

▮ Inheritance of Multiple Characters

In the foregoing section we considered the simplest case, namely that in which a single character is taken at a time—i.e., one parent has some character that the other lacks. We have now to consider the cases which are still commoner in nature where the parents differ in respect to two independent characters. Let, for example, the two characters be eye-pigment and hair curliness. Then each one of the six matings given in Table I for eye-color may occur combined with any one of the six matings for hair form; so that there would be a total of 6 times 6 or 36 possible

TABLE I Laws of Inheritance of Characters Based on Conditions of the Determiners in the Parental Germ Plasms

	Determiners			
Case	One Parent	Other Parent	Offspring	Characteristics of Offspring
1	PP	PP	PP, PP	All with pigmented iris (brown-eyed)
2	PP	Pp	PP, Pp	All pigmented, but half simplex
3	PP	pp	Pp, Pp	All pigmented and all simplex
4	Pp	Pp	PP, Pp, pP, pp	¼ duplex pigmented; ½ simplex; ¼ unpigmented (blue-eyed)
5	Pp	pp	Pp, pp	½ simplex; ½ unpigmented (blue-eyed)
6	pp	pp	pp, pp	All unpigmented (blue-eyed)

TABLE II Law of Condition of Eye-Characters in Children Based on the Characters of Their Parents

One Parent	Other Parent	Cases	Offspring
brown	brown	1, 2, 4	Either all of the children have brown eyes, or one fourth have blue eyes
brown	blue	3, 5	Either all children brown-eyed (though simplex) or half blue-eyed
blue	blue	6	All blue-eyed

combinations of matings. Similarly Table II would be replaced by one of 9 entries as follows.

The lessons that this enforces are: first, that characters are often and, indeed, usually, inherited independently and, secondly, that the outcome of a particular mating may be predicted with some precision; indeed, in many matings with certainty.

This study might be extended to cases of three or more independent characters but the tables in such cases become more complex and little would be gained by making them as the principle has been learned by the cases already given. In view of the great diversity of parents in respect to their visible characters the variability of children is readily accounted for.

■ Heredity of Sex and of "Sex-Limited" Characters

In most species, as in man, there are two sexes, and they are equally numerous. For a long time this equality has been a mystery; but of late years,

through the studies of McClung, Wilson, Stevens and Morgan, the mystery has been cleared up. For there has been discovered in the germ plasm a mechanism adequate for bringing about the observed results. We now know that sex is probably determined strictly by the laws of chance, like the turn of a penny. The cytological theory of the facts is as follows. One sex, usually (and herein taken as) the female, has all cells, even those of the young ovary, with a pair of each kind of chromosome, of which one pair is usually smaller than the others and more centrally placed. The chromosomes of this pair are called the X chromosomes. In the male, on the other hand, the forerunners of the sperm cells have one less chromosome, making the number odd. This odd chromosome [exceptionally paired] is usually of small size and is also known as an X chromosome. In the cell-division that leads to the formation of the mature spermatozoon, this odd chromosome goes *in toto* to one of the two daughter cells. The X chromosomes are commonly regarded as the "sex-chromosomes." With them are associated various characters that are either secondary sex characters or "sex-limited" characters. Consequently in respect to each and every such character the primordial egg cells are duplex and all the ripe eggs have one sex determiner and its associated characters. The primordial male cells are simplex and consequently, after segregation has occurred, the spermatozoa are of two equally numerous kinds—with and without the sex-determiner. The fertilization of a number of eggs by a number of sperm will result in two equally common conditions—namely a fertilized egg, called *zygote*, that contains *two* sex determiners—such develops into a female; and a zygote that contains only one sex determiner—such develops into a male. The nature

TABLE III Law of Combined Inheritance of Eye-Color and Hair Form

One Parent	Other Parent	Offspring
Brown eye, curly hair	Brown eye, curly hair	Either all brown-eyed and curly-haired; or one-fourth blue-eyed and also one-fourth of all straight-haired (with or without blue eyes)
Brown eye, curly hair	Brown eye, straight hair	All (or all but one-fourth) brown-eyed, and either all or one-half straight-haired
Brown eye, straight hair	Brown eye, straight hair	All (or all but one-fourth) brown-eyed; all straight-haired
Brown eye, curly hair	Blue eye, curly hair	All (or one-half) brown-eyed; all (or three-fourths) curly-haired
Brown eye, curly hair	Blue eye, straight hair	All (or one-half) brown-eyed; all (or one-half) curly-haired
Brown eye, straight hair	Blue eye, straight hair	All (or one-half) brown-eyed; all straight-haired
Blue eye, curly hair	Blue eye, curly hair	All blue-eyed; all (or three-fourths) curly-haired
Blue eye, curly hair	Blue eye, straight hair	All blue-eyed; all (or one-half) curly-haired
Blue eye, straight hair	Blue eye, straight hair	All blue-eyed; all straight-haired

of the germ cells in the germ gland of the future child and of the associated secondary sex-characters thus depend on which of the two sorts of sperm cells go into the make-up of the zygote.

Whenever the male parent is characterized by the absence of some character of which the determiner is typically lodged in the sex chromosome a remarkable sort of inheritance is to be expected. This is called sex-limited inheritance. The striking feature of this sort of heredity is that the trait appears only in males of the family, is not transmitted by them, but is transmitted through normal females of the family. Striking examples of this sort of heredity are considered later in the cases of multiple sclerosis; atrophy of optic nerve; color blindness; myopia; ichthyosis; muscular atrophy; and haemophilia.

The explanation is the same in all cases. The abnormal condition is due to the absence of a determiner from the male X chromosome.

If the trait be a positive sex-limited one, originating either on the father's or the mother's side, its inheritance will be more irregular.

■ The Application of the Laws of Hereditary to Eugenics

If one is provided with a knowledge of the methods of inheritance of unit characters it might seem to be an easy matter to state how each human trait is inherited and to show how any undesirable condition might be eliminated from the offspring and any wished for character introduced. Unfortunately, such a consummation cannot for some time be achieved. The reason for the delay is twofold. First, we do not yet know all of the unit characters in man; second, we can hardly know in advance which of them are due to positive determiners and which to the absence of such.

Unit characters can rarely be recognized by inspection. For example the white coat color of a horse is apparently a simple character, but experimental breeding shows that it is really due to several independently inheritable factors. The popular classification of traits is often crude, lagging far behind scientific knowledge. Thus insanity is frequently referred to a single trait. It is clear, however, that insanity is a *result* merely and not a specific trait. Some cases of insanity indicate an innate weakness of the nervous system such as leads it to break down under the incidence of heavy stress; other cases of insanity are due to a destruction of a part of the brain by a wound as, for instance, of a bullet. In some cases, through infection a wide-spread deterioration of the brain occurs; in other cases a clot in a cerebral blood vessel

may occlude it, cut off nutrition from a single locality of the brain and interfere with movements that have their centres at the affected point. Now these four results cannot be said to be due to the same unit defect; and they can hardly be compared in the study of heredity.

On the other hand, the original expectation that progress must wait on a complete analysis of unit characters proves not to be correct. There are a number of forms of insanity that are sharply separable symptomatically and structurally which have a common basis in that they are due to a nervous weakness; and "nervous weakness" may behave in heredity with relation to "nervous strength" like a lower grade, or the absence, of a highly developed character. Even without a complete analysis of a trait into its units we may still make practically important studies by using the principle that when both parents have low grades of a trait-complex the children will have low grades of that complex.

The matter of dependence of a character on a determiner or its absence is of great importance and is not easy to anticipate. For instance, long hair as in angora cats, sheep or guinea pigs is apparently not due to a factor added to short hair but rather to the absence of the determiner that stops growth in short-haired animals. One can only conclude whether a character is due to a determiner or to its absence by noting the effect of breeding likes in respect to the given trait. If all offspring are like the parents in respect to a trait, the trait (if simple) is probably a negative one. But if the offspring are very diverse, the trait (if simple) is probably due to a positive determiner and the germ cells of the parents are of two kinds; some with and some without the determiner.

The determination of unit characters is complicated by the fact that a character due to a simplex determiner often differs from one due to a duplex determiner. In the former case the character is slow in developing and frequently fails of reaching a stage of development found in the latter case. The offspring of red and black-eyed birds may have at first a light iris which gradually darkens. This fact is spoken of as the imperfection of dominance in the simplex condition.

Despite the difficulties in analysis of units of heredity and despite the complications in characters it is possible to see clearly the method of inheritance of a great number of human traits and to predict that many more will become analyzed in the near future.

Name: _____ **Date:** _____

1. What is the definition of eugenics?

2. What is the goal of eugenics?

3. What is a sex-limited charater?

4. What is the process by which knowledge from the science of heredity can be used by eugenicists?

Madison Grant

The Passing of the Great Race, 1916

Grant (1865-1937) was one of the most ardent and aggressive proponents of eugenics in the United States. Throughout the first third of the twentieth century, he argued for immigration restriction on the grounds that, if the U.S. continued to allow immigration from eastern Europe, southern Europe, and Asia, it would dilute the genetic quality of the citizenry. This selection is taken from his *Passing of the Great Race,* a book widely criticized today for its use of racism and its claims that western Europeans were inherently superior to other peoples.

RACE AND DEMOCRACY

Failure to recognize the clear distinction between race and nationality and the still greater distinction between race and language, the easy assumption that the one is indicative of the other, has been in the past a serious impediment to an understanding of racial values. Historians and philologists have approached the subject from the view-point of linguistics, and as a result we have been burdened with a group of mythical races, such as the Latin, the Aryan, the Caucasian, and, perhaps, most inconsistent of all, the "Celtic" race.

Man is an animal differing from his fellow inhabitants of the globe, not in kind but only in degree of development, and an intelligent study of the human species must be preceded by an extended knowledge of other mammals, expecially the primates. Instead of such essential training, anthropologists often seek to qualify by research in linguistics, religion, or marriage customs, or in designs of pottery or blanket weaving, all of which relate to ethnology alone.

The question of race has been further complicated by the effort of old-fashioned theologians to cramp all mankind into the scant six thousand years of Hebrew chronology, as expounded by Archbishop Ussher. Religious teachers have also maintained the proposition not only that man is something fundamentally distinct from other living creatures, but that there are no inherited differences in humanity that cannot be obliterated by education and environment.

It is, therefore, necessary at the outset for the reader to thoroughly appreciate that race, language, and nationality are three separate and distinct things, and that in Europe these three elements are only occasionally found persisting in combination, as in the Scandinavian nations.

To realize the transitory nature of political boundaries, one has only to consider the changes of the past century, to say nothing of those which may occur at the end of the present war. As to language, here in America we daily hear the English language spoken by many men who possess not one drop of English blood, and who, a few years since, knew not one word of Saxon speech.

As a result of certain religious and social doctrines, now happily becoming obsolete, race consciousness has been greatly impaired among civilized nations, but in the beginning all differences of class, of caste, and of color, marked actual lines of race cleavage.

In many countries the existing classes represent races that were once distinct. In the city of New York, and elsewhere in the United States, there is a native American aristocracy resting upon layer after layer of immigrants of lower races, and the native American, while, of course, disclaiming the distinction of a patrician class, nevertheless has, up to this time, supplied the leaders of thought and the control of capital, of education, and of the religious ideals and altruistic bias of the community.

In the democratic forms of government the operation of universal suffrage tends toward the selection

From *Passing of the Great Race: Or, the Racial Basis of European History,* New York: Charles Scribner's Sons, 1916.

of the average man for public office rather than the man qualified by birth, education, and integrity. How this scheme of administration will ultimately work out remains to be seen, but from a racial point of view, it will inevitably increase the preponderance of the lower types and cause a corresponding loss of efficiency in the community as a whole.

The tendency in a democracy is toward a standardization of type and a diminution of the influence of genius. A majority must of necessity be inferior to a picked minority, and it always resents specializations in which it cannot share. In the French Revolution the majority, calling itself "the people," deliberately endeavored to destroy the higher type, and something of the same sort was, in a measure, done after the American Revolution by the expulsion of the Loyalists and the confiscation of their lands.

In America we have nearly succeeded in destroying the privilege of birth; that is, the intellectual and moral advantage a man of good stock brings into the world with him. We are now engaged in destroying the privilege of wealth; that is, the reward of successful intelligence and industry, and in some quarters there is developing a tendency to attack the privilege of intellect and to deprive a man of the advantages of an early and thorough education. Simplified spelling is a step in this direction. Ignorance of English grammar or classic learning must not be held up as a reproach to the political and social aspirant.

Mankind emerged from savagery and barbarism under the leadership of selected individuals whose personal prowess, capacity, or wisdom gave them the right to lead and the power to compel obedience. Such leaders have always been a minute fraction of the whole, but as long as the tradition of their predominance persisted they were able to use the brute strength of the unthinking herd as part of their own force, and were able to direct at will the blind dynamic impulse of the slaves, peasants, or lower classes. Such a despot had an enormous power at his disposal which, if he were benevolent or even intelligent, could be used, and most frequently was used, for the general uplift of the race. Even those rulers who most abused this power put down with merciless rigor the antisocial elements, such as pirates, brigands, or anarchists, which impair the progress of a community, as disease or wounds cripple an individual.

True aristocracy is government by the wisest and best, always a small minority in any population. Human society is like a serpent dragging its long body on the ground, but with the head always thrust a little in advance and a little elevated above the earth. The serpent's tail, in human society represented by the antisocial forces, was in the past dragged by sheer force along the path of progress. Such has been the organization of mankind from the beginning, and such it still is in older communities than ours. What progress humanity can make under the control of universal suffrage, or the rule of the average, may find a further analogy in the habits of certain snakes which wiggle sideways and disregard the head with its brains and eyes. Such serpents, however, are not noted for their ability to make rapid progress.

To use another simile, in an aristocratic as distinguished from a plutocratic, or democratic organization, the intellectual and talented classes form the point of the lance, while the massive shaft represents the body of the population and adds by its bulk and weight to the penetrative impact of the tip. In a democratic system this concentrated force at the top is dispersed throughout the mass, supplying, to be sure, a certain amount of leaven, but in the long run the force and genius of the small minority is dissipated, if not wholly lost. *Vox populi*, so far from being *Vox Dei*, thus becomes an unending wail for rights, and never a chant of duty.

Where a conquering race is imposed on another race the institution of slavery often arises to compel the servient race to work, and to introduce it forcibly to a higher form of civilization. As soon as men can be induced to labor to supply their own needs slavery becomes wasteful and tends to vanish. Slaves are often more fortunate than freemen when treated with reasonable humanity, and when their elemental wants of food, clothing, and shelter are supplied.

The Indians around the fur posts in northern Canada were formerly the virtual bond slaves of the Hudson Bay Company, each Indian and his squaw and pappoose being adequately supplied with simple food and equipment. He was protected as well against the white man's rum as the red man's scalping parties, and in return gave the Company all his peltries—the whole product of his year's work. From an Indian's point of view this was nearly an ideal condition, but was to all intents serfdom or slavery. When, through the opening up of the country, the continuance of such an archaic system became an impossibility, the Indian sold his furs to the highest bidder, received a large price in cash, and then wasted the proceeds in trinkets instead of blankets, and in rum instead of flour, with the result that he is now gloriously free, but is on the highroad to becoming a diseased outcast. In this case of the Hudson Bay Indian the advantages of the upward step from serfdom to freedom are not altogether clear. A very similar condition of vassalage existed until recently among the peons of Mexico, but without the compensation of an intelligent and provident ruling class.

In the same way serfdom in mediæval Europe apparently was a device through which the landowners overcame the nomadic instincts of their tenantry. Years are required to bring land to its highest productivity, and agriculture cannot be successfully practised even in well-watered and fertile districts by farmers who continually drift from one locality to another. The serf or villein was, therefore, tied by law to the land, and could not leave except with his master's consent. As soon as these nomadic instincts ceased to exist serfdom vanished. One has only to read the severe laws against vagrancy in England, just before the Reformation, to realize how widespread and serious was this nomadic instinct. Here in America we have not yet forgotten the wandering instincts of our Western pioneers, which in that case proved to be beneficial to every one except the migrants.

Name: _____ **Date:** _____

1. How, according to Grant, have religious thinkers furthered the confusion over the differences between *race* and *nationality?*

2. What does Grant argue democracy tends to do to the average intelligence and ability within a given society?

Herbert Spencer Jennings

"Undesirable Aliens," 1923

Jennings (1868-1947) was one of the few American biologists who openly criticized the American eugenics movement. He was not an outright opponent of eugenics; in fact, he supported certain aspects of the movement. Rather, Jennings argued that the scientific study of eugenics, which would later be called genetics, ought to be kept independent of the propaganda surrounding the application of that knowledge to help solve social and political problems. In this piece, Jennings attacked Harry Laughlin's testimony before the House Committee on Immigration and Naturalization, which considered limiting immigration from certain parts of the world. Note that while he argued against many of Laughlin's conclusions, he also posited his own hierarchy of humans.

The Congressional Committee on Immigration has published an extensive investigation[1] by H. H. Laughlin, of the Carnegie Institution's Eugenics Record Office, on degeneracy and social inadequacy in relation to immigration, a document that is bound to influence greatly discussion and legislation on immigration. The main purpose of the work is "to gauge the relative soundness and stability of the different racial groups in the United States, which gauge, in turn would constitute a measure of their relative long time value to the Nation, especially when viewed in the light of the inborn quality of future generations" (page 731). After presenting the data, Laughlin concludes (page 755) that *"the recent immigrants, as a whole, present a higher percentage of inborn socially inadequate qualities than do the older stocks,"* and proposes measures for preventing the continuance of this introduction of inferior stocks.

On what is this conclusion based and how fully is it established?

Laughlin examined 445 of the existing 667 state and federal custodial institutions, with relation to the nativity and descent of their 210,855 inmates. The relative degeneracy of the different groups of native and foreign-born citizens is expressed by

[1]Analysis of America's Modern Melting Pot. Hearings before the Committee on Immigration and Naturalization, House of Representatives, Sixty-Seventh Congress. Third Session. Serial 7-C. Pages 725-831. Washington, 1923.

From *Survey* 51, 1923

comparing for the chief classes of defeats the quotas furnished by each group. A group that furnishes inmates of these institutions in the same proportion as it furnishes inhabitants to the United states is said to fulfill its quota by 100 per cent; if it furnishes inmates in larger proportion its quota fulfillment is above 100 per cent; if in smaller it is below 100 per cent. These percentages of quota fulfilment are the yard sticks for comparing different groups. Thus the Swiss fill but 27 per cent of their quota for criminality while the Italians yield 219 per cent of theirs, so that in the latter the proportion of criminals is eight times as great as in the former. Quota fulfilments by groups are thus worked out for feeblemindedness, insanity, crime, epilepsy, tuberculosis, blindness, deafness, deformity, pauperism of dependence on the community; and for all these types of defect taken as a unit. A number of these categories are subclassified further. In a set of eight striking diagrams the percentages of quota fulfilment are represented by the lengths of heavy black bars, so that he who runs may read. The report deals thus with the relative values of the different groups of the population, but solely from the standpoint of relative defectiveness. It requires to be supplemented, as Laughlin rewards, by a study of the valuable contributions from the same groups. As to the various sorts of defects, conspicuous differences appear in the diverse groups of the population.

What now is here demonstrated as to relative racial values; as to peculiarities native in the differ-

Quota Fulfilment: Percentages

	Actual Numbers Included	Native White, Both Parents Native	Foreign Born White Immigrants	Native White, Both Parents Foreign	Native White One Parent Foreign
Insanity	91954	73	226	108	104
Crime	63923	82	86	91	116
Feeblemindedness	15656	108	30	165	190
Dependency	14811	104	138	102	102
Tuberculosis	10101	89	133	123	123
Epilepsy	6233	93	72	180	200
Deafness	5093	134	15	82	76
Blindness	2388	156	11	57	81
Deformity	676	66	12	364	145
All defects together	210835	84	146	109	117

ent stocks, descending by inheritance into our population? In the groups making oup our population do we find strains characterized by the prevalence of particular defects? This is the question that Laughlin's data are designed to answer.

Compare first the immigrants as a whole, and their immediate offspring, with the native population. From Laughlin's summary table we may extract the more important facts. The figures are the percentages of the avereage allowance that are contributed by each group. Lower quota fulfilment of course indicates superiority.

In five of the nine categories—in feeblemindedness, epilepsy, deafness, blindness and deformity—the foreign-born are superior to the natives born of native parents; in four of these the superiority is very great. This is of course because our immigration laws exclude individuals having those defects. The cases still found have either escaped detection at entrance to the county, or have developed since entrance. In four categories the foreign-born are inferior to the natives born of native parents; in one of these—crime—but slightly inferior; in insanity, tuberculosis and pauperism or dependency, much inferior.

But this superficially favorable showing of the immigrants largely disappears when we examine the numbers of individuals in the different categories. Almost half of all the defectives fall in the single class of the insane, and it is in this class that the immigrants make their worst showing—three times as large a proportion of them falling in this class as of the natives born from native parents. Since case for case insanity is as great a defect as any other, the comparison becomes very unfavorable to

the foreign-born. For all defects taken together, the foreign-born show almost double the proportion yielded by the natives born of native parents. Of the 210,835 defectives, the latter supply 95,666, the immigrants 44,587; while in proportion to their numbers in th population we should expect 113,446 from the natives born of native parents, and but 30,592 from the foreign-born. It is mainly in insanity that the inferiority of the immigrants is shown (30,123 foreign-born insane); in respect to dependency (2961 foreign-born cases) and tuberculosis (1954 cases) it is relatively of less consequence.

What is the significance of this on the whole markedly unfavorable balance of the statistics against the foreign-born? Does it show a defective inheritance, an inferior racial constitution, in the immigrants?

As to this, two main questions arise: one relates to the possible role of diverse environments in the two cases; the other to possible differential representation of native and foreign-born in the custodial institutions.

As to the first point, the four categories in which the comparison is unfavorable to the immigrants—insanity, crime, pauperism and tuberculosis—may all be characterized as mental, moral or physical breakdowns. In determining whether these shall occur, either diverse inheritance or diverse environments may play the deciding role. The two sets of individuals compared have had extremely different effective environments. The foreign-born have come through the soul-searching ordeal of immigration; the natives have not. The immigrants have come from countries where their opportunities were less than those enjoyed by the natives of America; under the heavy handicap of ignorance of the language, customs and laws of the country in which they arrive, often also under the handicaps of poverty and lack of education, they have tried to make their way in our fierce competitive life. Will not mental, moral and physical breakdown occur more frequently in that class than in the other—even if the inheritance in the two cases be equal? Beyond question; the immigrant class are bound to show a greater proportion of defects due to environmental pressure than the native class. But how much greater? Is the total observed diversity to be so accounted for, without relation to diverse inheritances? Would an equal number of average Americans put through the process of immigration under the same conditions, show an equal number of breakdowns? No one knows. But an affirmative answer to these questions is not excluded by the data.

But, coming to the second point, do the statistics give a correct picture of the relative frequency of occurrence of the defects? Do native and foreign-born

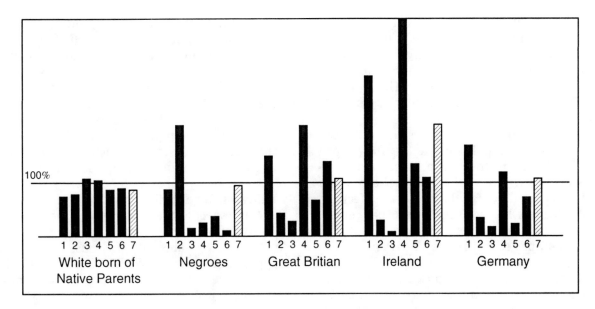

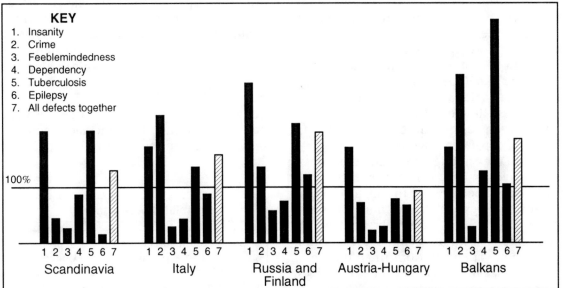

KEY

1. Insanity
2. Crime
3. Feeblemindedness
4. Dependency
5. Tuberculosis
6. Epilepsy
7. All defects together

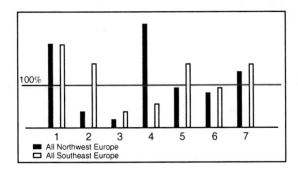

■ All Northwest Europe
□ All Southeast Europe

THESE THREE CHARTS taken together indicate the degree of "quota fulfillment" by each of the numerically important groups of immigrants studied by Laughlin, or, roughly speaking, their relative contribution to the population of institutions for the defective and dependent. For figures and a fuller explanation see the table at the foot of page 312. The column for dependency among Irish immigrants is broken by the border of the chart; it should run 1¾ inches higher. The lower chart opposite compares all the groups from northwest Europe with all those from southeast Europe for each of the seven categories of disability. Charts based on Laughlin data.

detectives find their way in the same relative proportions into the state and federal custodial institutions? Or is there possibly a differential representation of the two groups? The detectives in these institutions are but a small proportion of those that exist, even of the same types. Laughlin estimates (page 736) that only about 5 per cent of the feebleminded needing custodial care are actually receiving it in institutions. Somewhat less than 5 per cent would then be represented in his statistics. For the other classes of detectives, detailed estimates are not given. Laughlin, however, does estimate (page 749) that about one million defectives are cared for in institutions of some sort. His survey would include about 20 per cent of these. The other 80 per cent would be mainly in private or possibly in municipal institutions.

Now, it is clear from the statistics given that certain classes of the population are less fully represented than others in the state and federal institutions which Laughlin studied. The Negro is far below his quota in most of the classes of defects: in feeblemindedness he furnishes but 16 per cent of his allowance; in insanity but 53 per cent, in tuberculosis but 40 per cent (in spite of his known susceptibility to tuberculosis); in epilepsy but 12 per cent, and so on. This cannot represent the actual incidence of these defects in the Negro. Obviously the Negro does not readily find his way into public institutions (except prisons). Again, in pauperism or dependency on the community, the immigrants from the north and west of Europe give a quota fulfillment of 234 per cent, those from the south and east of Europe of but 50 per cent; in senile insanity the former section yields 311 per cent, the latter but 82 per cent. These differences seem obviously due to some diversity in customs in the two sections as to family care of dependent members.

As between the immigrants and the long-established native families, is it not probable that the former, through poverty and the absence of ties uniting them to the social fabric, must have recourse more frequently, in case of breakdown, to the governmental institutions? Would not statistics from expensive private institutions in all probability show a reversal in the proportions of native-born and foreign-born, as compared with the governmental institutions? It should be possible to collect statistics from such private institutions; until this is done, it cannot be held established that the occurrence of the defects is actually so much greater in the foreign-born as the face of the present statistics seems to show.

So far, therefore, as the direct comparison of immigrants with the natives born of native parents is concerned, it does not appear to be established that the recent immigrants are inferior in their inherited qualities. But further evidence on the matter is yielded by Laughlin's statistics summarized in the last two columns of the table given above. Here we have the proportions of detectives yielded by the first generation descendants of immigrants; natives with one or both parents foreign-born. A number of notable facts appear here. The proportion of insane (108 per cent) has fallen to less than one half what it was in the immigrants themselves (226 per cent)—in harmony with the presumption that in

them it was due largely to the conditions involved in immigration; but it is still much above the proportion found in natives born of native parents (73 per cent). As to dependency on the community, deafness, and blindness, this second generation is superior to the natives of older stock.

But feeblemindedness, epilepsy and deformity rise far above the proportions shown in the immigrants themselves; in these defects, as in insanity, the children of immigrants present a much worse record than do those born of native parents. To what can this be attributed?

With respect to the extraordinary increase in "deformity" (from 12 per cent to 364 per cent) Laughlin (page 746) states that this class includes those crippled as a result of accident and that "doubtless much of the high incidence of quota fulfillment by the children of immigrants is caused by their hazardous occupation and other dangerous features of their environment." Thus the inferiority of environment persists into the second generation; this fact may well account also for the higher percentage of crime, insanity and tuberculosis among the children of the immigrants.

But feeblemindedness and epilepsy are less dependent on environmental conditions than are the other defects: their high incidence among the second generation immigrants cannot plausibly be

---

▮ The Disability Sweepstakes

Groups of the foreign-born who, in proportion to their share in the total population of the United States, contribute the largest numbers of inmates to custodial institutions, as indicated by the Laughlin survey. Classified by types of disability.

Insanity	**Dependency**
1. Ireland	1. Ireland
2. Russia-Finland	2. Great Britain
3. Scandinavia	3. Balkans

Crime	**Tuberculosis**
1. Balkans	1. Balkans
2. Italy	2. Scandinavia
3. Russia-Finland	3. Russia-Finland

Feeblemindedness	**Epilepsy**
1. Russia-Finland	1. Great Britain
2. Great Britain	2. Russia-Finland
3. Tie between Italy and Balkans	3. Ireland

All Defects Together

1. Ireland   2. Russia-Finland   3. Balkans

Northern-western Europe takes four firsts, three seconds and two thirds. Southern-eastern Europe takes three firsts, three seconds and five thirds.

accounted for by difference in environment. This yields therefore a positive indication of greater defectiveness in the immigrant stock as compared with the native stock. There does however remain the possibility, or probability, discussed above, that the members of immigrant families have recourse more frequently to public institutions than do older native families; this, along with their inferior environment, may account for a part or all of the inferiority in their record. This is in urgent need of investigation: until this is carried out, it stands in the way of Laughlin's conclusion that "the recent immigrants as a whole present a higher percentage of inborn socially inadequate qualities than do the older stocks."

But whether this conclusion be admitted or not, some defective stocks, whether in greater or less proportion than among the natives, undoubtedly do come in with the immigrant stream. Can we discover what group or groups are chiefly responsible for this introduction of defective inheritance into our population? There are difficulties. Laughlin gives the percentage of quota fulfilment in each class of detectives for the foreign-born from the nations and geographical regions from which our immigrants come. But the real evidence of defective inheritance comes in the first native-born generation, and he does not give us data as to the specific parentage (by nationality) of the detectives in these. We know only that they came on one or both sides from immigrant parents. Further, these are children of immigrants who arrived, not recently, but according to Laughlin's calculations, in the period from 1880 to 1900, or earlier. Since that time the composition of the immigrant stream has changed. We can, therefore, get only indirect evidence, by examining the relative frequency of the various defects in the different groups of the recent immigrants, and by considering which of these groups prevailed in the immigrant stream that produced the defective offspring now in our institutions.

For this purpose Laughlin's data for the more important groups of the foreign-born may be summarized in a table. This will be confined to the European immigrants, and, in order to emphasize salient features, to the main large regions from which our immigrants come. Each of the regions or nations included is represented by at least a million foreign-born Americans, save the Balkans, with 220,000: this region is included on account of its recent importance as a source of immigrants. The classes of detectives are given in order of size, the small and unimportant classes of the deaf, blind and deformed being omitted. For comparison, the figures are given also for the native whites born of native parents, and for the Negroes.

This table will repay study. It shows that, among the European regions forming the chief sources of our immigrants, the highest proportion of defectives comes from Ireland, with a quota fulfilment of 209 per cent. Russia is second with 184 per cent, and the Balkans third with 175 per cent. In the single categories (in order of the numbers contained), for insanity Ireland is again the leader, yielding over three times its allowance (305 per cent), followed by Russia (266 per cent), with Scandinavia third (193 per cent). In crime the Balkans comes first (278 per cent), Italy next (218 per cent), Russia third (126 per cent). Owing to the very effective exclusion of the feebleminded, the quotas from all countries are small and the order of precedence perhaps without significance: as we find it, the order is, Russia first, Great Britain second, Italy and the Balkans tied for third place. In dependency, Ireland is overwhelmingly preeminent, with a quota of fulfilment (634 per cent) more than six times her allowance; followed afar off by Great Britain (218 per cent), with the Balkans a distant third (121 per cent). For tuberculosis the Balkans are first (379 per cent), Scandinavia second (214 per cent), Russia third (200 per cent). Finally, in epilepsy Great Britain is first (146

Comparative Quota Fulfilments of the Major Racial Groups in American Custodial Institutions (Percentages)

If the ratio of German-born epileptics to the total number of epileptics in the custodial institutions studied was the same as the ratio of German-born residents in the United States to the total population, the German quota fulfilment in epilepsy would be 100 per cent. Lower quota fulfilment of course indicates superiority.

	Insanity	Crime	Feeble-mindedness	Dependency	Tuberculosis	Epilepsy	All Defects Together
Native whites born of native parents	73	82	108	104	89	93	84
Negroes	52	208	16	25	40	12	93
Great Britain	157	44	27	218	72	146	113
Ireland	305	31	8	634	136	108	209
Germany	175	35	20	120	25	76	107
Scandinavia	193	35	20	76	214	14	119
Italy	158	218	25	40	124	82	145
Russia and Finland	266	126	51	72	200	117	184
Austria-Hungary	134	68	21	25	71	65	92
Balkans	163	278	25	121	379	75	175
All North and West Europe	198	38	19	234	94	80	130
All South and East Europe	189	141	33	50	148	89	143

per cent), Russia second (117 per cent), Ireland third (108 per cent).

Summarizing in sporting parlance the nations that are "placed" first, second or third in this competition, Ireland has three "firsts," including that for total detectives, and one "third." The Balkans have two "firsts and two "thirds" (including that for total detectives); Russia has one "first," three "seconds" (including that for total detectives), and one "third." Great Britain has one "first" and two "seconds"; Scandinavia and Italy have each one "second" and one "third." Unplaced are Austria-Hungary and Germany. The lowest score for total detectives falls to Austria-Hungary (92 per cent)—the only large region that yields less than its allowance. At some distance follows Germany (107) and Great Britain (113).

This showing hardly confirms the impression that Europe falls into two contrasted regions, one desirable, the other undesirable—the north and west on the one hand, the south and east on the other. The country with the worst record falls in the north and west division; that with the best record in the south and east. To the north and west division fall in the competitive scoring for high proportions of defectives, four first places, three "seconds" and two "thirds"; to the south and east division three "firsts," three "seconds" and five "thirds." Comparing the north and west division as a whole with the south and east as a whole, the former has the better record as to crime, feeblemindedness, epilepsy and tuberculosis, the latter as to insanity and dependency. For total defectives, the north and west has a small but distinct advantage, a fulfilment of 130 per cent, as against 143 for the south and east.

If we are required to draw conclusions respecting these main sources of immigrants, it is clear that these data present immigration as least desirable from Ireland, the Balkans and Russia, in that order; most desirable from Austria-Hungary (including the present Czecho-Slovakia and parts of Jugoslavia and Poland), Germany, and Great Britain, in that order.

Laughlin's figures for the smaller subdivisions of Europe, and for non-European countries, are of great interest; only certain points can be mentioned as to the proportions of all classes of defectives together. In Austria-Hungary, Austria (which included Czecho-Slovakia) with a quota fulfilment of 82 per

cent, has a better record than Hungary (115 per cent). Still smaller proportions of defectives than Austria are given by Switzerland (54), Japan (58), Wales (61). Greece (191 per cent for all defectives together) yields a worse record than the Balkans as a whole in all classes except feeblemindedness and epilepsy. Larger proportions of defectives than Ireland (209 per cent) are yielded by Australia (1,000), Serbia (600), Spain (400), India (400) Bulgaria (227) and Mexico (210); but in most of these cases the numbers involved are so small as to make the figures unreliable.

What may be concluded as to the groups that are responsible for the large proportion of apparently heritable defects appearing in the native-born offspring of immigrants (as seen in the last two columns of our first table)? Laughlin draws no explicit conclusion, but from the average ages of defectives of that group he shows that their parents arrived in the years 1880 to 1900 or earlier; also that the prevailing immigrant nations at that period were Germany and Ireland. All the lines of evidence presented thus converge upon Ireland as the chief source of defectives.

The general upshot is of a character to discourage attempts to regulate immigration on the basis of race and nationality, so far as Europeans are concerned. He would be a hardy politician who framed a law designed to discriminate against Ireland and Greece. Possibly this result is fortunate. But what should be done? At one extreme it is held, as Mr. Zangwill recently put it, that nationality is the ill with which the world is afflicted; the only remedy is to break down all barriers. A defective individual harms the world equally wherever he is; he should be allowed to go where he is best off. The nationalistic view, on the other hand, is that the United States can consider only its own welfare. To this end, Laughlin recommends not racial discrimination, but a more careful examination of the prospective immigrant in the country of origin, taking into consideration his inheritance, as indicated by the defectiveness or otherwise, of the family to which he belongs. The unit of admittance would be the family rather than the individual. If the nationalistic view is to prevail, this appears to be the only practicable method—if indeed this method itself is practicable!

Name: _____ **Date:** _____

1. What, according to Jennings, was Laughlin's conclusion in his testimony before the Congressional Committee on Immigration?

2. In challenging Laughlin's conclusions, what two questions does Jennings pose?
   1.

   2.

3. According to Jennings' analysis of Laughlin's data, from what countries do the most disabled immigrants originate?

4. What does Jennings conclude is the solution to the problems he identifies with national differences in immigration?

Harry H. Laughlin

Eugenical Sterilization in America, 1926

Laughlin (1880-1943) was the single most influential proponent of eugenics in the United States. Hired by Charles Davenport to head the Eugenics Record Office in 1910, Laughlin gave speeches, wrote books and articles, and organized both the research into eugenics and the promotion of it to social and political leaders. Throughout the early 1920s he served as the "Expert Eugenical Agent" to the United States House of Representatives and provided scientific justification to limit immigration into the United States. Laughlin was also a staunch advocate of sterilization, both voluntary and coerced, to limit the increase in "feebleminded" citizens.

One purpose of this investigation into eugenical sterilization in the United States is to determine whether a state can employ sexual sterilization for the purpose of eliminating from its family stocks certain degenerate strains. These studies were conducted primarily from the standpoint of biology, in which study the reactions of the state as an organic entity were made the basis of consideration. From this viewpoint eugenical sterilization may be defined as a purposeful attempt, consciously made by a group of the species man, to direct, in some small degree, their own evolution. Thus while it properly enters the field of public policy, and consequently of politics, it is an equally proper and possible subject for research. It is for scientific study to find the facts and to analyze the processes involved, and for the establishers of public policy to use the facts as they see fit.

As a fundamental biological study the investigation of eugenical sterilization may be made as definite as trying to determine how any other given organism, whether an individual or a group, might try to cast off handicapping influences. Such eliminative efforts have to be measured, their processes traced, and their results evaluated. With sterilization research it is particularly difficult to establish the unbiased attitude, always demanded by science, because it is a study made about the species man by

members of the same species, but this is one of the difficulties, not necessarily insuperable, always inherent in all research in eugenics. Furthermore, for the most part, unlike the case in many researches in physics or chemistry, the factors which determine eugenical conditions are usually not subject to laboratory control; but more like other investigations, many in astronomy for example, the uncontrolled subject processes of eugenical research are measured and analyzed as found. But this limitation is not always present, for oftentimes in studying individual traits and reactions which have eugenical bearings, laboratory or field control can be established. However, as in the present study of the behavior of a state, or of a large group of families, as an organic entity, such control is not feasible for experimental purposes.

Many eugenical problems are essentially those of the family, or of associated groups of families such as a state. In the present study a number of states of the American Union were found, under a definite order of society, trying to apply sexual sterilization in selected cases. A scientific analysis of this attempt called for definite biological, statistical, legislative and legal studies. Researches in these several phases were reported in "Eugenical Sterilization in the United States."* Some of these earlier studies dealt with such problems as eugenical diagnosis for use in establishing and applying the criteria of selection for eugenical sterilization, the physiological effect of definite types of sexual sterilization on definite types and ages of individuals of each sex, and the

From *Eugenical Sterilization: 1926*. Published by The American Eugenics Society, 1926.

extent and eugenical efficacy of eugenical sterilization in achieving its attempted purpose to aid in the selective elimination of certain types of degenerate family strains. The essential statistical and legal data and the practical results of these researches are reported in the present paper.

PLACE OF EUGENICAL STERILIZATION IN STATE POLICY

Generally eugenical sterilization has been demonstrated, when devoid of punitive elements, to be consistent with the constitutions of the several states in which it has been tested. Too much cannot be expected from it. It has proven to be a possible agency in combatting degeneracy. But it is only one process in the system of conscious eugenical efforts which the nation is learning to use in its attempts to control both the quality and quantity of its future population. Its primary purpose is to prevent reproduction by the most degenerate and defective human family stocks of the particular state which is applying it. As the principles of eugenics become more definitely incorporated into the general policy of the state, eugenical sterilization will have to be applied still more consistently to the lowest natural or hereditary physical, mental, and temperamental or moral levels; because, as a rule, such inadequates and producers of inadequates in the body politic are not capable of obeying, on their own initiative, laws concerning mate selection and human reproduction. These lowest human family strains must, therefore, be taken in hand by the state, for the promotion of the general welfare.

Recent history has demonstrated that in the practical application of eugenical sterilization, effectiveness from the eugenical point of view, and legal soundness in applying the bill of rights, work hand in hand. Thus eugenical sterilization is becoming a conservative and settled principle in attempts to promote the general welfare of the state.

EARLY EXPERIMENTAL LAWS

Since 1907, when eugenical sterilization was first legalized by an American state, several different types of laws have been enacted and tried out. The result has been a great deal of litigation, much of which has served to determine the constitutionality of different features in sterilization legislation. In these tests the so-called bill of rights, or the fundamental principles of Anglo-Saxon liberty, have demonstrated their soundness and their real basic character. The result has been that sterilization as a punitive measure has generally (but not always) been held to be *cruel and unusual punishment.* As a punishment, even in cases when not cruel and unusual, with the

greatest insistence, it has been held by the courts that such punishment must be administered so as not to constitute a *bill of attainder,* nor must it be *ex post facto.* It is held that every right of the defendant in criminal procedure, to defense and protection, must be applied against an order for punitive sterilization, the same as against any other legal punishment. There must be *due process of law.* But the whole tendency is to sweep aside punitive sterilization as repugnant to the spirit of our institutions because, if the cruel punishment, it is at least unusual, and there is not always a direct correspondence between hereditary degeneracy and a specific crime. The only non-therapeutic justification for sexual sterilization is to prevent reproduction on the part of persons whose offspring, according to the demonstrated rules of heredity, would probably be highly inadequate or degenerate. Discarding punitive sterilization, different states continue to legalize sexual sterilization on the purely eugenical basis. This tendency is not only sound biologically, but is sound legally. Sterilization cannot be used as a punishment; it should therefore be administered only in the interests of general racial welfare, regardless of the criminalistic tendencies of the person operated upon. Therefore the ordinary legal procedure demanded in criminal cases does not rigidly apply in non-punitive sterilization cases. Legally the closest analogy which does apply is the commitment, voluntarily or involuntarily, of defectives or other inadequates to state custodial institutions.

Recent court decisions in Virginia and Michigan uphold the right of the state to enact eugenical sterilization statutes in the interests of the general welfare. They hold also that the means employed is demonstrated to be consistent with the implied purpose, namely, the improvement of the hereditary qualities of the future population, and the benefit of the particular individual.

It is needless to say that surgical operations for pathological reasons, which incidentally destroy the reproductive function, do not come under the subject of eugenical sterilization. Such operations are fully covered in their legal aspect by the laws regulating surgical practice in general. If an operation, primarily for eugenical purposes, is intended upon either the human male or female, it is necessary that such operation be regulated by a statute on the subject of eugenical sterilization. Socially, the only valid excuse for sterilization is the eugenical purpose.

CLASS LEGISLATION

In the early laws the principal difficulty was to write a statute which would not constitute *class legislation.* This, indeed, was the principal concern of the courts in interpreting the eugenical statutes. The courts have held quite uniformly that eugenical sterilization is well within the police power of the state in promoting the general welfare. It must, however, in order to avoid class legislation, be rigidly applicable to all members of the same natural classes in the whole population. The definition of the class to which eugenical sterilization is to be applied constitutes the principal legislative responsibility. After the many laws which have already been enacted and tried out, and tested from many legal points of view, it is now clear that any state in the Union can, if it desires, enact a eugenical sterilization law which the courts will hold constitutionally sound. Enough has been learned also about the practical administration, so that adequate machinery can be set up for enforcing the statute. But the principal advance has been made by the practical eugenicist, who, by means of intensive study of defective and degenerate individuals and their family histories, is becoming expert in locating certain individuals as "potential parents of socially inadequate offspring." For some time to come, the standard for sterilization should continue to remain very low and thus avoid the possibility of biological, and consequently legal, injustice in doubtful cases. Sound family stocks must not be destroyed. As eugenical diagnosis makes headway, in the future, and the legislative form and administrative procedure in eugenical sterilization become more definitely worked out, it should be possible to raise the standard in the direction of more certain and more radical elimination of constitutionally inferior stocks.

STATE-WIDE APPLICATION

Another feature in the matter of persons subject deserves especial attention. The early eugenical sterilization laws were applicable only to inmates of the larger state institutions. The fact is that while social inadequates are in the custody of modern state institutions, they do not reproduce. Modern segregation is an effective eugenical means for preventing reproduction. Thus it was illogical to apply eugenical sterilization to institutional inmates so long as they were in the custody of the state. On the other hand, the inmates of the smaller municipal and private institutions, which are less well administered, and which inmates are admitted for a shorter period of time, are not so carefully protected against reproduction. It is now appropriate that, for eugenical purposes, the inmates of institutions, who are found to be cacogenic, should be sterilized, with ample time for convalescence, only when about to be released into the population at large. This is becoming the common state policy.

Thus in order to prevent class legislation from the legal point of view, and in order to insure eugenical effectiveness, an important reclassification of persons subjectable was found necessary. All persons in the state who are legally proven to be cacogenics (that is, to be, within the probabilities stated in the law, potential parents of socially inadequate offspring), regardless of whether such persons are inmates of state, municipal or private institutions, or in the population at large, should be equally subjectable to eugenical sterilization. The only saving conditions, which should be amply defined by law, should be those which, in a given case, amply guarantee that the particular cacogenic person will not become a parent. If the state finds it eugenically necessary to sterilize a person characterized by a given type of hereditary degeneracy, who is of a given age, and of a given likelihood of reproducing defective offspring, such person should be sterilized regardless of the wealth or social position of such person or of his near kin, and regardless also of the relation of the particular person to economic independence or state charity or custody.

In order to apply eugenical sterilization to the natural class defined in the statutes, it is necessary to have state-wide machinery. Thus, in the new laws enacted by South Dakota, Michigan and Maine, it is not presumed that all of the defectives of a certain degree of degeneracy are in state institutions. Acknowledging this fact, the law applies not only to inmates of institutions about to be released, but also to equally cacogenic members of the population at large. In some of these states, a measure of eugenical authority has been granted to the central board of charities or commission of welfare. The states of Oregon, Idaho and Montana have established State Boards of Eugenics.

LEGAL PARALLELS TO COURT PROCEDURE FOR STERILIZATION

Just as it required some time to work out the legal basis for commitment to custodial institutions for the defective classes, so now the laws and administrative procedure are about to be perfected for eugenical sterilization. Just as the commitment to custodial institutions, whether voluntary or involuntary, is an established practice in all states, so eugenical sterilization is finding its legal place. As in the case of commitment to an institution, the individual, even if he does not consent, may be seized and treated for his own benefit and for the protection of society. Also, as in the marriage laws of different states, one principal feature is the regulation of mate selection in the interests of sound offspring in the next generation. As in the case of quarantine, the so-called personal liberty of a definitely diagnosed class is restricted in the interests of the individual and of the general welfare. As in the case of vaccination, which most recently has found its legal and medical place in American life, so in eugenical sterilization the state may seize the individual and, either voluntarily or involuntarily on the subject's part, perform a surgical operation upon him. Sterilization has something of the nature of each of these processes, and in legal practice has drawn upon all of their legal procedures for its proper place in legislation, jurisprudence and administration.

COURT PROCEDURE OR ADMINISTRATIVE ORDER?

The question has many times arisen whether eugenical sterilization, duly authorized by statute, should be applied by administrative order in selected cases, or whether the matter is serious enough to demand that, in each case, a court order be issued only after proper hearings in which the subject has had ample opportunity to demonstrate his eugenical soundness. While the matter is not generally analogous to criminal procedure, it is quite parallel to commitment to custodial institutions for the insane and the feeble-minded. The tendency, which seems sound both biologically and legally, is to declare the matter a chronic and not an acute condition, and to be so important, both to the individual and to the state, that a proper hearing in court should precede every order for eugenical sterilization. Thus again the bill of rights throws its protection about the citizen in every step during the development and application of this new legal attempt to aid population conservation.

CODIFICATION OF EUGENICAL STATUTES

Ultimately, when the laws of the different states which bear upon eugenics become extensive, it will be necessary to establish a eugenical code, the same as has already been worked out for the regulation of education, of health, and of other phases of public welfare, because coördination and system are considered necessary in any well-organized modern legislative scheme with many ramifications. The future eugenical code will cover such features as human migration, marriage and mate selection, eugenical sterilization, birth control, eugenical education, and many other factors in the regulation of quality and quantity of population.

MODEL EUGENICAL STERILIZATION LAW

Both the long and the short model laws, given in Section F of this pamphlet, have been worked out after very careful consideration of all legislation, lit-

igation and administration which have characterized eugenical sterilization in the United States since its legalized beginning in Indiana in 1907. Also the eugenical and medical phases of the problem have been given due study. It is felt that the statutes outlined are sound, and that any state, in enacting either of them, would add, in some degree, to its control of future population, in the interest of a better endowed population from the physical, mental, temperamental, and moral points of view.

THE FEDERAL GOVERNMENT AND EUGENICAL STERILIZATION

In the United States, for the most part, eugenical sterilization, the same as marriage laws, is a function of the several state governments, rather than of the Federal Government. Following this division of responsibility, twenty-three of the forty-eight different states have enacted eugenical sterilization statutes of one sort or another. The District of Columbia, the outlying territories of Alaska, Hawaii, Porto Rico, and the Federal Government are without laws in this particular field. For the District of Columbia and the outlying territories, legislation logically would be enacted as in other domestic matters, particularly those relating to mate selection. For the United States Government, however, the situation is a little different. The Federal Government, except in the matter of immigration control, plays a relatively small part in population control. Indeed the states have so assumed and exercised responsibility in relation to population that the several state governments are beginning to chafe under the authority of the Federal Government in cases in which the latter admits into the United States, and consequently into the territory of some particular state, a social inadequate who does not add to the family-stock values of the state, but who, on the other hand, is a defective or degenerate and must, therefore, be maintained in a custodial institution at the expense of the state. Thus the Federal Government exercises the authority to admit an individual, while the local government must maintain any defectives which the Federal Government may have admitted. In order to correct this particular evil, either the Federal Government must select much more radically and effectively among the candidates for admission as immigrants, or, if there is no improvement in selection in the admission process, then the state governments will perhaps ask the Federal Government for permission to sue for reimbursement for the care of foreign-born defectives. The insistence on this latter proposition would serve to bring the matter to a head and thus demand a decision which would be sound both eugenically and legally.

But, including immigration control, the Federal Government has several important jurisdictions, within which, if eugenical sterilization becomes a national policy by states, the general government would have to collaborate by providing for the eugenical sterilization of certain classes. These classes are: (1) Immigrants who personally are eligible to admission, but whose family-stock standards are such that, under the model state law, they would be considered potential parents of socially inadequate offspring; (2) all persons, below the standards of parenthood set in the model state law, who are beyond the jurisdiction of the state laws, including the inhabitants of the District of Columbia, the organized and outlying territories, and the Indian reservations, also, inmates of federal institutions, and soldiers and sailors.

Among the federal agencies which could administer this law, the government could choose among the United States Public Health Service, the Children's Bureau, or the Women's Bureau of the Department of Labor. Or in case a Federal Department of Welfare were established, a Bureau of Eugenics in such department would constitute the logical executive agency. A federal eugenicist attached to any of these services could administer the law to the limited extent which the Federal Government will probably find itself ultimately called upon to apply in order to collaborate with the increasing number of state governments which are establishing the policy of eugenical sterilization. The eugenical basis and the general procedure in a federal statute should be approximately the same as that provided in the model state law.

Name: _____ **Date:** _____

1. What, according to Laughlin, is the primary purpose of eugenical sterilization?

2. Does Laughlin believe that sterilization should be used as a form of punishment? Why or why not?

3. Why is it, according to Laughlin, illogical to sterilize only those persons in the custody of state institutions?

4. Why is eugenical sterilization primarily an issue for states governments and not the federal government?

Oliver Wendell Holmes, Jr.

BUCK v. BELL,
Superintendent of State Colony Epileptics and Feeble Minded.

Argued April 22, 1927.
Decided May 2, 1927.

Holmes (1841-1935) wrote the majority opinion for the landmark U.S. Supreme Court case Buck v. Bell in 1927. In it, the Court supported the use of involuntary sterilization to prevent prisoners and mental health patients from having children and, in their opinion, producing more socially defective citizens. By the time the Court had heard this case, over half of the states in America had legalized the involuntary sterilization of people who were wards of the state, including underage children. In Buck v. Bell, Carrie Buck, a "feeble-minded" woman who had been committed to a state-run mental health facility in Virginia, had been ordered sterilized along with her mother and infant daughter. She challenged the order, and the case went all the way to the highest court in the land. The Court ruled that the state was within its right to sterilize all three women, along with any other individual it considered genetically inferior, because, "Three generations of imbeciles are enough."

Mr. Justice HOLMES delivered the opinion of the Court.

This is a writ of error to review a judgment of the Supreme Court of Appeals of the State of Virginia, affirming a judgment of the Circuit Court of Amherst County, by which the defendant in error, the superintendent of the State Colony for Epileptics and Feeble Minded, was ordered to perform the operation of salpingectomy upon Carrie Buck, the plaintiff in error, for the purpose of making her sterile. 143 Va. 310, 130 S. E. 516. The case comes here upon the contention that the statute authorizing the judgment is void under the Fourteenth Amendment as denying to the plaintiff in error due process of law and the equal protection of the laws.

Carrie Buck is a feeble-minded white woman who was committed to the State Colony above mentioned in due form. She is the daughter of a feeble-minded mother in the same institution, and the mother of an illegitimate feeble-minded child.

She was eighteen years old at the time of the trial of her case in the Circuit Court in the latter part of 1924. An Act of Virginia approved March 20, 1924 (Laws 1924, c. 394) recites that the health of the patient and the welfare of society may be promoted in certain cases by the sterilization of mental defectives, under careful safeguard, etc.; that the sterilization may be effected in males by vasectomy and in females by salpingectomy, without serious pain or substantial danger to life; that the Commonwealth is supporting in various institutions many defective persons who if now discharged would become *206 a menace but if incapable of procreating might be discharged with safety and become self-supporting with benefit to themselves and to society; and that experience has shown that heredity plays an important part in the transmission of insanity, imbecility, etc. The statute then enacts that whenever the superintendent of certain institutions including the abovenamed State Colony shall be of opinion that it is for the best interest of the patients and of society that an inmate under his care should be sexually sterilized, he may have the operation performed

Buck v. Bell US Supreme Court Decision, 1927.

upon any patient afflicted with hereditary forms of insanity, imbecility, etc., on complying with the very careful provisions by which the act protects the patients from possible abuse.

The superintendent first presents a petition to the special board of directors of his hospital or colony, stating the facts and the grounds for his opinion, verified by affidavit. Notice of the petition and of the time and place of the hearing in the institution is to be served upon the inmate, and also upon his guardian, and if there is no guardian the superintendent is to apply to the Circuit Court of the County to appoint one. If the inmate is a minor notice also is to be given to his parents, if any, with a copy of the petition. The board is to see to it that the inmate may attend the hearings if desired by him or his guardian. The evidence is all to be reduced to writing, and after the board has made its order for or against the operation, the superintendent, or the inmate, or his guardian, may appeal to the Circuit Court of the County. The Circuit Court may consider the record of the board and the evidence before it and such other admissible evidence as may be offered, and may affirm, revise, or reverse the order of the board and enter such order as it deems just. Finally any party may apply to the Supreme Court of Appeals, which, if it grants the appeal, is to hear the case upon the record of the trial in the Circuit Court and may enter such order as it thinks the Circuit Court should have entered. There can be no doubt that so far as procedure is concerned the rights of the patient are most carefully considered, and as every step in this case was taken in scrupulous compliance with the statute and after months of observation, there is no doubt that in that respect the plaintiff in error has had due process at law.

The attack is not upon the procedure but upon the substantive law. It seems to be contended that in no circumstances could such an order be justified. It certainly is contended that the order cannot be justified upon the existing grounds. The judgment finds the facts that have been recited and that Carrie Buck, is the probable potential parent of so-cially inadequate offspring, likewise afflicted, that she may be sexually sterilized without detriment to her general health and that her welfare and that of society will be promoted by her sterilization, and thereupon makes the order. In view of the general declarations of the Legislature and the specific findings of the Court obviously we cannot say as matter of law that the grounds do not exist, and if they exist they justify the result. We have seen more than once that the public welfare may call upon the best citizens for their lives. It would be strange if it could not call upon those who already sap the strength of the State for these lesser sacrifices, often not felt to be such by those concerned, in order to prevent our being swamped with incompetence. It is better for all the world, if instead of waiting to execute degenerate offspring for crime, or to let them starve for their imbecility, society can prevent those who are manifestly unfit from continuing their kind. The principle that sustains compulsory vaccination is broad enough to cover cutting the Fallopian tubes. Jacobson v. Massachusetts, 197 U.S. 11, 25 S. Ct. 358, 49 L. Ed. 643, 3 Ann. Cas. 765. Three generations of imbeciles are enough.

But, it is said, however it might be if this reasoning were applied generally, it fails when it is confined to the small number who are in the institutions named and is not applied to the multitudes outside. It is the usual last resort of constitutional arguments to point out shortcomings of this sort. But the answer is that the law does all that is needed when it does all that it can, indicates a policy, applies it to all within the lines, and seeks to bring within the lines all similarly situated so far and so fast as its means allow. Of course so far as the operations enable those who otherwise must be kept confined to be returned to the world, and thus open the asylum to others, the equality aimed at will be more nearly reached.

Judgment affirmed.

Mr. Justice BUTLER dissents.

END OF DOCUMENT

Name: _____ **Date:** _____

1. What does the 1924 Virginia law on sterilization require?

2. What is the process by which a Virginian is to be sterilized?

3. In affirming the constitutionality of the law, Holmes gives several examples of other situations in which citizens give up individual rights for the betterment of society. Describe at least two of these situations.

1.

2.

4. To what other medical situation does Holmes refer in upholding the validity of coerced sterilization?

Margaret Sanger

"No Healthy Race without Birth Control," 1921

Sanger (1879-1966) was the premier American proponent of birth control. She worked with other American progressive reformists to encourage the widespread use of family planning and the open availability of birth control to anyone who wanted access to it. From the late nineteenth century through the mid-twentieth century, obscenity laws limited women's access to birth control, classifying it alongside pornography and outlawing its sale through the U.S. mail. Working primarily in immigrant communities and among the American poor, Sanger taught women where to obtain birth control and how to use it. In this piece, she demonstrated the relationship between the eugenics movement and the birth control movement. As you read it, keep in mind the fact that many eugenicists believed that birth control was actually dysgenic (the opposite of eugenic) because it was more likely to be used by "good quality" people and less likely to be used by the "feebleminded."

Our girls must be brought up to realize that Motherhood is the most sacred profession in the world, and that it is a profession that requires more preparation than any other open to women. This preparation must be begun in infancy; but unlike much of the dull routine of what passes for preliminary education' to-day, the prerequisites' for motherhood should be made, and luckily for us, are being made more and more interesting for girls and young women. The first requisite is, of course, sound healthy bodies—and incidentally sound healthy minds—built up by play and sport and work of the right kind.

One of the most encouraging signs to-day is that more and more girls and women are entering into sports that build up strong bodies—swimming, diving, skating, tennis and many others—and that the old ideals and fashions of the all-too-ladylike are disappearing. The old-time fashion of fainting or swooning we read about in the novels of the nineteenth century is dead. The wasp' waist is gone; and if the corset has not completely gone, it is going rapidly, with the long skirts that hampered the limbs, and the high heels that make walking a caricature. Once freed of these silly impediments women can never again give up their freedom. And if these styles

are fatal to the flaws of obesity and thinness, those defects will somehow also disappear.

I place this stress upon healthy bodies for the future mothers of the race, because I am firmly convinced that strong healthy women will not choose as the fathers of their children puny, anemic men; and thus if our girls become more and more gloriously healthy, the boys will likewise have to be. The day is passing when any puny, under-developed male can choose the mother of his children.' The new, strong young woman will only be attracted to the physically fit young man. In this matter, we may trust the girl more than the young man.

Beauty is no longer skin deep. Nothing could be more false than that silly adage. Beauty, as we are more and more coming to recognize, is not a matter of a pair of blue eyes or brown, of Mary Pickford curls, or a skilfully imposed mask of make-up. Beauty is bone deep. Beauty is health and strength and soundness of limb and body. Take care of the body and the complexion will take care of itself. Develop your body and beauty, the real beauty, not the conventional and artificial, will inevitably result.

The well-developed, strong, healthy body is the first requisite for motherhood. And that includes brain development, intelligence and spirituality as well. These latter qualities are needed in the choosing of the husband. But once these problems are sat-

From *Physical Culture*, March 1921

367

isfactorily solved, the young woman may yet be un-prepared for motherhood. If she has been a working woman, she will probably need rest and relaxation before undertaking the supreme task of maternity. Modern life, especially modern city life, is becoming more and more complex. Living conditions are diffi-cult. New homes are hard to find; they are moreover expensive. Under such conditions, while it may be most advisable for the young couple to marry, it may be financially impossible or impractical to bring children into the world the first years of marriage. This is especially true of city dwellers, where high rents and the high cost of living must first be met and mastered. Birth control, in one form or another, is then the most practical solution of this difficulty, and intelligent and irreproachable young married people are, more and more, in the interest of their children and the proper spacing' of their families, becoming adherents of this doctrine.

Even after marriage many young women nowa-days are continuing their professional or business careers because they wish to share the burden of homemaking with their husbands, and because they are no longer content to be mere household drudges in a two-by-four flat. They are ambitious. They want to welcome their children into a real home with real advantages. Physical fitness being the first great requirement for parenthood, the young married woman cannot be too selfish regard-ing her own health. She must guard it jealously; and she is always justified in refusing to sacrifice this health for sentimental reasons. It is her own most precious treasure as well as that of the whole race. With the physical exercises and sports I men-tioned above, there is an equal and no less impor-tant complementary need of complete relaxation and rest. Too much importance cannot be put on the value of deep untroubled sleep as the com-pletest and sweetest restorer of tired nerves and muscles.

Only secondary to the menace of the great racial diseases is the danger of fatigue to potential moth-erhood. This truth was brought home to me last summer when I went to Scotland to find out for myself the conditions surrounding motherhood among the workers there. I visited Rosythe, a village made during the war for the housing of dockwork-ers of the river Forth. Housing conditions there were of course far above the average in comfort and cleanliness. They were occupied for the most part by dockworkers and their wives who had come from Lancashire.

Now under the admirable conditions prevailing there, one had good reason to expect that the babies—and there were hundreds of them—would be at least a bit above the average in health and live-liness. But there were large numbers of them who, in spite of their appearance of being well fed and well cared for, nevertheless, were wistfully lack-adaisical and lazy. They were not so lively as regu-lar' babies. Nor were they, I was assured by nurses and physicians, the victims of any hereditary dis-eases. What then was the matter?

They were born tired. Their mothers were tired. These women, as I soon found out once I began to follow this interesting clue, had been tired practi-cally all their lives. Obliged at the age of nine or ten to put in long, monotonous, fatiguing hours in the mills and factories of Lancashire, their bodies be-came misshapen. And these poor women had prac-tically upon their marriage, been plunged directly into the task of motherhood. There had been no in-terval of rest and relaxation, no recovery from the permanent fatigue of mill and factory. Their chil-dren were born tired. There is a temporary fatigue and a permanent fatigue. The influence of the mother on her child is one so obvious that it is evi-dent to all, and yet only now are we beginning to wake up to its tremendous, its almost overwhelm-ing importance to the next generation and the whole future of our race.

The whole tendency of the new psychology is to trace the troubles and the weaknesses of our adult life (the physical and the psychical always closely interacting) back to the shocks, the hurts, the mis-eries of childhood. More and more infancy and childhood are becoming the most important period of life. If we take care of the children, we may be sure that they will soon take care of themselves. It is in the realization of the tremendous importance of each and every child brought in to this world, that the exponents of birth control emphasize the ne-cessity, by means of the limitation of parenthood, of expending a thousand times more care and at-tention upon every child than is the good fortune of any child to receive now.

Every mother and mother-to-be should protect the fundamental rights of her babies and in fact of all babies. Baby's rights' have been well formulated by my friend Marie Carmichael Stopes: They are:

1. To be wanted.
2. To be loved before birth as well as after birth.
3. To be given a body untainted by a heritable disease, uncontaminated by any of the racial poisons.
4. To be fed on the food that nature supplies, or, if that fails, the very nearest substitute that can be discovered.
5. To have fresh air to breathe; to play in the sun-shine with his limbs free in the air; to crawl about on sweet clean grass.

6. When he is good to do what a baby wants to do and not what his parents want; for instance, to sleep most of his time, not to sit up and crow in response to having his cheeks pinched or his sides tickled.

7. When he is naughty, to do what his parents want and not what he wants; to be made to understand the law of the jungle.' From his earliest days he must be disciplined in relation to the great physical facts of existence, to which he will always hereafter have to bow. The sooner he comprehends this, the better for his future.

If intelligent and wide awake mothers of these United States would protect these rights not only for their own children but for all, motherhood would then be truly mobilized. When we see little children occasionally cuffed, kicked, dragged, pulled, shoved, and cursed through the streets or crowds of our great cities, our blood boils and we are often thoughtlessly angered. But look into the situation. You will find, as so often I have found, that the poor mother is the victim of fatigue. Her family is too large; she is distracted; and the unfortunate child becomes the butt of the poor woman's nervous, mental and physical fatigue. It is better to prevent the recurrence of this overworked and overtired motherhood than to place the blame on these victims of our present legalized barbarism.

Here is another grave danger that confronts even the physically fit young mother. Few women are strong enough to retain their normal health and strength under the ordeal of rapid successions of pregnancy, childbearing and child rearing with no well-spaced intervals of rest and relaxation. This is a point that most opponents of Birth Control forget or ignore, failing absolutely to note the inevitable and unavoidable fatigue of the poor mother and the deplorable reaction of this fatigue upon her children. In the supreme self-sacrifice of motherhood, women often forget their duty to the children they have already brought into the world, and in submitting to successive pregnancies, find that they have wrecked their own youth and health and thus become themselves prematurely old and worn out.

If the healthy and intelligent motherhood that is now becoming a hopeful reality in our society were the only factor in the situation to reckon with, all would be well. But to-day, as always in the past, such mothers find themselves surrounded by less healthy, less intelligent, less discriminating mothers. And the children of feeble-minded, the diseased and the mentally dwarfed drag down the standards of schools and society. It is one of the strange paradoxes of human existence that while health itself is not contagious or infectious, diseases—the great social scourges—are. So that health, so precious to the individual and the race, must continually defend itself, defend itself against the inroads of disease and its baneful train of evils and miseries.

Therefore, if motherhood is to be mobilized for the protection of the children, the intelligent mother cannot and will not confine her attention and interest merely to her own home. It is to her interest that all the children of the families of her community and country be endowed with the birthright of health and happiness. Neither in the neighborhood nor the school should the progress of the normal, healthy, growing child be impeded by those poor little victims of hereditary disease whose bodies and brains are incurably subnormal from the start. While everything must be done to right the wrong that was committed in bringing them with such tragic handicaps into this world, it is certainly not the children of the next generation—the veritable torchbearers of the race—upon whose shoulders this load should be placed.

Many fine women in America to-day are courageously facing this problems of less fortunate mothers and children, are realizing that motherhood to be true and beautiful must extend its power beyond the individual home, are realizing that motherhood must be a socialized force, and are seeking to express this feeling in various charities.

They support milk stations, nutrition clinics, charitable institutions of all kinds, and advocate maternity bills in the state and federal legislatures which seek to improve the conditions under which children are brought into the world. But none of these measures, I am convinced really strikes at the root of the evil. Legislation may do something to lessen evils, but it cannot by itself prevent them. The crying need is not for palliatives but for prevention, for the dissemination of knowledge of Birth Control.

What we need is the spread, gradual but sure, of intelligence to all mothers. This can be done only by the co-operation of the awakened mothers of America, counseling and helping the less fortunate and unenlightened mothers with whom they come in contact. It will be a day -[by]- day, unending and often thankless task, [but] gradually the woman who courageously undertakes it will see the beneficial results of her influence, and the growth of a true hygienic and healthful power. She will discover that the response among the poor women of her acquaintance is truly touching and their immense gratitude will be her great reward.

Understand that I do not mean by this a prying into the lives and affairs of other women. I object to "butting in." Tact is one of the first essentials in these matters as in everything else. But on the basis of the eternal dignity of motherhood, in the interests of the children, you will find that there is a strong bond between all mothers. It is an easy thing to inspire the confidence of the mother who is now the victim of a grave social injustice.

Speak always of the sacred and moral value of health, both for the mother and the child. Is it not possible that out of this spirit of mobilized motherhood, there may grow up a great power among women which can be so organized as to prevent the repetition of all these menaces to the next generation? I am optimistic enough to believe so.

I am convinced that the question of Birth Control most dramatically illuminates the present slavery of motherhood in America. Whatever your present ideas on this pressing problem are, however unimportant it may seem to you personally, try to understand its relation to the great problems that confront the whole world to-day.

I have discovered that many who oppose it are not in the least informed on the great problems of parenthood and population. Therefore, aiming for the true mobilization of motherhood, let me make these few suggestions to every mother and every other woman in the country.

Find out for yourself the laws in your State concerning the dissemination of Birth Control information.

Find out for yourself the opinion of your family physician concerning the wisdom of such statutes.

Find out for yourself the feelings of the women of your acquaintance and the neighborhood concerning the wisdom of Birth Control and the circulation of information concerning it.

Before condemning it, let the problem be thoroughly, frankly and openly discussed.

If you are a member of a woman's club or organization, demand that the matter be presented by competent speakers on Birth Control. In this way, you can inform yourself on all the phases of Birth Control, from the point of social hygiene, eugenics, individual health of mother and child, and as a factor in fighting those great plagues of tuberculosis and venereal diseases.

This knowledge will be of the greatest aid to you in another direction. More and more we Americans, both individually and as a nation, are asked to support charities and philanthropies. Without questioning the worthiness or the value of these efforts to ameliorate the miseries of the world, we may and should make sure that we are not dropping our dollars into a bottomless pit. Therefore we are all of us justified in answering each of these appeals for charitable purposes by asking the following pertinent questions:

1. What is your organization doing in addition to alleviating the miseries you describe, toward preventing a recurrence of such conditions?
2. Do you consider the dissemination of knowledge of Birth Control as an effective factor toward the prevention of heritable diseases or conditions unfavorable to the next generation?

Many philanthropies and charitable enterprises, while admitting the efficacy of Birth Control toward the prevention of miseries in the immediate future, nevertheless cannot spread this knowledge because the supporters of the charities, they point out, do not believe in it.

An awakened and enlightened public opinion, particularly of a mobilized and militant motherhood, might accomplish in this field invaluable benefits and put us on the surest and straightest road to radiant racial health.

Name: _____ **Date:** _____

1. List three things that according to Sanger, a woman needs to do in order to be a good mother?

    1.

    2.

    3.

2. What benefits do women and children receive from the increased number of women working outside the home?

3. What problems result for women and children because of the increased number of women working outside the home?

4. What role does Sanger believe birth control plays in the health of women and children in the United States?

5. What do you think Sanger means in saying that she is concerned that we are not "dropping our dollars into a bottomless pit." What is this "pit?"

Section VI

The Scopes Trial

Butler Act

PUBLIC ACTS OF THE STATE OF TENNESSEE
PASSED BY THE SIXTY-FOURTH GENERAL ASSEMBLY
1925

Following the World War I and the widespread belief that Darwinism somehow incited at least some of the carnage that resulted from it, many Americans believed that evolutionary theory ought not be taught in public schools. By the mid-twenties, many states had considered laws that would forbid the teaching of evolution in public schools.

CHAPTER NO. 27

House Bill No. 185

(By Mr. Butler)

AN ACT prohibiting the teaching of the Evolution Theory in all the Universities, Normals and all other public schools of Tennessee, which are supported in whole or in part by the public school funds of the State, and to provide penalties for the violations thereof.

Section 1. *Be it enacted by the General Assembly of the State of Tennessee,* That it shall be unlawful for any teacher in any of the Universities, Normals and all other public schools of the State which are supported in whole or in part by the public school funds of the State, to teach any theory that denies the story of the Divine Creation of man as taught in the Bible, and to teach instead that man has descended from a lower order of animals.

Section 2. *Be it further enacted,* That any teacher found guilty of the violation of this Act, Shall be guilty of a misdemeanor and upon conviction, shall be fined not less than One Hundred $ (100.00) Dollars nor more than Five Hundred ($ 500.00) Dollars for each offense.

Section 3. *Be it further enacted,* That this Act take effect from and after its passage, the public welfare requiring it.

Passed March 13, 1925

W. F. Barry,
Speaker of the House of Representatives

L. D. Hill,
Speaker of the Senate

Approved March 21, 1925.

Austin Peay,
Governor.

Butler Act, Tennessee Law enacted in 1925.

Name: _____ **Date:** _____

1. Specifically what did the Butler Act forbid?

2. What was the penalty for teachers who violated the law?

3. How long did it take for the Governor to sign the bill once it was passed by the state House and Senate?

H. L. Mencken

"Obituary for William Jennings Bryan," 1925

Mencken (1880-1956) was an author, journalist for the Baltimore, and editor of the *American Mercury*. An outspoken elitist, Mencken was sharply critical of the "common man," and he railed against the dangers of democracy, which he called a "boobocracy" because it lowered every individual to the same level by giving each person the same rights and abilities to control the political leaders. He attended the 1925 trial in which John T. Scopes was tried for teaching evolution in a public school, and his caustic and snobby reports shaped American's notions of what happened there. A harsh critic of William Jennings Bryan, Mencken wrote this mock obituary of him in the days following Bryan's death. It demonstrated both his hatred for Bryan and his sense of superiority over all of Bryan's supporters.

Has it been marked by historians that the late William Jennings Bryan's last secular act on this earth was to catch flies? A curious detail, and not without its sardonic overtones. He was the most sedulous flycatcher in American history, and by long odds the most successful. His quarry, of course, was not *Musca domestica* but *Homo neandertalensis*. For forty years he tracked it with snare and blunderbuss, up and down the backways of the Republic. Wherever the flambeaux of Chautauqua smoked and guttered, and the bilge of Idealism ran in the veins, and Baptist pastors dammed the brooks with the saved, and men gathered who were weary and heavy laden, and their wives who were unyieldingly multiparous and full of Peruna—there the indefatigable Jennings set up his traps and spread his bait.

He knew every forlorn country town in the South and West, and he could crowd the most remote of them to suffocation by simply winding his horn. The city proletariat, transiently flustered by him in 1896, quickly penetrated his buncombe and would have no more of him; the gallery jeered him at every Democratic national convention for twenty-five years. But out where the grass grows high, and the horned cattle dream away the lazy days, and men still fear the powers and principalities of the air—out there between the corn-rows he held his old puissance to the end. There was no need of beaters to

drive in his game. The news that he was coming was enough. For miles the flivver dust would choke the roads. And when he rose at the end of the day to discharge his Message there would be such breathless attention, such a rapt and enchanted ecstasy, such a sweet rustle of amens as the world had not known since Johanan fell to Herod's headsman.

There was something peculiarly fitting in the fact that his last days were spent in a one-horse Tennessee village, and that death found him there. The man felt at home in such scenes. He liked people who sweated freely, and were not debauched by the refinements of the toilet. Making his progress up and down the Main street of little Dayton, surrounded by gaping primates from the upland valleys of the Cumberland Range, his coat laid aside, his bare arms and hairy chest shining damply, his bald head sprinkled with dust—so accoutred and on display he was obviously happy. He liked getting up early in the morning, to the tune of cocks crowing on the dunghill. He liked the heavy, greasy victuals of the farmhouse kitchen. He liked country lawyers, country pastors, all country people. I believe that this liking was sincere—perhaps the only sincere thing in the man.

His nose showed no uneasiness when a hillman in faded overalls and hickory shirt accosted him on the street, and besought him for light upon some mystery of Holy Writ. The simian gabble of a country town was not gabble to him, but wisdom of an occult and superior sort. In the presence of city

From *American Mercury*, October 1925 by H.L. Mencken. Published by The American Mercury Reader.

folks he was palpably uneasy. Their clothes, I suspect, annoyed him, and he was suspicious of their too delicate manners. He knew all the while that they were laughing at him—if not at his baroque theology, then at least at his alpaca pantaloons. But the yokels never laughed at him. To them he was not the huntsman but the prophet, and toward the end, as he gradually forsook mundane politics for purely ghostly concerns, they began to elevate him in their hierarchy. When he died he was the peer of Abraham. Another curious detail: his old enemy, Wilson, aspiring to the same white and shining robe, came down with a thump. But Bryan made the grade. His place in the Tennessee hagiocracy is secure. If the village barber saved any of his hair, then it is curing gallstones down there today. But what label will he bear in more urban regions? One, I fear, of a far less flattering kind. Bryan lived too long, and descended too deeply into the mud, to be taken seriously hereafter by fully literate men, even of the kind who write schoolbooks. There was a scattering of sweet words in his funeral notices, but it was no more than a response to conventional sentimentality. The best verdict the most romantic editorial writer could dredge up, save in the eloquent South, was to the general effect that his imbecilities were excused by his earnestness—that under his clowning, as under that of the juggler of Notre Dame, there was the zeal of a steadfast soul. But this was apology, not praise; precisely the same thing might be said of Mary Baker G. Eddy, the late Czar Nicholas, or Czolgosz. The truth is that even Bryan's sincerity will probably yield to what is called, in other fields, definitive criticism. Was he sincere when he opposed imperialism in the Philippines, or when he fed it with deserving Democrats in Santo Domingo? Was he sincere when he tried to shove the Prohibitionists under the table, or when he seized their banner and began to lead them with loud whoops? Was he sincere when he bellowed against war, or when he dreamed of himself as a tin-soldier in uniform, with a grave reserved among the generals? Was he sincere when he denounced the late John W. Davis, or when he swallowed Davis? Was he sincere when he fawned over Champ Clark, or when he betrayed Clark? Was he sincere when he pleaded for tolerance in New York, or when he bawled for the fagot and the stake in Tennessee?

This talk of sincerity, I confess, fatigues me. If the fellow was sincere, then so was P. T. Barnum. The word is disgraced and degraded by such uses. He was, in fact, a charlatan, a mountebank, a zany without shame or dignity. What animated him from end to end of his grotesque career was simply ambition—the ambition of a common man to get his hand upon the collar of his superiors, or, failing that, to get his thumb into their eyes.

He was born with a roaring voice, and it had the trick of inflaming half-wits. His whole career was devoted to raising these half-wits against their betters, that he himself might shine. His last battle will be grossly misunderstood if it is thought of as a mere exercise in fanaticism—that is, if Bryan the Fundamentalist Pope is mistaken for one of the bucolic Fundamentalists. There was much more in it than that, as everyone knows who saw him on the field. What moved him, at bottom, was simply hatred of the city men who had laughed at him so long, and brought him at last to so tatterdemalion an estate. He lusted for revenge upon them. He yearned to lead the anthropoid rabble against them, to set *Homo neandertalensis* upon them, to punish them for the execution they had done upon him by attacking the very vitals of their civilization. He went far beyond the bounds of any merely religious frenzy, however inordinate. When he began denouncing the notion that man is a mammal even some of the hinds at Dayton were agape. And when, brought upon Darrow's cruel hook, he writhed and tossed in a very fury of malignancy, bawling against the baldest elements of sense and decency like a man frantic—when he came to that tragic climax there were snickers among the hinds as well as hosannas.

Upon that hook, in truth, Bryan committed suicide, as a legend as well as in the body. He staggered from the rustic court ready to die, and he staggered from it ready to be forgotten, save as a character in a third-rate farce, witless and in execrable taste. The chances are that history will put the peak of democracy in his time; it has been on the downward curve among us since the campaign of 1896.

He will be remembered, perhaps, as its supreme impostor, the *reductio ad absurdum* of its pretension. Bryan came very near being President of the United States. In 1896, it is possible, he was actually elected. He lived long enough to make patriots thank the inscrutable gods for Harding, even for Coolidge. Dullness has got into the White House, and the smell of cabbage boiling, but there is at least nothing to compare to the intolerable buffoonery that went on in Tennessee. The President of the United States doesn't believe that the earth is square, and that witches should be put to death, and that Jonah swallowed the whale. The Golden Text is not painted weekly on the White House wall, and there is no need to keep ambassadors waiting while Pastor Simpson, of Smithsville, prays for rain in the Blue Room. We have escaped something—by a narrow margin, but still safely.

That is, so far. The Fundamentalists continue at the wake, and sense gets a sort of reprieve. The legislature of Georgia, so the news comes, has shelved the anti-evolution bill, and turns its back upon the legislature of Tennessee. Elsewhere minorities prepare for battle—here and there with some assurance of success. But it is too early, it seems to me, to send the firemen home; the fire is still burning on many a far-flung hill, and it may begin to roar again at any moment. The evil that men do lives after them. Bryan, in his malice, started something that it will not be easy to stop. In ten thousand country towns his old heelers, the evangelical pastors, are propagating his gospel, and everywhere the yokels are ready for it. When he disappeared from the big cities, the big cities made the capital error of assuming that he was done for. If they heard of him at all, it was only as a crimp for real-estate speculators— the heroic foe of the unearned increment hauling it in with both hands. He seemed preposterous, and hence harmless. But all the while he was busy among his old lieges, preparing for a *jacquerie* that should floor all his enemies at one blow. He did the job competently. He had vast skill at such enterprises. Heave an egg out of a Pullman window, and you will hit a Fundamentalist almost anywhere in the United States today. They swarm in the country towns, inflamed by their pastors, and with a saint, now, to venerate. They are thick in the mean streets behind the gasworks. They are everywhere that learning is too heavy a burden for mortal minds, even the vague, pathetic learning on tap in little red schoolhouses. They march with the Klan, with the Christian Endeavor Society, with the Junior Order of United American Mechanics, with the Epworth League, with all the rococo bands that poor and unhappy folk organize to bring some light of purpose into their lives. They have had a thrill, and they are ready for more.

Such is Bryan's legacy to his country. He couldn't be President, but he could at least help magnificently in the solemn business of shutting off the Presidency from every intelligent and self-respecting man. The storm, perhaps, won't last long, as time goes in history. It may help, indeed, to break up the democratic delusion, now already showing weakness, and so hasten its own end. But while it lasts it will blow off some roofs and flood some sanctuaries.

Name: _____ **Date:** _____

1. List five words that Mencken used in this piece that were unfamiliar to you. Look up these five words in the dictionary and write the definitions after each.

1.

2.

3.

4.

5.

2. Why do you think Mencken used terminology that is not well-known?

3. According to Mencken, what kinds of people did Bryan enjoy spending time with?

4. Do you think the Mencken believed that Bryan was harmless? Why?

William Jennings Bryan

"The Origin of Man," 1924

Bryan (1860-1925) was an American pacifist, Nebraska congressman, three-time Democratic presidential nominee, and Secretary of State under President Wilson. In the years following World War I he campaigned in favor of laws that would restrict the teaching of evolution in public schools. Concerned about the caustic effects of evolutionary theory on children and believing that the content of public school curriculum should be controlled by the will of the people, Bryan argued that evolutionary theory did not have a place in American public classrooms. In this piece, he presented his evidence for the menace that evolution represented to modern civilization.

When astronomers discover an eccentricity in the orbit of a planet, they turn their telescopes in that direction in search of the celestial body that is drawing the planet out of its regular course. The evolutionary hypothesis is the unseen influence—not celestial by any means—which is making eccentricities in the religious orbit of Christians.

Or, to use an illustration nearer home, physicians, when they find certain diseases, arthritis, for instance, institute a search for the source of the poison that brings disorder into the body—the teeth, the tonsils, and the sinus being examined first. The evolutionary hypothesis is the source of the poison which is bringing disorder into the Church. Scratch a critic of the Bible and you are sure to find an evolutionist.

In view of the grave importance of the issue raised, let us first consider the meaning of the word evolution. It is quite evident that many believers in evolution do not understand just what the evolutionary hypothesis is. One university professor thought it meant the development of a plant from the seed. This is not evolution, but growth, the development being in a circle from seed, through plant, to seed again, just as the egg develops from egg, through chicken, to egg again.

Another professor used the development of the automobile to illustrate evolution; he said it grew from two cylinders to four cylinders, and so on.

From *Seven Questions in Dispute* by William Jennings Bryan, publisher by Fleming H. Revel Company. 1924.

This is not evolution, but invention. Man can construct a machine and improve it indefinitely, but the machine can neither construct itself nor improve upon itself. This development of the telephone was used by another evolutionist, but the illustration is faulty for the same reason. A short while ago an evolutionist, calling at my house, referred to the progress of man from a state of ignorance to a state of education, as evolution—another error in definition. Man's education is the result of training given by others according to an educational system established by people long since dead. Education does not pass from generation to generation by inheritance; it is acquired by each individual for himself with the aid of others.

WHAT EVOLUTION HAS COME TO MEAN

Evolution, in so far as it enters into the present religious controversy, means one thing and one thing only, namely, that every living thing in the vegetable and animal world is related to every other living thing, directly or collaterally; that is, that all living things are descended from a common ancestor and, therefore, those on each line are "cousins" to everything descended from the same ancestor along a different line. Darwin taught that all living things developed from "one or a few germs of life" that "appeared" on this planet about two hundred millions of years ago. Some believe that all life descended originally from a single germ. Darwin's son estimated the time at fifty-seven million years; others have estimated it differently, the estimates varying from twenty-four millions to three hundred and six millions. The central thought in evolution is, as Professor LeConte expresses it, "continuous progressive change, according to certain laws and by means of resident forces."

We cannot play fast and loose with evolution. It is a definite system although merely a hypothesis. If we accept evolution as an explanation of creation, we are not at liberty to choose our relatives. If we marry into the family of the underworld—or the world below man—we must accept kinship with every living thing—with animals that are hated as well as animals that are admired, with the reptiles that are despised as well as with the birds that delight us—even with the pestiferous insects and the loathsome vermin—with the noxious weed as well as with the palatable vegetable and the fragrant flower. Evolution is presented as a world scheme—unless it explains everything, it explains nothing.

Evolutionists are divided into two classes, atheistic and theistic. The atheistic evolutionist has evolution begin at the beginning and account for all development, including life. Theistic evolutionists begin with God, but differ as to the amount of interference they concede to the Almighty. At best, they put God so far away as to rob man of the consciousness of His presence in the life; they weaken, if not destroy, the sense of responsibility; and they discourage prayer. At present the theistic evolutionists are doing more harm than the atheists; they loudly proclaim their belief in God while they discredit the Bible, our only infallible standard of faith and conduct—the Book that gives us our conception of God and our only knowledge of the Saviour. Theistic evolution might be defined as an anæsthetic that deadens the Christian's pain while his religion is being removed.

Before considering the effect of evolution, when accepted as if it were a fact, let us inquire whether it is supported by sufficient evidence to compel a reasonable person to accept it.

First: What is a hypothesis? It is merely a guess—perfectly legitimate as a guess, but entirely different from a truth or a fact. If Darwin had called his hypothesis a guess it would not have lived a year; but the idea expressed briefly by the word "guess," when inflated into the four-syllable word "hypothesis," has floated for some sixty years upon the surface of public thought. And what is offered as proof that the evolutionary hypothesis, or guess, furnishes an explanation of the origin of the more than a million species to be found in the animal and vegetable world? (Darwin estimated the number of species at from two to three millions.) Nothing but resemblances,—and these resemblances are insignificant when compared with admitted differences.

"EACH AFTER ITS OWN ORDER"

There is enough similarity between man and the mammals to have raised the question of kinship thousands of years ago, but the proof furnished by resemblances is completely over-thrown by one fact, namely, that it has been impossible to trace any species to any other, notwithstanding the number of species and the resemblances between them. A thousand witnesses may testify to resemblances between a person at the bar and a murderer, but they are of no value if the accused can prove that he was a thousand miles away when the crime was committed. Of what weight, we may likewise inquire, are resemblances when Darwin admitted that he had never been able to connect any species with any other? Huxley declared that no connecting link had ever been found; and only two years ago the same statement was made by Professor Bateson, of Great Britain, who came all the way across the Atlantic to give that information to the scientists of America. Similarity puts us on inquiry, but it does not reveal origins. If we see houses of different sizes, built of exactly the same material, we do not say that the larger grew out of the smaller; we say that the same architect planned them all. Why deny to God the credit for originating species—at last, until one species can be traced to another?

Darwin, impressed by similarity in appearance, thought man a descendant of the monkey family. So many of the evolutionists, even teachers in our colleges, are now denying that Darwin ever hung man on the monkey family's tree that it may be worth while to give his exact words. He was far more honest than some of his apologists. Here is what Darwin said:

The most ancient progenitors in the kingdom of the Vertebrata, at which we are able to obtain an obscure glance, apparently consisted of a group of marine animals, resembling the larvæ of existing Ascidians. These animals probably gave rise to a group of fishes, as lowly organized as the lancelot; and from these the Ganoids, and other fishes like the Lepidosiren, must have been developed. From such fish a very small advance would carry us on to the Amphibians. We have seen that birds and reptiles were once intimately connected together; and the Monotremata now connect mammals with reptiles in a slight degree. But no one can at present say by what line of descent the three higher and related classes, namely, mammals, birds, and reptiles, were derived from the two lower vertebrate classes, namely, amphibians and fishes. In the class of mammals the steps are not difficult to conceive which led from the ancient Monotremata to the ancient Marsupials; and from these to the early progenitors of the placental mammals. We may thus ascend to the Lemuridæ, and the interval is not very wide from these to the Simiidæ. The Simiidæ then branched off into two great stems, the New World and Old World monkeys; and from the latter, at a remote period, Man, the wonder and glory of the Universe, proceeded. Thus we have given to man a pedigree of prodigious length, but not, it may be said, of noble quality.

Darwin went so far as to express the opinion that the chimpanzee was more likely than the gorilla to have been the ancestor of man. He says:

In regard to bodily size or strength, we do not know whether man is descended from some small species, like the chimpanzee, or from one as powerful as the gorilla; and, therefore, we cannot say whether man has become larger and stronger, or smaller and weaker, than his ancestors. We should, however, bear in mind that an animal possessing great size, strength, and ferocity, and which, like the gorilla, could defend itself from all enemies, would not perhaps have become social; and this would most effectually have checked the acquirement of the higher mental qualities, such as sympathy and the love of his fellows. Hence it might have been an immense advantage to man to have sprung from some comparatively weak creature.

While the evolutionist is prolific in fine-spun theories, there are few better illustrations of attenuated reasoning than the above quotations afford. After locating our first parents in Central Africa, Darwin asks, "But why speculate?" If he had thought of that in the beginning, he would have been saved the trouble of writing the *Origin of Species* and *The Descent of Man,* both of which are made up of speculations. He used the phrase, "We may well suppose," over and over again, and employed every word in the dictionary that means uncertainty.

At the present time, there is a tendency among scientists to get away from the explanations that Darwin formulated, such as Natural Selection and Sexual Selection, but they accept the same conclusions without giving any explanations whatever. I venture to reproduce on the following page a drawing taken from a recent book, *The Antiquity of Man,* by Arthur Keith. (Lippincott.)

It would be hard to conceive of anything more purely imaginative than this drawing. Without being able to find a single species that can be traced to any other species, these writers of scientific fiction trace relationship and picture lines of descent as if they were abundantly supplied with facts that had come under their own observation. Without being able to establish kinship between any two animals—for instance, the dog and the cat, or the sheep and the goat—they are audacious enough to attempt to connect man with all the animals below

him, and then proceed to build a philosophy of life on their unverified guesses.

Of all the arguments that evolutionists use, they seem to rely most confidently on what is known as the recapitulation argument. The fact that the fœtus (the unborn child) of a human being passes through certain changes from the time of conception until birth has been seized upon by evolutionists as conclusive proof that man has come up through the forms of life to which the fœtus-changes bear resemblance. The argument is not entitled to the weight that is given to it.

First, because the changes in the fœtus do not present a complete recapitulation of the forms through which, according to evolutionists, man has passed; the record is so incomplete that one of the proponents of this argument felt it necessary to forge fictitious proofs in the way of manufactured photographs.

But even if the record were complete, the force of the fact as testimony would be completely overthrown by a more important fact, namely, that each living thing is traceable to a single cell, and that these cells are so identical in appearance that no scientist has yet been able to detect the difference between the first cell of an elephant, a worm, an eagle, and a man. There is a difference, as shown by the development that follows—each developing according to a law impressed upon it at the beginning of its existence—although the difference cannot be found. As there is no place along this line, from the first cell on to the perfectly developed creature that comes from it, where one living thing can be transformed into another, one is driven to the seemingly necessary conclusion that each species is created distinct and separate by the Author of the Universe.

Evolutionists try to trace evolution in everything, whether physical, mental, or moral, but there is no proof that man advances toward perfection by any fixed law of nature. There is no natural law that insures an improved physical development. What civilized race is a physical improvement on the savage? What race to-day is stronger than the Grecian athletes? President Angell of Yale, himself an evolutionist, even denies that the average man of to-day surpasses the ancients in intellectual capacity. He says:

So far as we can judge by the evidence in historic times, there is no reason whatever to suppose that the native intellectual abilities of the average American citizen are in any way superior to those of the Egyptians four thousand years before Christ, or to the Homeric Greeks, or to others of the peoples of that general period in the Mediterranean basin, records of whose civilization have come more or less completely to our knowledge. ("The Evolution of Man.")

And so in morals; is that sacred unit of society, the home, better safeguarded to-day from its greatest enemy, adultery?

Christ Himself was not a product of evolution. He appeared suddenly after a barren period of four hundred years, during which time the Jewish race had not produced a great man. Even those evolutionists who regard Him as a superior teacher do not put Him at the top of an ascending scale; they do not claim that He was the outgrowth of, and a slight improvement on, some one nearly as good. He came like lightning out of a clear sky. He revolutionized the philosophy of life and introduced a new era. He had no predecessor; He has no successor. He saves, not by the slow process of education, but by a change of heart—the New Birth.

But the case against the evolutionary hypothesis is even stronger. There is not only an entire absence of evidence sufficient to support the hypothesis, but there is positive evidence that overthrows all the presumptions that have been built upon similarity.

PRESUMPTION—NOT EVIDENCE

Chemistry is the science that gives us our most intimate acquaintance with nature. It is the business of chemistry to resolve all matter into its constituent elements and to give us the characteristics and combining powers of these elements. Ninety-two original elements have been discovered, analyzed, and tabulated; so far as we know, every form of matter on the earth and in the earth is one of these elements or a combination of two or more of them. As these elements are isolated so that chemistry can, so to speak, walk all around them, it is, therefore, in position to discover every relationship that exists between particles, atoms, and electrons. If there were in nature such a force as evolution is described as being—a pushing force—an internal urge—that tends to lift all matter from lower to higher forms, chemistry would discover it. The fact that chemistry has never discovered the slightest trace or faintest suggestion of such an upward tendency is proof that it is not there—does not exist.

All of the formulæ of chemistry are mathematically exact and permanent. Take water, for instance; it is a combination of hydrogen and oxygen, H_2O. Water was on earth before any form of life appeared—we know this because no living thing can exist without water. No matter how far back the guessers may go in estimating the time that has elapsed since life appeared on the planet—no matter how many ciphers they use in estimating the vastness of the period—water was here first, and water has not changed. Neither has anything else changed, so far as chemistry can ascertain. Chemistry places

an insuperable obstruction in the path of the evolutionists—it supplies facts that more than answer all the arguments advanced in support of evolution.

The poison-bag of the serpent, the structure of the bird's wing, the battery in the electric ray, and a multitude of other characteristics in animate things cannot be explained by evolution. Anatomy presents convincing evidence that man's body was designed by an Infinite Intelligence and carefully adapted to the work required of him. His eyes, his ears, his heart, his lungs, his stomach, his arteries, his veins, his ducts, his nerves, his muscles—all his parts show that man is not a haphazard development of chance, but a creation, constructed for a purpose.

The evolutionists not only reason without facts, but they reason ridiculously. No book of fiction can compare in imaginativeness with the sober explanations of these guessing scientists. Having rejected the Bible record of creation, they find it necessary to fashion fanciful accounts of impossible changes.

Darwin, for instance, accepting as if true the proposition that man's brain is superior to woman's brain, attempted to explain it on the ground that man's intellectual powers were developed while he was still a brute by fighting for the female he preferred. Then, forgetting that he had represented the males as selecting the females, he explained that man (whom he supposes to have been once a hairy animal) became a hairless animal—how? By the females selecting the males with the least hair, it being assumed that the females, by unanimous agreement, preferred the males with the least hair; they thus bred the hair off! Must we consider this science, or just a guess?

Evolutionists attempt to explain the eye as a development by chance. The imaginary process by which the first eye developed was as follows: An animal without any eyes happened to discover one day that there was a piece of pigment or freckle on one spot on the skin. The sun's rays also discovered this piece of pigment or freckle as they travelled over the body and, converging there more than elsewhere, made it warmer there than elsewhere; this produced an irritation there instead of elsewhere, and this irritation, in turn, produced a nerve there instead of elsewhere, and the nerve developed into an eye. Then another freckle and another eye. Does any one think I am trying to libel the intelligence of the evolutionists? Dr. Fosdick, in his little book, *The Meaning of Faith*, says:

Man has grown up in this universe gradually developing his powers and functions as responses to his environment. If he has eyes, so the biologists assure us, it is because light waves played upon the skin and eyes came out in answer; if he has ears, it is because the air waves were there first, and the ears came out to hear. Man never yet, according to the evolutionist, has developed any power save as a reality called it into being. There would be no fins if there were no water, no wings if there were no air, no legs if there were no land.

Why did not the light waves keep on playing until eyes came out all over the body? There are those who can believe that an eye—that wonderful and beautiful organ—came into being in this way, and yet they cannot believe the miracles of the Bible!

The leg, according to evolutionists, developed also by chance. One guess is that a little animal without any legs one day discovered a wart on the belly—it had come without notices or premonitory symptoms; if it had come on the back instead of the belly, the whole history of the world might have been different. But fortunately this wart came on the belly, and the little animal, finding that it could use the wart to work itself along, used it until it developed into a leg. And then another wart, and another leg. Why did man stop at two legs while the centipede kept on till it got a hundred?

Not very long ago, a professor in a Pennsylvania college explained to an audience in Philadelphia that we dream of falling because our ancestors fell out of trees fifty thousand years ago; but, he says, we never dream of being hurt when we fall—his explanation being that those who fell and were killed had no descendants, and that we must, therefore, have descended from those who fell and were not killed.

Another scientist announced that the great day in history was the day when a water puppy crawled upon the land, and, deciding to remain there, became a land animal, and man's first progenitor. A dispatch from France announces that a prominent scientist has communicated with the soul of a dog and found that the dog was happy.

They are even trying to bring evolution down to the comprehension of children. Graebner, in his book, *Evolution*, quotes from *Home Geography for Primary Grades* (page 143) an evolutionist's guess about birds, as follows:

Ever so long ago, their grandfathers were not birds at all. Then they could not fly, for they had neither wings nor feathers. These grandfathers of our birds had four legs, a long tail, and jaws with teeth. After a time feathers grew upon their bodies and their front legs became changed for flying. These were strange looking creatures. There are none living like them now.

Is it necessary to believe all this tomfoolery at the risk of being called ignorant if we reject it? Evolutionists, having adopted the hypothesis that everything has developed from one or a few invisible germs of life, feel that it is necessary to explain everything, no matter how fanciful the explanation is. Don't laugh at them; they are doing the best they can; but why do they accept such a hypothesis?

Christianity does not fear any truth that science has discovered or may discover. All truth is of God, whether it is revealed in the Bible or by nature; therefore, truths cannot conflict. It is not truth that Christians object to; they object to guesses put forward without verification and substituted for "Thus saith the Lord." Newton's definition of the law of gravitation deals with a fact, and that fact has done Christianity no harm. It does not contravene a single Bible truth. So with the roundness of the earth; it is a fact, and provable, and it does not disturb Christianity. But evolution is not a fact; it is not probable; it is merely a guess, and a guess that is disastrous to religion. It leads those who accept it to look downward to the brute for interpretations of themselves. Those who believe in evolution regard man as "a bundle of inherited tendencies"—inherited from the beast. A man's whole thought and view of life is revolutionized when he looks to the jungle for his ancestry. He is none too strong when he finds inspiration in the belief that God made him for a purpose, as part of a Divine plan; made him to have dominion, and therefore responsible for every thought and word and deed.

THE LOGICAL RESULT OF A BELIEF IN EVOLUTION

The objection to evolution, however, as an explanation of life is not, primarily, that it is not true—many things that are false are scarcely deserving of attention. Neither is the ridiculousness of the explanations of evolutionists the chief reason for rejecting it, although there is more unintentional humour in these explanations than in any intended fun. The principal objection to evolution is that it is highly harmful to those who accept it and attempt to conform their thought to it. Evolution does not ruin all who accept it, neither does smallpox kill all who take it. In fact, only five per cent of those who take smallpox die of it. The spiritual mortality among evolutionists is greater than that. Bishop Candler says that a man can be both an evolutionist and a Christian, if he is not much of either.

Darwin furnishes a convincing illustration of the logical result of evolution upon man's thought and life. He began life a Christian, but in order to hold to his hypothesis he found it necessary to discard every vital truth of the Christian religion. In a letter written in his old age and published in his *Life and Letters* he tells the whole story.

He declares that, at the time he wrote this letter, he did not believe there had ever been any revelation, thus rejecting the Bible as the inspired Word of God and Christ as Son and Saviour. But he says in the letter that when (as a young man) he went south on the *Beagle* he was laughed at and called orthodox because he quoted the Bible as "an unanswerable authority on a question of mortality." Note the change. In the same letter he also declared himself an Agnostic, adding that "the beginning of all things is a mystery insoluble by us," but he explains that about the time he wrote the *Origin of Species* he believed in a First Great Cause. In this letter he asks a question which throws some light upon the pathway that he followed in his journey from Christianity to Agnosticism. He inquires:

> Can the mind of man, which has, as I fully believe, been developed from a mind as low as that possessed by the lowest animals, be trusted when it draws such grand conclusions [in regard to God and Immortality]?

He drags man down to a brute level; then he judges man by brute standards and shuts the door of heaven against him. When he first announced his hypothesis he gave God credit for placing the first germs of life upon our planet; later, when he became an Agnostic, he apologized for yielding too much to public sentiment, omitted the word "God," and changed the word "placed" to the word "appeared,"—a word which suits the atheistic evolutionist as well as the theistic evolutionist.

Benjamin Kidd, in his *Science of Power*, says that Bernhardi built his doctrine, "Might makes Right," on Darwin's doctrine, "The Survival of the Fittest." Nietzsche carried Darwinism to its logical conclusion and denied the existence of God, denounced Christianity as the doctrine of the degenerate, and democracy as the refuge of the weakling; he overthrew all standards of mortality and eulogized war as necessary to man's development.

Prof. James H. Leuba, of Bryn Mawr College, in a book entitled *Belief in God and Immortality*, asserts that religion is dying out among the educated in this country. To prove it, he sent a questionnaire to the scientists whose names he found in a book which he declares contained the name of practically every scientist of prominence. Relying upon the answers received from those selected in the ordinary way, he declares that more than half the prominent scientists do not believe in a personal God or a personal immortality. Selecting nine representative colleges and universities, he questioned students in the same way and declares that their answers show that only fifteen per cent of the freshmen had abandoned Christianity, while thirty per cent. of the juniors and forty to forty-five per cent. of the men who graduated had discarded the cardinal principles of the Christian faith. This change toward unbelief was due, in his opinion, to the influence of the cultured men under whose instruction the students passed.

Fairhurst, in his book, *Atheism in Our Universities*, gives evidence of widespread attacks on the Christ-

ian religion by teachers in our colleges and universities. Innumerable instances could be given of the influence of this sort of teaching upon young men and young women who have gone from Christian homes, Christian Sunday schools, and Christian churches into our colleges and universities, only to return with their hearts barren of faith—cynics, agnostics, or atheists. This is the poison which is thinning the ranks of the candidates for the ministry, more than half of whom lose their message while in college and turn from the highest of callings to some line of work that does not require a spiritual vision or the seeming sacrifices that ministers gladly endure because of their love for Christ and zeal for souls.

I recently heard an evolutionist, the head of the Department of Biology, in one of the most prominent colleges in the United States, say in the presence of students that he did not pray and did not believe in revealed religion. One of the leading religious papers reports a survey of one of the large universities which shows that sixty-two per cent. of the men drink, fifty per cent. gamble, and that only ten per cent. are interested in religion. The president of another college is quoted as saying that college students do not pray any more and do not understand the meaning of a personal God.

Within a few months I received a letter from a professor in one of the leading colleges for women in the East enclosing a list of questions that were to be discussed at a conference there. One question reads as follows: "Is it taken for granted that religion is an obsolescent function which should be allowed to atrophy quietly without arousing the passionate prejudice of outworn superstition?" Shortly afterwards I received a letter from a father (whose daughter attends this college) complaining of the irreligious atmosphere of the institution. Four parents, two fathers and two mothers, have complained to me that their daughters had their faith undermined in another woman's college. What shall it profit a student, boy or girl, if he gain an education and lose a soul?

What the Church especially needs, to-day, is to have its educated boys and girls return from the institutions of learning with their spiritual enthusiasm increased, so that with consecrated hearts and minds they can become the religious leaders of their respective communities. As it is, many if not most return with their interest in the Church lessened or destroyed.

The Church's ministry is suffering because of the paralyzing influence of the brute doctrine of evolution. Where do the modernists begin when they make their attacks upon the trustworthiness of the Bible? They commence with the Mosaic account of man's creation. This, they say, is antagonistic to scientific thought. To what scientific thought? To the evolutionary hypothesis. Man, according to evolutionists, was not fashioned by the Creator by a separate act, but is a lineal descendant of lower forms of life. The Bible is condemned as false because it is not in harmony with supposed evolutionary processes.

When a modernist attacks the deity of Christ, it is because the evolutionary hypothesis has no place for a Son of God, incarnate in the flesh; the supernatural and the miraculous are rejected because inconsistent with the evolutionary hypothesis. Why is the Virgin Birth disputed? Because it is miraculous and involves the supernatural; it is, therefore, in conflict with the evolutionary hypothesis.

On what ground do the modernists reject blood atonement? Because there is no place in the evolutionary hypothesis for the fall of man. Evolution teaches that man has been rising all the time, and that, therefore, there was never any need of a Saviour, but only a continuity of natural law.

And so with the bodily resurrection of Christ; it is not a matter of interpretation; the language is plain and unmistakable. The bodily resurrection of Christ is denied by modernists because, if admitted, it would make a break in the slow and continuous development which the evolutionary hypothesis assumes.

When one adopts the evolutionary hypothesis as the basis of his calculations he will, if consistent, progressively reject every vital passage in the Bible and thus drag the Bible down from its exalted position and put it in the class with man-made books. The evolutionist robs the Bible of all authority and makes it but "a scrap of paper," to be accepted, rejected, or amended according to the whim of the reader. That this is the natural and logical effect of the evolutionary hypothesis is becoming more and more apparent as the lines are being drawn in the various churches for the conflict which is to decide whether the churches will defend the Bible as the Word of God and, therefore, authoritative, or make it subject to revision by those who are described as scientists and elevated to the position of a court of last resort. H. G. Wells' *Outline of History* and Van Loon's books show what devastation may be expected when an evolutionist undertakes to rewrite the Bible.

What is the remedy? The right way is so simple that there ought to be universal agreement in adopting it.

WHAT COURSE OUGHT CHRISTIANS TO ADOPT?

First: Let the questions at issue be openly and freely discussed in every church and before every church unit, from the lowest to the supreme council of the church. Let each church member state his or her position candidly and honestly, leaving the majority to decide what the position of the church shall be. Each church has as much right to determine its position in accordance with the laws governing it as the individual has to determine his position.

There should be no bitterness. Freedom of conscience is guaranteed in this country and the guarantee should never be weakened. Freedom of speech is also guaranteed, and no restrictions on it should be permitted. The individual has a right to think for himself, to believe what he likes, and to express himself as he pleases. But freedom of conscience and freedom of speech are individual rights and belong only to individuals, as individuals. The moment one takes on a representative character, he becomes obligated to represent faithfully and loyally those who have commissioned him to represent them. A man has no more right to misrepresent a church than he has to misrepresent a political party or to misrepresent a business firm that has conferred authority upon him—no more right to embezzle power than to embezzle money. In proportion as the Church has a higher standard of morals than a political party or a business corporation, just in that proportion should the representative of a religious organization be more scrupulously loyal.

The majority has a right to rule; the minority must acquiesce in the decision rendered, or withdraw and set up its own organization with its own creed or principles or platform—three words that have substantially the same meaning. No evangelical church has ever endorsed the modernist side of any of the issues now before the Church. Until the modernist side is endorsed, the modernists, and not the orthodox members, are responsible for any discord that may enter the Church. Those who stand where the Church has stood for centuries can answer the modernists as Elijah answered Ahab when the idolatrous king upbraided the prophet of fire: "Art thou he that troubleth Israel?" The reply was, "I have not troubled Israel; but thou, and thy father's house, in that ye have forsaken the commandments of the Lord, and thou hast followed Baalim."

Second: Stop the teaching of evolution—not as a mere hypothesis, but as a fact—in church schools. It is not a fact, but merely a hypothesis. It is the Church's fault if this poisonous doctrine spreads through schools that are under church control. One test of sanity is to put the suspected person in a tank into which a full stream of water is running and tell him to dip out the water. If he has not sense enough to turn off the inflowing stream of water before he begins to dip, he is declared insane. Can the churches escape a similar judgment if they permit church schools to discredit, during the week, the Bible used in Sunday-school and church?

Likewise with public schools; teachers in public schools must teach what the taxpayers desire taught—the hand that writes the pay check rules the school. A scientific soviet is attempting to dictate what shall be taught in our schools and, in so doing, is attempting to mould the religion of the nation. It is the smallest, the most impudent, and the most tyrannical oligarchy that ever attempted to exercise arbitrary power. Dr. Steinmetz estimated the number of scientists in the United States at five thousand; Professor Leuba puts the number at fifty-five hundred; the American Society for the Advancement of Science claims less than twelve thousand members—that is about one in one hundred of our college graduates, and about one in ten thousand of our population. These scientists are undermining the Bible by teaching daily that which cannot be true if the Bible is true. These assaults upon the Bible are not based upon established facts or demonstrated truths, but, as has been shown, are built upon cobweb theories as unsubstantial as "the fabric of a dream."

If a teacher of evolution insists that he should be permitted to teach whatever he pleases, regardless of the wishes of the taxpayers, the answer is obvious. He should teach what he is employed to teach, just as a painter uses the colours that his employer desires; just as the army or navy officer uses the equipment provided by the government and directs it against those whom the government desires attacked; just as the public official carries out the will of his constituents. Would a teacher be permitted to teach in any public school in the United States that a monarchy is superior to a government in which the people rule, or to advise pupils that they should not obey the law? If we are so careful not to permit employees of the public to do other things that are objectionable, why should we permit teachers employed by the State to deny the existence of God, whose name we stamp upon our coin—"In God We Trust"—or scoff at the Bible, which our President uses when he takes the oath of office?

The Legislature of Florida, at its last session, adopted by unanimous vote a joint resolution declaring it contrary to the public welfare for teachers paid by taxation to teach as a fact any hypothesis that links man in blood relationship with any lower form of life.

The Board of the University of Texas has recently resolved that no atheist, agnostic or infidel shall teach in that university. The Governor of North Carolina has refused to allow two biologies to be used in State schools because they taught, one that man came from the ape and the other that man is a cousin of the ape.

We do not interfere with freedom of conscience or with freedom of speech when we refuse to pay a man for teaching things that we think are injurious, especially to the young. Christians are required to build their own colleges in which to teach Christianity; why should not atheists be required to build their own colleges in which to teach atheism? And the same question can be applied to agnosticism, or to any other kind of teaching objectionable to the taxpayers. If the scientists contend that they are simply teaching a scientific interpretation of the Bible, the same question arises: Why should a few people demand pay from the public for teaching a scientific interpretation of the Bible when teachers in public institutions are not permitted to teach the orthodox interpretation of the Bible? By what logic can the minority demand privileges that are denied to the majority?

EVOLUTION THE MENACE OF CIVILIZATION

In conclusion, let me add that there never was a time when the world could less afford to permit the brute doctrine of evolution to go unchallenged; it is the greatest menace to civilization as well as to religion. Belief in God is the fundamental fact in society; upon it rest all the controlling influences of life. Anything that weakens man's faith in God imperils the future of the race. That this is the natural and logical tendency of the evolutionary hypothesis must be apparent to any one; that it is the actual result in many, if not most cases, is proved by Darwin's experience, by the statistics collected by Leuba, and by the observation of any one who has mingled with the students of universities, of colleges, and even of high schools. It is time for the spiritual forces of the nation and the world to unite in opposing the teaching of evolution as a fact; all who give a spiritual interpretation to life are vitally interested in combating materialistic influences and in defending belief in God, the foundation of all religious faith. The future of the race is at stake.

Darwin's God was nowhere—he could not find him; Darwin's Bible was nothing—it had lost its inspiration; Darwin's Christ was nobody—he had an ape for an ancestor on both his father's and his mother's side. Such a Christ is impotent to save.

Evolution, theistic as well as atheistic, when carried to its logical conclusion, robs Christ of the glory of the Virgin Birth, of the majesty of His deity, and of the triumph of His resurrection. Such a Christ cannot meet the world's needs. Society, brought to the verge of ruin by a godless philosophy—by mind-worship—by learning unsanctified by love—can be revived and reconstructed only by the salvation and leadership of a full-statured Christ, whose code of morality is to endure for all ages, whose Gospel is for all mankind, and whose teachings will establish a universal brotherhood and usher in the day when swords shall be beaten into ploughshares and nations learn war no more.

Name: _____ **Date:** _____

1. What, according to Bryan, is an atheistic evolutionist?

2. What is a theistic evolutionist?

3. What evidence does Bryan present in opposition to the belief that evolution drives every living thing closer and closer to perfections?

4. What, according to Bryan, is the logical conclusion that the belief in evolution eventually leads to?

5. What does Bryan argue that a true Christian ought to believe?

Section VII

The Modern Evolutionary Synthesis

Julian Huxley

Evolution: The Modern Synthesis, 1942

Huxley (1887-1975) was an English biologist, the grandson of T. H. Huxley and the brother of novelist Aldous Huxley. In the mid-twentieth century he helped organize what he termed "the modern evolutionary synthesis," a multi-disciplinary attempt to synthesize the existing knowledge, identify shortcomings and conflicts, and agree on the essential elements of evolutionary theory. The modern evolutionary synthesis brought together statisticians, paleontologists, geneticists, and organismal biologists to present a coherent explanation for evolution. In this selection, Huxley explains the confused state of evolutionary science as it existed in the first half of the twentieth century.

THE THEORY OF NATURAL SELECTION

Evolution may lay claim to be considered the most central and the most important of the problems of biology. For an attack upon it we need facts and methods from every branch of the science—ecology, genetics, paleontology, geographical distribution, embryology, systematics, comparative anatomy—not to mention reinforcements from other disciplines such as geology, geography, and mathematics.

Biology at the present time is embarking upon a phase of synthesis after a period in which new disciplines were taken up in turn and worked out in comparative isolation. Nowhere is this movement towards unification more likely to be valuable than in this many-sided topic of evolution; and already we are seeing the first-fruits in the re-animation of Darwinism.

By Darwinism I imply that blend of **induction and deduction** which Darwin was the first to apply to the study of evolution. He was concerned both to establish the fact of evolution and to discover the mechanism by which it operated; and it was precisely, because he attacked both aspects of the problem simultaneously, that he was so successful. On the one hand he amassed enormous quantities of facts from which inductions concerning the

evolutionary process could be drawn; and on the other, starting from a few general principles, he deduced the further principle of natural selection.

It is as well to remember the strong deductive element in Darwinism. Darwin based his theory of natural selection on three observable facts of nature and two deductions from them. The first fact is the tendency of all organisms to increase in a geometrical ratio. The tendency of all organisms to increase is due to the fact that offspring, in the early stages of their existence, are always more numerous than their parents; this holds good whether reproduction is sexual or asexual, by fission or by budding, by means of seeds, spores, or eggs.[1] The second fact is that, in spite of this tendency to progressive increase, the numbers of a given species actually remain more or less constant.

The first deduction follows. From these two facts he deduced the struggle for existence. For since more young are produced than can survive, there must be competition for survival. In amplifying his theory, he extended the concept of the struggle for existence to cover reproduction. The struggle is in point of fact for survival of the stock; if its survival is aided by greater fertility, an earlier breeding season, or other reproductive function, these should be included under the same head.

[1] The only exception, so far as I am aware, is to be found in certain human populations which fall far short of replacing themselves.

Darwin's third fact of nature was variation: all organisms vary appreciably. And the second and final deduction, which he deduced from the first deduction and third fact, was Natural Selection. Since there is a struggle for existence among individuals, and since these individuals are not all alike, some of the variations among them will be advantageous in the struggle for survival, others unfavourable. Consequently, a higher proportion of individuals with favourable variations will on the average survive, a higher proportion of those with unfavourable variations will die or fail to reproduce themselves. And since a great deal of variation is transmitted by heredity, these effects of differential survival will in large measure accumulate from generation to generation. Thus natural selection will act constantly to improve and to maintain the adjustment of animals and plants to their surroundings and their way of life.

A few comments on these points in the light of the historical development of biology since Darwin's day will clarify both his statement of the theory and the modern position in regard to it.

His first fact has remained unquestioned. All organisms possess the potentiality of geometric increase. We had better perhaps say *increase of geometric type,* since the ratio of offspring to parents may vary considerably from place to place, and from season to season. In all cases, however, the tendency or potentiality is not merely to a progressive increase, but to a multiplicative and not to an additive increase.

Equally unquestioned is his second fact, the actual constancy of numbers of any species. As he himself was careful to point out, the constancy is only approximate. At any one time, there will always be some species that are increasing in their numbers, others that are decreasing. But even when a species is increasing, the actual increase is never as great as the potential: some young will fail to survive. Again, with our much greater knowledge of ecology, we know to-day that many species undergo cyclical and often remarkably regular fluctuations, frequently of very large extent, in their numbers (see Elton, 1927). But this fact, although it has certain interesting evolutionary consequences does not invalidate the general principle.

The first two facts being accepted, the deduction from them also holds: a struggle for existence, or better, a struggle for survival, must occur.

The difficulties of the further bases of the theory are greater, and it is here that the major criticisms have fallen. In the first place, Darwin assumed that the bulk of variations were inheritable. He expressly stated that any which were not inheritable would be irrelevant to the discussion; but he continued in the

assumption that those which are inheritable provide an adequate reservoir of potential improvement.[2]

As Haldane (1938, p. 107) has pointed out, the decreased interest in England in plant-breeding, caused by the repeal of the Corn Laws, led Darwin to take most of his evidence from animal-breeders. This was much more obscure than what the plant-breeders in France had obtained: in fact Vilmorin, before Darwin wrote, had fully established the roles of heritable and non-heritable variation in wheat.

Thus in Darwin's time, and still more in England than in France, the subject of inheritance was still very obscure. In any case the basic laws of heredity, or, as we should now say, the principles of genetics, had not yet emerged. In a full formulation of the theory of Natural Selection, we should have to add a further fact and a further deduction. We should begin, as he did, with the fact of variation, and deduce from it and our previous deduction of the struggle for existence that there must be a *differential survival* of different types of offspring in each generation. We should then proceed to the fact of inheritance. *Some* variation is inherited: and that fraction will be available for transmission to later generations. Thus our final deduction is that the result will be a differential transmission of inherited variation. The term Natural Selection is thus seen to have two rather different meanings. In a broad sense it covers all cases of differential survival: but from the evolutionary point of view it covers only the differential transmission of inheritable variations.

Mendelian analysis has revealed the further fact, unsuspected by Darwin, that recombination of existing genetic units may both produce and modify new inheritable variations. And this, as we shall see later, has important evolutionary consequences.

Although both the principle of differential survival and that of its evolutionary accumulation by Natural Selection were for Darwin essentially deductions, it is important to realize that, if true, they are also facts of nature capable of verification by observation and experiment. And in point of fact differential mortality, differential survival, and differential multiplication among variants of the same species are now known in numerous cases.

The criticism, however, was early made that a great deal of the mortality found in nature appeared to be accidental and nonselective. This would hold

---

[2] *Origin of Species* (6th ed., one vol. ed., p. 9): ". . . any variation which is not inherited is unimportant for us. But the number and diversity of inheritable deviations of structure, both those of slight and those of considerable physiological importance, are endless. No breeder doubts how strong is the tendency to inheritance: that like produces like is his fundamental belief." And so on.

for the destruction of the great majority of eggs and larvae of prolific marine animals, or the death of seeds which fell on stony ground or other unsuitable habitats. It remains true that we require many more quantitative experiments on the subject before we can know accurately the extent of non-selective elimination. Even a very large percentage of such eliminations, however, in no way invalidates the selection principle from holding for the remaining fraction (see p. 467). The very fact that it is accidental and non-selective ensures that the residue shall be a random sample, and will therefore contain any variation of selective value in the same proportions as the whole population. It is, I think, fair to say that the fact of differential survival of different variations is generally accepted, although it still requires much clarification, especially on the quantitative side. In other words, natural selection within the bounds of the single generation is an active factor in biology.

THE NATURE OF VARIATION

The really important criticisms have fallen upon Natural Selection as an evolutionary principle, and have centred round the nature of inheritable variation.

Darwin, though his views on the subject did not remain constant, was always inclined to allow some weight to Lamarckian principles, according to which the effects of use and disuse and of environmental influences were supposed to be in some degree inherited. However, later work has steadily reduced the scope that can be allowed to such agencies: Weismann drew a sharp distinction between soma and germplasm, between the individual body which was not concerned in reproduction, and the hereditary constitution contained in the germ-cells, which alone was transmitted in heredity. Purely somatic effects, according to him, could not be passed on: the sole inheritable variations were variations in the hereditary constitution.

Although the distinction between soma and germplasm is not always so sharp as Weismann supposed, and although the principle of Baldwin and Lloyd Morgan, usually called Organic Selection, shows how Lamarckism may be simulated by the later replacement of adaptive modifications by adaptive mutations, Weismann's conceptions resulted in a great clarification of the position. It is owing to him that we to-day classify variations into two fundamentally distinct categories—modifications and mutations (together with new arrangements of mutations, or recombinations; see below, p. 20). Modifications are produced by alterations in the environment (including modifications of the internal environment such as are brought about by use and disuse), mutations by alterations in the substance of the hereditary constitution. The distinction may be put in a rather different but perhaps more illuminating way. Variation is a study of the differences between organisms. On analysis, these differences may turn out to be due to differences in environment (as with an etiolated plant growing in a cellar as against a green one in light; or a sun-tanned sailor as against a pale slum-dweller); or they may turn out to be due to differences in hereditary constitution (as between an albino and a green seedling in the same plot, or a negro and a white man in the same city); or of course to a simultaneous difference both in environment and in constitution (as with the difference in stature between an undernourished pigmy and a well-nourished negro). Furthermore, only the latter are inherited. We speak of them as genetic differences: at their first origin they appear to be due to mutations in the hereditary constitution. The former we call modifications, and are not inheritable.

The important fact is that only experiment can decide between the two. Both in nature and in the laboratory, one of two indistinguishable variants may turn out to be due to environment, the other to genetic peculiarity. A particular shade of human complexion may be due to genetic constitution making for fair complexion plus considerable exposure to the sun, or to a genetically dark complexion plus very little tanning: and similarly for stature, intelligence, and many other characters.

This leads to a further important conclusion: characters as such are not and cannot be inherited. For a character is always the joint product of a particular genetic composition and a particular set of environmental circumstances. Some characters are much more stable in regard to the normal range of environmental variation than are others—for instance, human eye-colour or hair-form as against skin-colour or weight. But these too are in principle similar. Alter the environment of the embryo sufficiently, and eyeless monsters with markedly changed brain-development are produced.

In the early days of Mendelian research, phrases such as "in fowls, the character rose-comb is inherited as a Mendelian dominant" were current. So long as such phrases are recognized as mere convenient shorthand, they are harmless; but when they are taken to imply the actual genetic transmission of the characters, they are wholly incorrect.

Even as shorthand, they may mislead. To say that rose-comb is inherited as a dominant, even if we know that we mean the genetic factor for rose-comb, is likely to lead to what I may call the one-to-one or billiard-ball view of genetics. There are assumed to be a large number of characters in the organism, each one represented in a more or less invariable way by a particular factor or gene, or a combination of a few factors. This crude particulate view is a mere restatement of the preformation theory of development: granted the rose-comb factor, the rose-comb character, nice and clear-cut, will always appear. The rose-comb factor, it is true, is not regarded as a sub-microscopic replica of the actual rose-comb, but is taken to represent it by some form of unanalysed but inevitable correspondence.

The fallacy in this view is again revealed by the use of the difference method. In asserting that rose-comb is a dominant character, we are merely stating in a too abbreviated form the results of experiments to determine what constitutes the difference between fowls with rose-combs and fowls with single combs. In reality, what is inherited as a Mendelian dominant is the gene in the rose-combed stock which differentiates it from the single-combed stock: we have no right to assert anything more as a result of our experiments than the existence of such a differential factor.

Actually, every character is dependent on a very large number (possibly all) of the genes in the hereditary constitution: but some of these genes exert marked differential effects upon the visible appearance. Both rose- and single-comb fowls contain all the genes needed to build up a full-sized comb: but "rose" genes build it up according to one growth-pattern, "single" genes according to another.

This principle is of great importance. For instance, up till very recently the chief data in human genetics have been pedigrees of abnormalities of diseases collected by medical men. And in collecting these data, medical men have usually been obsessed with the implications of the ideas of "character-inheritance". When the character has not appeared in orthodox and classical Mendelian fashion they have tended to dismiss it with some such phrase as "inheritance irregular", whereas further analysis might have shown a perfectly normal *inheritance* of the gene concerned, but an irregular *expression* of the character, dependent on the other genes with which it was associated and upon differences in environment (see discussion in Hogben, 1933).

This leads on to a further and very vital fact, namely, the existence of a type of genetic process undreamt of until the Mendelian epoch. In Darwin's day biological inheritance meant the reappearance of similar characters in offspring and parent, and implied the physical transmission of some material basis for the characters. What would Darwin or any nineteenth-century biologist say to facts such as the following, which now form part of any elementary course in genetics? A black and an albino mouse are mated. All their offspring are grey, like wild mice: but in the second generation greys, blacks, and albinos appear in the ratio $9:3:4$. Or again, fowls with rose-comb and pea-comb mated together produce nothing but so-called walnut combs: but in the next generation, in addition to walnut, rose, and pea, some single combs are produced.

To the biologist of the Darwinian period the production of the grey mice would have been not inheritance, but "reversion" to the wild type, and the reappearance of the blacks and whites in the next generation would have been "atavism" or "skipping a generation". Similarly the appearance of single combs in the fowl cross would have been described as reversion, while the production of walnut combs would have been regarded as some form of "sport."

In reality, the results are in both cases immediately explicable on the assumption of two pairs of genes, each transmitted from parent to offspring by the same fundamental genetic mechanism. The "reversions", "atavisms", and "sports" are all due to new combinations of old genes. Thus, although all the facts are in one sense phenomena of inheritance, it is legitimate and in some ways desirable to distinguish those in which the same characters reappear generation after generation from those in which new characters are generated. As Haldane has put it, modern genetics deals not only with inheritance, but with recombination.

Thus the raw material available for evolution by natural selection falls into two categories—mutation and recombination. Mutation is the only begetter of intrinsic change in the separate units of the hereditary constitution: it alters the nature of genes.[3]

Recombination, on the other hand, though it may produce quite new combinations with quite new effects on characters, only juggles with existing genes. It is, however, almost as important for evolution. It cannot occur without sexual reproduction: and its importance in providing the possibility of speedily combining several favourable mutations doubtless accounts for the all-but-universal presence of the sexual process in the life-cycle or organisms. We shall in later chapters see its importance for adjusting mutations to the needs of the organism.

Darwinism to-day thus still contains an element of deduction, and is none the worse for that as a sci-

---

[3]Strictly speaking, this applies only to gene-mutation. Chromosome-mutation, whether it adds or subtracts chromosome-sets, whole chromosomes, or parts of chromosomes, or inverts sections of chromosomes, merely provides new quantitative or positional combinations of old genes. However, chromosome-mutation may alter the *effects* of genes. Thus we are covered if we say that mutation alters either the qualitative nature or the effective action of the hereditary constitution.

entific theory. But the facts available in relation to it are both more precise and more numerous, with the result that we are able to check our deductions and to make quantitative prophecies with much greater fullness than was possible to Darwin. This has been especially notable as regards the mathematical treatment of the problem, which we owe to R. A. Fisher, J. B. S. Haldane, Sewall Wright, and others. We can now take mutation-rates and degrees of advantage of one mutation or combination over another, which are within the limits actually found in genetic experiments, and can calculate the rates of evolution which will then occur.

If mutation had a rate that was very high it would neutralize or over-ride selective effects: if one that was very low, it would not provide sufficient raw material for change; if it were not more or less at random in many directions, evolution would run in orthogenetic grooves. But mutation being in point of fact chiefly at random, and the mutation-rate being always moderately low, we can deduce that the struggle for existence should be effective in producing differential survival and evolutionary change.

THE ECLIPSE OF DARWINISM

The death of Darwinism has been proclaimed not only from the pulpit, but from the biological laboratory; but, as in the case of Mark Twain, the reports seem to have been greatly exaggerated, since to-day Darwinism is very much alive.

The reaction against Darwinism set in during the nineties of last century. The youngest zoologists of that time were discontented with the trends of their science. The major school still seemed to think that the sole aim of zoology was to elucidate the relationship of the later groups. Had not Kovalevsky demonstrated the vertebrate affinities of the sea-squirts, and did not comparative embryology prove the common ancestry of groups so unlike as worms and molluscs? Intoxicated with such earlier successes of evolutionary phylogeny, they proceeded (like some Forestry Commission of science) to plant wildernesses of family trees over the beauty-spots of biology.

A related school, a little less prone to speculation, concentrated on the pursuit of comparative morphology within groups. This provides one of the most admirable of intellectual trainings for the student, and has yielded extremely important results for science. But if pursued too exclusively for its own sake, it leads, as Radl has pithily put it in his *History of Biological Theories,* to spending one's time comparing one thing with another without ever troubling about what either of them really is. In other words,

zoology, becoming morphological, suffered divorce from physiology. And finally Darwinism itself grew more and more theoretical. The paper demonstration that such and such a character was or might be adaptive was regarded by many writers as sufficient proof that it must owe its origin to Natural Selection. Evolutionary studies became more and more merely case-books of real or supposed adaptations. Late nineteenth-century Darwinism came to resemble the early nineteenth-century school of Natural Theology. Paléy *redivivus,* one might say, but philosophically upside down, with Natural Selection instead of a Divine Artificer as the *Deus ex machina.* There was little contact of evolutionary speculation with the concrete facts of cytology and heredity, or with actual experimentation.

A major symptom of revolt was the publication of William Bateson's *Materials for the Study of Variation* in 1894. Bateson had done valuable work on the embryology of *Balanoglossus;* but his sceptical and concrete mind found it distasteful to spend itself on speculations on the ancestry of the vertebrates, which was then regarded as the outstanding topic of evolution, and he turned to a task which, however different it might seem, he rightly regarded as piercing nearer to the heart of the evolutionary problems. Deliberately he gathered evidence of variation which was discontinuous, as opposed to the continuous variation postulated by Darwin and Weismann. The resultant volume of material, though its gathering might fairly be called biassed, was impressive in quantity and range, and deeply impressed the more active spirits in biology. It was the first symptom of what we may call the period of mutation theory, which postulated that large mutations, and not small "continuous variations", were the raw material of evolution, and actually determined most of its course, selection being relegated to a wholly subordinate position.

This was first formally promulgated by de Vries (1901, 1905) as a result of his work with the evening primroses, *Oenothera,* and was later adopted by various other workers, notably T. H. Morgan, in his first genetical phase. The views of the early twentieth-century geneticists, moreover, were coloured by the rediscovery of Mendel's laws by Correns, de Vries, and Tschermak in the spring of 1900, and the rapid generalization of them, notably by Bateson.

Naturally, the early Mendelians worked with clear-cut differences of large extent. As it became clearer that Mendelian inheritance was universal, it was natural to suppose that all Mendelian factors produced large effects, that therefore mutation was sharp and discontinuous, and that the continuous variation which is obviously widespread in nature is not heritable.

Bateson did not hesitate to draw the most devastating conclusions from his reading of the Mendelian facts. In his Presidential Address to the British Association in 1914, assuming first that change in the germplasm is always by large mutation and secondly that all mutation is loss, from a dominant something to a recessive nothing, he concluded that the whole of evolution is merely an unpacking. The hypothetical ancestral amoeba contained—actually and not just potentially—the entire complex of life's hereditary factors. The jettisoning of different portions of this complex released the potentialities of this, that, and the other group and form of life. Selection and adaptation were relegated to an unconsidered background.

Meanwhile the true-blue Darwinian stream, leaving Weismannism behind, had reached its biometric phase. Tracing its origin to Galton, biometry blossomed under the guidance of Karl Pearson and Weldon. Unfortunately this, the first thorough application of mathematics to evolution, though productive of many important results and leading to still more important advances in method, was for a considerable time rendered sterile by its refusal to acknowledge the genetic facts discovered by the Mendelians. Both sides, indeed, were to blame. The biometricians stuck to hypothetical modes of inheritance and genetic variation on which to exercise their mathematical skill; the Mendelians refused to acknowledge that continuous variation could be genetic, or at any rate dependent on genes, or that a mathematical theory of selection could be of any real service to the evolutionary biologist.

It was in this period, immediately prior to the war, that the legend of the death of Darwinism acquired currency. The facts of Mendelism appeared to contradict the facts of paleontology, the theories of the mutationists would not square with the Weismannian views of adaptation, the discoveries of experimental embryology seemed to contradict the classical recapitulatory theories of development. Zoologists who clung to Darwinian views were looked down on by the devotees of the newer disciplines, whether cytology or genetics, *Entwicklungs-mechanik* or comparative physiology, as old-fashioned theorizers; and the theological and philosophical antipathy to Darwin's great mechanistic generalization could once more raise its head without fearing too violent a knock.

But the old-fashioned selectionists were guided by a sound instinct. The opposing factions became reconciled as the younger branches of biology achieved a synthesis with each other and with the classical disciplines: and the reconciliation converged upon a Darwinian centre.

It speedily became apparent that Mendelism applied to the heredity of all many-celled and many single-celled organisms, both animals and plants. The Mendelian laws received a simple and general interpretation: they were due in the first place to inheritance being particulate, and in the second place to the particles being borne on the chromosomes, whose behaviour could be observed under the microscope. Many apparent exceptions to Mendelian rules turned out to be due to aberrations of chromosome-behaviour. Segregation and recombination, the fundamental Mendelian facts, are all but universal, being co-extensive with sexual reproduction; and mutation, the further corollary of the particulate theory of heredity, was found to occur even more widely, in somatic tissues and in parthenogenetic and sexually-reproducing strains as well as in the germtrack of bisexual species. Blending inheritance as originally conceived was shown not to occur, and cytoplasmic inheritance to play an extremely subsidiary role.

The Mendelians also found that mutations could be of any extent, and accordingly that apparently continuous as well as obviously discontinuous variation had to be taken into account in discussing heredity and evolution. The mathematicians found that biometric methods could be applied to neo-Mendelian postulates, and then become doubly fruitful. Cytology became intimately linked with genetics. Experimental embryology and the study of growth illuminated heredity, recapitulation, and palcontology. Ecology and systematics provided new data and new methods of approach to the evolutionary problem. Selection, both in nature and in the laboratory, was studied quantitatively and experimentally. Mathematical analysis showed that only particulate inheritance would permit evolutionary change: blending inheritance, as postulated by Darwin, was shown by R. A. Fisher (1930a) to demand mutation-rates enormously higher than those actually found to occur. Thus, though it may still be true in a formal sense that, as such an eminent geneticist as Miss E. R. Saunders said at the British Association meeting in 1920, "Mendelism is a theory of heredity: it is not a theory of evolution", yet the assertion is purely formal. Mendelism is now seen as an essential part of the theory of evolution. Mendelian analysis does not merely explain the distributive hereditary mechanism: it also, together with selection, explains the progressive mechanism of evolution.

Biology in the last twenty years, after a period in which new disciplines were taken up in turn and worked out in comparative isolation, has become a more unified science. It has embarked upon a period of synthesis, until to-day it no longer presents the spectacle of a number of semi-independent and largely contradictory sub-sciences, but is coming to rival the unity of older sciences like physics, in which advance in any one branch leads almost at once to advance in all other fields, and theory and experiment march hand-in-hand. As one chief result, there has been a rebirth of Darwinism. The historical facts concerning this trend are summarized by Shull in a recent book (1936). It is noteworthy that T. H. Morgan, after having been one of the most extreme critics of selectionist doctrine, has recently, as a result of modern work in genetics (to which he has himself so largely contributed), again become an upholder of the Darwinian point of view (T. H. Morgan, 1925, and later writings); while his younger colleagues, notably Muller and Sturtevant, are strongly selectionist in their evolutionary views.

The Darwinism thus reborn is a modified Darwinism, since it must operate with facts unknown to Darwin; but it is still Darwinism in the sense that it aims at giving a naturalistic interpretation of evolution, and that its upholders, while constantly striving for more facts and more experimental results, do not, like some cautious spirits, reject the method of deduction.

Hogben (1931, p. 145 seq.) disagrees with this conclusion. He accepts the findings of neo-Mendelism and the mathematical conclusions to be drawn from them; but, to use his own words, "the essential difference between the theory of natural selection expounded by such contemporary writers as J. B. S. Haldane, Sewall Wright, and R. A. Fisher, as contrasted with that of Darwin, resides in the fact that Darwin interpreted the process of artificial selection in terms of a theory of 'blending inheritance' universally accepted by his own generation, whereas the modern view is based on the Theory of Particulate Inheritance. The consequences of the two views are very different. According to the Darwinian doctrine, evolution is an essentially continuous process, and selection is essentially creative in the sense that no change would occur if selection were removed. According to the modern doctrine, evolution is discontinuous. The differentiation of varieties or species may suffer periods of stagnation. Selection is a destructive agency."

Accordingly, Hogben would entirely repudiate the title of Darwinism for the modern outlook, and would prefer to see the term Natural Selection replaced by another to mark the new connotations it has acquired, although on this latter point he is prepared to admit the convenience of retention.

These objections, coming from a biologist of Hogben's calibre, must carry weight. On the other hand we shall see reason in later chapters for finding them ungrounded. In the first place, evolution, as revealed in fossil trends, *is* "an essentially continuous process". The building-blocks of evolution, in the shape of mutations, are, to be sure, discrete quanta of change. But firstly, the majority of them (and the very great majority of those which survive to become incorporated in the genetic constitution of living things) appear to be of small extent; secondly, the effect of a given mutation will be different according to the combinations of modifying genes present (pp. 68 seq.); and thirdly, its effect may be masked or modified by environmental modification. The net result will be that, for all practical purposes, most of the variability of a species at any given moment will be continuous, however accurate are the measurements made; and that most evolutionary change will be gradual, to be detected by a progressive shifting of a mean value from generation to generation.

In the second place, the statement that selection is a destructive agency is not true, if it is meant to imply that it is *merely* destructive. It is also directive, and because it is directive, it has a share in evolutionary creation. Neither mutation nor selection alone is creative of anything important in evolution; but the two in conjunction are creative.

Hogben is perfectly right in stressing the fact of the important differences in content and implication between the Darwinism of Darwin or Weismann and that of Fisher or Haldane. We may, however, reflect that the term *atom* is still in current use and the atomic theory not yet rejected by physicists, in spite of the supposedly indivisible units having been divided. This is because modern physicists still find that the particles called atoms by their predecessors do play an important role, even if they are compound and do occasionally lose or gain particles and even change their nature. If this is so, biologists may with a good heart continue to be Darwinians and to employ the term Natural Selection, even if Darwin knew nothing of mendelizing mutations, and if selection is by itself incapable of changing the constitution of a species or a line.

It is with this reborn Darwinism, this mutated phoenix risen from the ashes of the pyre kindled by men so unlike as Bateson and Bergson, that I propose to deal in succeeding chapters of this book.

Name: _____ **Date:** _____

1. How, according to Huxley, is Darwinism a "blend of induction and deduction?"

2. How have critiques of the theory of natural selection used the problems of inheritable variation to attack Darwinism?

3. What was the "Eclipse of Darwinism" as Huxley described it?

4. What had to happen, according to Huxley, for Darwinism to be reborn like a "mutated phoenix risen from the ashes?"

Theodosius Dobzhansky

"Nothing in Biology Makes Sense Except in the Light of Evolution," 1973

Dobzhansky (1900-1975) was geneticist and a key figure in the modern evolutionary synthesis. A Russian immigrant, he came to the United States in 1927 and spent his career using insects to study genetics. In this piece, Dobzhansky demonstrated the concern that many American biologists had about the widespread public animosity toward evolutionary science and explained why evolutionary science was vital to the progress of modern biology.

As recently as 1966, sheik Abd el Aziz bin Baz asked the king of Saudi Arabia to suppress a heresy that was spreading in his land. Wrote the sheik:

"The Holy Koran, the Prophet's teaching, the majority of Islamic scientists, and the actual facts all prove that the sun is running in its orbit . . . and that the earth is fixed and stable, spread out by God for his mankind . . . . Anyone who professed otherwise would utter a charge of falsehood toward God, the Koran, and the Prophet."

The good sheik evidently holds the Copernican theory to be a "mere theory," not a "fact." In this he is technically correct. A theory can be verified by a mass of facts, but it becomes a proven theory, not a fact. The sheik was perhaps unaware that the Space Age had begun before he asked the king to suppress the Copernican heresy. The sphericity of the earth has been seen by astronauts, and even by many earth-bound people on their television screens. Perhaps the sheik could retort that those who venture beyond the confines of God's earth suffer hallucinations, and that the earth is really flat.

Parts of the Copernican world model, such as the contention that the earth rotates around the sun, and not vice versa, have not been verified by direct observations even to the extent the sphericity of the earth has been. Yet scientists accept the model as an accurate representation of reality. Why? Because it makes sense of a multitude of facts which are otherwise meaningless or extravagant. To nonspecialists most of these facts are unfamiliar. Why then do we accept the "mere theory" that the earth is a sphere revolving around a spherical sun? Are we simply submitting to authority? Not quite: we know that those who took the time to study the evidence found it convincing.

The good sheik is probably ignorant of the evidence. Even more likely, he is so hopelessly biased that no amount of evidence would impress him. Anyway, it would be shear waste of time to attempt to convince him. The Koran and the Bible do not contradict Copernicus, nor does Copernicus contradict them. It is ludicrous to mistake the Bible and the Koran for primers of natural science. They treat of matters even more important: the meaning of man and his relations to God. They are written in poetic symbols that were understandable to people of the age when they were written, as well as to peoples of all other ages. The king of Arabia did not comply with the sheik's demand. He knew that some people fear enlightenment, because enlightenment threatens their vested interests. Education is not to be used to promote obscurantism.

The earth is not the geometric center of the universe, although it may be its spiritual center. It is a mere speck of dust in the cosmic spaces. Contrary to Bishop Ussher's calculations, the world did not appear in approximately its present state in 4004 BC. The estimates of the age of the universe given by modern cosmologists are still only rough approximations, which are revised (usually upward) as the methods of estimation are refined. Some cosmologists take the universe to be about 10 billion years old; others suppose that it may have existed, and will continue to exist, eternally. The origin of life on earth is dated tentatively between 3 and 5 billion years ago; manlike beings appeared relatively quite recently, between 2 and 4 million years ago. The estimates of the age of the earth, of the duration of the geologic and paleontologic eras, and of the antiquity of man's ancestors are now based mainly on radiometric evidence the proportions of isotopes of certain chemical elements in rocks suitable for such studies.

Shiek bin Baz and his like refuse to accept the radiometric evidence, because it is a "mere theory." What is the alternative? One can suppose that the Creator saw fit to play deceitful tricks on geologists and biologists. He carefully arranged to have various rocks provided with isotope ratios just right to mislead us into thinking that certain rocks are 2 billion years old, others 2 million, which in fact they are only some 6,000 years old. This kind of pseudo-explanation is not very new. One of the early anti-evolutionists, P. H. Gosse, published a book entitled *Omphalos* ("the Navel"). The gist of this amazing book is that Adam, though he had no mother, was created with a navel, and that fossils were placed by the Creator where we find them now—a deliberate act on his part, to give the appearance of great antiquity and geologic upheavals. It is easy to see the fatal flaw in all such notions. They are blasphemies, accusing God of absurd deceitfulness. This is as revolting as it is uncalled for.

DIVERSITY OF LIVING BEINGS

The diversity and the unity of life are equally striking and meaningful aspects of the living world. Between 1.5 and 2 million species of animals and plants have been described and studied; the number yet to be described is probably as great. The diversity of sizes, structures, and ways of life is staggering but fascinating. Here are just a few examples.

The foot-and-mouth disease virus is a sphere 8-12 mm in diameter. The blue whale reaches 30 m in length and 135 t in weight. The simplest viruses are parasites in cells of other organisms, reduced to barest essentials minute amounts of DNA or RNA, which subvert the biochemical machinery of the host cells to replicate their genetic information, rather than that of the host.

It is a matter of opinion, or of definition, whether viruses are considered living organisms or peculiar chemical substances. The fact that such differences of opinion can exist is in itself highly significant. It means that the borderline between living and inanimate matter is obliterated. At the opposite end of the simplicity complexity spectrum you have

vertebrate animals, including man. The human brain has some 12 billion neurons; the synapses between the neurons are perhaps a thousand times numerous.

Some organisms live in a great variety of environments. Man is at the top of the scale in this respect. He is not only a truly cosmopolitan species but, owing to his technologic achievements, can survive for at least a limited time on the surface of the moon and in cosmic spaces. By contrast, some organisms are amazingly specialized. Perhaps the narrowest ecologic niche of all is that of a species of the fungus family Laboulbeniaceae, which grows exclusively on the rear portion of the elytra of the beetle *Aphenops cronei*, which is found only in some limestone caves in southern France. Larvae of the fly *Psilopa petrolei* develop in seepages of crude oil in California oilfields; as far as is known they occur nowhere else. This is the only insect able to live and feed in oil, and its adult can walk on the surface of the oil only as long as no body part other than the tarsi are in contact with the oil. Larvae of the fly *Drosophila carciniphila* develop only in the nephric grooves beneath the flaps of the third maxilliped of the land crab *Geocarcinus ruricola*, which is restricted to certain islands in the Caribbean.

Is there an explanation, to make intelligible to reason this colossal diversity of living beings? Whence came these extraordinary, seemingly whimsical and superfluous creatures, like the fungus *Laboulbenia*, the beetle *Aphenops cronei*, the flies *Psilopa petrolei* and *Drosophila carciniphila*, and many, many more apparent biologic curiosities? The only explanation that makes sense is that the organic diversity has evolved in response to the diversity of environment on the planet earth. No single species, however perfect and however versatile, could exploit all the opportunities for living. Every one of the millions of species has its own way of living and of getting sustenance from the environment. There are doubtless many other possible ways of living as yet unexploited by any existing species; but one thing is clear: with less organic diversity, some opportunities for living would remain unexploited. The evolutionary process tends to fill up the available ecologic niches. It does not do so consciously or deliberately; the relations between evolution and environment are more subtle and more interesting than that. The environment does not impose evolutionary changes on its inhabitants, as postulated by the now abandoned neo-Lamarckian theories. The best way to envisage the situation is as follows: the environment presents challenges to living species, to which the later may respond by adaptive genetic changes.

An unoccupied ecologic niche, an unexploited opportunity for living, is a challenge. So is an environmental change, such as the Ice Age climate giving place to a warmer climate. Natural selection may cause a living species to respond to the challenge by adaptive genetic changes. These changes may enable the species to occupy the formerly empty ecologic niche as a new opportunity for living, or to resist the environmental change if it is unfavorable. But the response may or may not be successful. This depends on many factors, the chief of which is the genetic composition of the responding species at the time the response is called for. Lack of successful response may cause the species to become extinct. The evidence of fossils shows clearly that the eventual end of most evolutionary lines is extinction. Organisms now living are successful descendants of only a minority of the species that lived in the past and of smaller and smaller minorities the farther back you look. Nevertheless, the number of living species has not dwindled; indeed, it has probably grown with time. All this is understandable in the light of evolution theory; but what a senseless operation it would have been, on God's part, to fabricate a multitude of species ex nihilo and then let most of them die out!

There is, of course, nothing conscious or intentional in the action of natural selection. A biologic species does not say to itself, "Let me try tomorrow (or a million years from now) to grow in a different soil, or use a different food, or subsist on a different body part of a different crab." Only a human being could make such conscious decisions. This is why the species *Homo sapiens* is the apex of evolution. Natural selection is at one and the same time a blind and creative process. Only a creative and blind process could produce, on the one hand, the tremendous biologic success that is the human species and, on the other, forms of adaptedness as narrow and as constraining as those of the overspecialized fungus, beetle, and flies mentioned above.

Anti-evolutionists fail to understand how natural selection operates. They fancy that all existing species were generated by supernatural fiat a few thousand years ago, pretty much as we find them today. But what is the sense of having as many as 2 or 3 million species living on earth? If natural selection is the main factor that brings evolution about, any number of species is understandable: natural selection does not work according to a foreordained plan, and species are produced not because they are needed for some purpose but simply because there is an environmental opportunity and genetic wherewithal to make them possible. Was the Creator in a jocular mood when he made *Psilopa petrolei* for California oil fields and species of *Drosophila* to live exclusively on some body-parts of certain land crabs on only cer-

tain islands in the Caribbean? The organic diversity becomes, however, reasonable and understandable if the Creator has created the living world not by caprice but by evolution propelled by natural selection. It is wrong to hold creation and evolution as mutually exclusive alternatives. I am a creationist and an evolutionist. Evolution is God's, or Nature's method of creation. Creation is not an event that happened in 4004 BC; it is a process that began some 10 billion years ago and is still under way.

UNITY OF LIFE

The unity of life is no less remarkable than its diversity. Most forms of life are similar in many respects. The universal biologic similarities are particularly striking in the biochemical dimension. From viruses to man, heredity is coded in just two, chemically related substances: DNA and RNA. The genetic code is as simple as it is universal. There are only four genetic "letters" in DNA: adenine, guanine, thymine, and cytosine. Uracil replaces thymine in RNA. The entire evolutionary development of the living world has taken place not by invention of new "letters" in the genetic "alphabet" but by elaboration of ever-new combinations of these letters.

Not only is the DNA-RNA genetic code universal, but so is the method of translation of the sequences of the "letters" in DNA-RNA into sequences of amino acids in proteins. The same 20 amino acids compose countless different proteins in all, or at least in most, organisms. Different amino acids are coded by one to six nucleotide triplets in DNA and RNA. And the biochemical universals extend beyond the genetic code and its translation into proteins: striking uniformities prevail in the cellular metabolism of the most diverse living beings. Adenosine triphosphate, biotin, riboflavin, hemes, pyridoxin, vitamins K and B12, and folic acid implement metabolic processes everywhere.

What do these biochemical or biologic universals mean? They suggest that life arose from inanimate matter only once and that all organisms, no matter now diverse, in other respects, conserve the basic features of the primordial life. (It is also possible that there were several, or even many, origins of life; if so, the progeny of only one of them has survived and inherited the earth.) But what if there was no evolution and every one of the millions of species were created by separate fiat? However offensive the notion may be to religious feeling and to reason, the anti-evolutionists must again accuse the Creator of cheating. They must insist that He deliberately arranged things exactly as if his method of creation was evolution, intentionally to mislead sincere seekers of truth.

The remarkable advances of molecular biology in recent years have made it possible to understand how it is that diverse organisms are constructed from such monotonously similar materials: proteins composed of only 20 kinds of amino acids and coded only by DNA and RNA, each with only four kinds of nucleotides. The method is astonishingly simple. All English words, sentences, chapters, and books are made up of sequences of 26 letters of the alphabet. (They can be represented also by only three signs of the Morse code: dot, dash, and gap.) The meaning of a word or a sentence is defined not so much by what letters it contains as by the sequences of these letters. It is the same with heredity: it is coded by the sequences of the genetic "letters" the nucleotides in the DNA. They are translated into the sequences of amino acids in the proteins.

Molecular studies have made possible an approach to exact measurements of degrees of biochemical similarities and differences among organisms. Some kinds of enzymes and other proteins are quasi-universal, or at any rate widespread, in the living world. They are functionally similar in different living beings, in that they catalyze similar chemical reactions. But when such proteins are isolated and their structures determined chemically, they are often found to contain more or less different sequences of amino acids in different organisms. For example, the so-called alpha chains of hemoglobin have identical sequences of amino acids in man and the chimpanzee, but they differ in a single amino acid (out of 141) in the gorilla. Alpha chains of human hemoglobin differ from cattle hemoglobin in 17 amino acid substitutions, 18 from horse, 20 from donkey, 25 from rabbit, and 71 from fish (carp).

Cytochrome C is an enzyme that plays an important role in the metabolism of aerobic cells. It is found in the most diverse organisms, from man to molds. E. Margoliash, W. M. Fitch, and others have compared the amino acid sequences in cytochrome C in different branches of the living world. Most significant similarities as well as differences have been brought to light. The cytochrome C of different orders of mammals and birds differ in 2 to 17 amino acids, classes to vertebrates in 7 to 38, and vertebrates and insects in 23 to 41; and animals differ from yeasts and molds in 56 to 72 amino acids. Fitch and Margoliash prefer to express their findings in what are called "minimal mutational distances." It has been mentioned above that different amino acids are coded by different triplets of nucleotides in DNA of the genes; this code is now known. Most mutations involve substitutions of single nucleotides somewhere in the

Monkey	1	Chicken	18
Dog	13	Penguin	18
Horse	17	Turtle	19
Donkey	16	Rattlesnake	20
Pig	13	Fish (tuna)	31
Rabbit	12	Fly	33
Kangaroo	12	Moth	36
Duck	17	Mold	63
Pigeon	16	Yeast	56

DNA chain coding for a given protein. Therefore, one can calculate the minimum numbers of single mutations needed to change the cytochrome C of one organism into that of another. Minimal mutational distances between human cytochrome C and the cytochrome C of other living beings are as follows:

It is important to note that amino acid sequences in a given kind of protein vary within a species as well as from species to species. It is evident that the differences among proteins at the level of species, genus, family, order, class, and phylum are compounded of elements that vary also among individuals within a species. Individual and group differences are only quantitatively, not qualitatively, different. Evidence supporting the above propositions is ample and is growing rapidly. Much work has been done in recent years on individual variations in amino acid sequences of hemoglobin of human blood. More than 100 variants have been detected. Most of them involve substitutions of single amino acids—substitutions that have arisen by genetic mutations in the persons in whom they are discovered or in their ancestors. As expected, some of these mutations are deleterious to their carriers, but others apparently are neutral or even favorable in certain environments. Some mutant hemoglobins have been found only in one person or in one family; others are discovered repeatedly among inhabitants of different parts of the world. I submit that all these remarkable findings make sense in the light of evolution: they are nonsense otherwise.

COMPARATIVE ANATOMY AND EMBRYOLOGY

The biochemical universals are the most impressive and the most recently discovered, but certainly they are not the only vestiges of creation by means of evolution. Comparative anatomy and embryology proclaim the evolutionary origins of the present inhabitants of the world. In 1555 Pierre Belon established the presence of homologous bones in the superficially very different skeletons of man and bird. Later anatomists traced the homologies in the skeletons, as well as in other organs, of all vertebrates. Homologies are also traceable in the external skeletons of arthropods as seemingly unlike as a lobster, a fly, and a butterfly. Examples of homologies can be multiplied indefinitely.

Embryos of apparently quite diverse animals often exhibit striking similarities. A century ago these similarities led some biologists (notably the German zoologist Ernst Haeckel) to be carried by their enthusiasm as far as to interpret the embryonic similarities as meaning that the embryo repeats in its development the evolutionary history of its species: it was said to pass through stages in which it resembles its remote ancestors. In other words, early-day biologists supposed that by studying embryonic development one can, as it were, read off the stages through which the evolutionary development had passed. This so-called biogenetic law is no longer credited in its original form. And yet embryonic similarities are undeniable impressive and significant.

Probably everybody knows the sedentary barnacles which seem to have no similarity to free-swimming crustaceans, such as the copepods. How remarkable that barnacles pass through a free-swimming larval stage, the nauplius! At that stage of its development a barnacle and a Cyclops look unmistakably similar. They are evidently relatives. The presence of gill slits in human embryos and in embryos of other terrestrial vertebrates is another famous example. Of course, at no stage of its development is a human embryo a fish, nor does it ever have functioning gills. But why should it have unmistakable gill slits unless its remote ancestors did respire with the aid of gills? It is the Creator again playing practical jokes?

ADAPTIVE RADIATION: HAWAII'S FLIES

There are about 2,000 species of drosophilid flies in the world as a whole. About a quarter of them occur in Hawaii, although the total area of the archipelago is only about that of the state of New Jersey. All but 17 of the species in Hawaii are endemic (found nowhere else). Furthermore, a great majority of the Hawaiian endemics do not occur throughout the archipelago: they are restricted to single islands or even to a part of an island. What is the explanation of this extraordinary proliferation of drosophilid species in so small a territory? Recent work of H. L. Carson, H. T. Spieth, D. E. Hardy, and others makes the situation understandable.

The Hawaiian Islands are of volcanic origin; they were never parts of any continent. Their ages are between 5.6 and 0.7 million years. Before man came

there inhabitants were descendants of immigrants that had been transported across the ocean by air currents and other accidental means. A single drosophilid species, which arrived in Hawaii first, before there were numerous competitors, faced the challenge of an abundance of many unoccupied ecologic niches. Its descendants responded to this challenge by evolutionary adaptive radiation, the products of which are the remarkable Hawaiian drosophilids of today. To forestall a possible misunderstanding, let it be made clear that the Hawaiian endemics are by no means so similar to each other that they could be mistaken for variants of the same species; if anything, they are more diversified than are drosophilids elsewhere. The largest and the smallest drosophilid species are both Hawaiian. They exhibit an astonishing variety of behavior patterns. Some of them have become adapted to ways of life quite extraordinary for a drosophilid fly, such as being parasites in egg cocoons of spiders.

Oceanic islands other than Hawaii, scattered over the wide Pacific Ocean, are not conspicuously rich in endemic species of drosophilids. The most probable explanation of this fact is that these other islands were colonized by drosophilid after most ecologic niches had already been filled by earlier arrivals. This surely is a hypothesis, but it is a reasonable one. Anti-evolutionists might perhaps suggest an alternative hypothesis: in a fit of absentmindedness, the Creator went on manufacturing more and more drosophilid species for Hawaii, until there was an extravagant surfeit of them in this archipelago. I leave it up to you to decide which hypothesis makes sense.

STRENGTH AND ACCEPTANCE OF THE THEORY

Seen in the light of evolution, biology is, perhaps, intellectually the most satisfying and inspiring science. Without that light it becomes a pile of sundry facts some of them interesting or curious but making no meaningful picture as a whole.

This is not to imply that we know everything that can and should be known about biology and about evolution. Any competent biologist is aware of a multitude of problems yet unresolved and of questions yet unanswered. After all, biologic research shows no sign of approaching completion; quite the opposite is true. Disagreements and clashes of opinion are rife among biologists, as they should be in a living and growing science. Anti-evolutionists mistake, or pretend to mistake, these disagreements as indications of dubiousness of the entire doctrine of evolution. Their favorite sport is stringing together quotations, carefully and sometimes expertly taken out of context, to show that nothing is really established or agreed upon among evolutionists. Some of my colleagues and myself have been amused and amazed to read ourselves quoted in a way showing that we are really anti-evolutionists under the skin.

Let me try to make crystal clear what is established beyond reasonable doubt, and what needs further study, about evolution. Evolution as a process that has always gone on in the history of the earth can be doubted only by those who are ignorant of the evidence or are resistant to evidence, owing to emotional blocks or to plain bigotry. By contrast, the mechanisms that bring evolution about certainly need study and clarification. There are no alternatives to evolution as history that can withstand critical examination. Yet we are constantly learning new and important facts about evolutionary mechanisms.

It is remarkable that more than a century ago Darwin was able to discern so much about evolution without having available to him the key facts discovered since. The development of genetics after 1900 especially of molecular genetics, in the last two decades has provided information essential to the understanding of evolutionary mechanisms. But much is in doubt and much remains to be learned. This is heartening and inspiring for any scientist worth his salt. Imagine that everything is completely known and that science has nothing more to discover: what a nightmare!

Does the evolutionary doctrine clash with religious faith? It does not. It is a blunder to mistake the Holy Scriptures for elementary textbooks of astronomy, geology, biology, and anthropology. Only if symbols are construed to mean what they are not intended to mean can there arise imaginary, insoluble conflicts. As pointed out above, the blunder leads to blasphemy: the Creator is accused of systematic deceitfulness.

One of the great thinkers of our age, Pierre Teilhard de Chardin, wrote the following: "Is evolution a theory, a system, or a hypothesis? It is much more it is a general postulate to which all theories, all hypotheses, all systems much henceforward bow and which they must satisfy in order to be thinkable and true. Evolution is a light which illuminates all facts, a trajectory which all lines of though must follow this is what evolution is. Of course, some scientists, as well as some philosophers and theologians, disagree with some parts of Teilhard's teachings; the acceptance of his worldview falls short of universal. But there is no doubt at all that Teilhard was a truly and deeply religious man and that Christianity was the cornerstone of his worldview. Moreover, in his worldview science and faith were not segregated in watertight compartments, as they are with so many people. They were harmoniously fitting parts of his worldview. Teilhard was a creationist, but one who understood that the Creation is realized in this world by means of evolution.

Name: _____ **Date:** _____

1. List and explain in your own words three arguments that Dobzhansky offers against creationism.
    1.

    2.

    3.

2. List three ways, according to Dobzhansky, that all life is similar?
    1.

    2.

    3.

3. How does Dobzhansky use the example of drosophilid flies to support evolution?

4. How, according to Dobzhansky, can one be both a creationist and evolutionist?